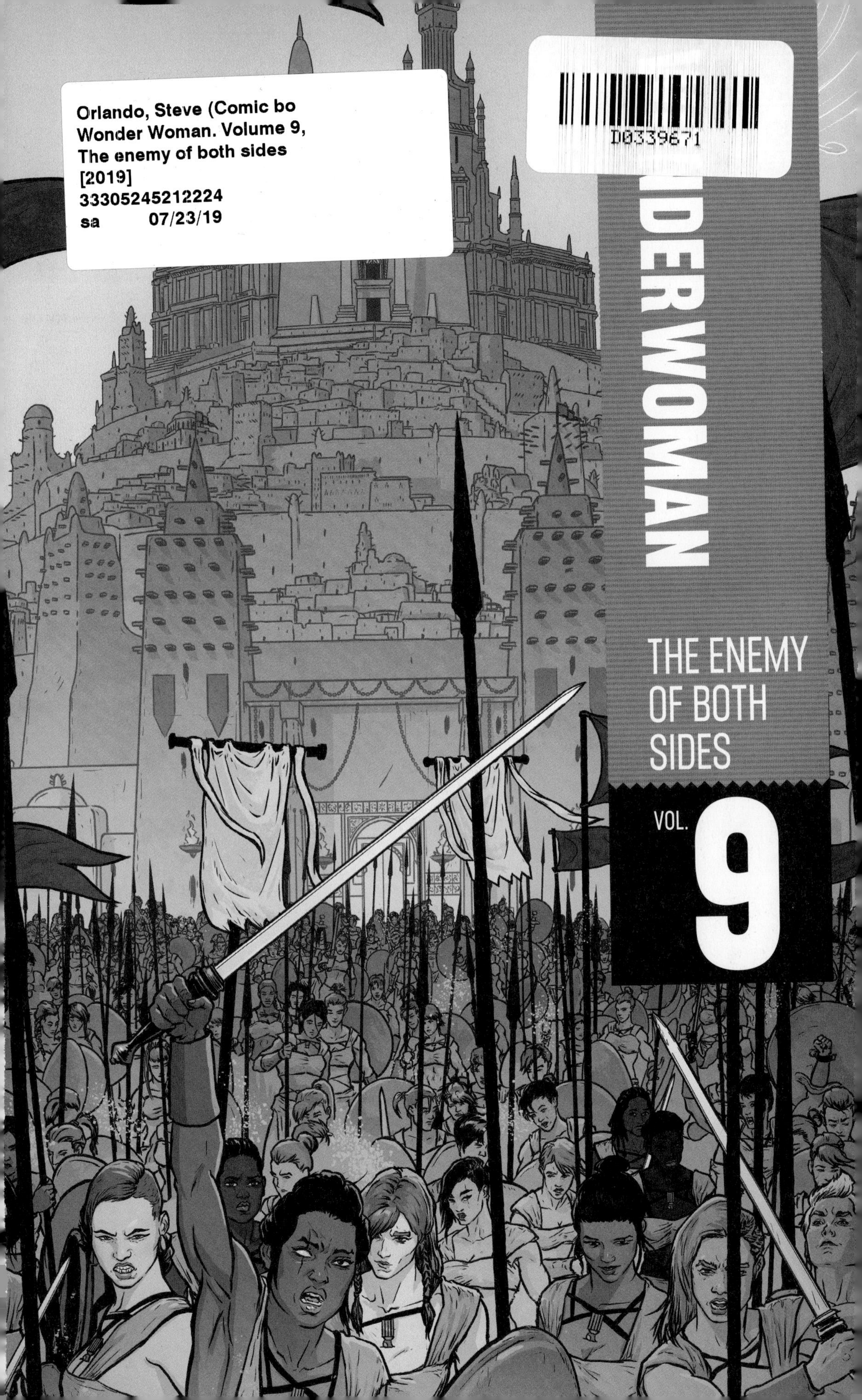
DER WOMAN
THE ENEMY OF BOTH SIDES
VOL. 9

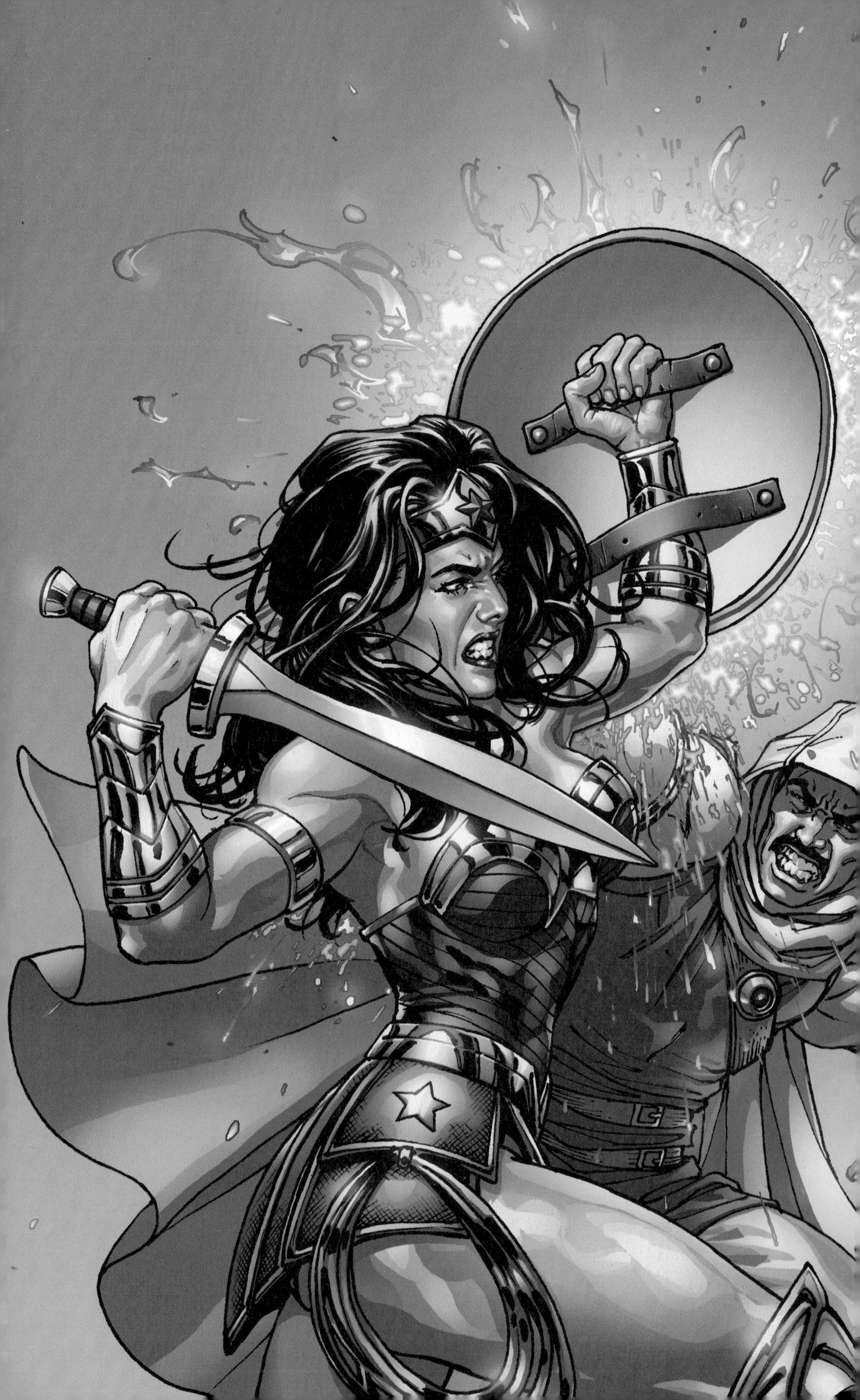

WONDER WOMAN
THE ENEMY OF BOTH SIDES

writers

STEVE ORLANDO
TIM SEELEY
RAFAEL SCAVONE
RAFAEL ALBUQUERQUE
BRENDEN FLETCHER
KARL KERSCHL
MAIRGHREAD SCOTT
GREG RUCKA
LIAM SHARP
FÁBIO MOON
MARGUERITE BENNETT
RENAE DE LIZ
JILL THOMPSON
HOPE LARSON
GAIL SIMONE

colorists

ROMULO FAJARDO JR.
BORJA PINDADO
STEVE BUCCELLATO
CHRIS SOTOMAYOR
DAVE McCAIG
MICHELE ASSARASAKORN
IVAN PLASCENCIA
FÁBIO MOON
MARGUERITE SAUVAGE
RAY DILLON
JILL THOMPSON
MAT LOPES
HI-FI

artists

LAURA BRAGA
ACO
DAVID LORENZO
HUGO PETRUS
RAÚL ALLÉN
PATRICIA MARTÍN
RICK LEONARDI
FELIPE WATANABE
JONAS TRINIDADE
RAFAEL ALBUQUERQUE
KARL KERSCHL
RILEY ROSSMO
LIAM SHARP
FÁBIO MOON
MARGUERITE SAUVAGE
RENAE DE LIZ
RAY DILLON
JILL THOMPSON
RAMON BACHS
COLLEEN DORAN

letterers

SAIDA TEMOFONTE
TRAVIS LANHAM
STEVE WANDS
JOSH REED
DERON BENNETT
JODI WYNNE
FÁBIO MOON
RAY DILLON
JASON ARTHUR
COREY BREEN
DAVE SHARPE

collection cover artist

STANLEY "ARTGERM" LAU

WONDER WOMAN created by
WILLIAM MOULTON MARSTON

VOL.
9

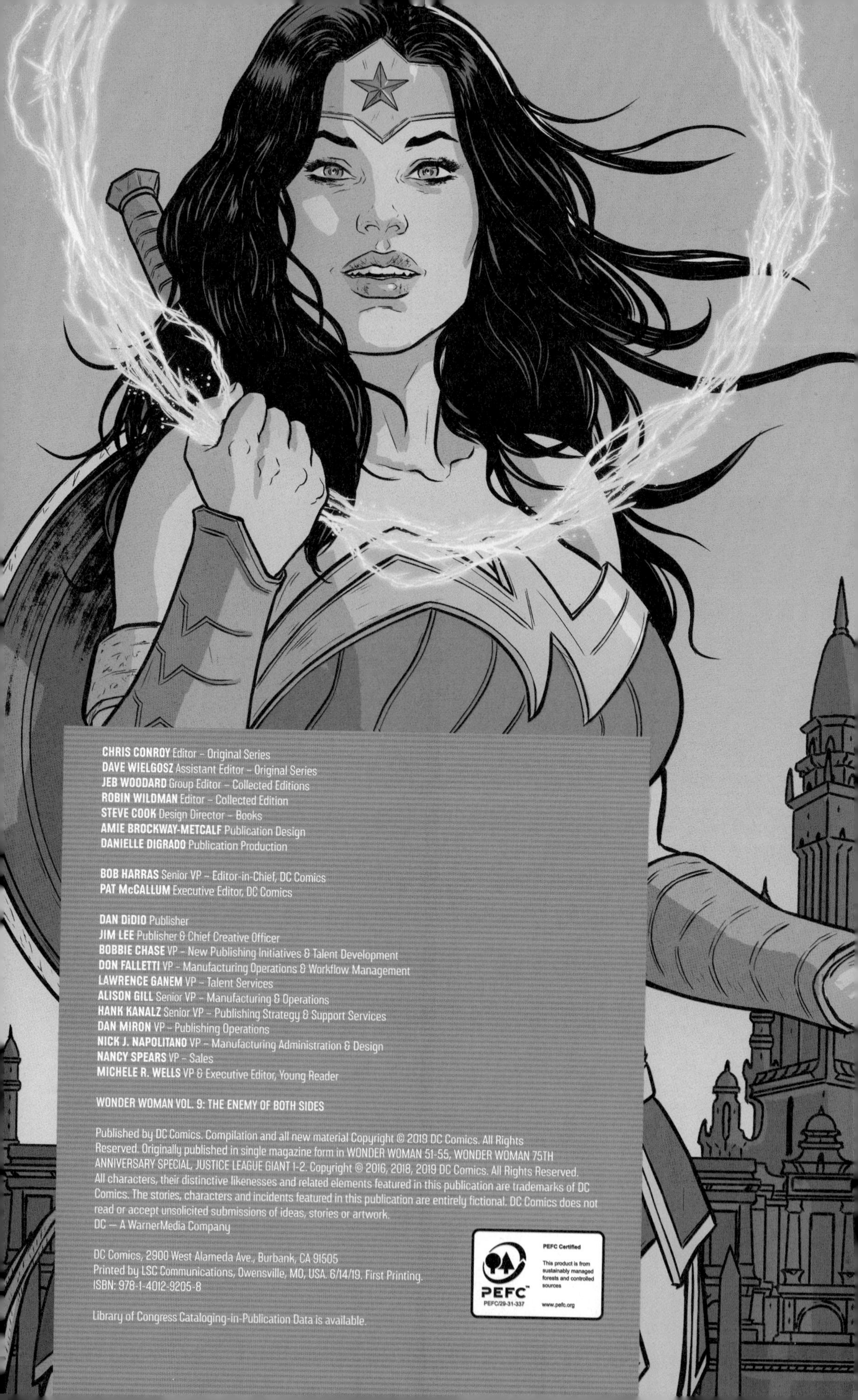

CHRIS CONROY Editor – Original Series
DAVE WIELGOSZ Assistant Editor – Original Series
JEB WOODARD Group Editor – Collected Editions
ROBIN WILDMAN Editor – Collected Edition
STEVE COOK Design Director – Books
AMIE BROCKWAY-METCALF Publication Design
DANIELLE DIGRADO Publication Production

BOB HARRAS Senior VP – Editor-in-Chief, DC Comics
PAT McCALLUM Executive Editor, DC Comics

DAN DiDIO Publisher
JIM LEE Publisher & Chief Creative Officer
BOBBIE CHASE VP – New Publishing Initiatives & Talent Development
DON FALLETTI VP – Manufacturing Operations & Workflow Management
LAWRENCE GANEM VP – Talent Services
ALISON GILL Senior VP – Manufacturing & Operations
HANK KANALZ Senior VP – Publishing Strategy & Support Services
DAN MIRON VP – Publishing Operations
NICK J. NAPOLITANO VP – Manufacturing Administration & Design
NANCY SPEARS VP – Sales
MICHELE R. WELLS VP & Executive Editor, Young Reader

WONDER WOMAN VOL. 9: THE ENEMY OF BOTH SIDES

DC Comics, 2900 West Alameda Ave., Burbank, CA 91505
Printed by LSC Communications, Owensville, MO, USA. 6/14/19. First Printing.
ISBN: 978-1-4012-9205-8

PEFC Certified
This product is from sustainably managed forests and controlled sources
PEFC/29-31-337
www.pefc.org

Library of Congress Cataloging-in-Publication Data is available.

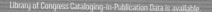

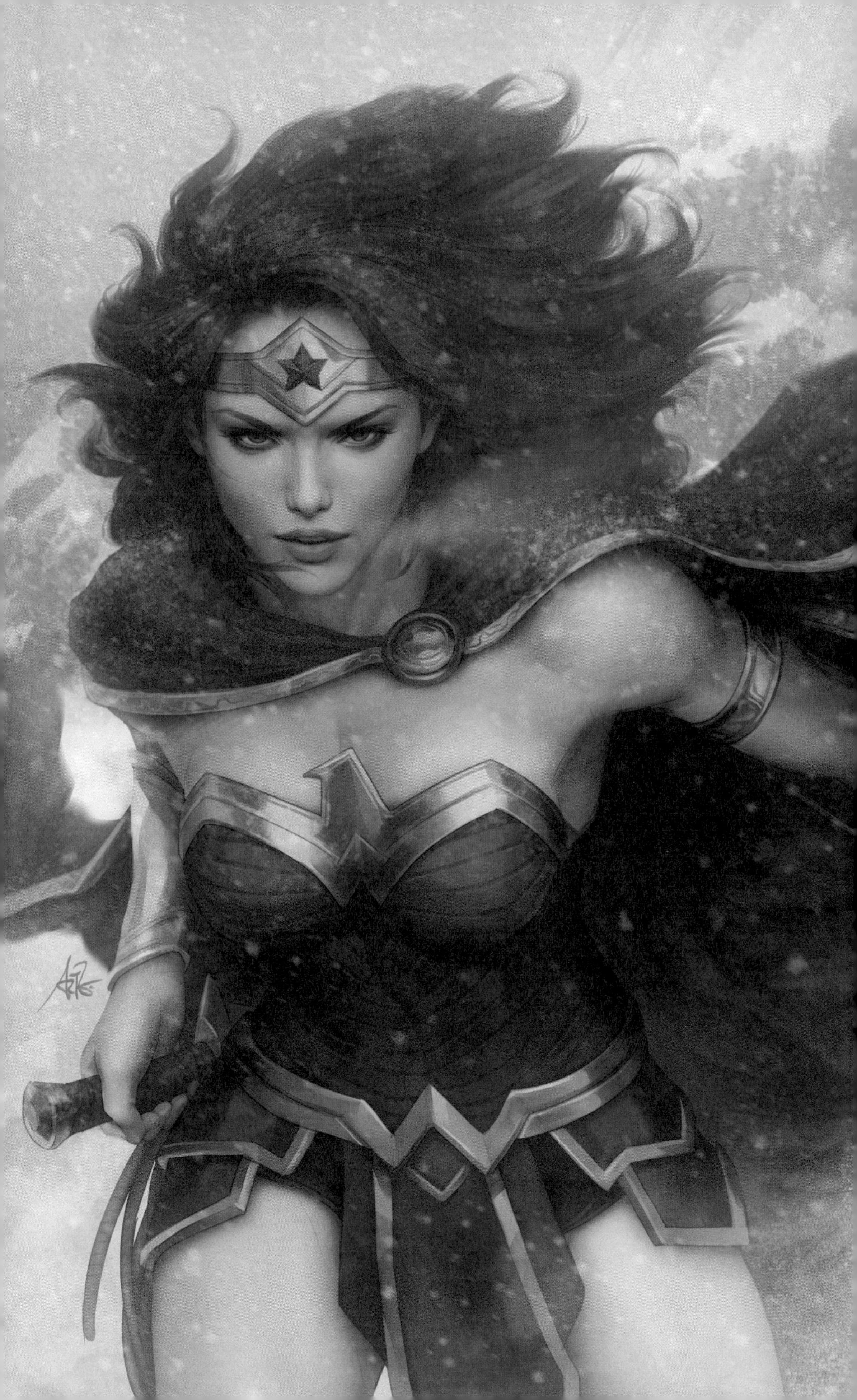

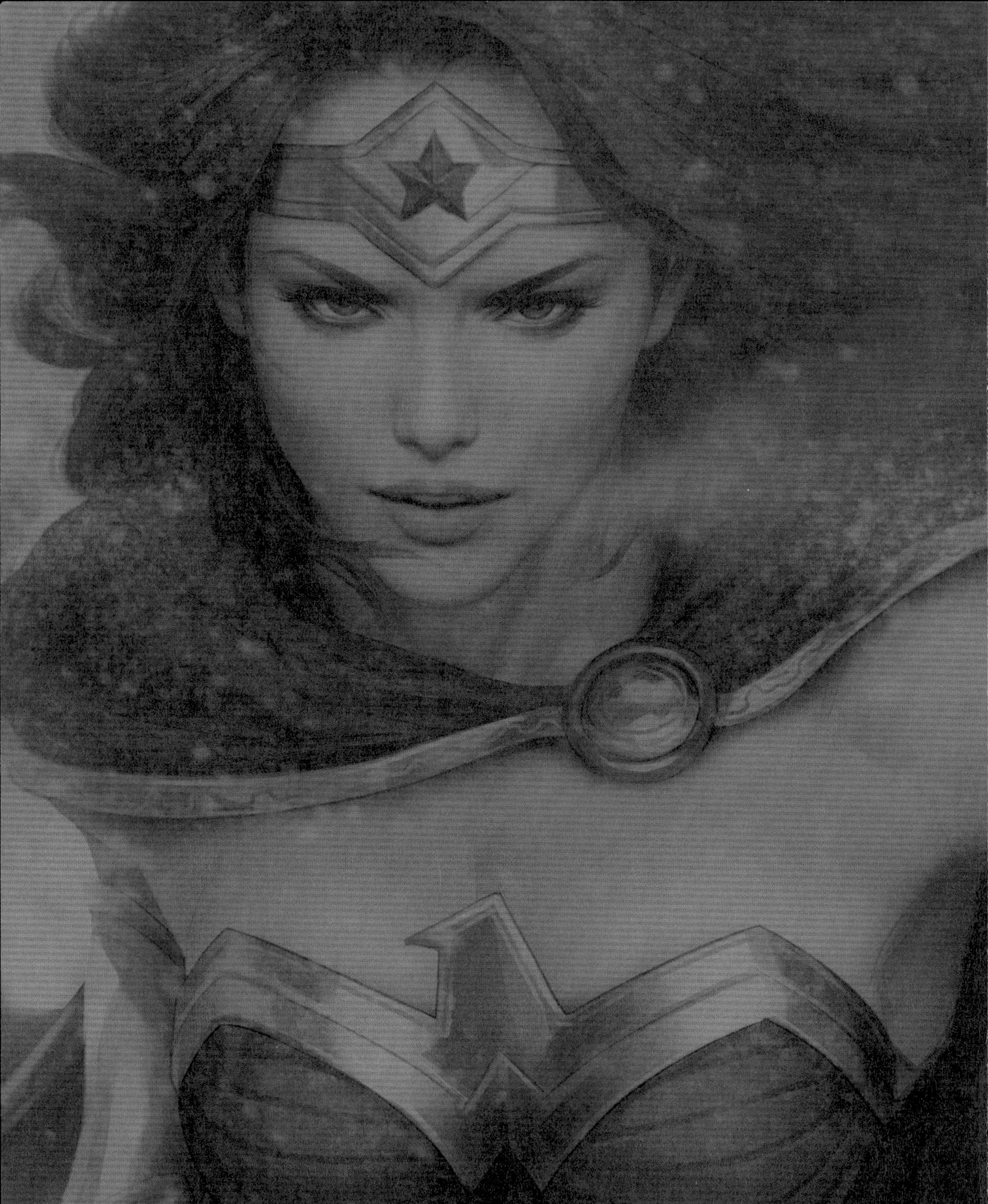

WONDER WOMAN
#51

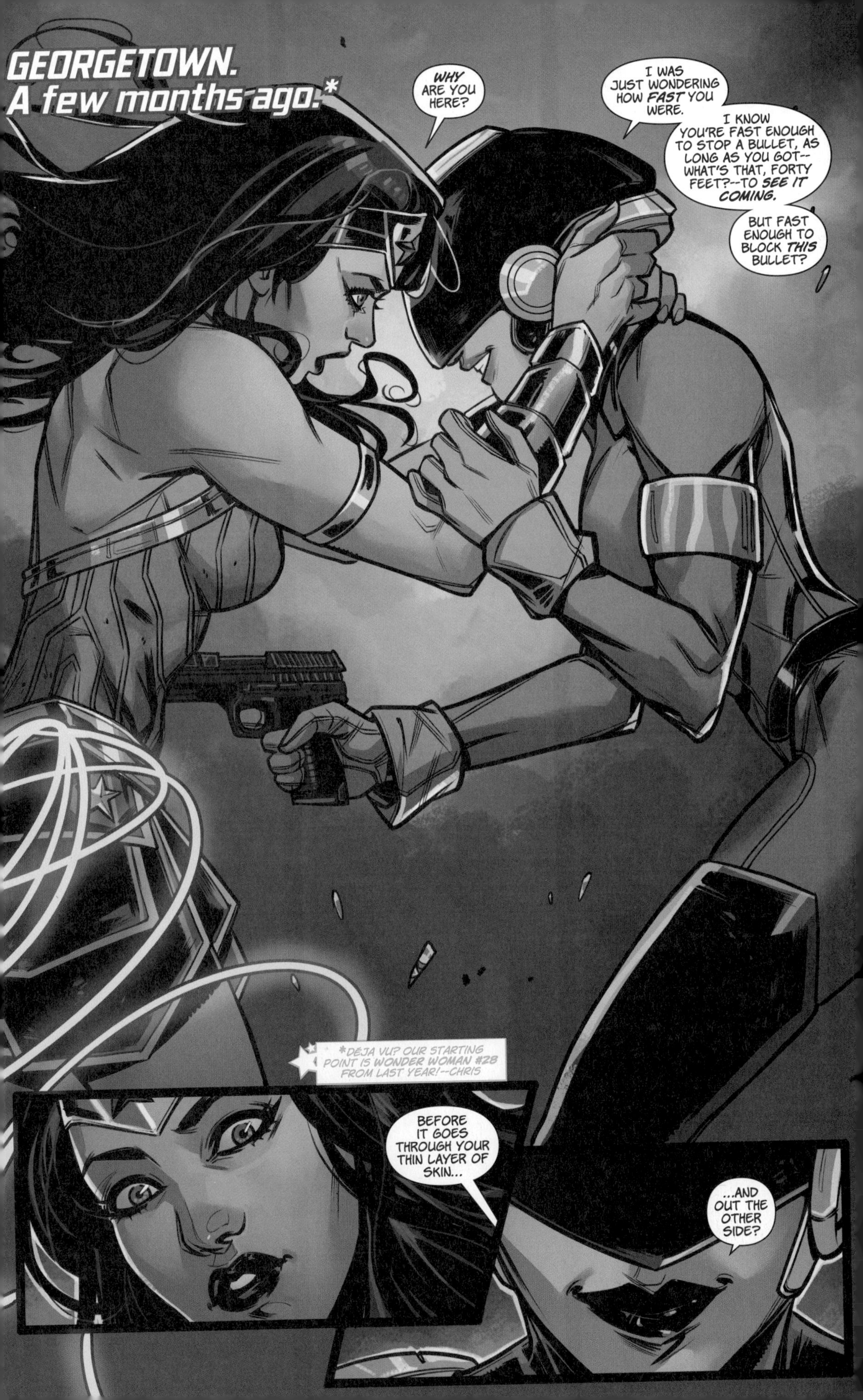
GEORGETOWN.
A few months ago.*
WHY ARE YOU HERE?
I WAS JUST WONDERING HOW FAST YOU WERE.
I KNOW YOU'RE FAST ENOUGH TO STOP A BULLET, AS LONG AS YOU GOT-- WHAT'S THAT, FORTY FEET?--TO SEE IT COMING.
BUT FAST ENOUGH TO BLOCK THIS BULLET?
*DÉJA VU? OUR STARTING POINT IS WONDER WOMAN #28 FROM LAST YEAR!--CHRIS
BEFORE IT GOES THROUGH YOUR THIN LAYER OF SKIN...
...AND OUT THE OTHER SIDE?

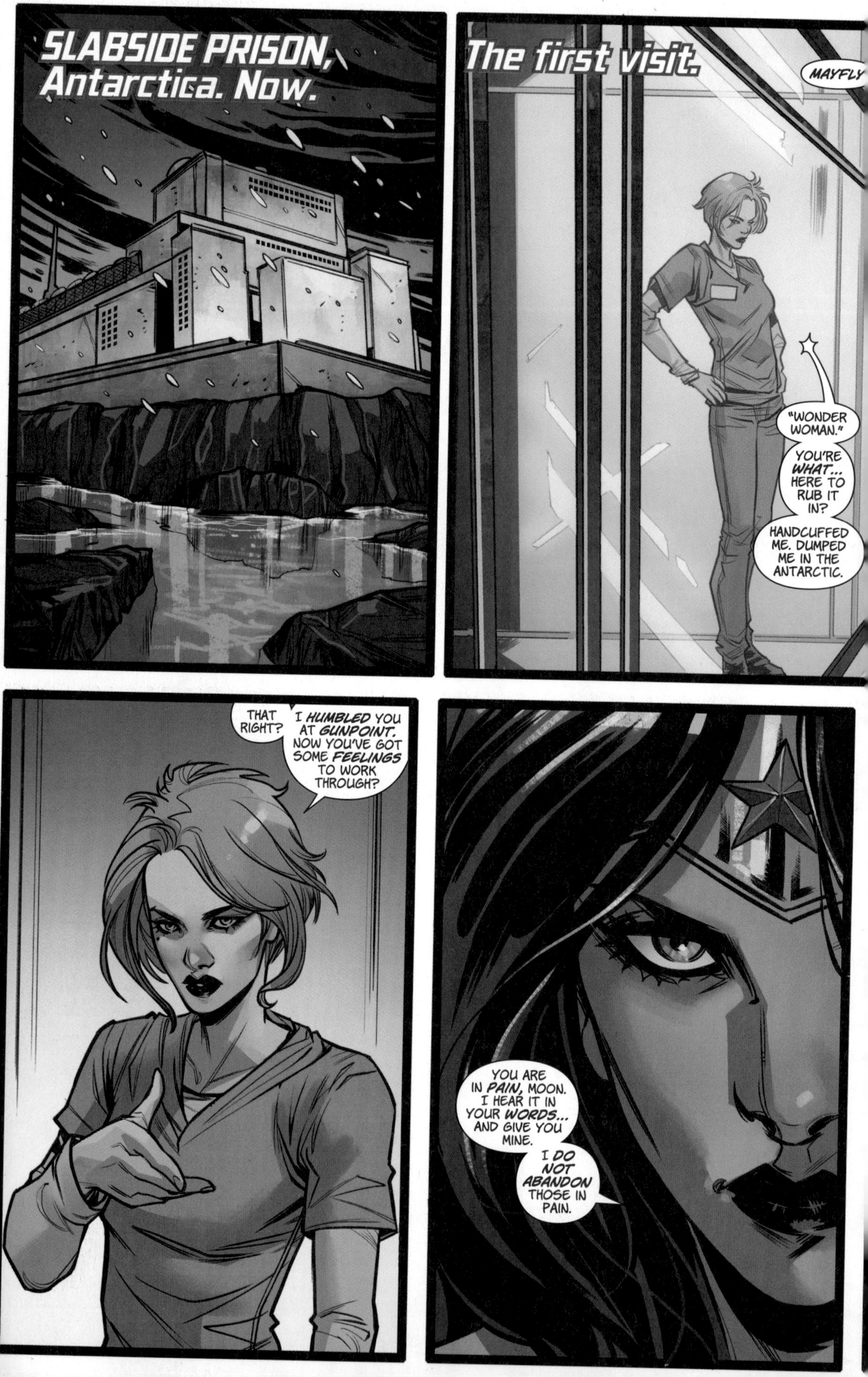
SLABSIDE PRISON, Antarctica. Now.
The first visit.
MAYFLY
"WONDER WOMAN."
YOU'RE WHAT... HERE TO RUB IT IN?
HANDCUFFED ME. DUMPED ME IN THE ANTARCTIC.
THAT RIGHT?
I HUMBLED YOU AT GUNPOINT. NOW YOU'VE GOT SOME FEELINGS TO WORK THROUGH?
YOU ARE IN PAIN, MOON. I HEAR IT IN YOUR WORDS... AND GIVE YOU MINE.
I DO NOT ABANDON THOSE IN PAIN.

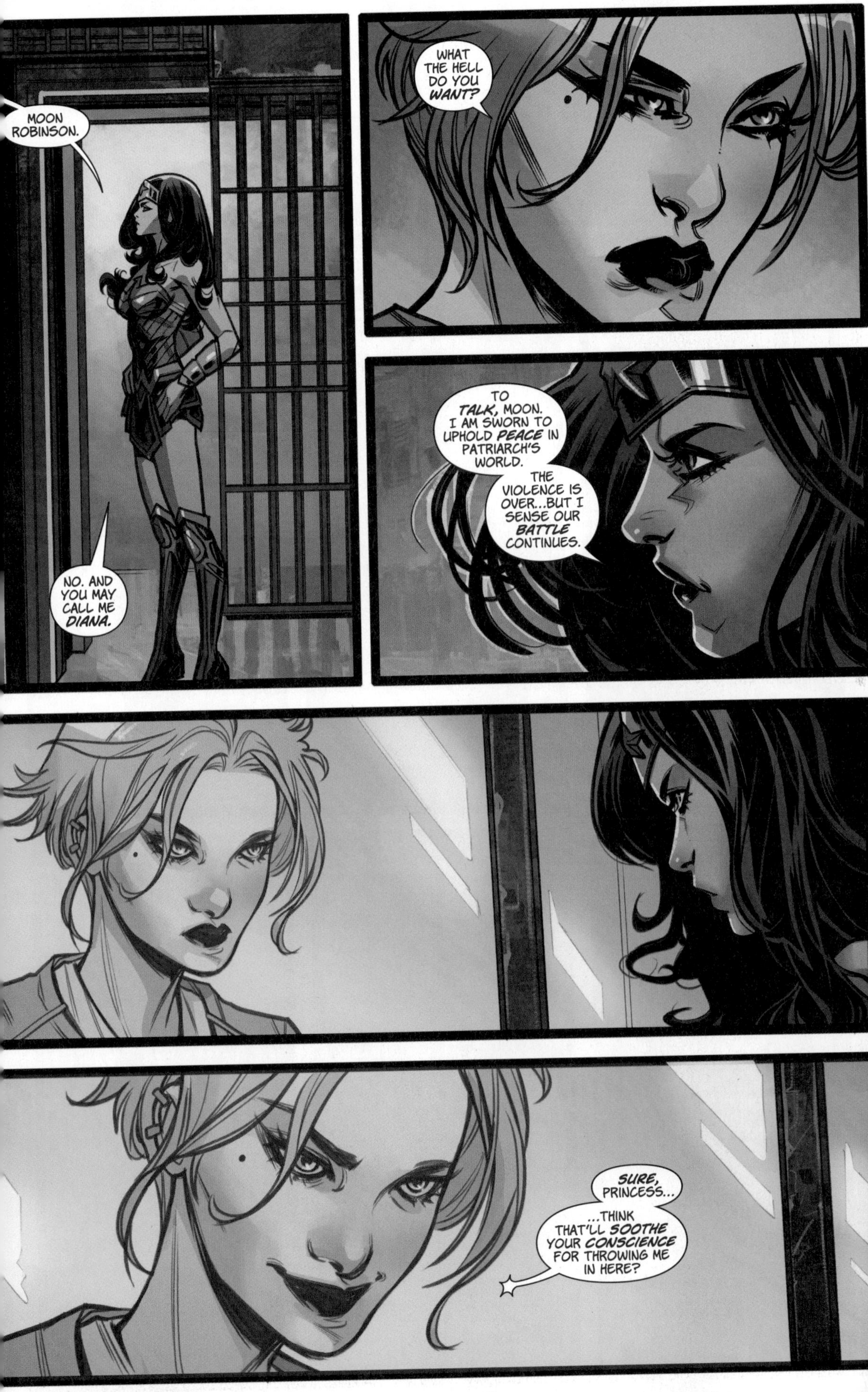
MOON ROBINSON.
WHAT THE HELL DO YOU *WANT?*
NO. AND YOU MAY CALL ME *DIANA.*
TO *TALK,* MOON. I AM SWORN TO UPHOLD *PEACE* IN PATRIARCH'S WORLD.
THE VIOLENCE IS OVER...BUT I SENSE OUR *BATTLE* CONTINUES.
SURE, PRINCESS...
...THINK THAT'LL *SOOTHE* YOUR *CONSCIENCE* FOR THROWING ME IN HERE?

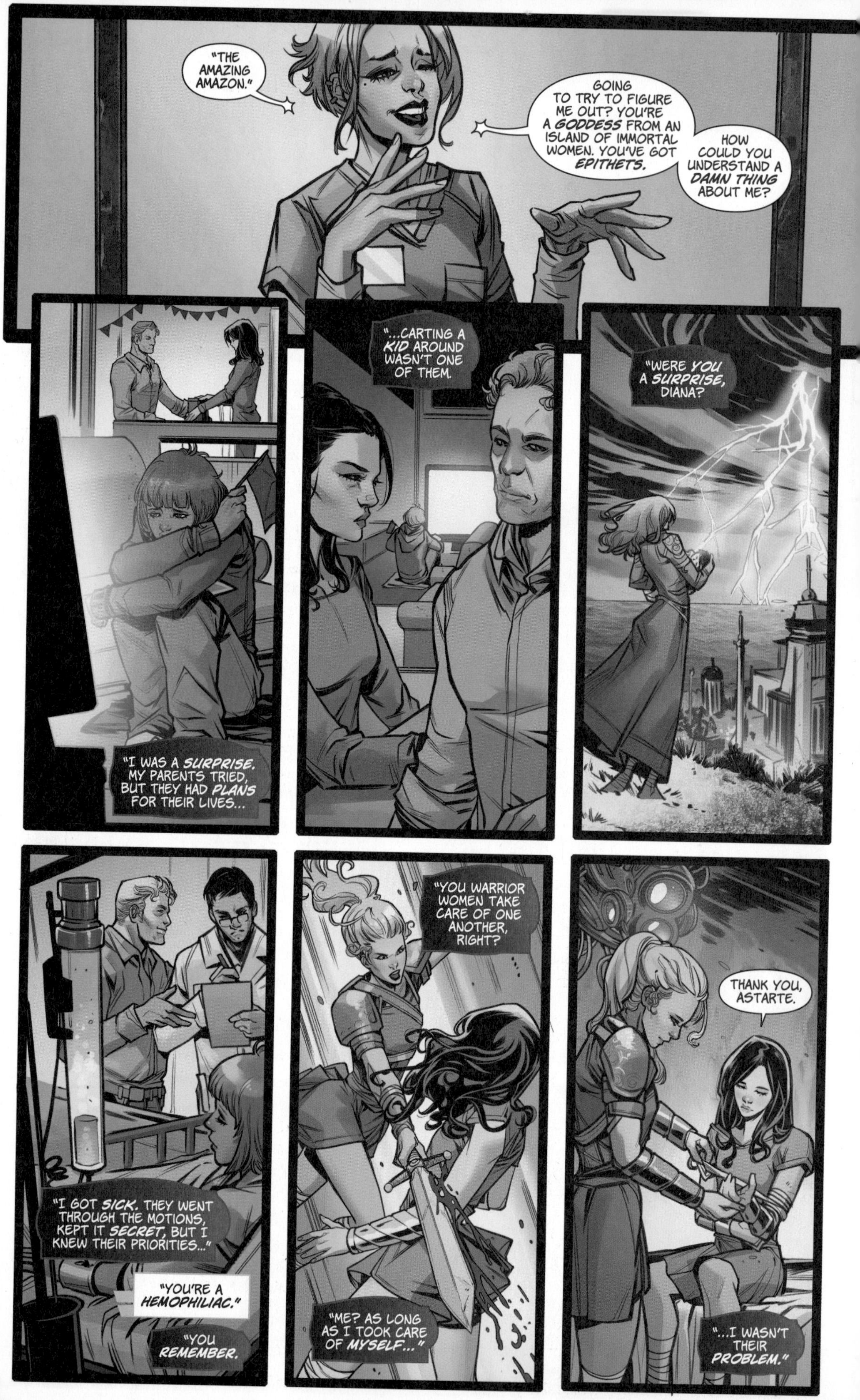
"THE AMAZING AMAZON."
GOING TO TRY TO FIGURE ME OUT? YOU'RE A GODDESS FROM AN ISLAND OF IMMORTAL WOMEN. YOU'VE GOT EPITHETS.
HOW COULD YOU UNDERSTAND A DAMN THING ABOUT ME?
"I WAS A SURPRISE. MY PARENTS TRIED, BUT THEY HAD PLANS FOR THEIR LIVES...
"...CARTING A KID AROUND WASN'T ONE OF THEM.
"WERE YOU A SURPRISE, DIANA?
"I GOT SICK. THEY WENT THROUGH THE MOTIONS, KEPT IT SECRET, BUT I KNEW THEIR PRIORITIES..."
"YOU'RE A HEMOPHILIAC."
"YOU REMEMBER.
"YOU WARRIOR WOMEN TAKE CARE OF ONE ANOTHER, RIGHT?
"ME? AS LONG AS I TOOK CARE OF MYSELF..."
THANK YOU, ASTARTE.
"...I WASN'T THEIR PROBLEM."

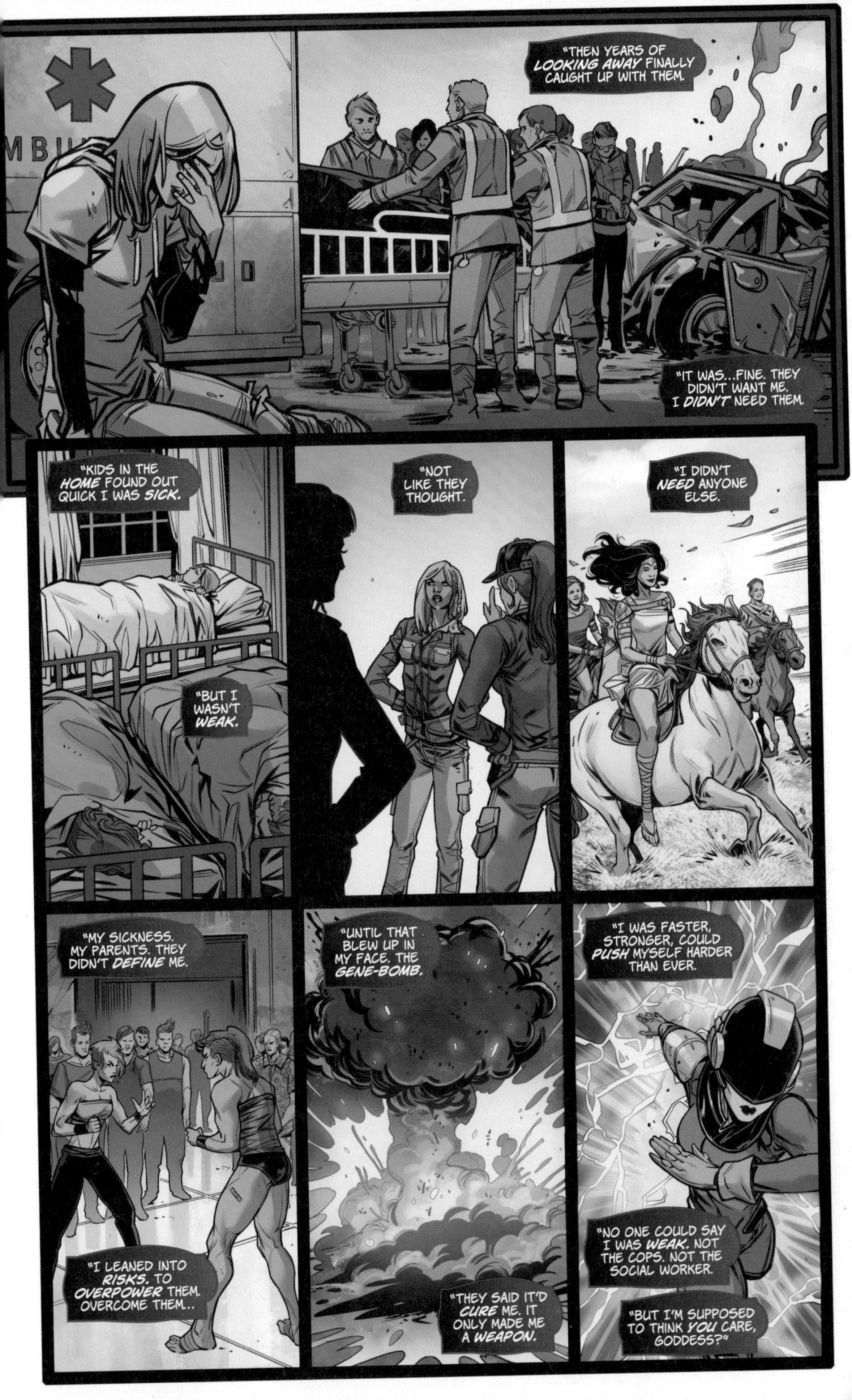
"THEN YEARS OF LOOKING AWAY FINALLY CAUGHT UP WITH THEM.
"IT WAS...FINE. THEY DIDN'T WANT ME. I DIDN'T NEED THEM.
"KIDS IN THE HOME FOUND OUT QUICK I WAS SICK.
"BUT I WASN'T WEAK.
"NOT LIKE THEY THOUGHT.
"I DIDN'T NEED ANYONE ELSE.
"MY SICKNESS. MY PARENTS. THEY DIDN'T DEFINE ME.
"I LEANED INTO RISKS. TO OVERPOWER THEM. OVERCOME THEM...
"UNTIL THAT BLEW UP IN MY FACE. THE GENE-BOMB.
"THEY SAID IT'D CURE ME. IT ONLY MADE ME A WEAPON.
"I WAS FASTER, STRONGER, COULD PUSH MYSELF HARDER THAN EVER.
"NO ONE COULD SAY I WAS WEAK. NOT THE COPS. NOT THE SOCIAL WORKER.
"BUT I'M SUPPOSED TO THINK YOU CARE, GODDESS?"

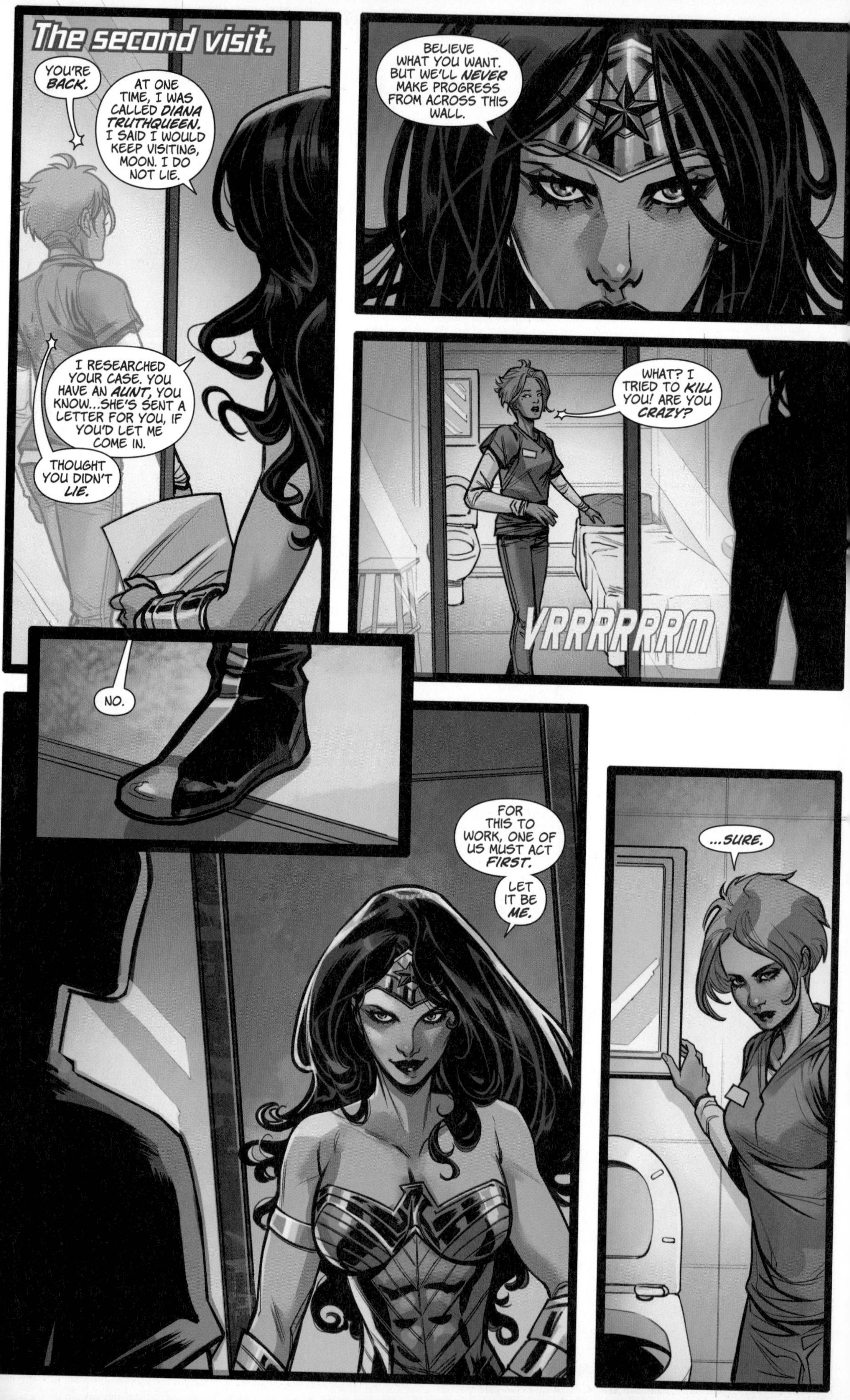

The second visit.
YOU'RE BACK.
AT ONE TIME, I WAS CALLED DIANA TRUTHQUEEN. I SAID I WOULD KEEP VISITING, MOON. I DO NOT LIE.
BELIEVE WHAT YOU WANT. BUT WE'LL NEVER MAKE PROGRESS FROM ACROSS THIS WALL.
I RESEARCHED YOUR CASE. YOU HAVE AN AUNT, YOU KNOW...SHE'S SENT A LETTER FOR YOU, IF YOU'D LET ME COME IN.
THOUGHT YOU DIDN'T LIE.
NO.
WHAT? I TRIED TO KILL YOU! ARE YOU CRAZY?
VRRRRRRM
FOR THIS TO WORK, ONE OF US MUST ACT FIRST.
LET IT BE ME.
...SURE.

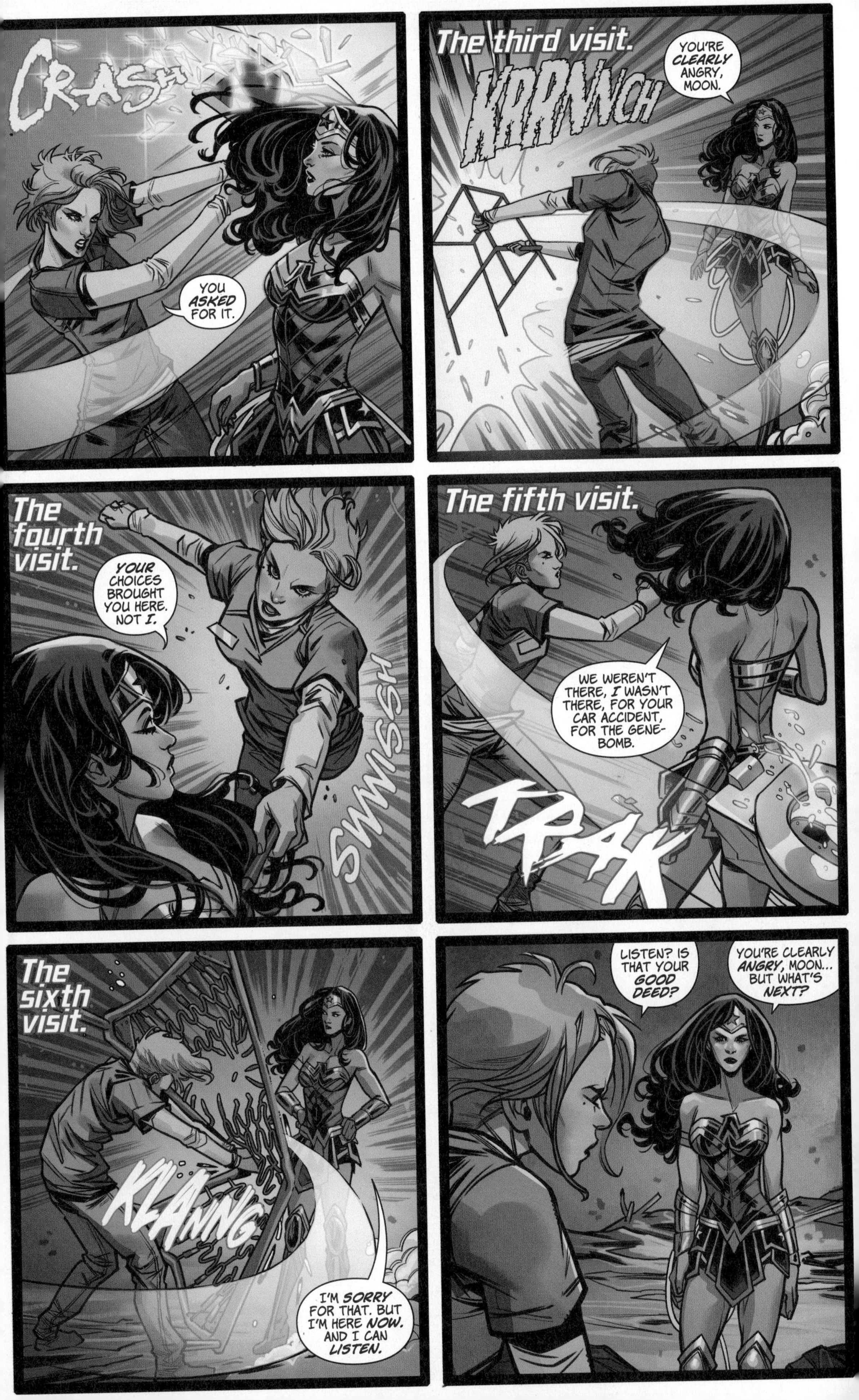
CRASH
YOU ASKED FOR IT.
The third visit.
KRRNNCH
YOU'RE CLEARLY ANGRY, MOON.
The fourth visit.
YOUR CHOICES BROUGHT YOU HERE. NOT I.
SWIISSH
The fifth visit.
WE WEREN'T THERE, I WASN'T THERE, FOR YOUR CAR ACCIDENT, FOR THE GENE-BOMB.
TRAK
The sixth visit.
KLANNG
I'M SORRY FOR THAT. BUT I'M HERE NOW. AND I CAN LISTEN.
LISTEN? IS THAT YOUR GOOD DEED?
YOU'RE CLEARLY ANGRY, MOON... BUT WHAT'S NEXT?

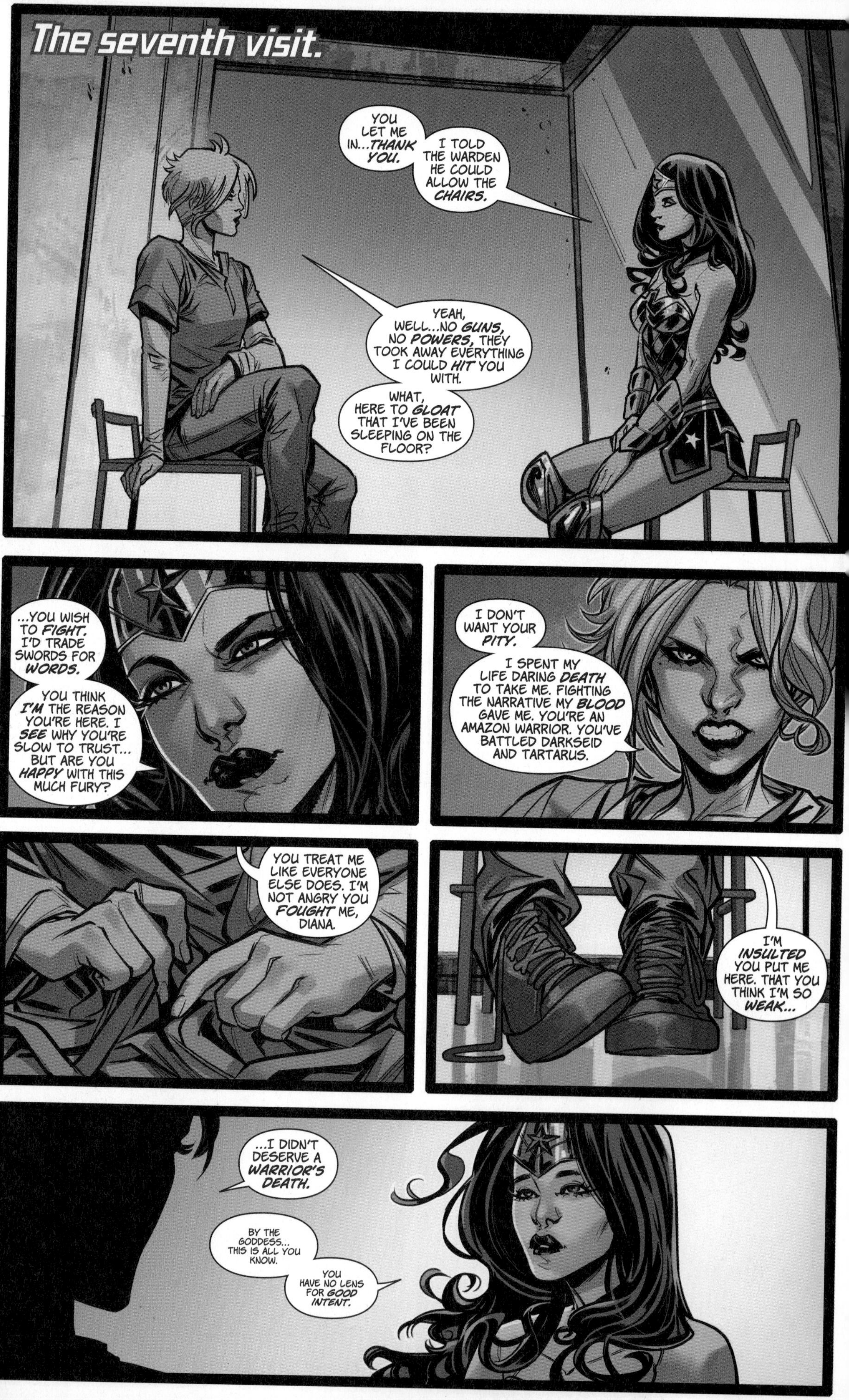
The seventh visit.
YOU LET ME IN...THANK YOU.
I TOLD THE WARDEN HE COULD ALLOW THE CHAIRS.
YEAH, WELL...NO GUNS, NO POWERS, THEY TOOK AWAY EVERYTHING I COULD HIT YOU WITH.
WHAT, HERE TO GLOAT THAT I'VE BEEN SLEEPING ON THE FLOOR?
...YOU WISH TO FIGHT. I'D TRADE SWORDS FOR WORDS.
YOU THINK I'M THE REASON YOU'RE HERE. I SEE WHY YOU'RE SLOW TO TRUST... BUT ARE YOU HAPPY WITH THIS MUCH FURY?
I DON'T WANT YOUR PITY.
I SPENT MY LIFE DARING DEATH TO TAKE ME. FIGHTING THE NARRATIVE MY BLOOD GAVE ME. YOU'RE AN AMAZON WARRIOR. YOU'VE BATTLED DARKSEID AND TARTARUS.
YOU TREAT ME LIKE EVERYONE ELSE DOES. I'M NOT ANGRY YOU FOUGHT ME, DIANA.
I'M INSULTED YOU PUT ME HERE. THAT YOU THINK I'M SO WEAK...
...I DIDN'T DESERVE A WARRIOR'S DEATH.
BY THE GODDESS... THIS IS ALL YOU KNOW.
YOU HAVE NO LENS FOR GOOD INTENT.

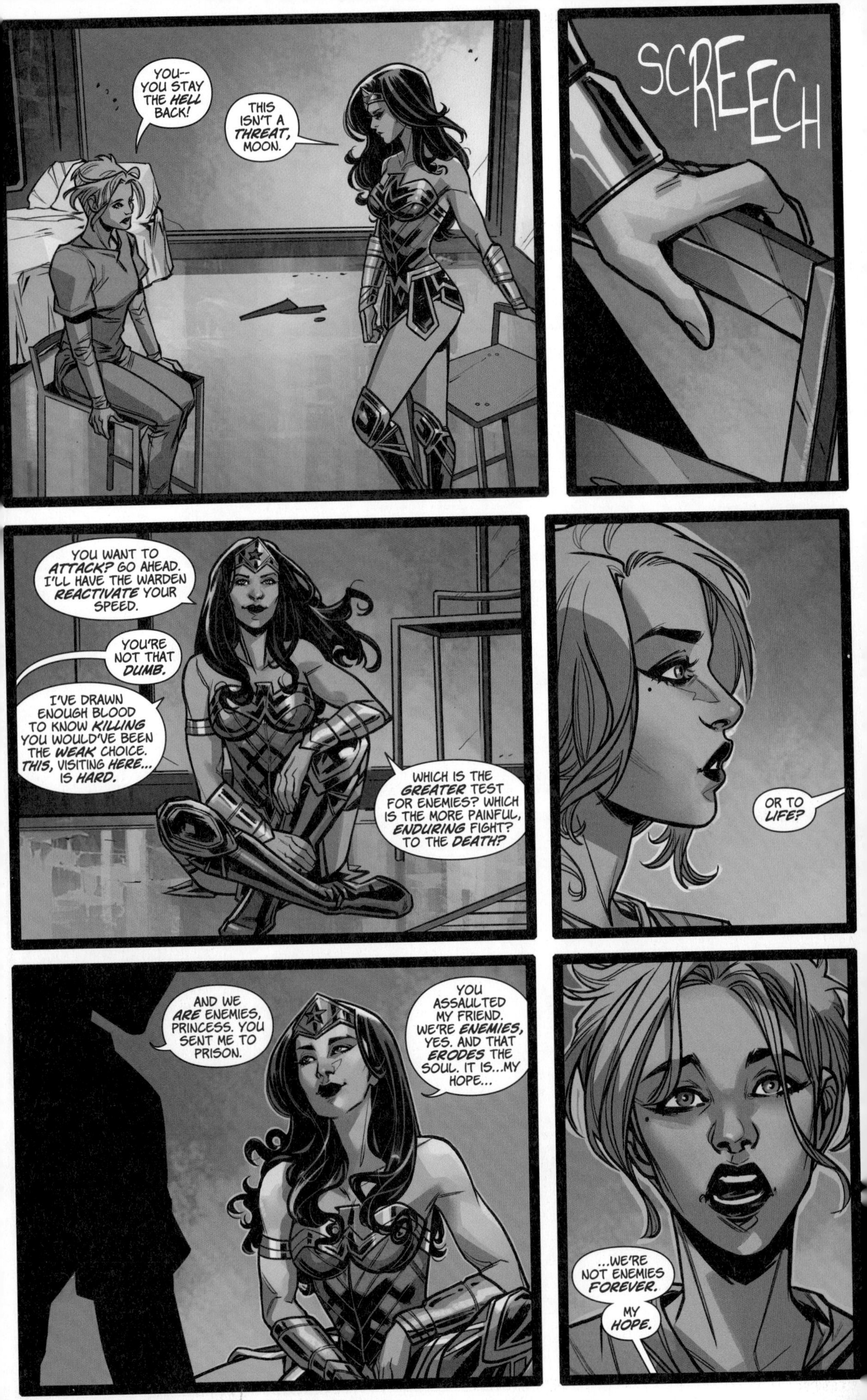
YOU--
YOU STAY THE HELL BACK!
THIS ISN'T A THREAT, MOON.
SCREEECH
YOU WANT TO ATTACK? GO AHEAD. I'LL HAVE THE WARDEN REACTIVATE YOUR SPEED.
YOU'RE NOT THAT DUMB.
I'VE DRAWN ENOUGH BLOOD TO KNOW KILLING YOU WOULD'VE BEEN THE WEAK CHOICE. THIS, VISITING HERE... IS HARD.
WHICH IS THE GREATER TEST FOR ENEMIES? WHICH IS THE MORE PAINFUL, ENDURING FIGHT? TO THE DEATH?
OR TO LIFE?
AND WE ARE ENEMIES, PRINCESS. YOU SENT ME TO PRISON.
YOU ASSAULTED MY FRIEND. WE'RE ENEMIES, YES. AND THAT ERODES THE SOUL. IT IS...MY HOPE...
...WE'RE NOT ENEMIES FOREVER.
MY HOPE.

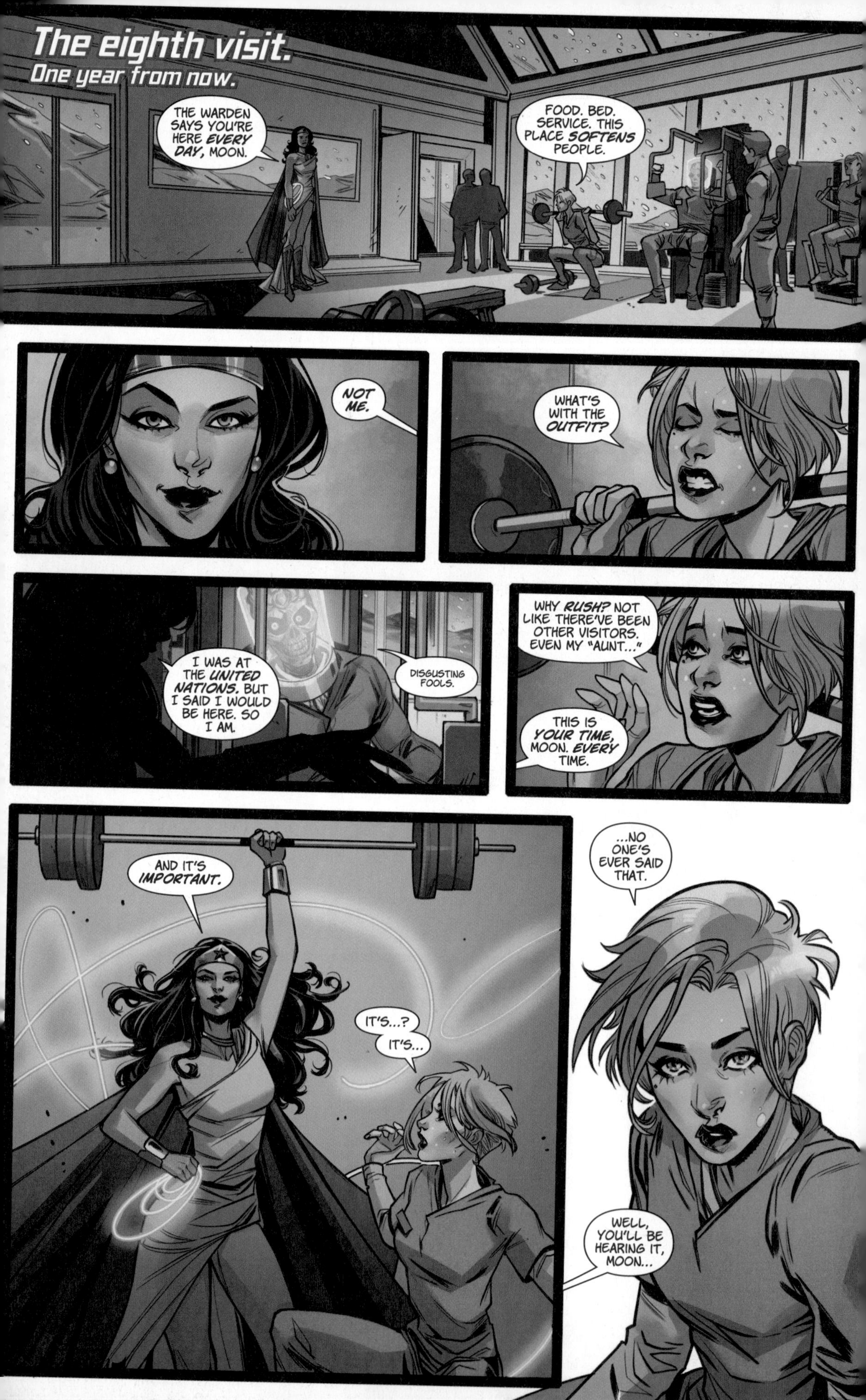
The eighth visit.
One year from now.
THE WARDEN SAYS YOU'RE HERE EVERY DAY, MOON.
FOOD. BED. SERVICE. THIS PLACE SOFTENS PEOPLE.
NOT ME.
WHAT'S WITH THE OUTFIT?
I WAS AT THE UNITED NATIONS. BUT I SAID I WOULD BE HERE. SO I AM.
DISGUSTING FOOLS.
WHY RUSH? NOT LIKE THERE'VE BEEN OTHER VISITORS. EVEN MY "AUNT..."
THIS IS YOUR TIME, MOON. EVERY TIME.
AND IT'S IMPORTANT.
IT'S...?
IT'S...
...NO ONE'S EVER SAID THAT.
WELL, YOU'LL BE HEARING IT, MOON...

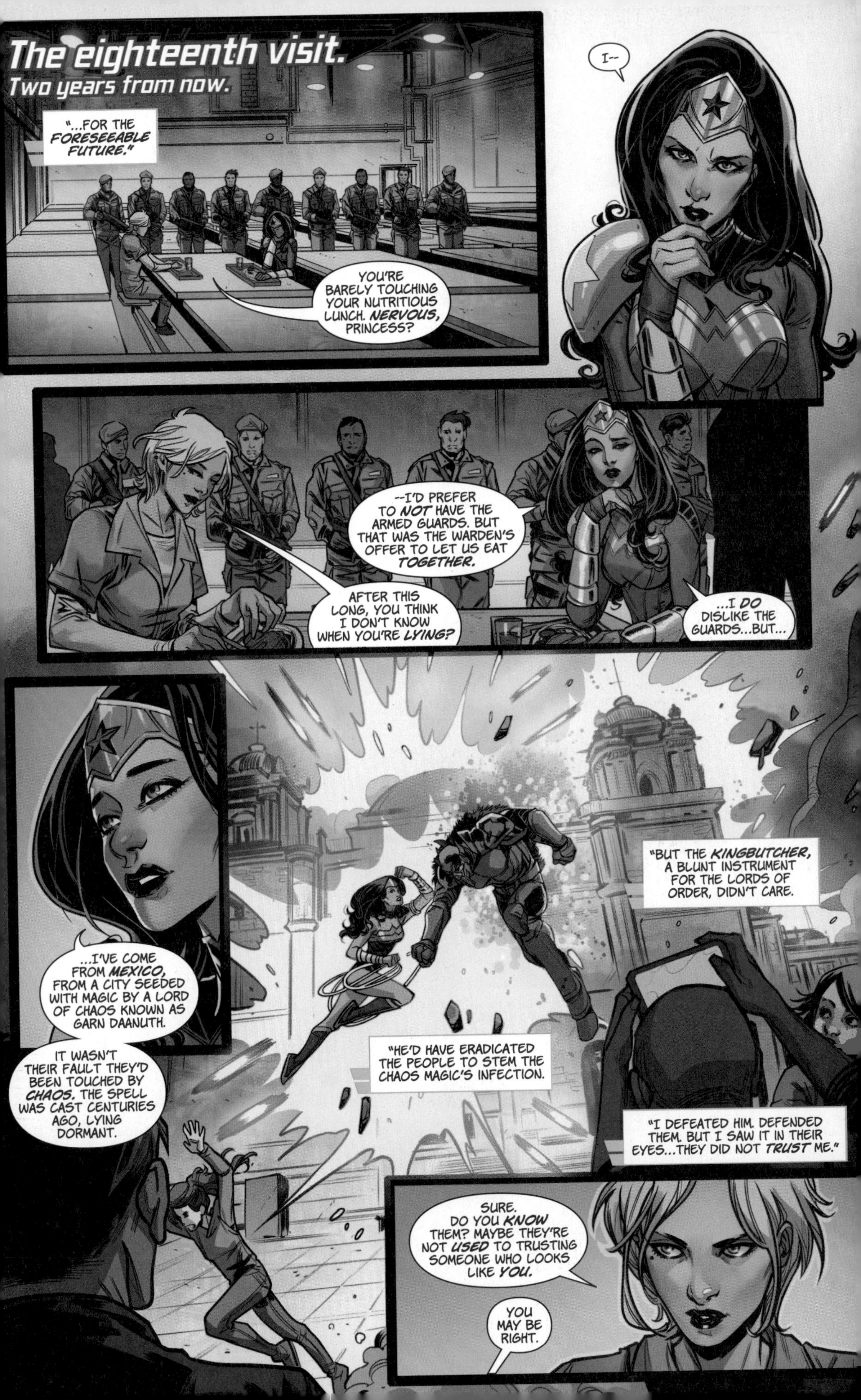

The eighteenth visit.
Two years from now.
"...FOR THE FORESEEABLE FUTURE."
YOU'RE BARELY TOUCHING YOUR NUTRITIOUS LUNCH. NERVOUS, PRINCESS?
I--
--I'D PREFER TO NOT HAVE THE ARMED GUARDS. BUT THAT WAS THE WARDEN'S OFFER TO LET US EAT TOGETHER.
AFTER THIS LONG, YOU THINK I DON'T KNOW WHEN YOU'RE LYING?
...I DO DISLIKE THE GUARDS...BUT...
...I'VE COME FROM MEXICO, FROM A CITY SEEDED WITH MAGIC BY A LORD OF CHAOS KNOWN AS GARN DAANUTH.
IT WASN'T THEIR FAULT THEY'D BEEN TOUCHED BY CHAOS. THE SPELL WAS CAST CENTURIES AGO, LYING DORMANT.
"BUT THE KINGBUTCHER, A BLUNT INSTRUMENT FOR THE LORDS OF ORDER, DIDN'T CARE.
"HE'D HAVE ERADICATED THE PEOPLE TO STEM THE CHAOS MAGIC'S INFECTION.
"I DEFEATED HIM. DEFENDED THEM. BUT I SAW IT IN THEIR EYES...THEY DID NOT TRUST ME."
SURE. DO YOU KNOW THEM? MAYBE THEY'RE NOT USED TO TRUSTING SOMEONE WHO LOOKS LIKE YOU.
YOU MAY BE RIGHT.

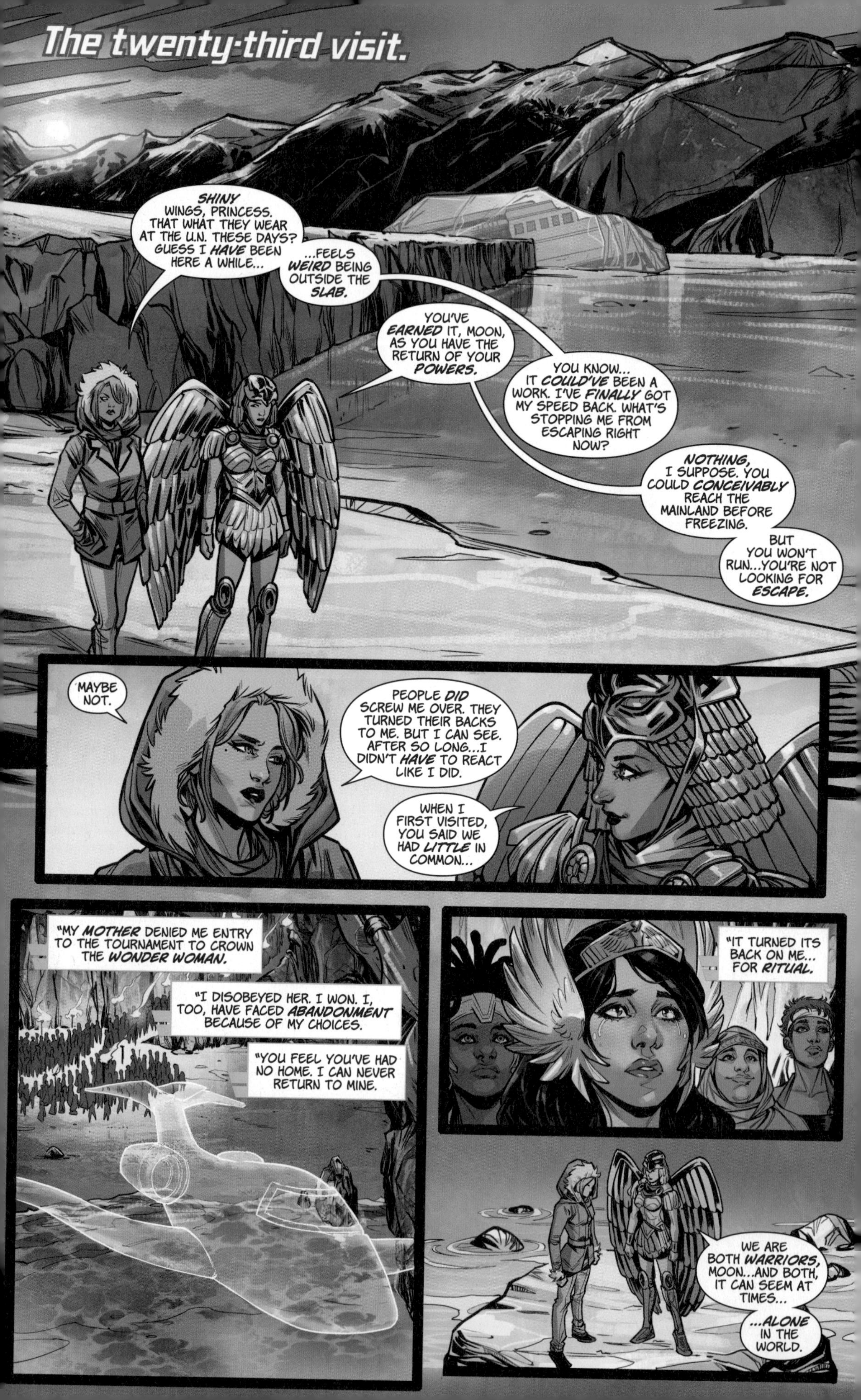
The twenty-third visit.
SHINY WINGS, PRINCESS. THAT WHAT THEY WEAR AT THE U.N. THESE DAYS? GUESS I HAVE BEEN HERE A WHILE...
...FEELS WEIRD BEING OUTSIDE THE SLAB.
YOU'VE EARNED IT, MOON, AS YOU HAVE THE RETURN OF YOUR POWERS.
YOU KNOW... IT COULD'VE BEEN A WORK. I'VE FINALLY GOT MY SPEED BACK. WHAT'S STOPPING ME FROM ESCAPING RIGHT NOW?
NOTHING, I SUPPOSE. YOU COULD CONCEIVABLY REACH THE MAINLAND BEFORE FREEZING.
BUT YOU WON'T RUN...YOU'RE NOT LOOKING FOR ESCAPE.
MAYBE NOT.
PEOPLE DID SCREW ME OVER. THEY TURNED THEIR BACKS TO ME. BUT I CAN SEE. AFTER SO LONG...I DIDN'T HAVE TO REACT LIKE I DID.
WHEN I FIRST VISITED, YOU SAID WE HAD LITTLE IN COMMON...
"MY MOTHER DENIED ME ENTRY TO THE TOURNAMENT TO CROWN THE WONDER WOMAN.
"I DISOBEYED HER. I WON. I, TOO, HAVE FACED ABANDONMENT BECAUSE OF MY CHOICES.
"YOU FEEL YOU'VE HAD NO HOME. I CAN NEVER RETURN TO MINE.
"IT TURNED ITS BACK ON ME... FOR RITUAL.
WE ARE BOTH WARRIORS, MOON...AND BOTH, IT CAN SEEM AT TIMES...
...ALONE IN THE WORLD.

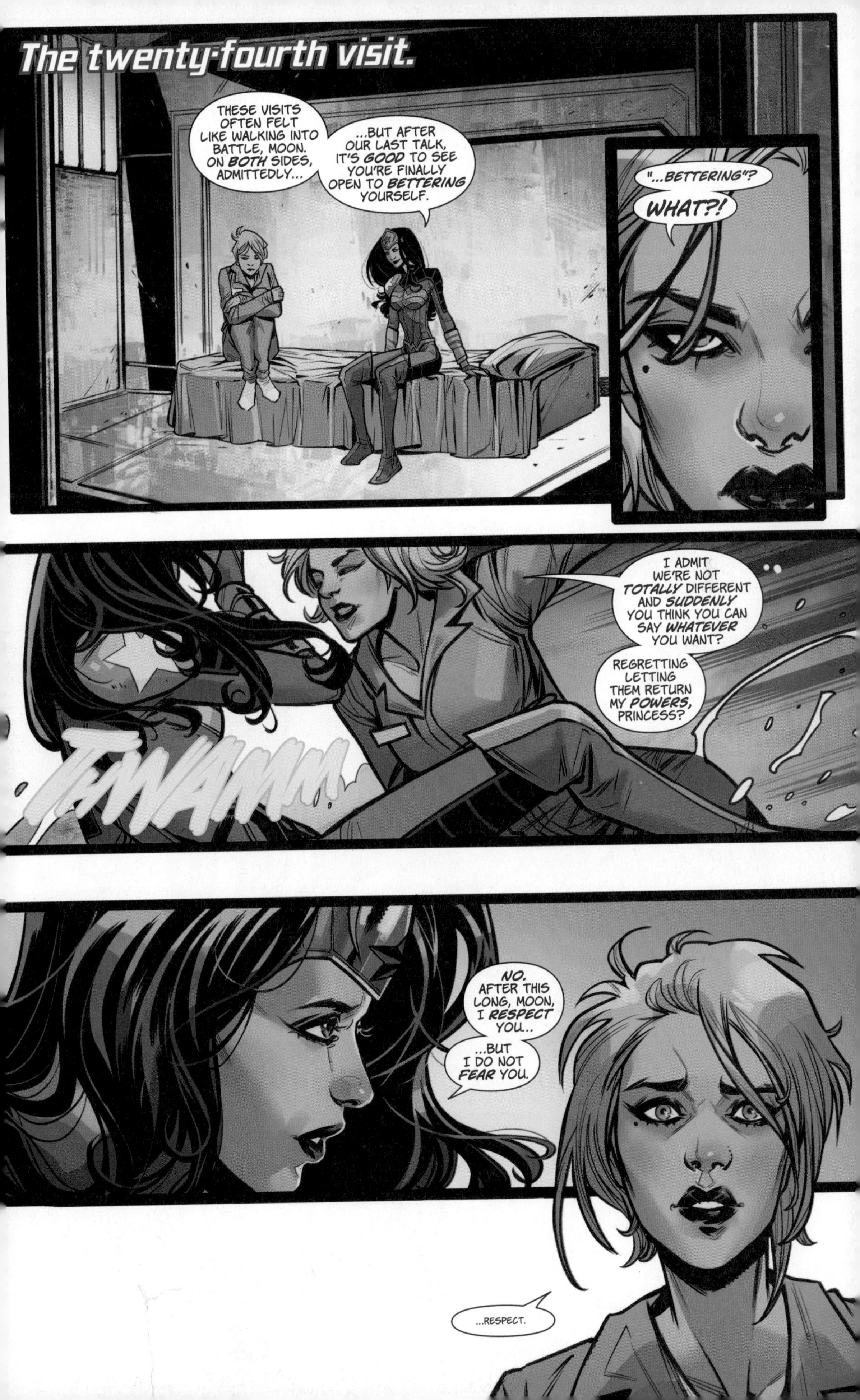
The twenty-fourth visit.
THESE VISITS OFTEN FELT LIKE WALKING INTO BATTLE, MOON. ON BOTH SIDES, ADMITTEDLY...
...BUT AFTER OUR LAST TALK, IT'S GOOD TO SEE YOU'RE FINALLY OPEN TO BETTERING YOURSELF.
"...BETTERING"?
WHAT?!
I ADMIT WE'RE NOT TOTALLY DIFFERENT AND SUDDENLY YOU THINK YOU CAN SAY WHATEVER YOU WANT?
REGRETTING LETTING THEM RETURN MY POWERS, PRINCESS?
THWAMM
NO. AFTER THIS LONG, MOON, I RESPECT YOU...
...BUT I DO NOT FEAR YOU.
...RESPECT.

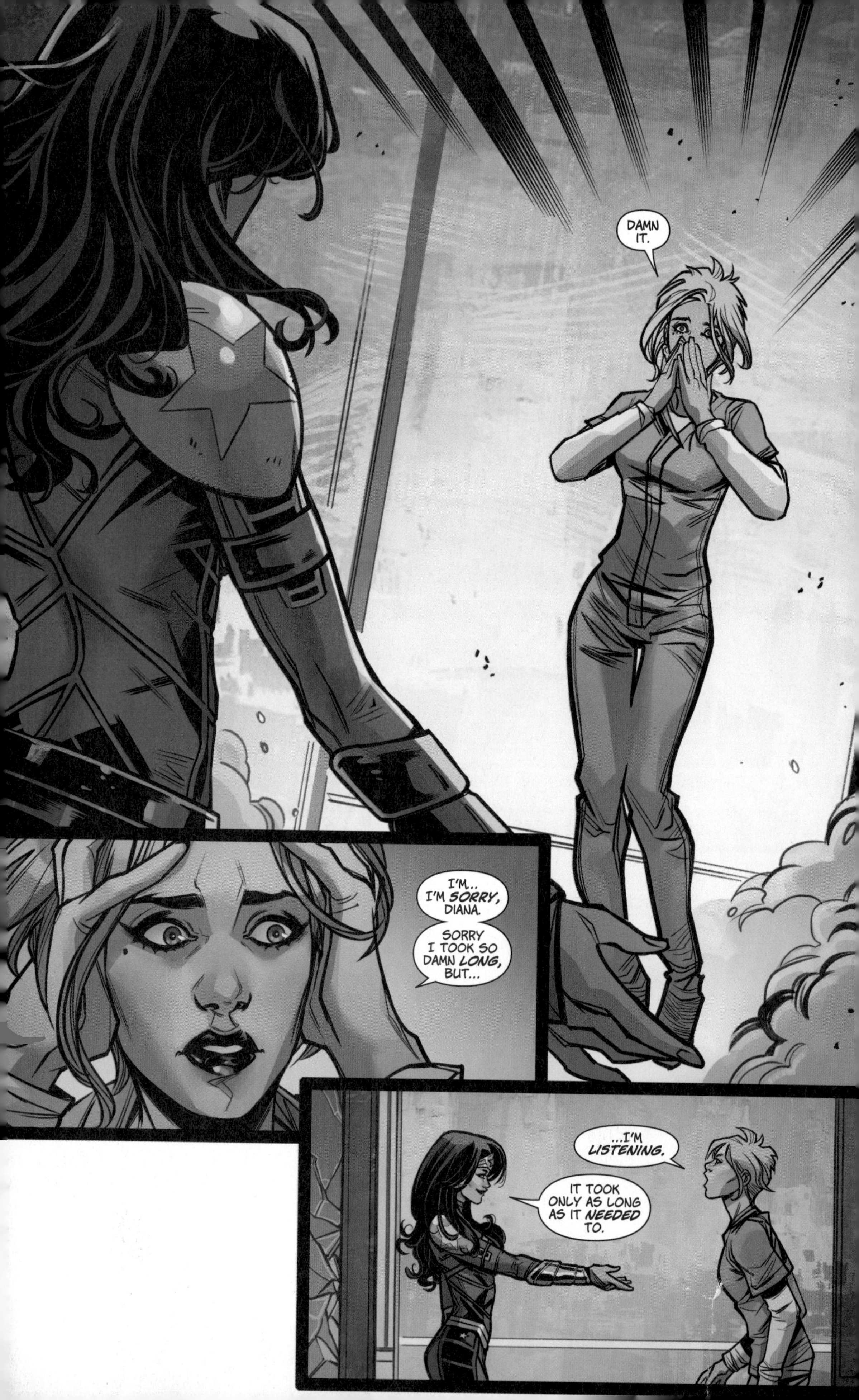
DAMN IT.
I'M... I'M SORRY, DIANA.
SORRY I TOOK SO DAMN LONG, BUT...
...I'M LISTENING.
IT TOOK ONLY AS LONG AS IT NEEDED TO.

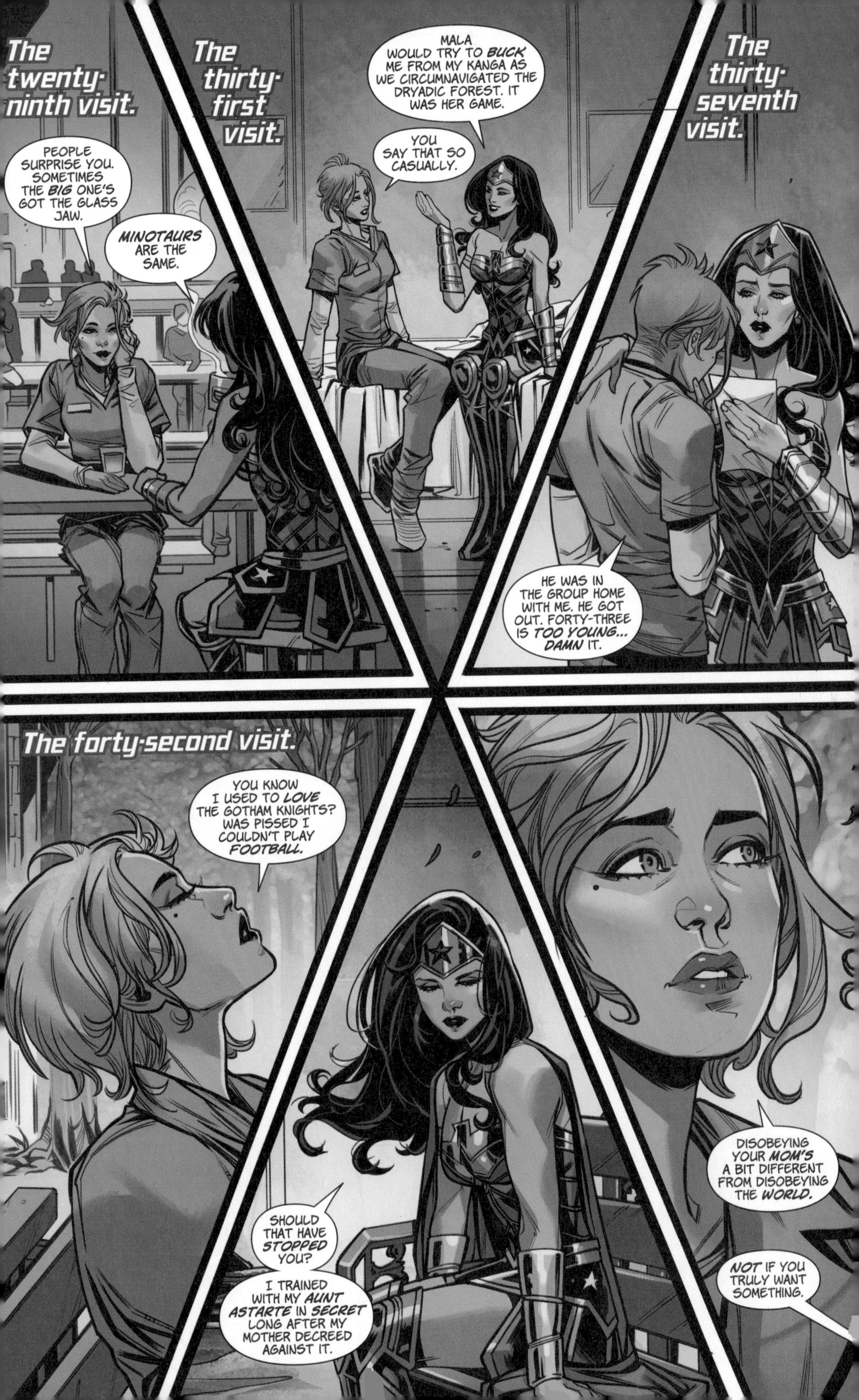
The twenty-ninth visit.
PEOPLE SURPRISE YOU. SOMETIMES THE BIG ONE'S GOT THE GLASS JAW.
MINOTAURS ARE THE SAME.
The thirty-first visit.
YOU SAY THAT SO CASUALLY.
MALA WOULD TRY TO BUCK ME FROM MY KANGA AS WE CIRCUMNAVIGATED THE DRYADIC FOREST. IT WAS HER GAME.
The thirty-seventh visit.
HE WAS IN THE GROUP HOME WITH ME. HE GOT OUT. FORTY-THREE IS TOO YOUNG... DAMN IT.
The forty-second visit.
YOU KNOW I USED TO LOVE THE GOTHAM KNIGHTS? WAS PISSED I COULDN'T PLAY FOOTBALL.
SHOULD THAT HAVE STOPPED YOU?
I TRAINED WITH MY AUNT ASTARTE IN SECRET LONG AFTER MY MOTHER DECREED AGAINST IT.
DISOBEYING YOUR MOM'S A BIT DIFFERENT FROM DISOBEYING THE WORLD.
NOT IF YOU TRULY WANT SOMETHING.

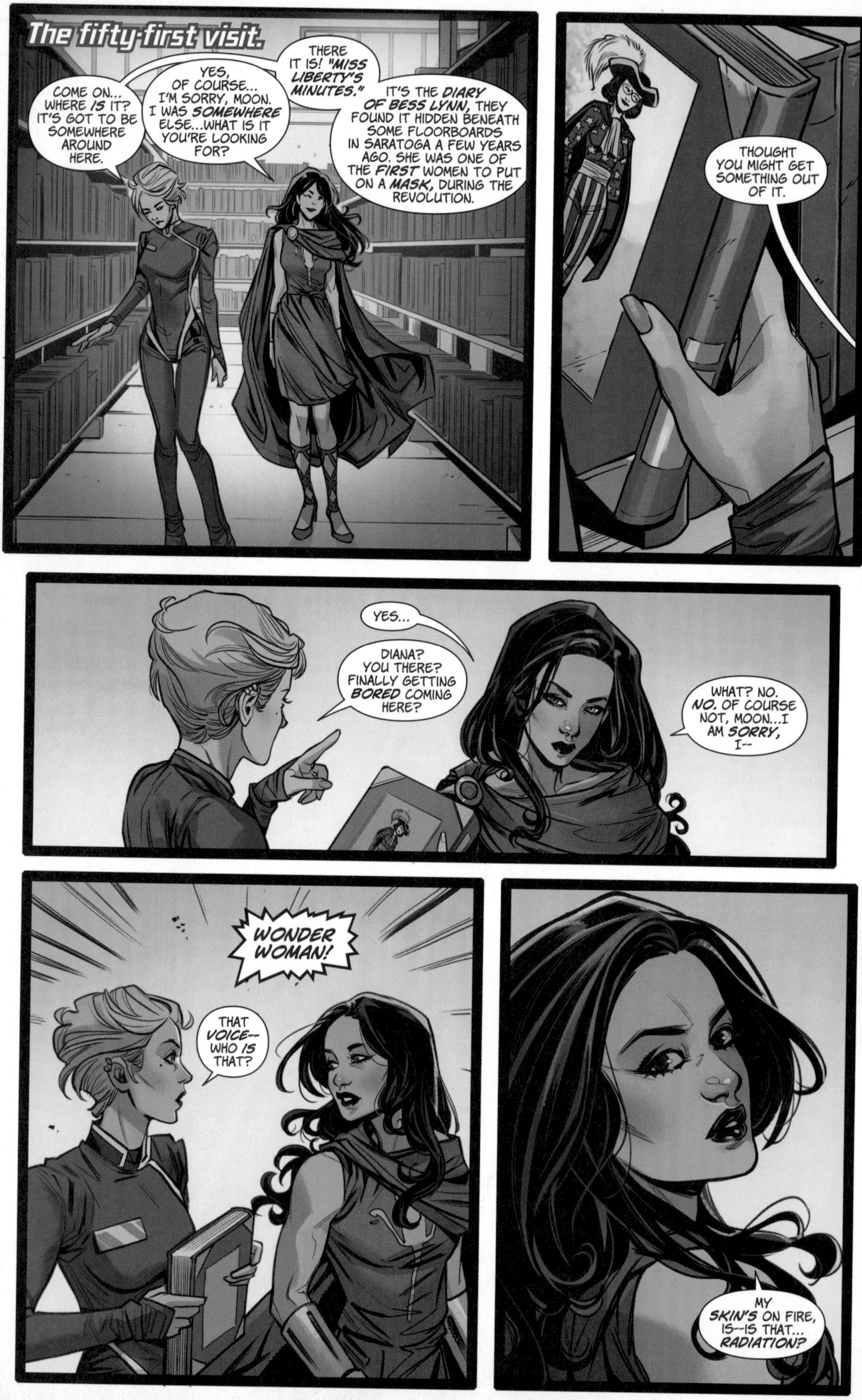
The fifty-first visit.
COME ON... WHERE IS IT? IT'S GOT TO BE SOMEWHERE AROUND HERE.
YES, OF COURSE... I'M SORRY, MOON. I WAS SOMEWHERE ELSE...WHAT IS IT YOU'RE LOOKING FOR?
THERE IT IS! "MISS LIBERTY'S MINUTES."
IT'S THE DIARY OF BESS LYNN, THEY FOUND IT HIDDEN BENEATH SOME FLOORBOARDS IN SARATOGA A FEW YEARS AGO. SHE WAS ONE OF THE FIRST WOMEN TO PUT ON A MASK, DURING THE REVOLUTION.
THOUGHT YOU MIGHT GET SOMETHING OUT OF IT.
YES...
DIANA? YOU THERE? FINALLY GETTING BORED COMING HERE?
WHAT? NO. NO. OF COURSE NOT, MOON...I AM SORRY, I--
WONDER WOMAN!
THAT VOICE-- WHO IS THAT?
MY SKIN'S ON FIRE, IS--IS THAT... RADIATION?

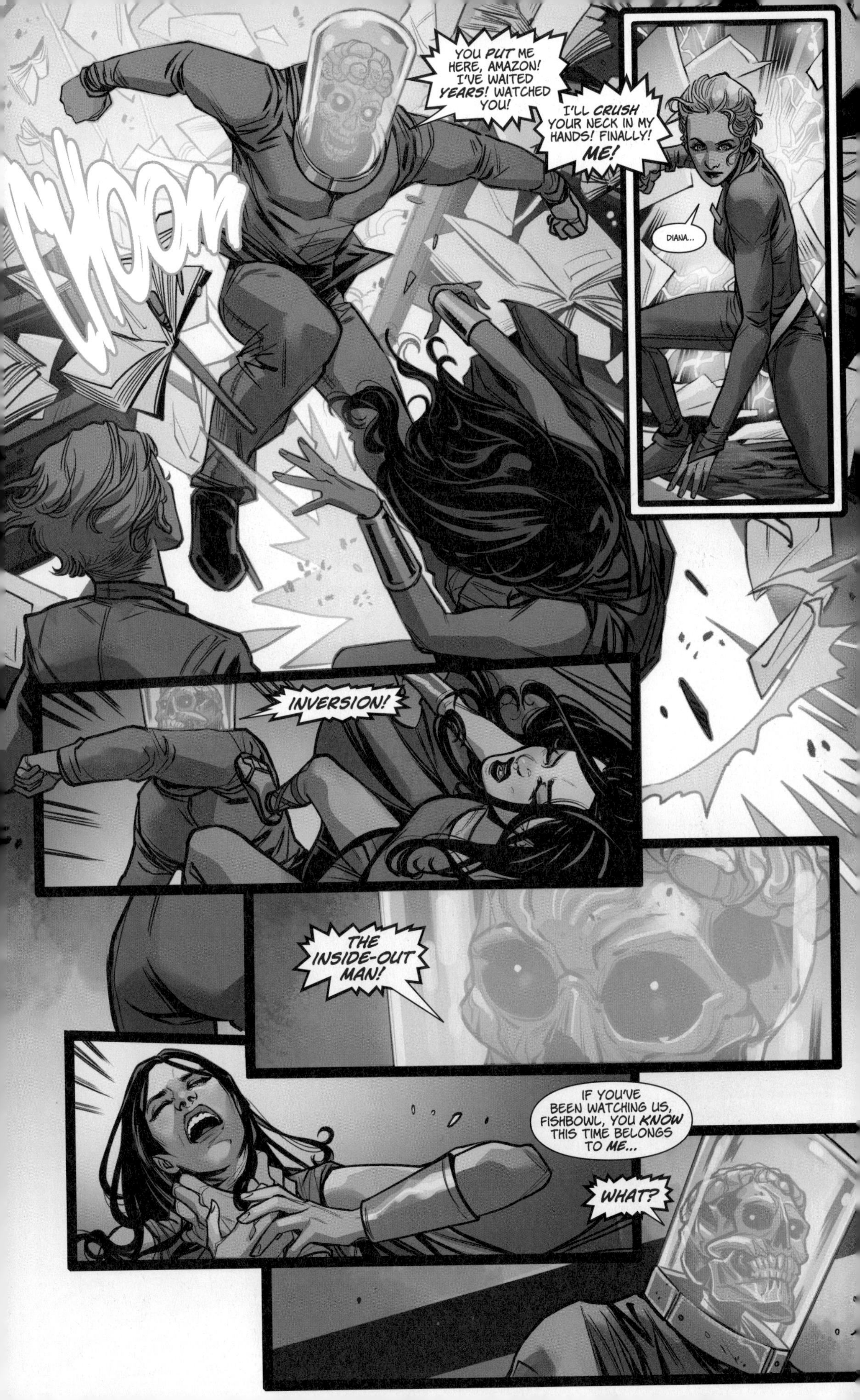

WHOOM
YOU PUT ME HERE, AMAZON! I'VE WAITED YEARS! WATCHED YOU!
I'LL CRUSH YOUR NECK IN MY HANDS! FINALLY! ME!
DIANA...
INVERSION!
THE INSIDE-OUT MAN!
IF YOU'VE BEEN WATCHING US, FISHBOWL, YOU KNOW THIS TIME BELONGS TO ME...
WHAT?

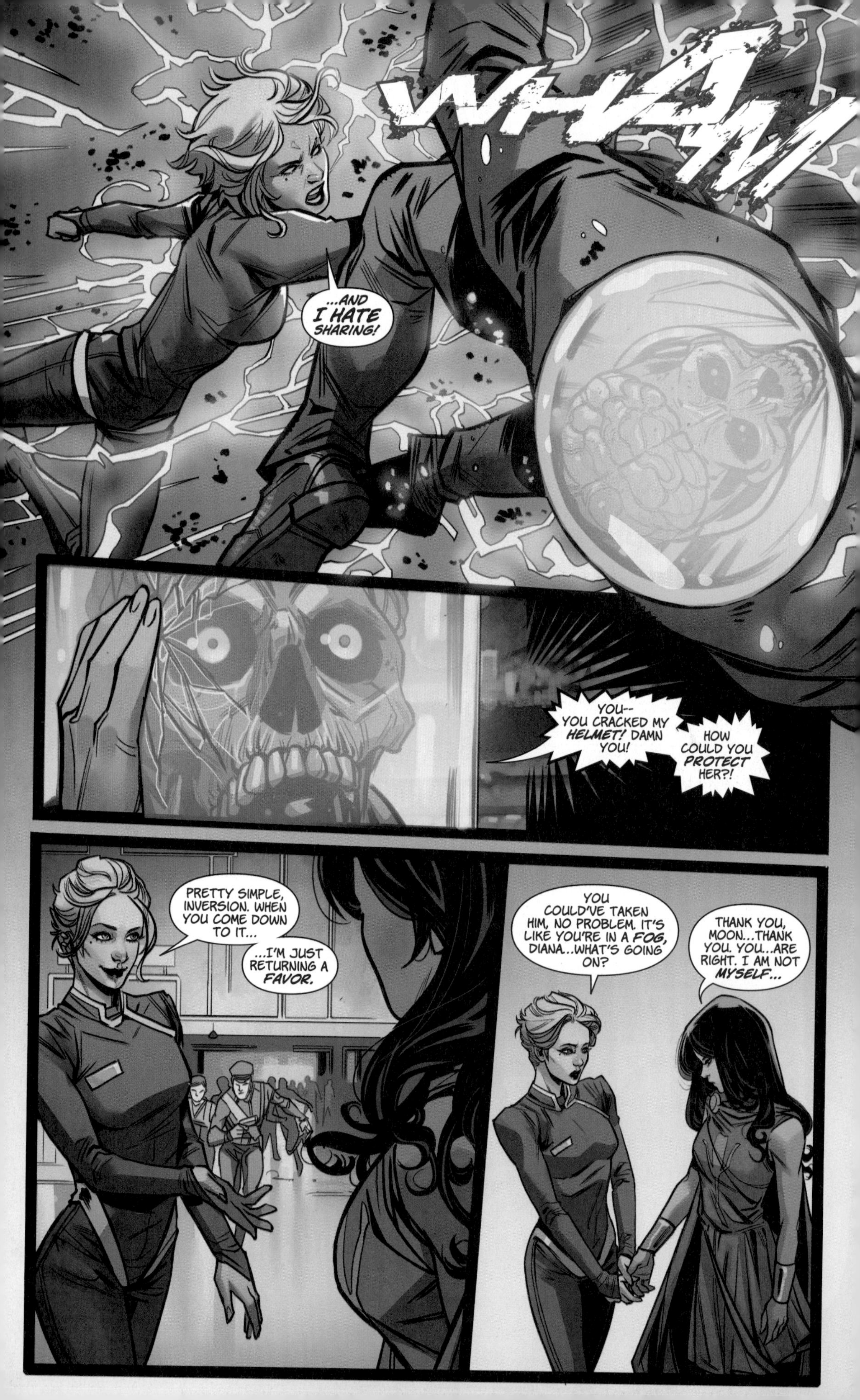
WHAM!
...AND I HATE SHARING!
YOU-- YOU CRACKED MY HELMET! DAMN YOU!
HOW COULD YOU PROTECT HER?!
PRETTY SIMPLE, INVERSION. WHEN YOU COME DOWN TO IT...
...I'M JUST RETURNING A FAVOR.
YOU COULD'VE TAKEN HIM, NO PROBLEM. IT'S LIKE YOU'RE IN A FOG, DIANA...WHAT'S GOING ON?
THANK YOU, MOON...THANK YOU. YOU...ARE RIGHT. I AM NOT MYSELF...

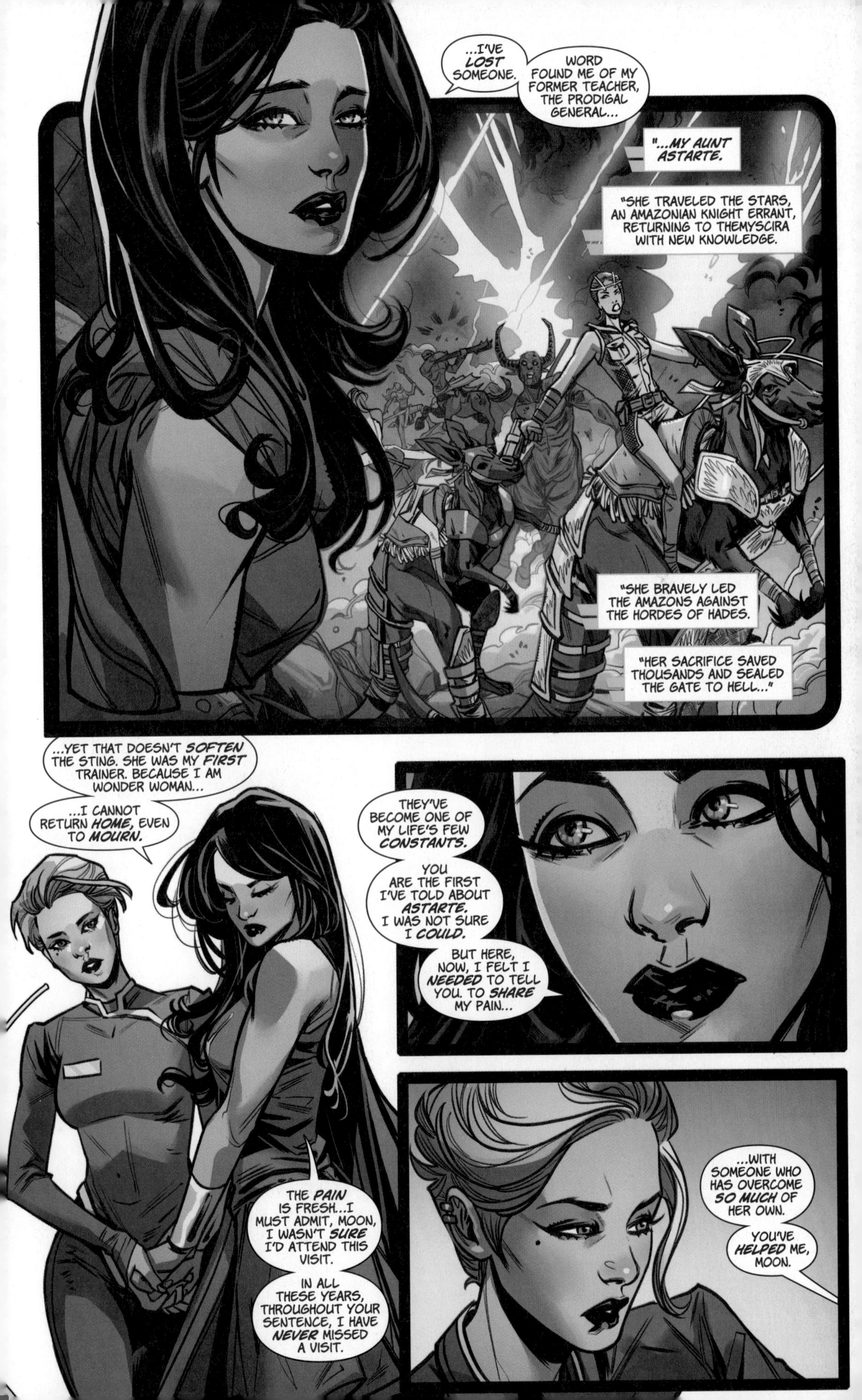

...I'VE LOST SOMEONE.
WORD FOUND ME OF MY FORMER TEACHER, THE PRODIGAL GENERAL...
"...MY AUNT ASTARTE.
"SHE TRAVELED THE STARS, AN AMAZONIAN KNIGHT ERRANT, RETURNING TO THEMYSCIRA WITH NEW KNOWLEDGE.
"SHE BRAVELY LED THE AMAZONS AGAINST THE HORDES OF HADES.
"HER SACRIFICE SAVED THOUSANDS AND SEALED THE GATE TO HELL..."
...YET THAT DOESN'T SOFTEN THE STING. SHE WAS MY FIRST TRAINER. BECAUSE I AM WONDER WOMAN...
...I CANNOT RETURN HOME, EVEN TO MOURN.
THE PAIN IS FRESH...I MUST ADMIT, MOON, I WASN'T SURE I'D ATTEND THIS VISIT.
IN ALL THESE YEARS, THROUGHOUT YOUR SENTENCE, I HAVE NEVER MISSED A VISIT.
THEY'VE BECOME ONE OF MY LIFE'S FEW CONSTANTS.
YOU ARE THE FIRST I'VE TOLD ABOUT ASTARTE. I WAS NOT SURE I COULD.
BUT HERE, NOW, I FELT I NEEDED TO TELL YOU. TO SHARE MY PAIN...
...WITH SOMEONE WHO HAS OVERCOME SO MUCH OF HER OWN.
YOU'VE HELPED ME, MOON.

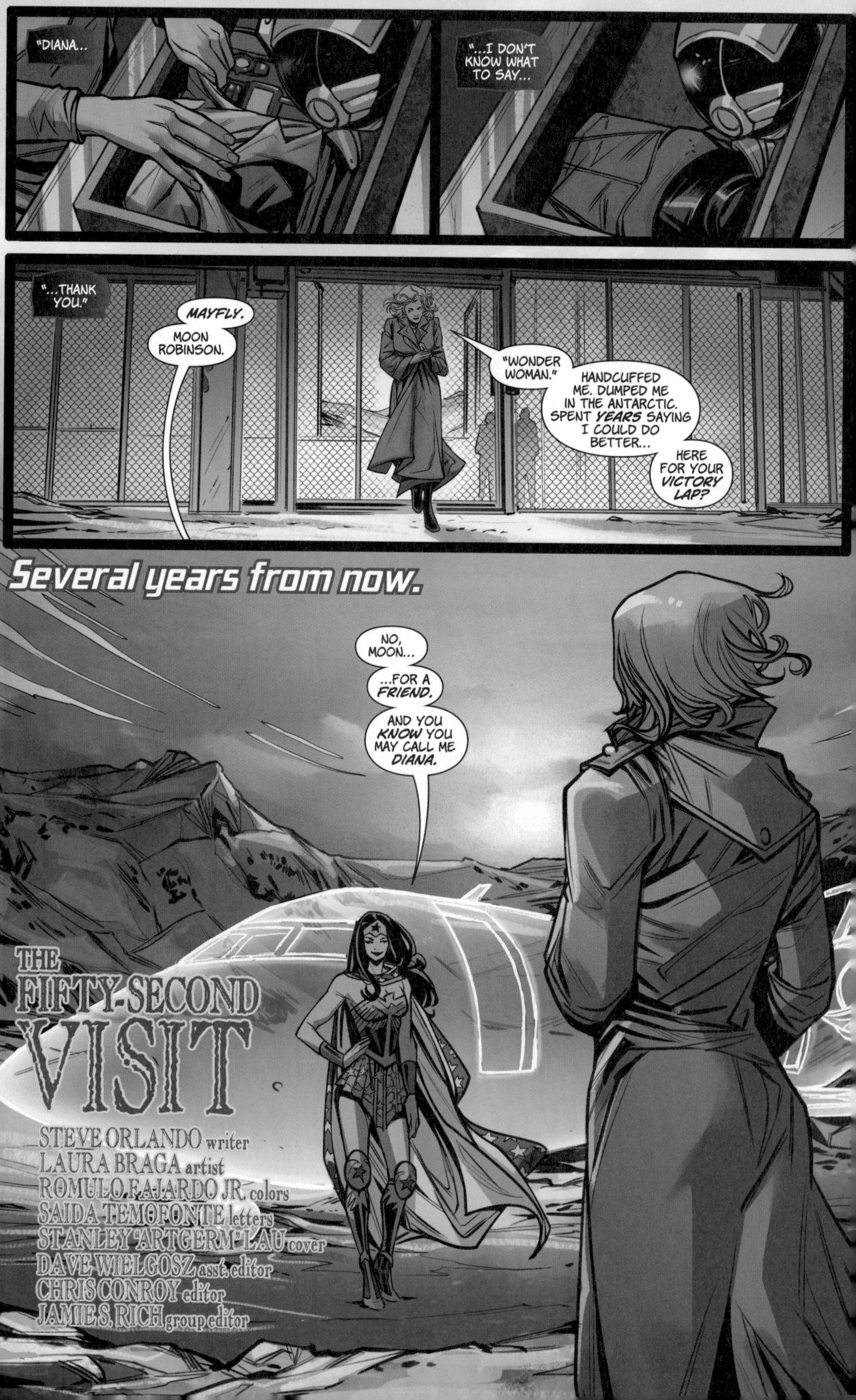
"DIANA...
"...I DON'T KNOW WHAT TO SAY...
"...THANK YOU."
MAYFLY.
MOON ROBINSON.
"WONDER WOMAN."
HANDCUFFED ME. DUMPED ME IN THE ANTARCTIC. SPENT YEARS SAYING I COULD DO BETTER...
HERE FOR YOUR VICTORY LAP?
Several years from now.
NO, MOON...
...FOR A FRIEND.
AND YOU KNOW YOU MAY CALL ME DIANA.
THE FIFTY-SECOND VISIT
STEVE ORLANDO writer
LAURA BRAGA artist
ROMULO FAJARDO JR. colors
SAIDA TEMOFONTE letters
STANLEY "ARTGERM" LAU cover
DAVE WIELGOSZ asst. editor
CHRIS CONROY editor
JAMIE S. RICH group editor

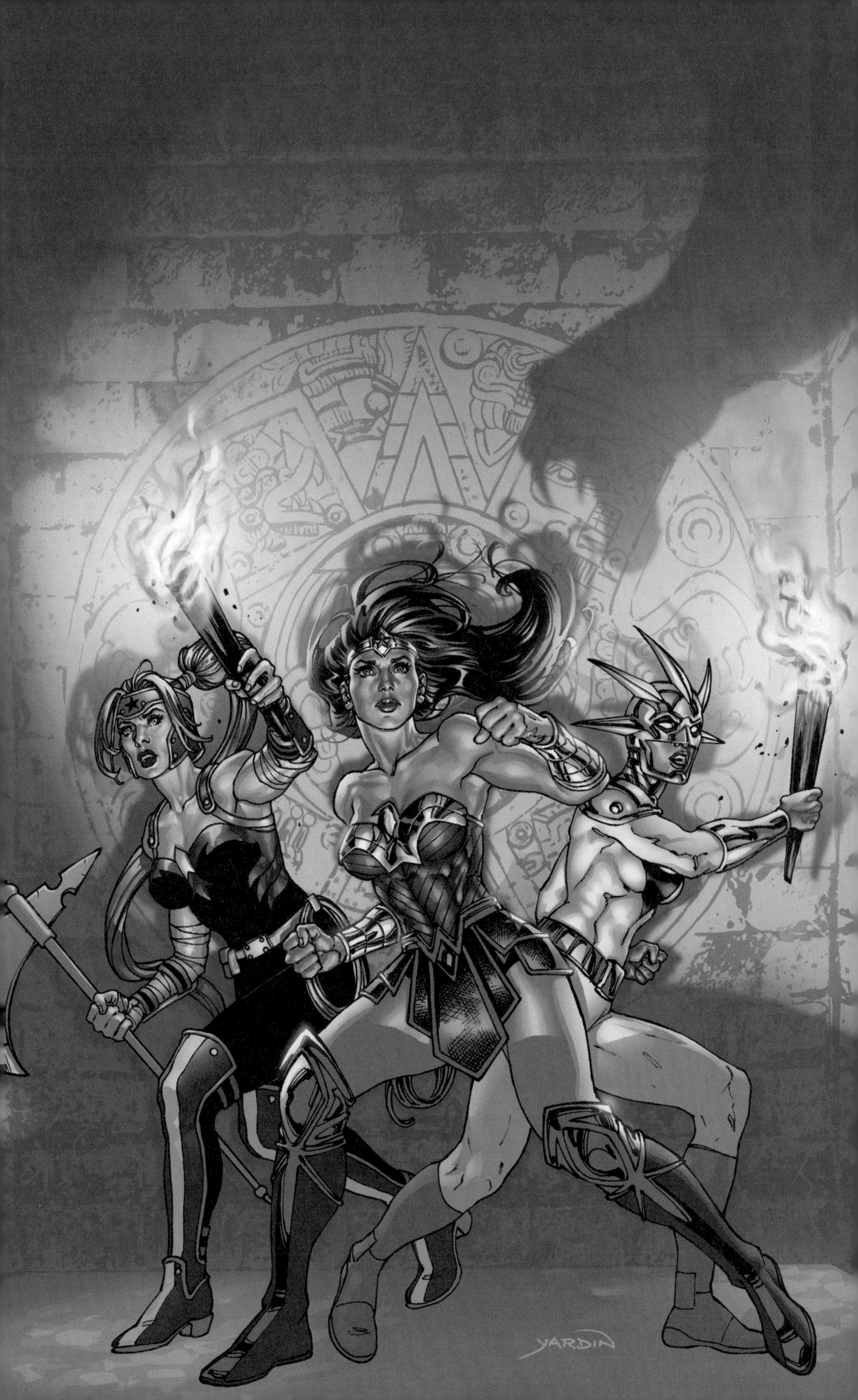

YARDIN

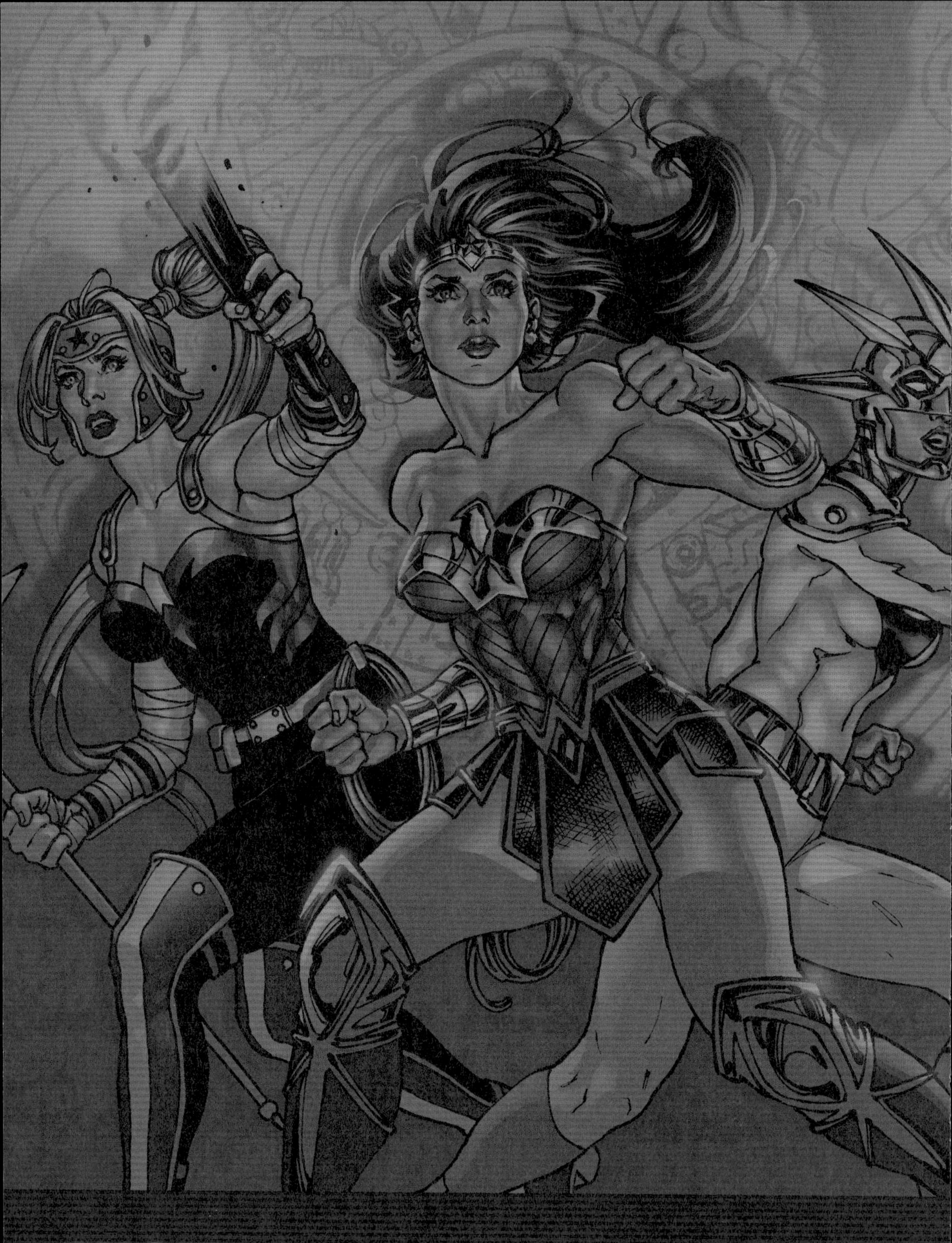

WONDER WOMAN
#52

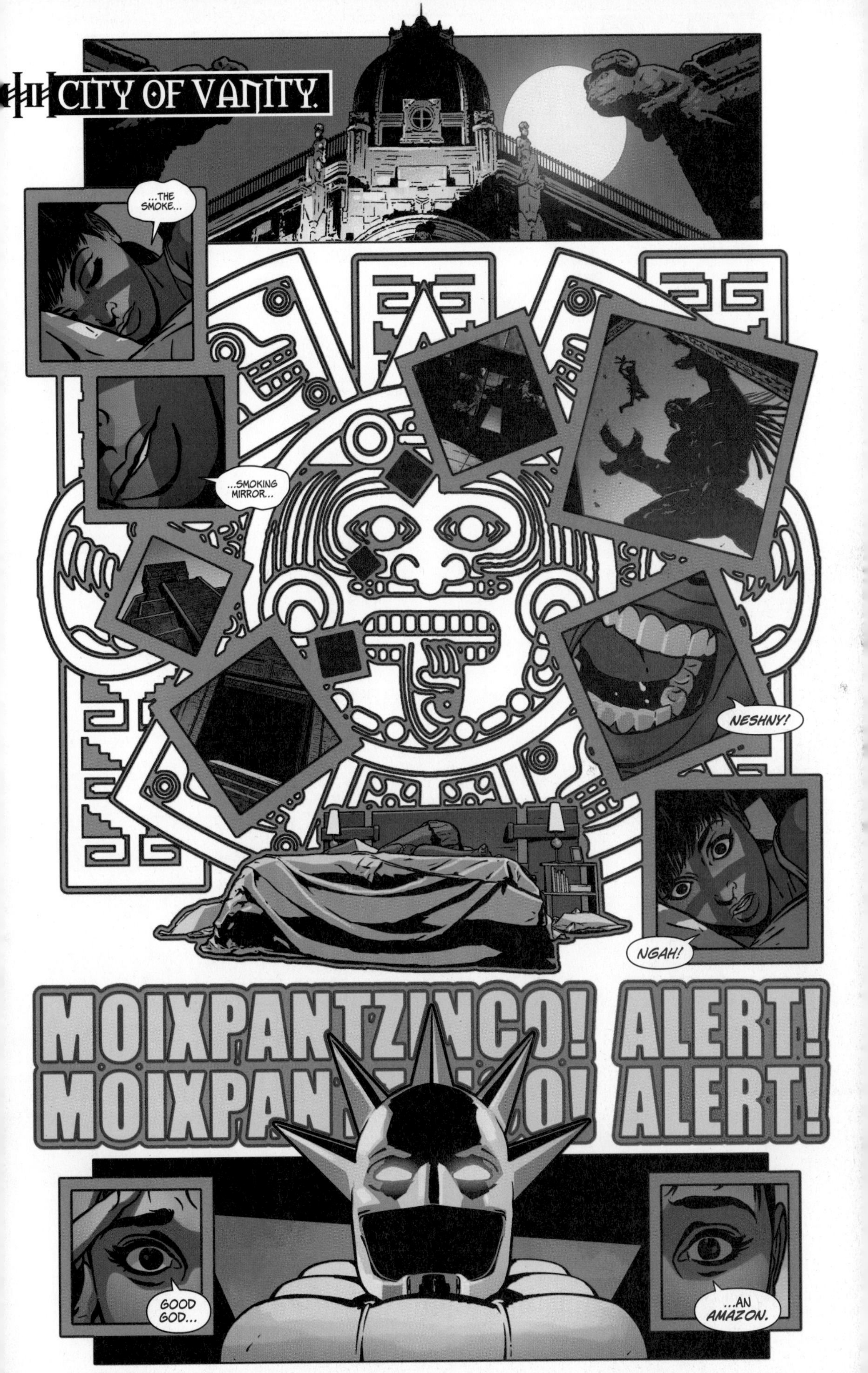
CITY OF VANITY.
...THE SMOKE...
...SMOKING MIRROR...
NESHNY!
NGAH!
MOIXPANTZINCO! ALERT!
ALERT!
GOOD GOD...
...AN AMAZON.

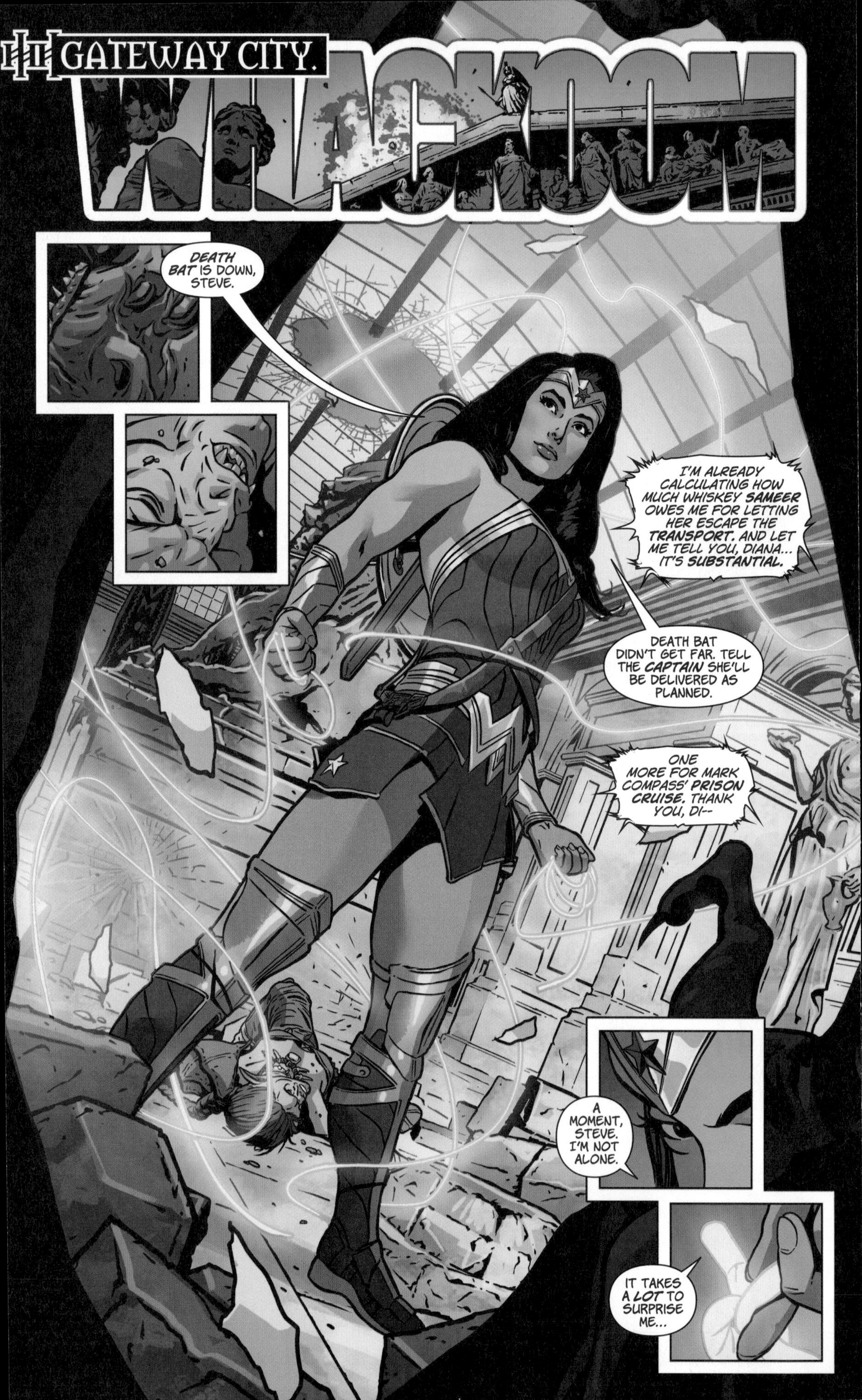

GATEWAY CITY.
WHACKOOM
DEATH BAT IS DOWN, STEVE.
I'M ALREADY CALCULATING HOW MUCH WHISKEY SAMEER OWES ME FOR LETTING HER ESCAPE THE TRANSPORT. AND LET ME TELL YOU, DIANA... IT'S SUBSTANTIAL.
DEATH BAT DIDN'T GET FAR. TELL THE CAPTAIN SHE'LL BE DELIVERED AS PLANNED.
ONE MORE FOR MARK COMPASS' PRISON CRUISE. THANK YOU, DI--
A MOMENT, STEVE. I'M NOT ALONE.
IT TAKES A LOT TO SURPRISE ME...

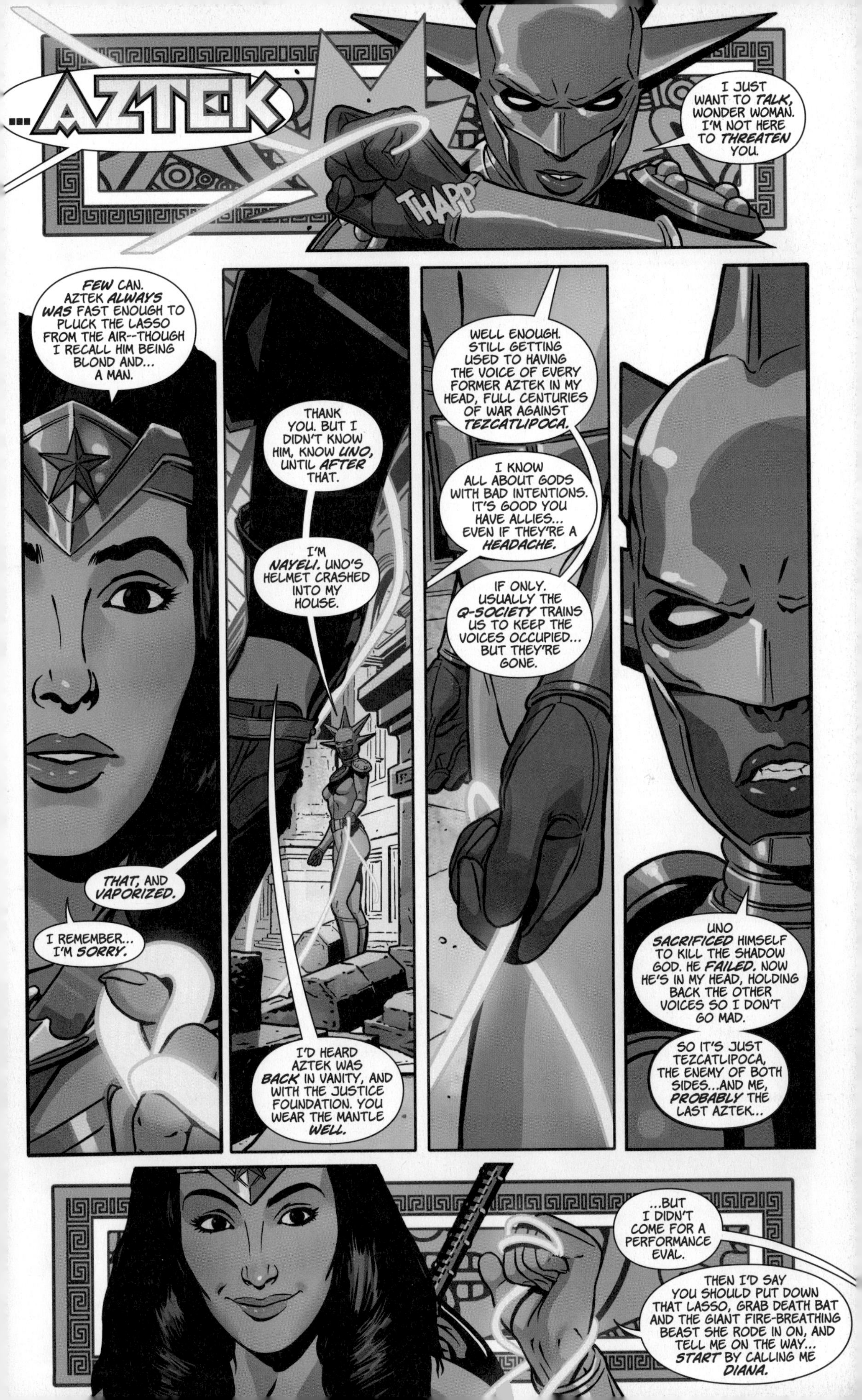

...AZTEK
I JUST WANT TO TALK, WONDER WOMAN. I'M NOT HERE TO THREATEN YOU.
THAPP
FEW CAN. AZTEK ALWAYS WAS FAST ENOUGH TO PLUCK THE LASSO FROM THE AIR--THOUGH I RECALL HIM BEING BLOND AND... A MAN.
THAT, AND VAPORIZED.
I REMEMBER... I'M SORRY.
THANK YOU. BUT I DIDN'T KNOW HIM, KNOW UNO, UNTIL AFTER THAT.
I'M NAYELI. UNO'S HELMET CRASHED INTO MY HOUSE.
I'D HEARD AZTEK WAS BACK IN VANITY, AND WITH THE JUSTICE FOUNDATION. YOU WEAR THE MANTLE WELL.
WELL ENOUGH. STILL GETTING USED TO HAVING THE VOICE OF EVERY FORMER AZTEK IN MY HEAD, FULL CENTURIES OF WAR AGAINST TEZCATLIPOCA.
I KNOW ALL ABOUT GODS WITH BAD INTENTIONS. IT'S GOOD YOU HAVE ALLIES... EVEN IF THEY'RE A HEADACHE.
IF ONLY. USUALLY THE Q-SOCIETY TRAINS US TO KEEP THE VOICES OCCUPIED... BUT THEY'RE GONE.
UNO SACRIFICED HIMSELF TO KILL THE SHADOW GOD. HE FAILED. NOW HE'S IN MY HEAD, HOLDING BACK THE OTHER VOICES SO I DON'T GO MAD.
SO IT'S JUST TEZCATLIPOCA, THE ENEMY OF BOTH SIDES...AND ME, PROBABLY THE LAST AZTEK...
...BUT I DIDN'T COME FOR A PERFORMANCE EVAL.
THEN I'D SAY YOU SHOULD PUT DOWN THAT LASSO, GRAB DEATH BAT AND THE GIANT FIRE-BREATHING BEAST SHE RODE IN ON, AND TELL ME ON THE WAY... START BY CALLING ME DIANA.

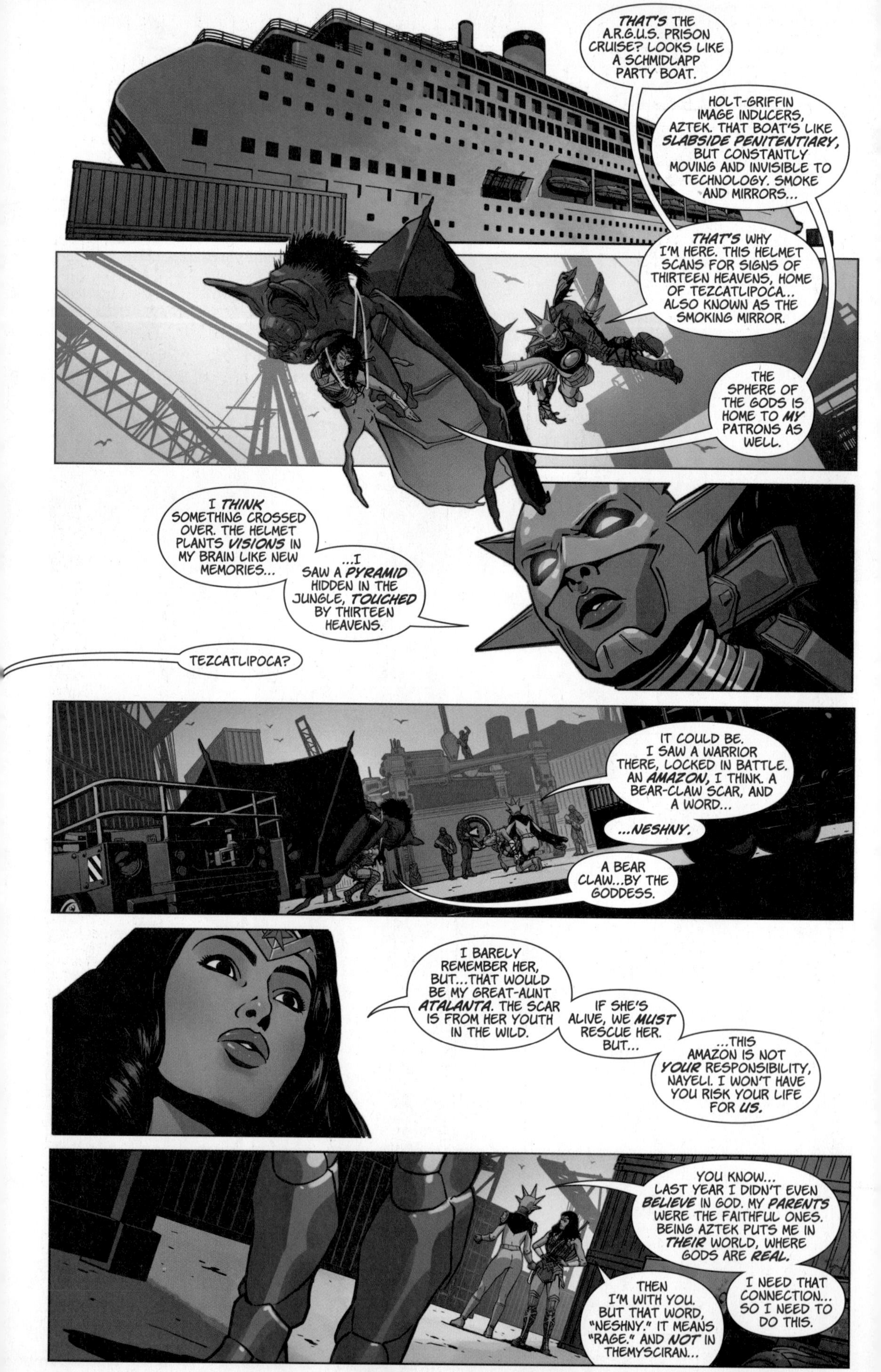
THAT'S THE A.R.G.U.S. PRISON CRUISE? LOOKS LIKE A SCHMIDLAPP PARTY BOAT.
HOLT-GRIFFIN IMAGE INDUCERS, AZTEK. THAT BOAT'S LIKE SLABSIDE PENITENTIARY, BUT CONSTANTLY MOVING AND INVISIBLE TO TECHNOLOGY. SMOKE AND MIRRORS...
THAT'S WHY I'M HERE. THIS HELMET SCANS FOR SIGNS OF THIRTEEN HEAVENS, HOME OF TEZCATLIPOCA... ALSO KNOWN AS THE SMOKING MIRROR.
THE SPHERE OF THE GODS IS HOME TO MY PATRONS AS WELL.
I THINK SOMETHING CROSSED OVER. THE HELMET PLANTS VISIONS IN MY BRAIN LIKE NEW MEMORIES...
...I SAW A PYRAMID HIDDEN IN THE JUNGLE, TOUCHED BY THIRTEEN HEAVENS.
TEZCATLIPOCA?
IT COULD BE. I SAW A WARRIOR THERE, LOCKED IN BATTLE. AN AMAZON, I THINK. A BEAR-CLAW SCAR, AND A WORD...
...NESHNY.
A BEAR CLAW...BY THE GODDESS.
I BARELY REMEMBER HER, BUT...THAT WOULD BE MY GREAT-AUNT ATALANTA. THE SCAR IS FROM HER YOUTH IN THE WILD.
IF SHE'S ALIVE, WE MUST RESCUE HER. BUT...
...THIS AMAZON IS NOT YOUR RESPONSIBILITY, NAYELI. I WON'T HAVE YOU RISK YOUR LIFE FOR US.
YOU KNOW... LAST YEAR I DIDN'T EVEN BELIEVE IN GOD. MY PARENTS WERE THE FAITHFUL ONES. BEING AZTEK PUTS ME IN THEIR WORLD, WHERE GODS ARE REAL.
I NEED THAT CONNECTION... SO I NEED TO DO THIS.
THEN I'M WITH YOU. BUT THAT WORD, "NESHNY." IT MEANS "RAGE." AND NOT IN THEMYSCIRAN...

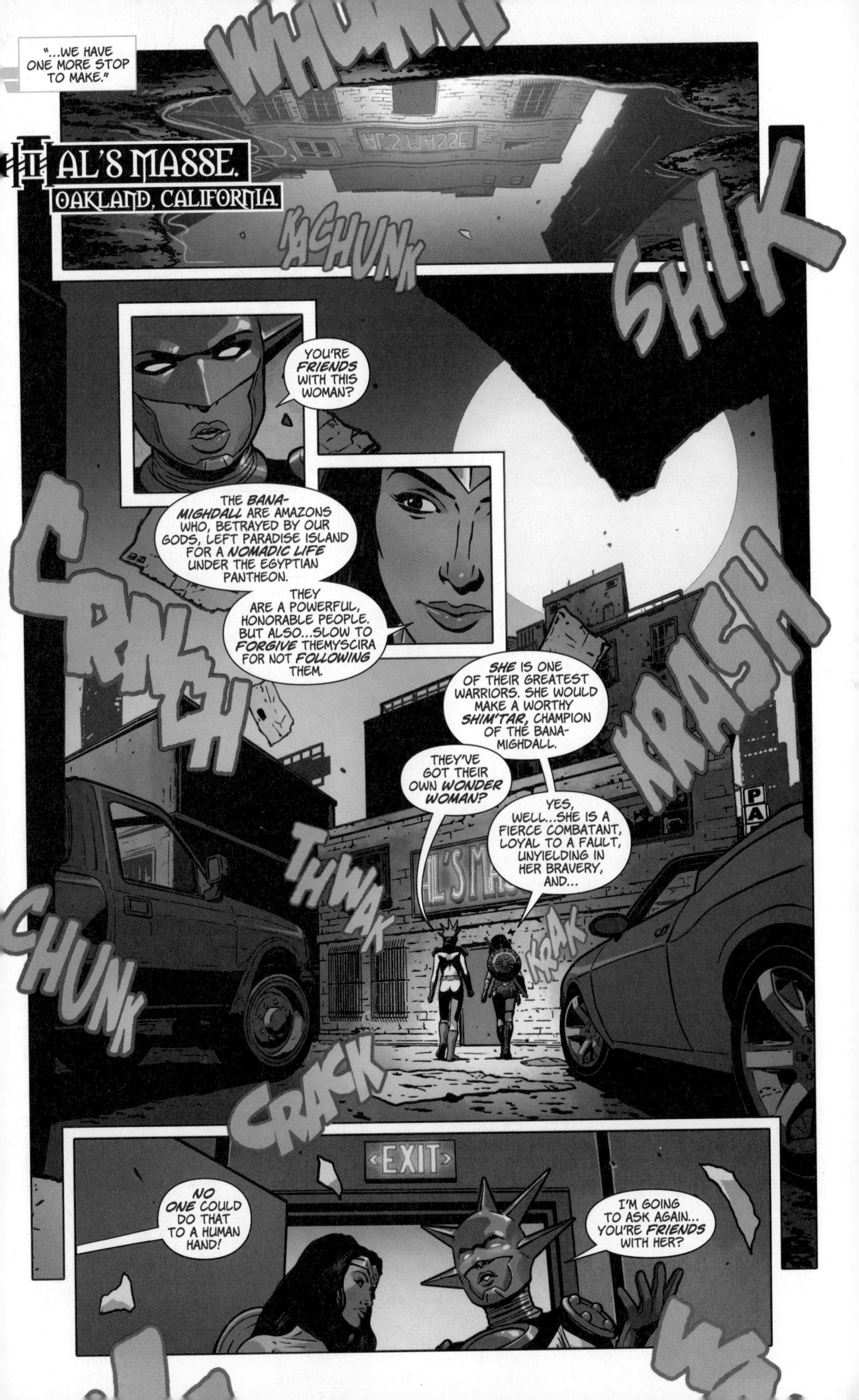

"...WE HAVE ONE MORE STOP TO MAKE."
WHUMM
AL'S MASSE. OAKLAND, CALIFORNIA.
KACHUNK
SHIK
YOU'RE *FRIENDS* WITH THIS WOMAN?
THE *BANA-MIGHDALL* ARE AMAZONS WHO, BETRAYED BY OUR GODS, LEFT PARADISE ISLAND FOR A *NOMADIC LIFE* UNDER THE EGYPTIAN PANTHEON.
THEY ARE A POWERFUL, HONORABLE PEOPLE. BUT ALSO...SLOW TO *FORGIVE* THEMYSCIRA FOR NOT *FOLLOWING* THEM.
CRANCH
KRASH
SHE IS ONE OF THEIR GREATEST WARRIORS. SHE WOULD MAKE A WORTHY *SHIM'TAR,* CHAMPION OF THE BANA-MIGHDALL.
THEY'VE GOT THEIR OWN *WONDER WOMAN?*
YES, WELL...SHE IS A FIERCE COMBATANT, LOYAL TO A FAULT, UNYIELDING IN HER BRAVERY, AND...
AL'S MASSE
THWAK
KRAK
CHUNK
CRACK
EXIT
NO ONE COULD DO THAT TO A HUMAN HAND!
I'M GOING TO ASK AGAIN... YOU'RE *FRIENDS* WITH HER?

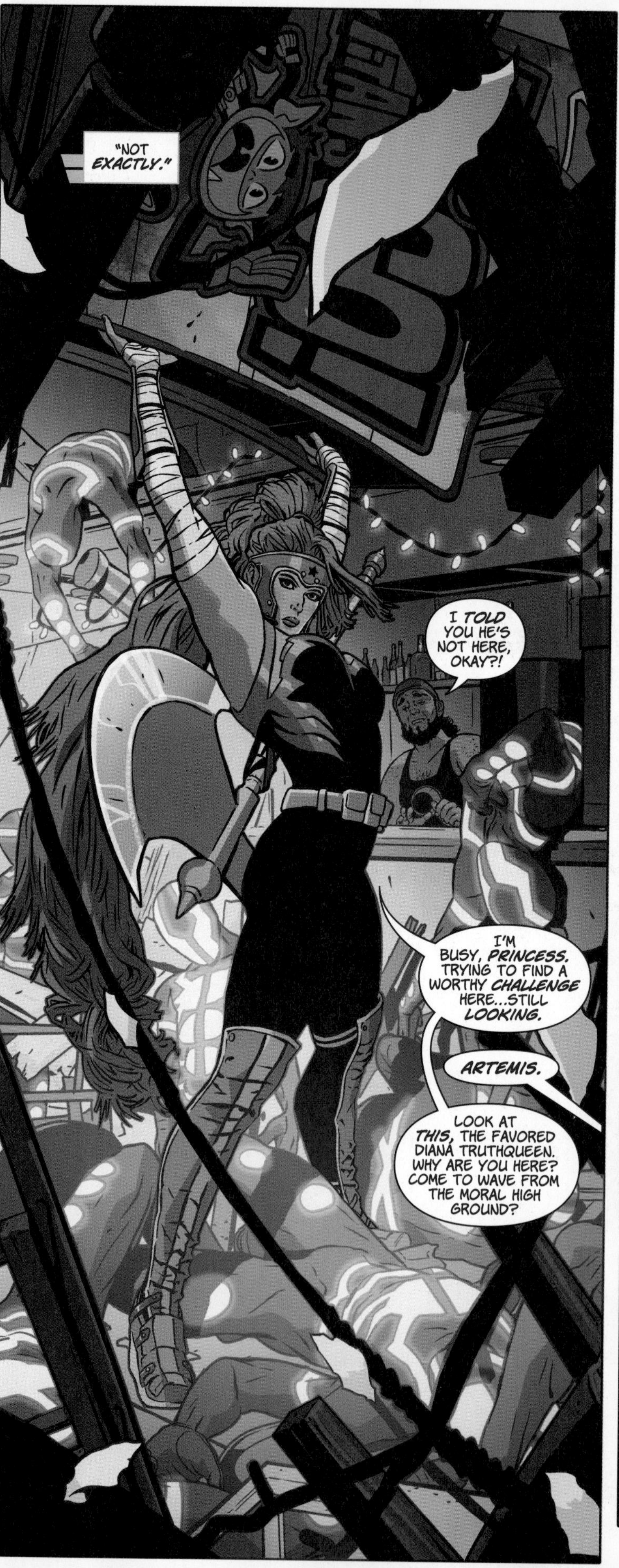
"NOT EXACTLY."
I TOLD YOU HE'S NOT HERE, OKAY?!
I'M BUSY, PRINCESS. TRYING TO FIND A WORTHY CHALLENGE HERE...STILL LOOKING.
ARTEMIS.
LOOK AT THIS, THE FAVORED DIANA TRUTHQUEEN. WHY ARE YOU HERE? COME TO WAVE FROM THE MORAL HIGH GROUND?

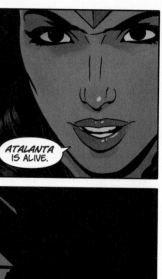

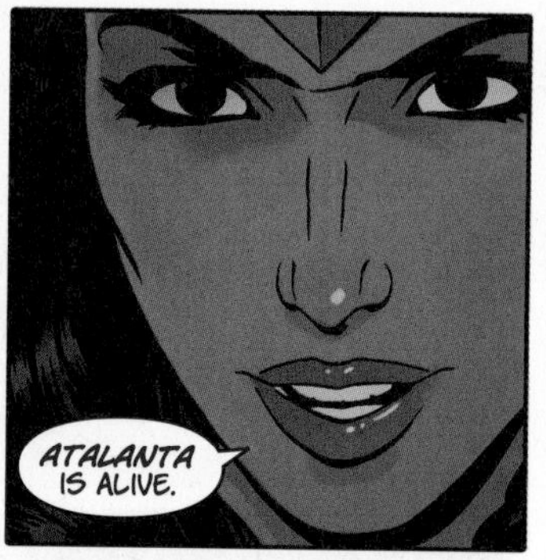
ATALANTA IS ALIVE.

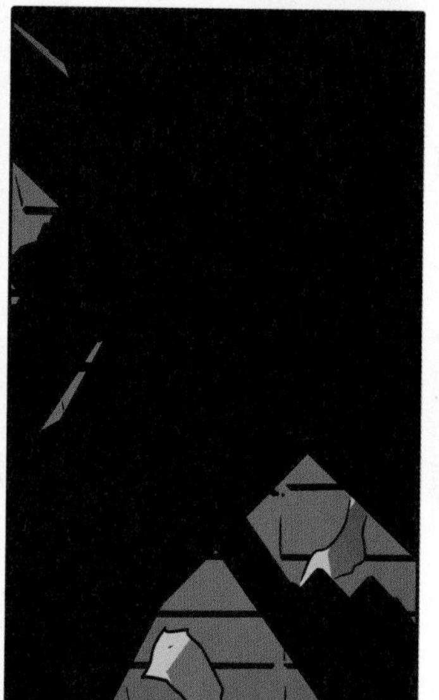
...

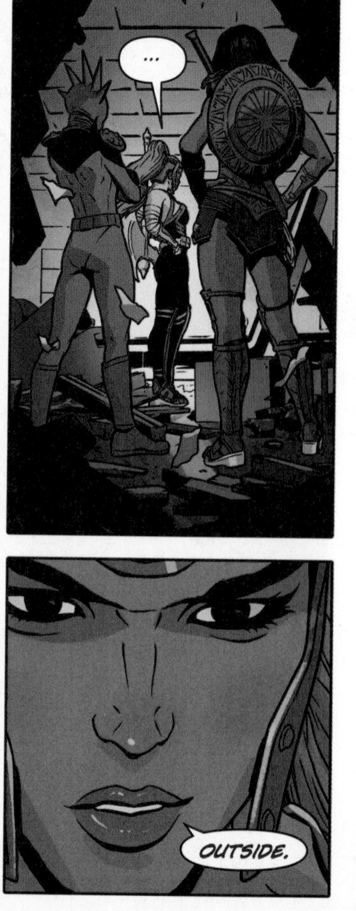
OUTSIDE.

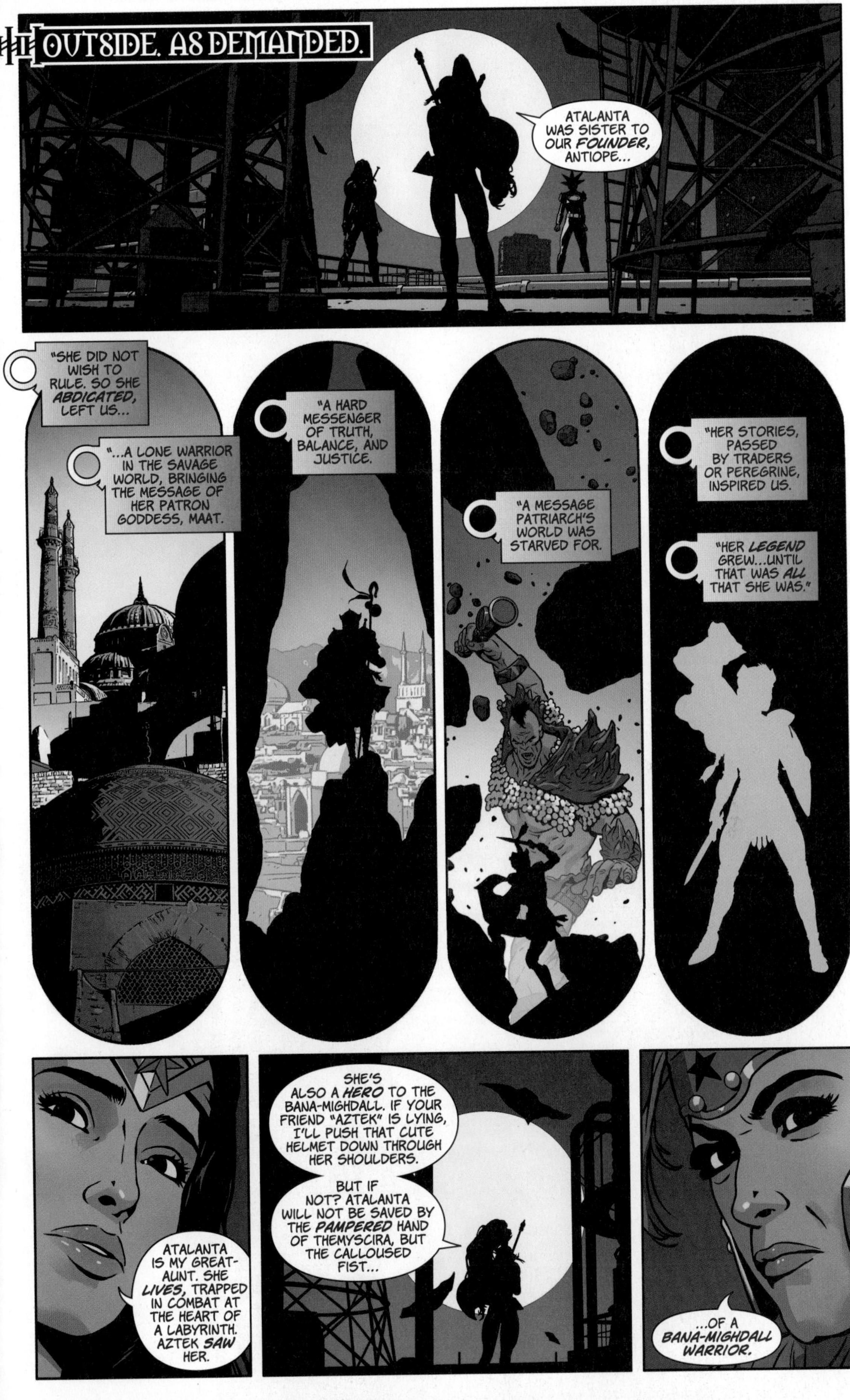
III OUTSIDE. AS DEMANDED.
ATALANTA WAS SISTER TO OUR *FOUNDER*, ANTIOPE...
"SHE DID NOT WISH TO RULE. SO SHE *ABDICATED*, LEFT US...
"...A LONE WARRIOR IN THE SAVAGE WORLD, BRINGING THE MESSAGE OF HER PATRON GODDESS, MAAT.
"A HARD MESSENGER OF TRUTH, BALANCE, AND JUSTICE.
"A MESSAGE PATRIARCH'S WORLD WAS STARVED FOR.
"HER STORIES, PASSED BY TRADERS OR PEREGRINE, INSPIRED US.
"HER *LEGEND* GREW...UNTIL THAT WAS *ALL* THAT SHE WAS."
ATALANTA IS MY GREAT-AUNT. SHE *LIVES*, TRAPPED IN COMBAT AT THE HEART OF A LABYRINTH. AZTEK *SAW* HER.
SHE'S ALSO A *HERO* TO THE BANA-MIGHDALL. IF YOUR FRIEND "AZTEK" IS LYING, I'LL PUSH THAT CUTE HELMET DOWN THROUGH HER SHOULDERS.
BUT IF NOT? ATALANTA WILL NOT BE SAVED BY THE *PAMPERED* HAND OF THEMYSCIRA, BUT THE CALLOUSED FIST...
...OF A *BANA-MIGHDALL WARRIOR.*

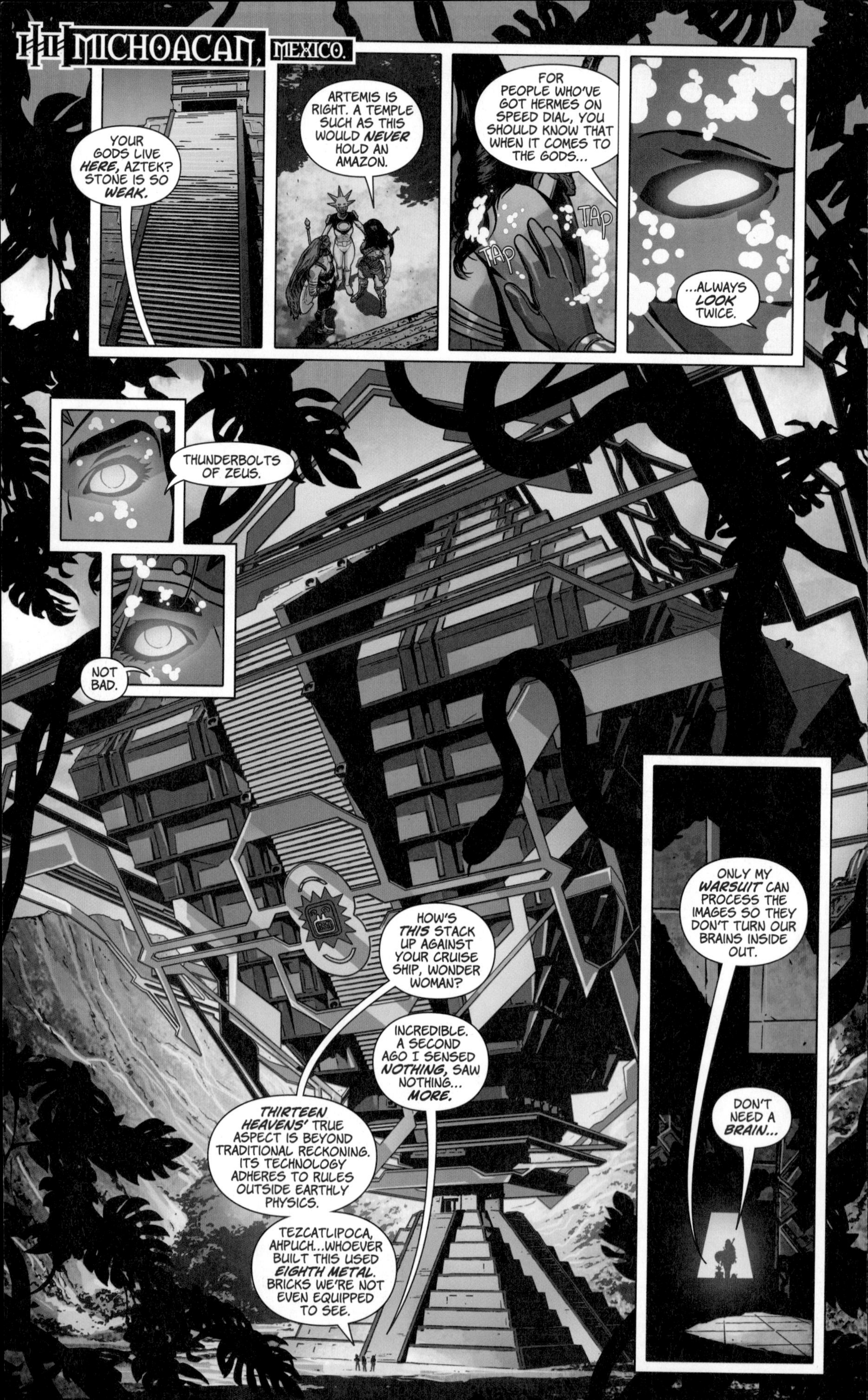
MICHOACAN, MEXICO.
YOUR GODS LIVE HERE, AZTEK? STONE IS SO WEAK.
ARTEMIS IS RIGHT. A TEMPLE SUCH AS THIS WOULD NEVER HOLD AN AMAZON.
FOR PEOPLE WHO'VE GOT HERMES ON SPEED DIAL, YOU SHOULD KNOW THAT WHEN IT COMES TO THE GODS...
TAP
TAP
...ALWAYS LOOK TWICE.
THUNDERBOLTS OF ZEUS.
NOT BAD.
HOW'S THIS STACK UP AGAINST YOUR CRUISE SHIP, WONDER WOMAN?
INCREDIBLE. A SECOND AGO I SENSED NOTHING, SAW NOTHING... MORE.
THIRTEEN HEAVENS' TRUE ASPECT IS BEYOND TRADITIONAL RECKONING. ITS TECHNOLOGY ADHERES TO RULES OUTSIDE EARTHLY PHYSICS.
TEZCATLIPOCA, AHPUCH...WHOEVER BUILT THIS USED EIGHTH METAL. BRICKS WE'RE NOT EVEN EQUIPPED TO SEE.
ONLY MY WARSUIT CAN PROCESS THE IMAGES SO THEY DON'T TURN OUR BRAINS INSIDE OUT.
DON'T NEED A BRAIN...

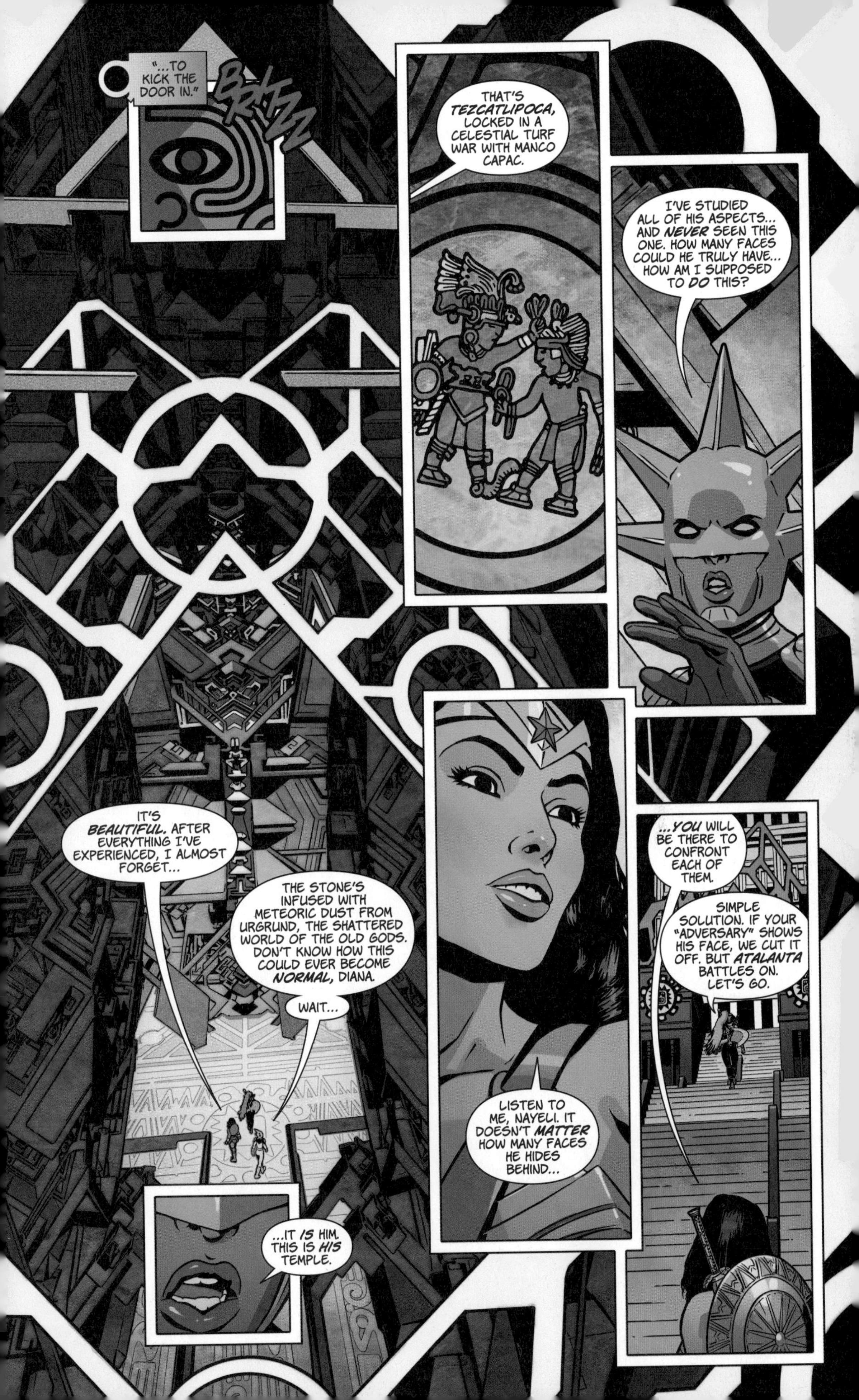
"...TO KICK THE DOOR IN."
BRKZZZ
THAT'S TEZCATLIPOCA, LOCKED IN A CELESTIAL TURF WAR WITH MANCO CAPAC.
I'VE STUDIED ALL OF HIS ASPECTS... AND NEVER SEEN THIS ONE. HOW MANY FACES COULD HE TRULY HAVE... HOW AM I SUPPOSED TO DO THIS?
IT'S BEAUTIFUL. AFTER EVERYTHING I'VE EXPERIENCED, I ALMOST FORGET...
THE STONE'S INFUSED WITH METEORIC DUST FROM URGRUND, THE SHATTERED WORLD OF THE OLD GODS. DON'T KNOW HOW THIS COULD EVER BECOME NORMAL, DIANA.
WAIT...
...IT IS HIM. THIS IS HIS TEMPLE.
LISTEN TO ME, NAYELI. IT DOESN'T MATTER HOW MANY FACES HE HIDES BEHIND...
...YOU WILL BE THERE TO CONFRONT EACH OF THEM.
SIMPLE SOLUTION. IF YOUR "ADVERSARY" SHOWS HIS FACE, WE CUT IT OFF. BUT ATALANTA BATTLES ON. LET'S GO.

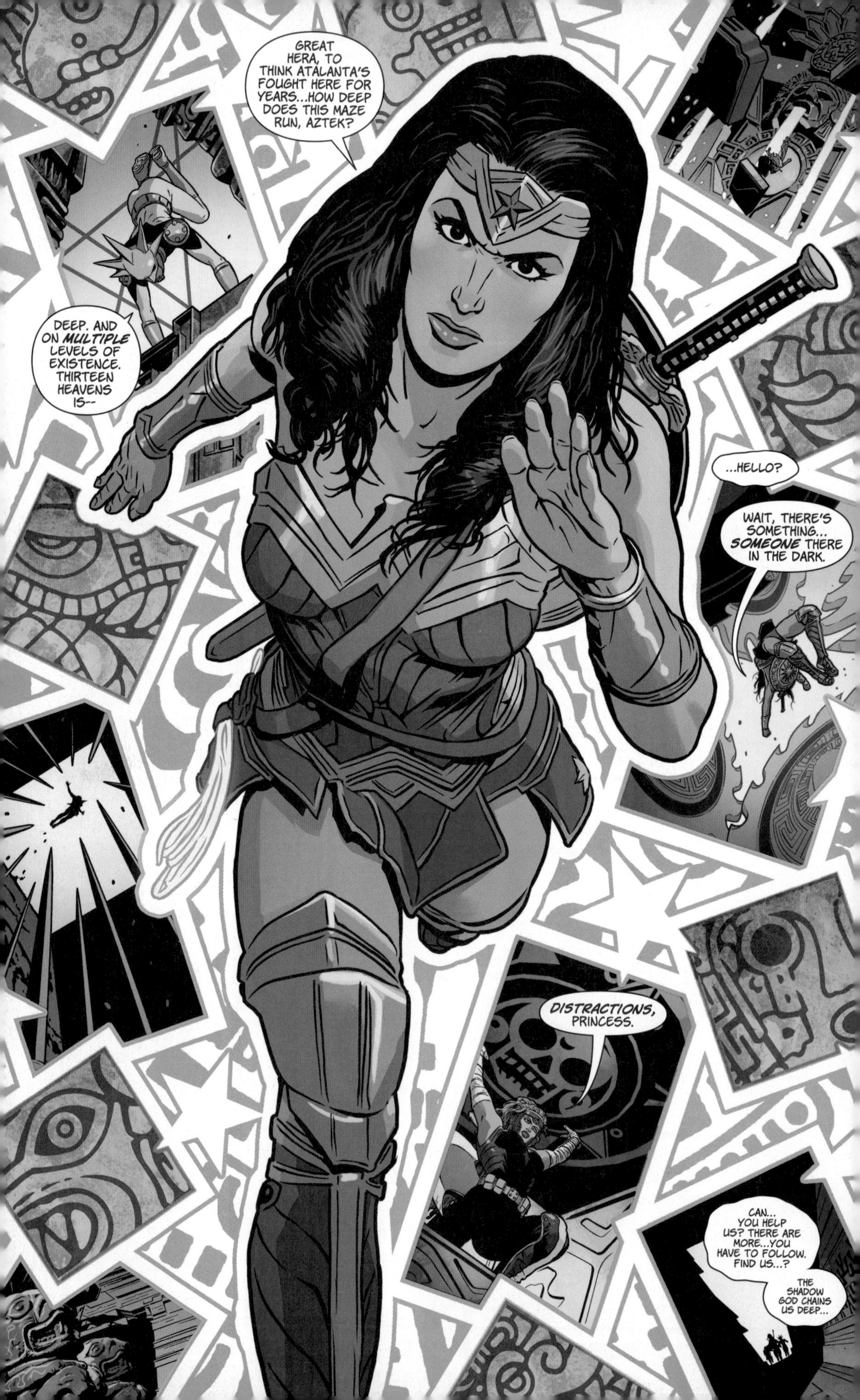
GREAT HERA, TO THINK ATALANTA'S FOUGHT HERE FOR YEARS...HOW DEEP DOES THIS MAZE RUN, AZTEK?
DEEP. AND ON MULTIPLE LEVELS OF EXISTENCE. THIRTEEN HEAVENS IS--
...HELLO?
WAIT, THERE'S SOMETHING... SOMEONE THERE IN THE DARK.
DISTRACTIONS, PRINCESS.
CAN... YOU HELP US? THERE ARE MORE...YOU HAVE TO FOLLOW. FIND US...?
THE SHADOW GOD CHAINS US DEEP...

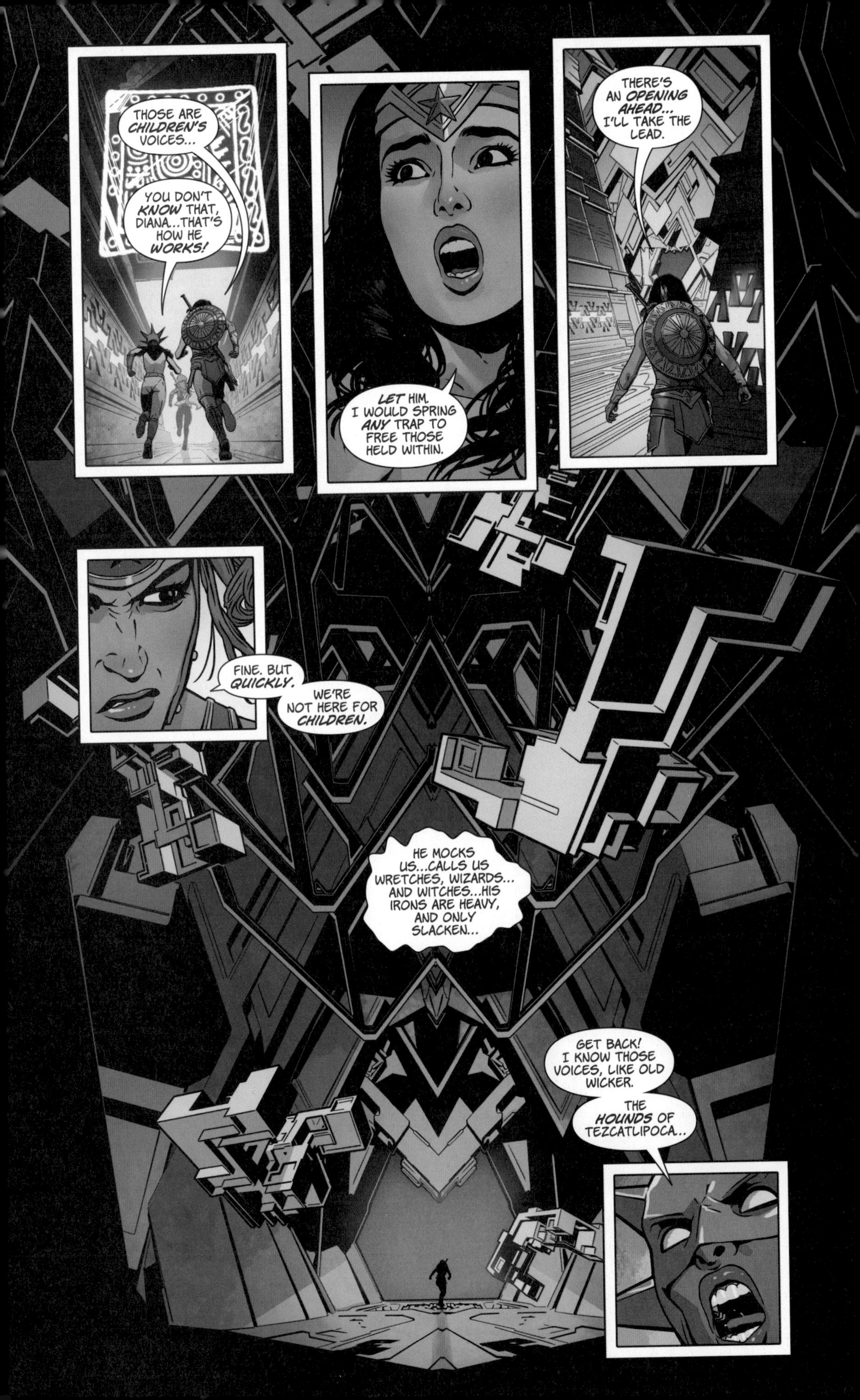
THOSE ARE CHILDREN'S VOICES...
YOU DON'T KNOW THAT, DIANA...THAT'S HOW HE WORKS!
LET HIM. I WOULD SPRING ANY TRAP TO FREE THOSE HELD WITHIN.
THERE'S AN OPENING AHEAD... I'LL TAKE THE LEAD.
FINE. BUT QUICKLY.
WE'RE NOT HERE FOR CHILDREN.
HE MOCKS US...CALLS US WRETCHES, WIZARDS... AND WITCHES...HIS IRONS ARE HEAVY, AND ONLY SLACKEN...
GET BACK! I KNOW THOSE VOICES, LIKE OLD WICKER.
THE HOUNDS OF TEZCATLIPOCA...

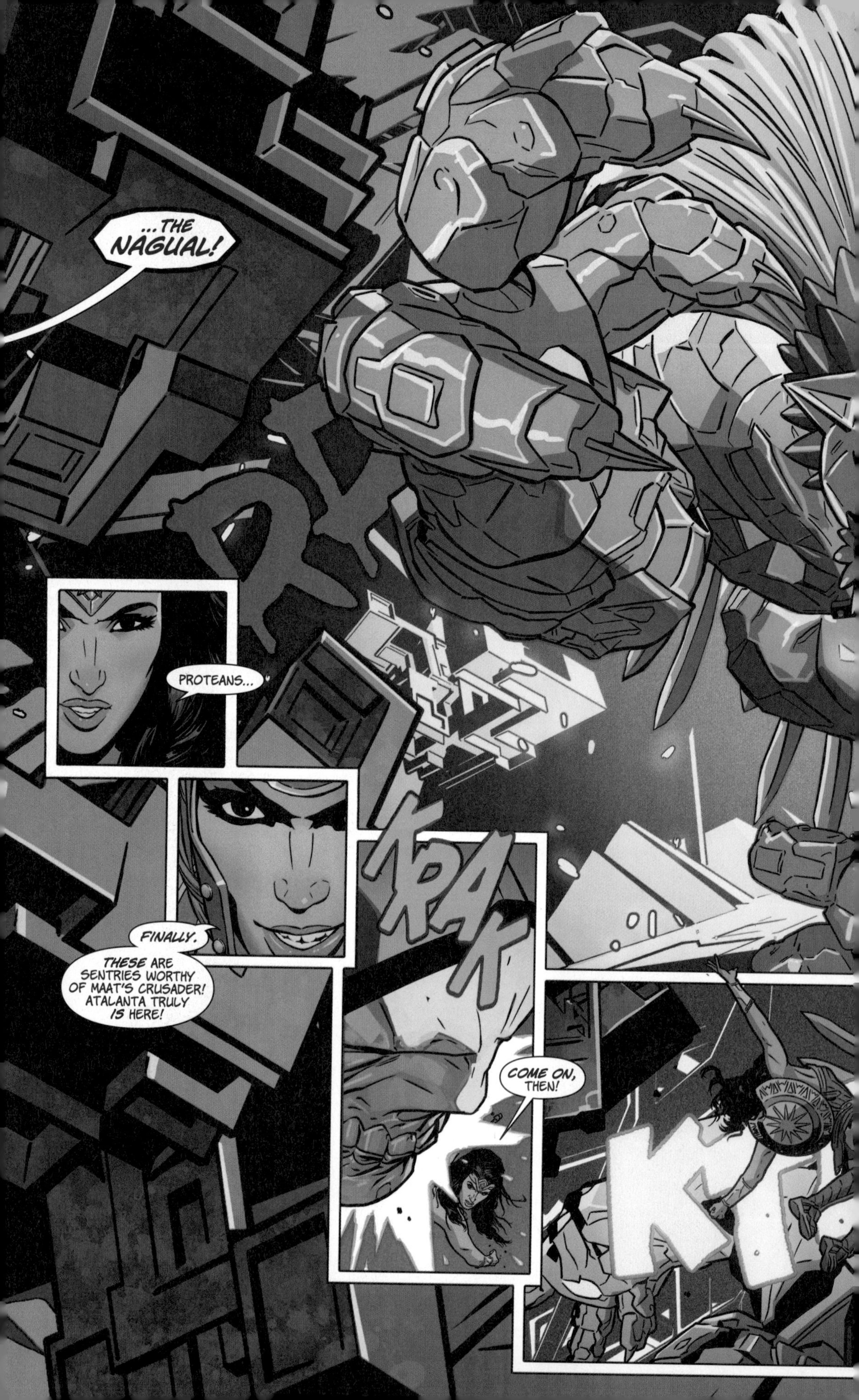
...THE NAGUAL!
PROTEANS...
FINALLY.
THESE ARE SENTRIES WORTHY OF MAAT'S CRUSADER! ATALANTA TRULY IS HERE!
KRAK
COME ON, THEN!

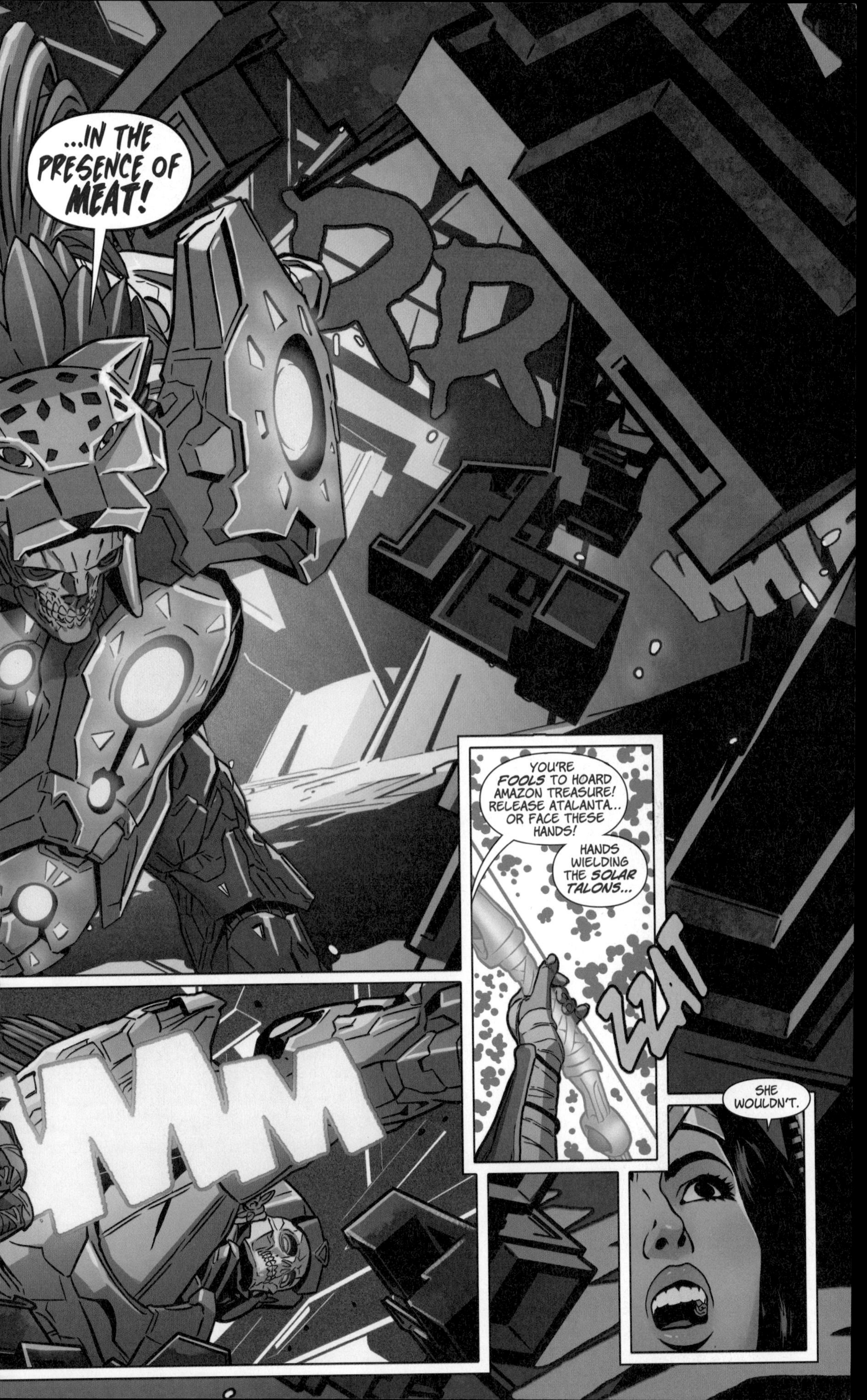
...IN THE PRESENCE OF MEAT!
RRR
WHA
YOU'RE FOOLS TO HOARD AMAZON TREASURE! RELEASE ATALANTA... OR FACE THESE HANDS!
HANDS WIELDING THE SOLAR TALONS...
ZZAT
MM
SHE WOULDN'T.

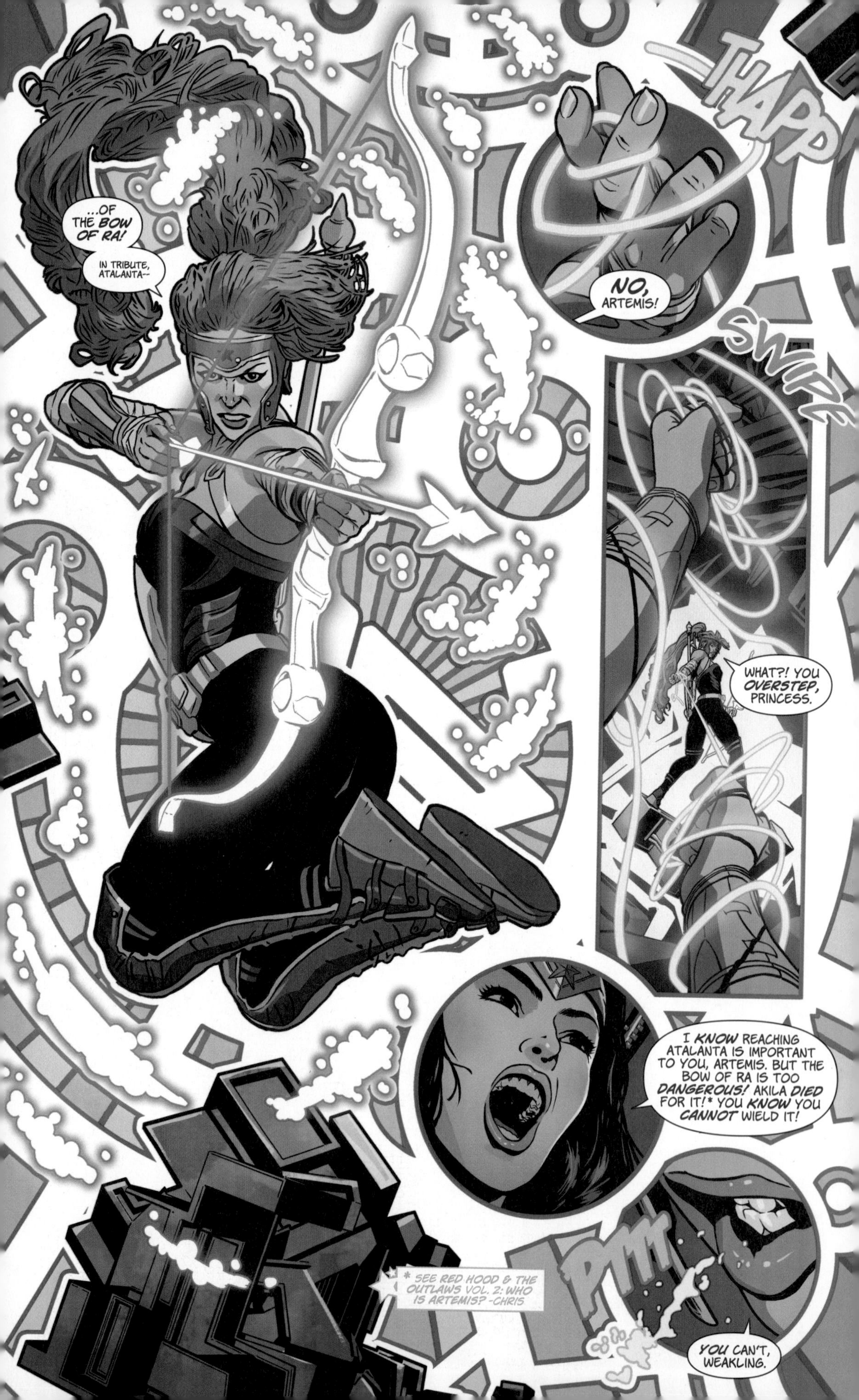
...OF THE BOW OF RA!
IN TRIBUTE, ATALANTA--
THAPP
NO, ARTEMIS!
SWIPE
WHAT?! YOU OVERSTEP, PRINCESS.
I KNOW REACHING ATALANTA IS IMPORTANT TO YOU, ARTEMIS. BUT THE BOW OF RA IS TOO DANGEROUS! AKILA DIED FOR IT!* YOU KNOW YOU CANNOT WIELD IT!
* SEE RED HOOD & THE OUTLAWS VOL. 2: WHO IS ARTEMIS? -CHRIS
PTTT
YOU CAN'T, WEAKLING.

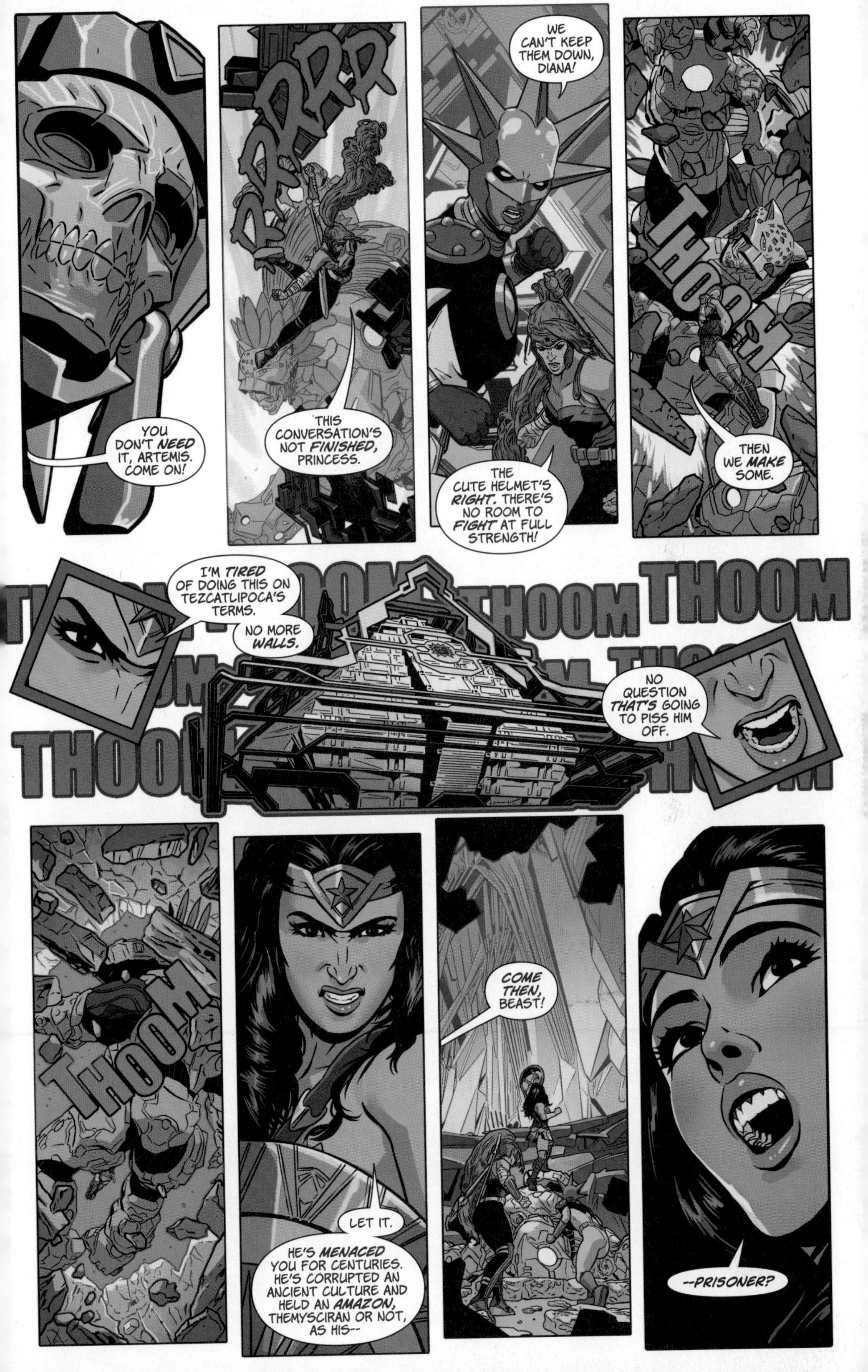
YOU DON'T *NEED* IT, ARTEMIS. COME ON!
RRRRR
THIS CONVERSATION'S NOT *FINISHED,* PRINCESS.
WE CAN'T KEEP THEM DOWN, DIANA!
THE CUTE HELMET'S *RIGHT.* THERE'S NO ROOM TO *FIGHT* AT FULL STRENGTH!
THOOM
THEN WE *MAKE* SOME.
THOOM THOOM THOOM
I'M *TIRED* OF DOING THIS ON TEZCATLIPOCA'S TERMS.
NO MORE *WALLS.*
NO QUESTION *THAT'S* GOING TO PISS HIM OFF.
THOOM
LET IT.
HE'S *MENACED* YOU FOR CENTURIES. HE'S CORRUPTED AN ANCIENT CULTURE AND HELD AN *AMAZON,* THEMYSCIRAN OR NOT, AS HIS--
COME THEN, BEAST!
--PRISONER?

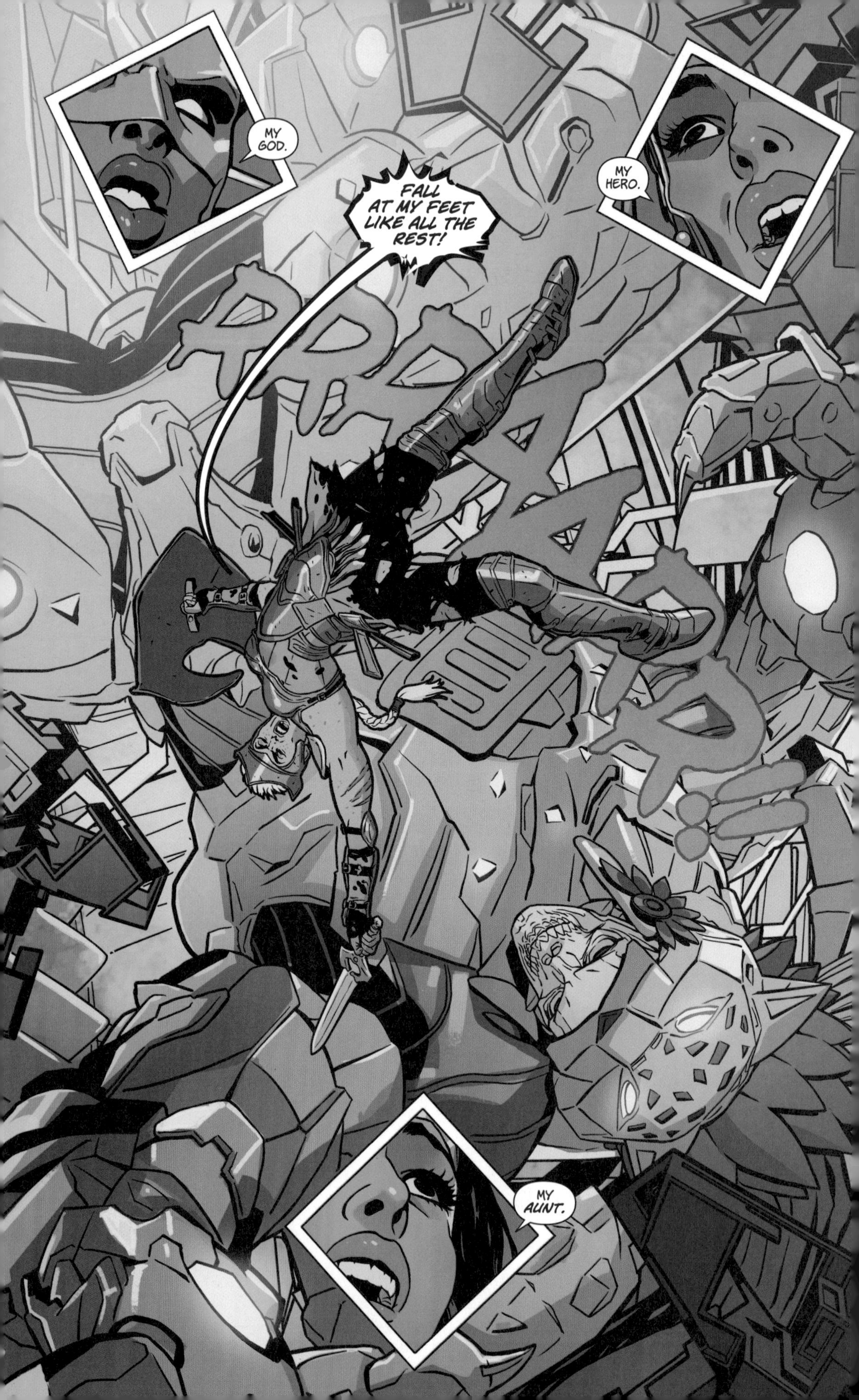
MY GOD.
FALL AT MY FEET LIKE ALL THE REST!
MY HERO.
MY AUNT.

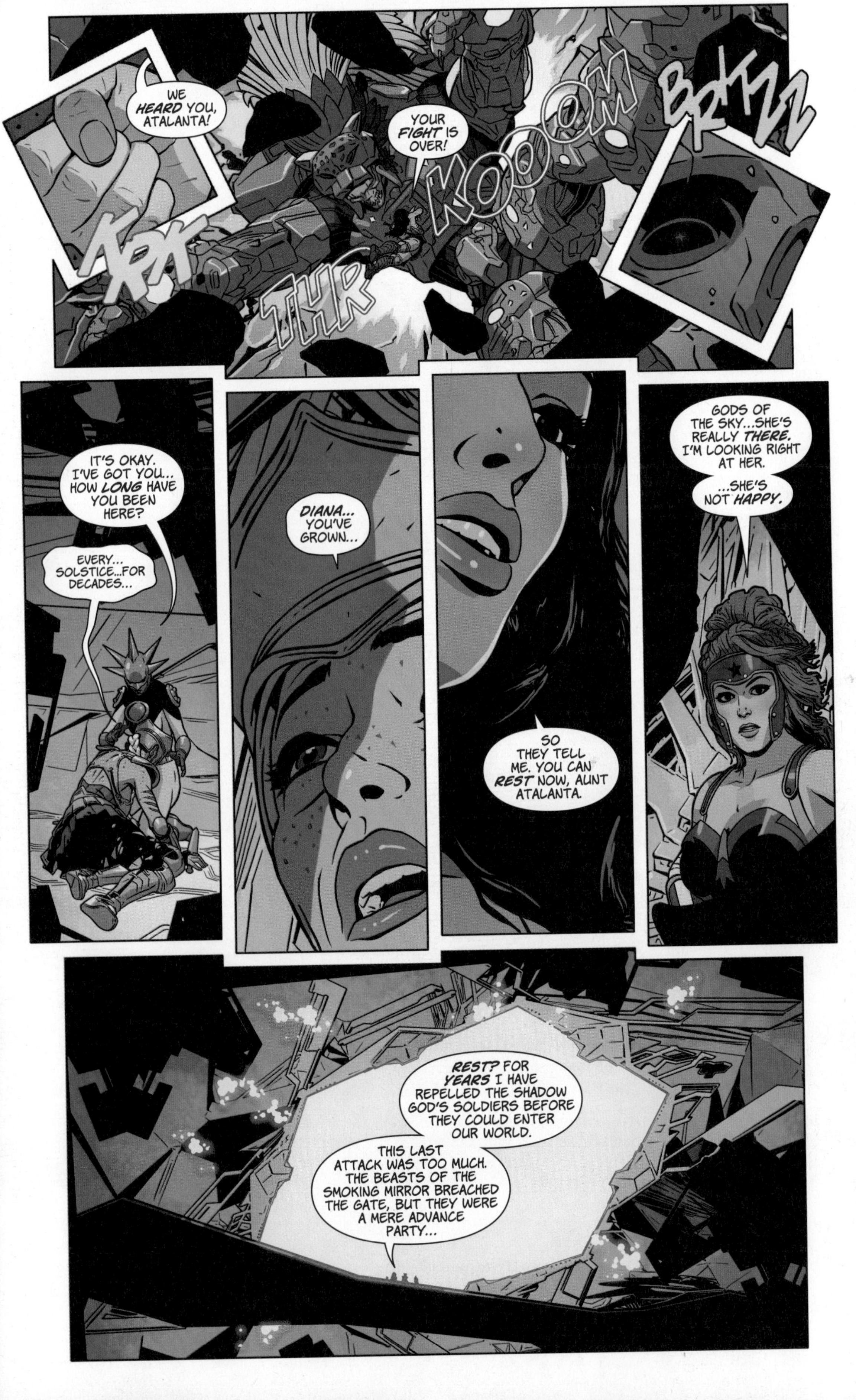
WE *HEARD* YOU, ATALANTA!
YOUR *FIGHT* IS OVER!
THR
KOOOOM
BRTZZ
IT'S OKAY. I'VE GOT YOU... HOW *LONG* HAVE YOU BEEN HERE?
EVERY... SOLSTICE...FOR DECADES...
DIANA... YOU'VE GROWN...
SO THEY TELL ME. YOU CAN *REST* NOW, AUNT ATALANTA.
GODS OF THE SKY...SHE'S REALLY *THERE.* I'M LOOKING RIGHT AT HER.
...SHE'S NOT *HAPPY.*
REST? FOR *YEARS* I HAVE REPELLED THE SHADOW GOD'S SOLDIERS BEFORE THEY COULD ENTER OUR WORLD.
THIS LAST ATTACK WAS TOO MUCH. THE BEASTS OF THE SMOKING MIRROR BREACHED THE GATE, BUT THEY WERE A MERE ADVANCE PARTY...

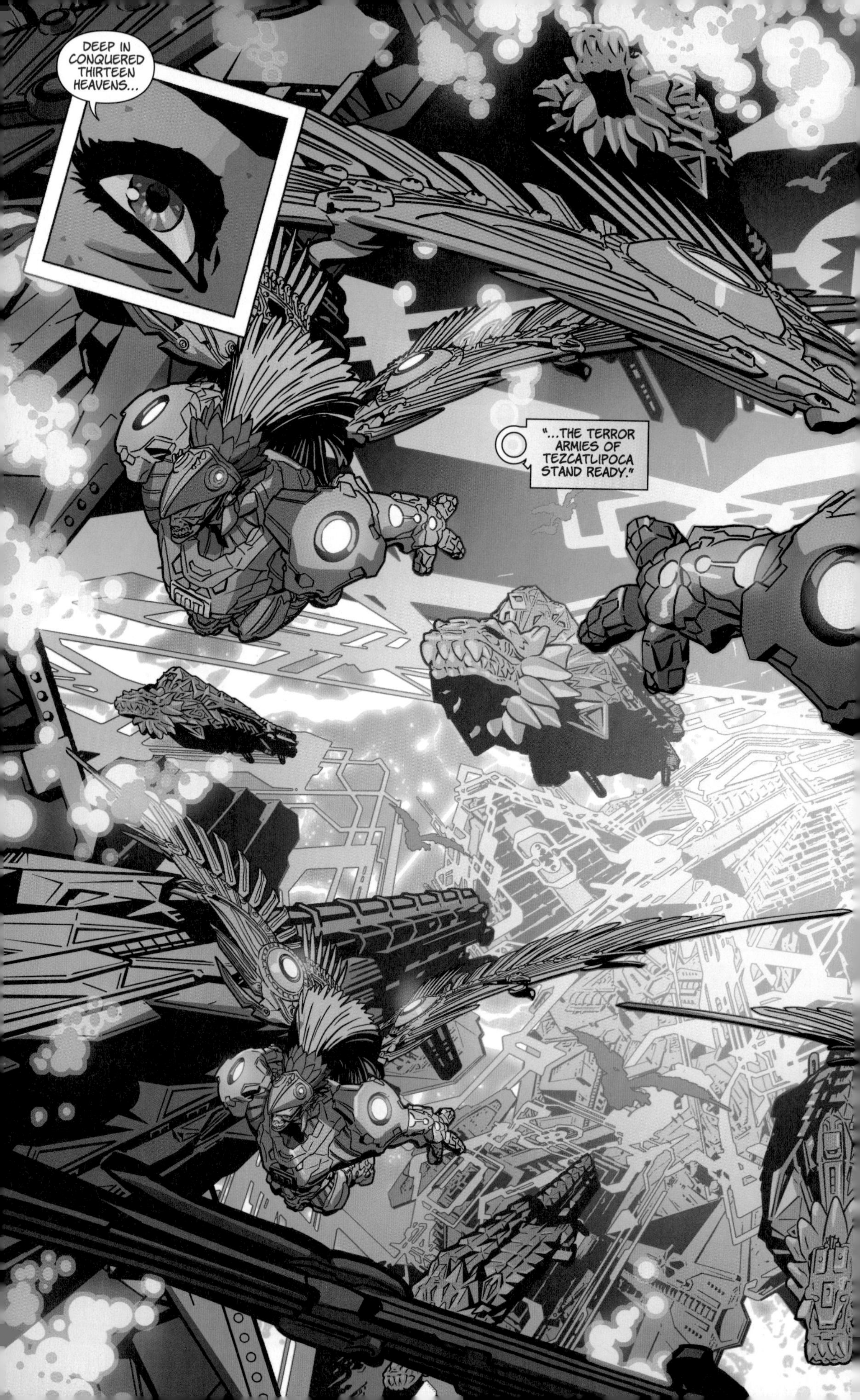
DEEP IN CONQUERED THIRTEEN HEAVENS...
"...THE TERROR ARMIES OF TEZCATLIPOCA STAND READY."

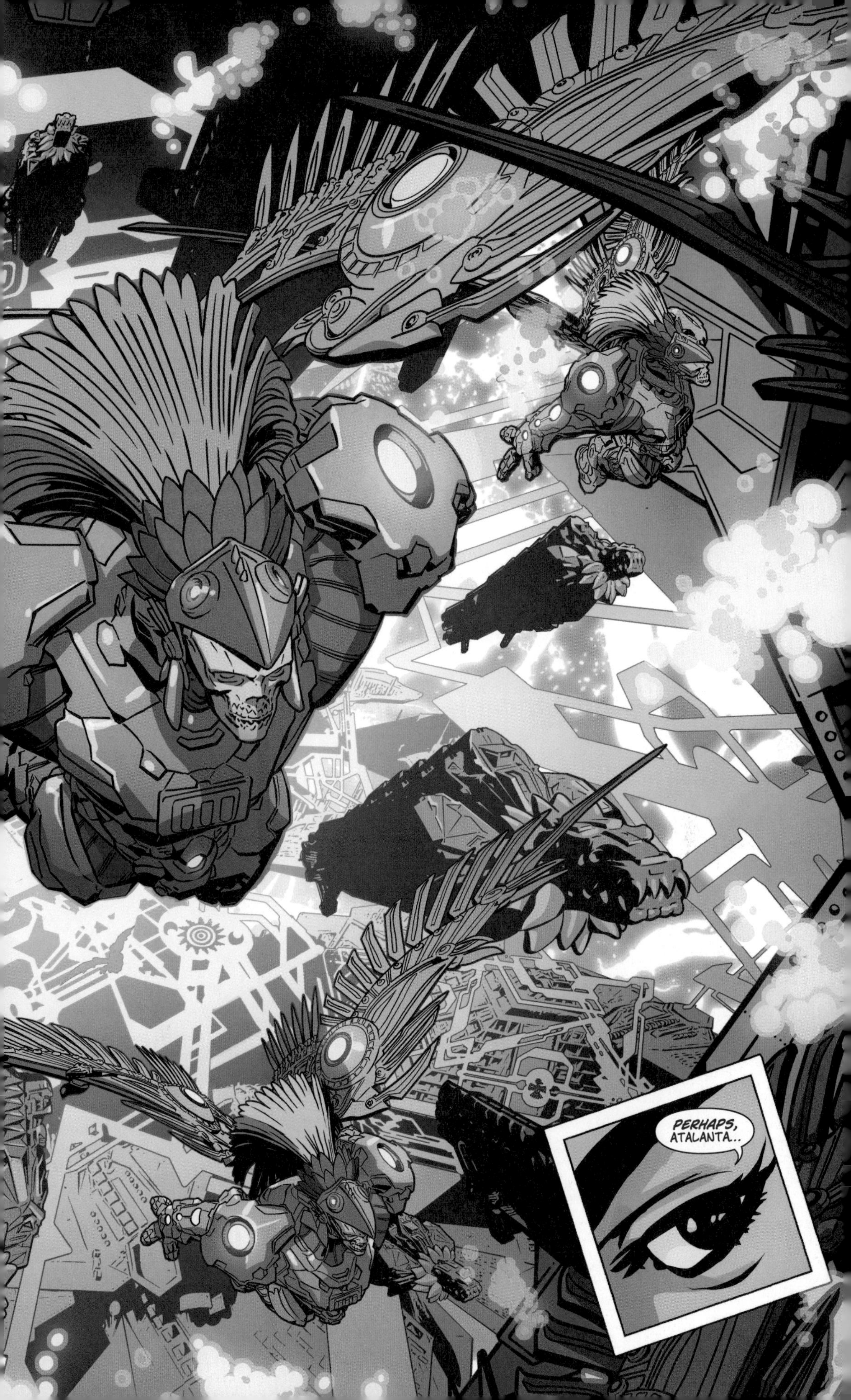
PERHAPS, ATALANTA...

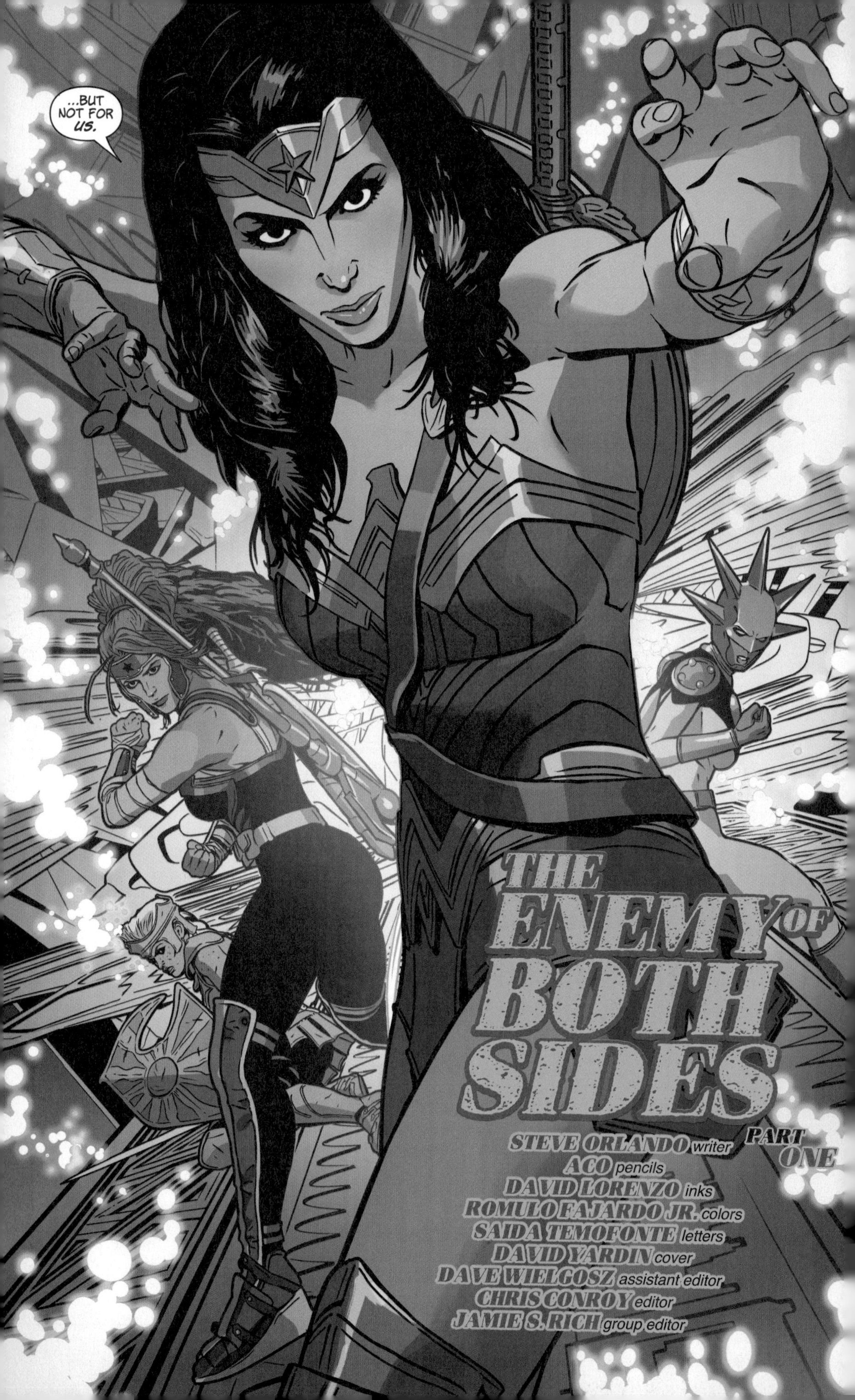
...BUT NOT FOR US.
THE ENEMY OF BOTH SIDES
PART ONE
STEVE ORLANDO writer
ACO pencils
DAVID LORENZO inks
ROMULO FAJARDO JR. colors
SAIDA TEMOFONTE letters
DAVID YARDIN cover
DAVE WIELGOSZ assistant editor
CHRIS CONROY editor
JAMIE S. RICH group editor

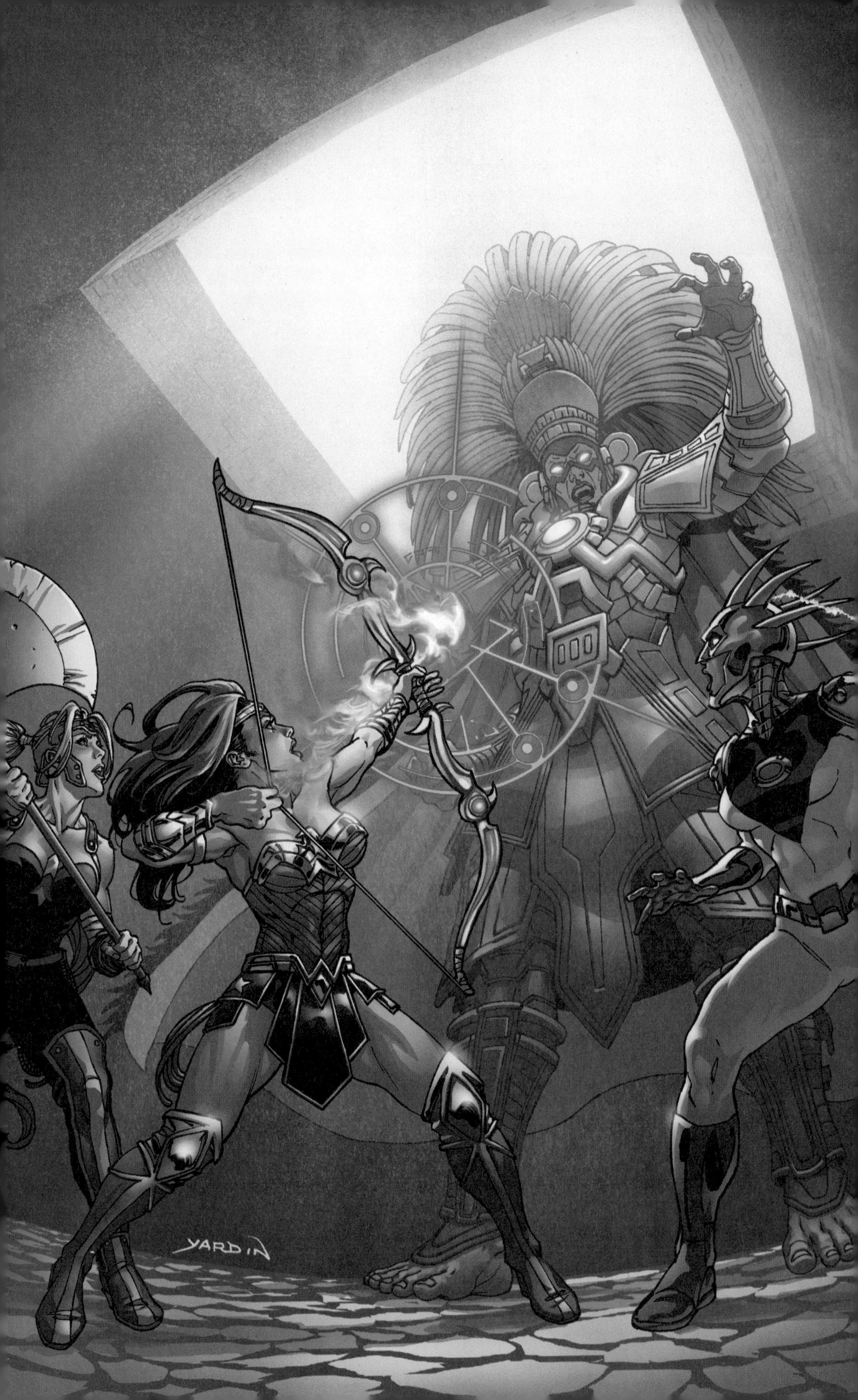
YARDIN

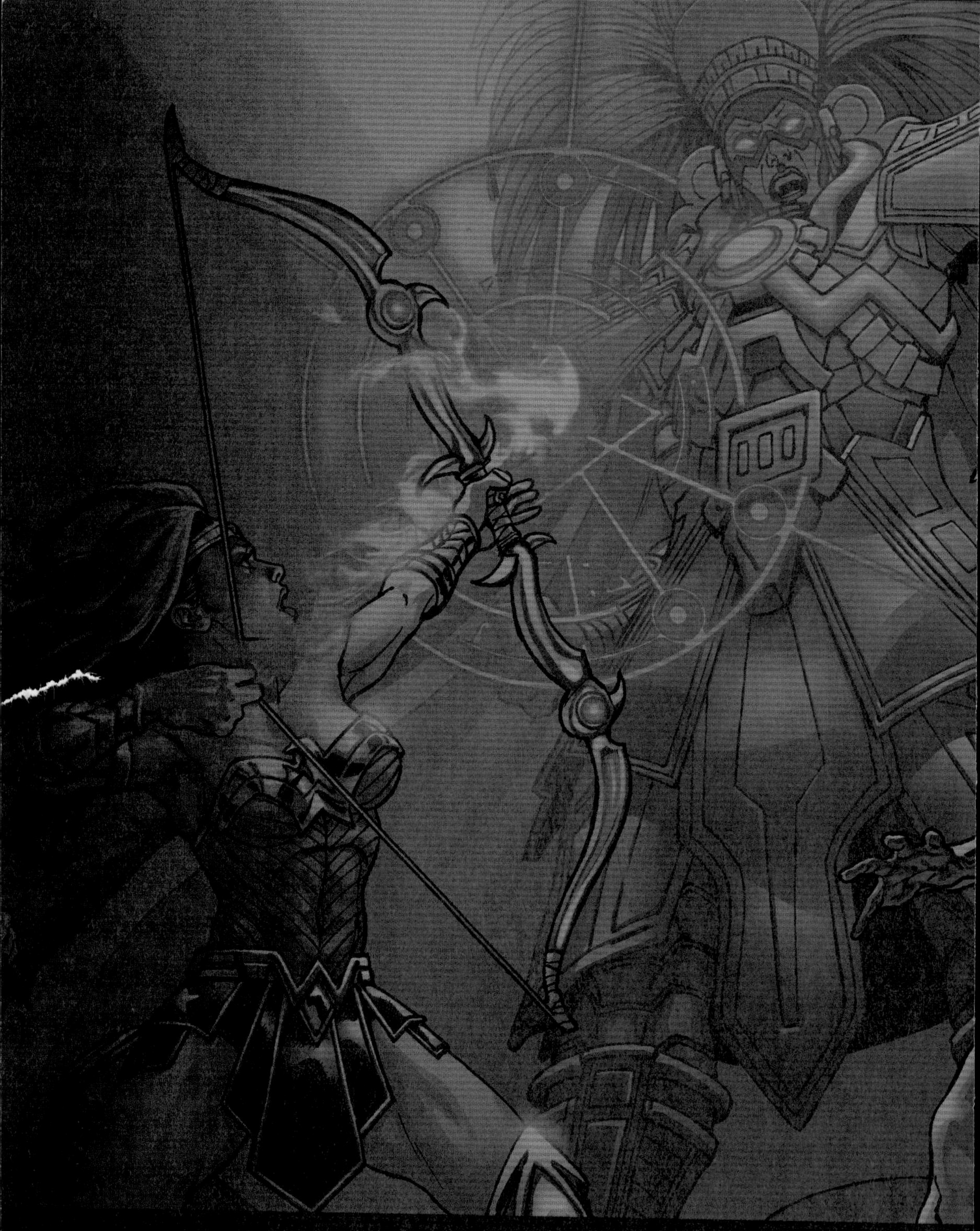

WONDER WOMAN
#53

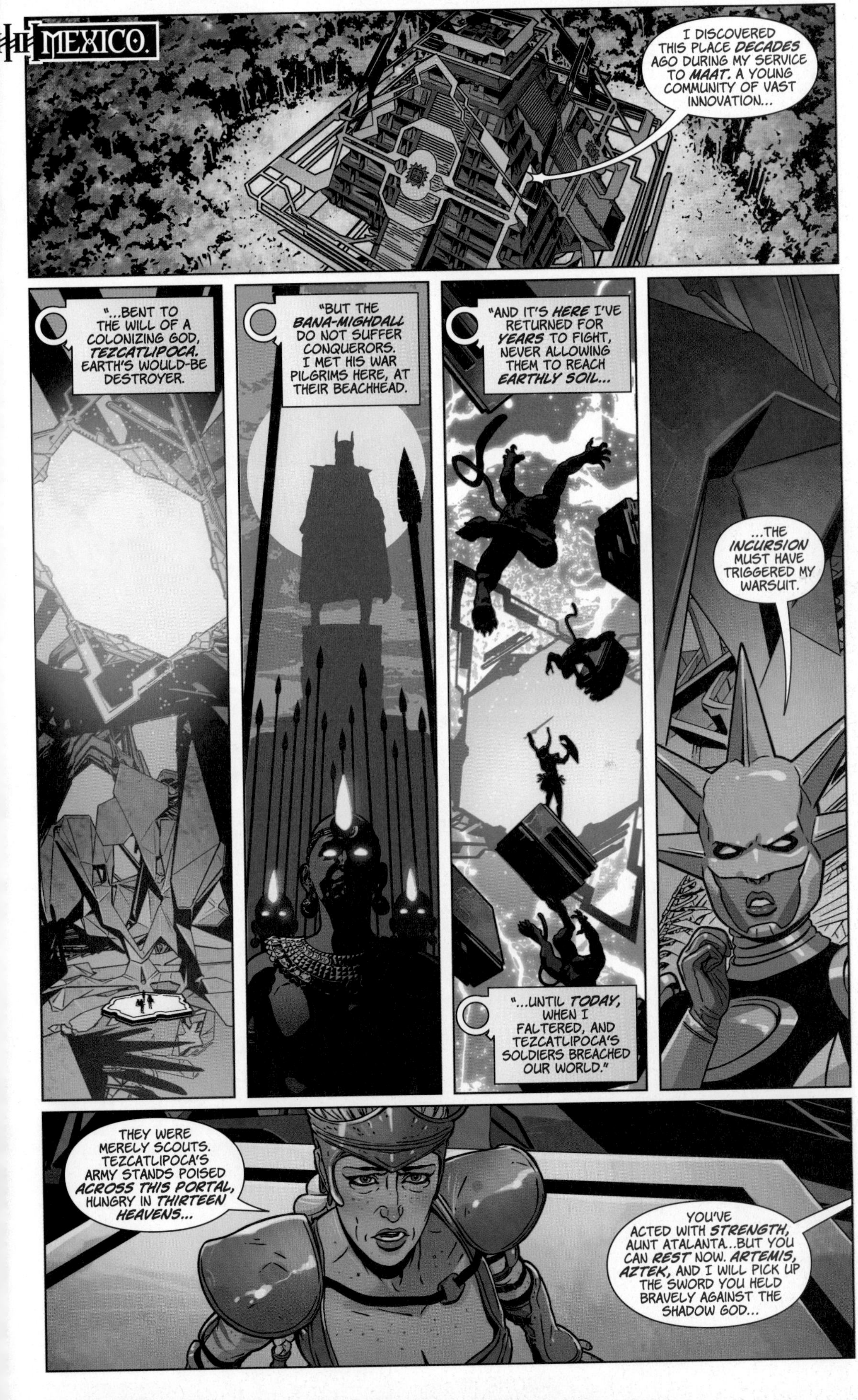
MEXICO.
I DISCOVERED THIS PLACE DECADES AGO DURING MY SERVICE TO MAAT. A YOUNG COMMUNITY OF VAST INNOVATION...
"...BENT TO THE WILL OF A COLONIZING GOD, TEZCATLIPOCA. EARTH'S WOULD-BE DESTROYER.
"BUT THE BANA-MIGHDALL DO NOT SUFFER CONQUERORS. I MET HIS WAR PILGRIMS HERE, AT THEIR BEACHHEAD.
"AND IT'S HERE I'VE RETURNED FOR YEARS TO FIGHT, NEVER ALLOWING THEM TO REACH EARTHLY SOIL...
"...UNTIL TODAY, WHEN I FALTERED, AND TEZCATLIPOCA'S SOLDIERS BREACHED OUR WORLD."
...THE INCURSION MUST HAVE TRIGGERED MY WARSUIT.
THEY WERE MERELY SCOUTS. TEZCATLIPOCA'S ARMY STANDS POISED ACROSS THIS PORTAL, HUNGRY IN THIRTEEN HEAVENS...
YOU'VE ACTED WITH STRENGTH, AUNT ATALANTA...BUT YOU CAN REST NOW. ARTEMIS, AZTEK, AND I WILL PICK UP THE SWORD YOU HELD BRAVELY AGAINST THE SHADOW GOD...

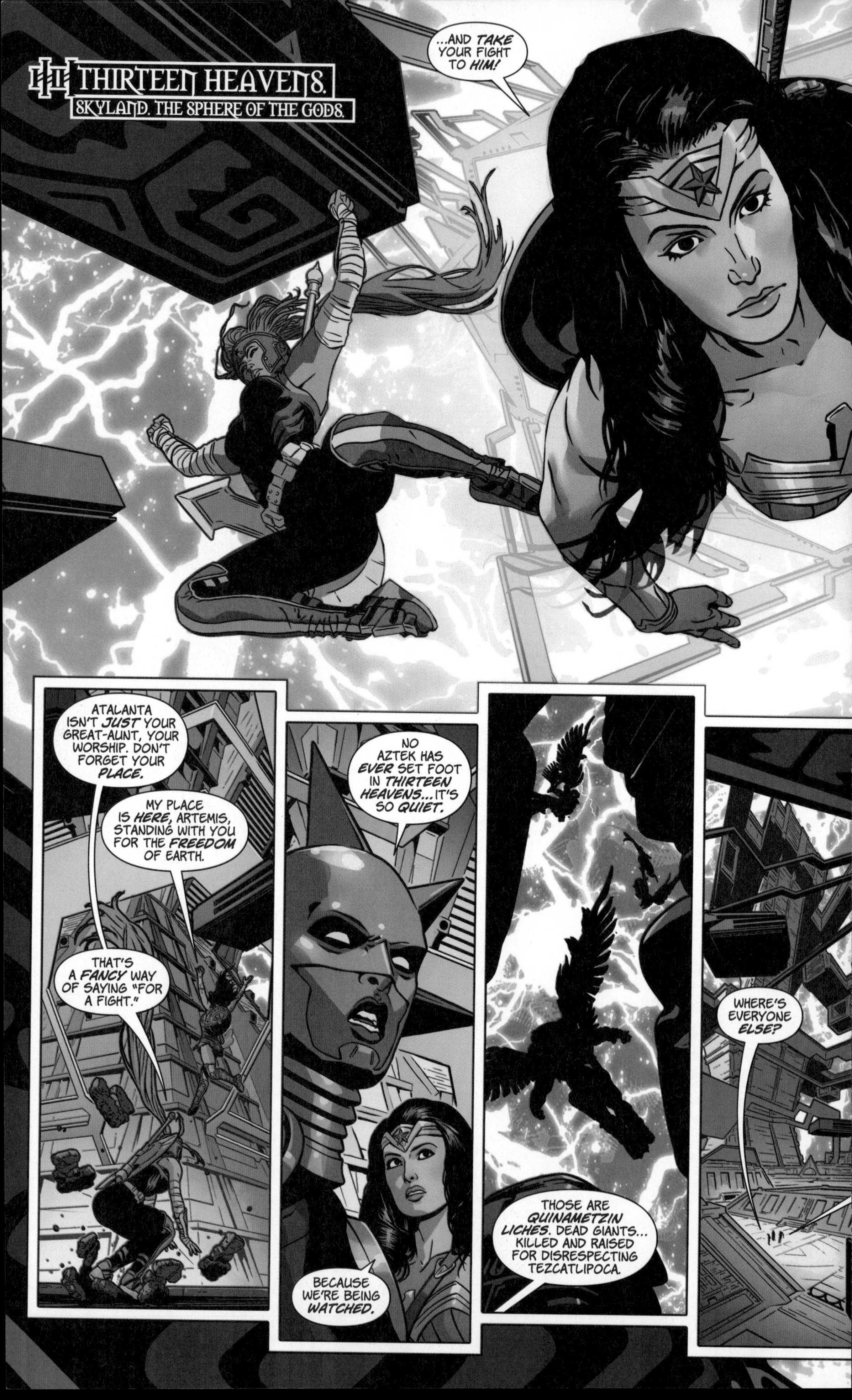
THIRTEEN HEAVENS.
SKYLAND. THE SPHERE OF THE GODS.
...AND TAKE YOUR FIGHT TO HIM!
ATALANTA ISN'T JUST YOUR GREAT-AUNT, YOUR WORSHIP. DON'T FORGET YOUR PLACE.
MY PLACE IS HERE, ARTEMIS, STANDING WITH YOU FOR THE FREEDOM OF EARTH.
THAT'S A FANCY WAY OF SAYING "FOR A FIGHT."
NO AZTEK HAS EVER SET FOOT IN THIRTEEN HEAVENS... IT'S SO QUIET.
BECAUSE WE'RE BEING WATCHED.
THOSE ARE QUINAMETZIN LICHES. DEAD GIANTS... KILLED AND RAISED FOR DISRESPECTING TEZCATLIPOCA.
WHERE'S EVERYONE ELSE?

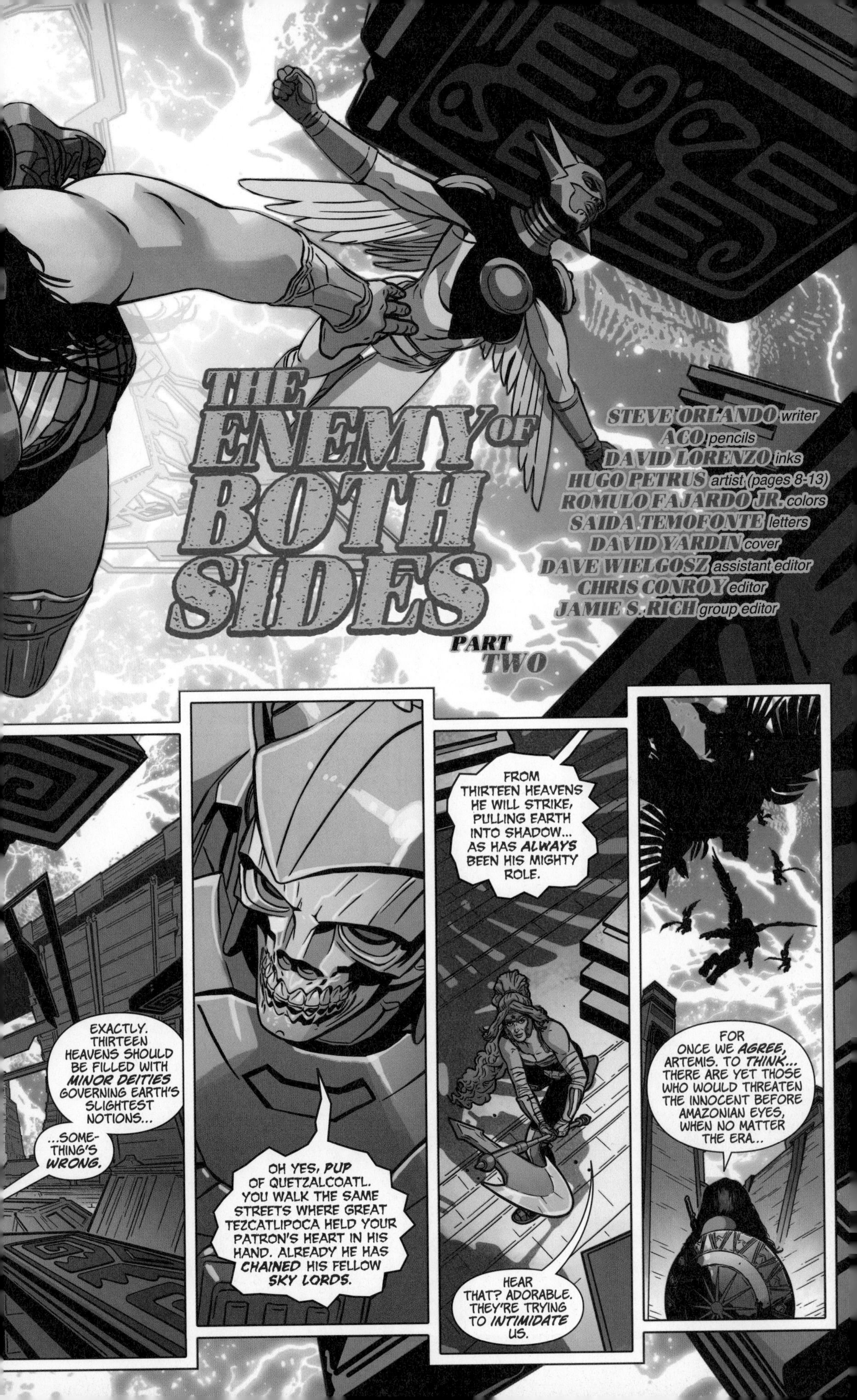
THE ENEMY OF BOTH SIDES
PART TWO
STEVE ORLANDO writer
ACO pencils
DAVID LORENZO inks
HUGO PETRUS artist (pages 8-13)
ROMULO FAJARDO JR. colors
SAIDA TEMOFONTE letters
DAVID YARDIN cover
DAVE WIELGOSZ assistant editor
CHRIS CONROY editor
JAMIE S. RICH group editor
EXACTLY. THIRTEEN HEAVENS SHOULD BE FILLED WITH MINOR DEITIES GOVERNING EARTH'S SLIGHTEST NOTIONS...
...SOME-THING'S WRONG.
OH YES, PUP OF QUETZALCOATL. YOU WALK THE SAME STREETS WHERE GREAT TEZCATLIPOCA HELD YOUR PATRON'S HEART IN HIS HAND. ALREADY HE HAS CHAINED HIS FELLOW SKY LORDS.
FROM THIRTEEN HEAVENS HE WILL STRIKE, PULLING EARTH INTO SHADOW... AS HAS ALWAYS BEEN HIS MIGHTY ROLE.
HEAR THAT? ADORABLE. THEY'RE TRYING TO INTIMIDATE US.
FOR ONCE WE AGREE, ARTEMIS. TO THINK... THERE ARE YET THOSE WHO WOULD THREATEN THE INNOCENT BEFORE AMAZONIAN EYES, WHEN NO MATTER THE ERA..

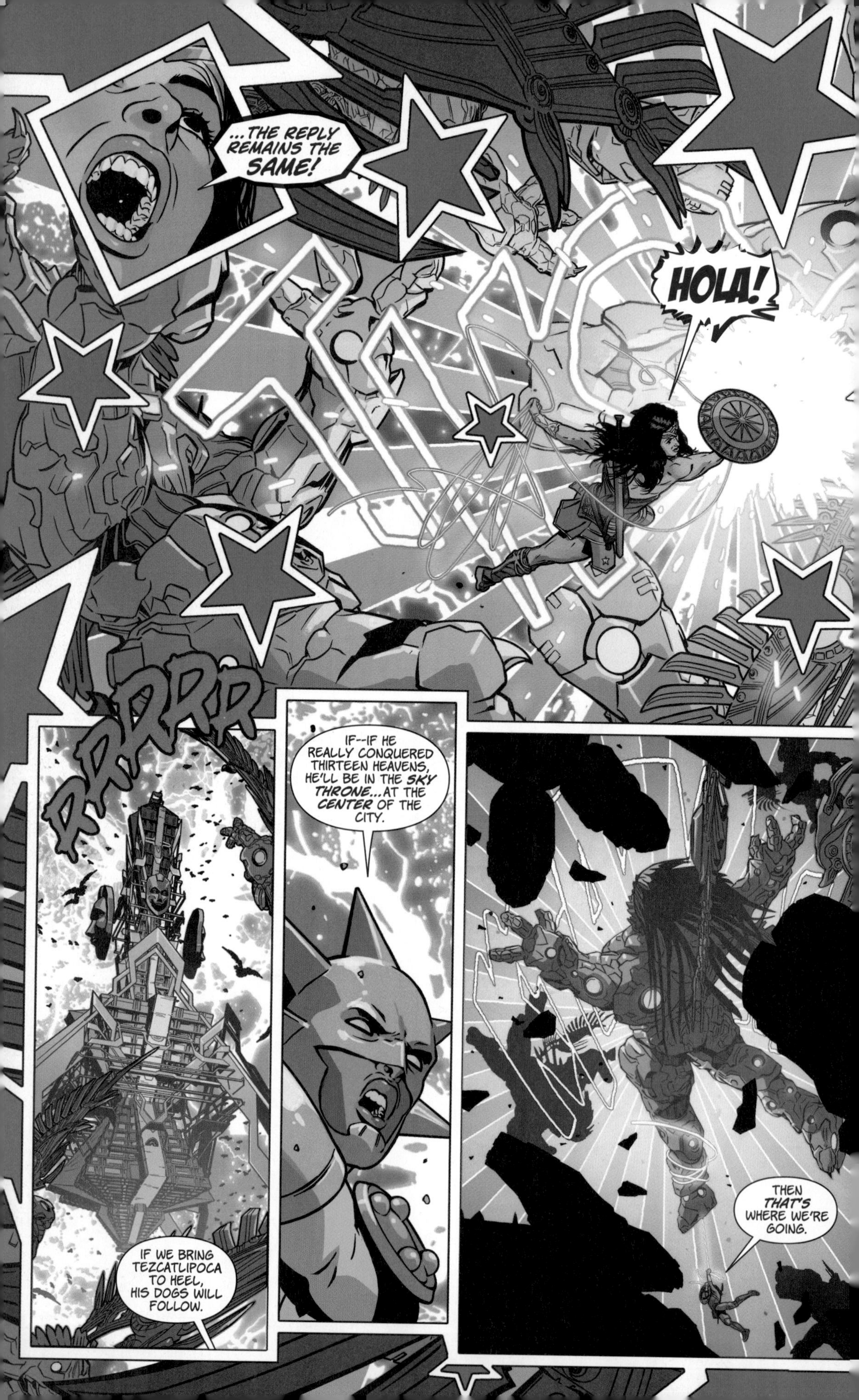

...THE REPLY REMAINS THE SAME!
HOLA!
RRRRR
IF WE BRING TEZCATLIPOCA TO HEEL, HIS DOGS WILL FOLLOW.
IF--IF HE REALLY CONQUERED THIRTEEN HEAVENS, HE'LL BE IN THE SKY THRONE...AT THE CENTER OF THE CITY.
THEN THAT'S WHERE WE'RE GOING.

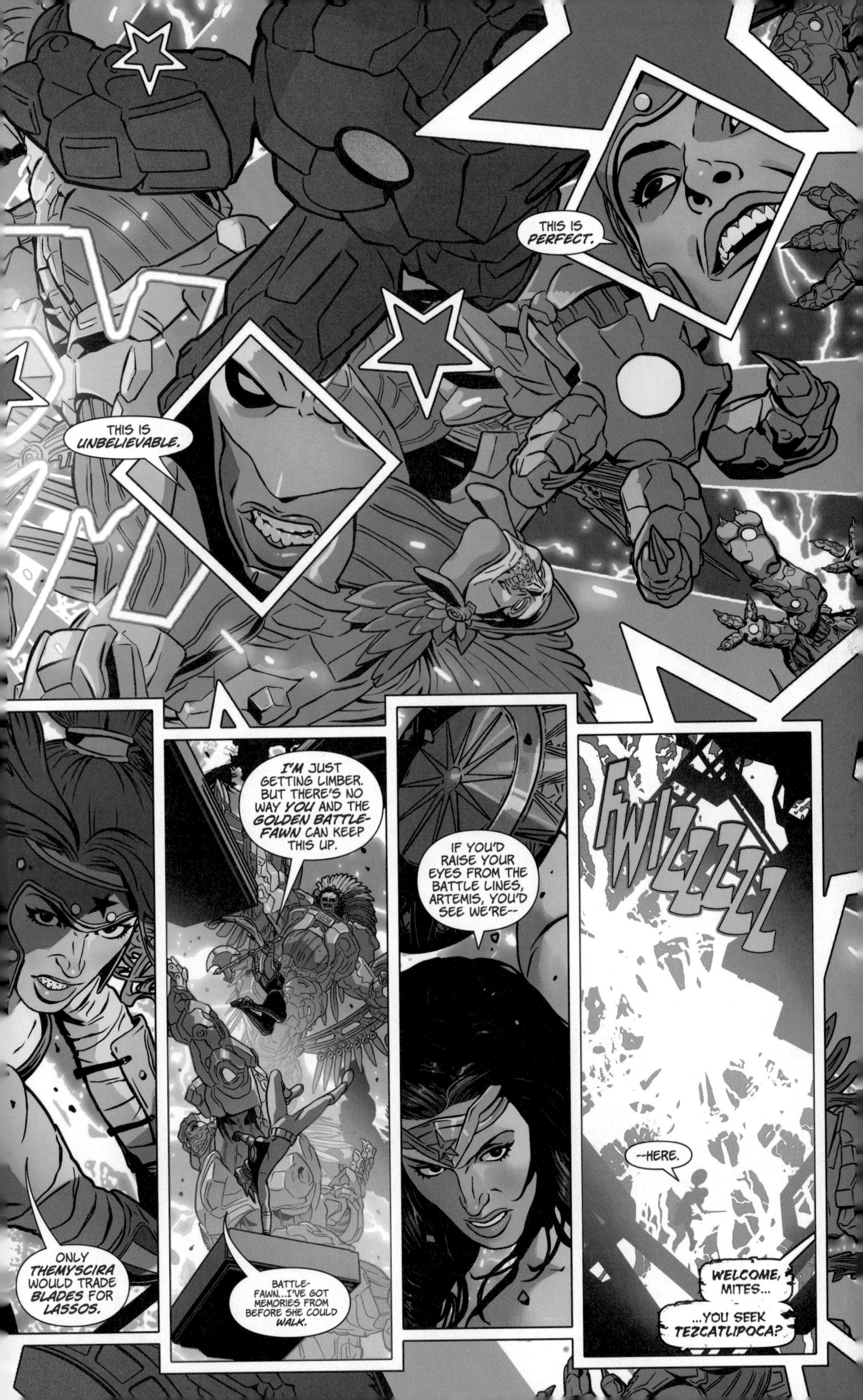
THIS IS PERFECT.
THIS IS UNBELIEVABLE.
ONLY THEMYSCIRA WOULD TRADE BLADES FOR LASSOS.
I'M JUST GETTING LIMBER. BUT THERE'S NO WAY YOU AND THE GOLDEN BATTLE-FAWN CAN KEEP THIS UP.
BATTLE-FAWN...I'VE GOT MEMORIES FROM BEFORE SHE COULD WALK.
IF YOU'D RAISE YOUR EYES FROM THE BATTLE LINES, ARTEMIS, YOU'D SEE WE'RE--
FWIZZZZZZ
--HERE.
WELCOME, MITES...
...YOU SEEK TEZCATLIPOCA?

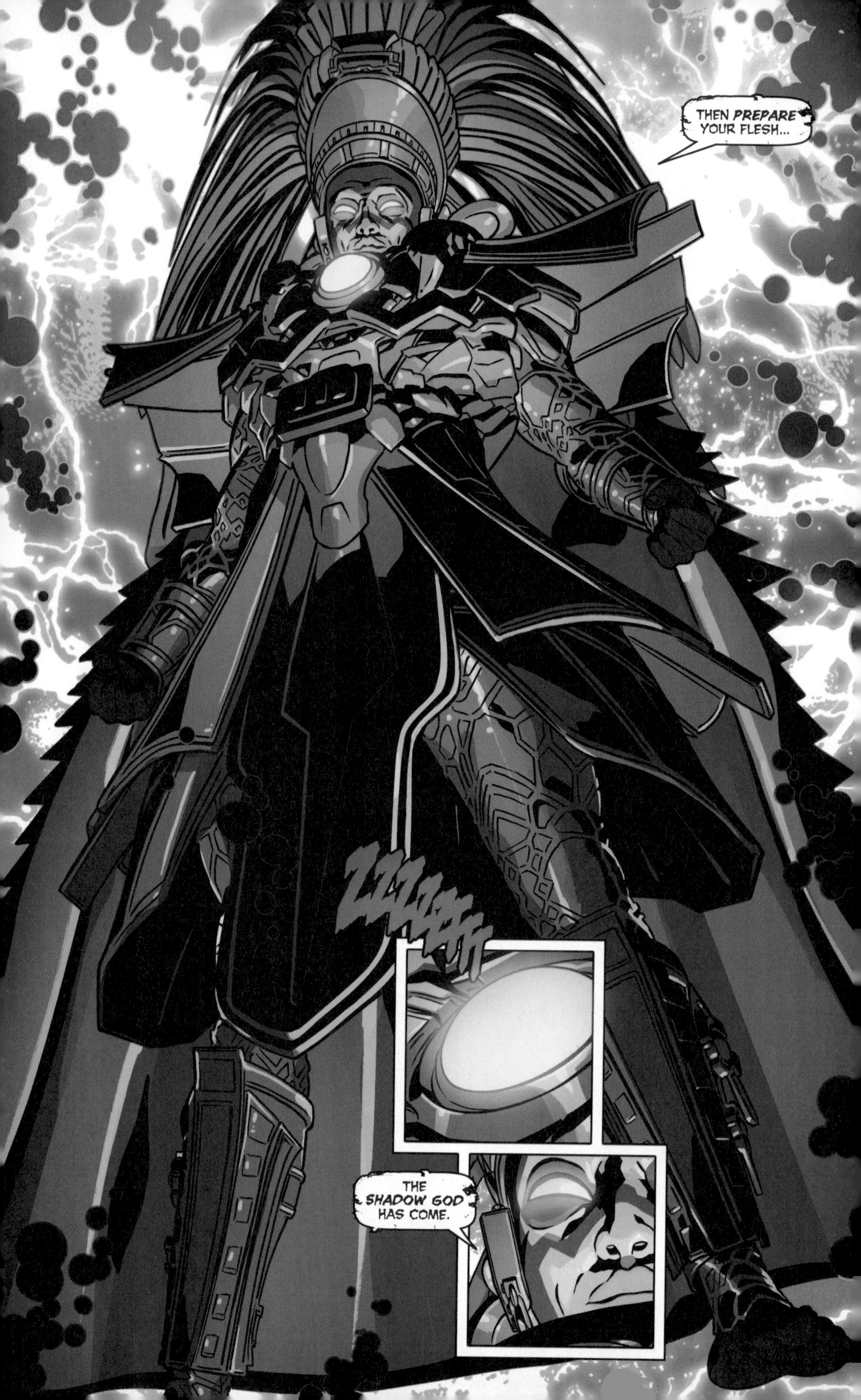
THEN PREPARE YOUR FLESH...
ZZZAKK
THE SHADOW GOD HAS COME.

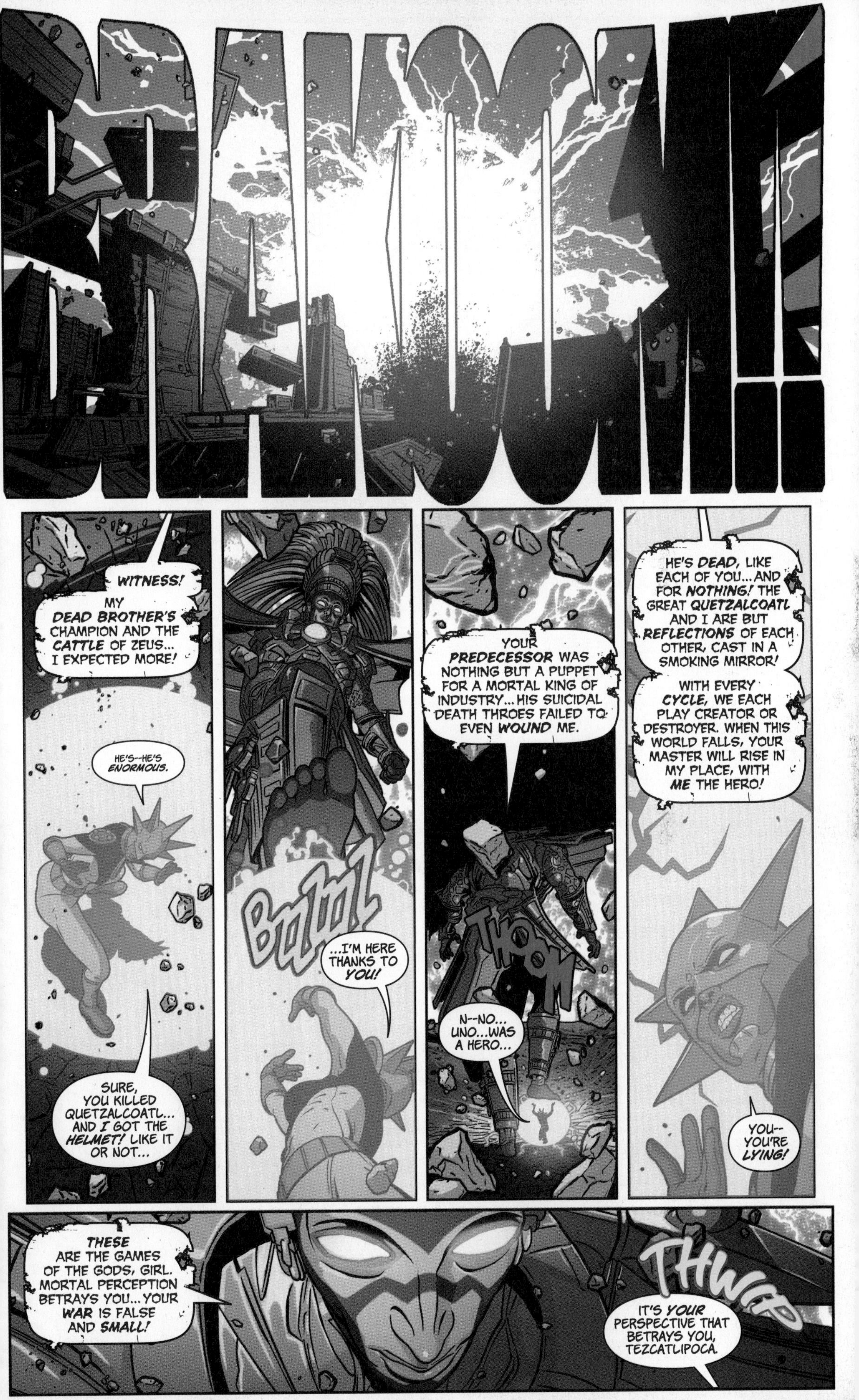
WITNESS! MY DEAD BROTHER'S CHAMPION AND THE CATTLE OF ZEUS... I EXPECTED MORE!
HE'S--HE'S ENORMOUS.
SURE, YOU KILLED QUETZALCOATL... AND I GOT THE HELMET! LIKE IT OR NOT...
...I'M HERE THANKS TO YOU!
YOUR PREDECESSOR WAS NOTHING BUT A PUPPET FOR A MORTAL KING OF INDUSTRY...HIS SUICIDAL DEATH THROES FAILED TO EVEN WOUND ME.
THOOM
N--NO... UNO...WAS A HERO...
HE'S DEAD, LIKE EACH OF YOU...AND FOR NOTHING! THE GREAT QUETZALCOATL AND I ARE BUT REFLECTIONS OF EACH OTHER, CAST IN A SMOKING MIRROR!
WITH EVERY CYCLE, WE EACH PLAY CREATOR OR DESTROYER. WHEN THIS WORLD FALLS, YOUR MASTER WILL RISE IN MY PLACE, WITH ME THE HERO!
YOU-- YOU'RE LYING!
THESE ARE THE GAMES OF THE GODS, GIRL. MORTAL PERCEPTION BETRAYS YOU...YOUR WAR IS FALSE AND SMALL!
THWIP
IT'S YOUR PERSPECTIVE THAT BETRAYS YOU, TEZCATLIPOCA.

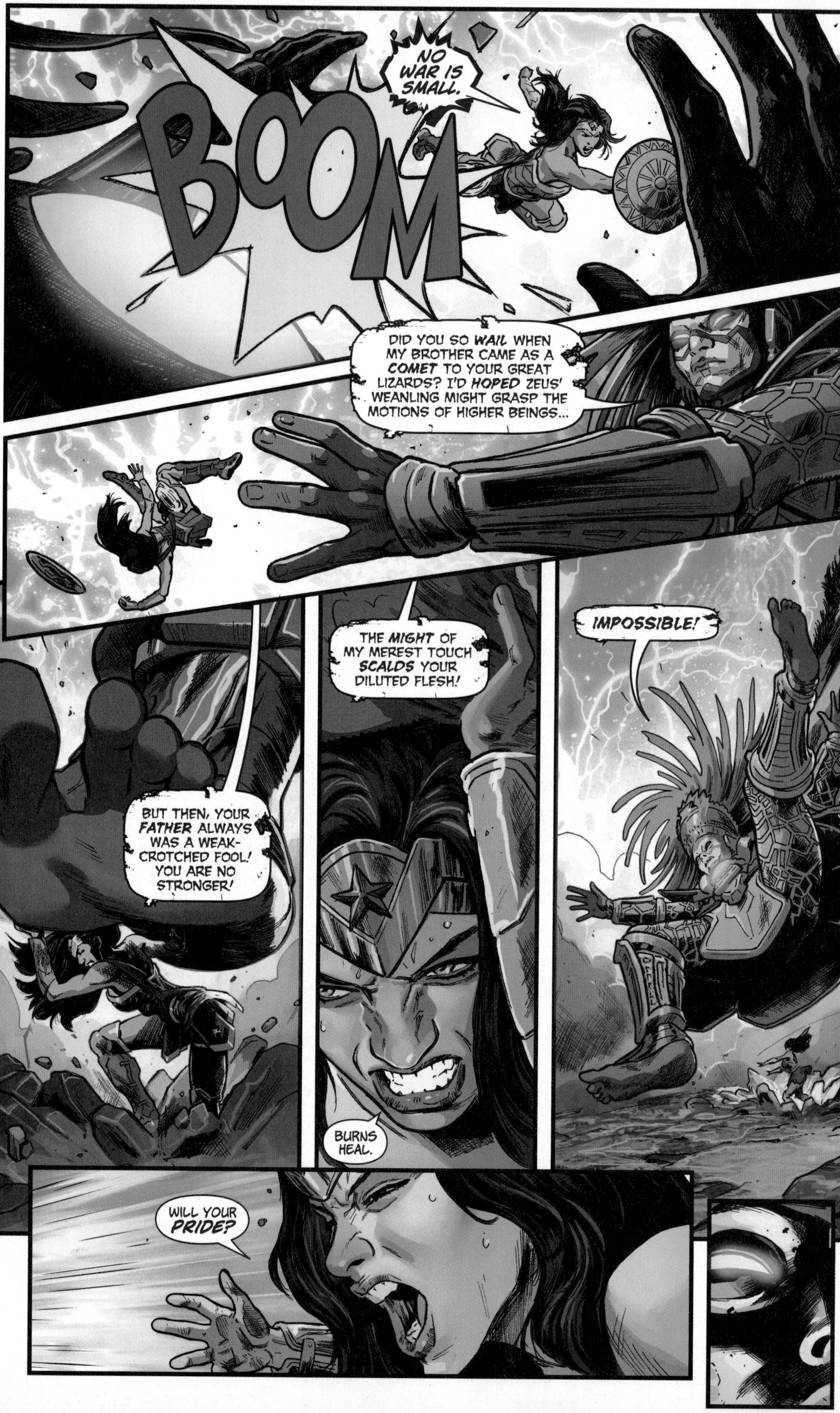
BOOM
NO WAR IS SMALL.
DID YOU SO WAIL WHEN MY BROTHER CAME AS A COMET TO YOUR GREAT LIZARDS? I'D HOPED ZEUS' WEANLING MIGHT GRASP THE MOTIONS OF HIGHER BEINGS...
BUT THEN, YOUR FATHER ALWAYS WAS A WEAK-CROTCHED FOOL! YOU ARE NO STRONGER!
THE MIGHT OF MY MEREST TOUCH SCALDS YOUR DILUTED FLESH!
BURNS HEAL.
IMPOSSIBLE!
WILL YOUR PRIDE?

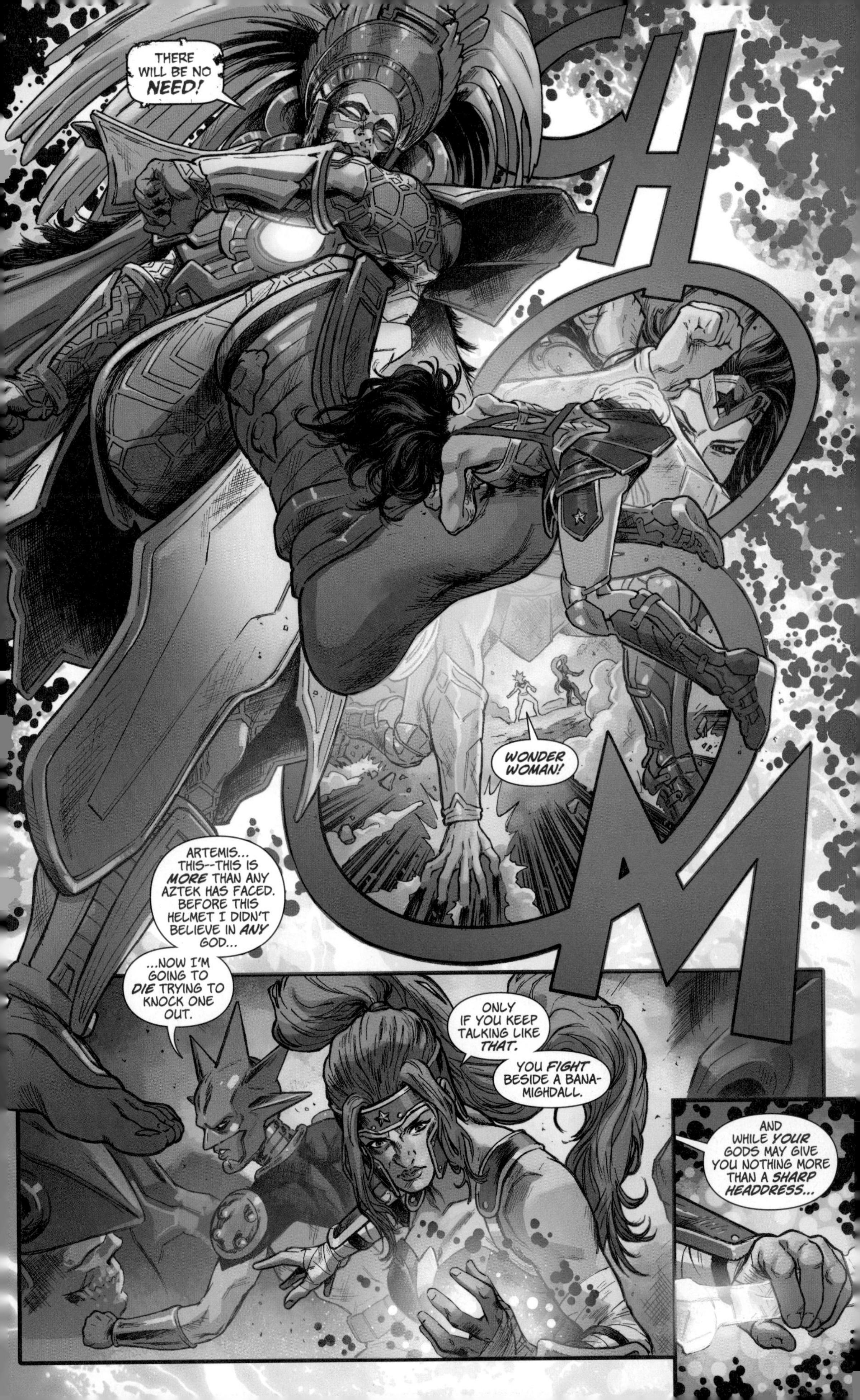
THERE WILL BE NO NEED!
CHOOM
WONDER WOMAN!
ARTEMIS... THIS--THIS IS MORE THAN ANY AZTEK HAS FACED. BEFORE THIS HELMET I DIDN'T BELIEVE IN ANY GOD...
...NOW I'M GOING TO DIE TRYING TO KNOCK ONE OUT.
ONLY IF YOU KEEP TALKING LIKE THAT.
YOU FIGHT BESIDE A BANA-MIGHDALL.
AND WHILE YOUR GODS MAY GIVE YOU NOTHING MORE THAN A SHARP HEADDRESS...

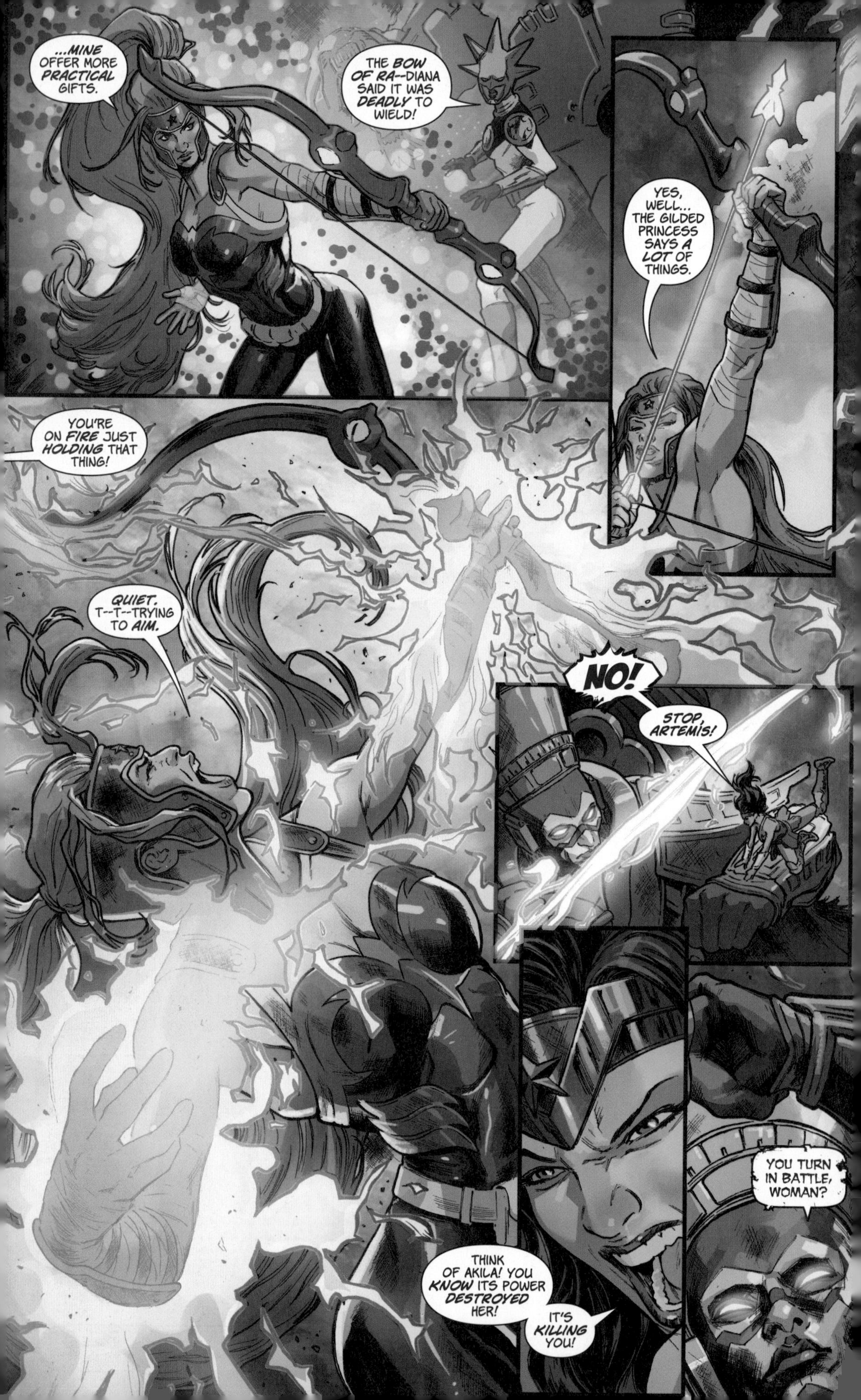
...MINE OFFER MORE PRACTICAL GIFTS.
THE BOW OF RA--DIANA SAID IT WAS DEADLY TO WIELD!
YES, WELL... THE GILDED PRINCESS SAYS A LOT OF THINGS.
YOU'RE ON FIRE JUST HOLDING THAT THING!
QUIET. T--T--TRYING TO AIM.
NO!
STOP, ARTEMIS!
YOU TURN IN BATTLE, WOMAN?
THINK OF AKILA! YOU KNOW ITS POWER DESTROYED HER!
IT'S KILLING YOU!

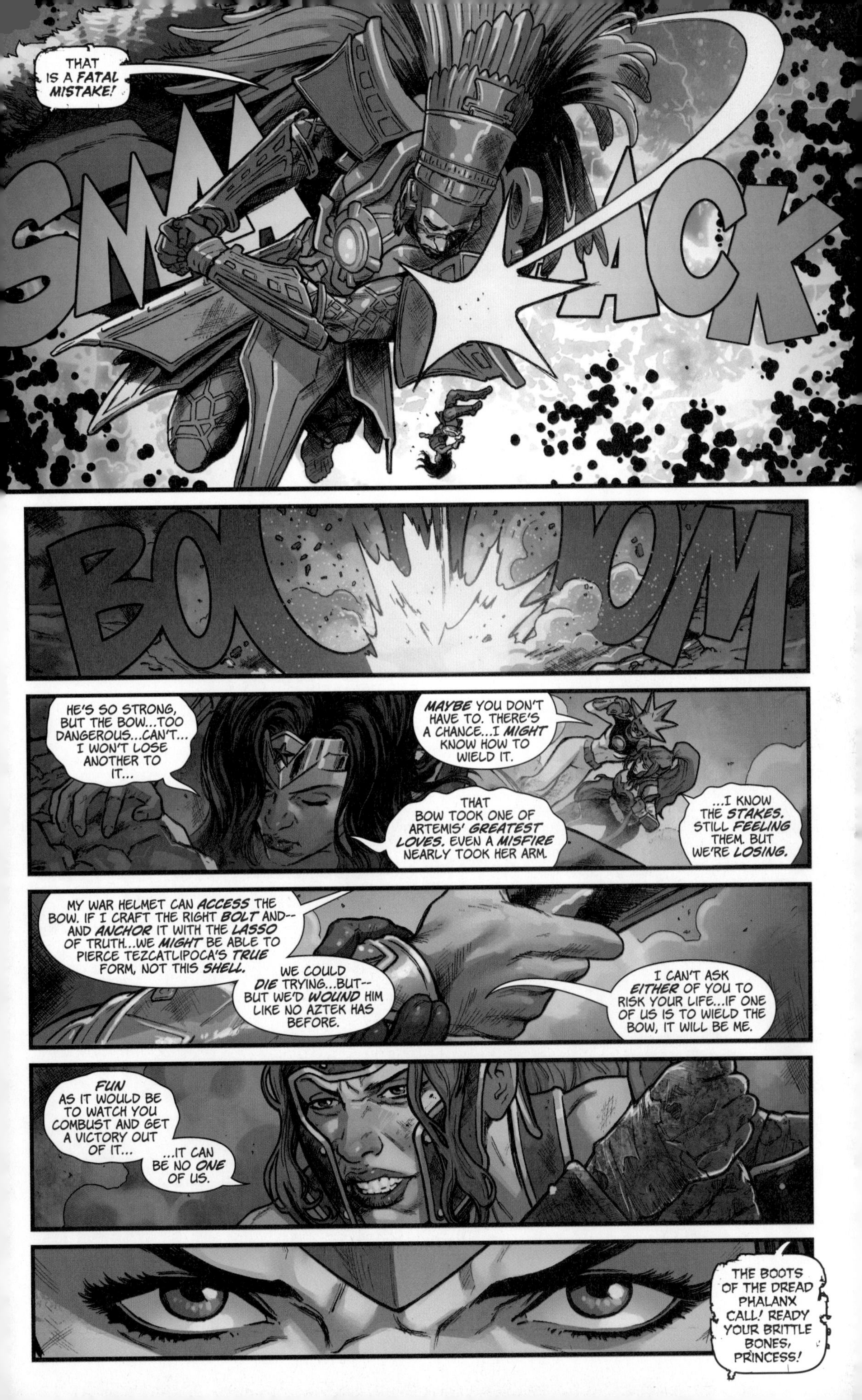
THAT IS A FATAL MISTAKE!
SMAAACK
BOOOM
HE'S SO STRONG, BUT THE BOW...TOO DANGEROUS...CAN'T... I WON'T LOSE ANOTHER TO IT...
MAYBE YOU DON'T HAVE TO. THERE'S A CHANCE...I MIGHT KNOW HOW TO WIELD IT.
THAT BOW TOOK ONE OF ARTEMIS' GREATEST LOVES. EVEN A MISFIRE NEARLY TOOK HER ARM.
...I KNOW THE STAKES. STILL FEELING THEM. BUT WE'RE LOSING.
MY WAR HELMET CAN ACCESS THE BOW. IF I CRAFT THE RIGHT BOLT AND--AND ANCHOR IT WITH THE LASSO OF TRUTH...WE MIGHT BE ABLE TO PIERCE TEZCATLIPOCA'S TRUE FORM, NOT THIS SHELL.
WE COULD DIE TRYING...BUT--BUT WE'D WOUND HIM LIKE NO AZTEK HAS BEFORE.
I CAN'T ASK EITHER OF YOU TO RISK YOUR LIFE...IF ONE OF US IS TO WIELD THE BOW, IT WILL BE ME.
FUN AS IT WOULD BE TO WATCH YOU COMBUST AND GET A VICTORY OUT OF IT...
...IT CAN BE NO ONE OF US.
THE BOOTS OF THE DREAD PHALANX CALL! READY YOUR BRITTLE BONES, PRINCESS!

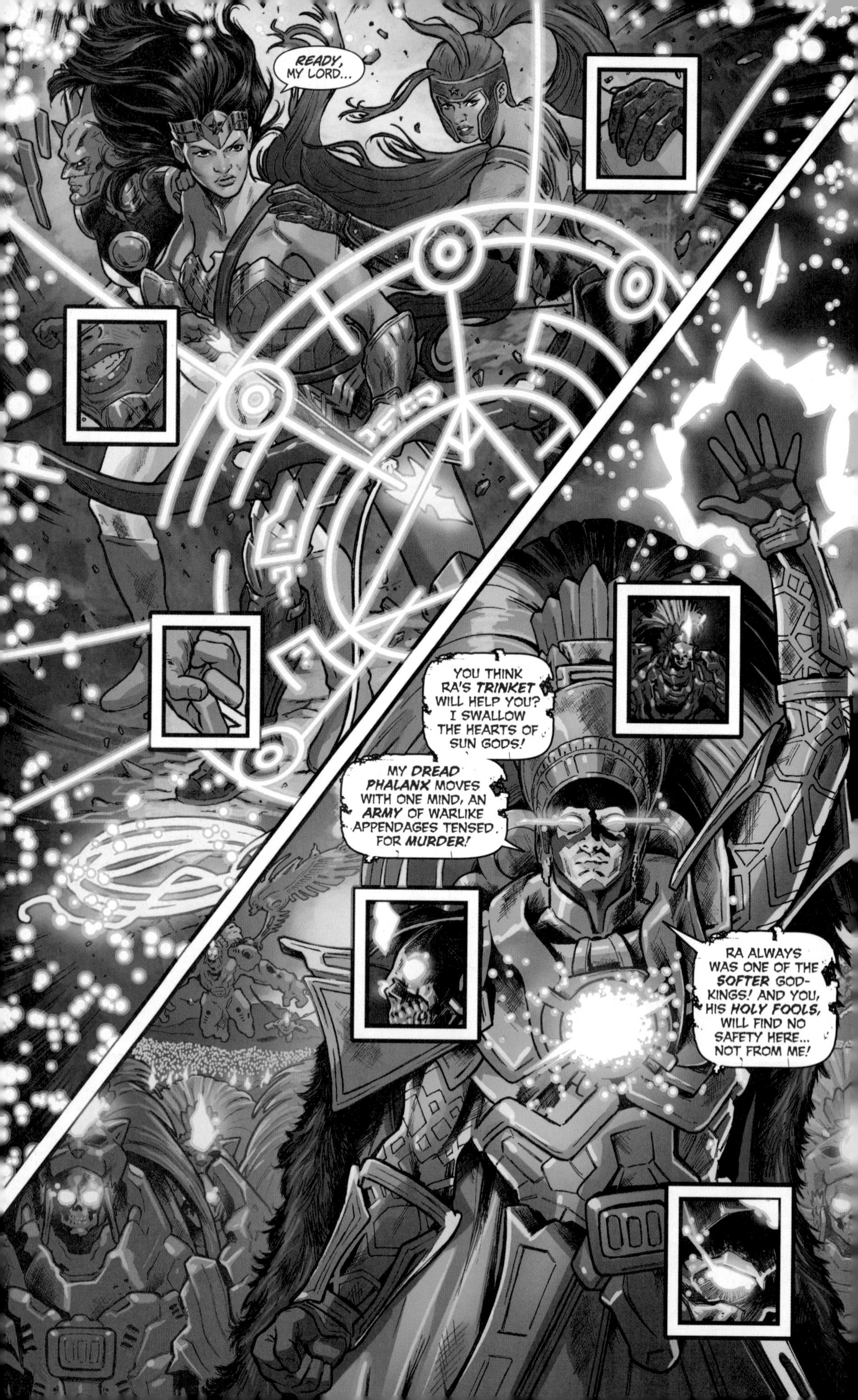
READY, MY LORD...
YOU THINK RA'S TRINKET WILL HELP YOU? I SWALLOW THE HEARTS OF SUN GODS!
MY DREAD PHALANX MOVES WITH ONE MIND, AN ARMY OF WARLIKE APPENDAGES TENSED FOR MURDER!
RA ALWAYS WAS ONE OF THE SOFTER GOD-KINGS! AND YOU, HIS HOLY FOOLS, WILL FIND NO SAFETY HERE... NOT FROM ME!

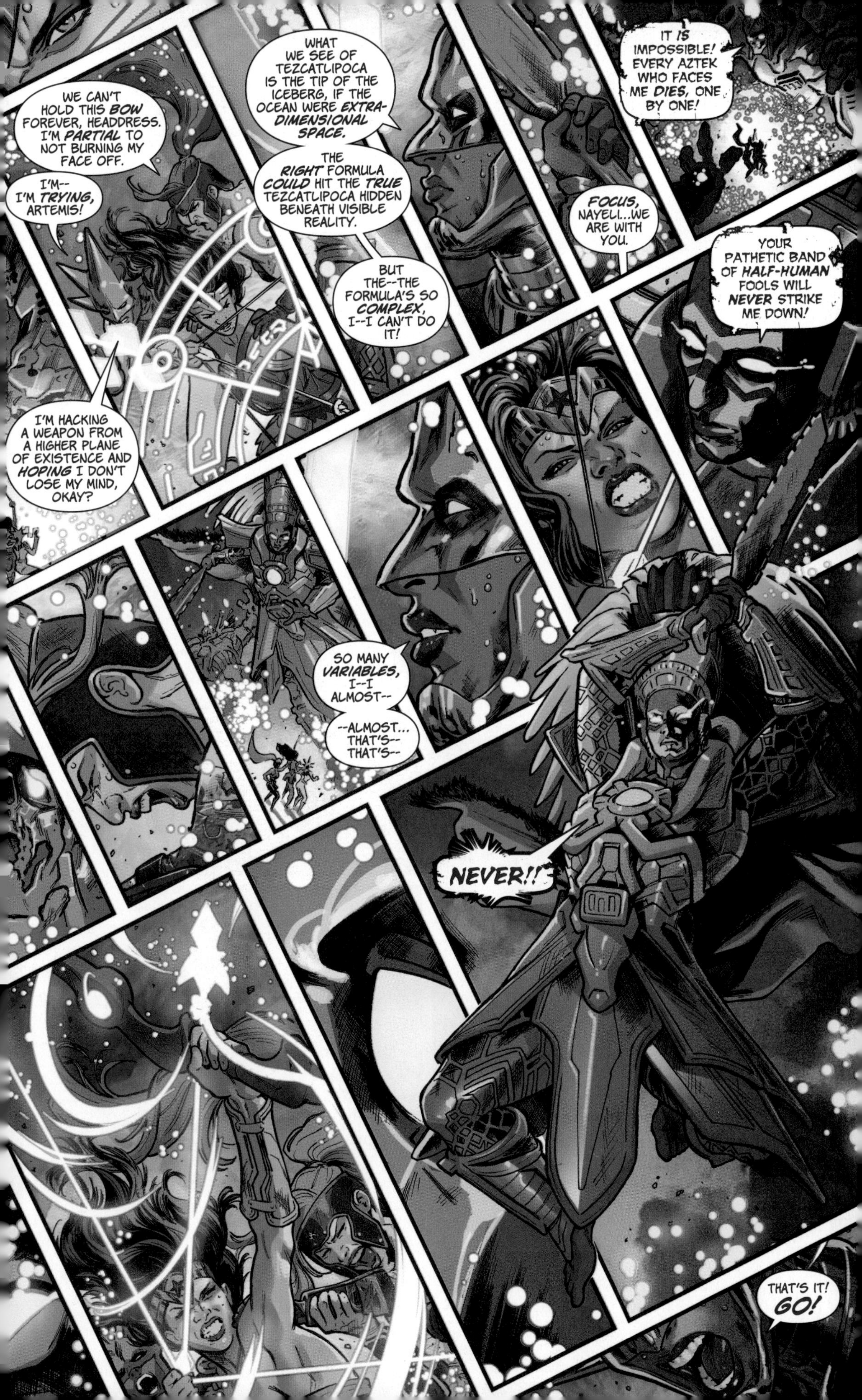
WE CAN'T HOLD THIS BOW FOREVER, HEADDRESS. I'M PARTIAL TO NOT BURNING MY FACE OFF.
I'M-- I'M TRYING, ARTEMIS!
I'M HACKING A WEAPON FROM A HIGHER PLANE OF EXISTENCE AND HOPING I DON'T LOSE MY MIND, OKAY?
WHAT WE SEE OF TEZCATLIPOCA IS THE TIP OF THE ICEBERG, IF THE OCEAN WERE EXTRA-DIMENSIONAL SPACE.
THE RIGHT FORMULA COULD HIT THE TRUE TEZCATLIPOCA HIDDEN BENEATH VISIBLE REALITY.
BUT THE--THE FORMULA'S SO COMPLEX, I--I CAN'T DO IT!
FOCUS, NAYELI...WE ARE WITH YOU.
IT IS IMPOSSIBLE! EVERY AZTEK WHO FACES ME DIES, ONE BY ONE!
YOUR PATHETIC BAND OF HALF-HUMAN FOOLS WILL NEVER STRIKE ME DOWN!
SO MANY VARIABLES, I--I ALMOST--
--ALMOST... THAT'S-- THAT'S--
NEVER!!
THAT'S IT! GO!

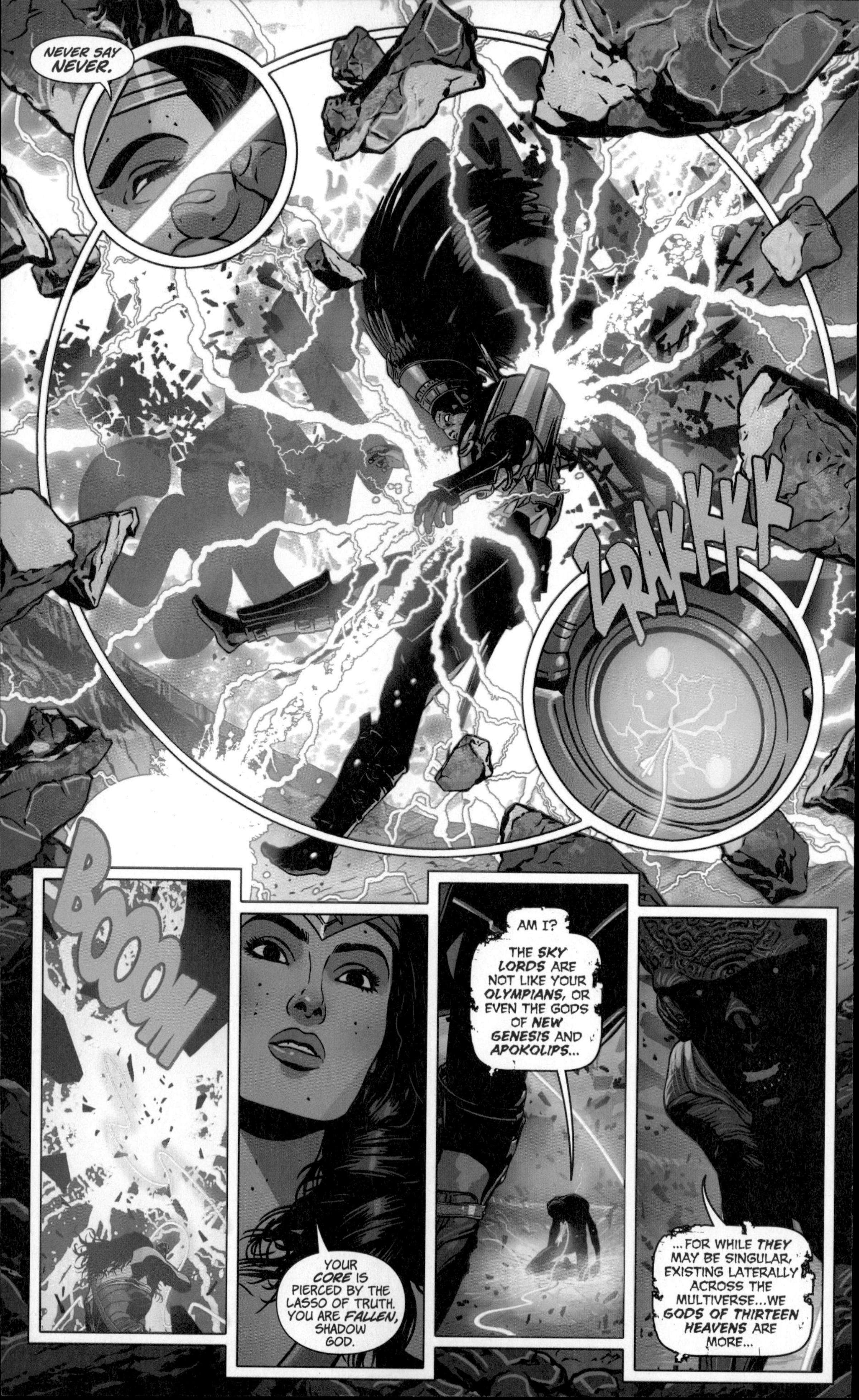
NEVER SAY NEVER.
ZRAKKKK
BOOOM
YOUR CORE IS PIERCED BY THE LASSO OF TRUTH. YOU ARE FALLEN, SHADOW GOD.
AM I?
THE SKY LORDS ARE NOT LIKE YOUR OLYMPIANS, OR EVEN THE GODS OF NEW GENESIS AND APOKOLIPS...
...FOR WHILE THEY MAY BE SINGULAR, EXISTING LATERALLY ACROSS THE MULTIVERSE...WE GODS OF THIRTEEN HEAVENS ARE MORE...

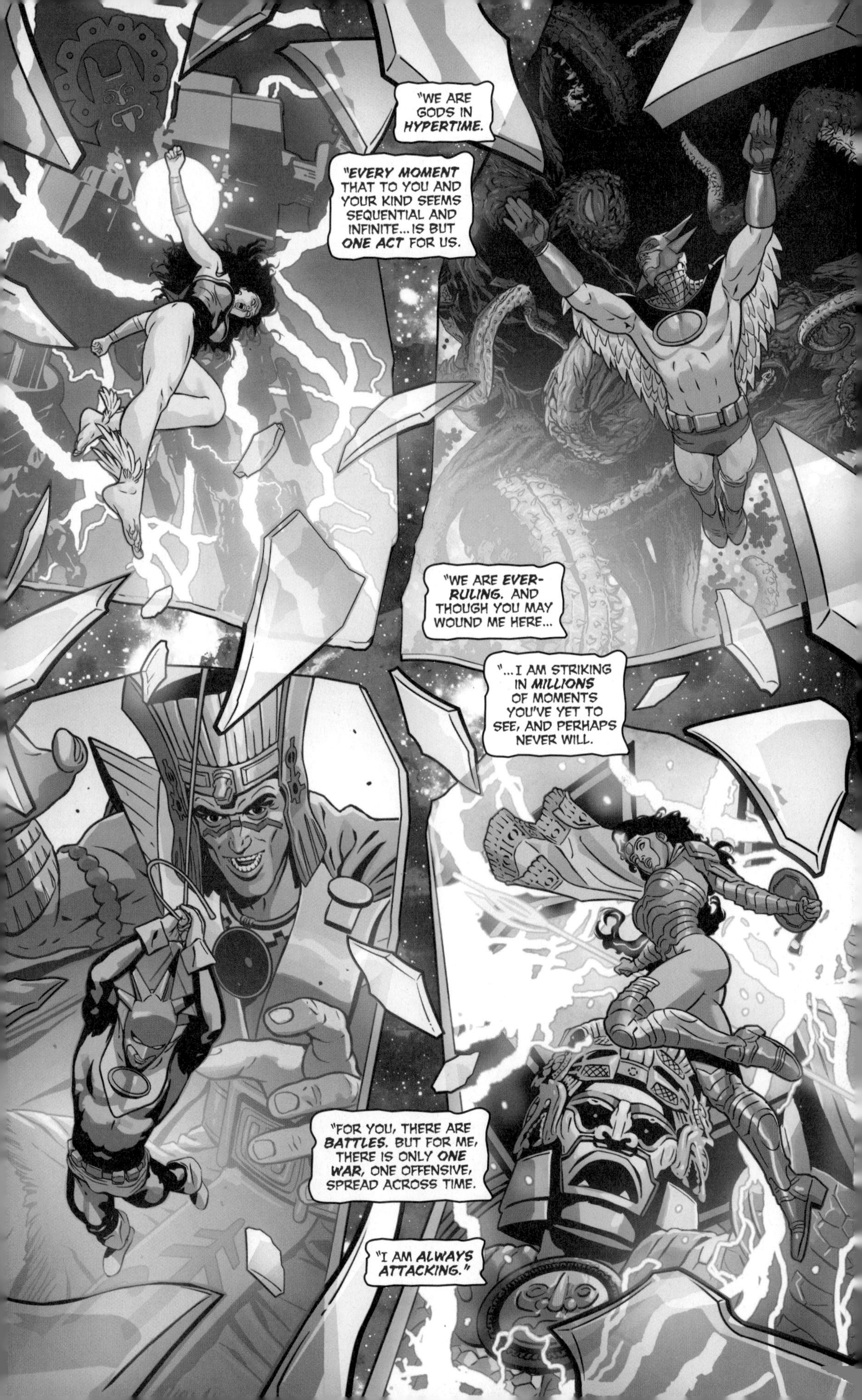
"WE ARE GODS IN HYPERTIME.
"EVERY MOMENT THAT TO YOU AND YOUR KIND SEEMS SEQUENTIAL AND INFINITE... IS BUT ONE ACT FOR US.
"WE ARE EVER-RULING. AND THOUGH YOU MAY WOUND ME HERE...
"...I AM STRIKING IN MILLIONS OF MOMENTS YOU'VE YET TO SEE, AND PERHAPS NEVER WILL.
"FOR YOU, THERE ARE BATTLES. BUT FOR ME, THERE IS ONLY ONE WAR, ONE OFFENSIVE, SPREAD ACROSS TIME.
"I AM ALWAYS ATTACKING."

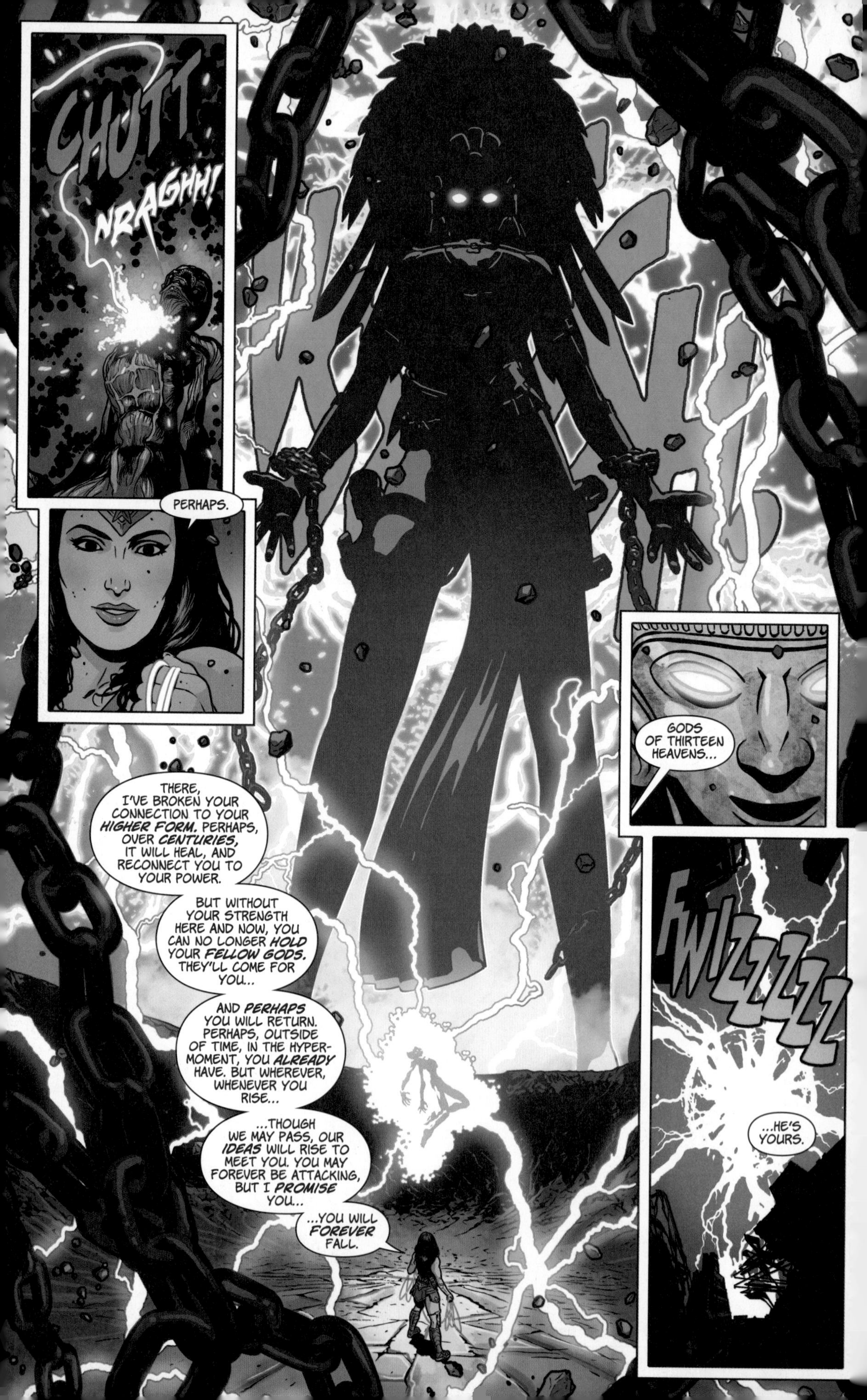
CHUTT
NRAGHH!
PERHAPS.
THERE, I'VE BROKEN YOUR CONNECTION TO YOUR HIGHER FORM. PERHAPS, OVER CENTURIES, IT WILL HEAL, AND RECONNECT YOU TO YOUR POWER.
BUT WITHOUT YOUR STRENGTH HERE AND NOW, YOU CAN NO LONGER HOLD YOUR FELLOW GODS. THEY'LL COME FOR YOU...
AND PERHAPS YOU WILL RETURN. PERHAPS, OUTSIDE OF TIME, IN THE HYPER-MOMENT, YOU ALREADY HAVE. BUT WHEREVER, WHENEVER YOU RISE...
...THOUGH WE MAY PASS, OUR IDEAS WILL RISE TO MEET YOU. YOU MAY FOREVER BE ATTACKING, BUT I PROMISE YOU...
...YOU WILL FOREVER FALL.
GODS OF THIRTEEN HEAVENS...
FWIZZZZZZ
...HE'S YOURS.

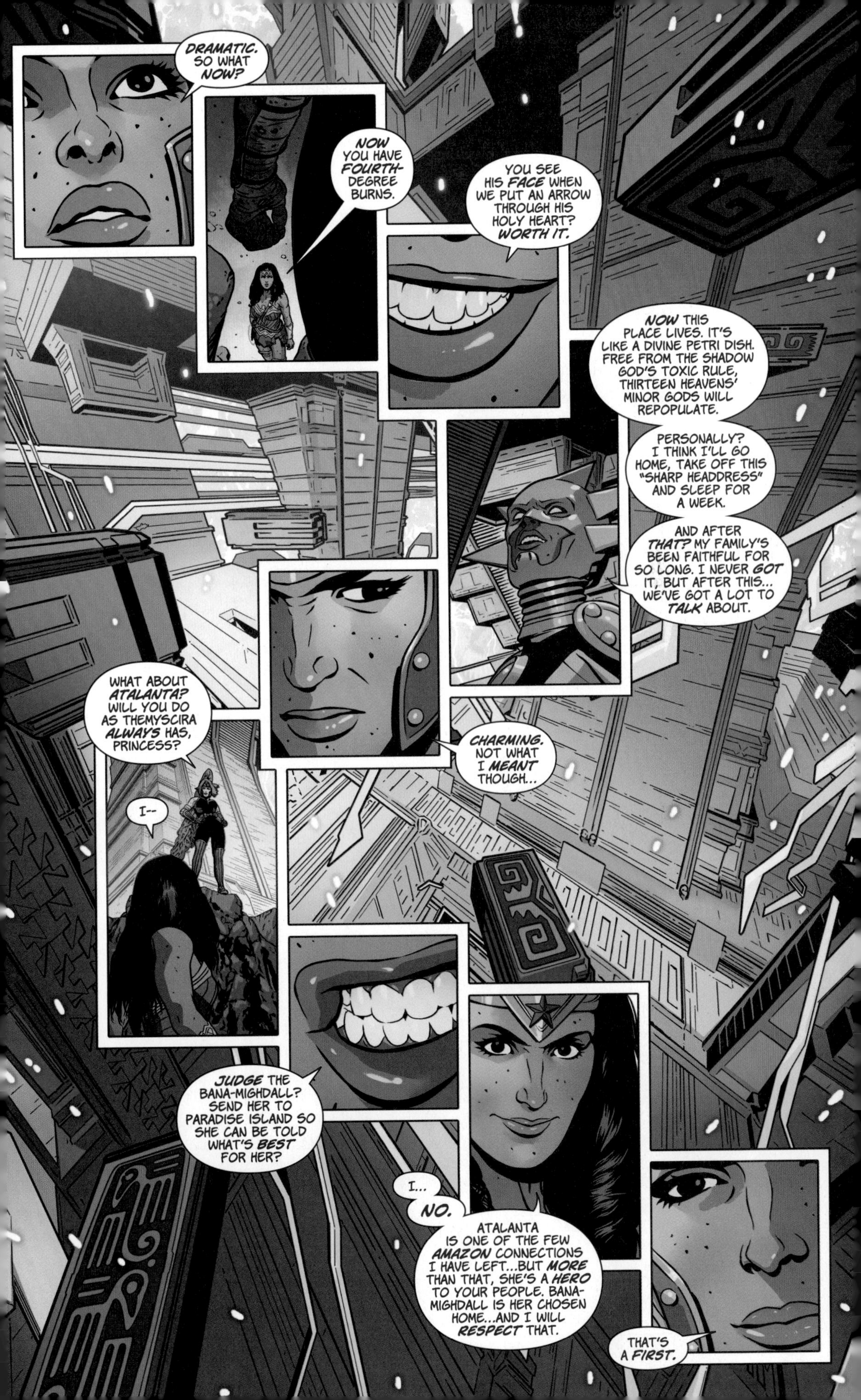
DRAMATIC. SO WHAT NOW?
NOW YOU HAVE FOURTH-DEGREE BURNS.
YOU SEE HIS FACE WHEN WE PUT AN ARROW THROUGH HIS HOLY HEART? WORTH IT.
NOW THIS PLACE LIVES. IT'S LIKE A DIVINE PETRI DISH. FREE FROM THE SHADOW GOD'S TOXIC RULE, THIRTEEN HEAVENS' MINOR GODS WILL REPOPULATE.
PERSONALLY? I THINK I'LL GO HOME, TAKE OFF THIS "SHARP HEADDRESS" AND SLEEP FOR A WEEK.
AND AFTER THAT? MY FAMILY'S BEEN FAITHFUL FOR SO LONG. I NEVER GOT IT, BUT AFTER THIS... WE'VE GOT A LOT TO TALK ABOUT.
CHARMING. NOT WHAT I MEANT THOUGH...
WHAT ABOUT ATALANTA? WILL YOU DO AS THEMYSCIRA ALWAYS HAS, PRINCESS?
I--
JUDGE THE BANA-MIGHDALL? SEND HER TO PARADISE ISLAND SO SHE CAN BE TOLD WHAT'S BEST FOR HER?
I...
NO.
ATALANTA IS ONE OF THE FEW AMAZON CONNECTIONS I HAVE LEFT...BUT MORE THAN THAT, SHE'S A HERO TO YOUR PEOPLE. BANA-MIGHDALL IS HER CHOSEN HOME...AND I WILL RESPECT THAT.
THAT'S A FIRST.

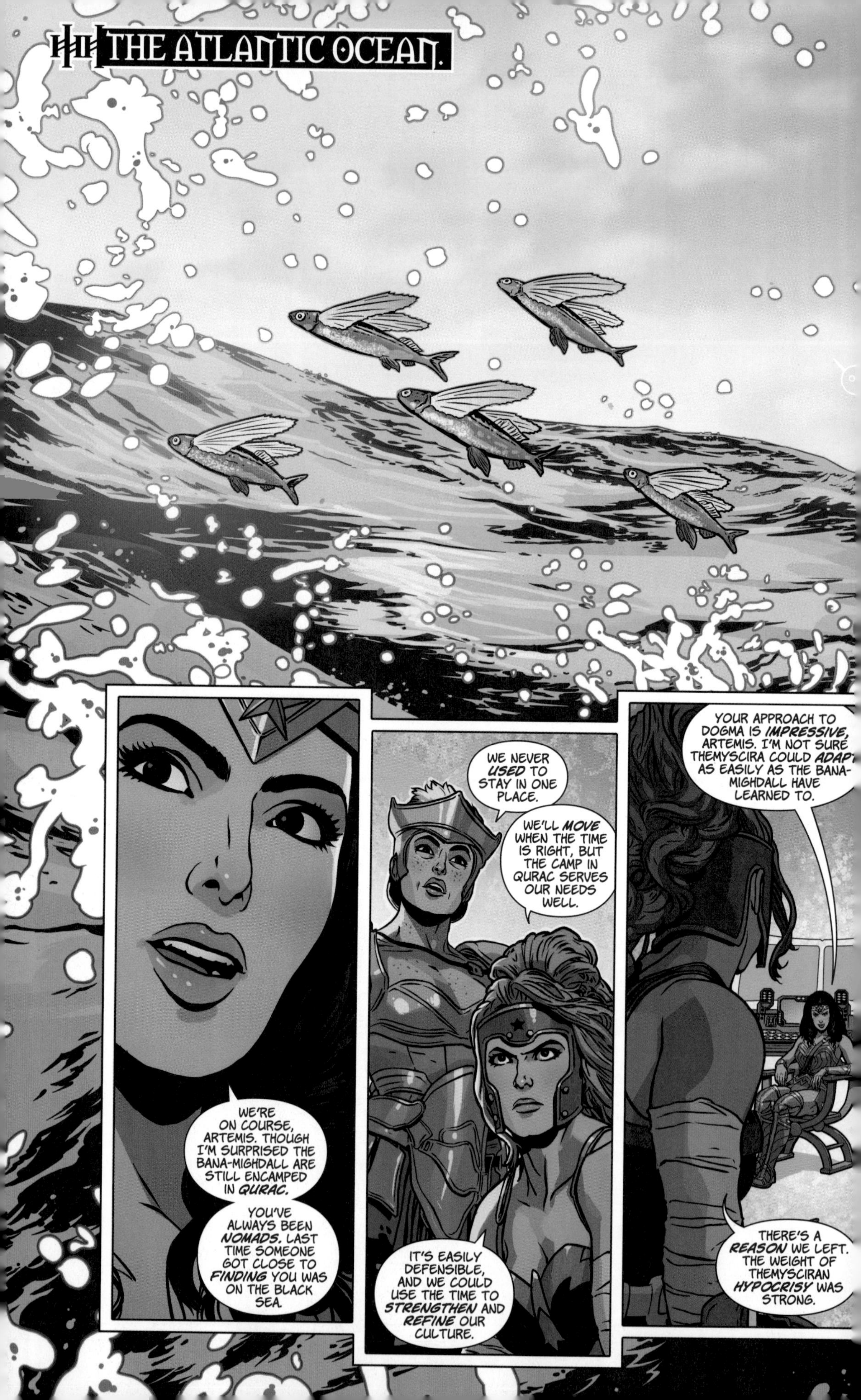
THE ATLANTIC OCEAN.
WE'RE ON COURSE, ARTEMIS. THOUGH I'M SURPRISED THE BANA-MIGHDALL ARE STILL ENCAMPED IN QURAC.
YOU'VE ALWAYS BEEN NOMADS. LAST TIME SOMEONE GOT CLOSE TO FINDING YOU WAS ON THE BLACK SEA.
WE NEVER USED TO STAY IN ONE PLACE.
WE'LL MOVE WHEN THE TIME IS RIGHT, BUT THE CAMP IN QURAC SERVES OUR NEEDS WELL.
IT'S EASILY DEFENSIBLE, AND WE COULD USE THE TIME TO STRENGTHEN AND REFINE OUR CULTURE.
YOUR APPROACH TO DOGMA IS IMPRESSIVE, ARTEMIS. I'M NOT SURE THEMYSCIRA COULD ADAPT AS EASILY AS THE BANA-MIGHDALL HAVE LEARNED TO.
THERE'S A REASON WE LEFT. THE WEIGHT OF THEMYSCIRAN HYPOCRISY WAS STRONG.

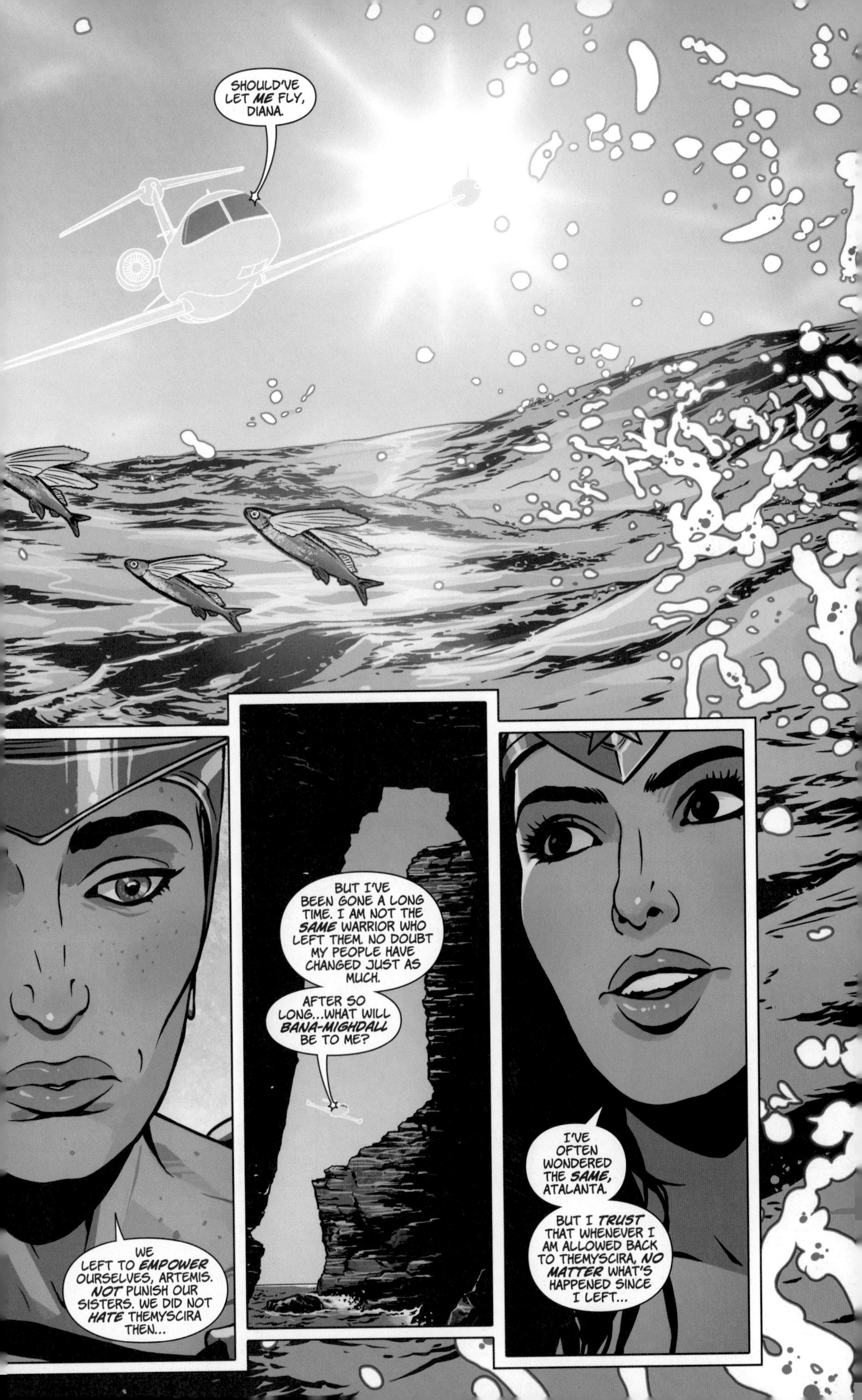
SHOULD'VE LET ME FLY, DIANA.
WE LEFT TO EMPOWER OURSELVES, ARTEMIS. NOT PUNISH OUR SISTERS. WE DID NOT HATE THEMYSCIRA THEN...
BUT I'VE BEEN GONE A LONG TIME. I AM NOT THE SAME WARRIOR WHO LEFT THEM. NO DOUBT MY PEOPLE HAVE CHANGED JUST AS MUCH.
AFTER SO LONG...WHAT WILL BANA-MIGHDALL BE TO ME?
I'VE OFTEN WONDERED THE SAME, ATALANTA.
BUT I TRUST THAT WHENEVER I AM ALLOWED BACK TO THEMYSCIRA, NO MATTER WHAT'S HAPPENED SINCE I LEFT...

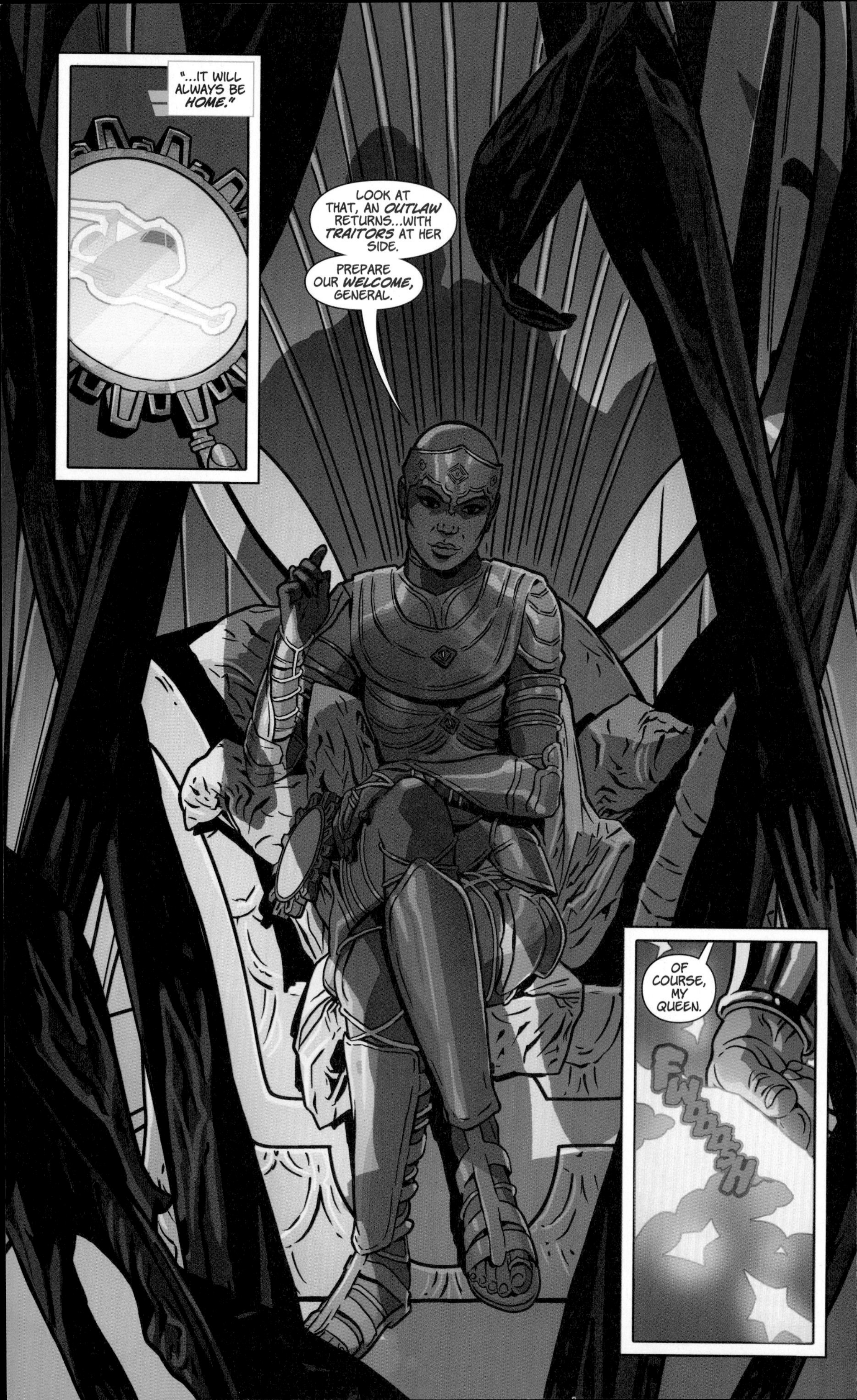
"...IT WILL ALWAYS BE *HOME.*"
LOOK AT THAT, AN *OUTLAW* RETURNS...WITH *TRAITORS* AT HER SIDE.
PREPARE OUR *WELCOME,* GENERAL.
OF COURSE, MY QUEEN.
FWOOOSH

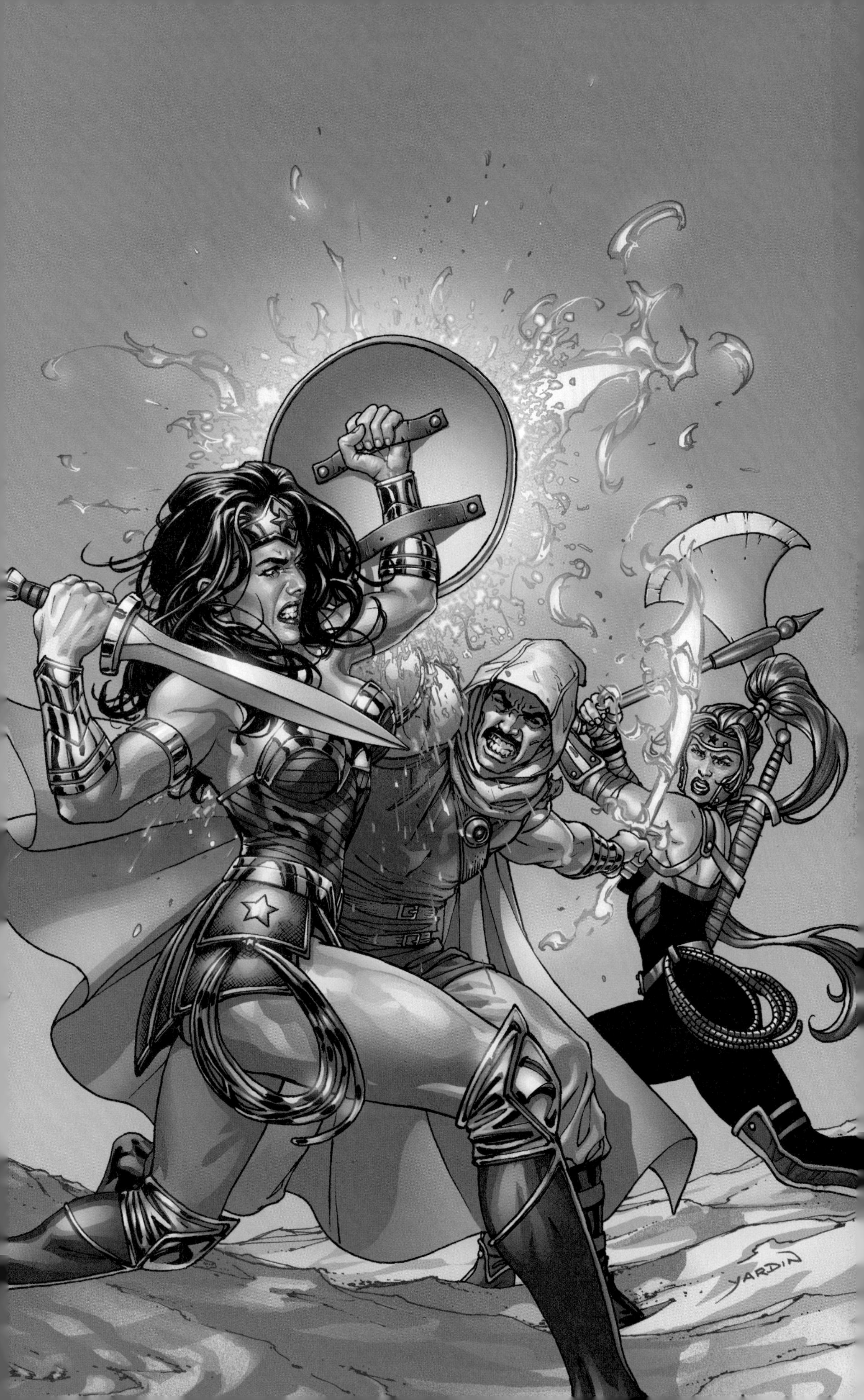
YARDIN

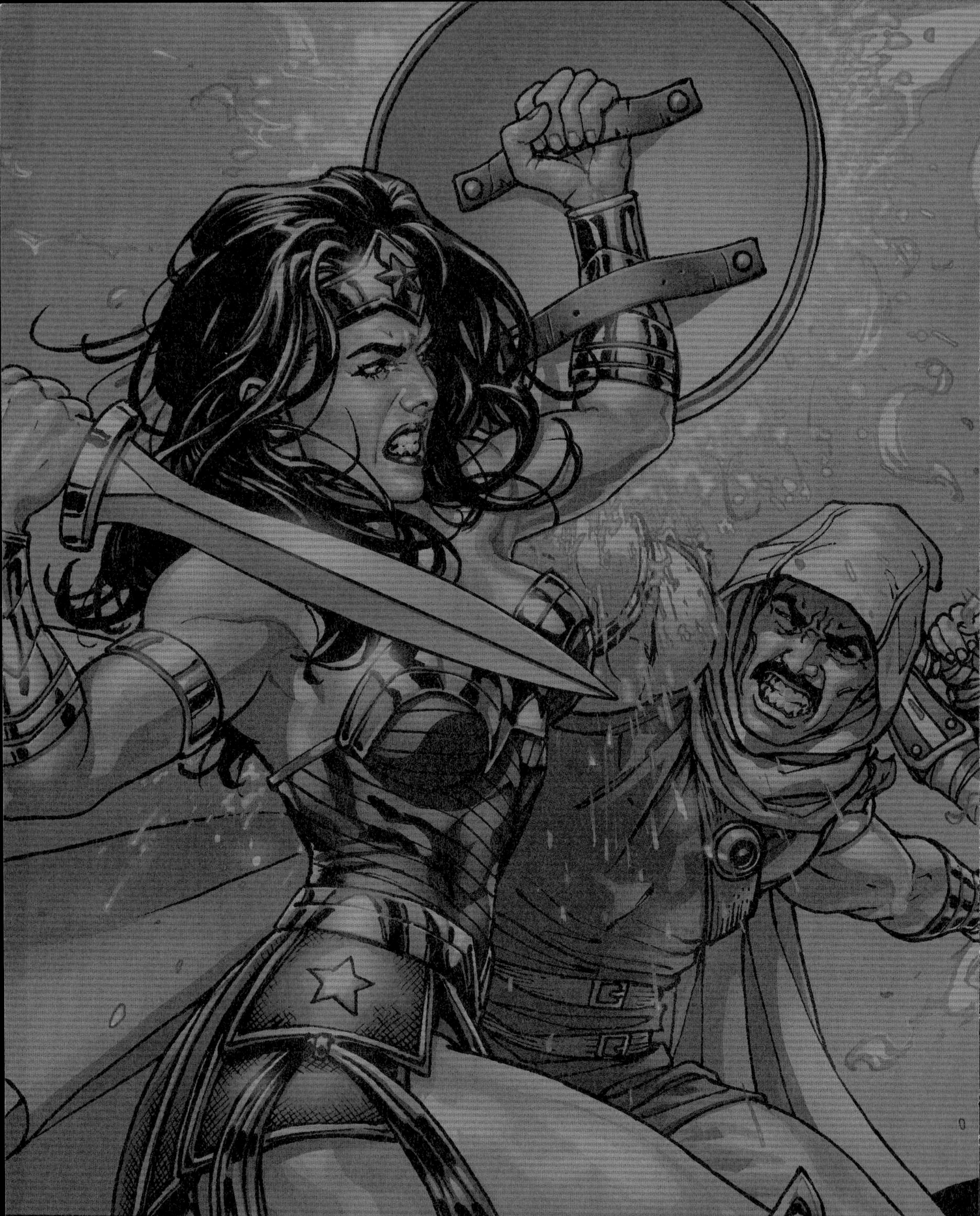

WONDER WOMAN
#54

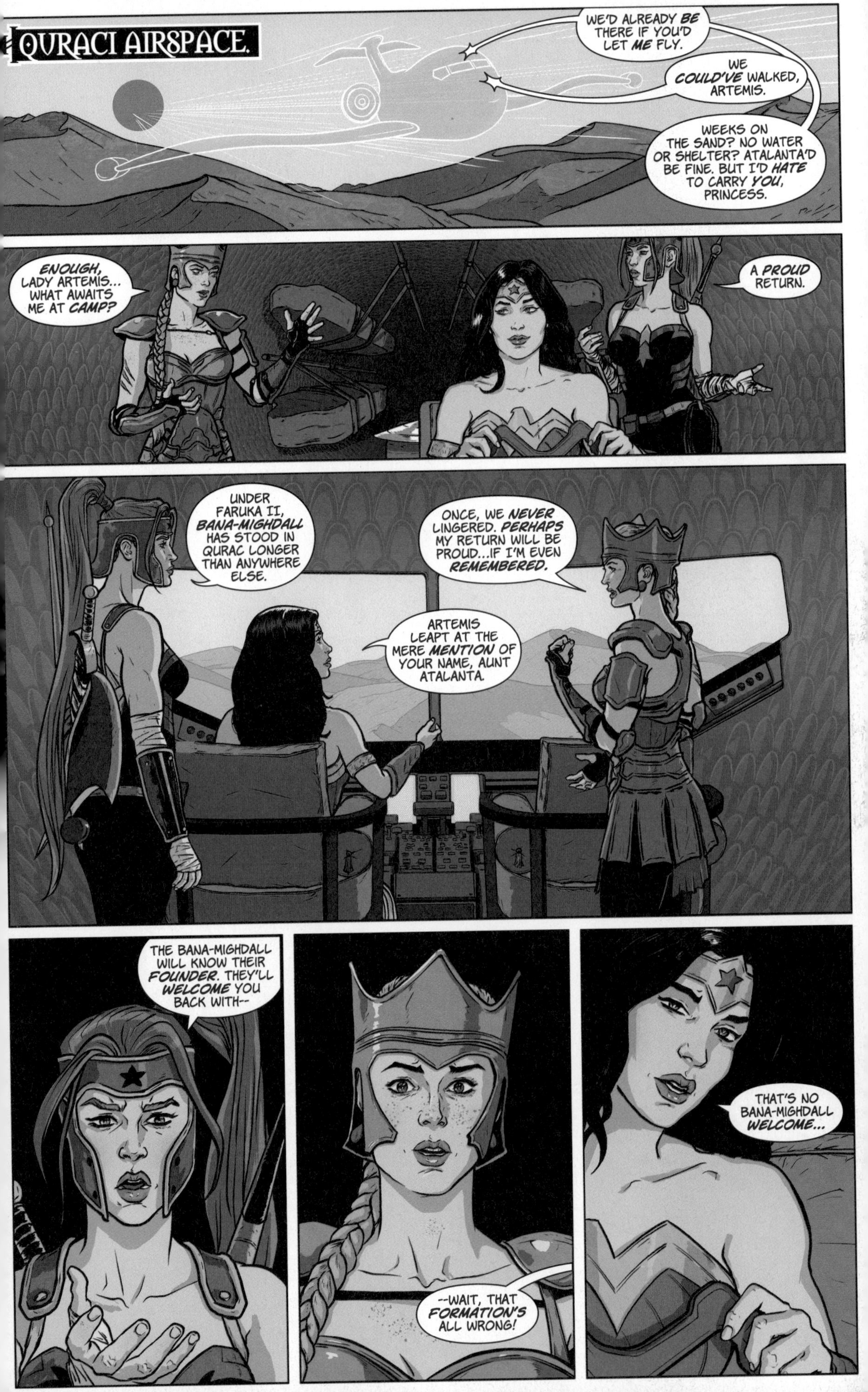
QURACI AIRSPACE.
WE'D ALREADY BE THERE IF YOU'D LET ME FLY.
WE COULD'VE WALKED, ARTEMIS.
WEEKS ON THE SAND? NO WATER OR SHELTER? ATALANTA'D BE FINE. BUT I'D HATE TO CARRY YOU, PRINCESS.
ENOUGH, LADY ARTEMIS... WHAT AWAITS ME AT CAMP?
A PROUD RETURN.
UNDER FARUKA II, BANA-MIGHDALL HAS STOOD IN QURAC LONGER THAN ANYWHERE ELSE.
ONCE, WE NEVER LINGERED. PERHAPS MY RETURN WILL BE PROUD...IF I'M EVEN REMEMBERED.
ARTEMIS LEAPT AT THE MERE MENTION OF YOUR NAME, AUNT ATALANTA.
THE BANA-MIGHDALL WILL KNOW THEIR FOUNDER. THEY'LL WELCOME YOU BACK WITH--
--WAIT, THAT FORMATION'S ALL WRONG!
THAT'S NO BANA-MIGHDALL WELCOME...

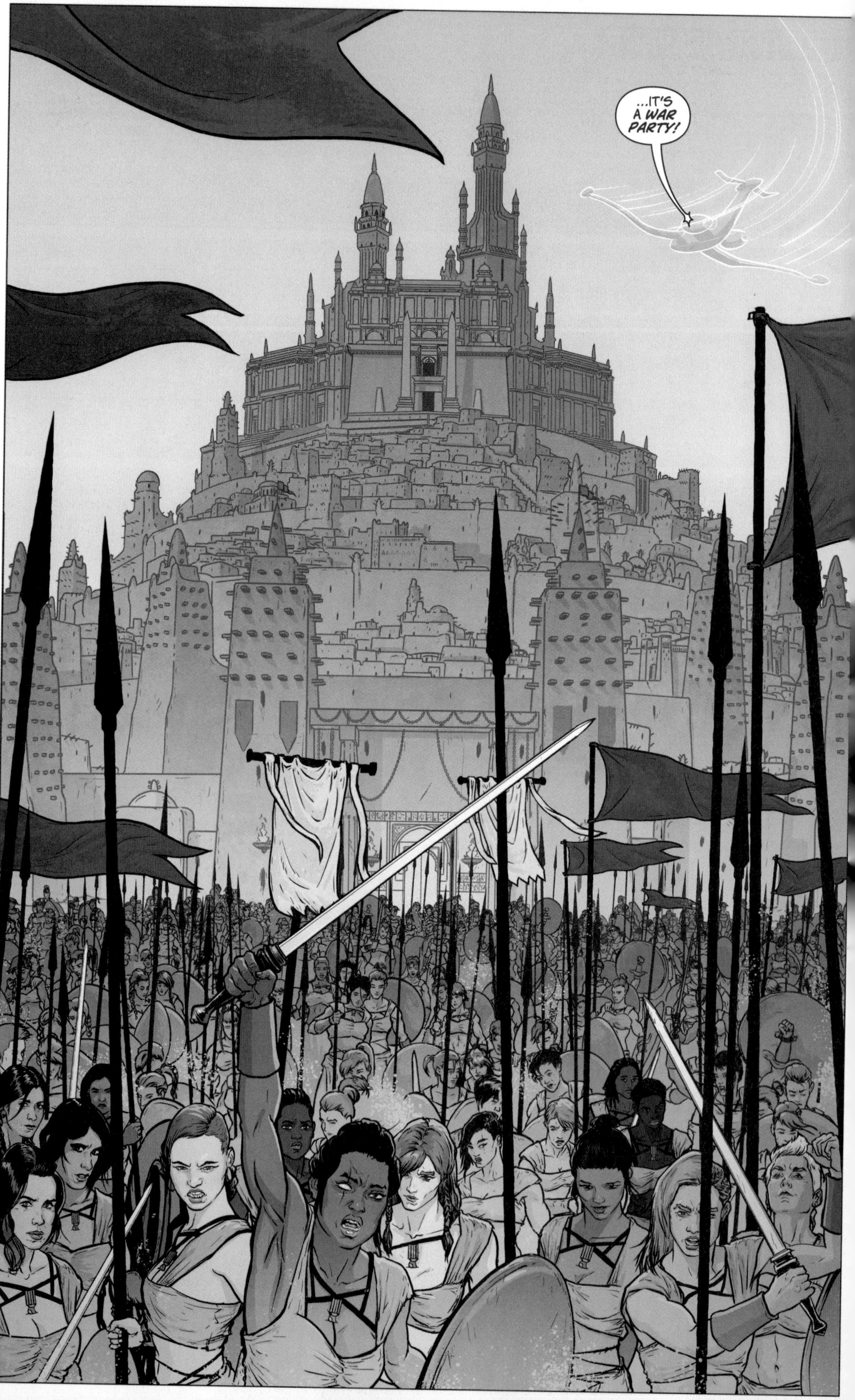
...IT'S A *WAR PARTY!*

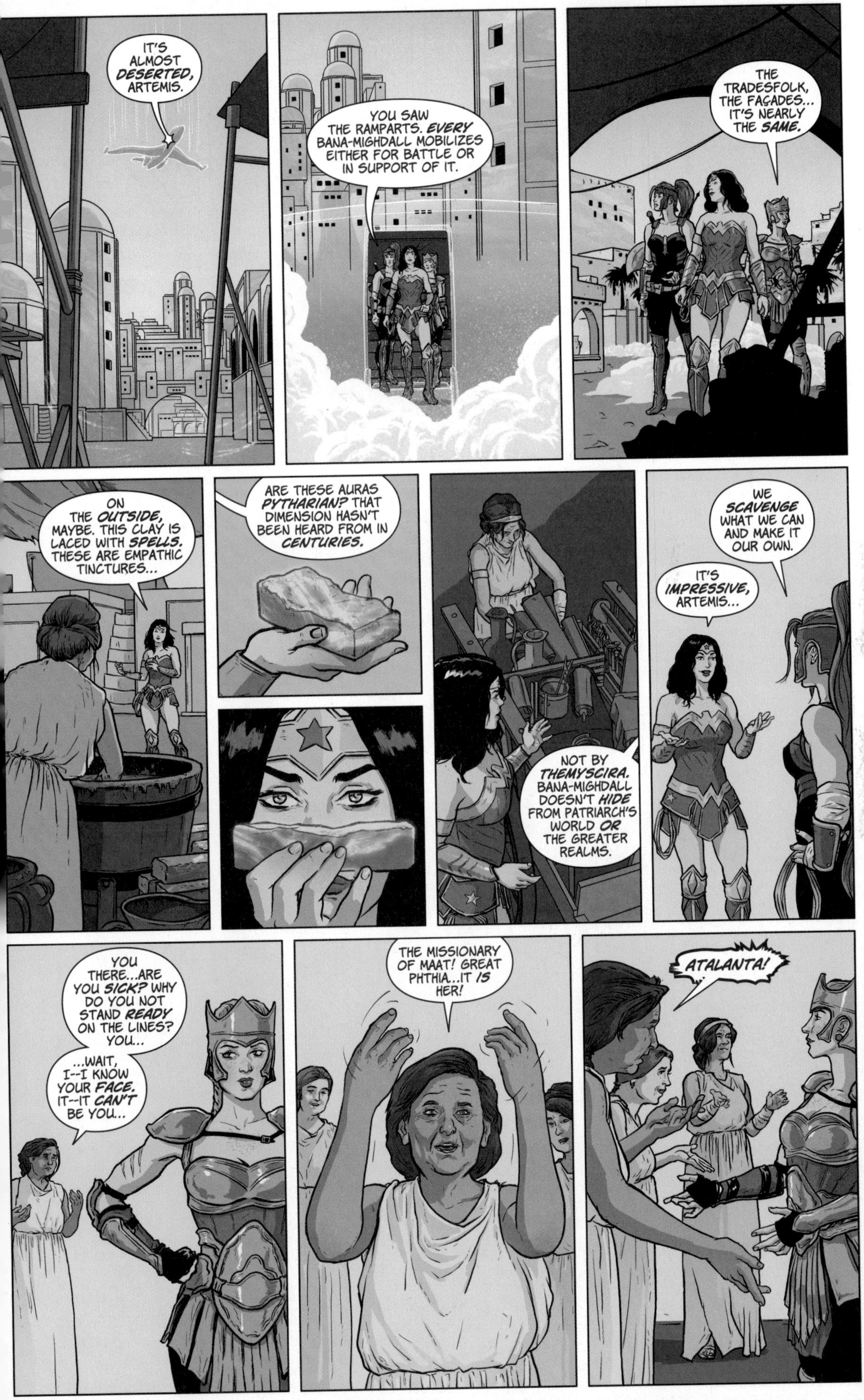
IT'S ALMOST DESERTED, ARTEMIS.
YOU SAW THE RAMPARTS. EVERY BANA-MIGHDALL MOBILIZES EITHER FOR BATTLE OR IN SUPPORT OF IT.
THE TRADESFOLK, THE FAÇADES... IT'S NEARLY THE SAME.
ON THE OUTSIDE, MAYBE. THIS CLAY IS LACED WITH SPELLS. THESE ARE EMPATHIC TINCTURES...
ARE THESE AURAS PYTHARIAN? THAT DIMENSION HASN'T BEEN HEARD FROM IN CENTURIES.
NOT BY THEMYSCIRA. BANA-MIGHDALL DOESN'T HIDE FROM PATRIARCH'S WORLD OR THE GREATER REALMS.
WE SCAVENGE WHAT WE CAN AND MAKE IT OUR OWN.
IT'S IMPRESSIVE, ARTEMIS...
YOU THERE...ARE YOU SICK? WHY DO YOU NOT STAND READY ON THE LINES? YOU...
...WAIT, I--I KNOW YOUR FACE. IT--IT CAN'T BE YOU...
THE MISSIONARY OF MAAT! GREAT PHTHIA...IT IS HER!
ATALANTA!

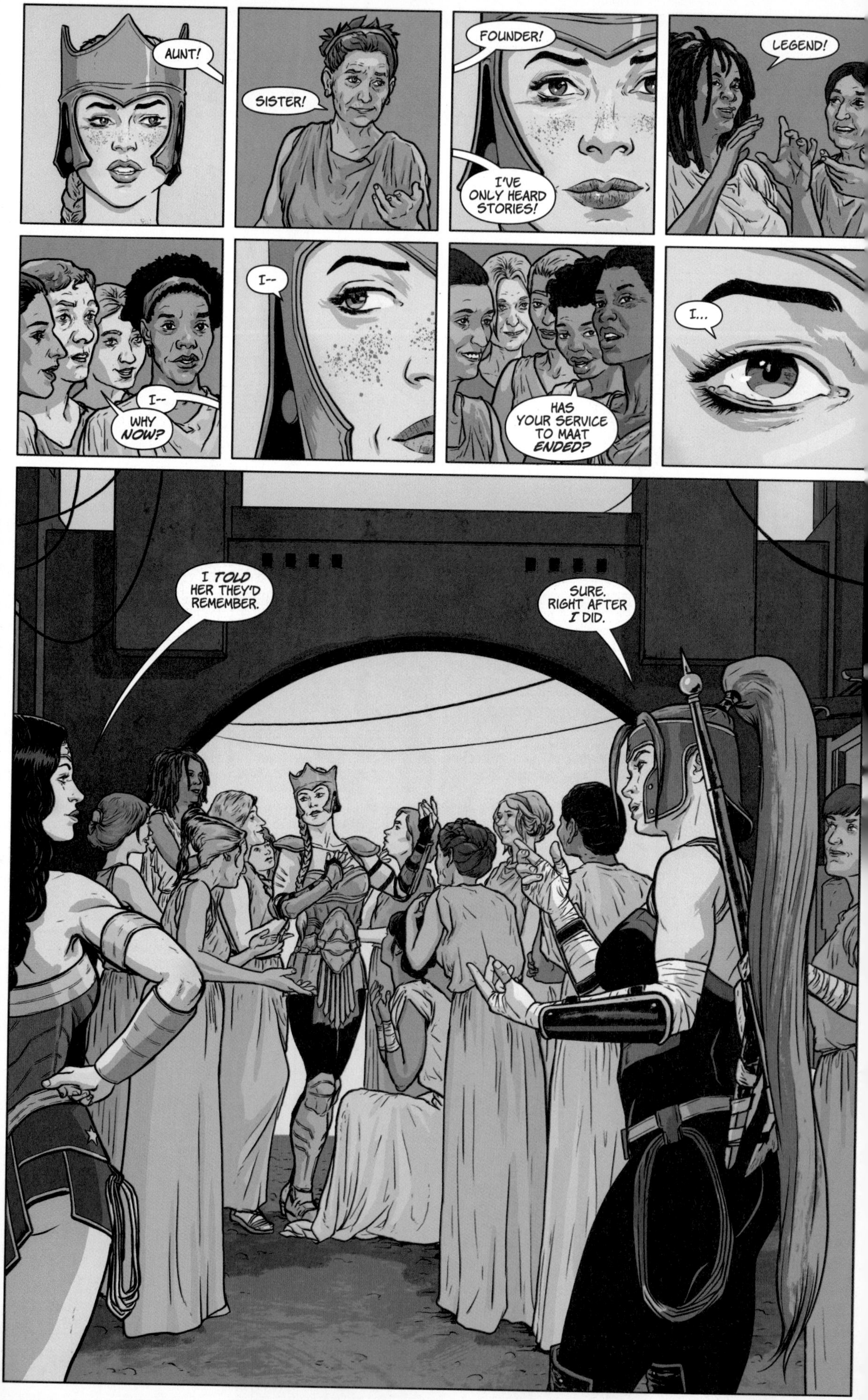
AUNT!
SISTER!
FOUNDER!
I'VE ONLY HEARD STORIES!
LEGEND!
I--
WHY NOW?
I--
HAS YOUR SERVICE TO MAAT ENDED?
I...
I TOLD HER THEY'D REMEMBER.
SURE. RIGHT AFTER I DID.

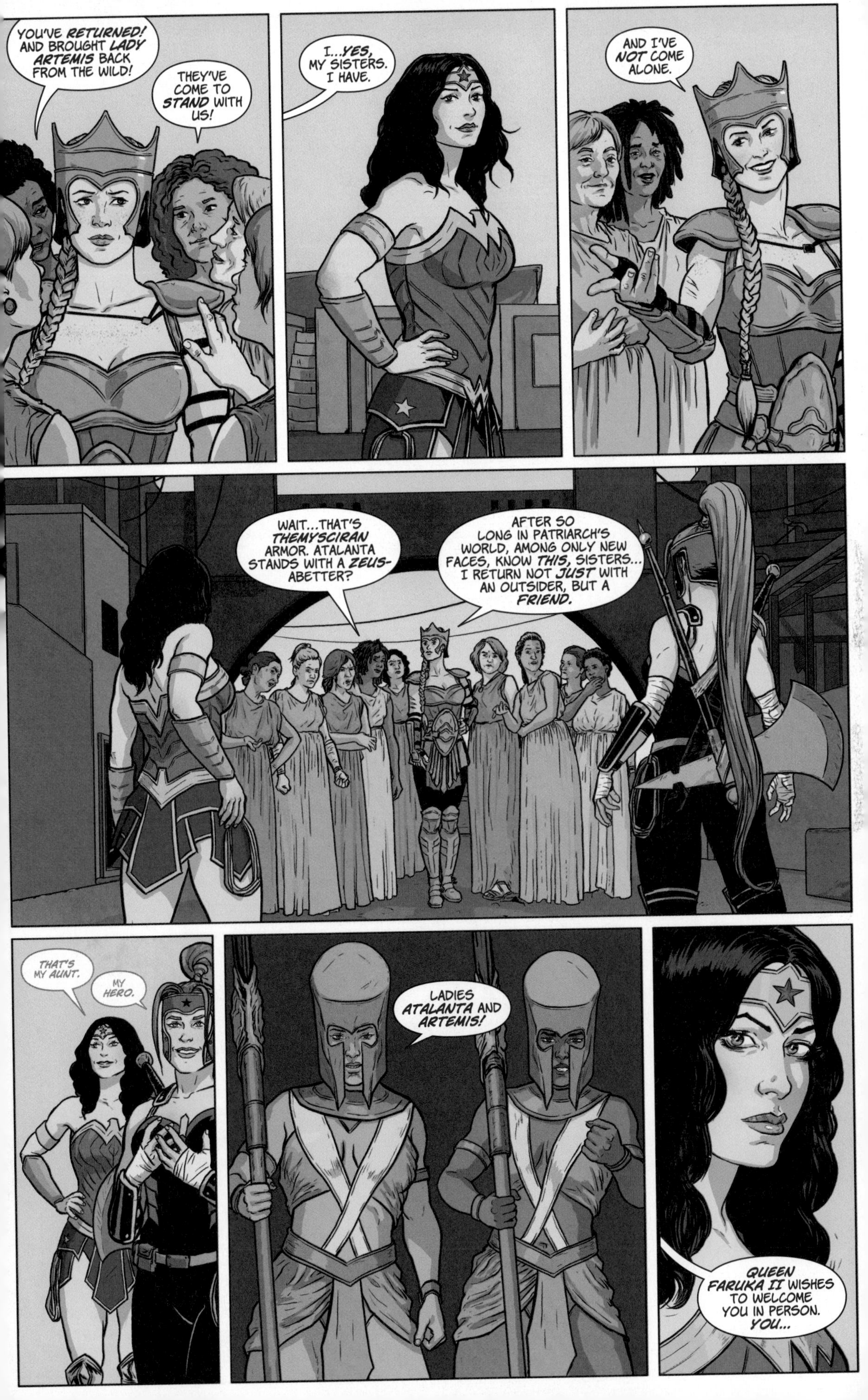
YOU'VE RETURNED! AND BROUGHT LADY ARTEMIS BACK FROM THE WILD!
THEY'VE COME TO STAND WITH US!
I...YES, MY SISTERS. I HAVE.
AND I'VE NOT COME ALONE.
WAIT...THAT'S THEMYSCIRAN ARMOR. ATALANTA STANDS WITH A ZEUS-ABETTER?
AFTER SO LONG IN PATRIARCH'S WORLD, AMONG ONLY NEW FACES, KNOW THIS, SISTERS... I RETURN NOT JUST WITH AN OUTSIDER, BUT A FRIEND.
THAT'S MY AUNT.
MY HERO.
LADIES ATALANTA AND ARTEMIS!
QUEEN FARUKA II WISHES TO WELCOME YOU IN PERSON. YOU...

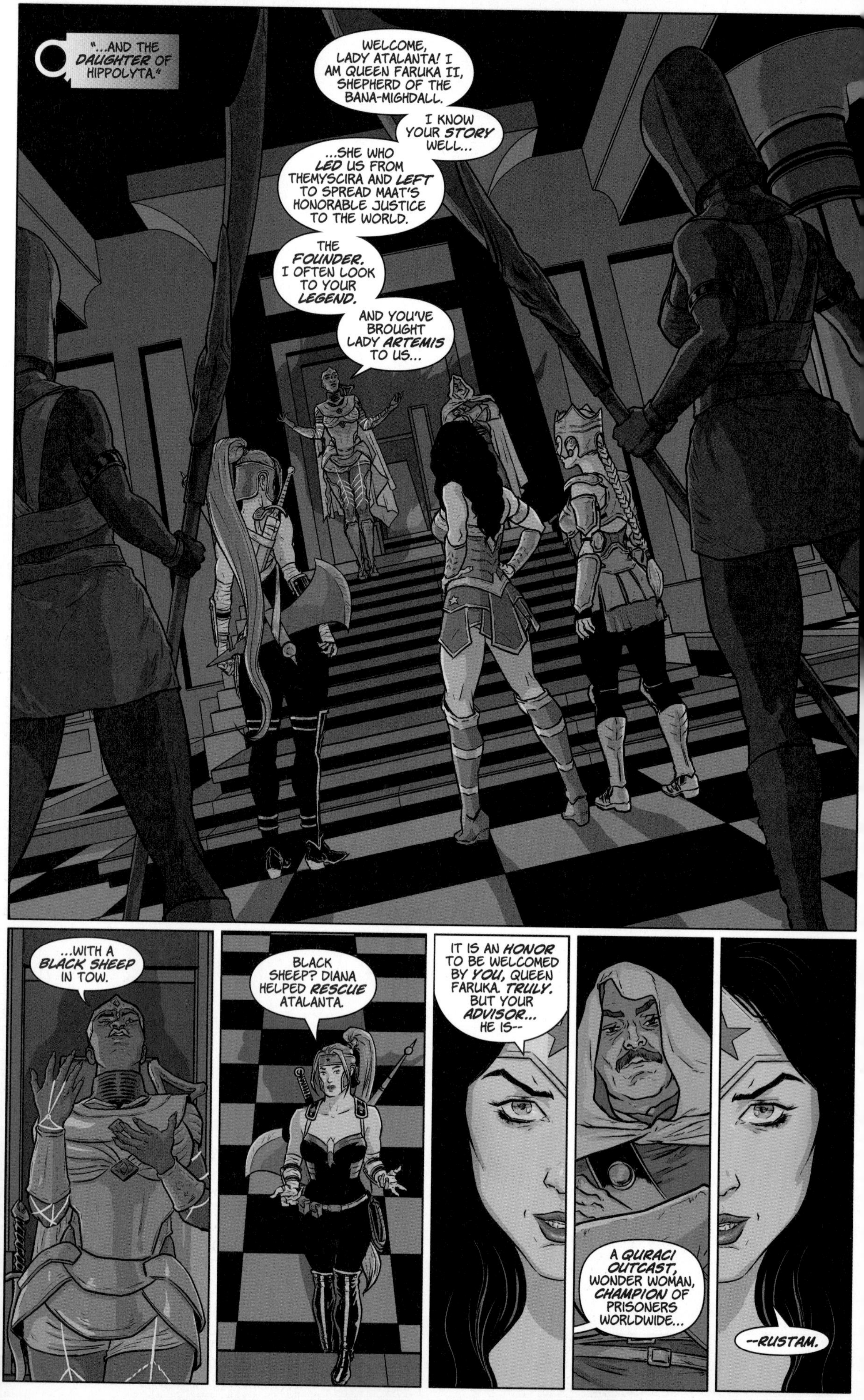
"...AND THE DAUGHTER OF HIPPOLYTA."
WELCOME, LADY ATALANTA! I AM QUEEN FARUKA II, SHEPHERD OF THE BANA-MIGHDALL.
I KNOW YOUR STORY WELL...
...SHE WHO LED US FROM THEMYSCIRA AND LEFT TO SPREAD MAAT'S HONORABLE JUSTICE TO THE WORLD.
THE FOUNDER. I OFTEN LOOK TO YOUR LEGEND.
AND YOU'VE BROUGHT LADY ARTEMIS TO US...
...WITH A BLACK SHEEP IN TOW.
BLACK SHEEP? DIANA HELPED RESCUE ATALANTA.
IT IS AN HONOR TO BE WELCOMED BY YOU, QUEEN FARUKA. TRULY. BUT YOUR ADVISOR... HE IS--
A QURACI OUTCAST, WONDER WOMAN, CHAMPION OF PRISONERS WORLDWIDE...
--RUSTAM.

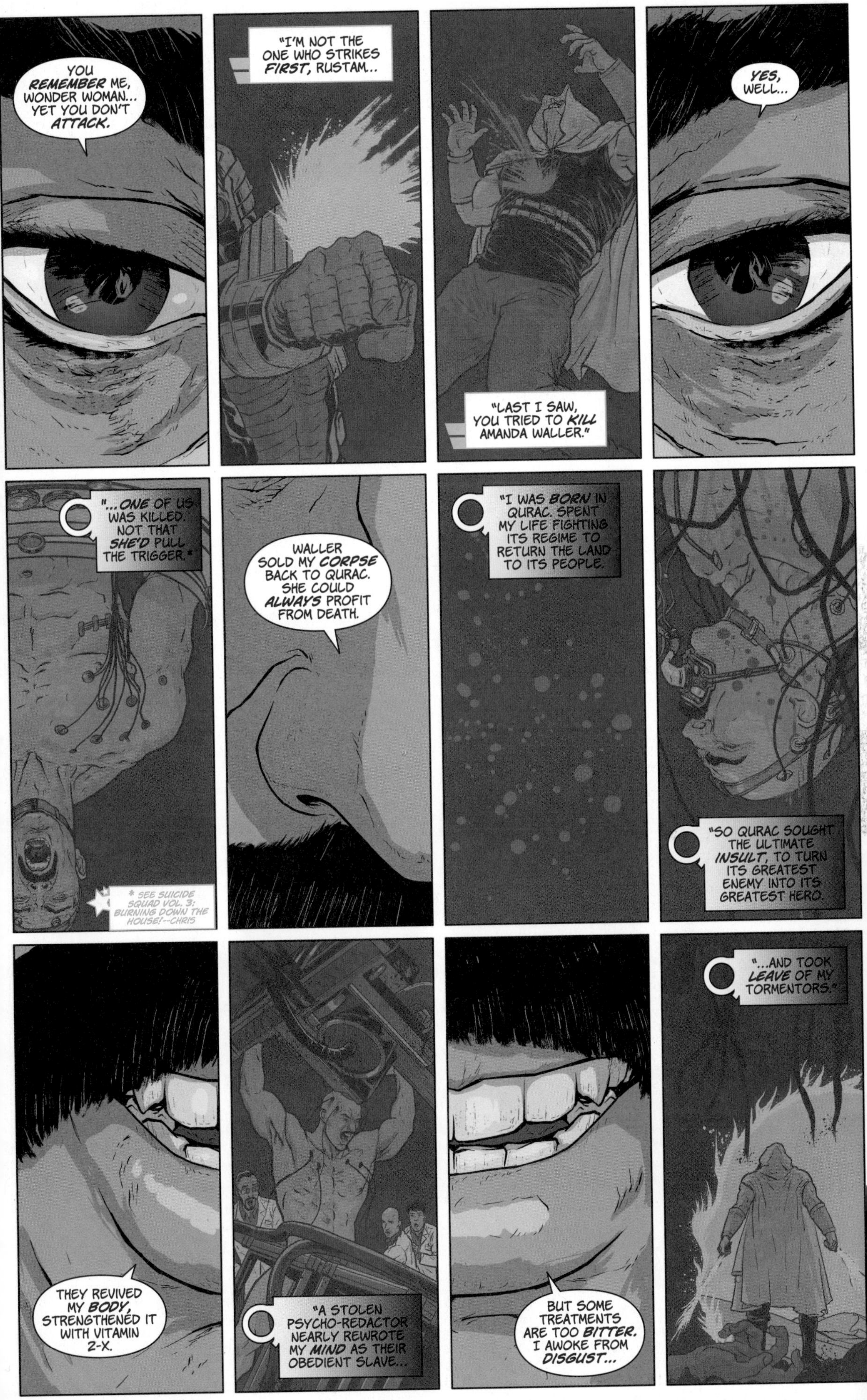
YOU REMEMBER ME, WONDER WOMAN... YET YOU DON'T ATTACK.
"I'M NOT THE ONE WHO STRIKES FIRST, RUSTAM...
"LAST I SAW, YOU TRIED TO KILL AMANDA WALLER."
YES, WELL...
"...ONE OF US WAS KILLED. NOT THAT SHE'D PULL THE TRIGGER.*
* SEE SUICIDE SQUAD VOL. 3: BURNING DOWN THE HOUSE! --CHRIS
WALLER SOLD MY CORPSE BACK TO QURAC. SHE COULD ALWAYS PROFIT FROM DEATH.
"I WAS BORN IN QURAC. SPENT MY LIFE FIGHTING ITS REGIME TO RETURN THE LAND TO ITS PEOPLE.
"SO QURAC SOUGHT THE ULTIMATE INSULT, TO TURN ITS GREATEST ENEMY INTO ITS GREATEST HERO.
THEY REVIVED MY BODY, STRENGTHENED IT WITH VITAMIN Z-X.
"A STOLEN PSYCHO-REDACTOR NEARLY REWROTE MY MIND AS THEIR OBEDIENT SLAVE...
BUT SOME TREATMENTS ARE TOO BITTER. I AWOKE FROM DISGUST...
"...AND TOOK LEAVE OF MY TORMENTORS."

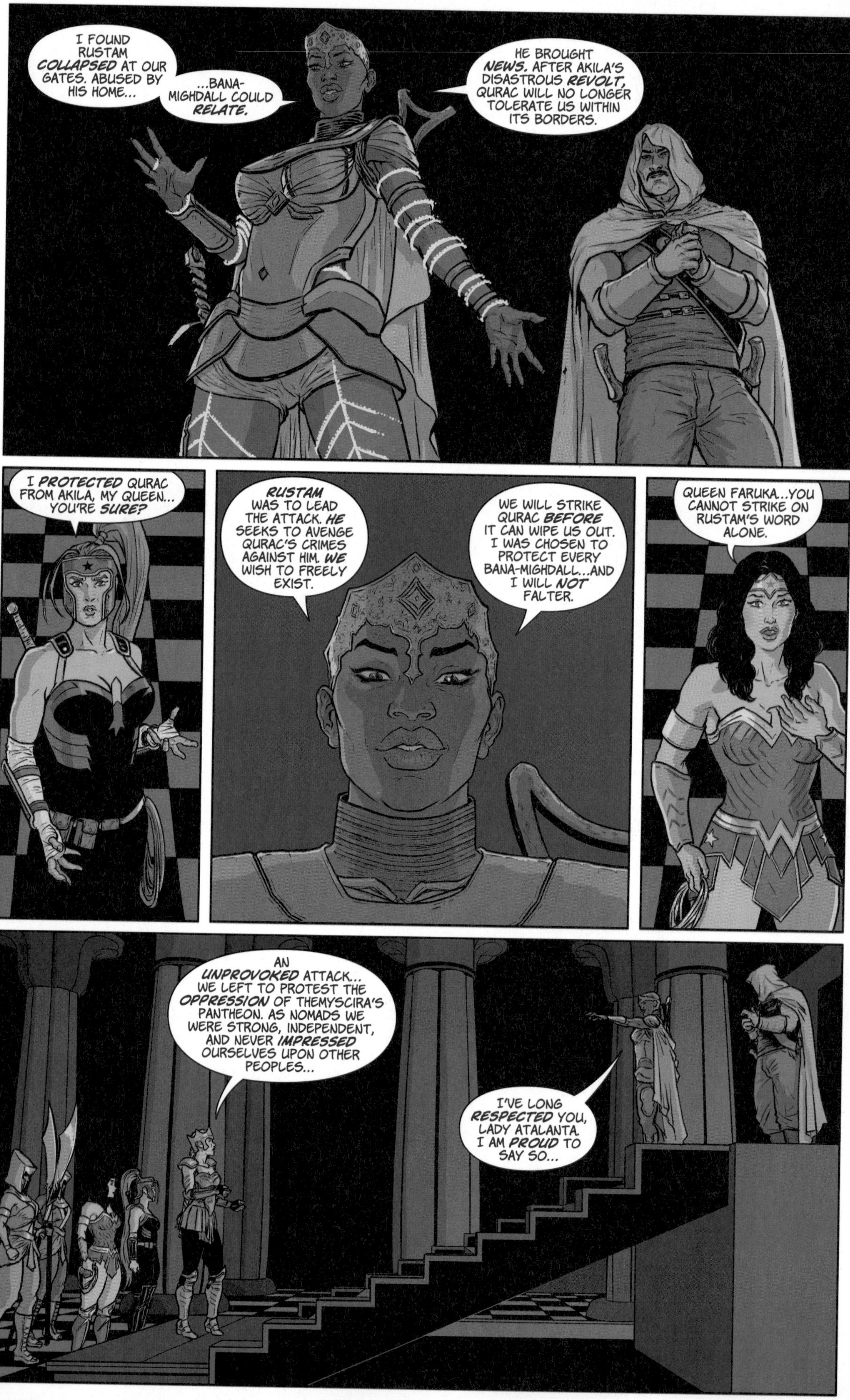

I FOUND RUSTAM COLLAPSED AT OUR GATES. ABUSED BY HIS HOME...
...BANA-MIGHDALL COULD RELATE.
HE BROUGHT NEWS. AFTER AKILA'S DISASTROUS REVOLT, QURAC WILL NO LONGER TOLERATE US WITHIN ITS BORDERS.
I PROTECTED QURAC FROM AKILA, MY QUEEN... YOU'RE SURE?
RUSTAM WAS TO LEAD THE ATTACK. HE SEEKS TO AVENGE QURAC'S CRIMES AGAINST HIM. WE WISH TO FREELY EXIST.
WE WILL STRIKE QURAC BEFORE IT CAN WIPE US OUT. I WAS CHOSEN TO PROTECT EVERY BANA-MIGHDALL...AND I WILL NOT FALTER.
QUEEN FARUKA...YOU CANNOT STRIKE ON RUSTAM'S WORD ALONE.
AN UNPROVOKED ATTACK... WE LEFT TO PROTEST THE OPPRESSION OF THEMYSCIRA'S PANTHEON. AS NOMADS WE WERE STRONG, INDEPENDENT, AND NEVER IMPRESSED OURSELVES UPON OTHER PEOPLES...
I'VE LONG RESPECTED YOU, LADY ATALANTA. I AM PROUD TO SAY SO...

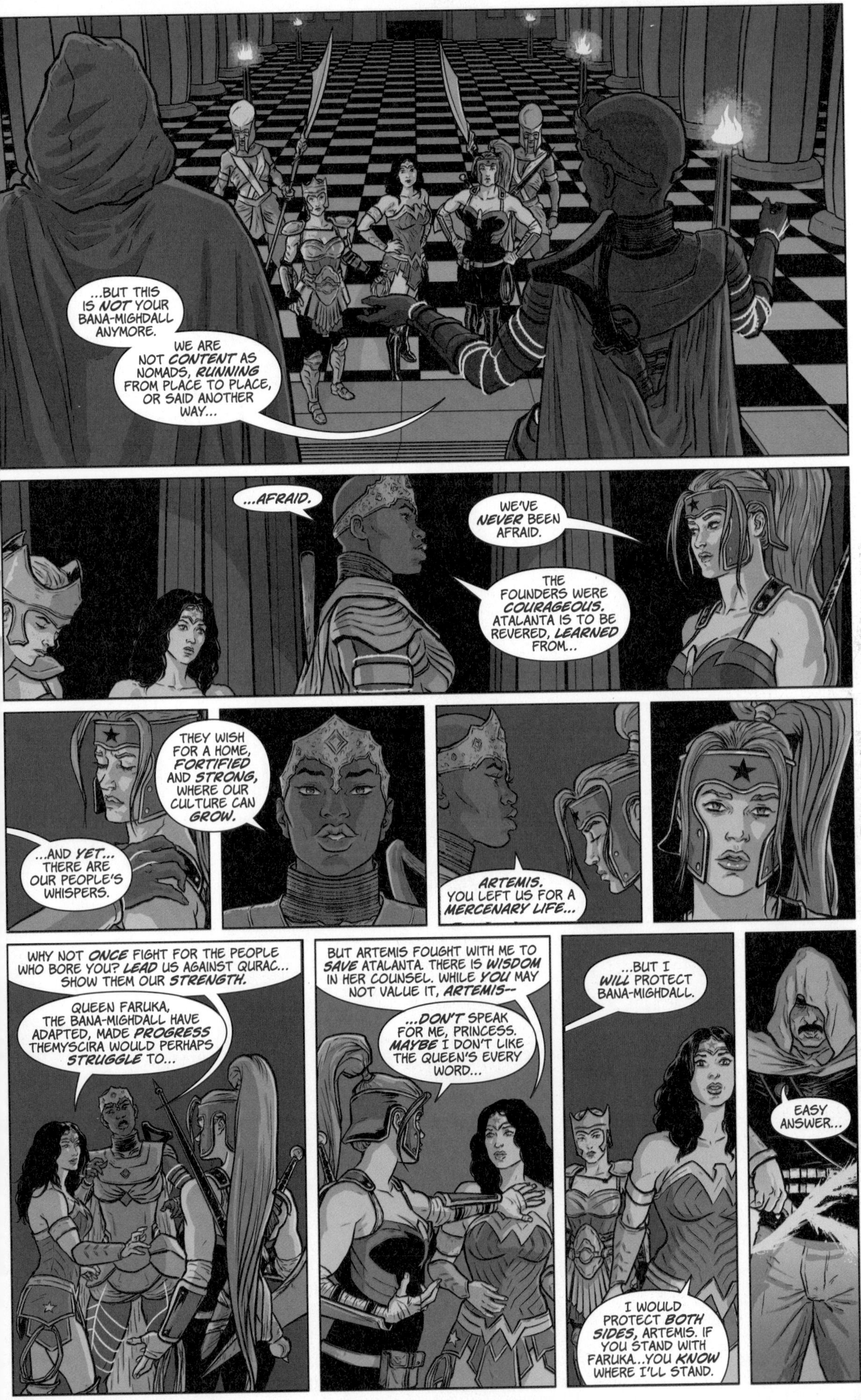
...BUT THIS IS NOT YOUR BANA-MIGHDALL ANYMORE.
WE ARE NOT CONTENT AS NOMADS, RUNNING FROM PLACE TO PLACE, OR SAID ANOTHER WAY...
...AFRAID.
WE'VE NEVER BEEN AFRAID.
THE FOUNDERS WERE COURAGEOUS. ATALANTA IS TO BE REVERED, LEARNED FROM...
...AND YET... THERE ARE OUR PEOPLE'S WHISPERS.
THEY WISH FOR A HOME, FORTIFIED AND STRONG, WHERE OUR CULTURE CAN GROW.
ARTEMIS. YOU LEFT US FOR A MERCENARY LIFE...
WHY NOT ONCE FIGHT FOR THE PEOPLE WHO BORE YOU? LEAD US AGAINST QURAC... SHOW THEM OUR STRENGTH.
QUEEN FARUKA, THE BANA-MIGHDALL HAVE ADAPTED, MADE PROGRESS THEMYSCIRA WOULD PERHAPS STRUGGLE TO...
BUT ARTEMIS FOUGHT WITH ME TO SAVE ATALANTA. THERE IS WISDOM IN HER COUNSEL. WHILE YOU MAY NOT VALUE IT, ARTEMIS--
...DON'T SPEAK FOR ME, PRINCESS. MAYBE I DON'T LIKE THE QUEEN'S EVERY WORD...
...BUT I WILL PROTECT BANA-MIGHDALL.
I WOULD PROTECT BOTH SIDES, ARTEMIS. IF YOU STAND WITH FARUKA...YOU KNOW WHERE I'LL STAND.
EASY ANSWER...

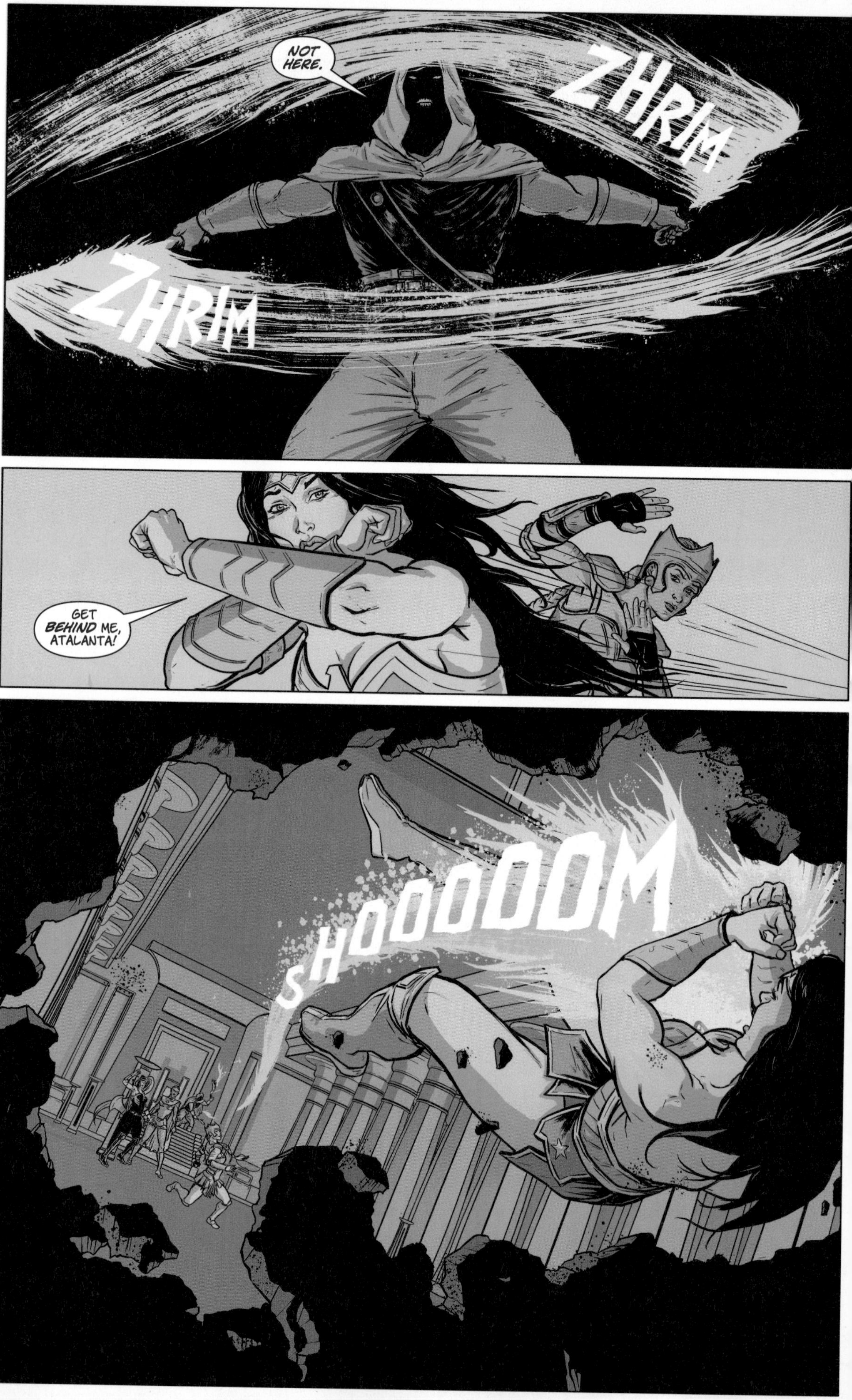
NOT HERE.
ZHRIM
ZHRIM
GET BEHIND ME, ATALANTA!
SHOOOOOOM

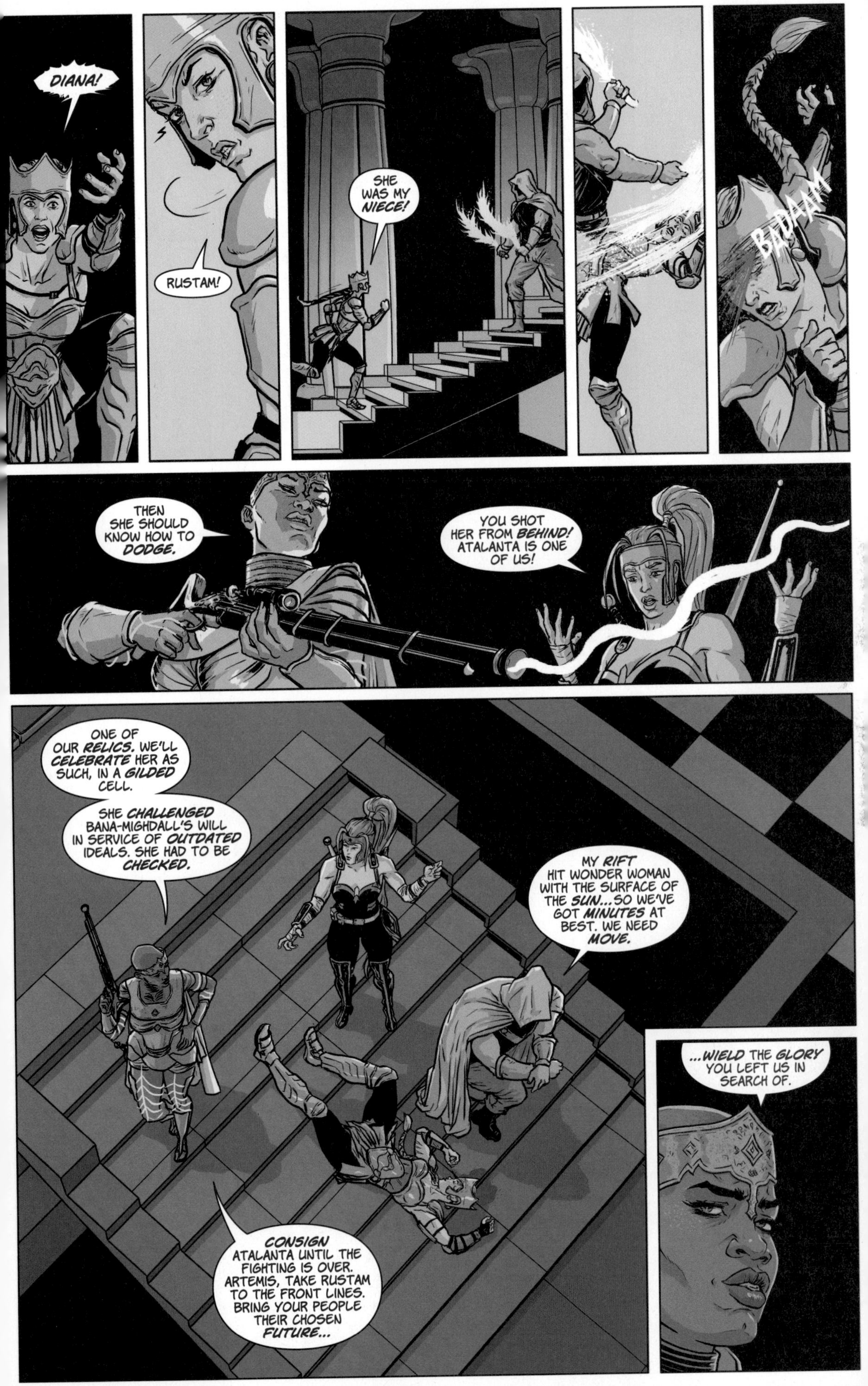
DIANA!
RUSTAM!
SHE WAS MY NIECE!
BADAAM
THEN SHE SHOULD KNOW HOW TO DODGE.
YOU SHOT HER FROM BEHIND! ATALANTA IS ONE OF US!
ONE OF OUR RELICS. WE'LL CELEBRATE HER AS SUCH, IN A GILDED CELL.
SHE CHALLENGED BANA-MIGHDALL'S WILL IN SERVICE OF OUTDATED IDEALS. SHE HAD TO BE CHECKED.
MY RIFT HIT WONDER WOMAN WITH THE SURFACE OF THE SUN...SO WE'VE GOT MINUTES AT BEST. WE NEED MOVE.
CONSIGN ATALANTA UNTIL THE FIGHTING IS OVER. ARTEMIS, TAKE RUSTAM TO THE FRONT LINES. BRING YOUR PEOPLE THEIR CHOSEN FUTURE...
...WIELD THE GLORY YOU LEFT US IN SEARCH OF.

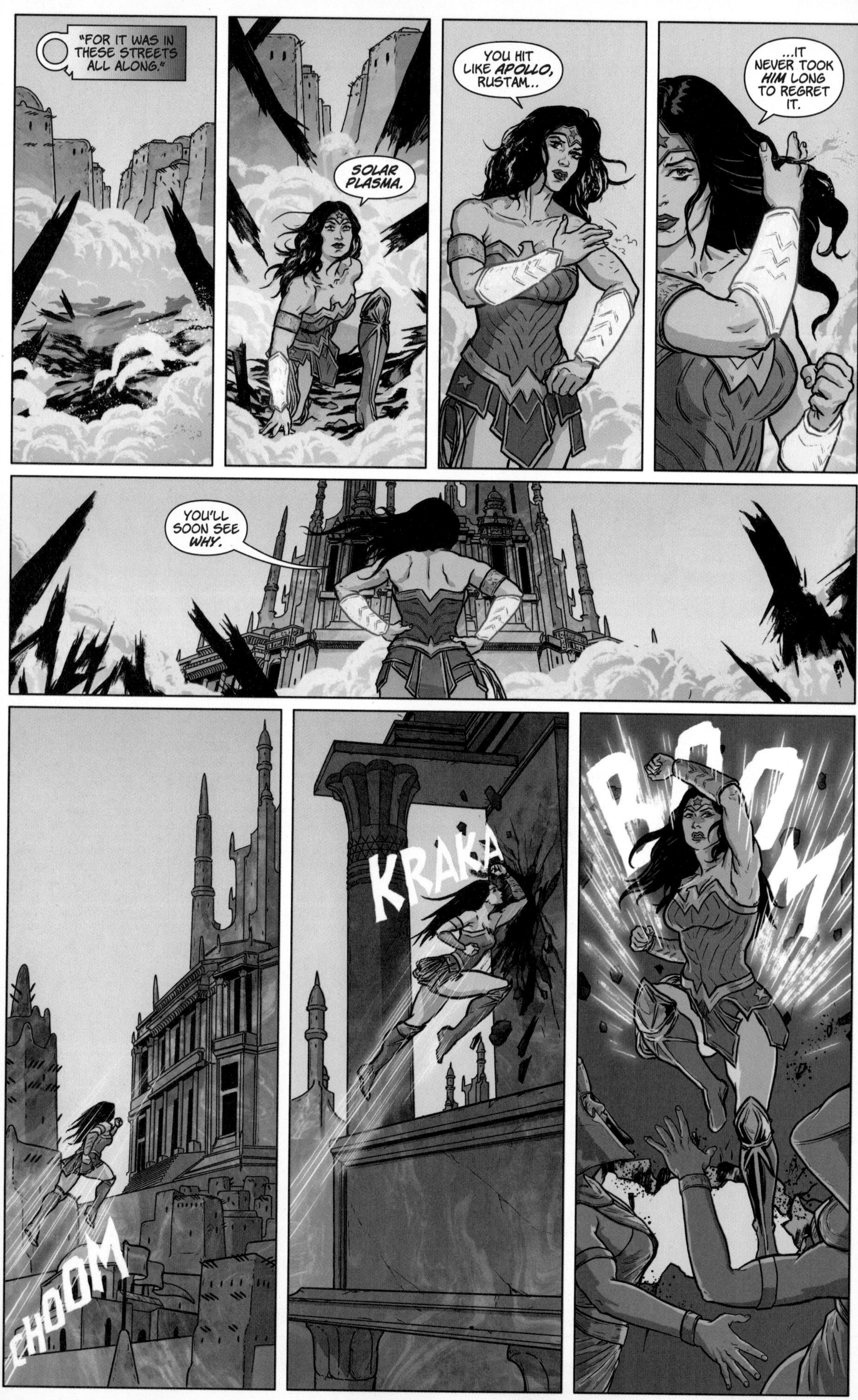
"FOR IT WAS IN THESE STREETS ALL ALONG."
SOLAR PLASMA.
YOU HIT LIKE APOLLO, RUSTAM...
...IT NEVER TOOK HIM LONG TO REGRET IT.
YOU'LL SOON SEE WHY.
CHOOM
KRAKA
BOOM

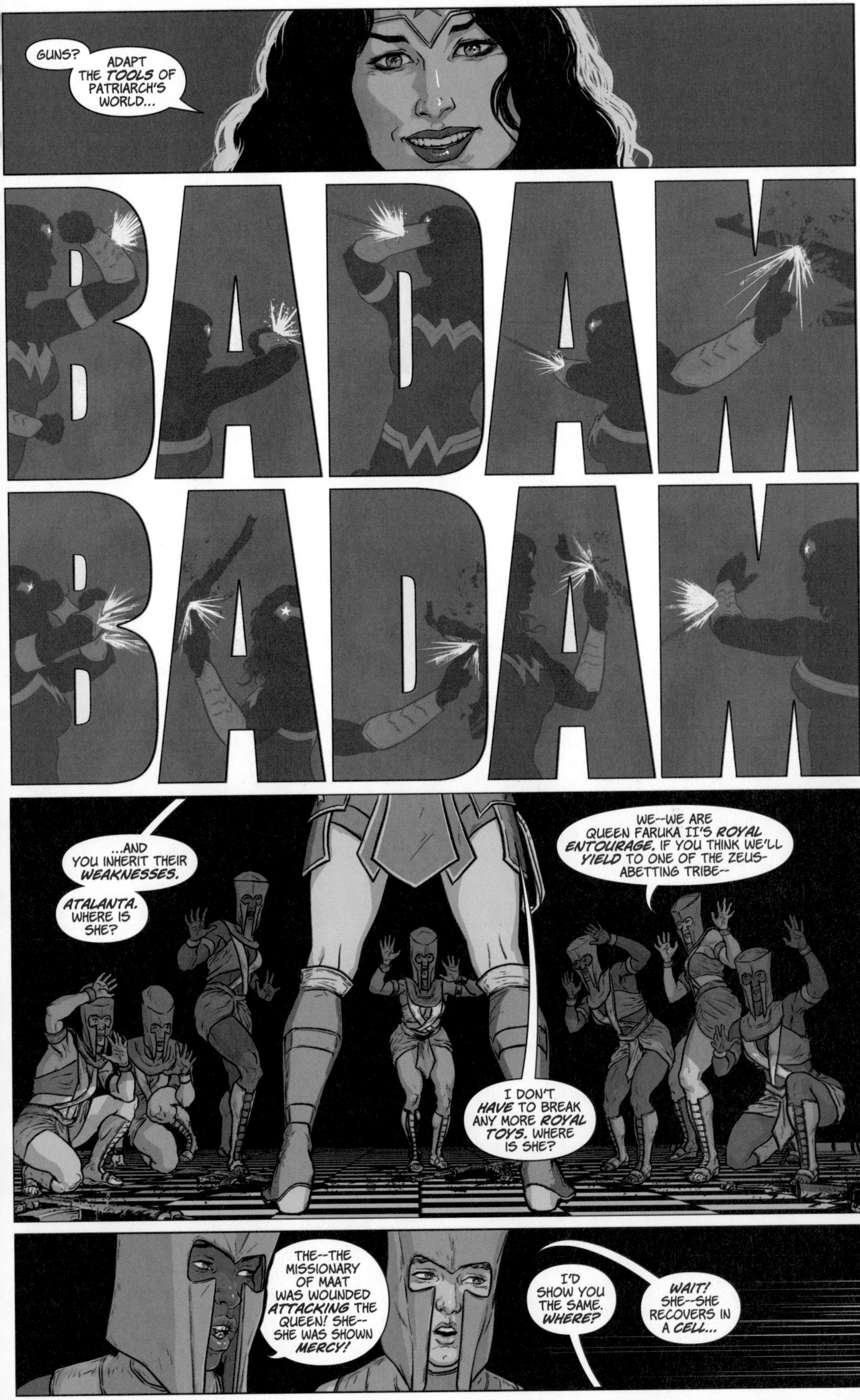
GUNS?
ADAPT THE TOOLS OF PATRIARCH'S WORLD...
BADAM
BADAM
...AND YOU INHERIT THEIR WEAKNESSES.
ATALANTA. WHERE IS SHE?
WE--WE ARE QUEEN FARUKA II'S ROYAL ENTOURAGE. IF YOU THINK WE'LL YIELD TO ONE OF THE ZEUS-ABETTING TRIBE--
I DON'T HAVE TO BREAK ANY MORE ROYAL TOYS. WHERE IS SHE?
THE--THE MISSIONARY OF MAAT WAS WOUNDED ATTACKING THE QUEEN! SHE--SHE WAS SHOWN MERCY!
I'D SHOW YOU THE SAME. WHERE?
WAIT! SHE--SHE RECOVERS IN A CELL...

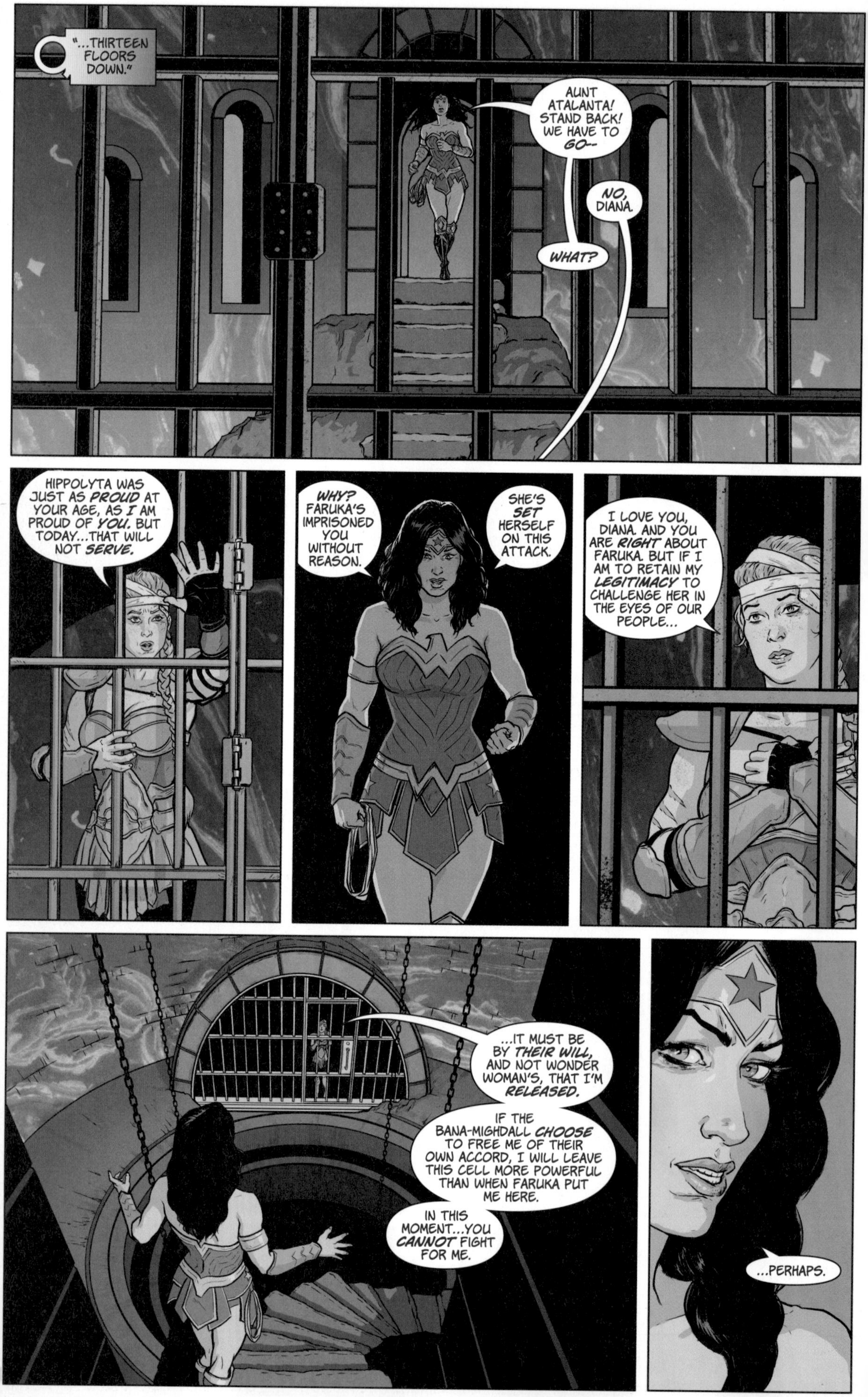
"...THIRTEEN FLOORS DOWN."
AUNT ATALANTA! STAND BACK! WE HAVE TO GO--
NO, DIANA.
WHAT?
HIPPOLYTA WAS JUST AS PROUD AT YOUR AGE, AS I AM PROUD OF YOU. BUT TODAY...THAT WILL NOT SERVE.
WHY? FARUKA'S IMPRISONED YOU WITHOUT REASON.
SHE'S SET HERSELF ON THIS ATTACK.
I LOVE YOU, DIANA. AND YOU ARE RIGHT ABOUT FARUKA. BUT IF I AM TO RETAIN MY LEGITIMACY TO CHALLENGE HER IN THE EYES OF OUR PEOPLE...
...IT MUST BE BY THEIR WILL, AND NOT WONDER WOMAN'S, THAT I'M RELEASED.
IF THE BANA-MIGHDALL CHOOSE TO FREE ME OF THEIR OWN ACCORD, I WILL LEAVE THIS CELL MORE POWERFUL THAN WHEN FARUKA PUT ME HERE.
IN THIS MOMENT...YOU CANNOT FIGHT FOR ME.
...PERHAPS.

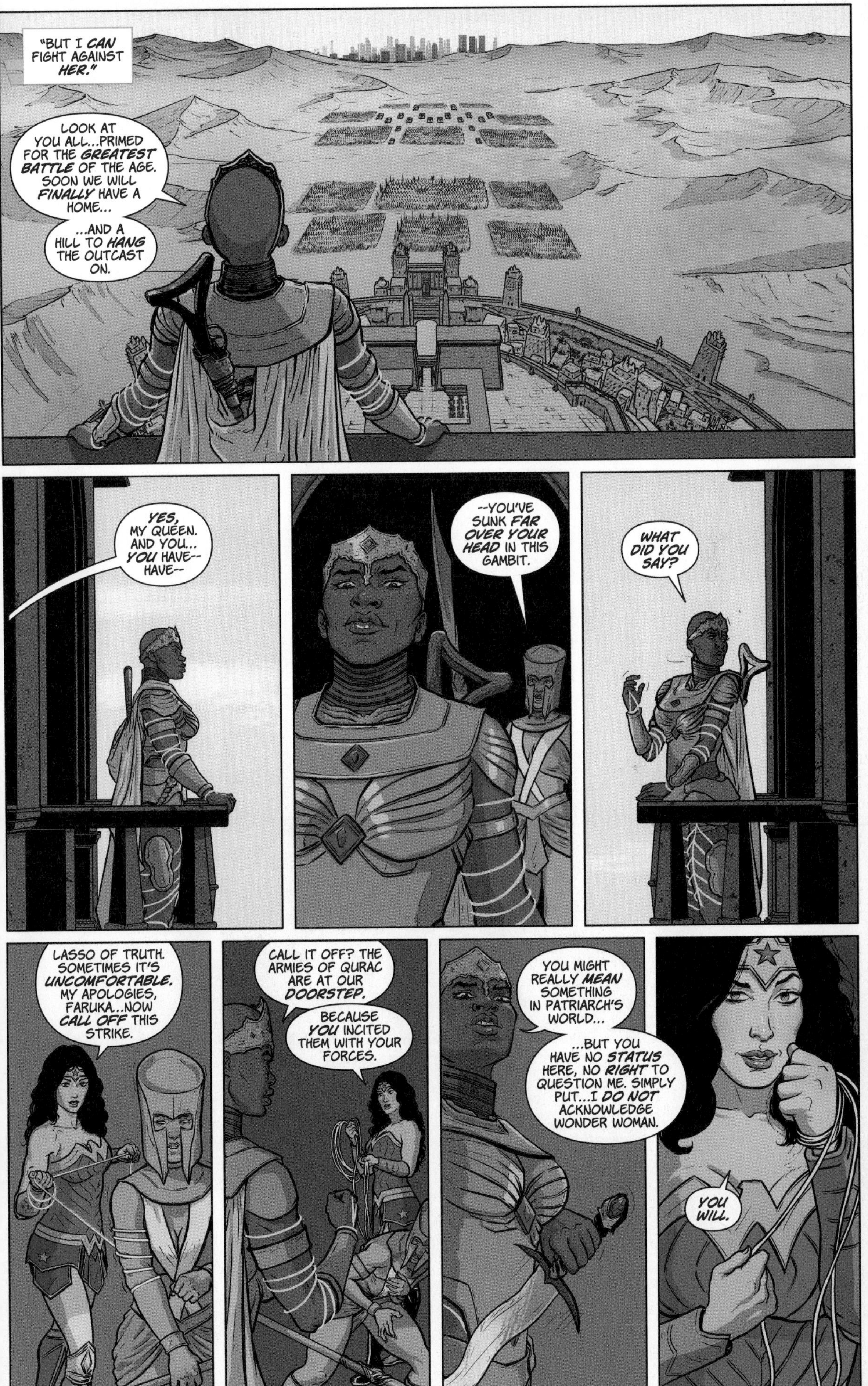
"BUT I CAN FIGHT AGAINST HER."
LOOK AT YOU ALL...PRIMED FOR THE GREATEST BATTLE OF THE AGE. SOON WE WILL FINALLY HAVE A HOME...
...AND A HILL TO HANG THE OUTCAST ON.
YES, MY QUEEN. AND YOU... YOU HAVE-- HAVE--
--YOU'VE SUNK FAR OVER YOUR HEAD IN THIS GAMBIT.
WHAT DID YOU SAY?
LASSO OF TRUTH. SOMETIMES IT'S UNCOMFORTABLE. MY APOLOGIES, FARUKA...NOW CALL OFF THIS STRIKE.
CALL IT OFF? THE ARMIES OF QURAC ARE AT OUR DOORSTEP.
BECAUSE YOU INCITED THEM WITH YOUR FORCES.
YOU MIGHT REALLY MEAN SOMETHING IN PATRIARCH'S WORLD...
...BUT YOU HAVE NO STATUS HERE, NO RIGHT TO QUESTION ME. SIMPLY PUT...I DO NOT ACKNOWLEDGE WONDER WOMAN.
YOU WILL.

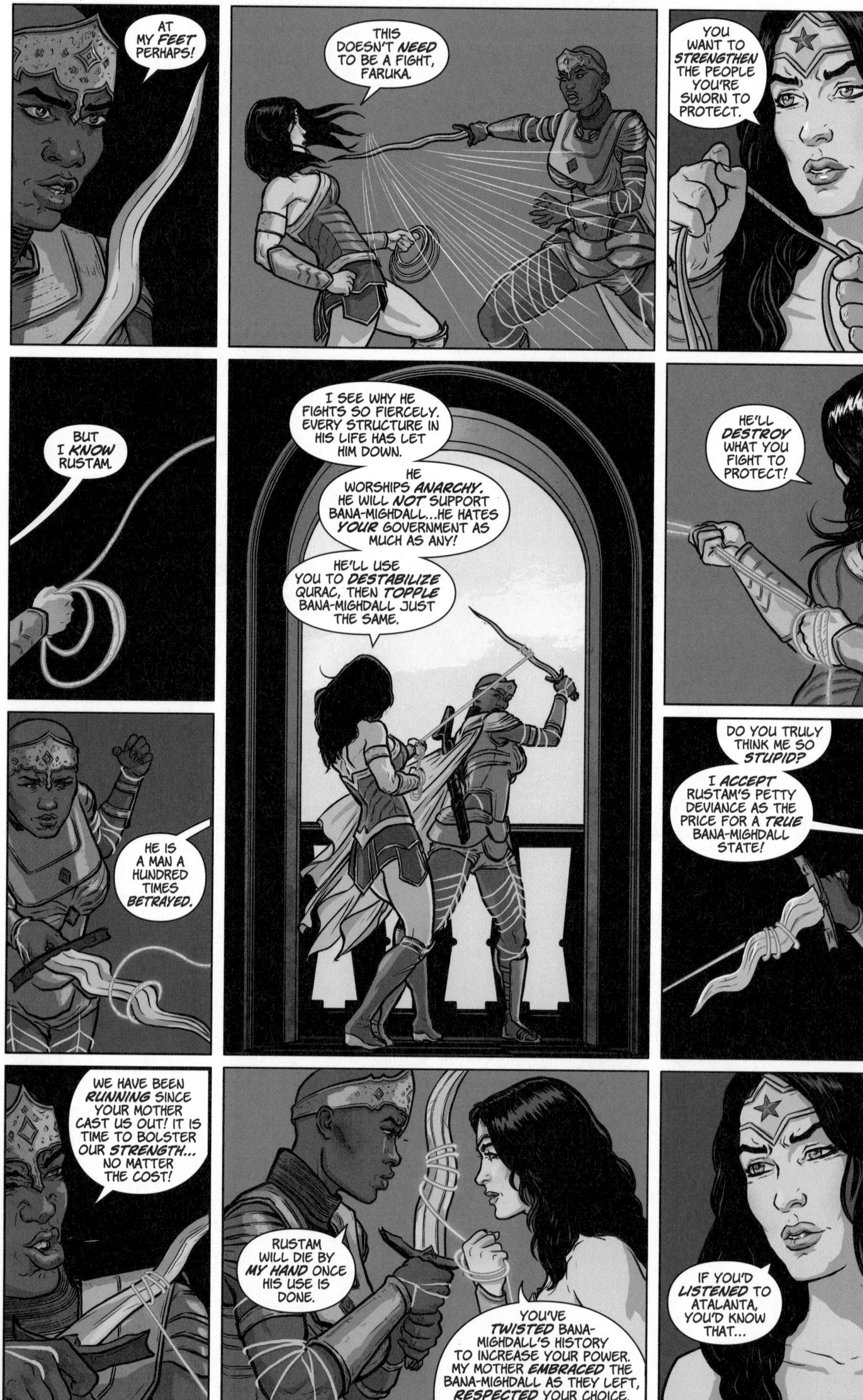
AT MY FEET PERHAPS!
THIS DOESN'T NEED TO BE A FIGHT, FARUKA.
YOU WANT TO STRENGTHEN THE PEOPLE YOU'RE SWORN TO PROTECT.
BUT I KNOW RUSTAM.
I SEE WHY HE FIGHTS SO FIERCELY. EVERY STRUCTURE IN HIS LIFE HAS LET HIM DOWN.
HE WORSHIPS ANARCHY. HE WILL NOT SUPPORT BANA-MIGHDALL...HE HATES YOUR GOVERNMENT AS MUCH AS ANY!
HE'LL USE YOU TO DESTABILIZE QURAC, THEN TOPPLE BANA-MIGHDALL JUST THE SAME.
HE'LL DESTROY WHAT YOU FIGHT TO PROTECT!
HE IS A MAN A HUNDRED TIMES BETRAYED.
DO YOU TRULY THINK ME SO STUPID?
I ACCEPT RUSTAM'S PETTY DEVIANCE AS THE PRICE FOR A TRUE BANA-MIGHDALL STATE!
WE HAVE BEEN RUNNING SINCE YOUR MOTHER CAST US OUT! IT IS TIME TO BOLSTER OUR STRENGTH... NO MATTER THE COST!
RUSTAM WILL DIE BY MY HAND ONCE HIS USE IS DONE.
YOU'VE TWISTED BANA-MIGHDALL'S HISTORY TO INCREASE YOUR POWER. MY MOTHER EMBRACED THE BANA-MIGHDALL AS THEY LEFT, RESPECTED YOUR CHOICE.
IF YOU'D LISTENED TO ATALANTA, YOU'D KNOW THAT...

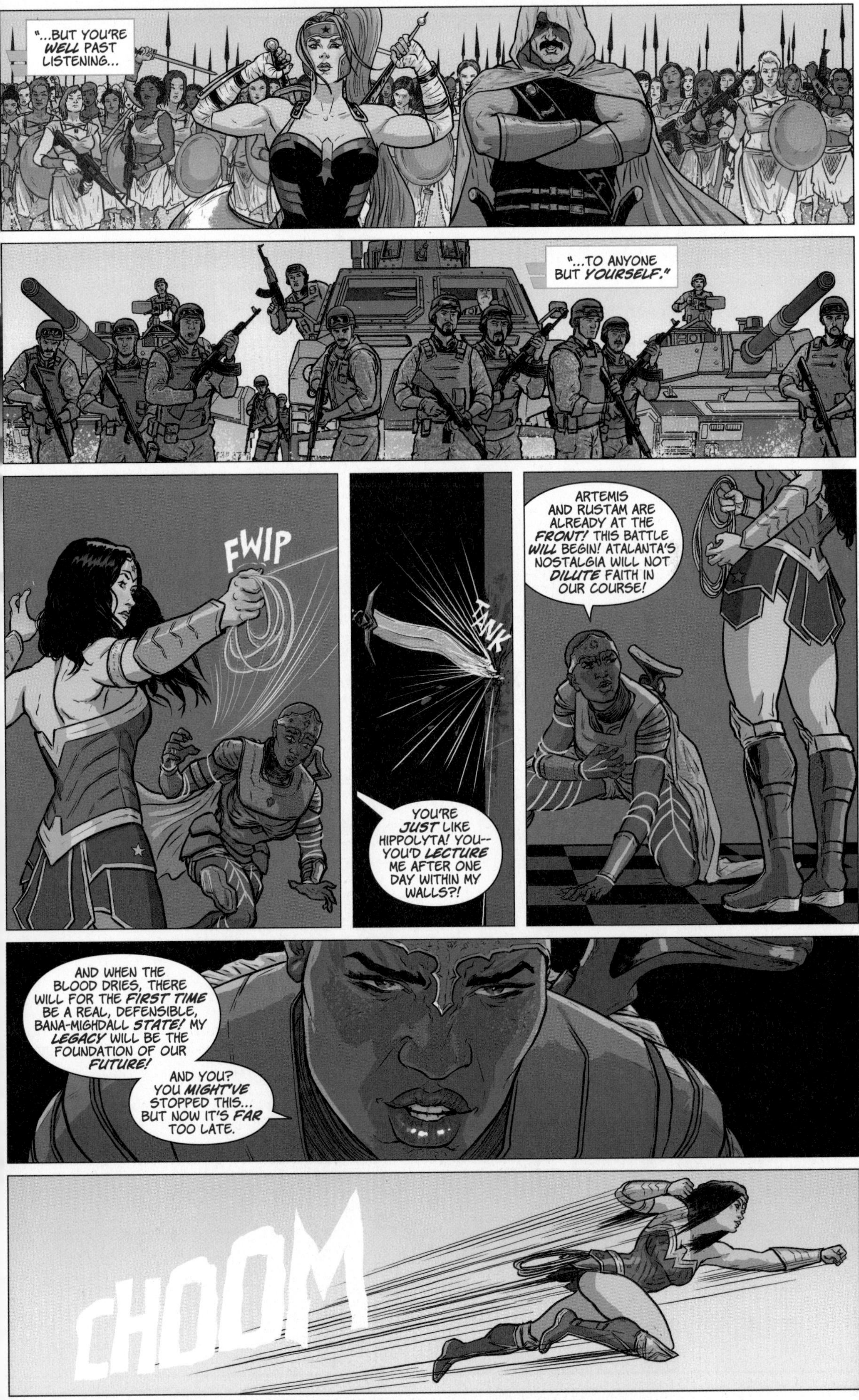
"...BUT YOU'RE *WELL* PAST LISTENING...
"...TO ANYONE BUT *YOURSELF.*"
FWIP
TANK
YOU'RE *JUST* LIKE HIPPOLYTA! YOU-- YOU'D *LECTURE* ME AFTER ONE DAY WITHIN MY WALLS?!
ARTEMIS AND RUSTAM ARE ALREADY AT THE *FRONT!* THIS BATTLE *WILL* BEGIN! ATALANTA'S NOSTALGIA WILL NOT *DILUTE* FAITH IN OUR COURSE!
AND WHEN THE BLOOD DRIES, THERE WILL FOR THE *FIRST TIME* BE A REAL, DEFENSIBLE, BANA-MIGHDALL *STATE!* MY *LEGACY* WILL BE THE FOUNDATION OF OUR *FUTURE!*
AND YOU? YOU *MIGHT'VE* STOPPED THIS... BUT NOW IT'S *FAR* TOO LATE.
CHOOM

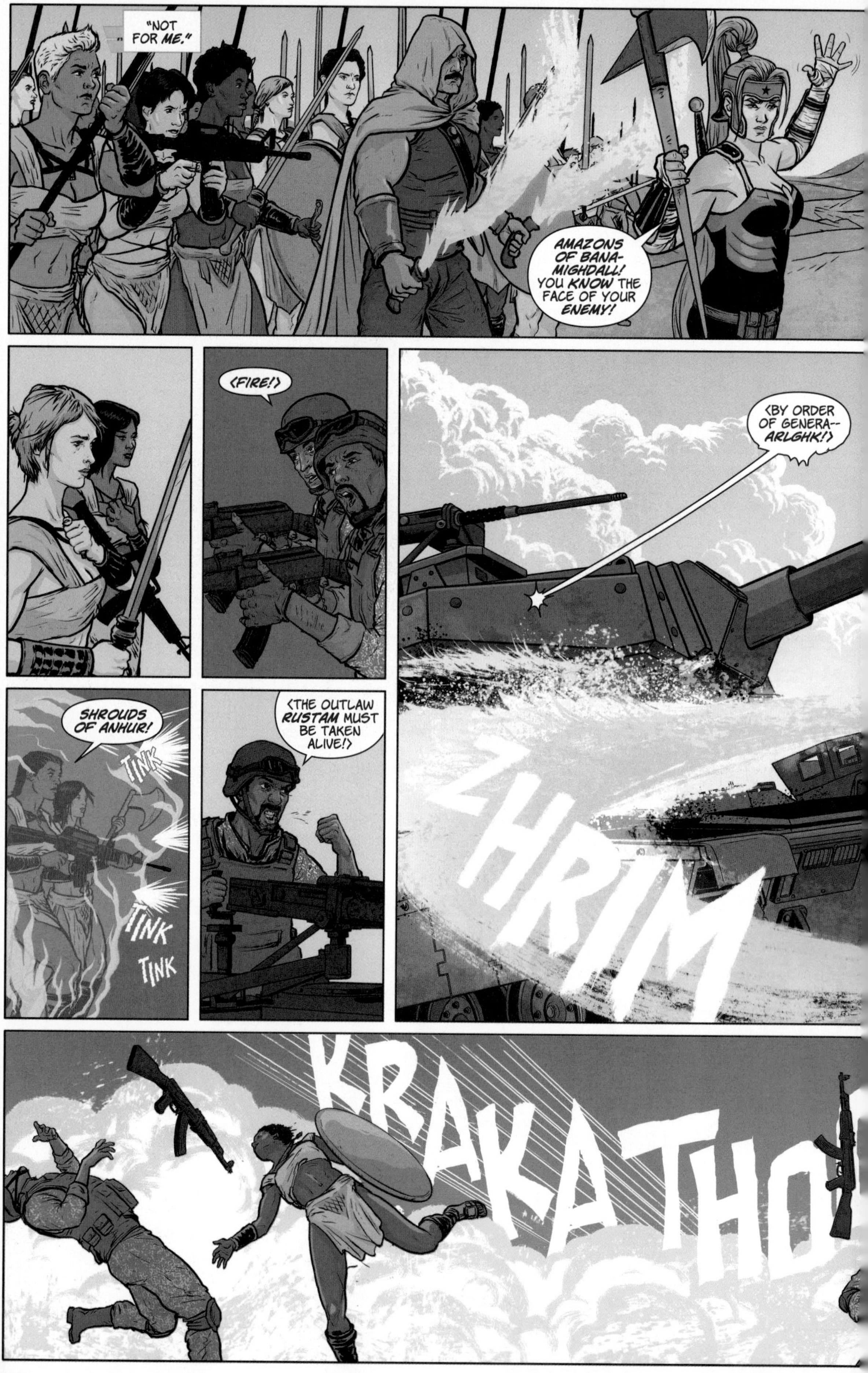
"NOT FOR ME."
AMAZONS OF BANA-MIGHDALL! YOU KNOW THE FACE OF YOUR ENEMY!
<FIRE!>
<BY ORDER OF GENERA-- ARLGHK!>
SHROUDS OF ANHUR!
TINK
TINK
TINK
<THE OUTLAW RUSTAM MUST BE TAKEN ALIVE!>
ZHRIM
KRAKATHO

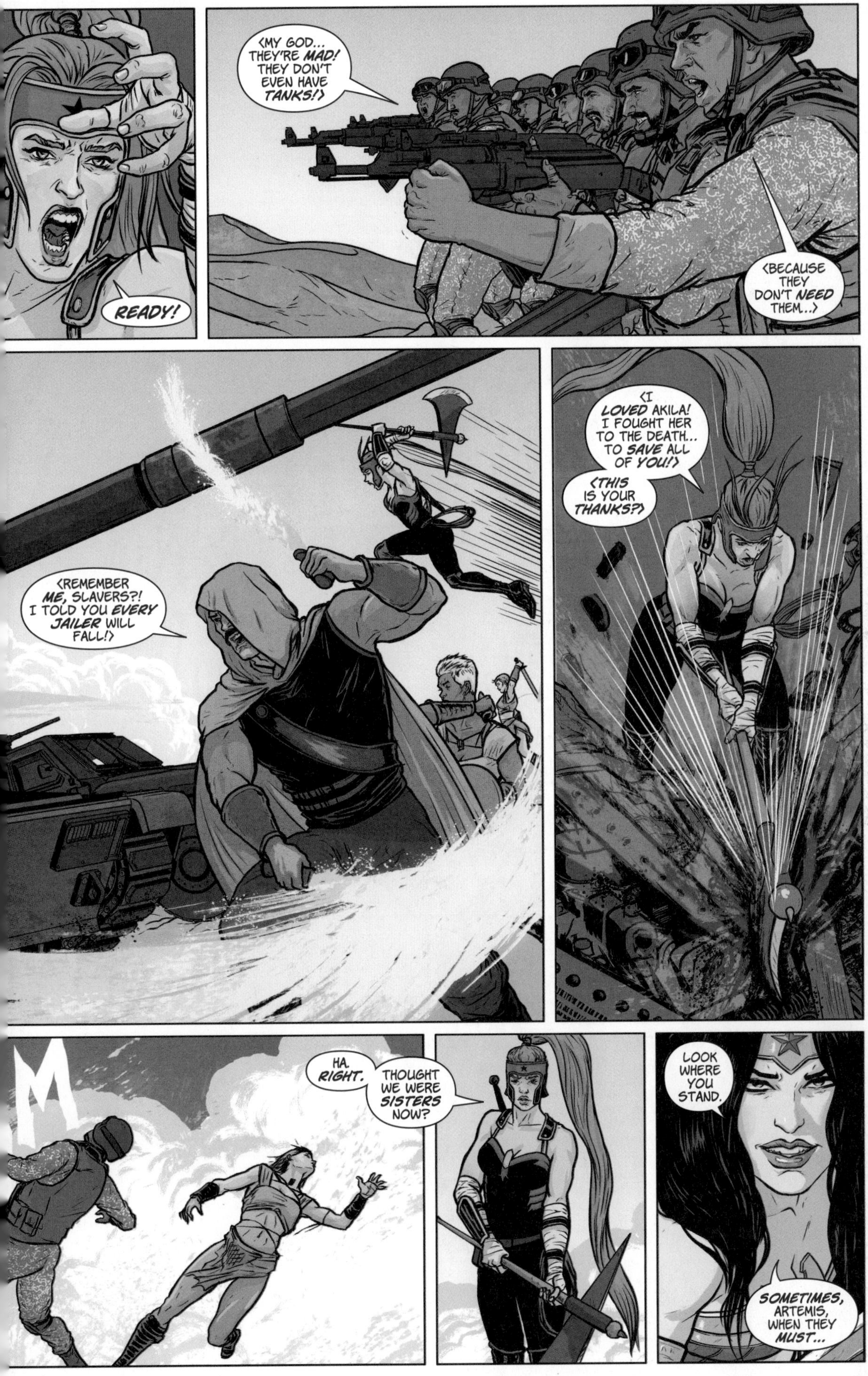
READY!
<MY GOD... THEY'RE MAD! THEY DON'T EVEN HAVE TANKS!>
<BECAUSE THEY DON'T NEED THEM...>
<REMEMBER ME, SLAVERS?! I TOLD YOU EVERY JAILER WILL FALL!>
<I LOVED AKILA! I FOUGHT HER TO THE DEATH... TO SAVE ALL OF YOU!>
<THIS IS YOUR THANKS?>
M
HA. RIGHT.
THOUGHT WE WERE SISTERS NOW?
LOOK WHERE YOU STAND.
SOMETIMES, ARTEMIS, WHEN THEY MUST...

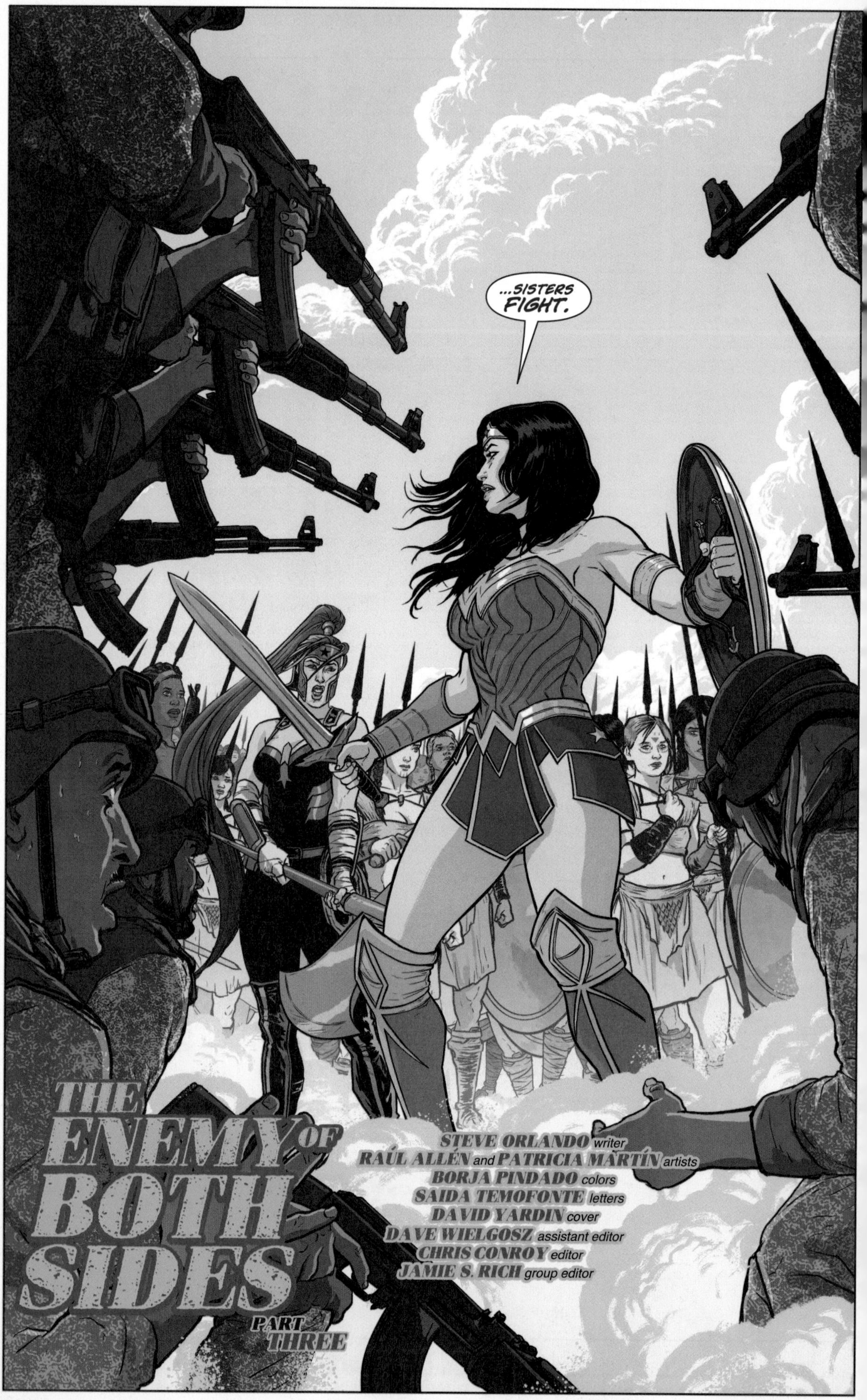
...SISTERS FIGHT.
THE ENEMY OF BOTH SIDES
PART THREE
STEVE ORLANDO writer
RAÚL ALLÉN and PATRICIA MÁRTÍN artists
BORJA PINDADO colors
SAIDA TEMOFONTE letters
DAVID YARDIN cover
DAVE WIELGOSZ assistant editor
CHRIS CONROY editor
JAMIE S. RICH group editor

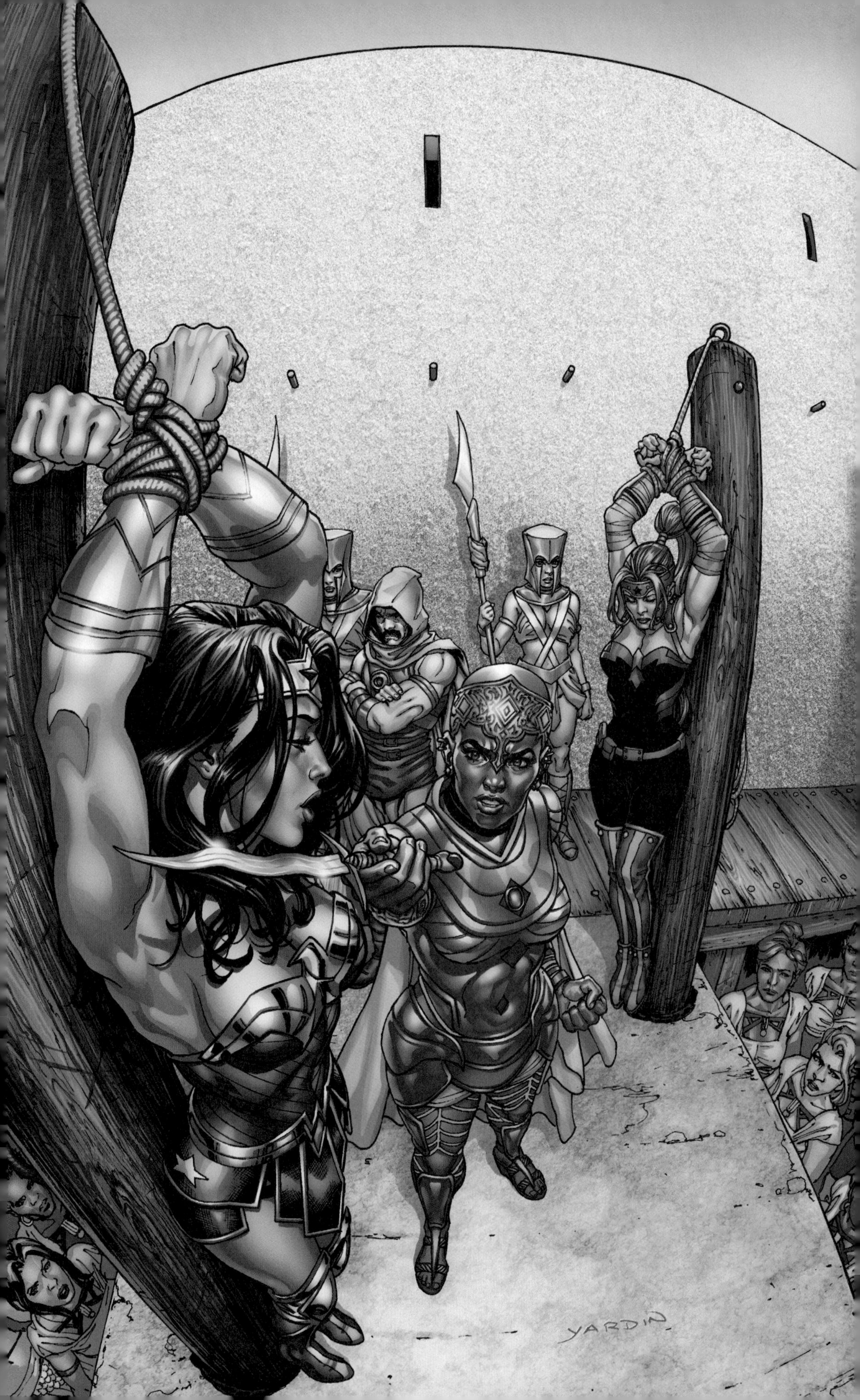
YARDIN

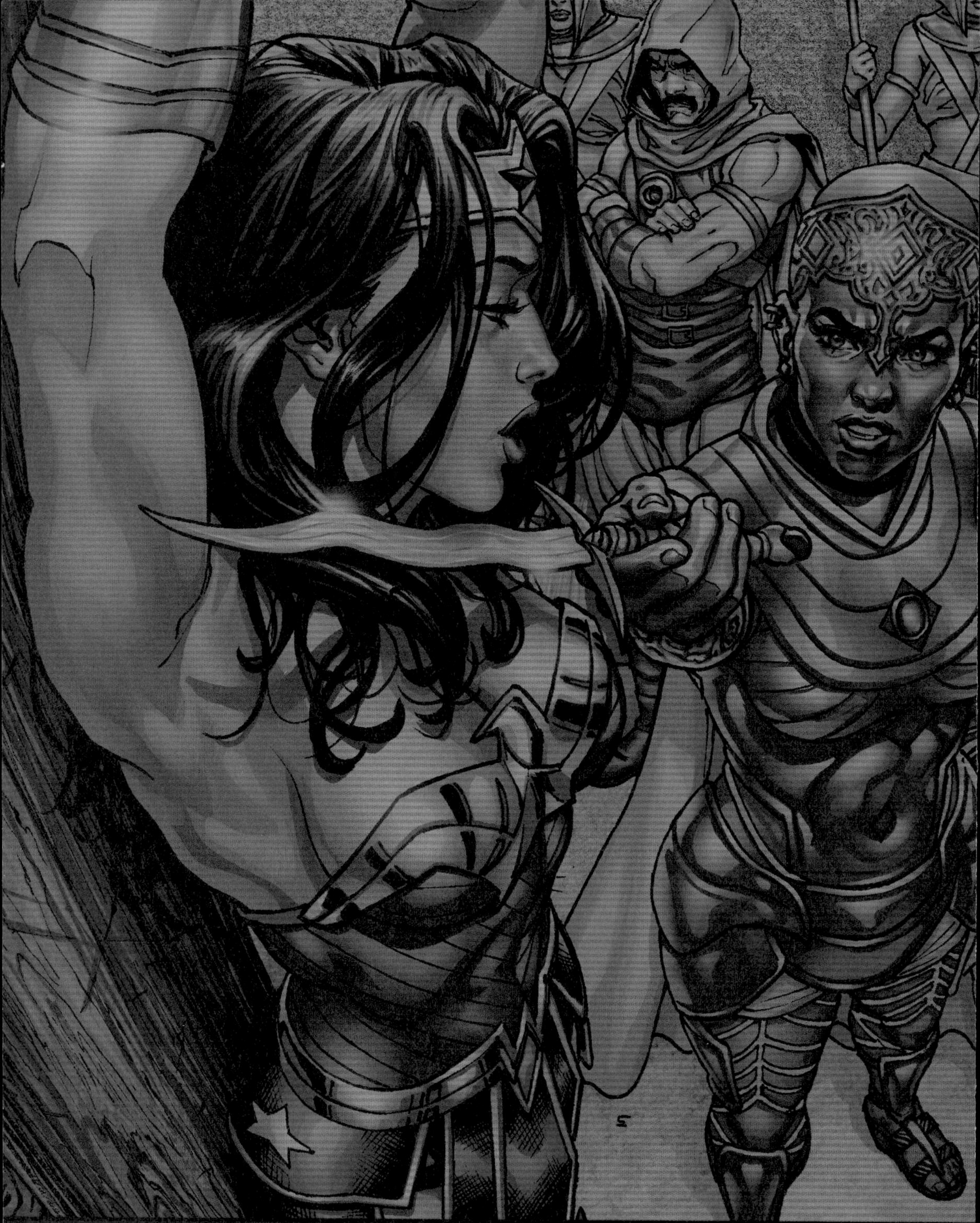

WONDER WOMAN

#55

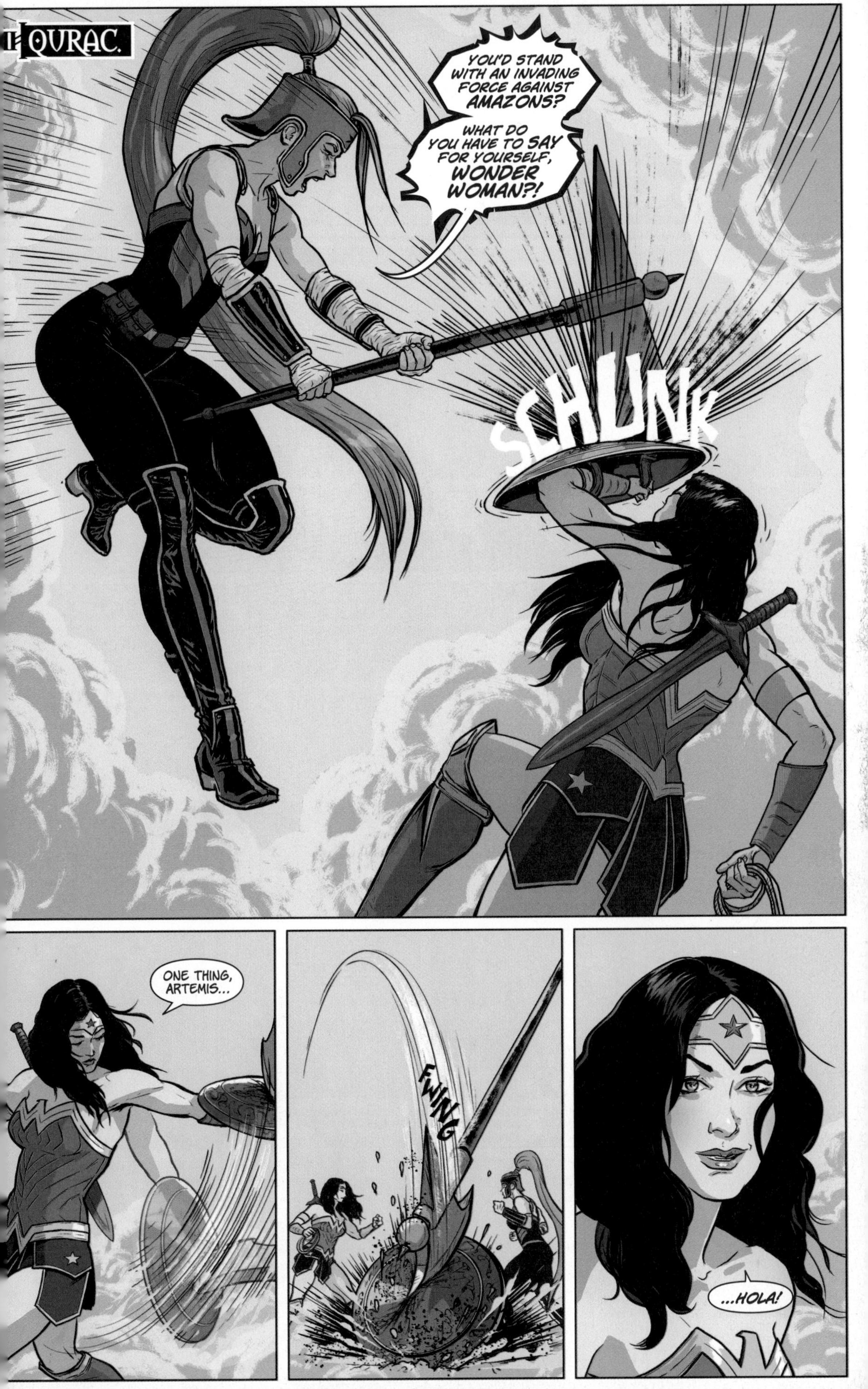
QURAC.
YOU'D STAND WITH AN INVADING FORCE AGAINST AMAZONS?
WHAT DO YOU HAVE TO SAY FOR YOURSELF, WONDER WOMAN?!
SCHUNK
ONE THING, ARTEMIS...
FWING
...HOLA!

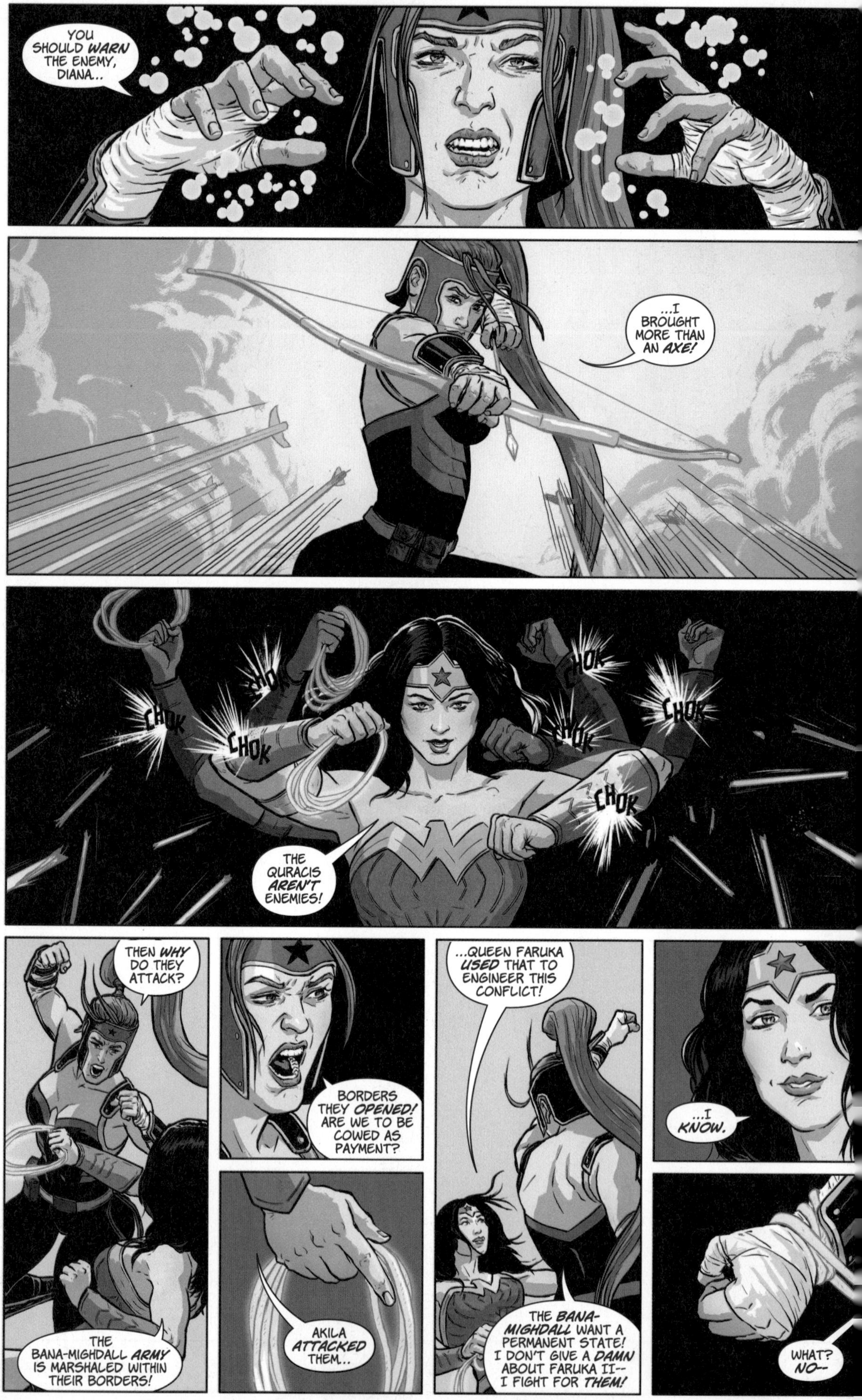
YOU SHOULD WARN THE ENEMY, DIANA...
...I BROUGHT MORE THAN AN AXE!
CHOK
CHOK
CHOK
CHOK
CHOK
CHOK
THE QURACIS AREN'T ENEMIES!
THEN WHY DO THEY ATTACK?
THE BANA-MIGHDALL ARMY IS MARSHALED WITHIN THEIR BORDERS!
BORDERS THEY OPENED! ARE WE TO BE COWED AS PAYMENT?
AKILA ATTACKED THEM...
...QUEEN FARUKA USED THAT TO ENGINEER THIS CONFLICT!
THE BANA-MIGHDALL WANT A PERMANENT STATE! I DON'T GIVE A DAMN ABOUT FARUKA II-- I FIGHT FOR THEM!
...I KNOW.
WHAT? NO--

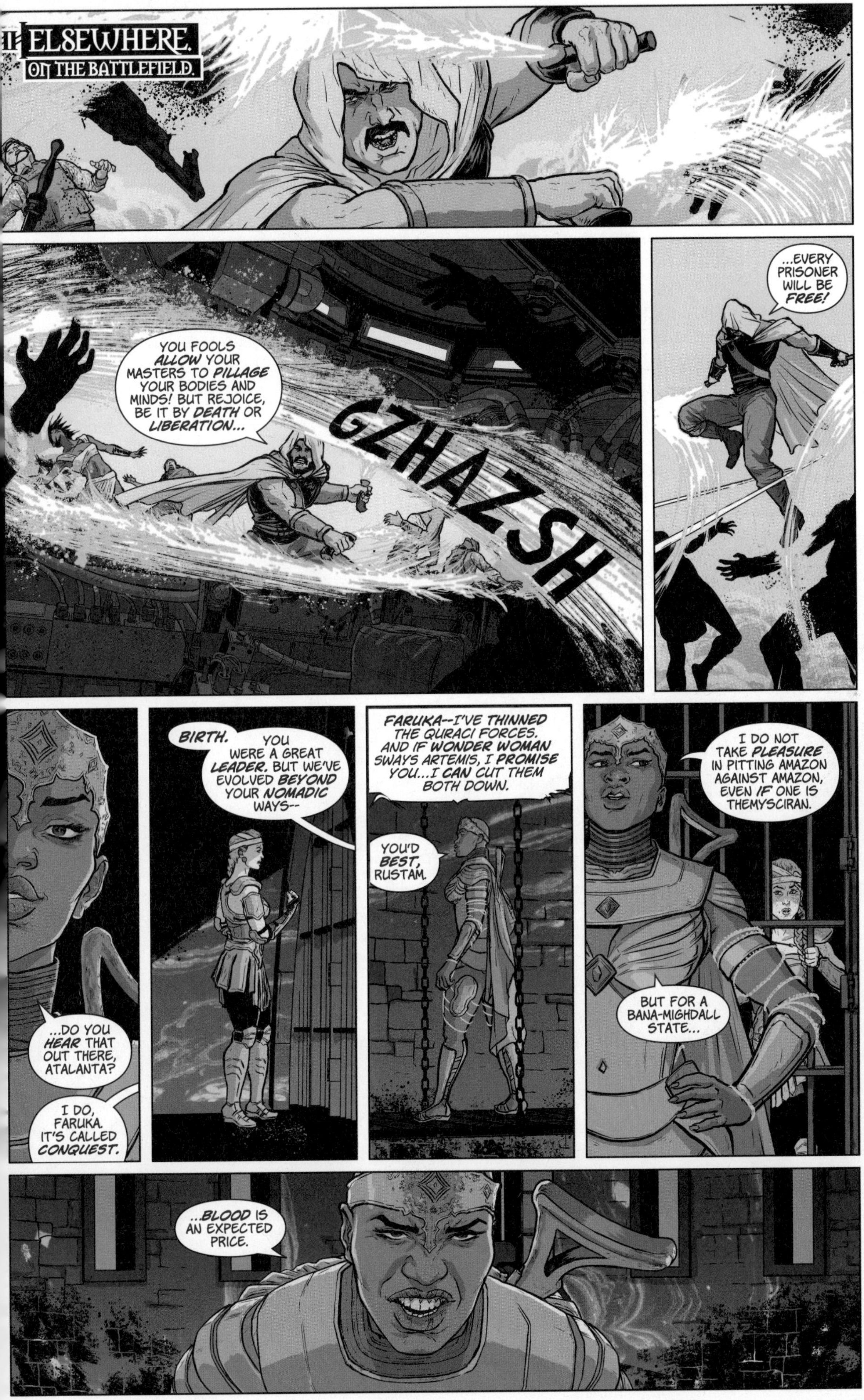
ELSEWHERE.
ON THE BATTLEFIELD.
YOU FOOLS ALLOW YOUR MASTERS TO PILLAGE YOUR BODIES AND MINDS! BUT REJOICE, BE IT BY DEATH OR LIBERATION...
GZHAZSH
...EVERY PRISONER WILL BE FREE!
...DO YOU HEAR THAT OUT THERE, ATALANTA?
I DO, FARUKA. IT'S CALLED CONQUEST.
BIRTH.
YOU WERE A GREAT LEADER. BUT WE'VE EVOLVED BEYOND YOUR NOMADIC WAYS--
FARUKA--I'VE THINNED THE QURACI FORCES. AND IF WONDER WOMAN SWAYS ARTEMIS, I PROMISE YOU...I CAN CUT THEM BOTH DOWN.
YOU'D BEST, RUSTAM.
I DO NOT TAKE PLEASURE IN PITTING AMAZON AGAINST AMAZON, EVEN IF ONE IS THEMYSCIRAN.
BUT FOR A BANA-MIGHDALL STATE...
...BLOOD IS AN EXPECTED PRICE.

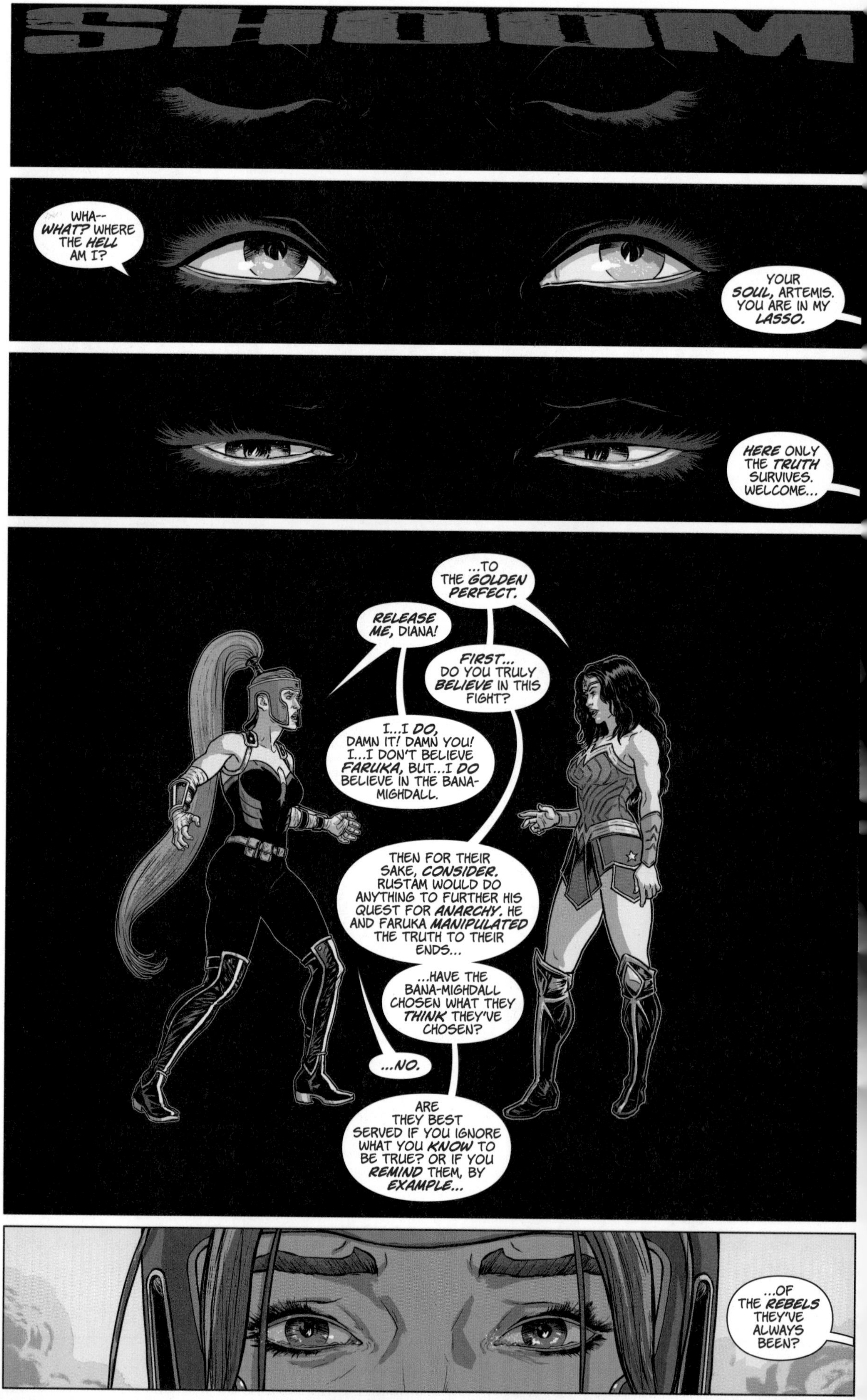
SHOOM
WHA-- WHAT? WHERE THE HELL AM I?
YOUR SOUL, ARTEMIS. YOU ARE IN MY LASSO.
HERE ONLY THE TRUTH SURVIVES. WELCOME...
...TO THE GOLDEN PERFECT.
RELEASE ME, DIANA!
FIRST... DO YOU TRULY BELIEVE IN THIS FIGHT?
I...I DO, DAMN IT! DAMN YOU! I...I DON'T BELIEVE FARUKA, BUT...I DO BELIEVE IN THE BANA-MIGHDALL.
THEN FOR THEIR SAKE, CONSIDER. RUSTAM WOULD DO ANYTHING TO FURTHER HIS QUEST FOR ANARCHY. HE AND FARUKA MANIPULATED THE TRUTH TO THEIR ENDS...
...HAVE THE BANA-MIGHDALL CHOSEN WHAT THEY THINK THEY'VE CHOSEN?
...NO.
ARE THEY BEST SERVED IF YOU IGNORE WHAT YOU KNOW TO BE TRUE? OR IF YOU REMIND THEM, BY EXAMPLE...
...OF THE REBELS THEY'VE ALWAYS BEEN?

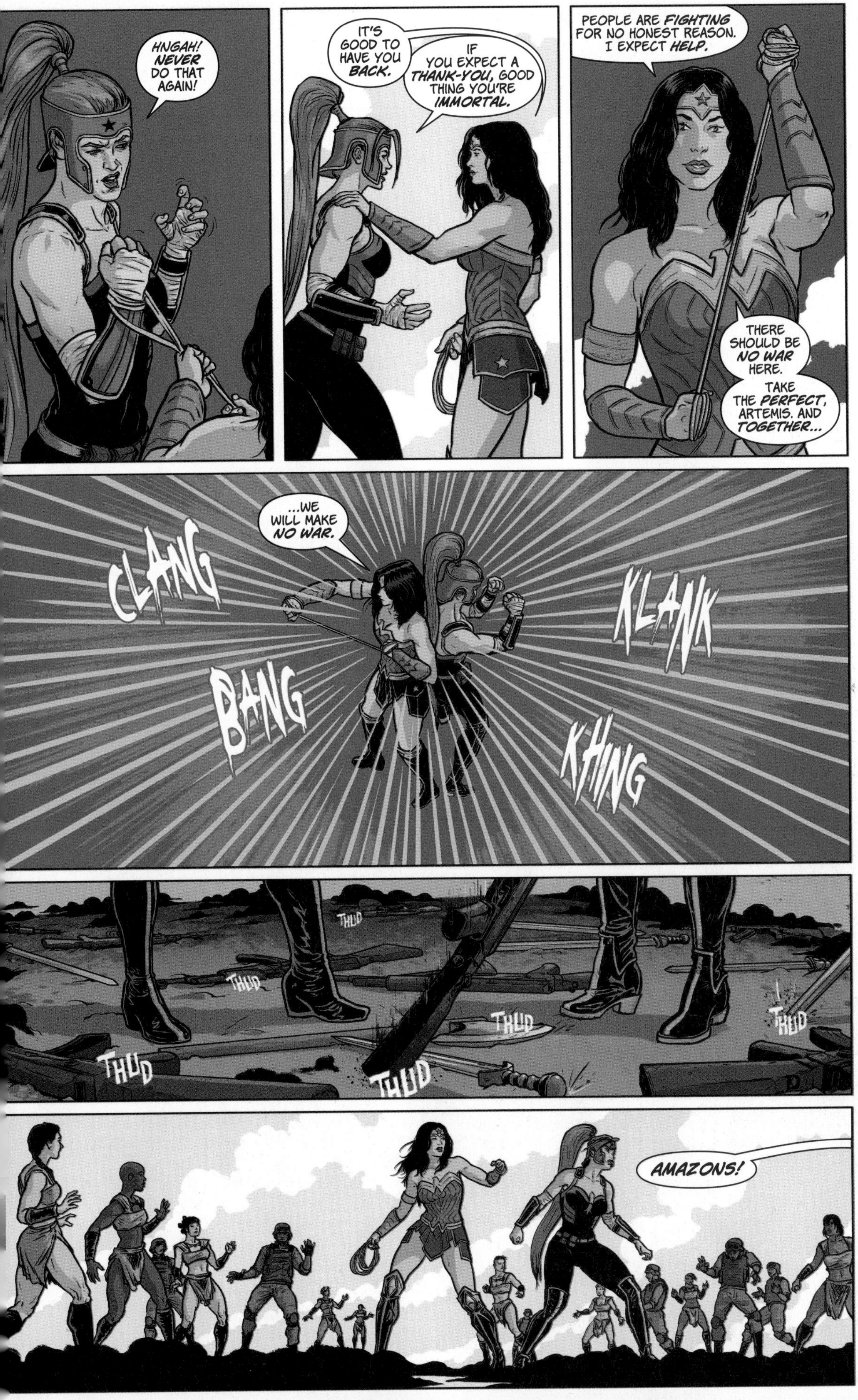
HNGAH! NEVER DO THAT AGAIN!
IT'S GOOD TO HAVE YOU BACK.
IF YOU EXPECT A THANK-YOU, GOOD THING YOU'RE IMMORTAL.
PEOPLE ARE FIGHTING FOR NO HONEST REASON. I EXPECT HELP.
THERE SHOULD BE NO WAR HERE.
TAKE THE PERFECT, ARTEMIS. AND TOGETHER...
...WE WILL MAKE NO WAR.
CLANG
BANG
KLANK
KHING
THUD
THUD
THUD
THUD
THUD
THUD
AMAZONS!

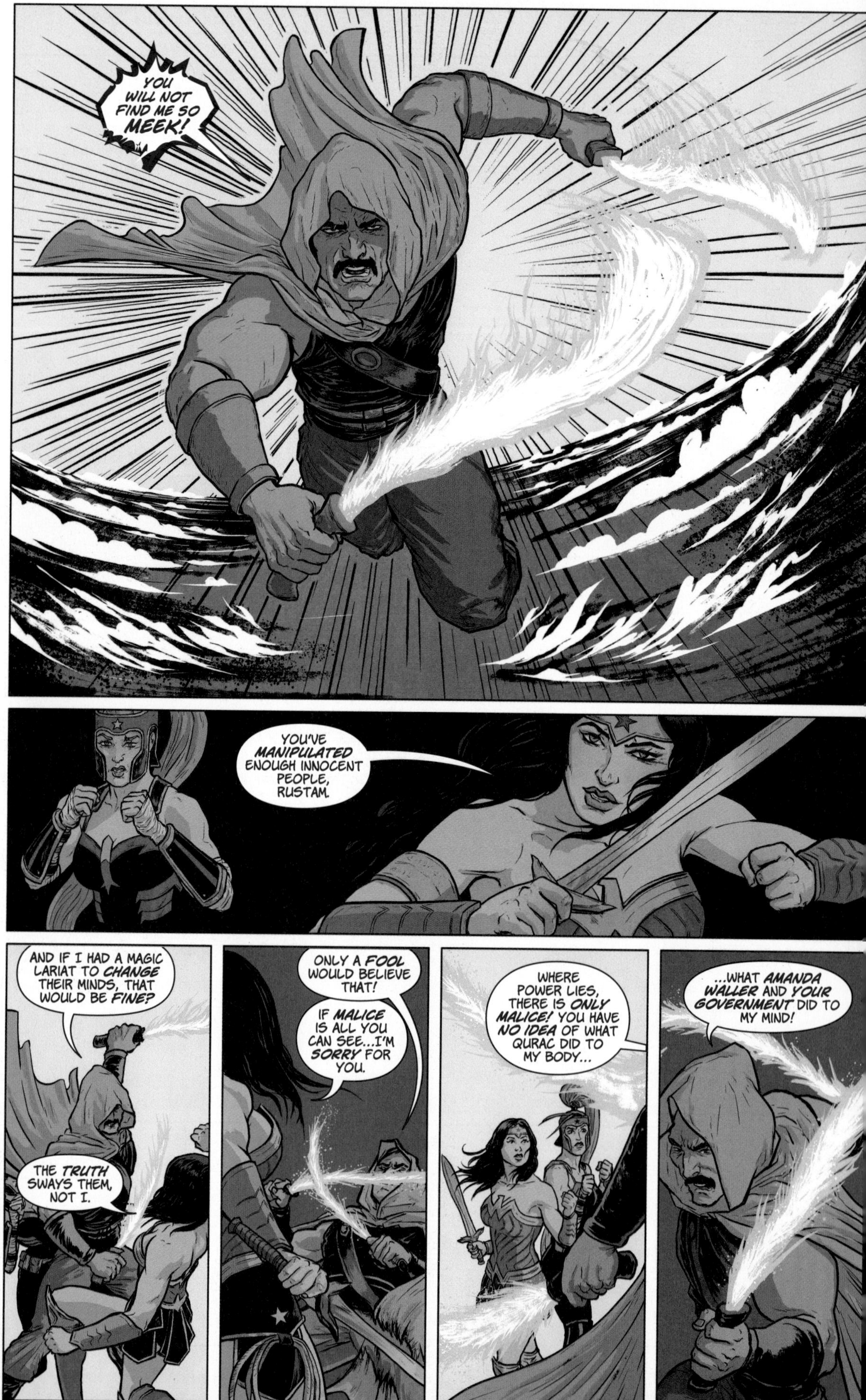
YOU WILL NOT FIND ME SO MEEK!
YOU'VE MANIPULATED ENOUGH INNOCENT PEOPLE, RUSTAM.
AND IF I HAD A MAGIC LARIAT TO CHANGE THEIR MINDS, THAT WOULD BE FINE?
THE TRUTH SWAYS THEM, NOT I.
ONLY A FOOL WOULD BELIEVE THAT!
IF MALICE IS ALL YOU CAN SEE...I'M SORRY FOR YOU.
WHERE POWER LIES, THERE IS ONLY MALICE! YOU HAVE NO IDEA OF WHAT QURAC DID TO MY BODY...
...WHAT AMANDA WALLER AND YOUR GOVERNMENT DID TO MY MIND!

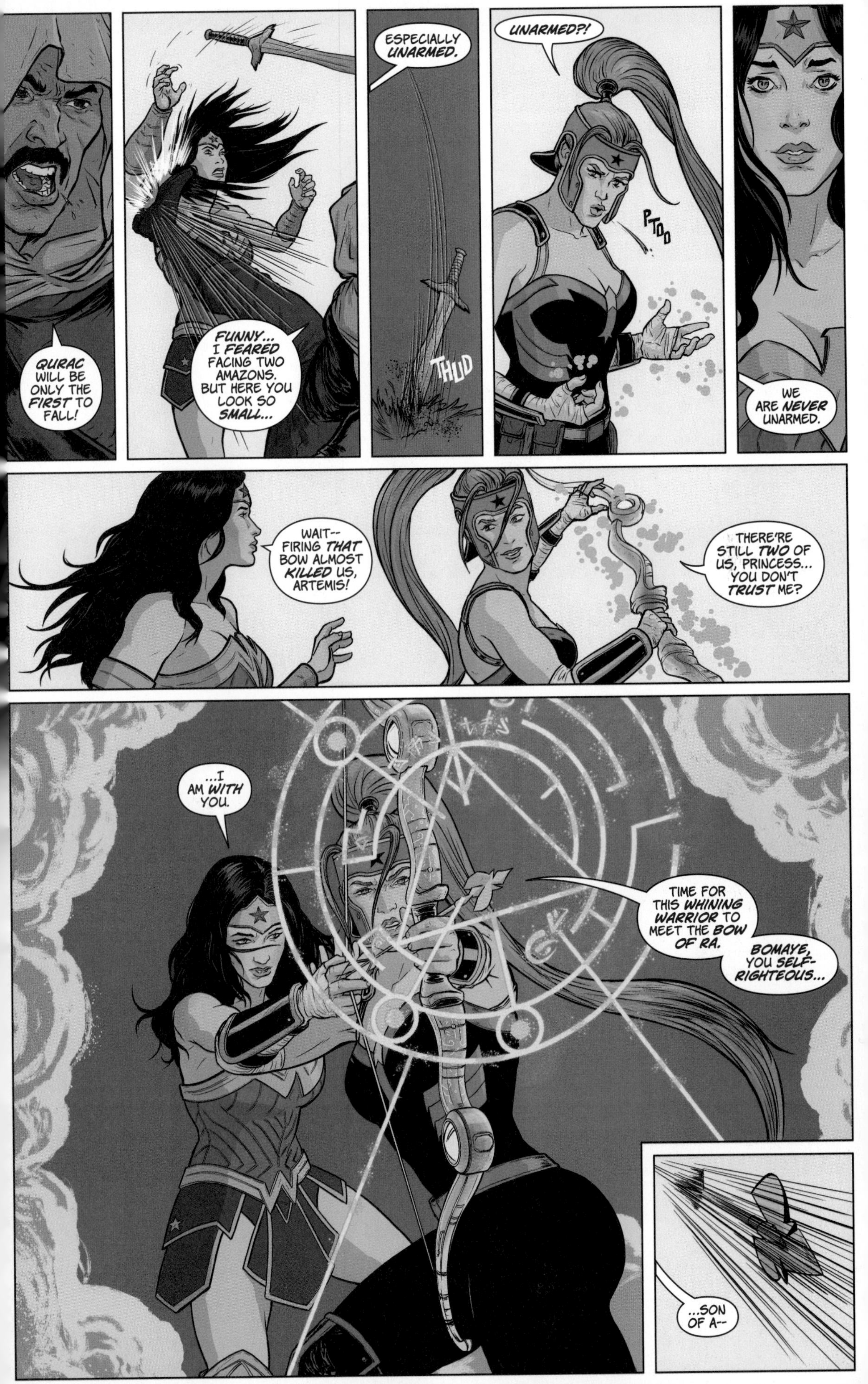

QURAC WILL BE ONLY THE FIRST TO FALL!
FUNNY... I FEARED FACING TWO AMAZONS. BUT HERE YOU LOOK SO SMALL...
ESPECIALLY UNARMED.
THUD
UNARMED?!
PTOO
WE ARE NEVER UNARMED.
WAIT-- FIRING THAT BOW ALMOST KILLED US, ARTEMIS!
THERE'RE STILL TWO OF US, PRINCESS... YOU DON'T TRUST ME?
...I AM WITH YOU.
TIME FOR THIS WHINING WARRIOR TO MEET THE BOW OF RA.
BOMAYE, YOU SELF-RIGHTEOUS...
...SON OF A--

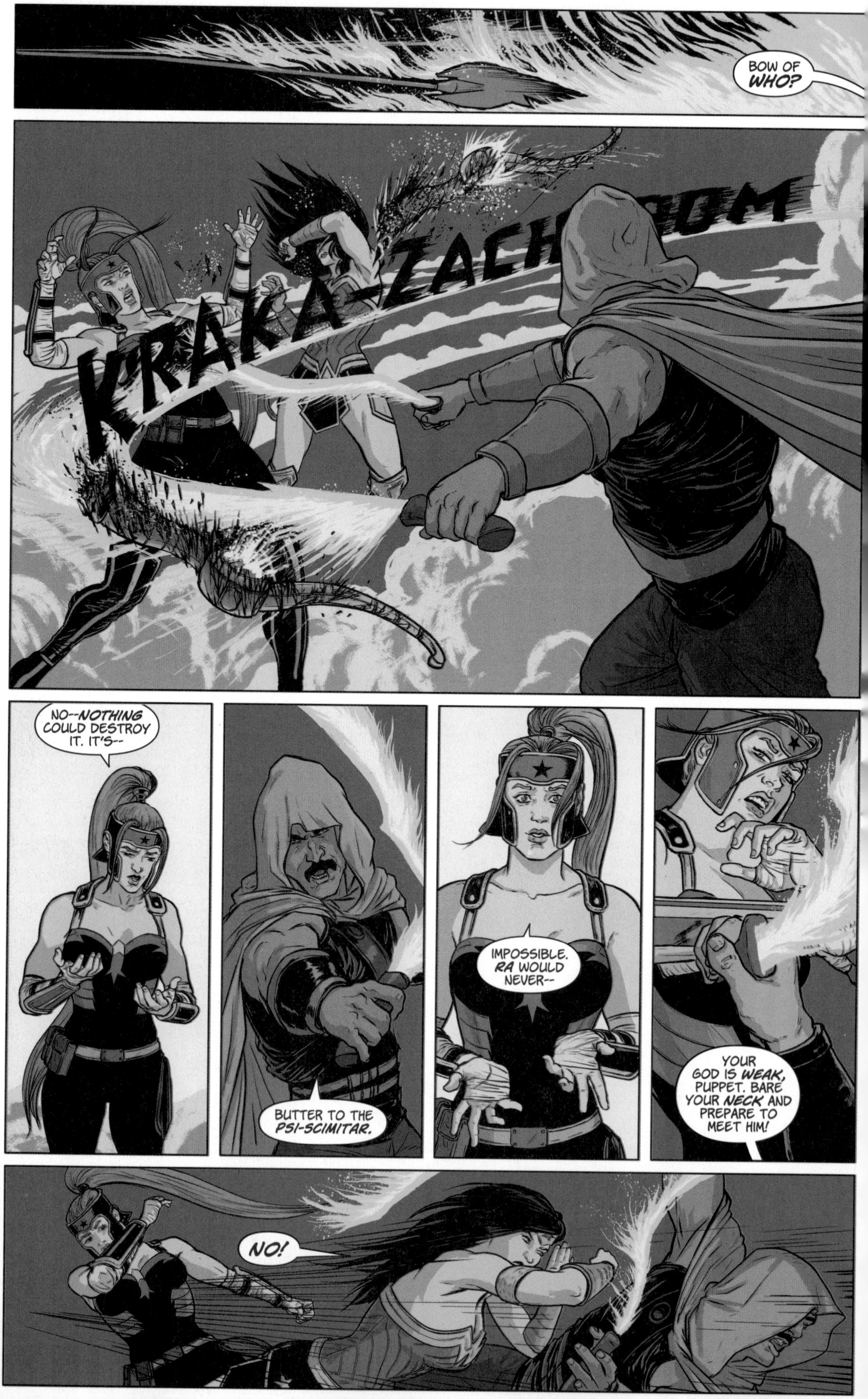
BOW OF WHO?
K'RAKA-ZACH
NO--NOTHING COULD DESTROY IT. IT'S--
BUTTER TO THE PSI-SCIMITAR.
IMPOSSIBLE. RA WOULD NEVER--
YOUR GOD IS WEAK, PUPPET. BARE YOUR NECK AND PREPARE TO MEET HIM!
NO!

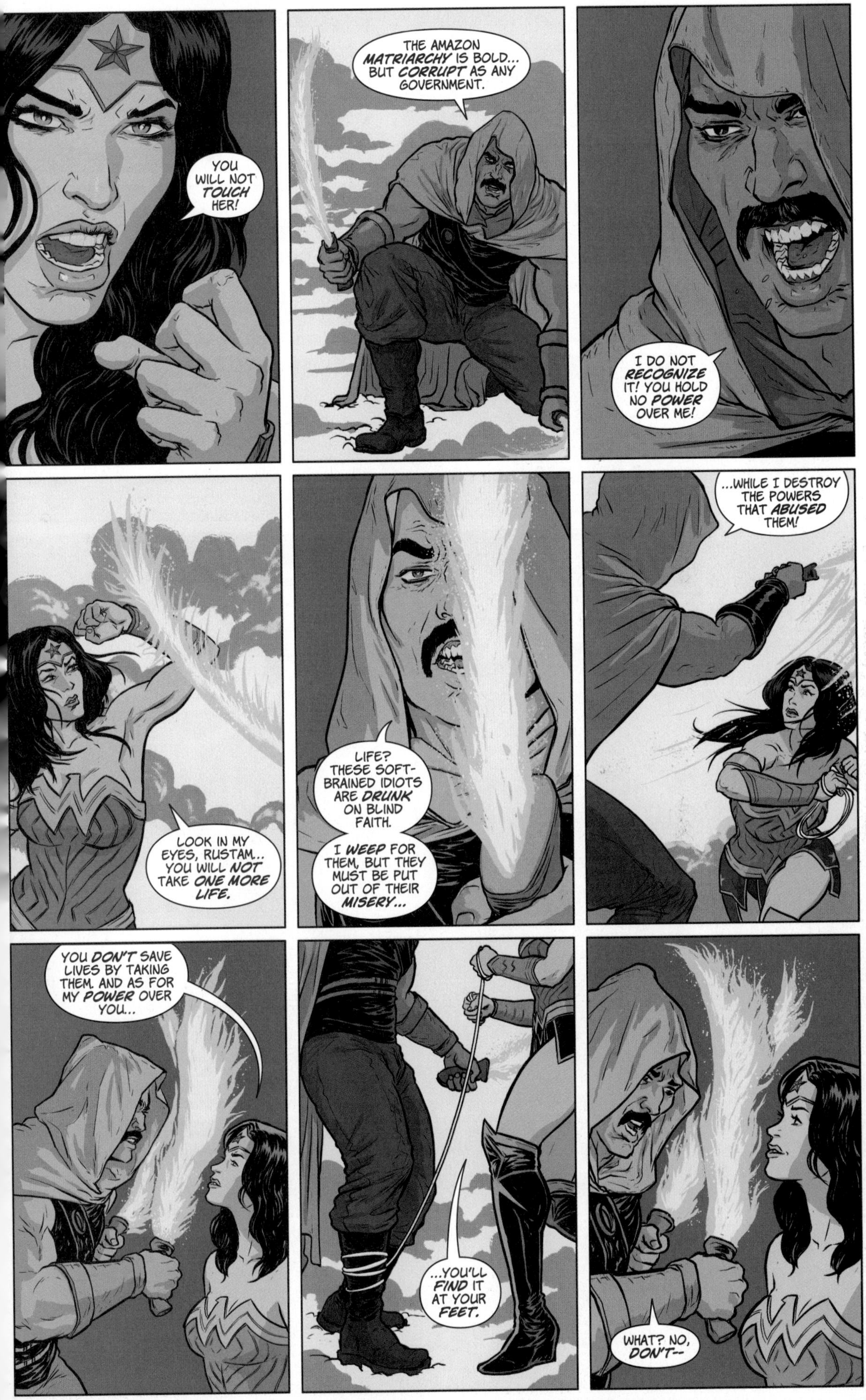
YOU WILL NOT TOUCH HER!
THE AMAZON MATRIARCHY IS BOLD... BUT CORRUPT AS ANY GOVERNMENT.
I DO NOT RECOGNIZE IT! YOU HOLD NO POWER OVER ME!
LOOK IN MY EYES, RUSTAM... YOU WILL NOT TAKE ONE MORE LIFE.
LIFE? THESE SOFT-BRAINED IDIOTS ARE DRUNK ON BLIND FAITH.
I WEEP FOR THEM, BUT THEY MUST BE PUT OUT OF THEIR MISERY...
...WHILE I DESTROY THE POWERS THAT ABUSED THEM!
YOU DON'T SAVE LIVES BY TAKING THEM. AND AS FOR MY POWER OVER YOU...
...YOU'LL FIND IT AT YOUR FEET.
WHAT? NO, DON'T--

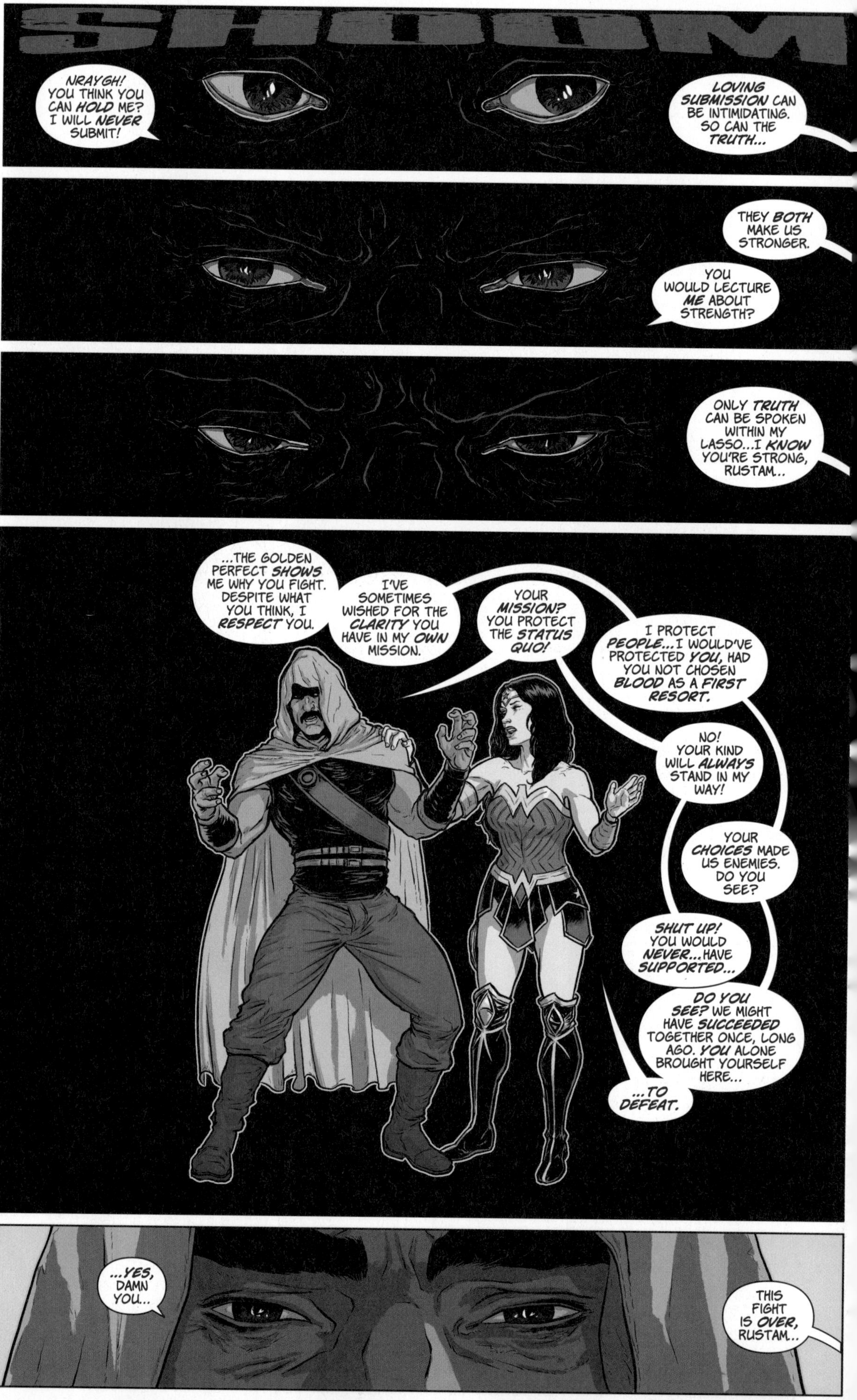
SHOOM
NRAYGH! YOU THINK YOU CAN HOLD ME? I WILL NEVER SUBMIT!
LOVING SUBMISSION CAN BE INTIMIDATING. SO CAN THE TRUTH...
THEY BOTH MAKE US STRONGER.
YOU WOULD LECTURE ME ABOUT STRENGTH?
ONLY TRUTH CAN BE SPOKEN WITHIN MY LASSO...I KNOW YOU'RE STRONG, RUSTAM...
...THE GOLDEN PERFECT SHOWS ME WHY YOU FIGHT. DESPITE WHAT YOU THINK, I RESPECT YOU.
I'VE SOMETIMES WISHED FOR THE CLARITY YOU HAVE IN MY OWN MISSION.
YOUR MISSION? YOU PROTECT THE STATUS QUO!
I PROTECT PEOPLE...I WOULD'VE PROTECTED YOU, HAD YOU NOT CHOSEN BLOOD AS A FIRST RESORT.
NO! YOUR KIND WILL ALWAYS STAND IN MY WAY!
YOUR CHOICES MADE US ENEMIES. DO YOU SEE?
SHUT UP! YOU WOULD NEVER...HAVE SUPPORTED...
DO YOU SEE? WE MIGHT HAVE SUCCEEDED TOGETHER ONCE, LONG AGO. YOU ALONE BROUGHT YOURSELF HERE...
...TO DEFEAT.
...YES, DAMN YOU...
THIS FIGHT IS OVER, RUSTAM...

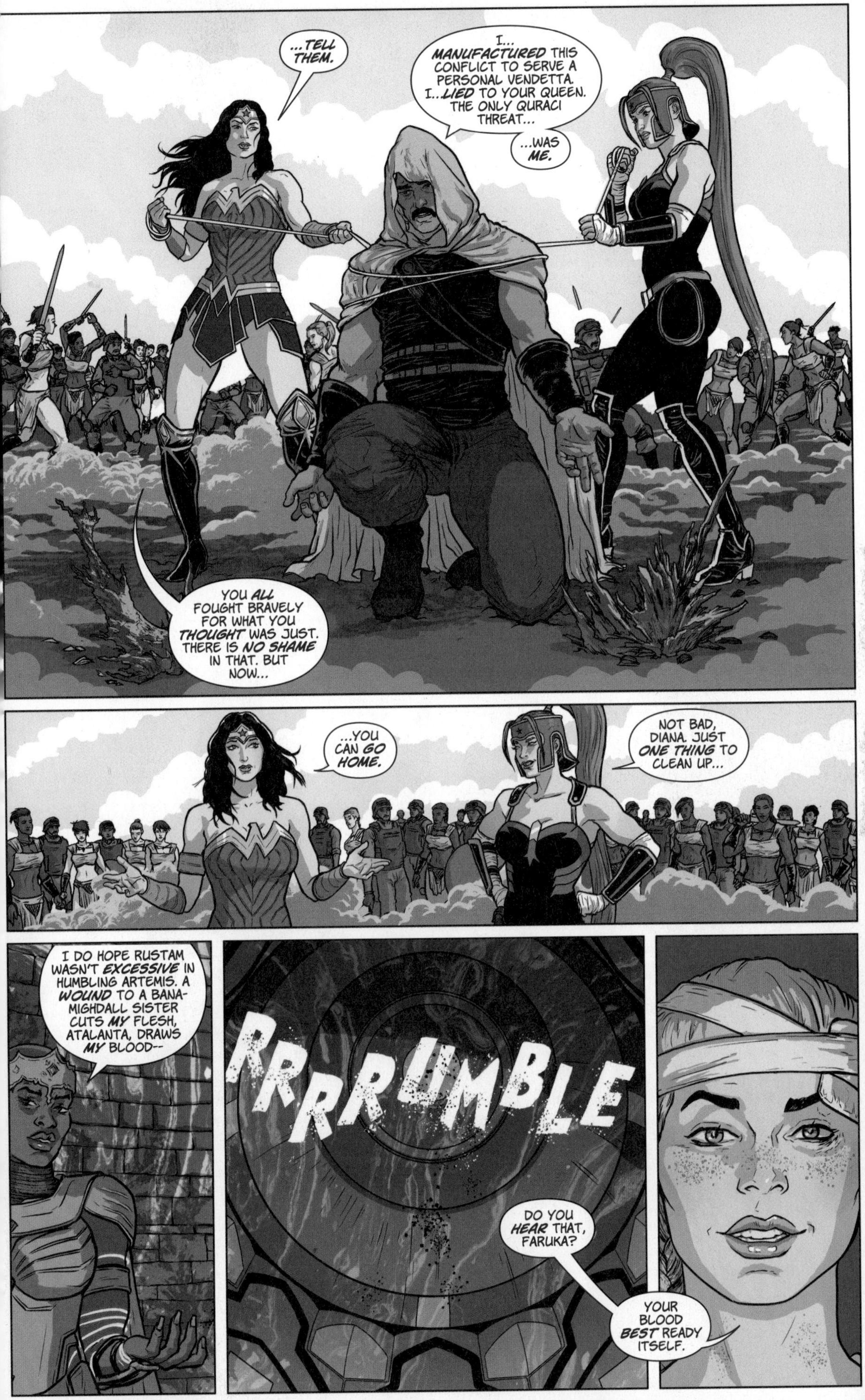
...TELL THEM.
I... MANUFACTURED THIS CONFLICT TO SERVE A PERSONAL VENDETTA. I...LIED TO YOUR QUEEN. THE ONLY QURACI THREAT...
...WAS ME.
YOU ALL FOUGHT BRAVELY FOR WHAT YOU THOUGHT WAS JUST. THERE IS NO SHAME IN THAT. BUT NOW...
...YOU CAN GO HOME.
NOT BAD, DIANA. JUST ONE THING TO CLEAN UP...
I DO HOPE RUSTAM WASN'T EXCESSIVE IN HUMBLING ARTEMIS. A WOUND TO A BANA-MIGHDALL SISTER CUTS MY FLESH, ATALANTA, DRAWS MY BLOOD--
RRRRUMBLE
DO YOU HEAR THAT, FARUKA?
YOUR BLOOD BEST READY ITSELF.

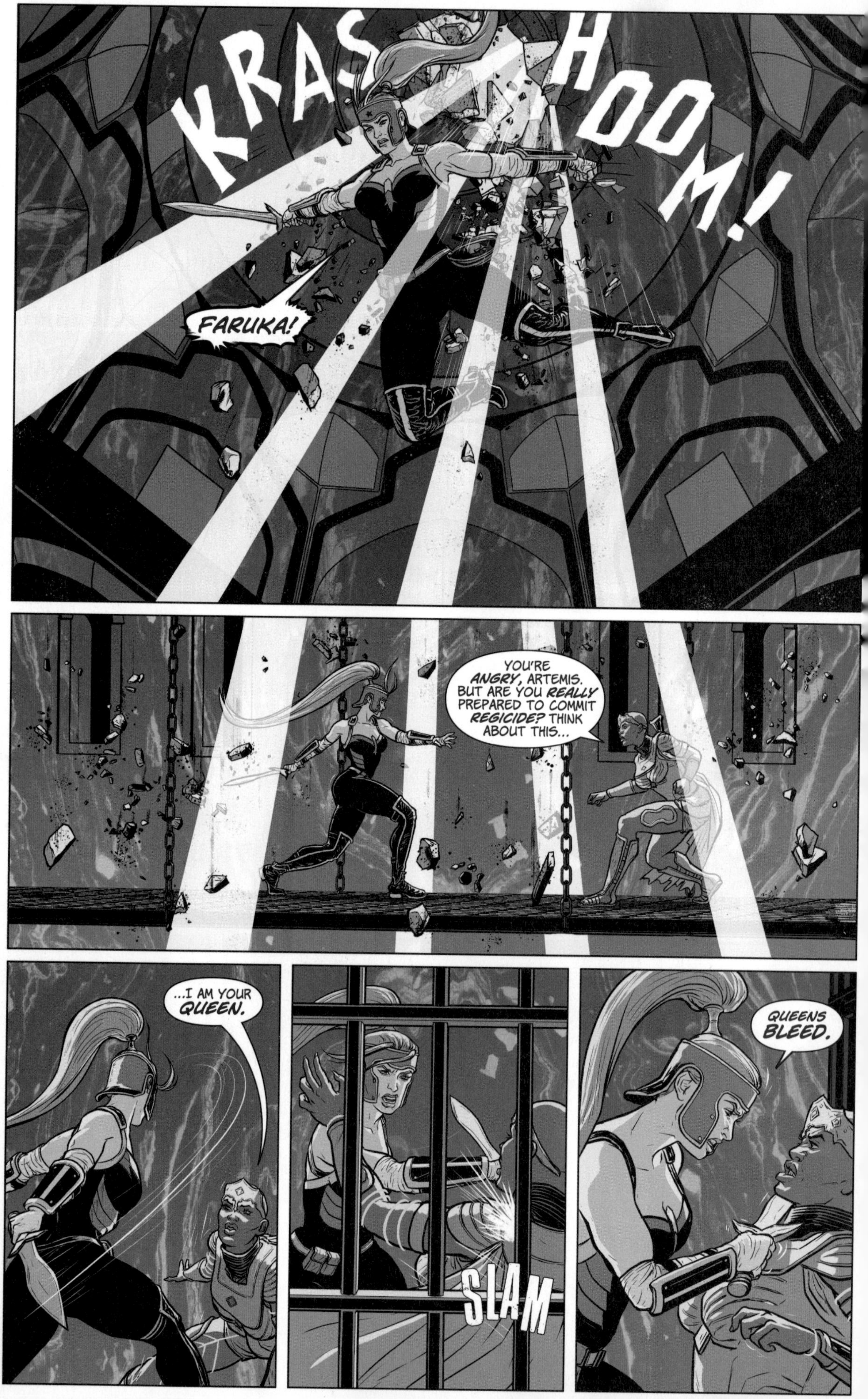
KRAS-HOOM!
FARUKA!
YOU'RE ANGRY, ARTEMIS. BUT ARE YOU REALLY PREPARED TO COMMIT REGICIDE? THINK ABOUT THIS...
...I AM YOUR QUEEN.
SLAM
QUEENS BLEED.

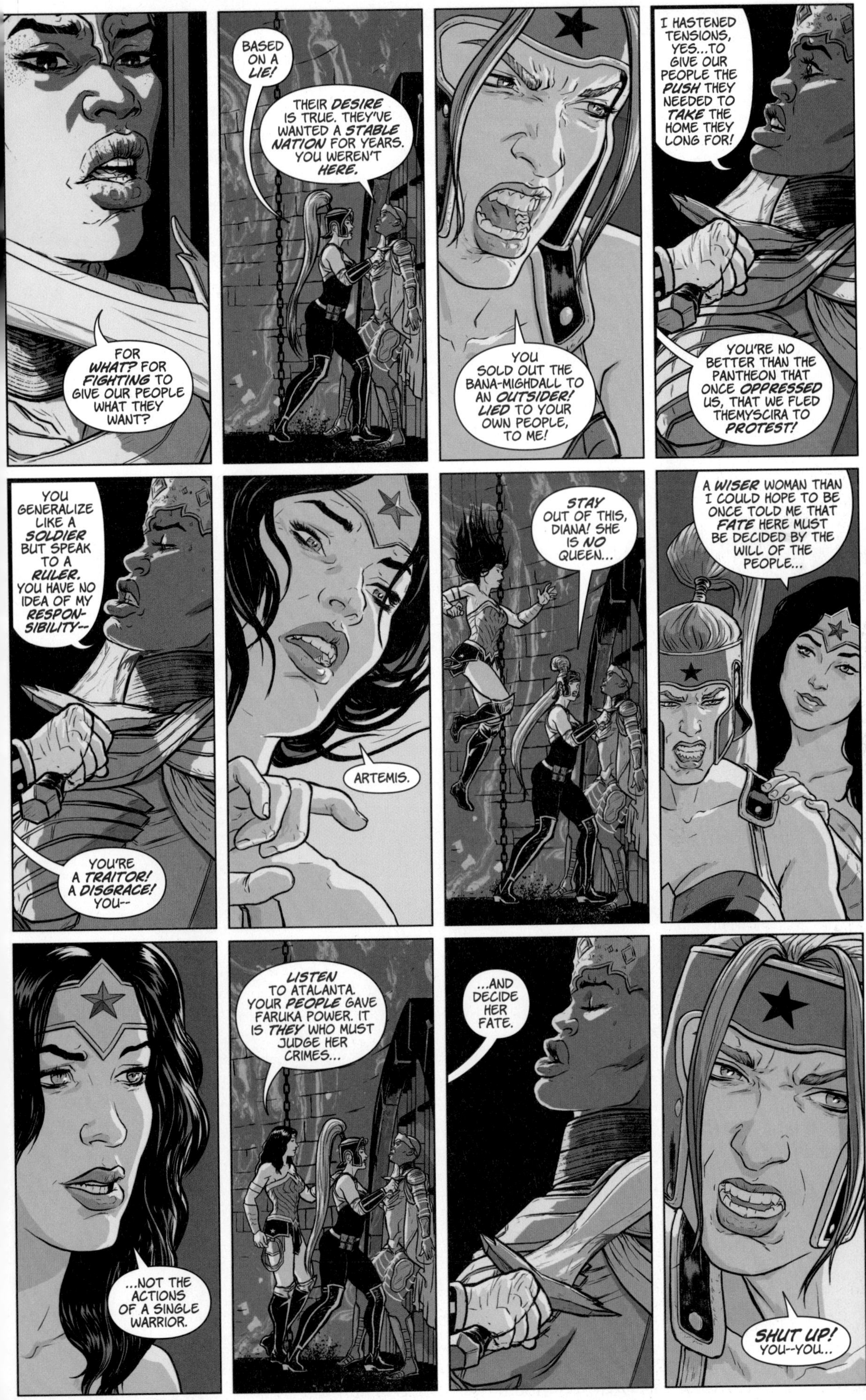
FOR WHAT? FOR FIGHTING TO GIVE OUR PEOPLE WHAT THEY WANT?
BASED ON A LIE!
THEIR DESIRE IS TRUE. THEY'VE WANTED A STABLE NATION FOR YEARS. YOU WEREN'T HERE.
YOU SOLD OUT THE BANA-MIGHDALL TO AN OUTSIDER! LIED TO YOUR OWN PEOPLE, TO ME!
I HASTENED TENSIONS, YES...TO GIVE OUR PEOPLE THE PUSH THEY NEEDED TO TAKE THE HOME THEY LONG FOR!
YOU'RE NO BETTER THAN THE PANTHEON THAT ONCE OPPRESSED US, THAT WE FLED THEMYSCIRA TO PROTEST!
YOU GENERALIZE LIKE A SOLDIER BUT SPEAK TO A RULER. YOU HAVE NO IDEA OF MY RESPON-SIBILITY--
YOU'RE A TRAITOR! A DISGRACE! YOU--
ARTEMIS.
STAY OUT OF THIS, DIANA! SHE IS NO QUEEN...
A WISER WOMAN THAN I COULD HOPE TO BE ONCE TOLD ME THAT FATE HERE MUST BE DECIDED BY THE WILL OF THE PEOPLE...
...NOT THE ACTIONS OF A SINGLE WARRIOR.
LISTEN TO ATALANTA. YOUR PEOPLE GAVE FARUKA POWER. IT IS THEY WHO MUST JUDGE HER CRIMES...
...AND DECIDE HER FATE.
SHUT UP! YOU--YOU...

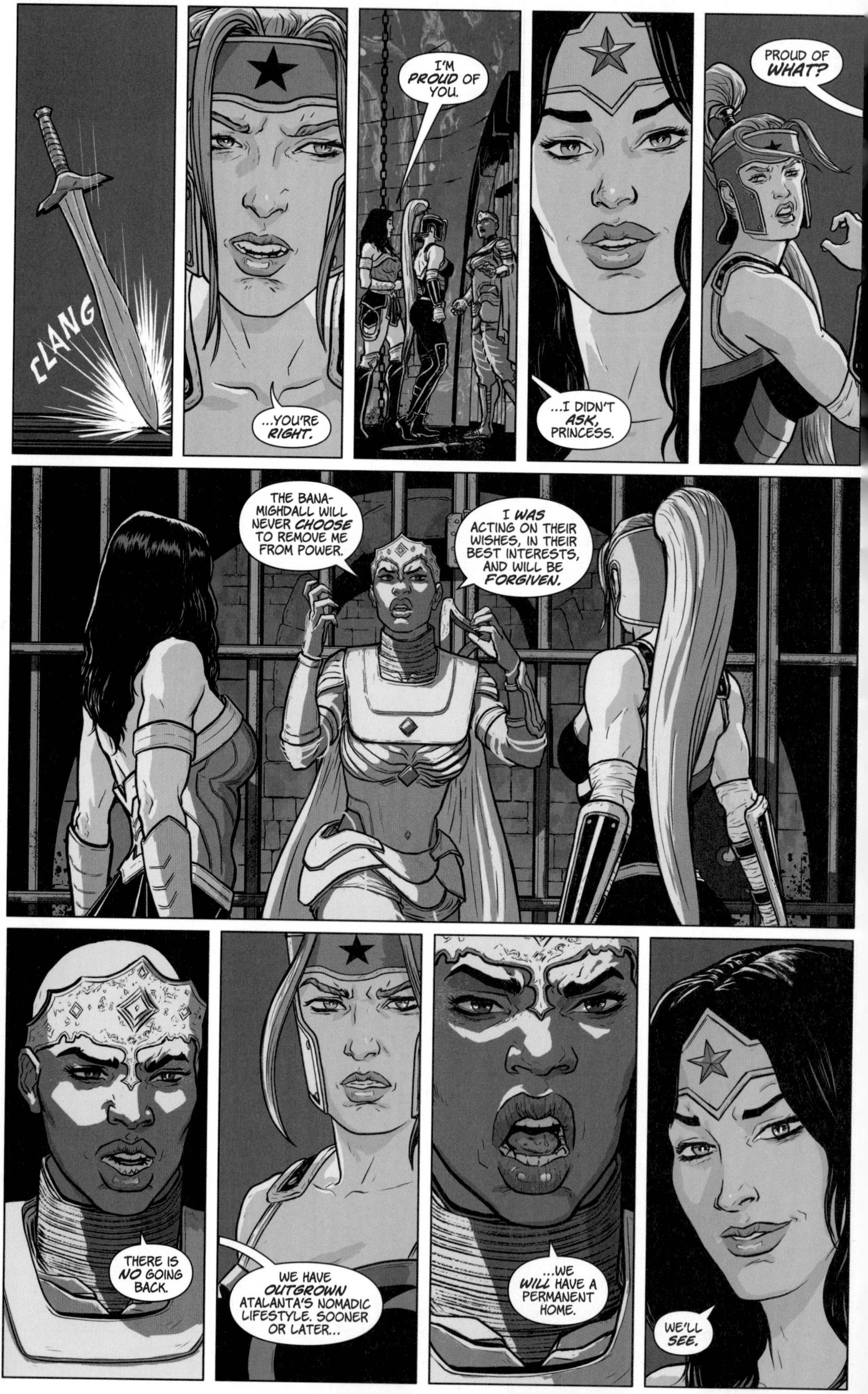
CLANG
...YOU'RE RIGHT.
I'M PROUD OF YOU.
...I DIDN'T ASK, PRINCESS.
PROUD OF WHAT?
THE BANA-MIGHDALL WILL NEVER CHOOSE TO REMOVE ME FROM POWER.
I WAS ACTING ON THEIR WISHES, IN THEIR BEST INTERESTS, AND WILL BE FORGIVEN.
THERE IS NO GOING BACK.
WE HAVE OUTGROWN ATALANTA'S NOMADIC LIFESTYLE. SOONER OR LATER...
...WE WILL HAVE A PERMANENT HOME.
WE'LL SEE.

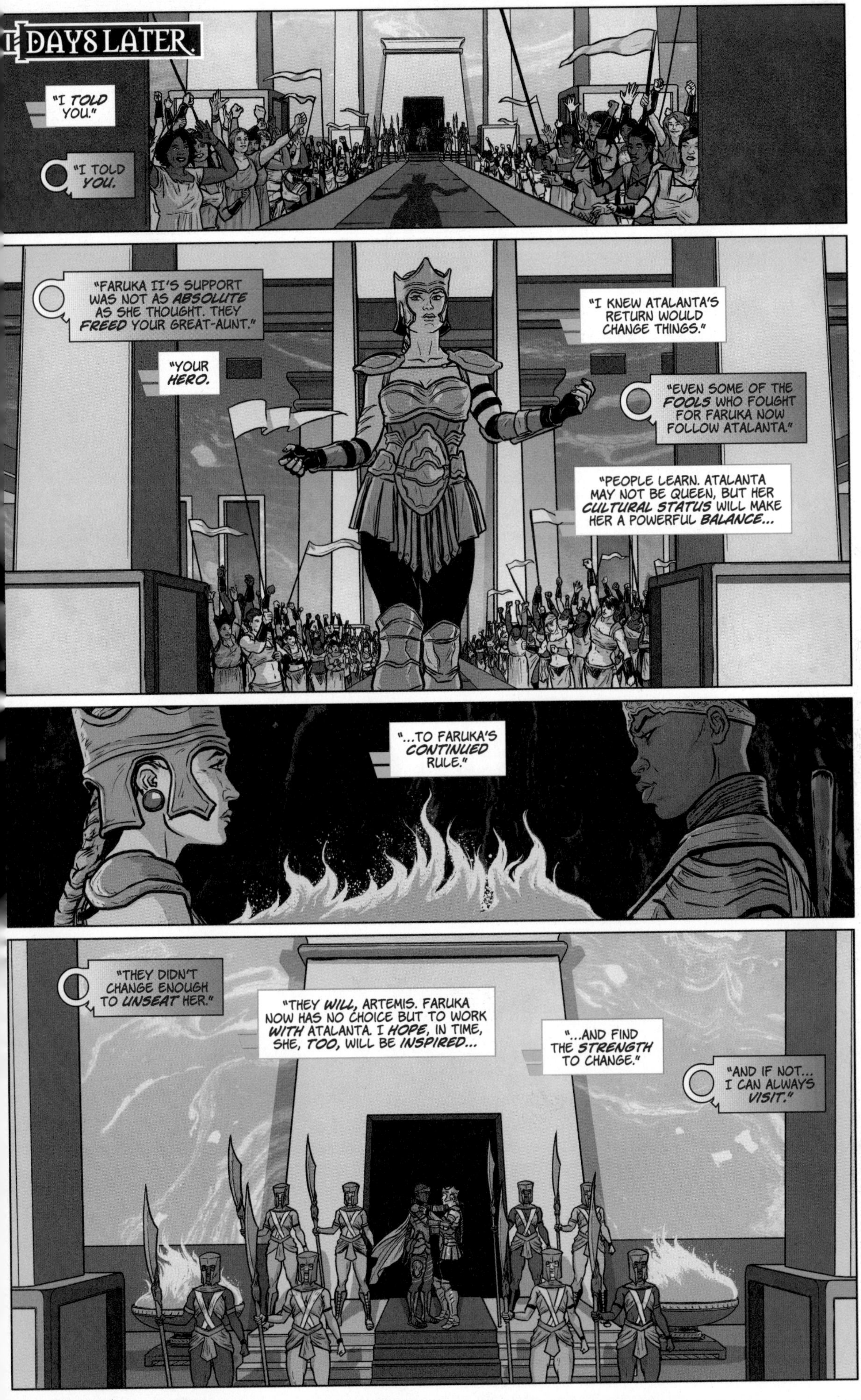
DAYS LATER.
"I TOLD YOU."
"I TOLD YOU.
"FARUKA II'S SUPPORT WAS NOT AS ABSOLUTE AS SHE THOUGHT. THEY FREED YOUR GREAT-AUNT."
"YOUR HERO.
"I KNEW ATALANTA'S RETURN WOULD CHANGE THINGS."
"EVEN SOME OF THE FOOLS WHO FOUGHT FOR FARUKA NOW FOLLOW ATALANTA."
"PEOPLE LEARN. ATALANTA MAY NOT BE QUEEN, BUT HER CULTURAL STATUS WILL MAKE HER A POWERFUL BALANCE...
"...TO FARUKA'S CONTINUED RULE."
"THEY DIDN'T CHANGE ENOUGH TO UNSEAT HER."
"THEY WILL, ARTEMIS. FARUKA NOW HAS NO CHOICE BUT TO WORK WITH ATALANTA. I HOPE, IN TIME, SHE, TOO, WILL BE INSPIRED...
"...AND FIND THE STRENGTH TO CHANGE."
"AND IF NOT... I CAN ALWAYS VISIT."

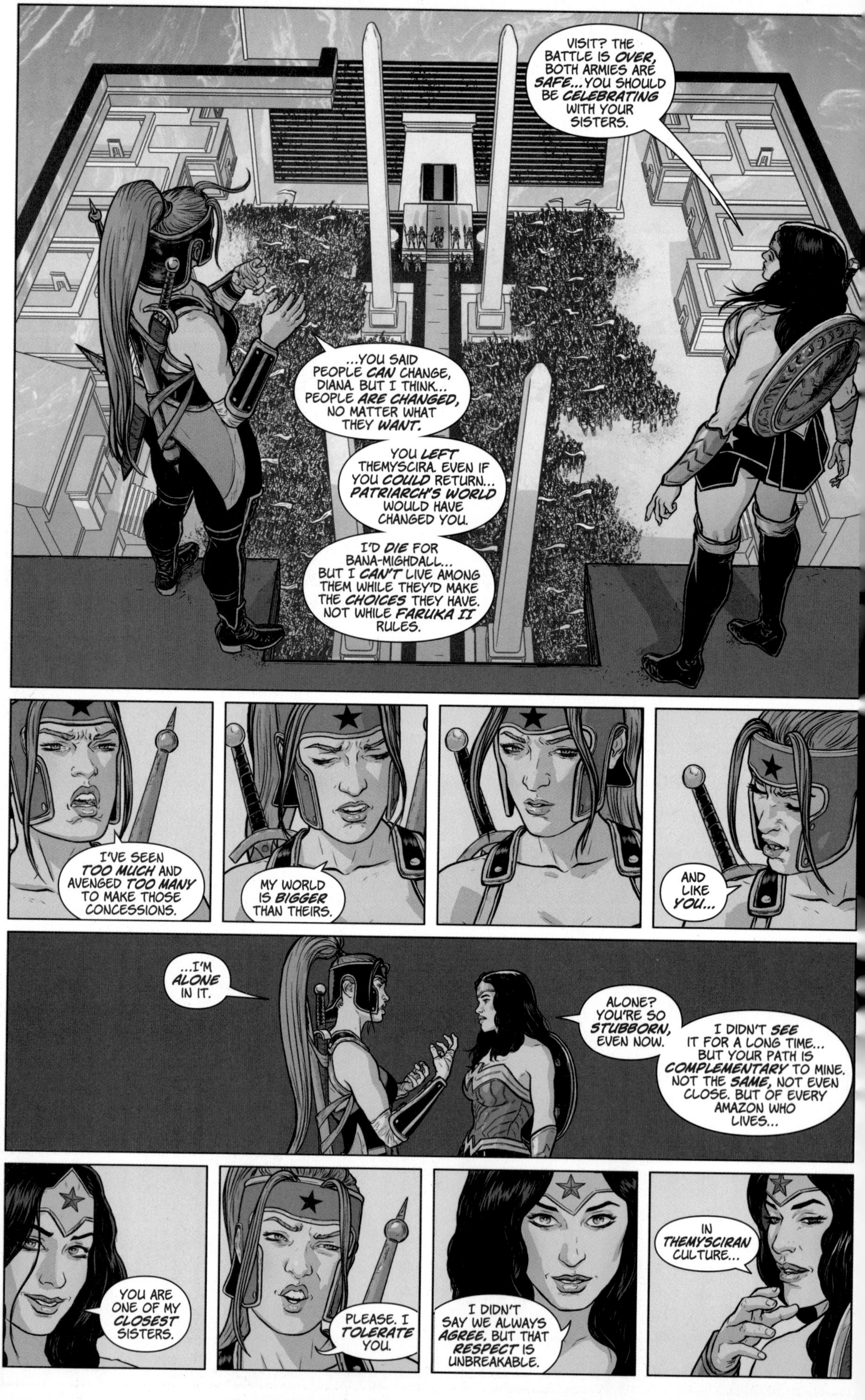
VISIT? THE BATTLE IS OVER, BOTH ARMIES ARE SAFE...YOU SHOULD BE CELEBRATING WITH YOUR SISTERS.
...YOU SAID PEOPLE CAN CHANGE, DIANA. BUT I THINK... PEOPLE ARE CHANGED, NO MATTER WHAT THEY WANT.
YOU LEFT THEMYSCIRA. EVEN IF YOU COULD RETURN... PATRIARCH'S WORLD WOULD HAVE CHANGED YOU.
I'D DIE FOR BANA-MIGHDALL... BUT I CAN'T LIVE AMONG THEM WHILE THEY'D MAKE THE CHOICES THEY HAVE. NOT WHILE FARUKA II RULES.
I'VE SEEN TOO MUCH AND AVENGED TOO MANY TO MAKE THOSE CONCESSIONS.
MY WORLD IS BIGGER THAN THEIRS.
AND LIKE YOU...
...I'M ALONE IN IT.
ALONE? YOU'RE SO STUBBORN, EVEN NOW.
I DIDN'T SEE IT FOR A LONG TIME... BUT YOUR PATH IS COMPLEMENTARY TO MINE. NOT THE SAME, NOT EVEN CLOSE. BUT OF EVERY AMAZON WHO LIVES...
YOU ARE ONE OF MY CLOSEST SISTERS.
PLEASE. I TOLERATE YOU.
I DIDN'T SAY WE ALWAYS AGREE. BUT THAT RESPECT IS UNBREAKABLE.
IN THEMYSCIRAN CULTURE...

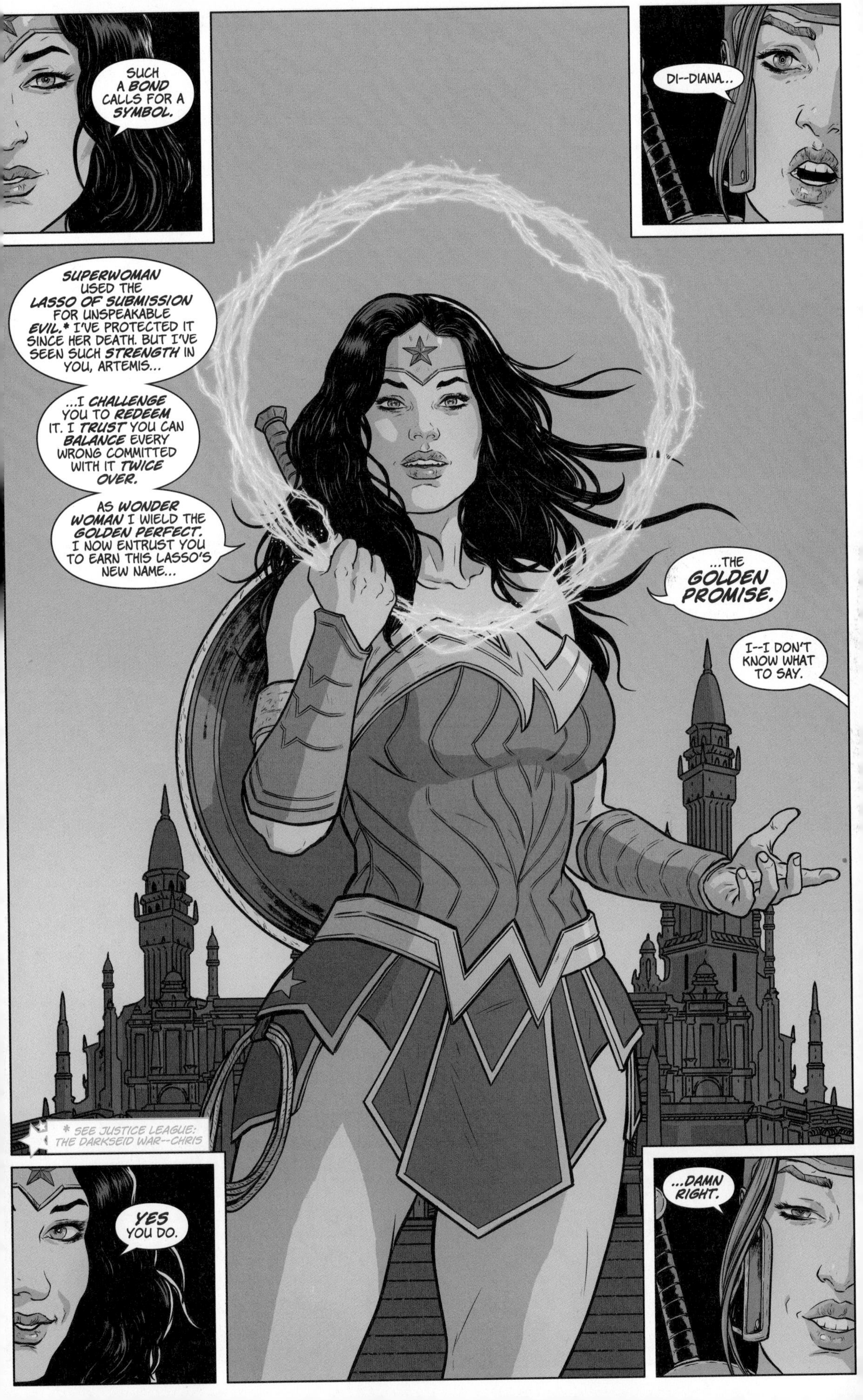
SUCH A BOND CALLS FOR A SYMBOL.
DI--DIANA..
SUPERWOMAN USED THE LASSO OF SUBMISSION FOR UNSPEAKABLE EVIL.* I'VE PROTECTED IT SINCE HER DEATH. BUT I'VE SEEN SUCH STRENGTH IN YOU, ARTEMIS...
...I CHALLENGE YOU TO REDEEM IT. I TRUST YOU CAN BALANCE EVERY WRONG COMMITTED WITH IT TWICE OVER.
AS WONDER WOMAN I WIELD THE GOLDEN PERFECT. I NOW ENTRUST YOU TO EARN THIS LASSO'S NEW NAME...
...THE GOLDEN PROMISE.
I--I DON'T KNOW WHAT TO SAY.
* SEE JUSTICE LEAGUE: THE DARKSEID WAR--CHRIS
YES YOU DO.
...DAMN RIGHT.

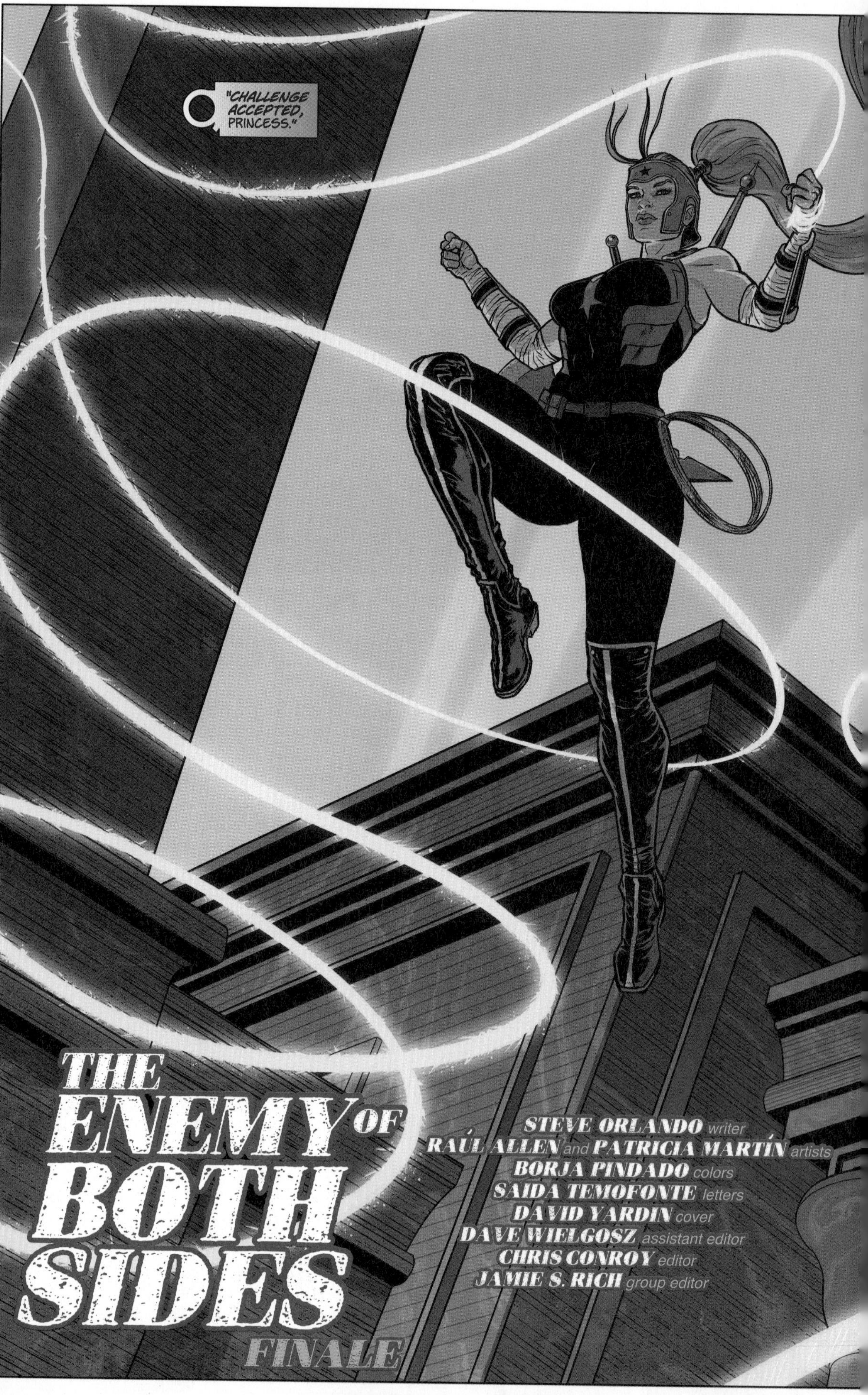
"CHALLENGE ACCEPTED, PRINCESS."
THE ENEMY OF BOTH SIDES FINALE
STEVE ORLANDO writer
RAÚL ALLEN and PATRICIA MARTÍN artists
BORJA PINDADO colors
SAIDA TEMOFONTE letters
DAVID YARDIN cover
DAVE WIELGOSZ assistant editor
CHRIS CONROY editor
JAMIE S. RICH group editor

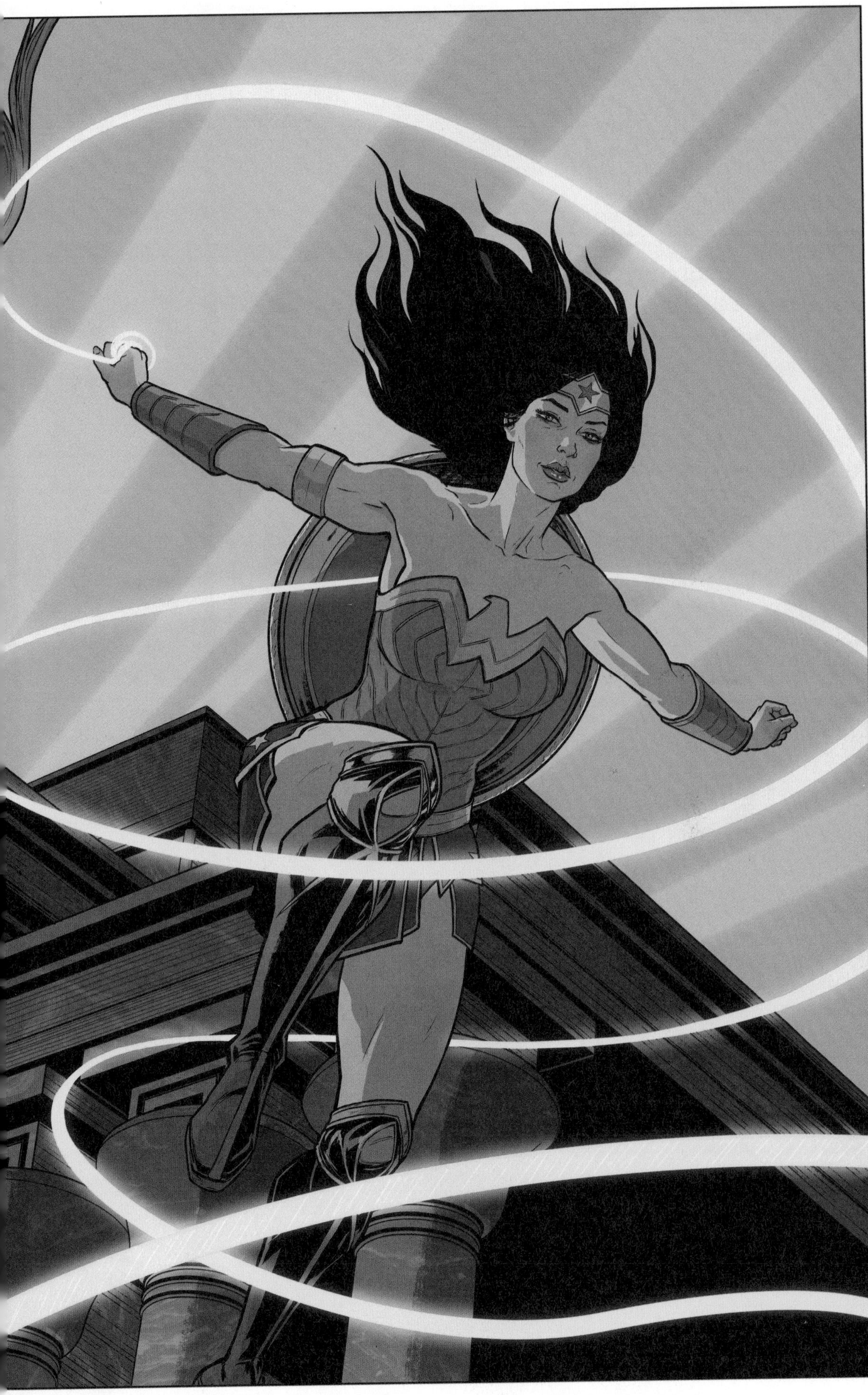

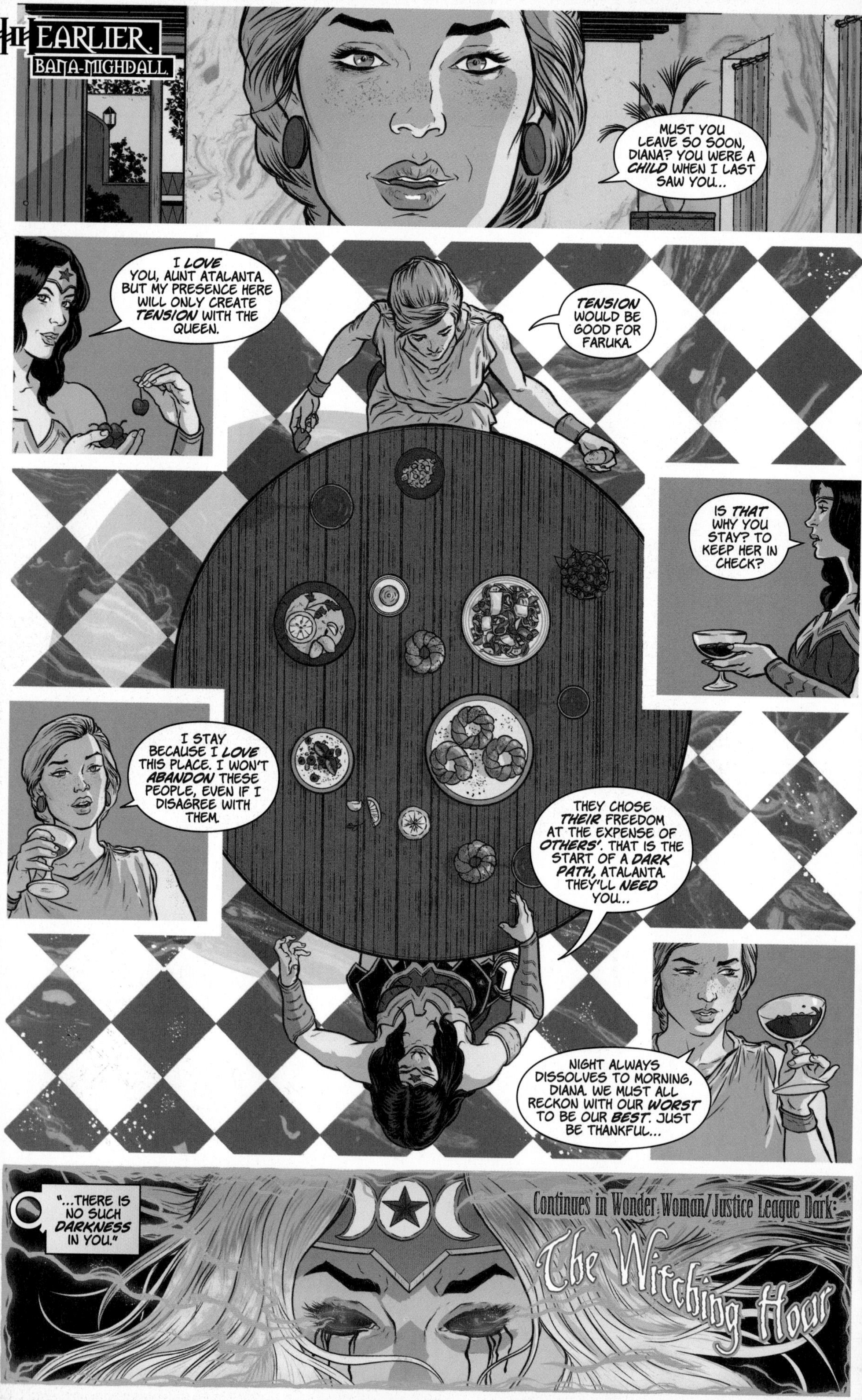
EARLIER.
BANA-MIGHDALL.
MUST YOU LEAVE SO SOON, DIANA? YOU WERE A CHILD WHEN I LAST SAW YOU...
I LOVE YOU, AUNT ATALANTA. BUT MY PRESENCE HERE WILL ONLY CREATE TENSION WITH THE QUEEN.
TENSION WOULD BE GOOD FOR FARUKA.
IS THAT WHY YOU STAY? TO KEEP HER IN CHECK?
I STAY BECAUSE I LOVE THIS PLACE. I WON'T ABANDON THESE PEOPLE, EVEN IF I DISAGREE WITH THEM.
THEY CHOSE THEIR FREEDOM AT THE EXPENSE OF OTHERS'. THAT IS THE START OF A DARK PATH, ATALANTA. THEY'LL NEED YOU...
NIGHT ALWAYS DISSOLVES TO MORNING, DIANA. WE MUST ALL RECKON WITH OUR WORST TO BE OUR BEST. JUST BE THANKFUL...
"...THERE IS NO SUCH DARKNESS IN YOU."
Continues in Wonder Woman/Justice League Dark:
The Witching Hour

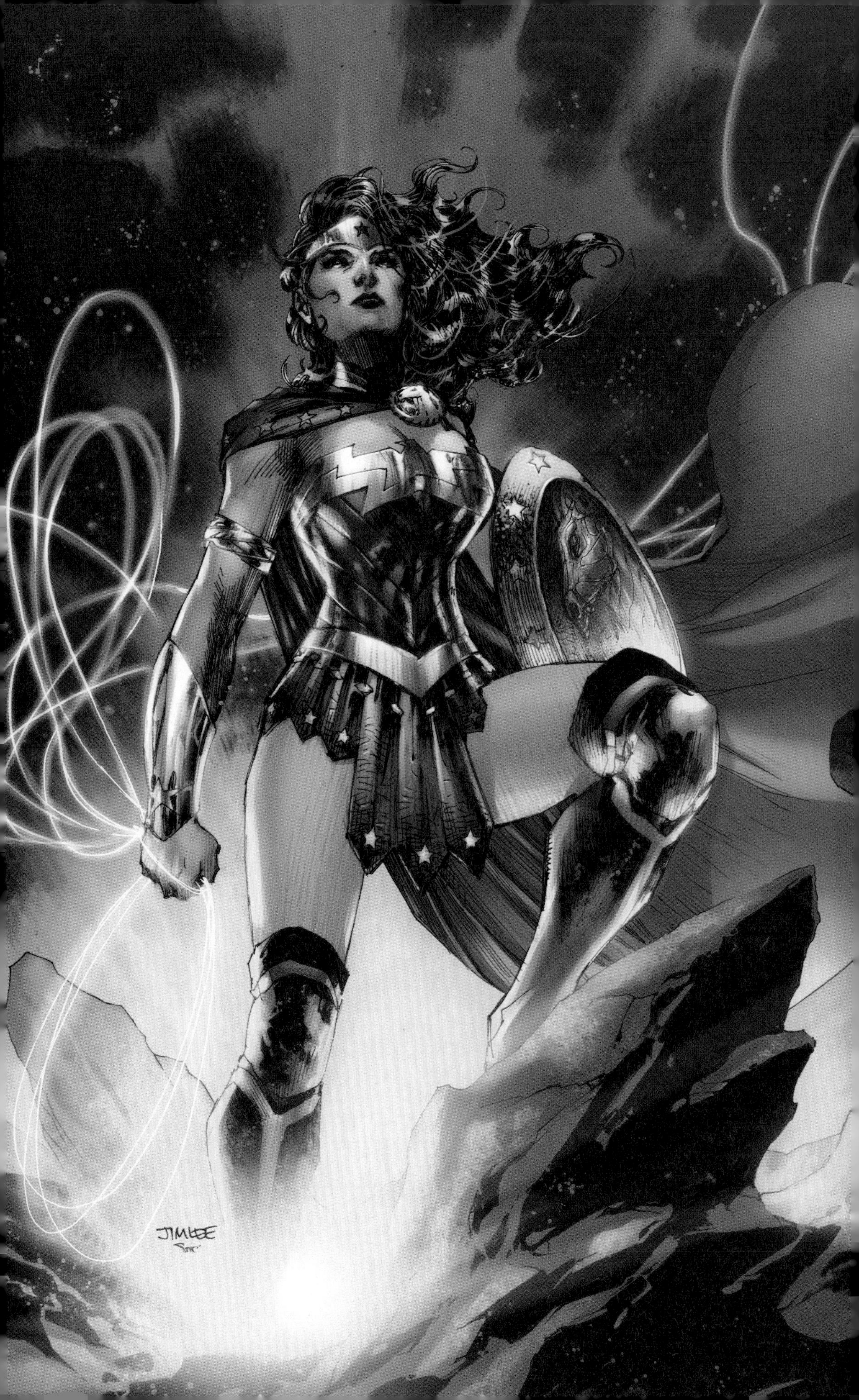
JIM LEE

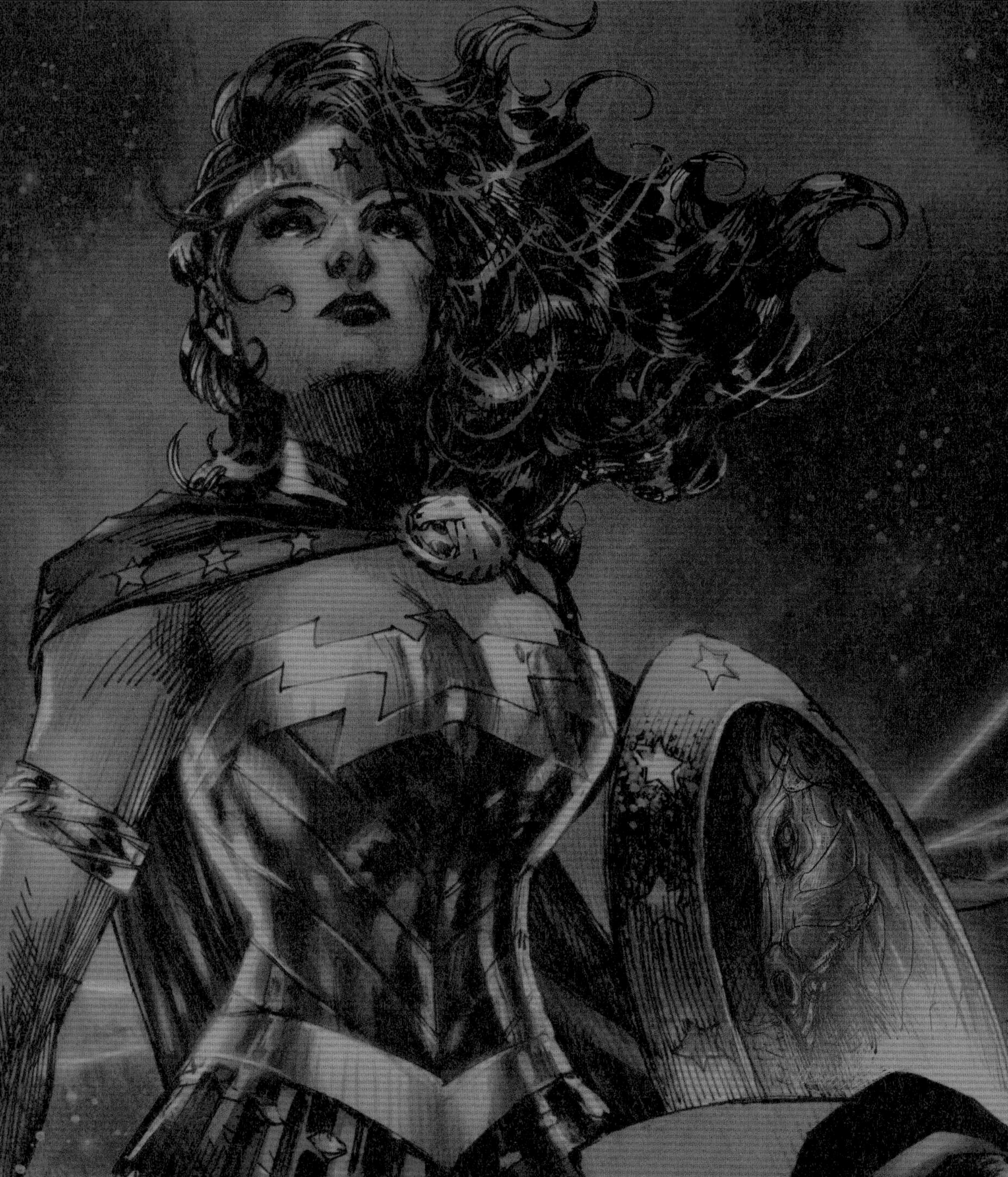

WONDER WOMAN

75TH ANNIVERSARY SPECIAL

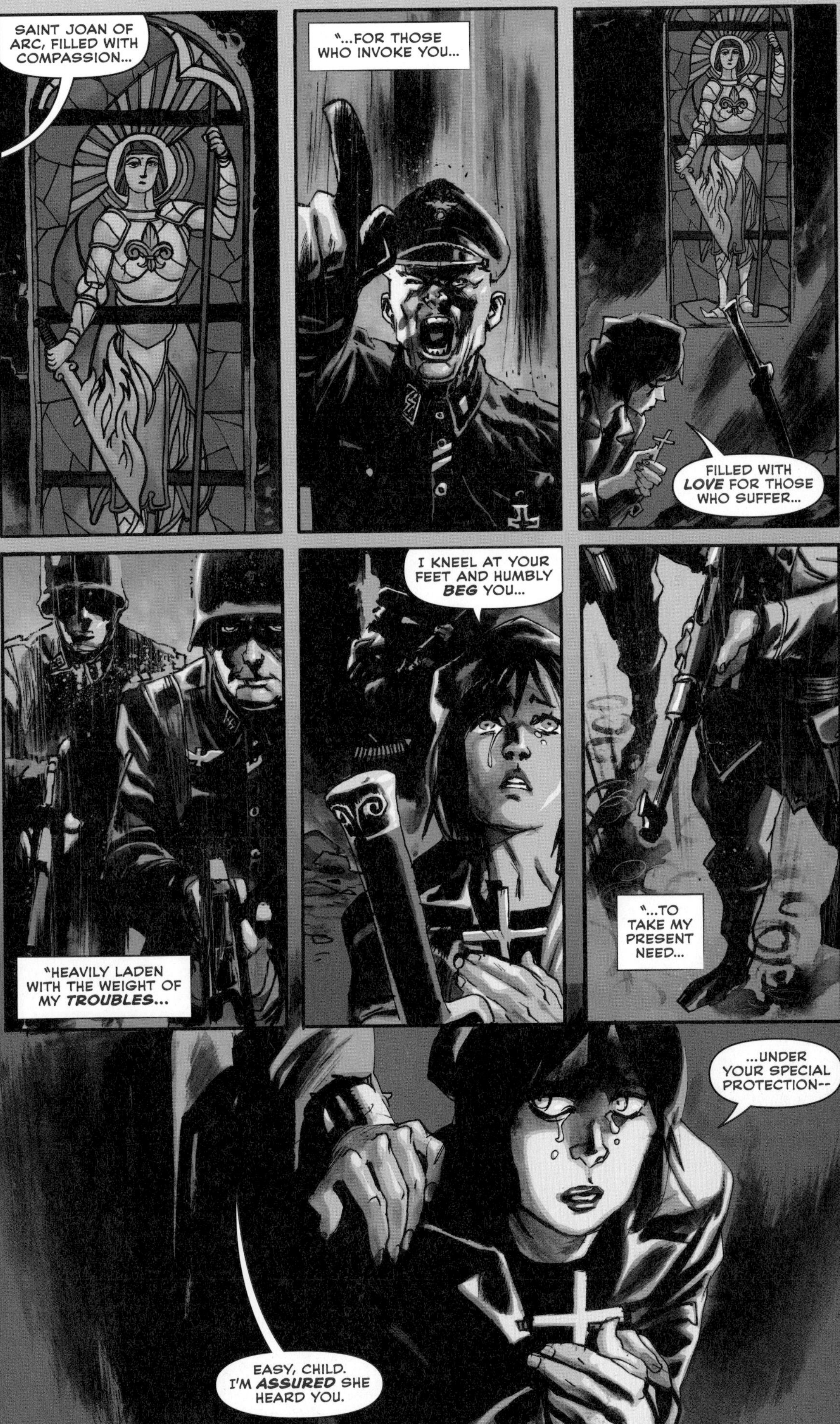
SAINT JOAN OF ARC, FILLED WITH COMPASSION...
"...FOR THOSE WHO INVOKE YOU...
FILLED WITH LOVE FOR THOSE WHO SUFFER...
"HEAVILY LADEN WITH THE WEIGHT OF MY TROUBLES...
I KNEEL AT YOUR FEET AND HUMBLY BEG YOU...
"...TO TAKE MY PRESENT NEED...
...UNDER YOUR SPECIAL PROTECTION--
EASY, CHILD. I'M ASSURED SHE HEARD YOU.

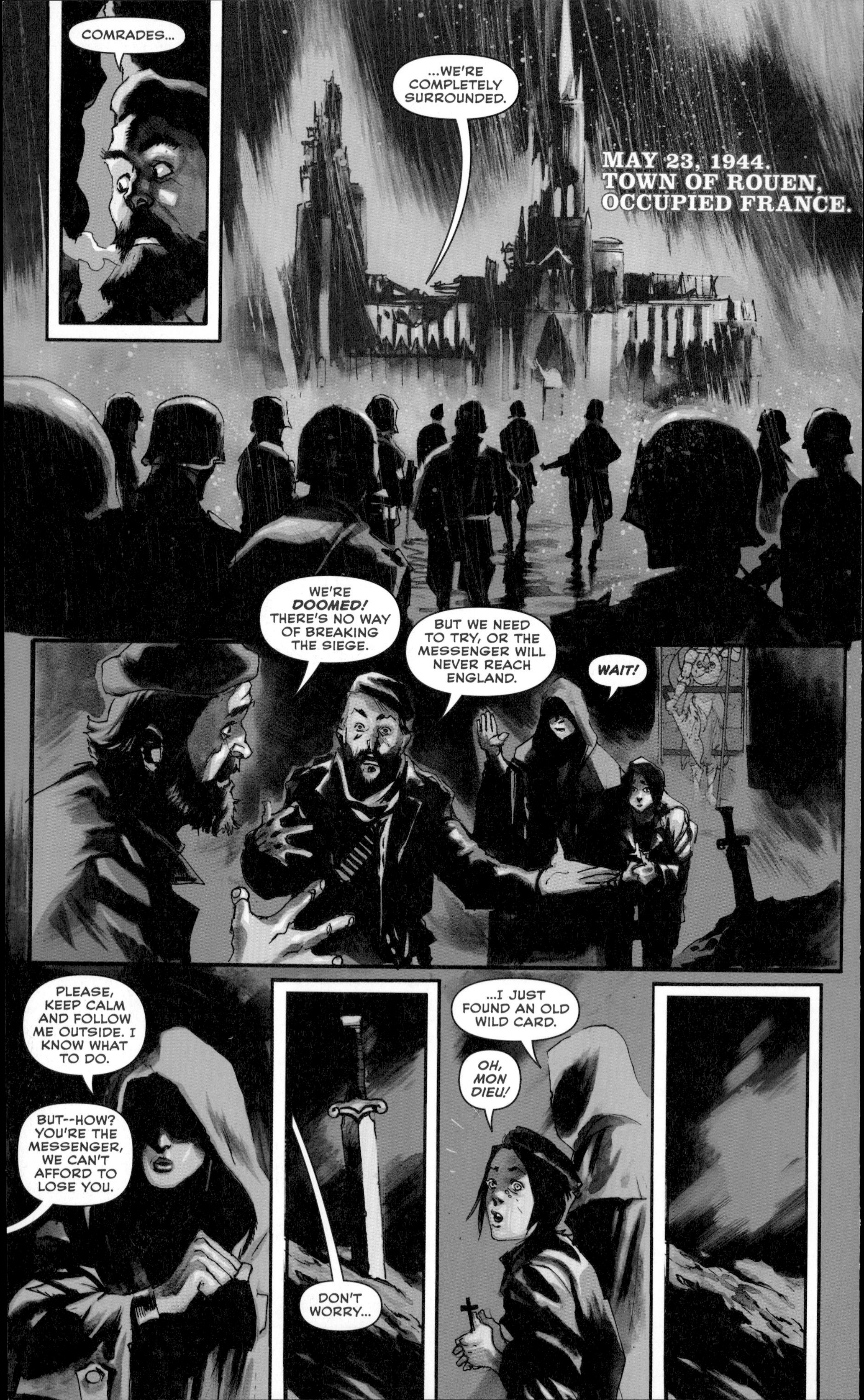
COMRADES...
...WE'RE COMPLETELY SURROUNDED.
MAY 23, 1944. TOWN OF ROUEN, OCCUPIED FRANCE.
WE'RE DOOMED! THERE'S NO WAY OF BREAKING THE SIEGE.
BUT WE NEED TO TRY, OR THE MESSENGER WILL NEVER REACH ENGLAND.
WAIT!
PLEASE, KEEP CALM AND FOLLOW ME OUTSIDE. I KNOW WHAT TO DO.
BUT--HOW? YOU'RE THE MESSENGER, WE CAN'T AFFORD TO LOSE YOU.
DON'T WORRY...
...I JUST FOUND AN OLD WILD CARD.
OH, MON DIEU!

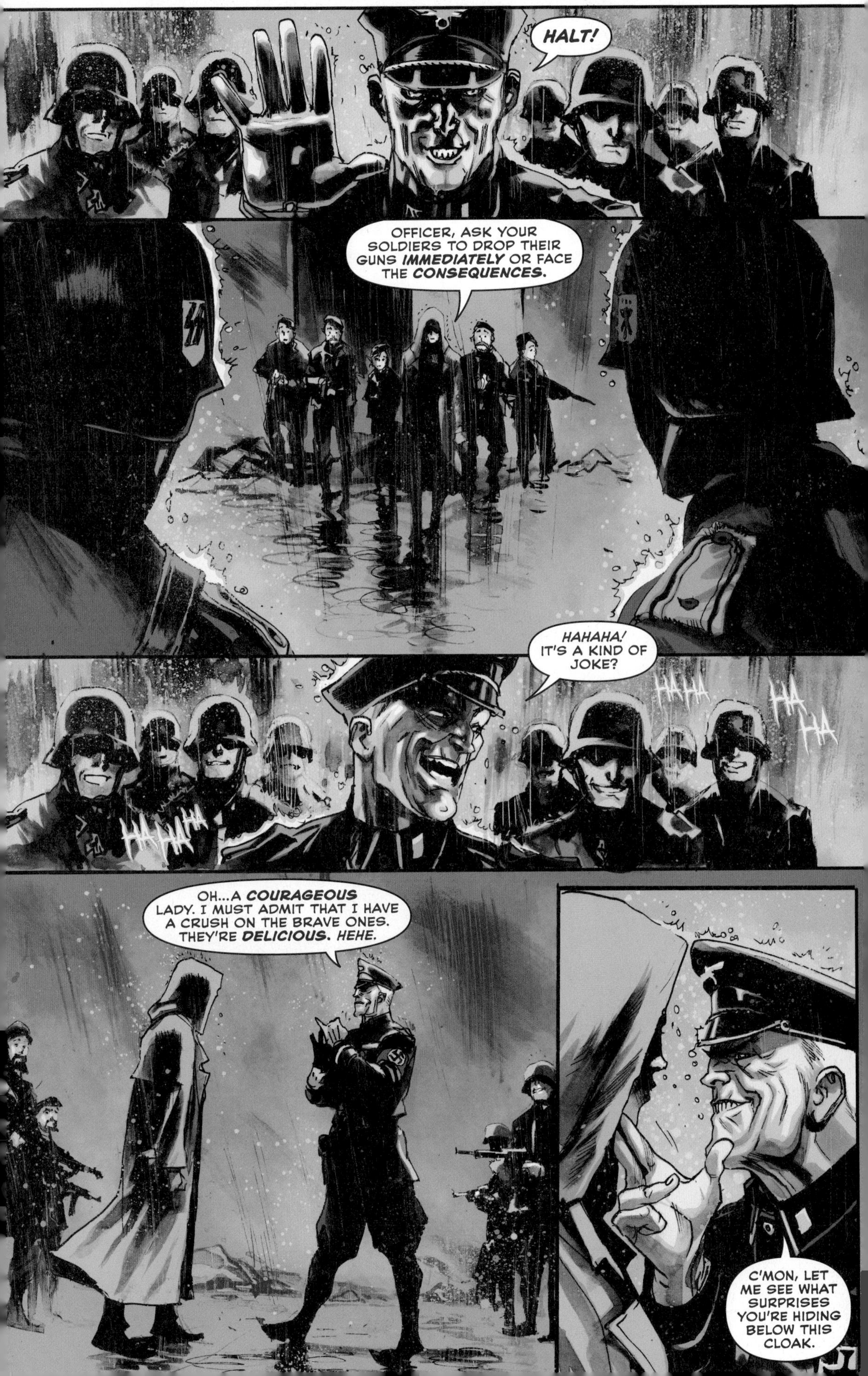
HALT!
OFFICER, ASK YOUR SOLDIERS TO DROP THEIR GUNS IMMEDIATELY OR FACE THE CONSEQUENCES.
HAHAHA! IT'S A KIND OF JOKE?
HA HA
HA HA
HA HA HA HA
OH...A COURAGEOUS LADY. I MUST ADMIT THAT I HAVE A CRUSH ON THE BRAVE ONES. THEY'RE DELICIOUS. HEHE.
C'MON, LET ME SEE WHAT SURPRISES YOU'RE HIDING BELOW THIS CLOAK.

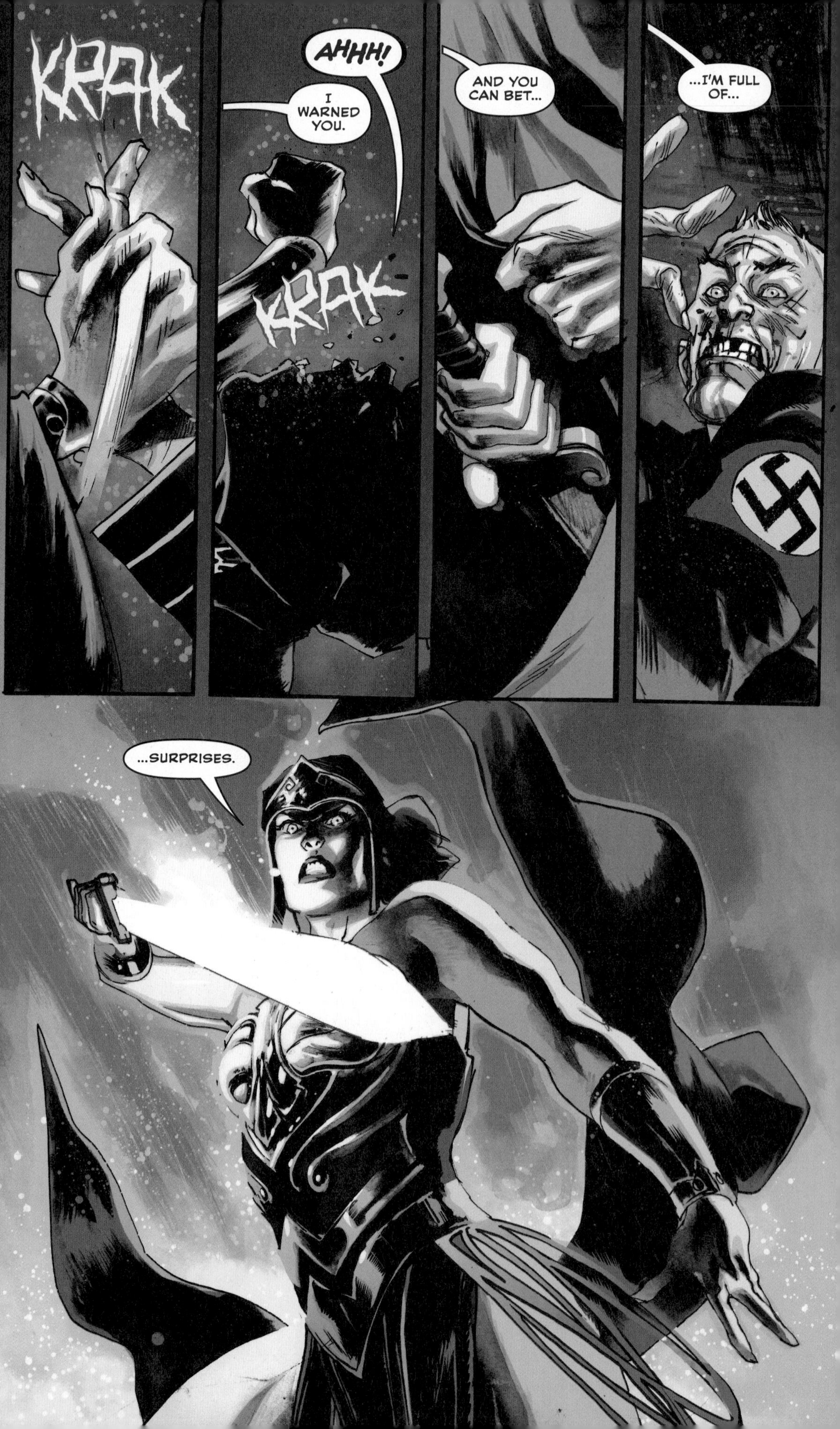
KRAK
AHHH!
I WARNED YOU.
KRAK
AND YOU CAN BET...
...I'M FULL OF...
...SURPRISES.

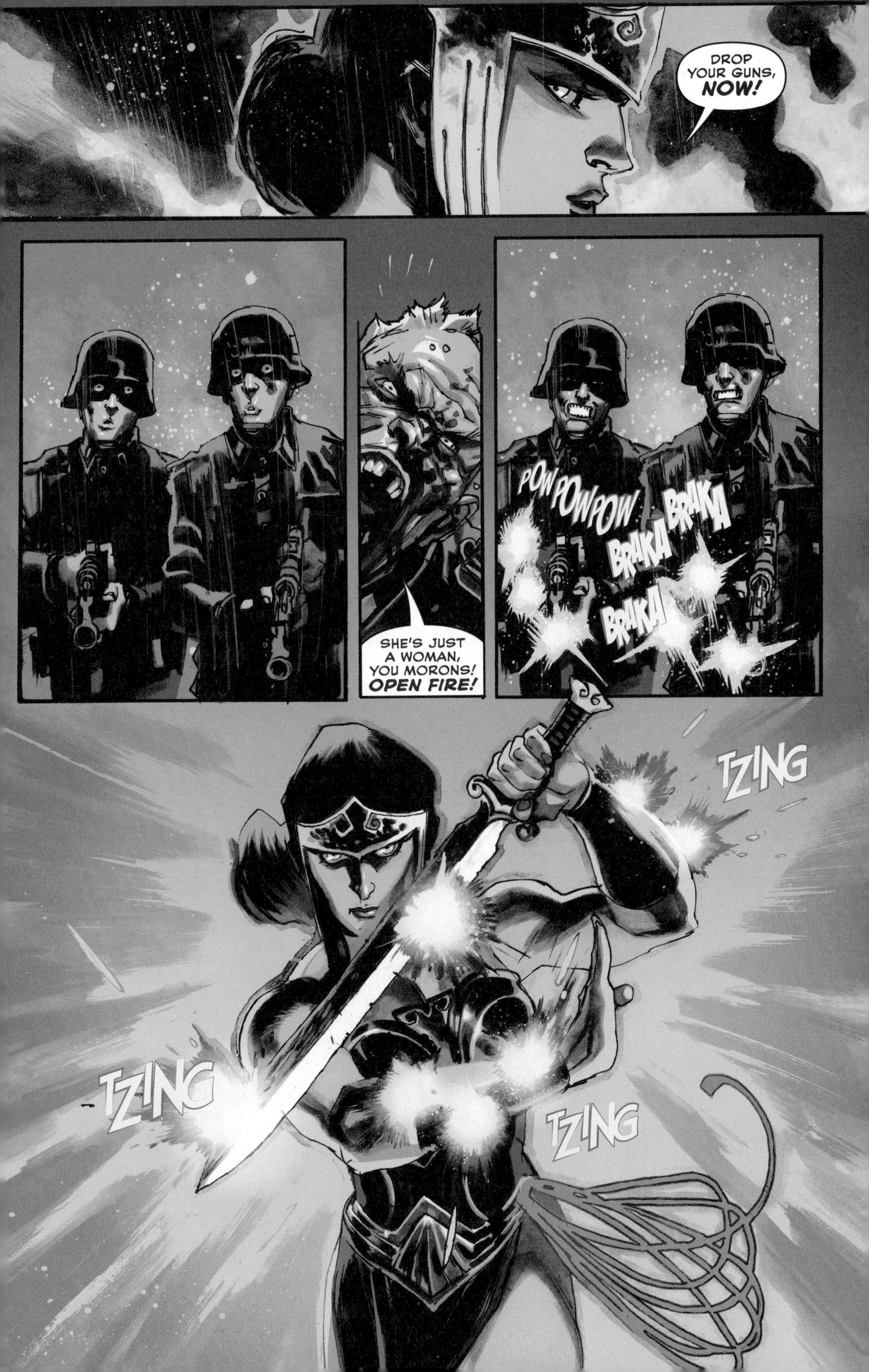
DROP YOUR GUNS, **NOW!**
SHE'S JUST A WOMAN, YOU MORONS! **OPEN FIRE!**
POW POW POW
BRAKA BRAKA
BRAKA
TZING
TZING
TZING

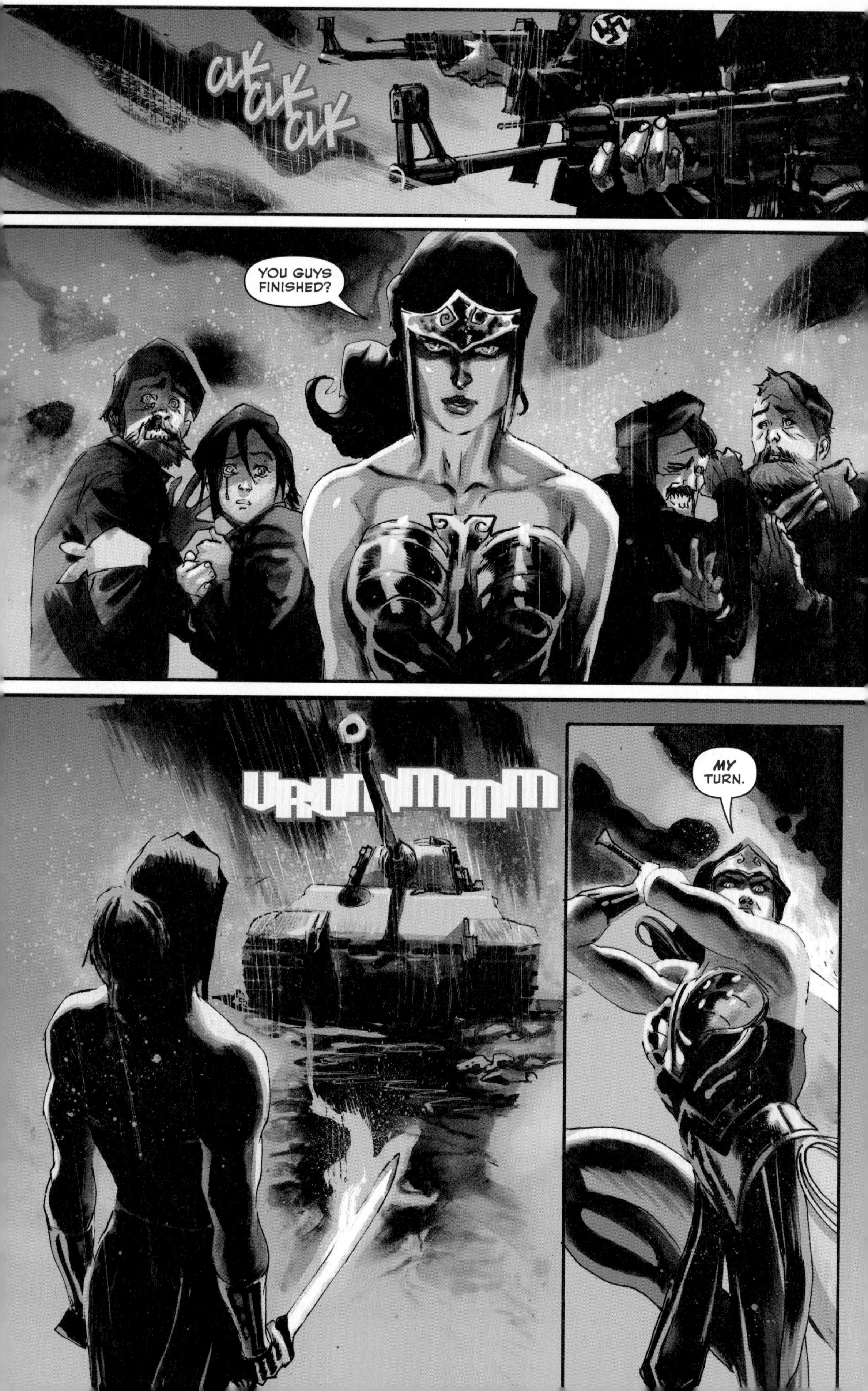
CLK CLK CLK
YOU GUYS FINISHED?
VRUMMMM
MY TURN.

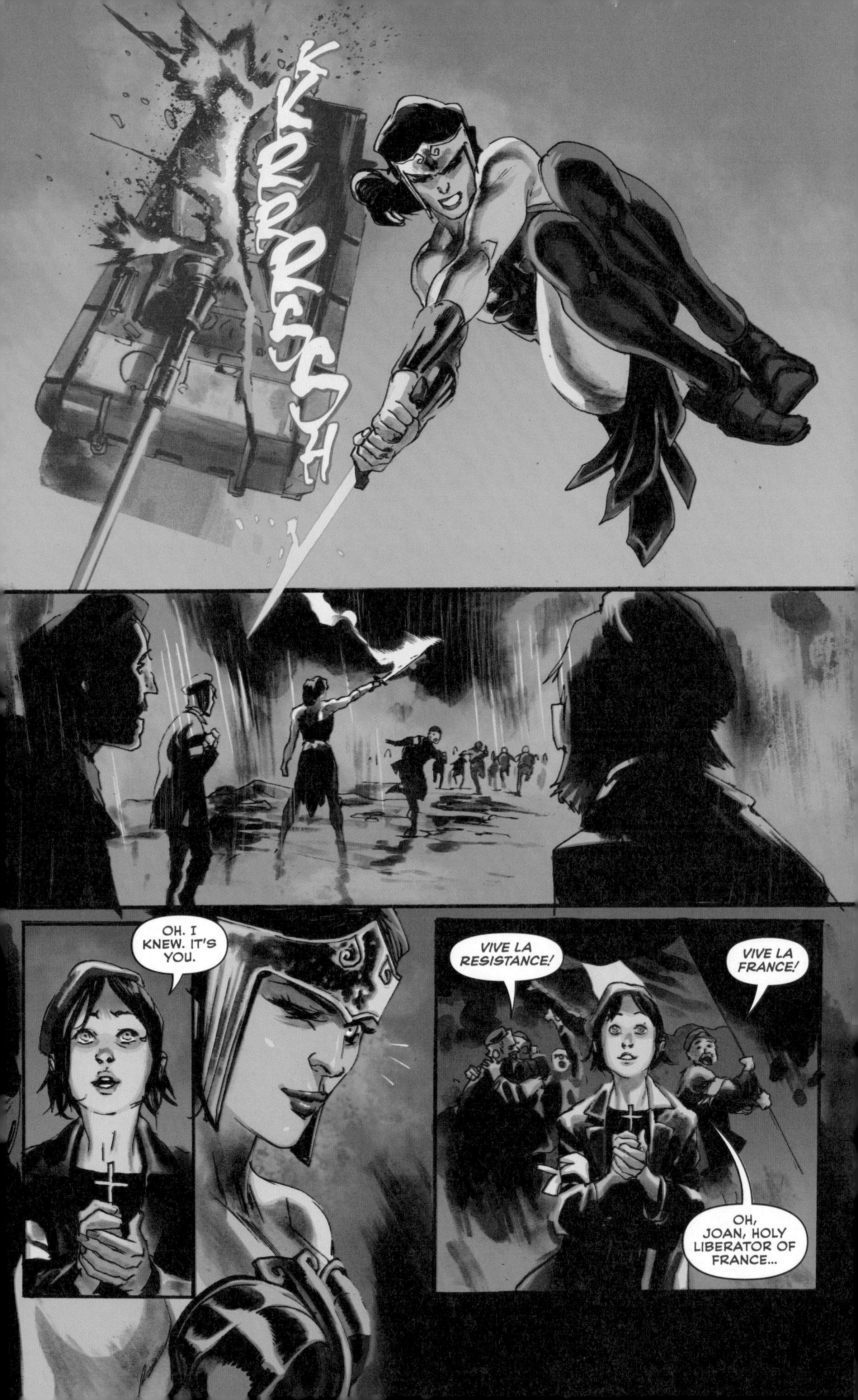
KKRRSSSH
OH. I KNEW. IT'S YOU.
VIVE LA RESISTANCE!
VIVE LA FRANCE!
OH, JOAN, HOLY LIBERATOR OF FRANCE...

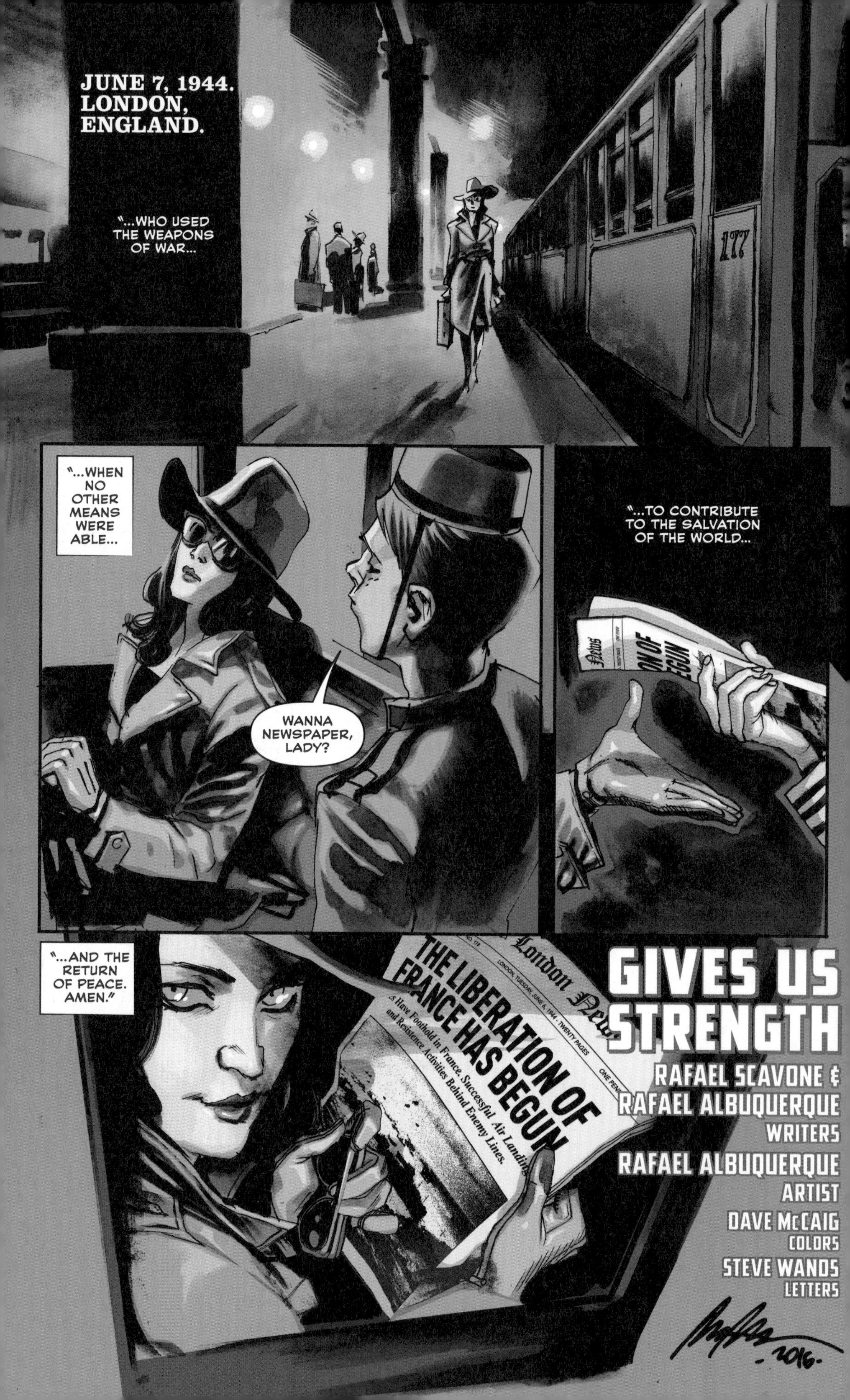
JUNE 7, 1944.
LONDON,
ENGLAND.
"...WHO USED THE WEAPONS OF WAR...
"...WHEN NO OTHER MEANS WERE ABLE...
WANNA NEWSPAPER, LADY?
"...TO CONTRIBUTE TO THE SALVATION OF THE WORLD...
"...AND THE RETURN OF PEACE. AMEN."
THE LIBERATION OF FRANCE HAS BEGUN
and Resistence Activities Behind Enemy Lines.
GIVES US STRENGTH
RAFAEL SCAVONE &
RAFAEL ALBUQUERQUE
WRITERS
RAFAEL ALBUQUERQUE
ARTIST
DAVE McCAIG
COLORS
STEVE WANDS
LETTERS
2016

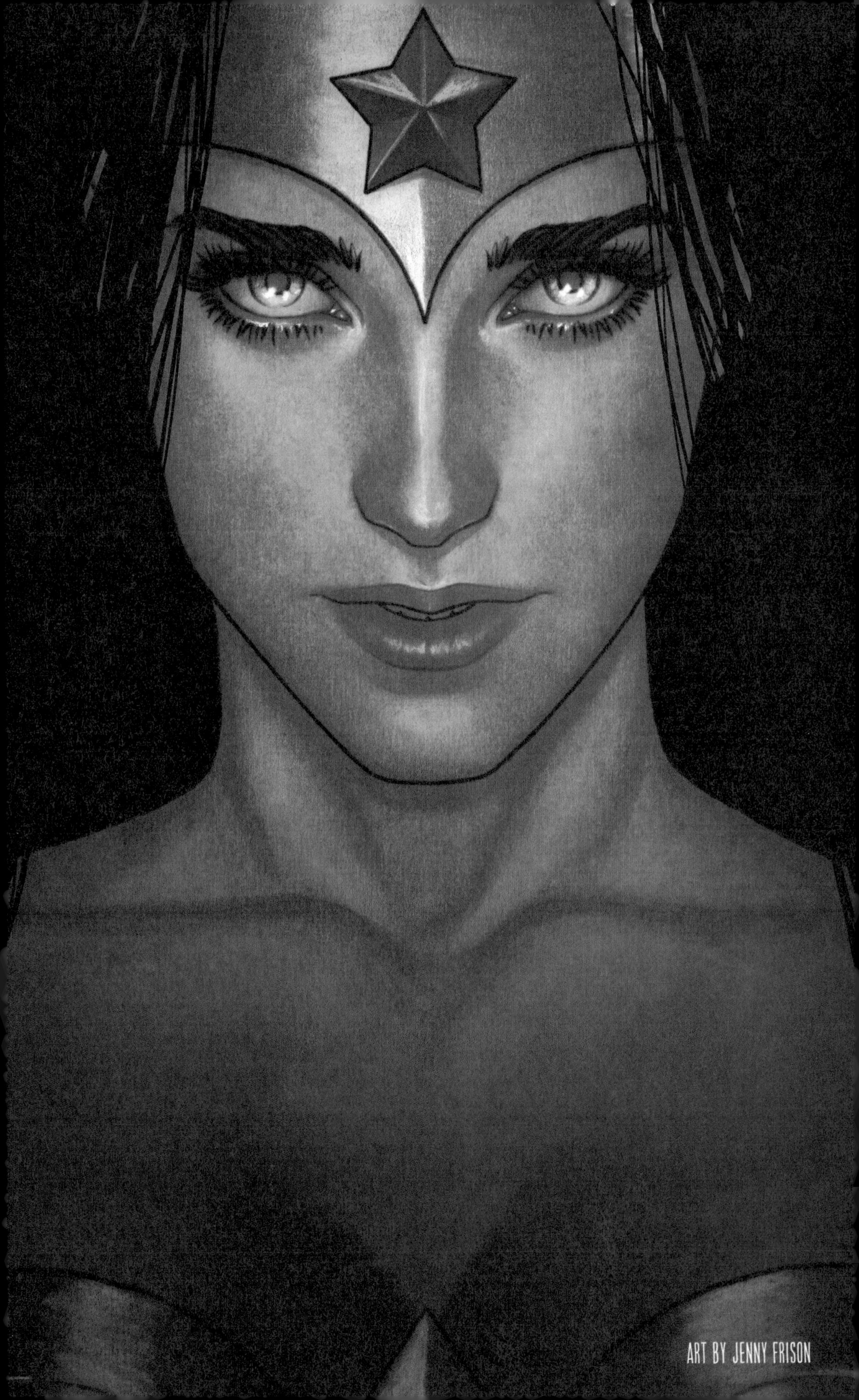
ART BY JENNY FRISON

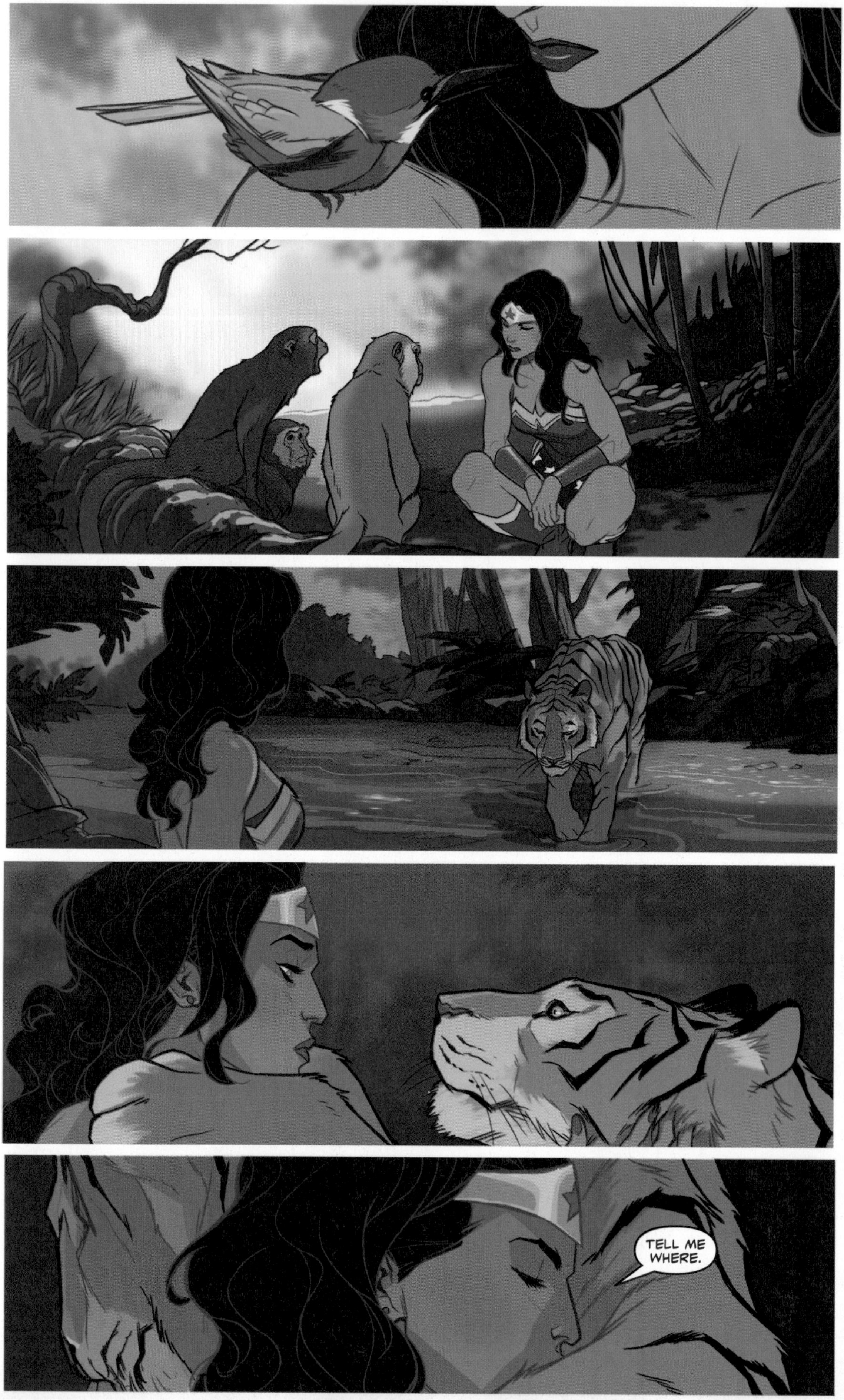
TELL ME
WHERE.

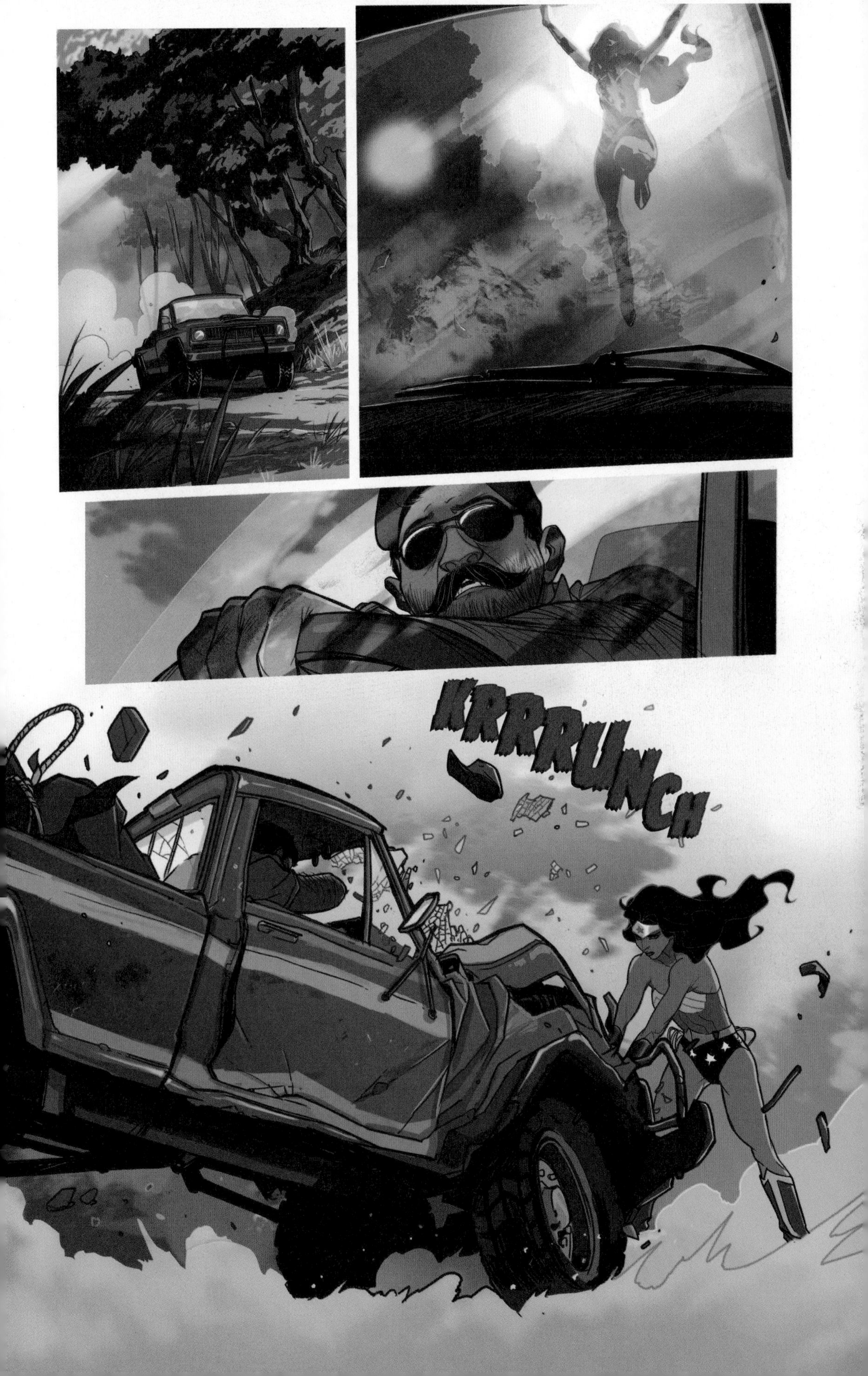
KRRRUNCH

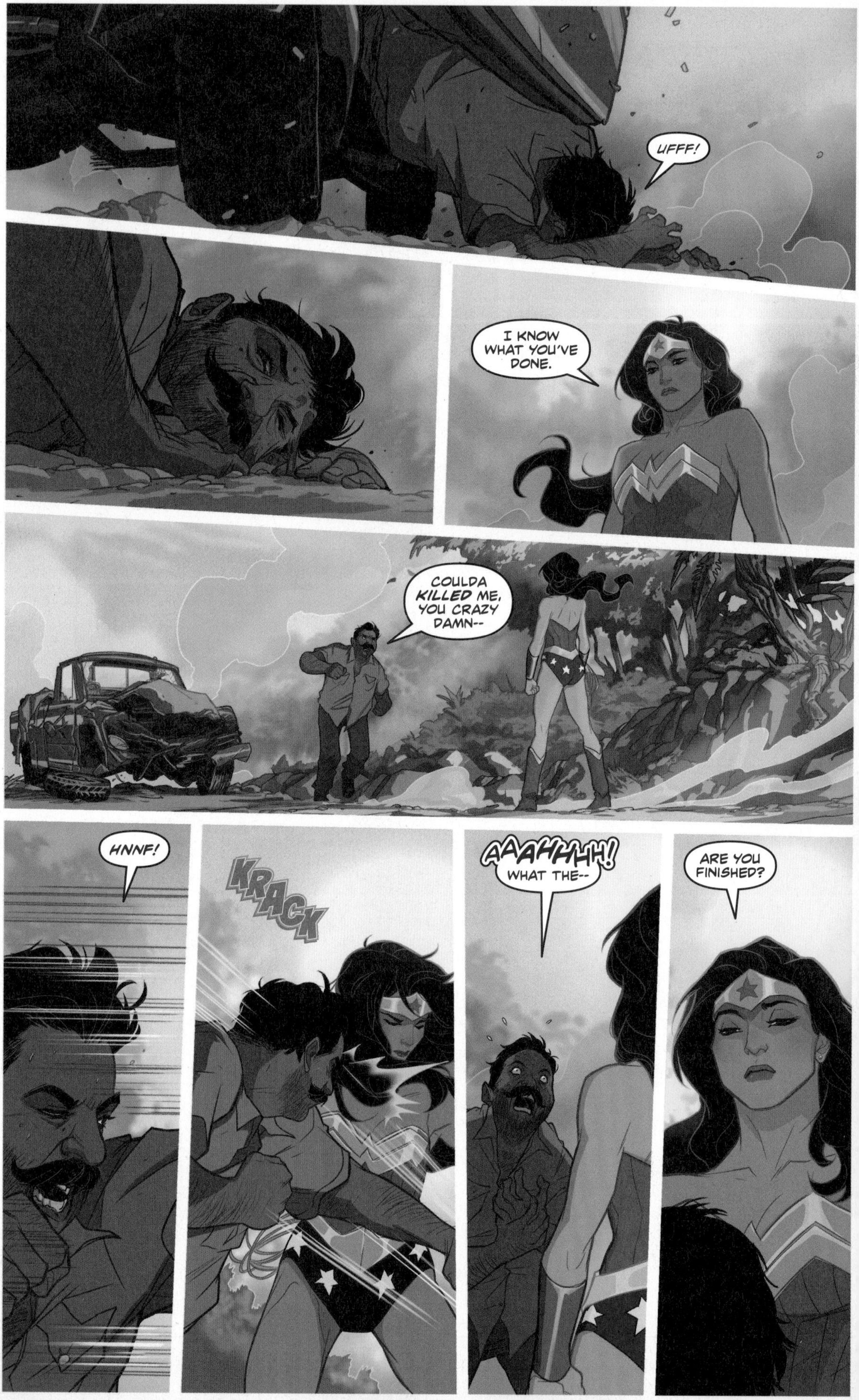
UFFF!
I KNOW WHAT YOU'VE DONE.
COULDA KILLED ME, YOU CRAZY DAMN--
HNNF!
KRACK
AAAHHHH! WHAT THE--
ARE YOU FINISHED?

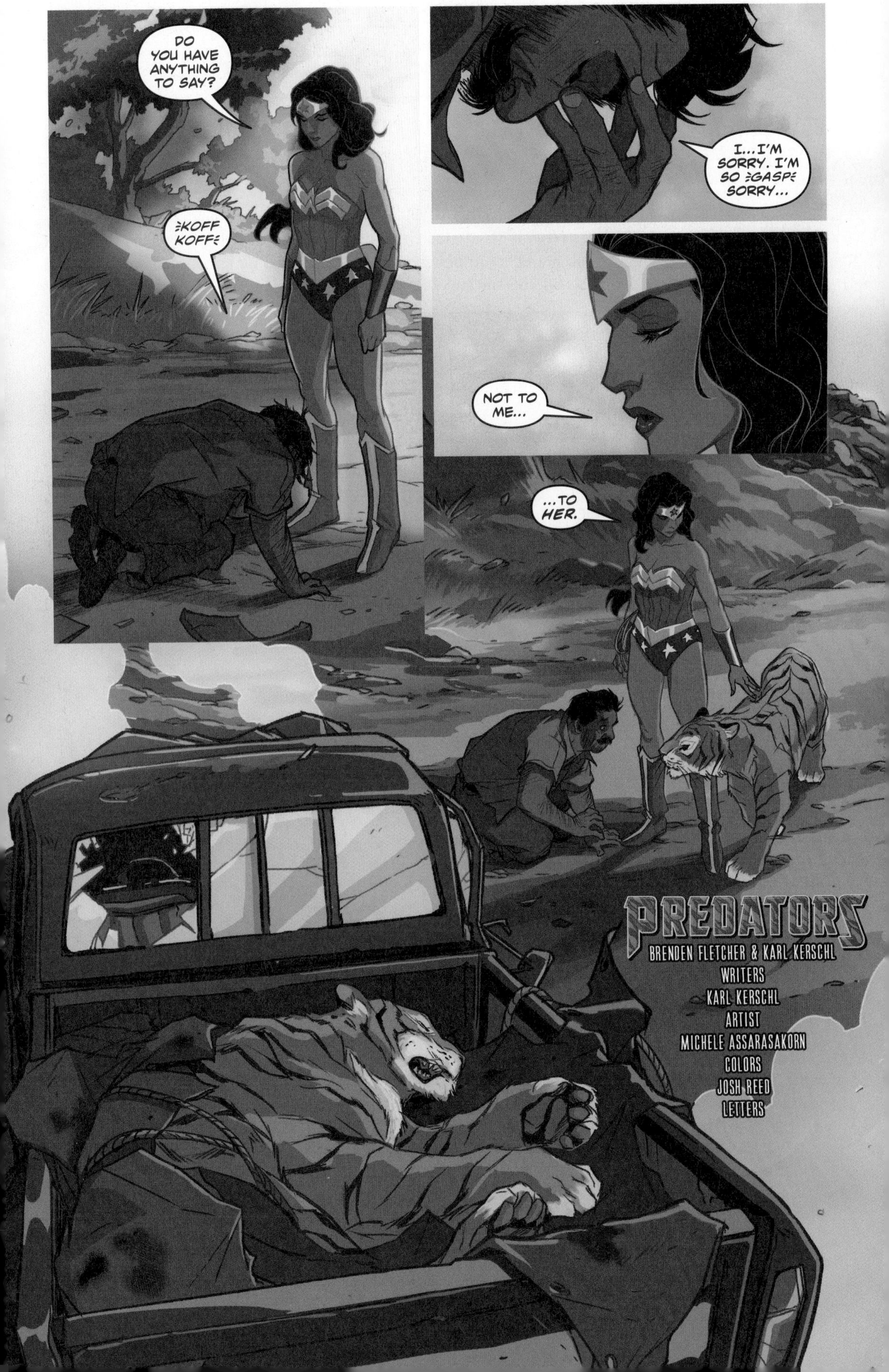
DO YOU HAVE ANYTHING TO SAY?
KOFF KOFF
I...I'M SORRY. I'M SO GASP SORRY...
NOT TO ME...
...TO HER.
PREDATORS
BRENDEN FLETCHER & KARL KERSCHL
WRITERS
KARL KERSCHL
ARTIST
MICHELE ASSARASAKORN
COLORS
JOSH REED
LETTERS

THE WONDER WOMAN COVERS OF BRIAN BOLLAND

BETWEEN 1992 AND 1995, LEGENDARY ARTIST BRIAN BOLLAND PRODUCED DOZENS OF SPECTACULAR COVERS FOR THE WONDER WOMAN ONGOING SERIES. Through twists, turns and costume redesigns, his renditions of Diana always showed off the character's natural grace, dignity and power, even when she was at her lowest ebb, or when she found herself in truly ridiculous situations (for example, as a waitress at a taco restaurant). Below, you'll find four of the WONDER WOMAN editors' favorite previously published Bolland images…followed by three rarely seen, unused pencil studies, developed during his original run for WONDER WOMAN covers that were never published!

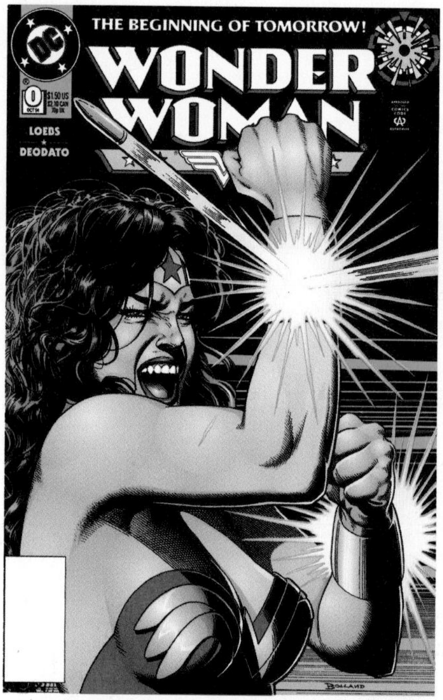
THE BEGINNING OF TOMORROW!
WONDER WOMAN
0
OCT 94
$1.50 US
LOEBS
DEODATO
BOLLAND

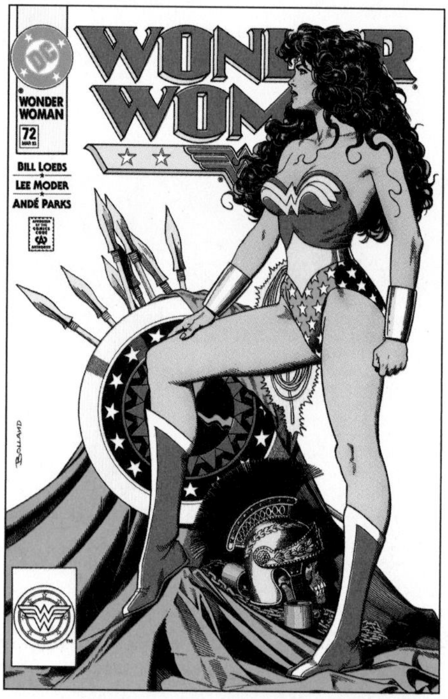
WONDER WOMAN
WONDER WOMAN
72
BILL LOEBS
LEE MODER
ANDÉ PARKS
BOLLAND

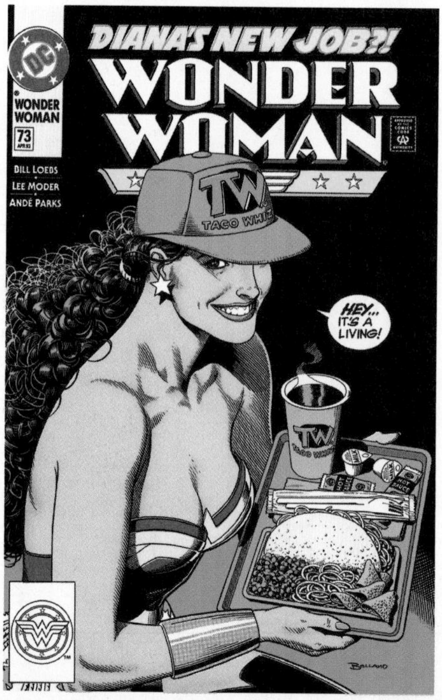
DIANA'S NEW JOB?!
WONDER WOMAN
WONDER WOMAN
73
BILL LOEBS
LEE MODER
ANDÉ PARKS
TW
TACO WHIZ
HEY... IT'S A LIVING!
BOLLAND

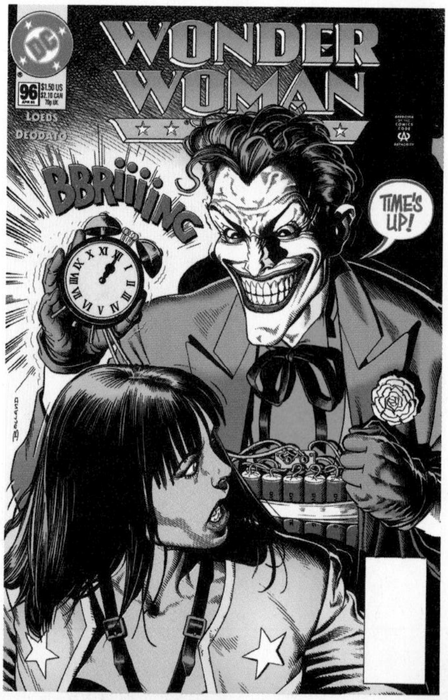
WONDER WOMAN
96
$1.50 US
LOEBS
DEODATO
BBRiiiiNG
TIME'S UP!
BOLLAND

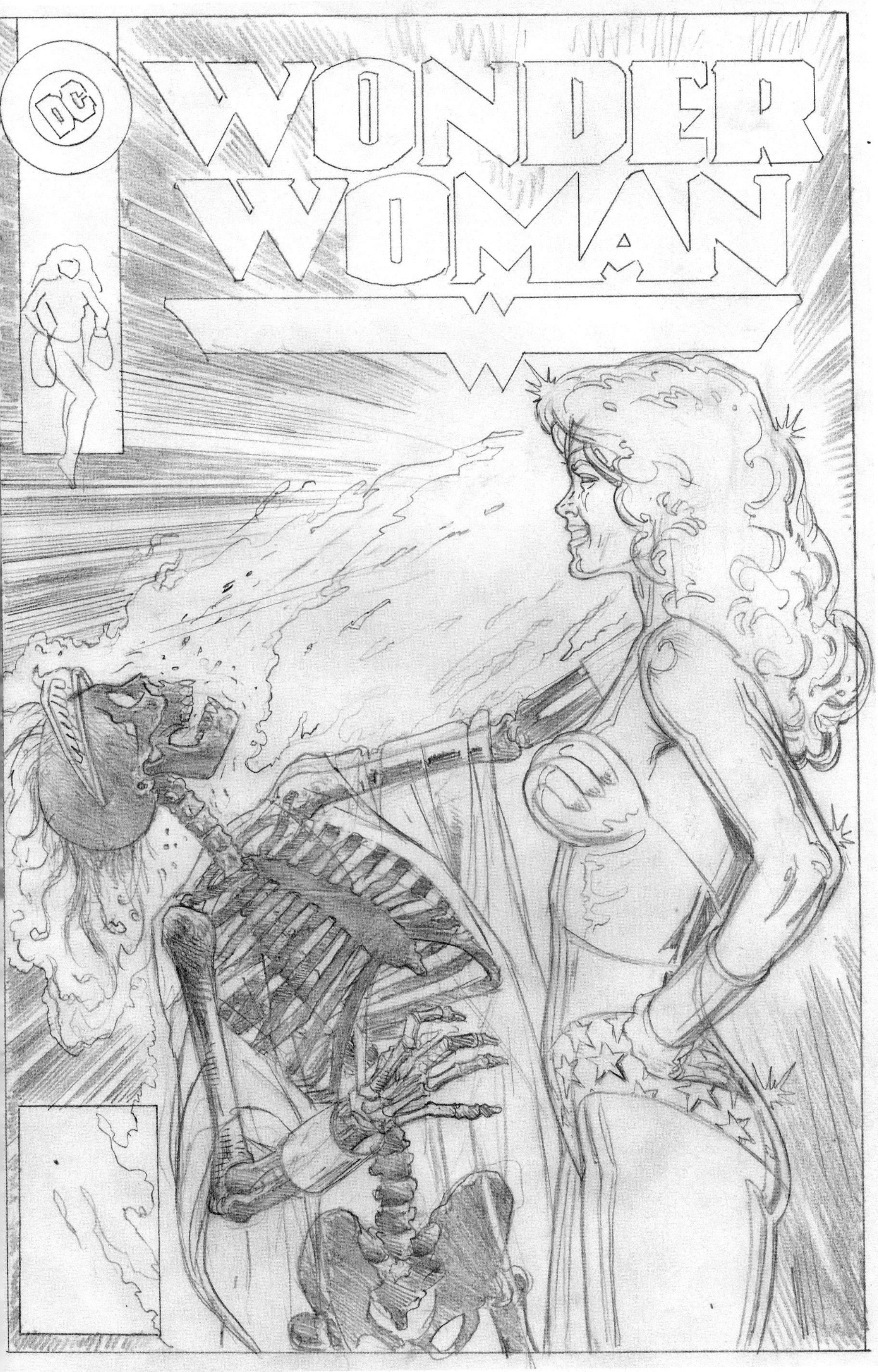
DC
WONDER
WOMAN

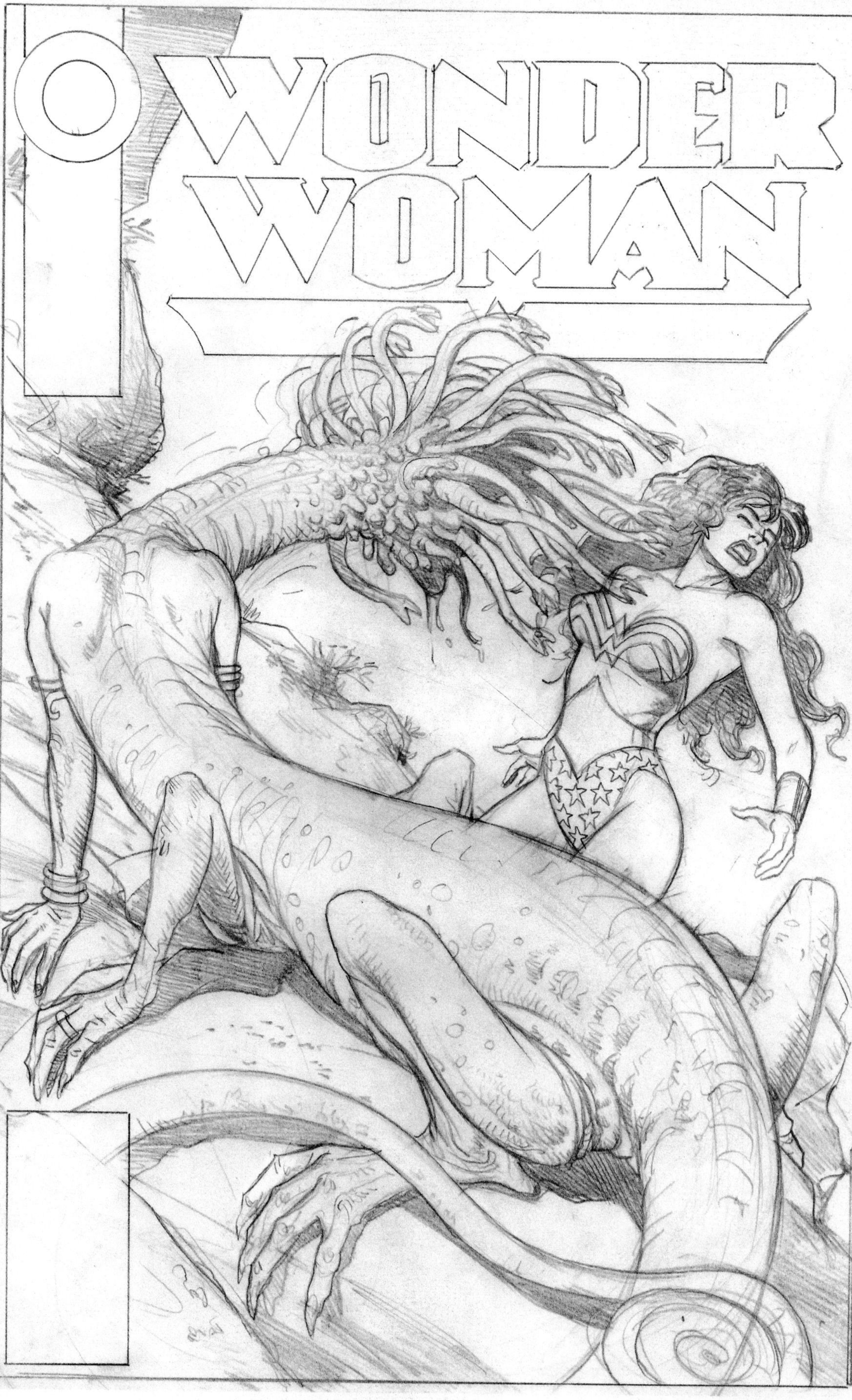
WONDER
WOMAN

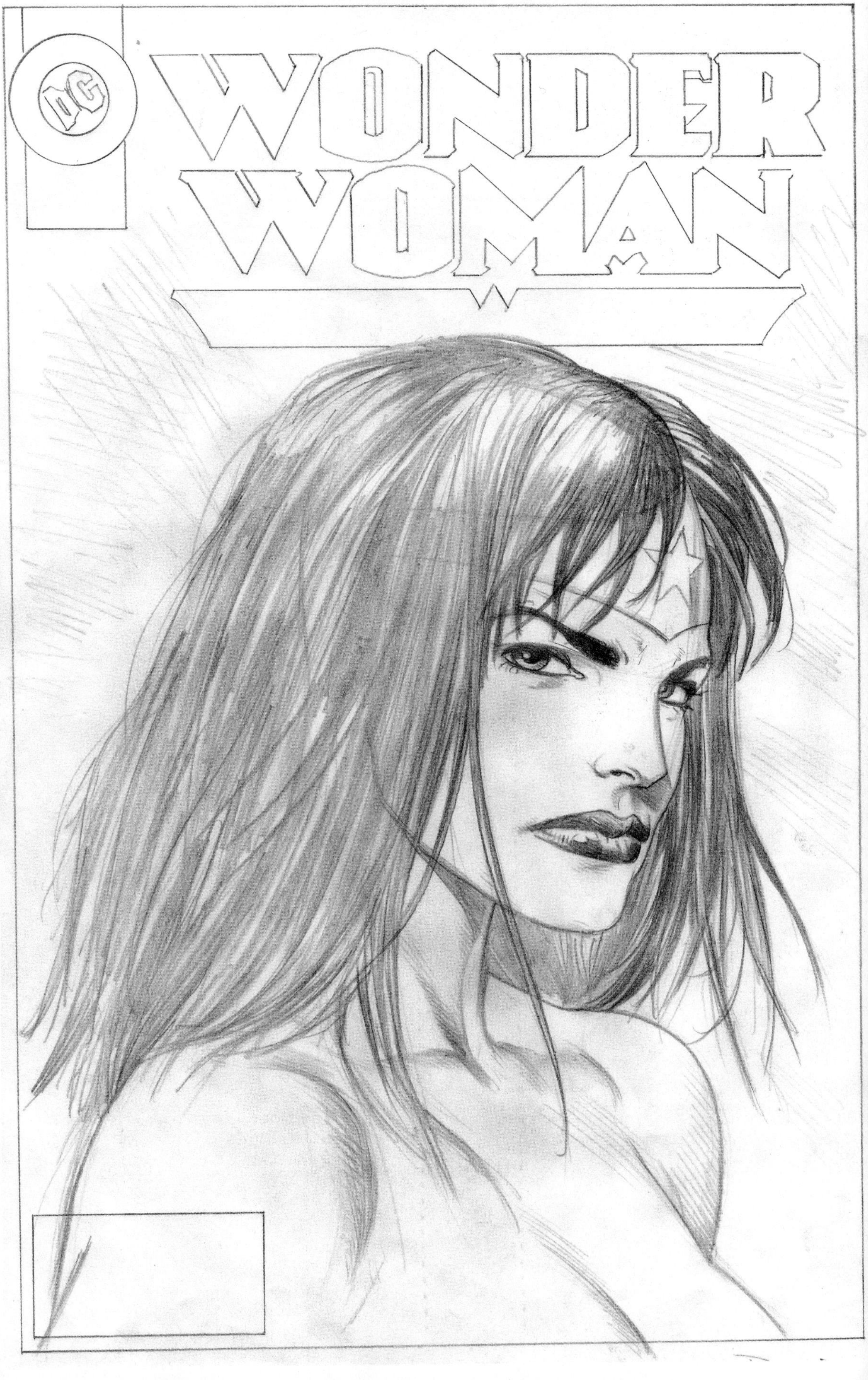
DC
WONDER
WOMAN

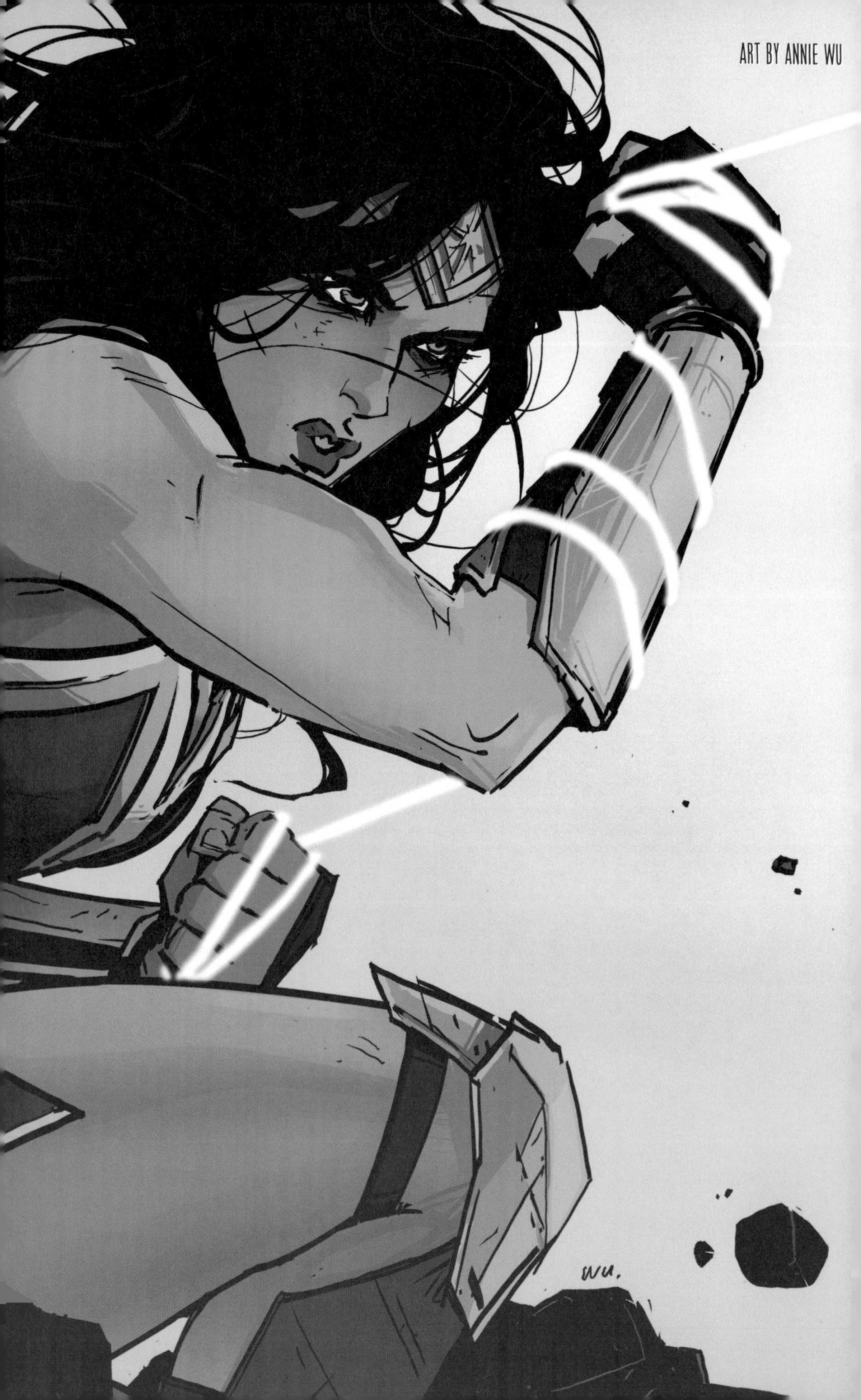
wu.
ART BY ANNIE WU

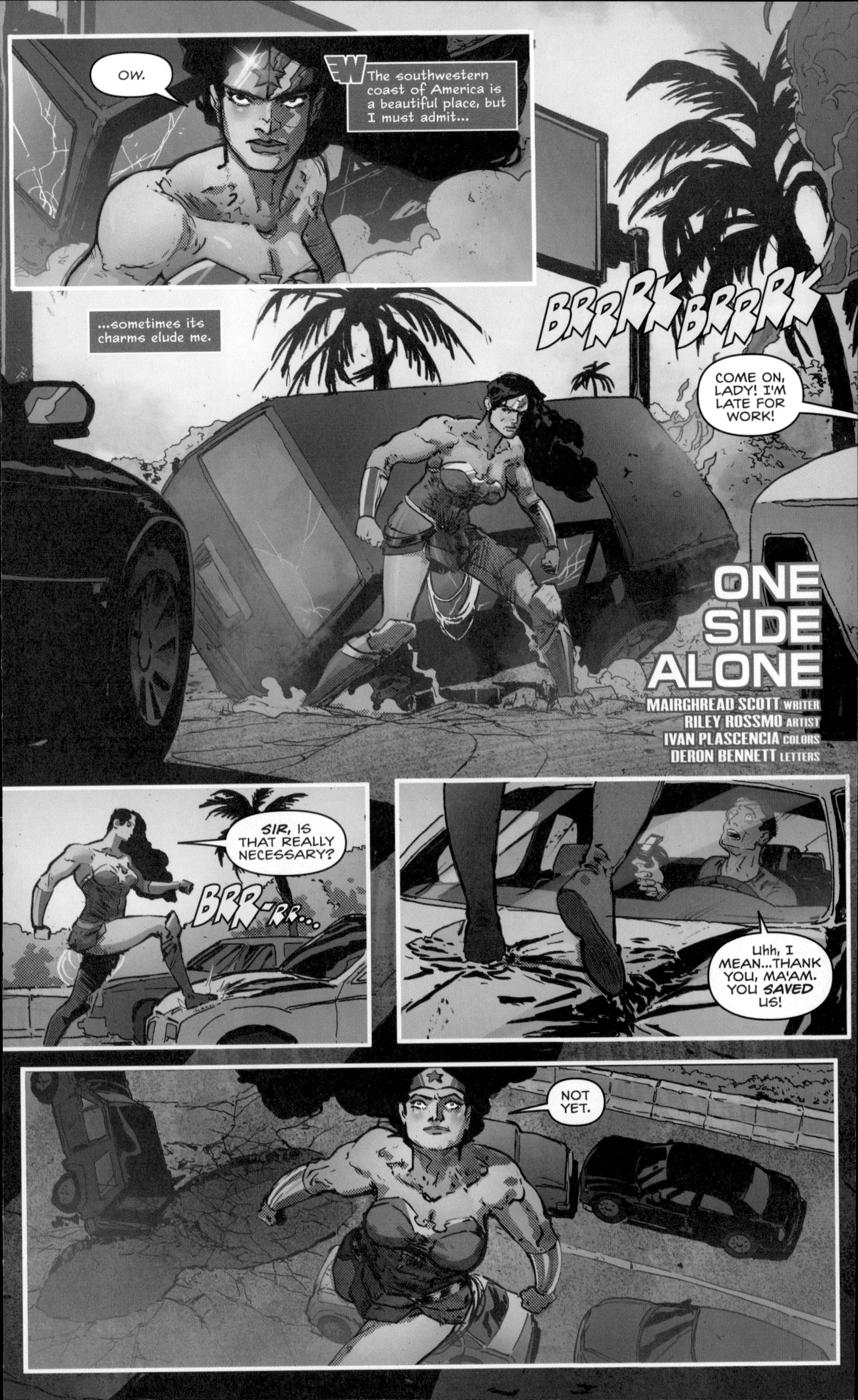
OW.
The southwestern coast of America is a beautiful place, but I must admit...
...sometimes its charms elude me.
BRRRK BRRRK
COME ON, LADY! I'M LATE FOR WORK!
ONE SIDE ALONE
MAIRGHREAD SCOTT WRITER
RILEY ROSSMO ARTIST
IVAN PLASCENCIA COLORS
DERON BENNETT LETTERS
SIR, IS THAT REALLY NECESSARY?
BRR-RR...
Uhh, I MEAN...THANK YOU, MA'AM. YOU SAVED US!
NOT YET.

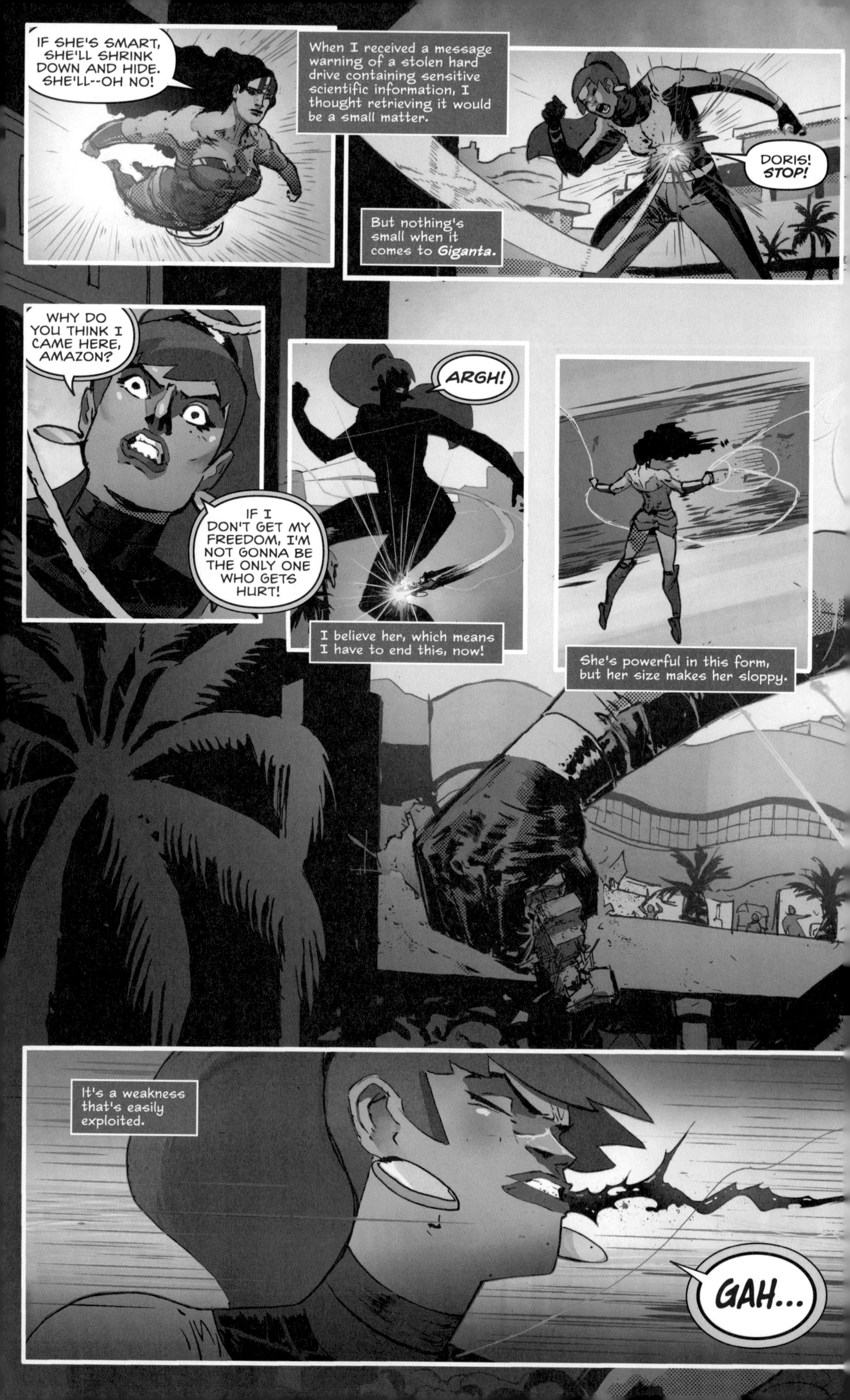
IF SHE'S SMART, SHE'LL SHRINK DOWN AND HIDE. SHE'LL--OH NO!
When I received a message warning of a stolen hard drive containing sensitive scientific information, I thought retrieving it would be a small matter.
But nothing's small when it comes to Giganta.
DORIS! STOP!
WHY DO YOU THINK I CAME HERE, AMAZON?
IF I DON'T GET MY FREEDOM, I'M NOT GONNA BE THE ONLY ONE WHO GETS HURT!
ARGH!
I believe her, which means I have to end this, now!
She's powerful in this form, but her size makes her sloppy.
It's a weakness that's easily exploited.
GAH...

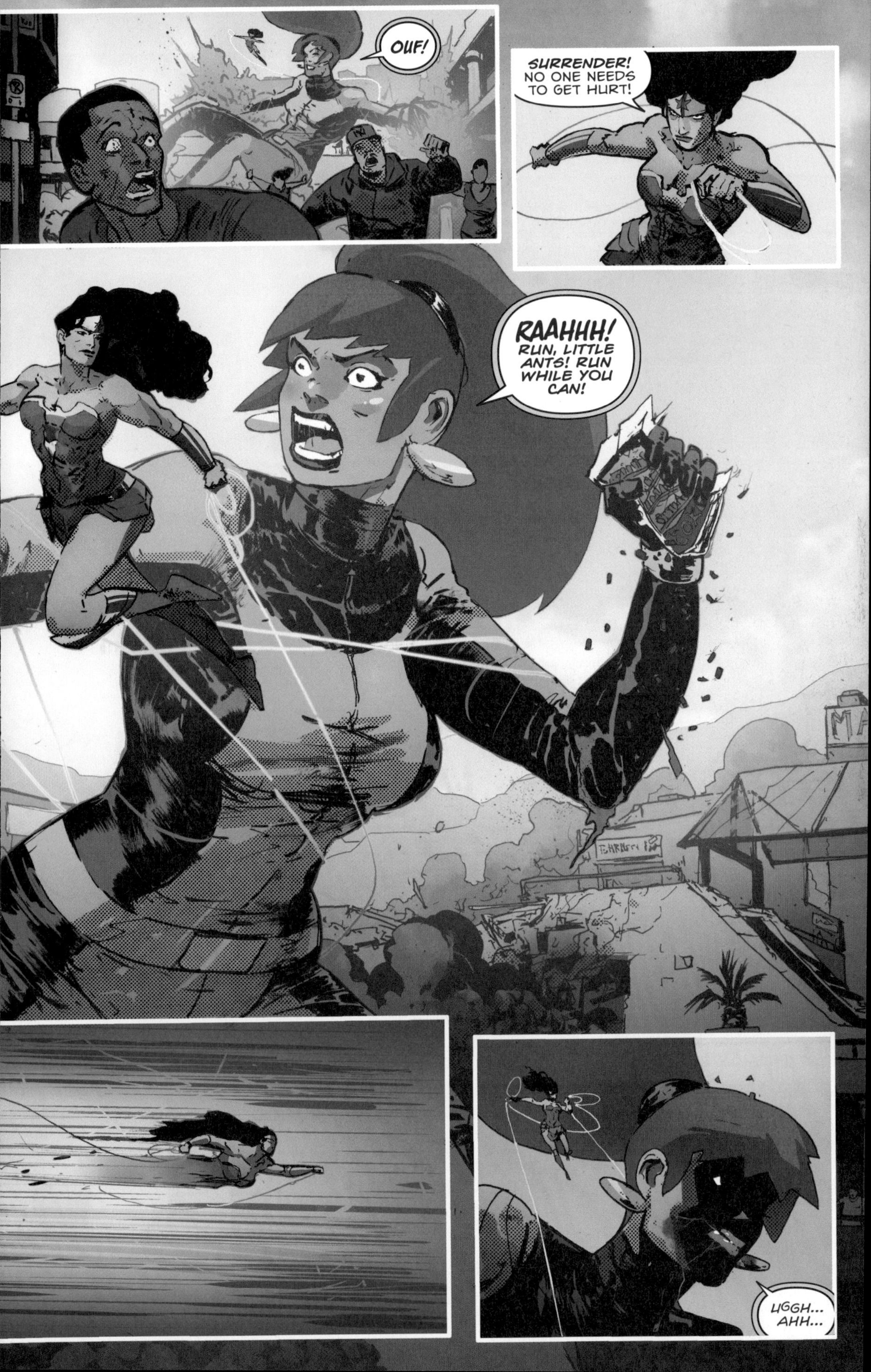
OUF!
SURRENDER! NO ONE NEEDS TO GET HURT!
RAAHHH! RUN, LITTLE ANTS! RUN WHILE YOU CAN!
UGGH... AHH...

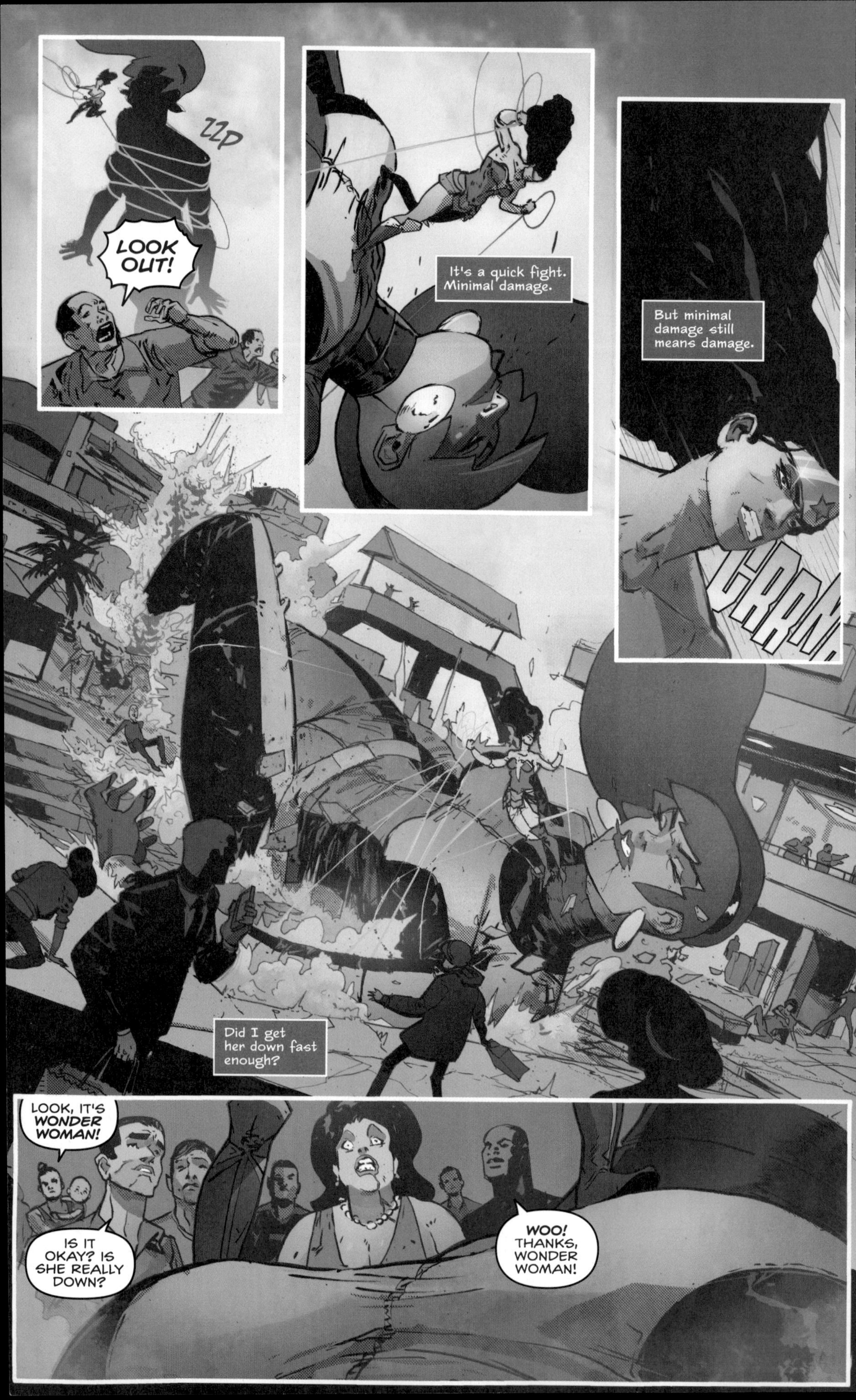
ZZP
LOOK OUT!
It's a quick fight. Minimal damage.
But minimal damage still means damage.
Did I get her down fast enough?
LOOK, IT'S WONDER WOMAN!
IS IT OKAY? IS SHE REALLY DOWN?
WOO! THANKS, WONDER WOMAN!

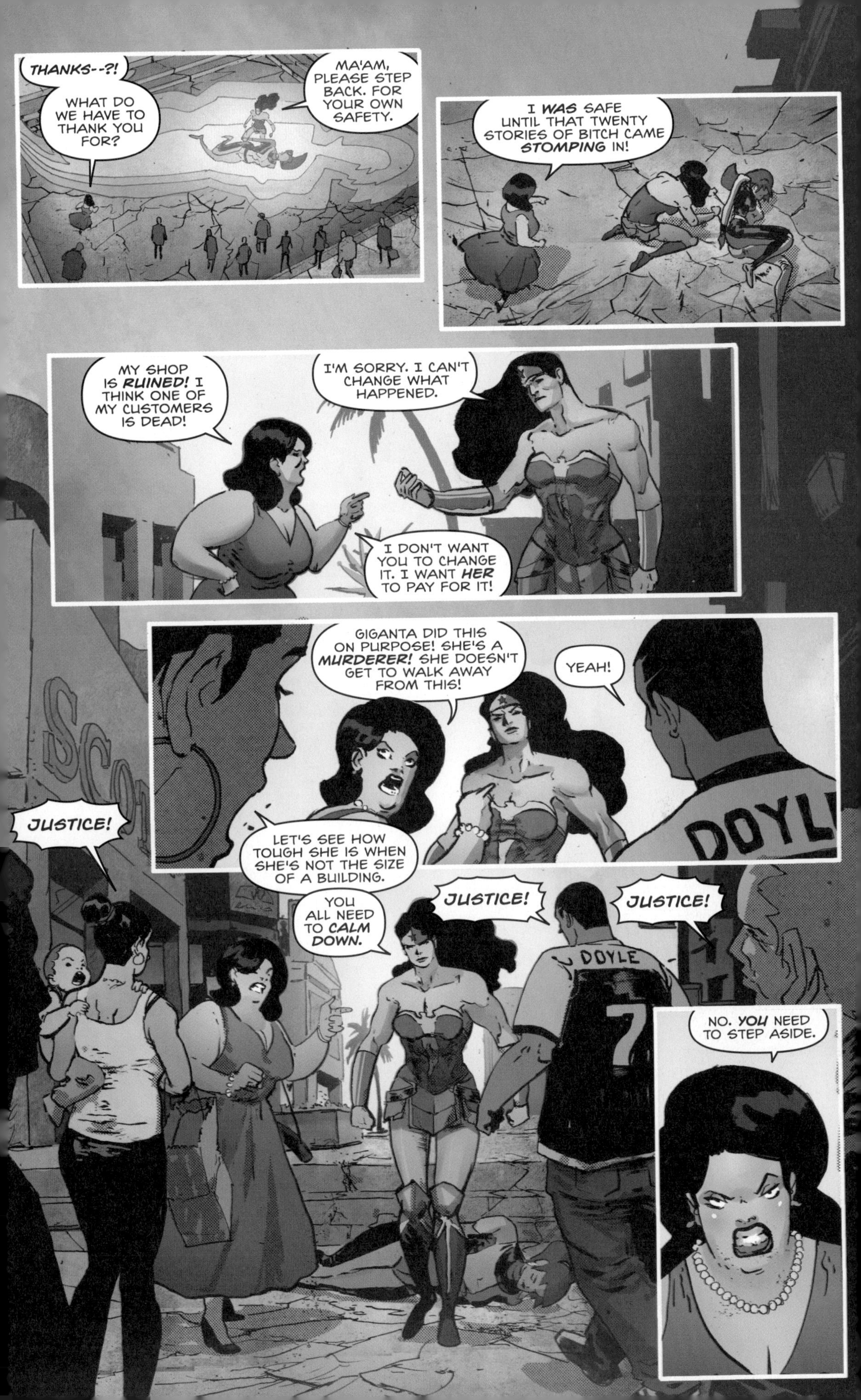
THANKS--?!
WHAT DO WE HAVE TO THANK YOU FOR?
MA'AM, PLEASE STEP BACK. FOR YOUR OWN SAFETY.
I WAS SAFE UNTIL THAT TWENTY STORIES OF BITCH CAME STOMPING IN!
MY SHOP IS RUINED! I THINK ONE OF MY CUSTOMERS IS DEAD!
I'M SORRY. I CAN'T CHANGE WHAT HAPPENED.
I DON'T WANT YOU TO CHANGE IT. I WANT HER TO PAY FOR IT!
GIGANTA DID THIS ON PURPOSE! SHE'S A MURDERER! SHE DOESN'T GET TO WALK AWAY FROM THIS!
YEAH!
DOYL
LET'S SEE HOW TOUGH SHE IS WHEN SHE'S NOT THE SIZE OF A BUILDING.
JUSTICE!
YOU ALL NEED TO CALM DOWN.
JUSTICE!
JUSTICE!
DOYLE
7
NO. YOU NEED TO STEP ASIDE.

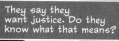They say they
want justice. Do they
know what that means?

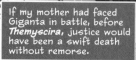If my mother had faced
Giganta in battle, before
Themyscira, justice would
have been a swift death
without remorse.

Even if she were incapacitated.
She would have been killed and
stripped of her trophies.

An offering to Pallas
Athena in thanks
for the victory.

If Giganta had killed someone on
Paradise Island, an Amazon raising
a hand against her own, we would
have called it a sickness.

All crimes can be
seen as cries for
help in time, and
time is all we had.

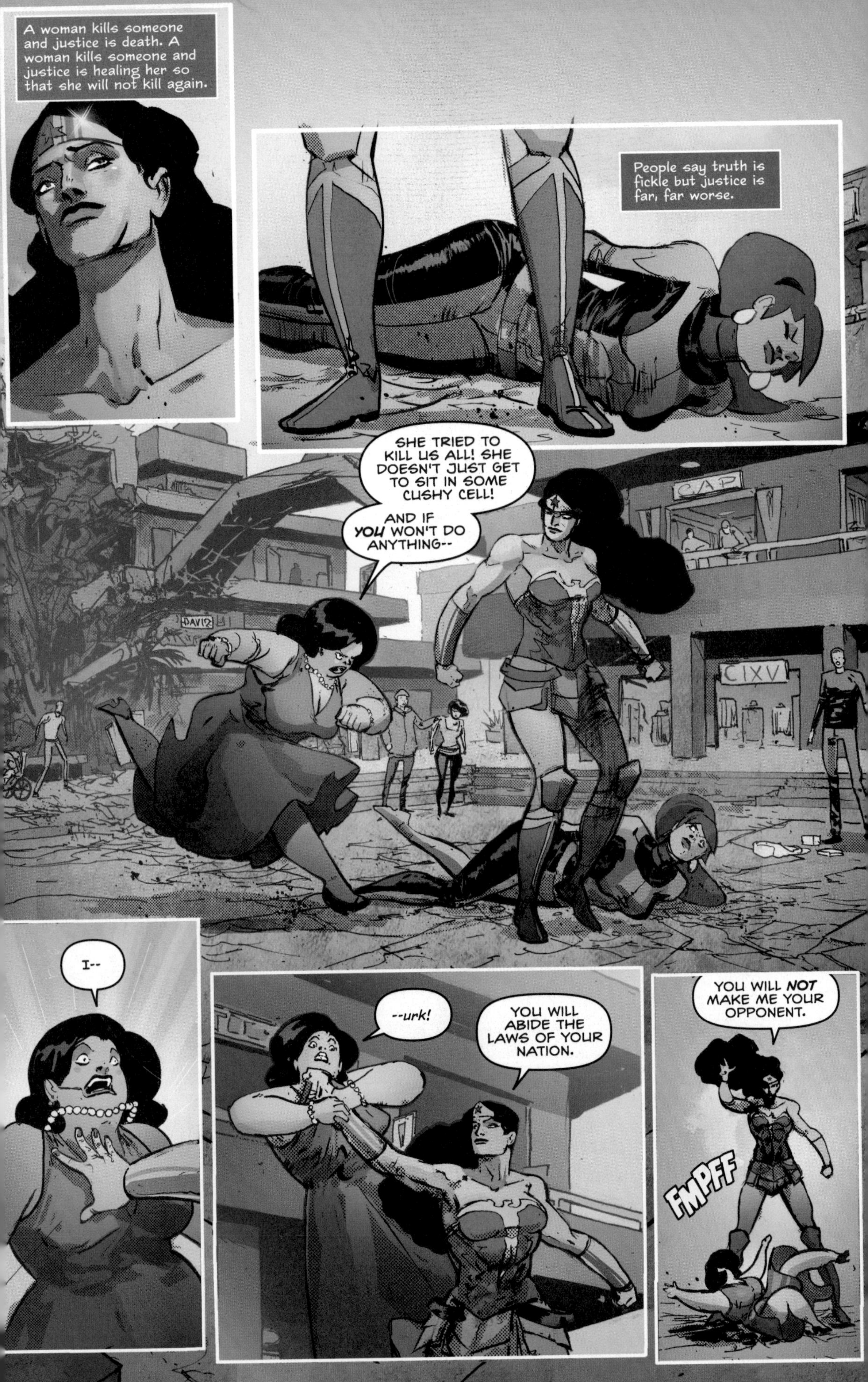
A woman kills someone and justice is death. A woman kills someone and justice is healing her so that she will not kill again.
People say truth is fickle but justice is far, far worse.
SHE TRIED TO KILL US ALL! SHE DOESN'T JUST GET TO SIT IN SOME CUSHY CELL!
AND IF YOU WON'T DO ANYTHING--
I--
--urk!
YOU WILL ABIDE THE LAWS OF YOUR NATION.
YOU WILL NOT MAKE ME YOUR OPPONENT.
FMPFF

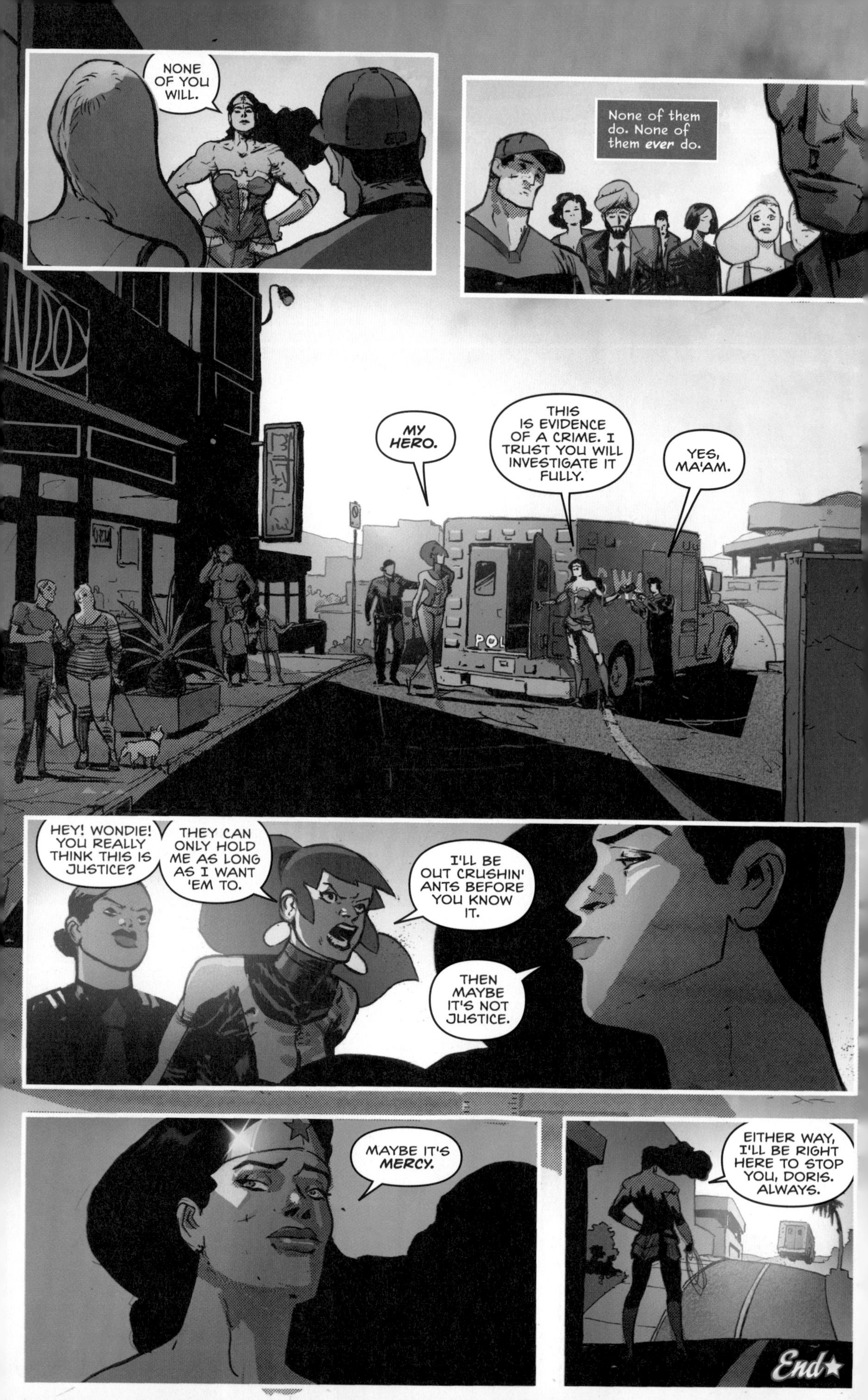
NONE OF YOU WILL.
None of them do. None of them *ever* do.
MY HERO.
THIS IS EVIDENCE OF A CRIME. I TRUST YOU WILL INVESTIGATE IT FULLY.
YES, MA'AM.
POL
HEY! WONDIE! YOU REALLY THINK THIS IS JUSTICE?
THEY CAN ONLY HOLD ME AS LONG AS I WANT 'EM TO.
I'LL BE OUT CRUSHIN' ANTS BEFORE YOU KNOW IT.
THEN MAYBE IT'S NOT JUSTICE.
MAYBE IT'S *MERCY.*
EITHER WAY, I'LL BE RIGHT HERE TO STOP YOU, DORIS. ALWAYS.
End

WONDER WOMAN
IN CONVERSATION
by *Lois Lane*

It's October in Manhattan, the kind of fall day where the sweaters have emerged and the scarves are starting to be wrapped instead of draped. I'm in town covering another story entirely, and in the middle of the press conference I get a text. "Coffee?"

The text is from Diana of Themyscira. The text is from Wonder Woman.

Twenty minutes later I'm at a café in the Village, and she's already there, sitting at a table off the sidewalk, book unopened in front of her. The staff knows who she is. Everyone knows who she is. She can dress down, but it makes no difference; your eye is drawn to her as if pulled on a fishing line. Pedestrians pause mid-stride, double-take. Some approach. Some continue on their way. She smiles. She is gracious. She signs napkins when people ask for autographs.

Some context. I've known Diana for the better part of a decade, first professionally and then—I'd like to think—as a friend. Roughly once a year she'll reach out to get together socially, just to catch up, and from the beginning (and with her consent) I've recorded our conversations. One day, in my dotage, I'll compile the whole mass of them and put out a book, a la Tuesdays with Morrie.

Details, for those who care about these things. Clothes: oversized wool sweater and corduroys. Drinks: green tea for her, double Americano for me. We shared a plate of biscotti. I will not list the author of the book, nor the manufacturer of the clothes, for reasons discussed below. We spent a few minutes playing catch-up on personal and social matters, which I am not including, before my first question.

I understand you just got back from Africa? I don't even know if you can talk about it.

I was in Bwunda for a little while.

And how was that?

I like Africa. I did not have much opportunity for sightseeing. I have been dealing with some personal issues and was looking for an old friend to help resolve them, and that led, as things often do, from one thing to another.

Did you find your friend?

I did, and she is doing very well now, for which I am grateful. I am hoping that she will be able to return the favor.

I've never known you to make a friend that wouldn't do their best.

(laughs) That is very flattering. I can say the same about you. I think, if we are fortunate, we surround ourselves with people who inspire us and lift us, and when they slip we catch them, and when we slip they catch us. And perhaps our judgment is not always flawless, but I would like to think that experience hones that, perhaps?

The personal stuff you've been dealing with, did you feel like you needed someone to catch you? Were we not there for you?

(pauses) You know how when people talk of depression, they talk of it both coming in storms and coming stealthily? So that, for many, it is the status quo, before they realize...that we lose our self-awareness in that. So I can't...I can't fault the people who love and care for me for not seeing what I did not myself see.

I think, again, when we have our moments of clarity, it is very easy to brush past them, to let the status quo continue. It can be very difficult and sometimes painful to turn and confront them. The only analogy I can think of is chronic pain. When that pain has been with you for so very long, it is background noise. And one is not aware of it until something happens that places it into relief.

But you're not talking about physical pain?

No. And I am not certain I am talking about emotional pain either. It has been difficult for me to untangle. I think there is a psychological element to it. I think it is important—and I think as a reporter

that you would be inclined to agree—that we question those basic assumptions that we often decide are true.

I have found myself in a position where a great deal of what I took as true no longer seems accurate.

That may be because I have changed. That may be because the world has changed. Or it may be because I was mistaken. And it is that last that is the most concerning. I put great stock in truth—I think that's one of the reasons why we get along.

Those of us who know you, and all of us who are watching you be "you," your facility for honesty, your inclination for honesty, it comes off of you in waves. It's kind of impossible to miss. I think people notice before they notice your beauty, or before they notice your clothes, or before they notice your strength. It emanates. It's hard to imagine—though when I stop and think about it I see it's absolutely possible—you not having a perfect assessment of what's going on with you. A perfect clarity. But I think that's something we put on you because we see you seeking clarity.

> ## "I have found myself in a position where a great deal of what I took as true no longer seems accurate."

Again, I think that is flattering.

Where I come from—or what I remember of where I come from—is that there is not much need nor cause for deception. People are honest with one another. It serves very little purpose to traffic in falsehoods. I think for my own purposes, I have always wanted to understand. I have always wanted to know more of the world, outside of those confines I was raised within. You cannot have, I think, a facility with or faith in truth if you do not start with a need to understand. That is, to understand the world around you, but also to have empathy for the people around you. Without that empathy how can you understand them?

I am perfectly capable of being deceptive. You are from a military background, you have seen this. The nature of combat, of warfare...deception is a large part of that. It is not simply a matter of martial skill. My culture certainly embraces the martial. That is not how we have defined ourselves. It would be the equivalent of saying that a cadet at West Point studies the history of warfare, battles and tactics, but nowhere in there learns to lie.

It seems to me that you would say there is a profound difference between, say, a feint in a fight, large or small, or withholding information about your troop movements, and, say, lying to a friend to gain a professional advantage.

Yes, though—

Though a lot of people would say—

—they are exactly the same, yes, and I would obviously disagree with that. There is a difference between artifice and mendacity, to use very expensive words.

They're cheaper now that everything's digital.

That is good to know. (*laughs*)

There seems to be a lot of mendacity about. Perhaps that is what troubles me. I have never had a problem with artifice. I am beginning to be concerned that I have been prey to mendacities. And if indeed I have been prey to them, have I participated in them? And if I have participated in them, have I done so tacitly? Or have I been manipulated? And that is always alarming.

We talk about manipulation...we tend to use it as a very pejorative word. At its root I do not think manipulation is by necessity pejorative. We seek the results we want. I do not call you and say, "Do you have time for coffee?" if I do not want you to say yes. Knowing that I am calling you, and knowing you as I do, I know your inclination is to say yes. Is that manipulative?

I don't know. Is it manipulative of me to look forward to meeting you for coffee, and to also know that someday there's a book in our conversations? You don't seem to mind and I don't seem to mind, and I don't think it inflects or impacts our friendship.

No, I do not think it does either. We are honest about such things. You are not hiding the recorder.

Right, but the recorder's on, so I'm also not bothering to talk about how long it took me to do my hair this morning.

(*laughs*)

There's no real reason to steer the conversation to things that I think aren't that interesting, or that I think some future eavesdropper will not find merit in. But that's for later in the elevator or whatever. I guess what I'm hearing, and what kind of alarms me, is the idea that there is someone out there who could manipulate you for very long. Do you...are we talking about gods, here? Ordinary humans?

This is interesting, and I think this is important. When we talk about the Patrons...outside of my culture, when the Patrons are discussed, they are always discussed as...they are granted an omnipotence that they do not have.

I think, perhaps, this is a result of the blurring of concepts of divinity versus godhood. There is a larger discussion to be had there, where a Judeo-Christian, monotheistic deity is presented as omnipotent, and may well be.

The Patrons are as—no, they are more flawed than—the people you will meet on the street. Thus they are as capable of, if not more capable because of their power, all the mendacity and cruelty and pettiness that you encounter in day-to-day life.

So I hesitate to think that...this is what I am trying to say. It does not take a god to deceive me. I have been deceived by plenty of mortals, flesh and blood. So I would not grant that it could only be a power on the scale of a Darkseid.

How are you feeling now?

Uncertain. Better. I have a course of action, and I feel that the course will bring resolution, and hopefully in resolution, that will bring understanding, and understanding will bring truth. It remains to be seen. I do not know how much further in this journey I have to go.

I do know that I am not my best self until I know myself. And I think that has been the most alarming aspect of this. But I think anyone can say that.

That actually does sound like a fair truism for most of us.

I am not dispensing great pearls of wisdom, I fear.

It saddens me. I think that is something that concerns me greatly. If I have deceived myself I do not know when I began to do it, nor do I know why. We tend to lie to ourselves because we are unhappy. I do not think I have been unhappy. But I am not certain I have been happy for a long time.

The happiness issue is an interesting one to me.

Are you happy?

I think so. Though I think you'll agree that when a person is busy, it's often very easy to forget to notice. To move from one thing to the next thing and not really take note. I know that when I'm not working, I'm unhappy.

Well, that is an answer in and of itself, is it not? When you are doing good work. I believe very strongly that doing good work is a source of happiness. Having a purpose to the days, and having goals, short- and long-term. I do not think either of us defines ourselves by our ability to meet these goals as much as the aspiration to reach for them.

> "I do not know how much further in this journey I have to go. I do know that I am not my best self until I know myself."

Right.

I do not expect the world to turn tomorrow to peace and harmony and walking hand in hand. That is certainly an aspiration, but I am not going to call myself a failure tomorrow morning if I do not read in the *Daily Planet* that world peace has been declared.

(laughs) Good. I can promise you we won't be printing it!

Pity.

I worry sometimes that it must be lonely.

I think sometimes that it is. There is the acute difference between loneliness and being alone. I am very fortunate, I have many, many people who are dear friends, and many people who love me.

But I have felt alone. More often than not, recently. Perhaps that is where this clarity has come from. We can walk through a city and still walk alone. I think that, more than anything else, is what I have begun to sense, that I feel...wrapped in an insulation, and separated. That may be it. Again, you cannot be honest if there is no connection. You cannot understand if there is no interaction.

And if you're not feeling like you've been knowing yourself well, who's connecting? Who's interacting?

Yes.

You know what you've never told me?

What have I never told you, Lois?

Wonder Woman spotted in the crowd at the Fashion Center in Arlington, Virginia earlier this week.

A thousand things! No, I've asked you before about your childhood and your culture and growing up, but I don't think I've ever asked you what you did for fun. Like, when you think about fun—

We played!

But in so many of our conversations you've talked about the purpose of play, games and contests, and it being geared toward the learning underneath. Which, as an education model, I can't argue with—that play is learning and learning is play—

And that education should be fun.

Right, but also...it just suddenly occurs to me to wonder what you think of when you think of doing something for fun.

Are you asking right now? Or are you asking then?

Maybe both? Maybe, is there a connection between now and then.

This is fun. This is fun, spending time with a friend is fun. Having a conversation with a friend, that is fun.

Play, in all of its forms, that is fun. I do not... there is not a lot of opportunity to play these days. That is actually a very difficult question. There are things that I enjoy. Reading, listening to music, meeting people. I enjoy being able to go pretty much wherever I want and see new things, and I enjoy those moments when I can stop and appreciate what is around me.

I am not certain at this point what I do for fun. That is rather sad, isn't it?

(laughs) Wasn't meant to be! I know a lot of busy people, I know a lot of busy women. I go to the gym to take care of myself, but I don't look forward to it. But I know some people who look forward to their run, because that's when they are alone in a good way, right? But you run plenty.

(laughs)

(laughs) I don't know what...I just can't even imagine you going out dancing.

Oh, I would like to do that.

But maybe that's because I don't see the world giving you a lot of time to do it and not feel bad that you're not doing something else.

That is part of it, I think. Also, it would be difficult...obviously, it is...it would be dishonest of me to say that if I go to a club with a friend I will not have an enormous impact on everything that thenhappens at that club. It does not matter what I wear or who I go with, if I am wearing my armor or an Eileen Fisher, it does not become about me dancing, it becomes about who I was dancing with, and what I wore, and what I did with my hair, and so forth.

Celebrity...I've interviewed a lot of celebrities.

Of all stripes.

Yes. It's interesting to me, there aren't a lot of people in your position, where there's celebrity next to a—I wouldn't say a religious mission—but combined spheres of influence, overlapping spheres of significance and weight that you bring with you. Because you showing up at a club...

I recently took a friend shopping. It was by necessity. She desperately needed new clothes. I was with another friend at the time, and the result... somebody saw us enter, and somebody got on Twitter...

Right, right...

...and somebody texted somebody else...

...and now suddenly there's a crowd-control issue outside the store.

Yes. I did not count, there were many people. Now, my friend just needed clothes. And frankly, needed some safety and privacy in which to buy them, and...

I guess it's interesting to me, I've met plenty of people who wouldn't hesitate to just call a store and say, "Can you shut down for two hours?"

Perhaps it would have been wiser to do that...

It just doesn't seem like something you would think about.

No, but perhaps I should have done. There is the ripple effect...I know that once we left, they were asked, that the young lady who helped us was put on camera. What did they buy? What were they doing? And I know that had an effect. I know that they probably ran out of the blue jeans that they sold.

And they weren't even for you.

And they were not even for me. So make of that as you will. I guess that goes back to your earlier point, it is hard to find fun.

An awful lot to think about.

I do not resent it. At least, I do not think I do. But there are days when...if I were honest, there are days when I would like to be able to...not be seen.

I can understand it. They tell me baseball hats and sunglasses work.

Yes, unfortunately I believe that is a known disguise.

(laughs)

I've tried. (laughs) I should go.

Yeah.

As always, it's nice to see you. Take care of yourself.

Always good to see you. And you.

I will try.

Let me know if you need me.

I will.

And she wouldn't let me pay—and the management insisted the drinks and the cookies be comped, and she insisted just as gently that she pay—and she went on her way, and I went back to mine.

And here's the thing. Every conversation we've had, it's always ended with me saying, "Let me know if you need me," and every time I've known that she would reach out if she ever did, however unlikely that might be. Same as I've known she would be there for me if I needed her.

This time, for the first time, I felt she might really need me.

And this time, for the first time, I felt she wouldn't call if she did.

I'm hoping that'll change by the next time she asks to meet me for coffee.

TRANSCRIPTION: Greg Rucka
PHOTOGRAPHY: Liam Sharp
with Romulo Fajardo Jr.
LAYOUT: Lori Jackson

Oh, Themyscira

LIAM SHARP Writer/Artist
ROMULO FAJARDO JR. Colors
JODI WYNNE Letters

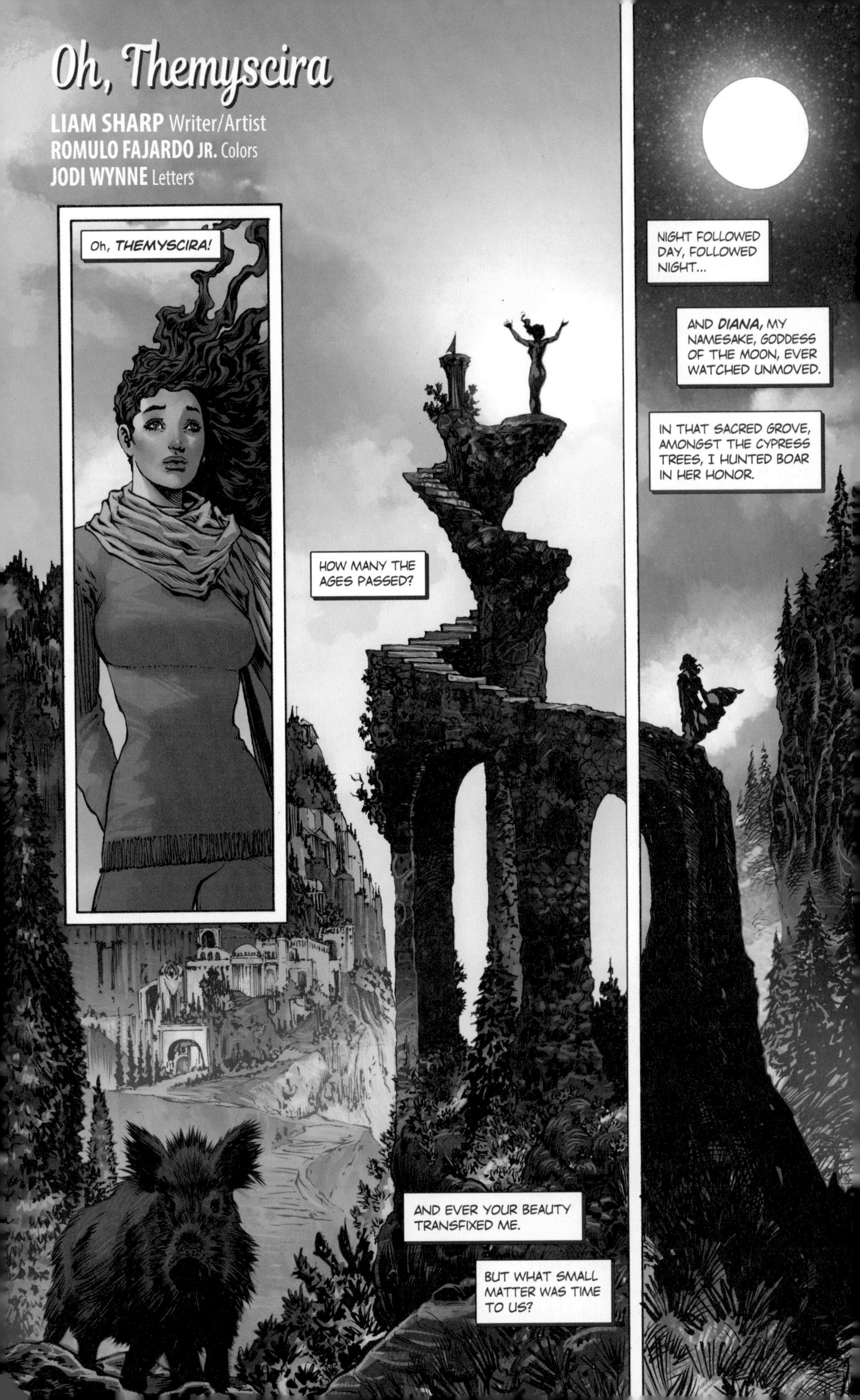
Oh, THEMYSCIRA!
HOW MANY THE AGES PASSED?
AND EVER YOUR BEAUTY TRANSFIXED ME.
BUT WHAT SMALL MATTER WAS TIME TO US?
NIGHT FOLLOWED DAY, FOLLOWED NIGHT...
AND DIANA, MY NAMESAKE, GODDESS OF THE MOON, EVER WATCHED UNMOVED.
IN THAT SACRED GROVE, AMONGST THE CYPRESS TREES, I HUNTED BOAR IN HER HONOR.

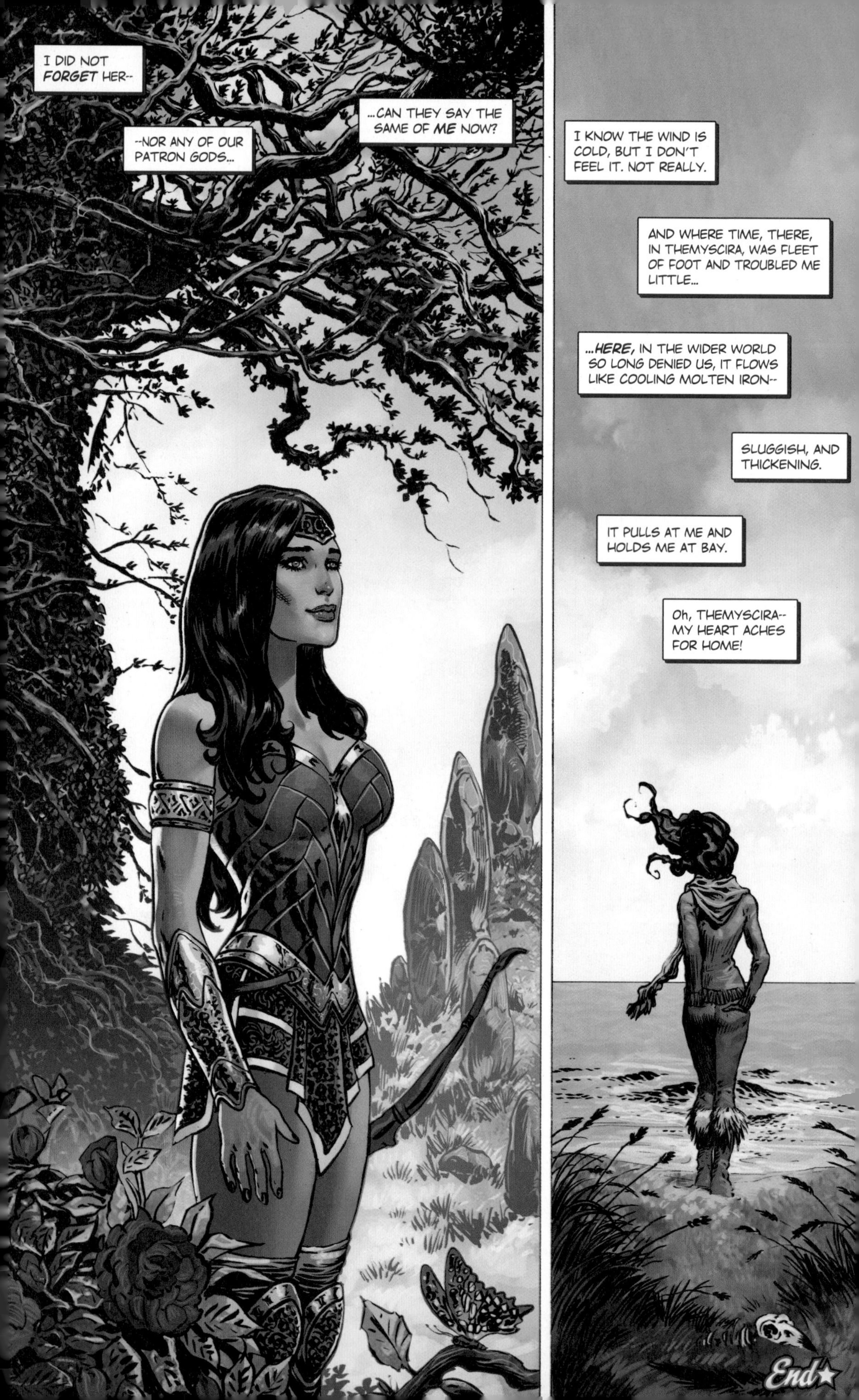
I DID NOT FORGET HER--
--NOR ANY OF OUR PATRON GODS...
...CAN THEY SAY THE SAME OF ME NOW?
I KNOW THE WIND IS COLD, BUT I DON'T FEEL IT. NOT REALLY.
AND WHERE TIME, THERE, IN THEMYSCIRA, WAS FLEET OF FOOT AND TROUBLED ME LITTLE...
...HERE, IN THE WIDER WORLD SO LONG DENIED US, IT FLOWS LIKE COOLING MOLTEN IRON--
SLUGGISH, AND THICKENING.
IT PULLS AT ME AND HOLDS ME AT BAY.
Oh, THEMYSCIRA-- MY HEART ACHES FOR HOME!
End

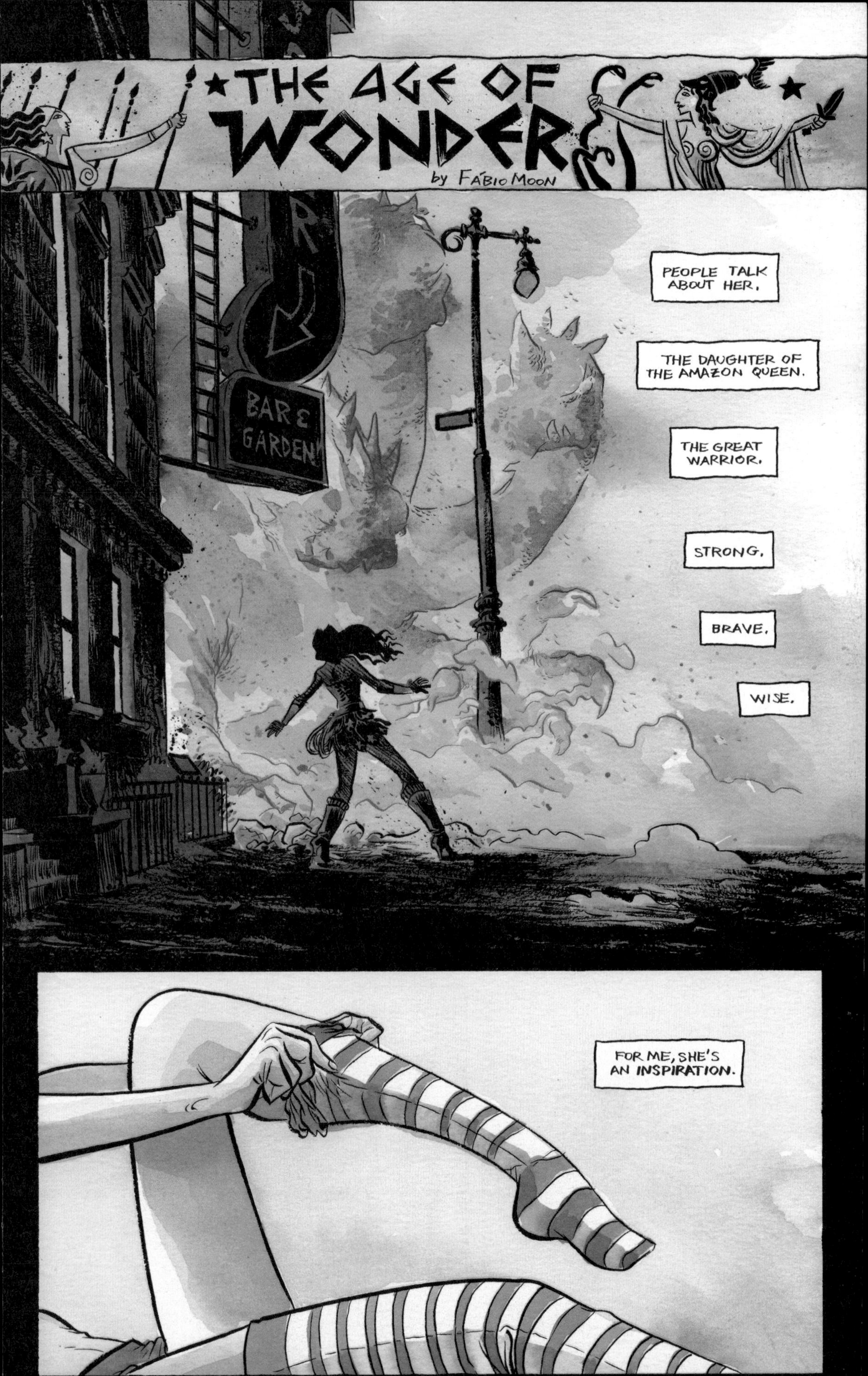

THE AGE OF WONDER
by FÁBIO MOON
BAR & GARDEN
PEOPLE TALK ABOUT HER.
THE DAUGHTER OF THE AMAZON QUEEN.
THE GREAT WARRIOR.
STRONG.
BRAVE.
WISE.
FOR ME, SHE'S AN INSPIRATION.

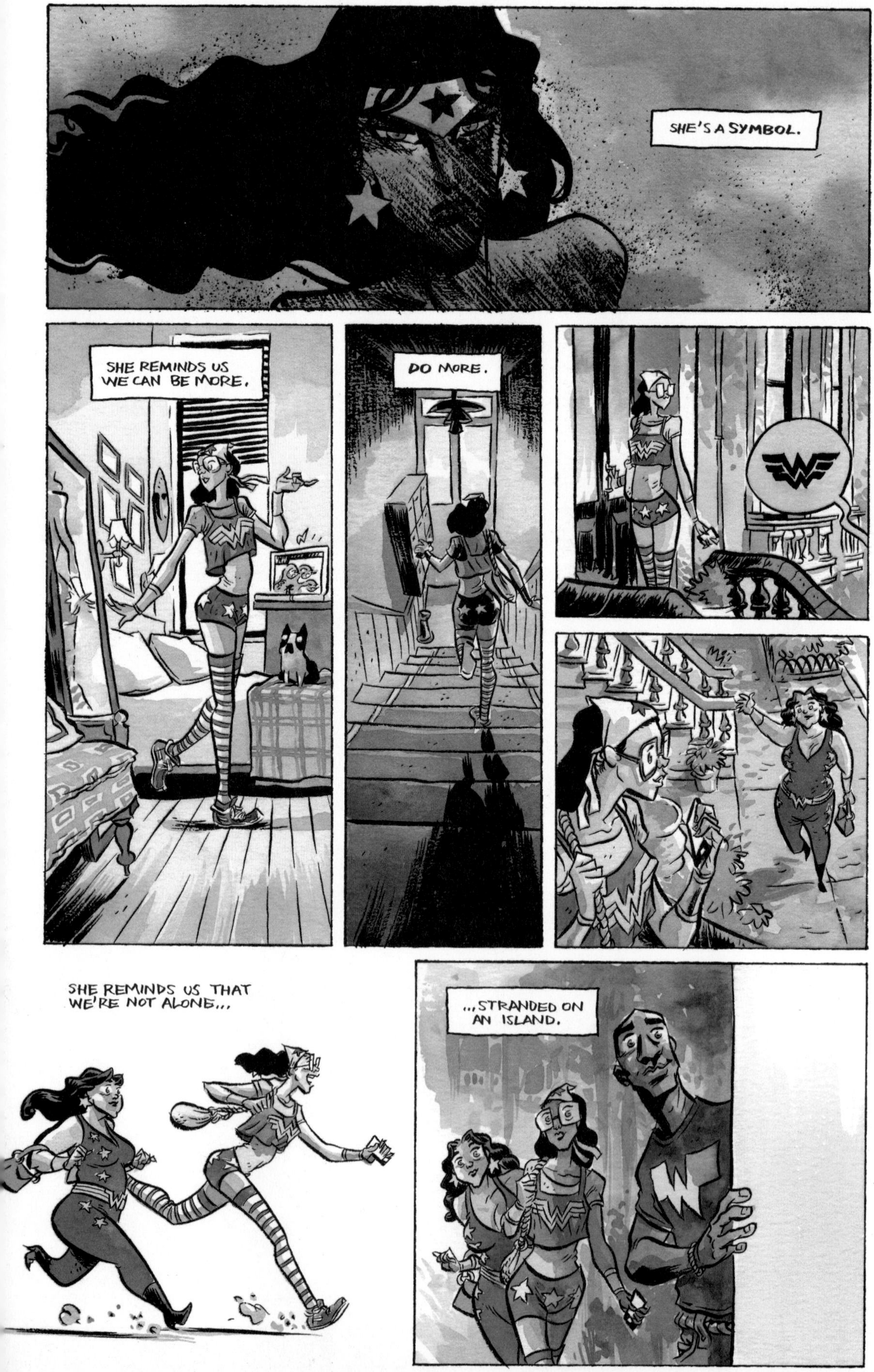
SHE'S A SYMBOL.
SHE REMINDS US WE CAN BE MORE.
DO MORE.
SHE REMINDS US THAT WE'RE NOT ALONE...
...STRANDED ON AN ISLAND.

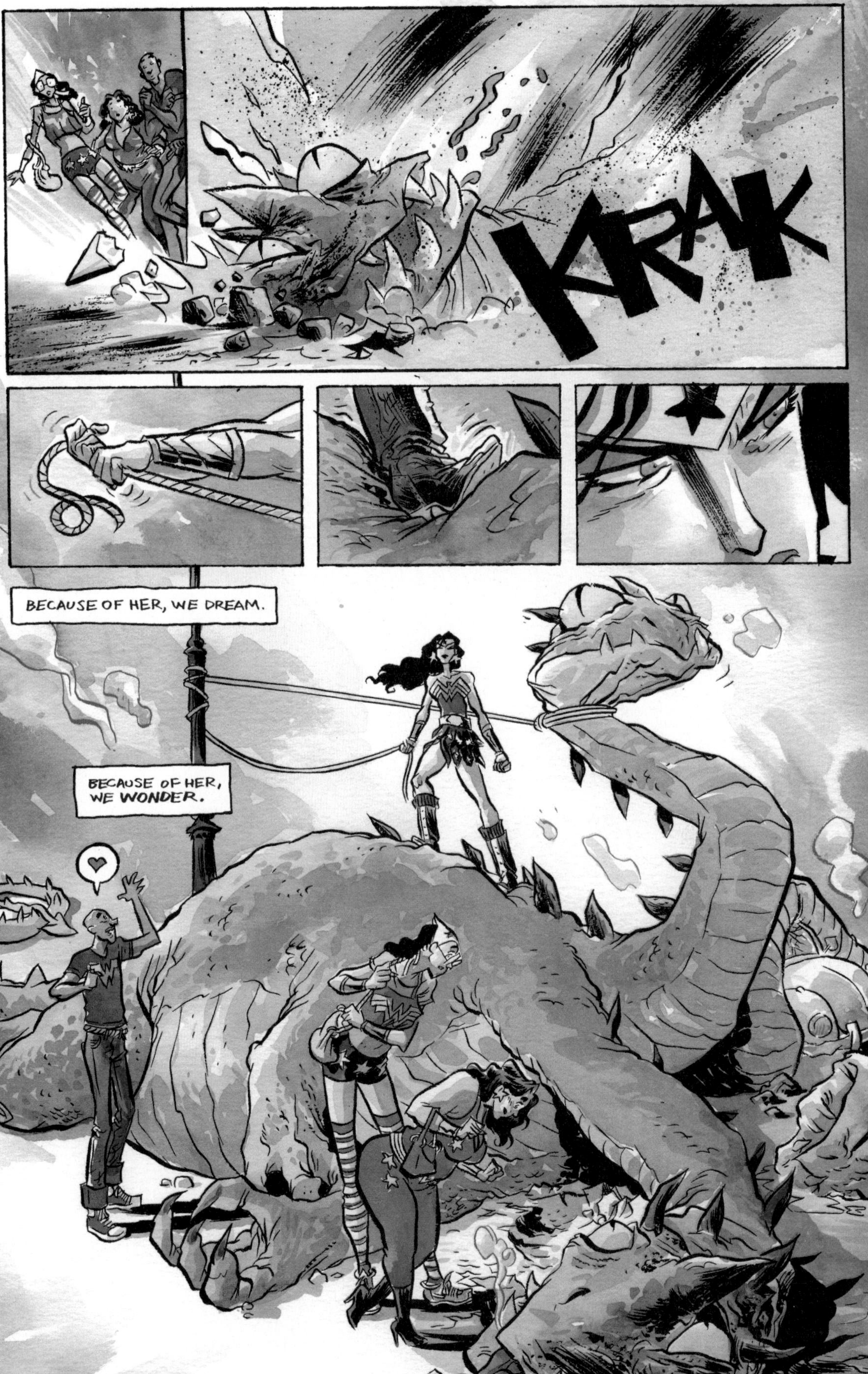
KRAK
BECAUSE OF HER, WE DREAM.
BECAUSE OF HER, WE WONDER.
End

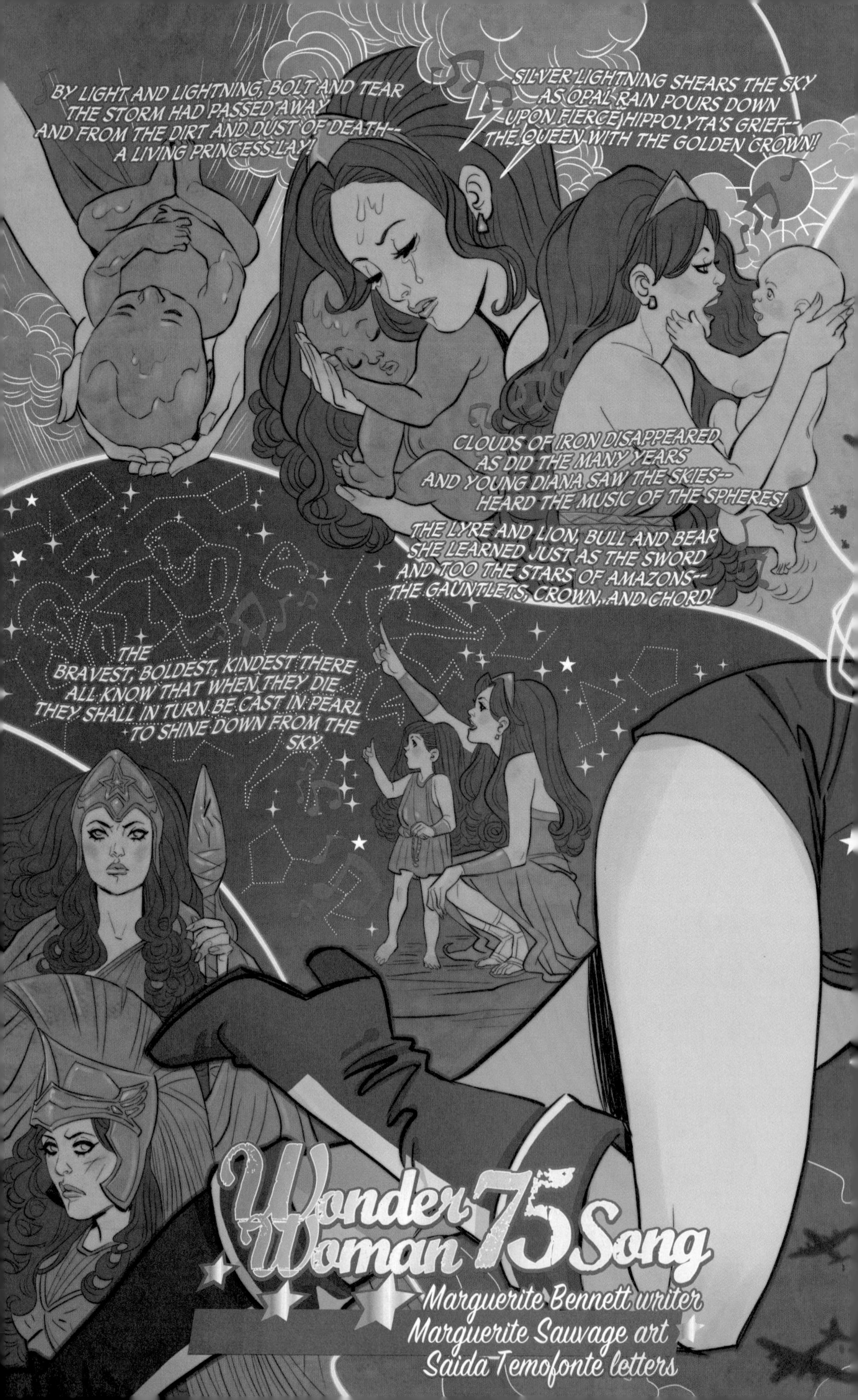
BY LIGHT AND LIGHTNING, BOLT AND TEAR
THE STORM HAD PASSED AWAY
AND FROM THE DIRT AND DUST OF DEATH--
A LIVING PRINCESS LAY!
SILVER LIGHTNING SHEARS THE SKY
AS OPAL RAIN POURS DOWN
UPON FIERCE HIPPOLYTA'S GRIEF--
THE QUEEN WITH THE GOLDEN CROWN!
CLOUDS OF IRON DISAPPEARED
AS DID THE MANY YEARS
AND YOUNG DIANA SAW THE SKIES--
HEARD THE MUSIC OF THE SPHERES!
THE LYRE AND LION, BULL AND BEAR
SHE LEARNED JUST AS THE SWORD
AND TOO THE STARS OF AMAZONS--
THE GAUNTLETS, CROWN, AND CHORD!
THE BRAVEST, BOLDEST, KINDEST THERE
ALL KNOW THAT WHEN THEY DIE
THEY SHALL IN TURN BE CAST IN PEARL
TO SHINE DOWN FROM THE SKY.
Wonder Woman 75 Song
Marguerite Bennett writer
Marguerite Sauvage art
Saida Temofonte letters

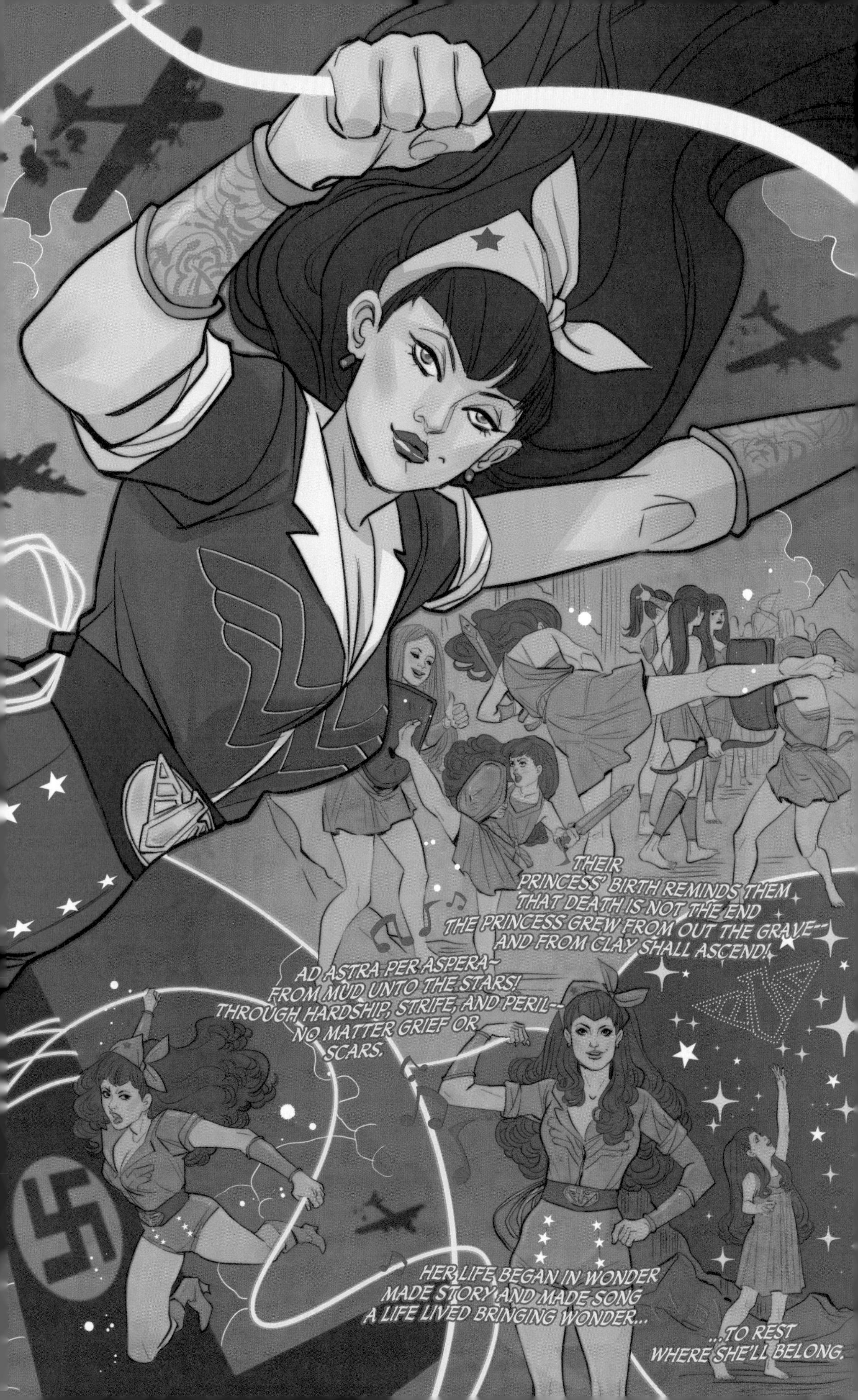
THEIR PRINCESS' BIRTH REMINDS THEM THAT DEATH IS NOT THE END
THE PRINCESS GREW FROM OUT THE GRAVE-- AND FROM CLAY SHALL ASCEND!
AD ASTRA PER ASPERA-- FROM MUD UNTO THE STARS! THROUGH HARDSHIP, STRIFE, AND PERIL-- NO MATTER GRIEF OR SCARS.
HER LIFE BEGAN IN WONDER MADE STORY AND MADE SONG A LIFE LIVED BRINGING WONDER...
...TO REST WHERE SHE'LL BELONG.

ART BY YANICK PAQUETTE & NATHAN FAIRBAIRN

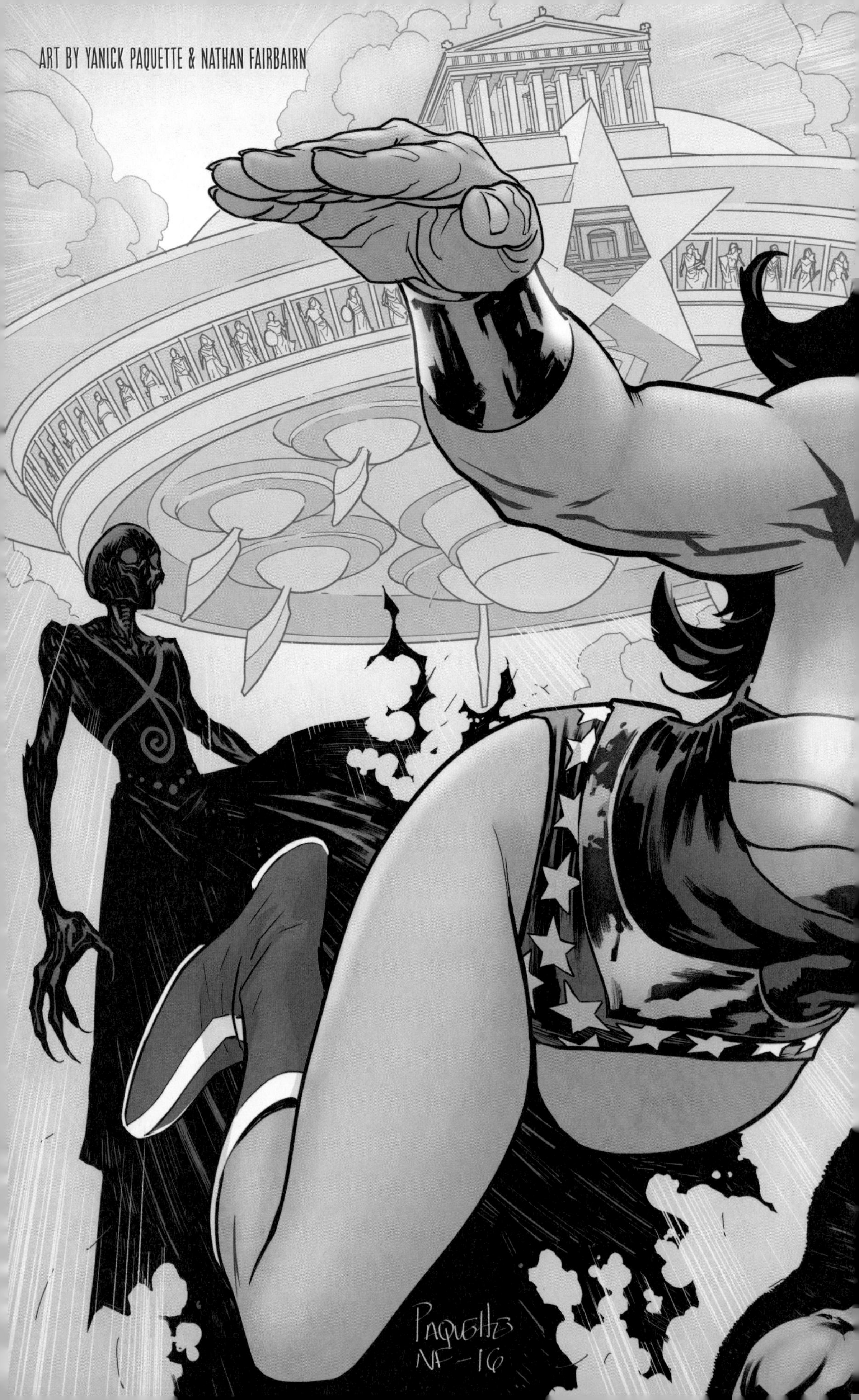

PAQUETTE
NF-16

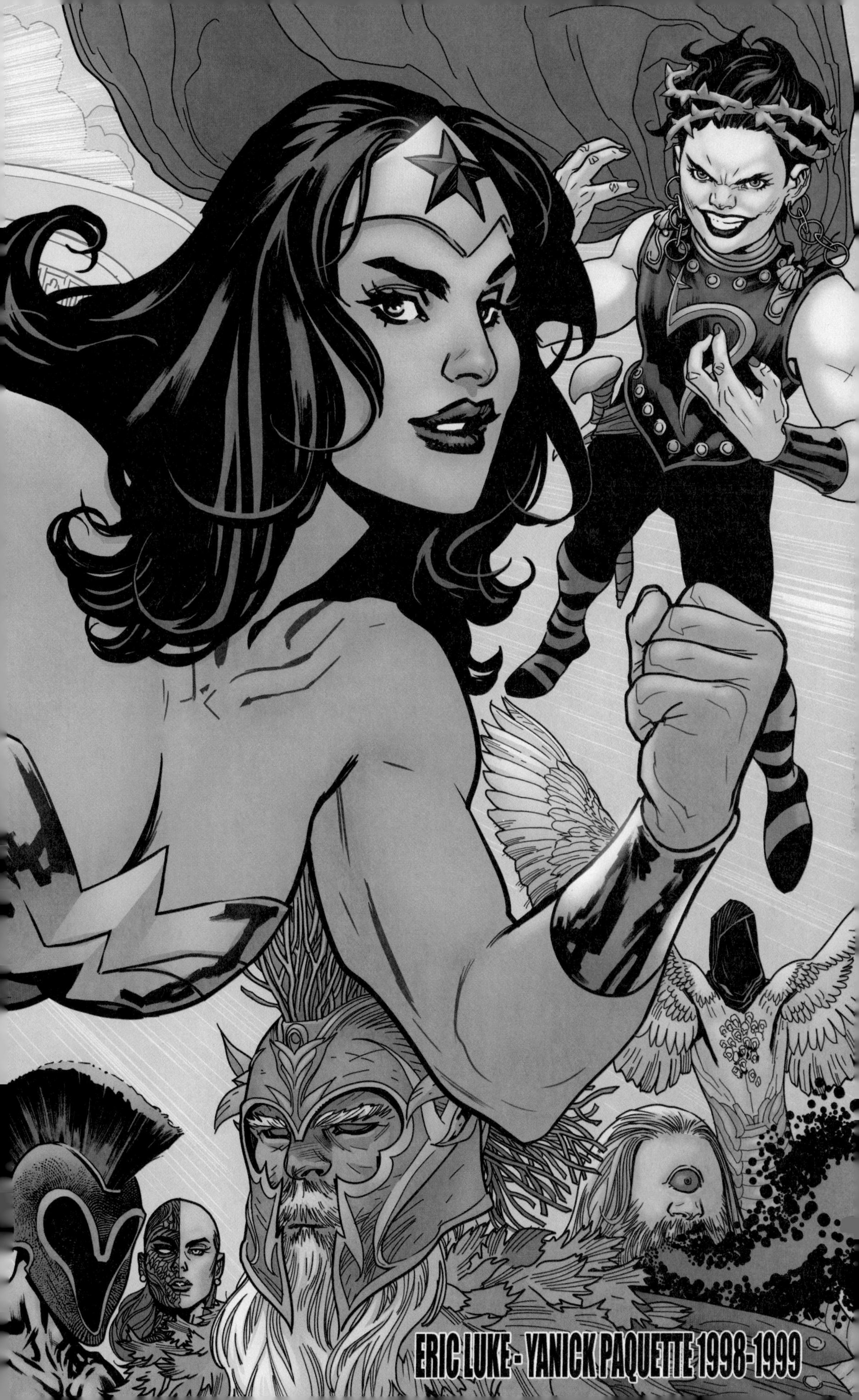
ERIC LUKE - YANICK PAQUETTE 1998-1999

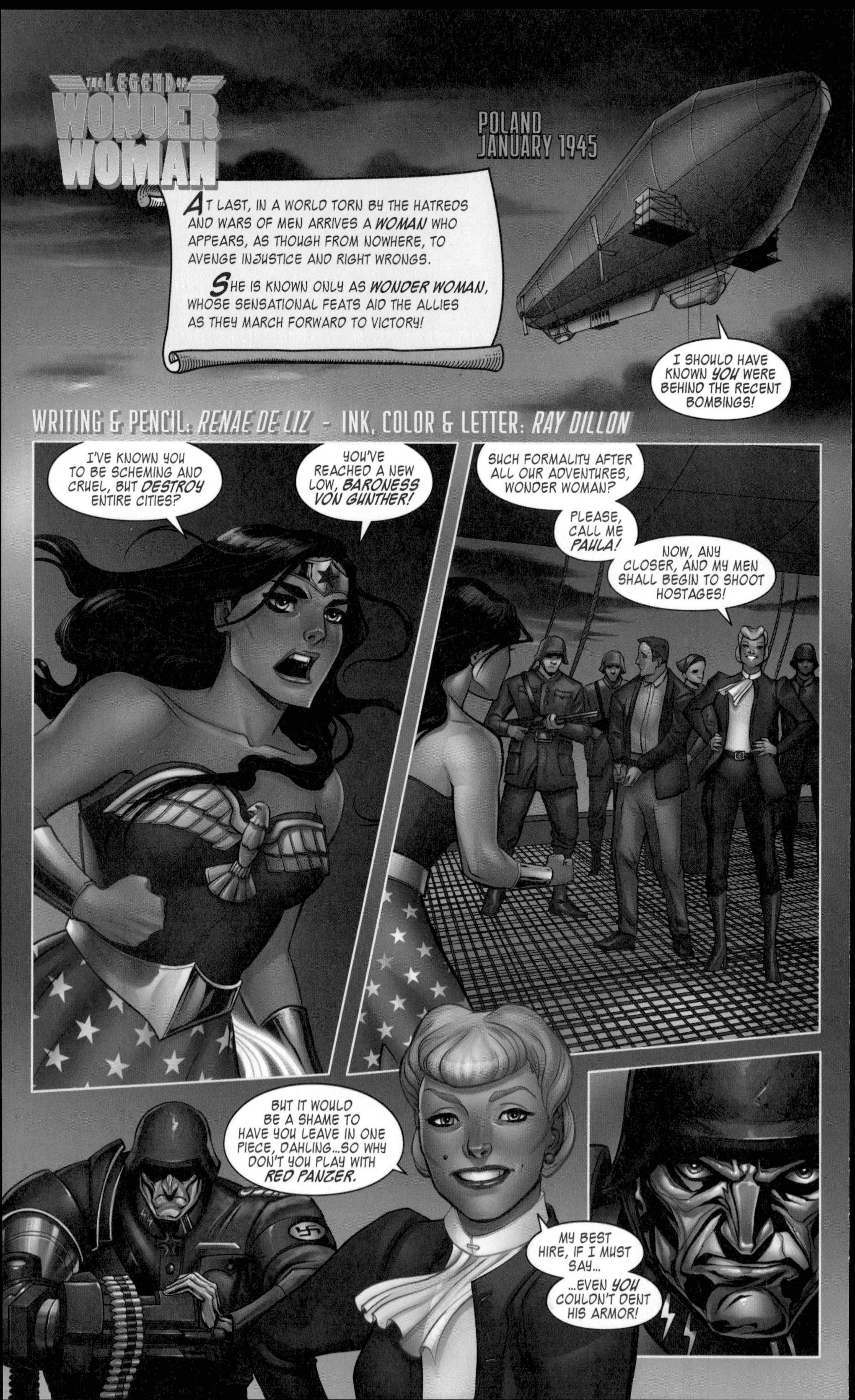
THE LEGEND OF WONDER WOMAN
POLAND JANUARY 1945
AT LAST, IN A WORLD TORN BY THE HATREDS AND WARS OF MEN ARRIVES A WOMAN WHO APPEARS, AS THOUGH FROM NOWHERE, TO AVENGE INJUSTICE AND RIGHT WRONGS.
SHE IS KNOWN ONLY AS WONDER WOMAN, WHOSE SENSATIONAL FEATS AID THE ALLIES AS THEY MARCH FORWARD TO VICTORY!
I SHOULD HAVE KNOWN YOU WERE BEHIND THE RECENT BOMBINGS!
WRITING & PENCIL: RENAE DE LIZ - INK, COLOR & LETTER: RAY DILLON
I'VE KNOWN YOU TO BE SCHEMING AND CRUEL, BUT DESTROY ENTIRE CITIES?
YOU'VE REACHED A NEW LOW, BARONESS VON GUNTHER!
SUCH FORMALITY AFTER ALL OUR ADVENTURES, WONDER WOMAN?
PLEASE, CALL ME PAULA!
NOW, ANY CLOSER, AND MY MEN SHALL BEGIN TO SHOOT HOSTAGES!
BUT IT WOULD BE A SHAME TO HAVE YOU LEAVE IN ONE PIECE, DAHLING...SO WHY DON'T YOU PLAY WITH RED PANZER.
MY BEST HIRE, IF I MUST SAY...
...EVEN YOU COULDN'T DENT HIS ARMOR!

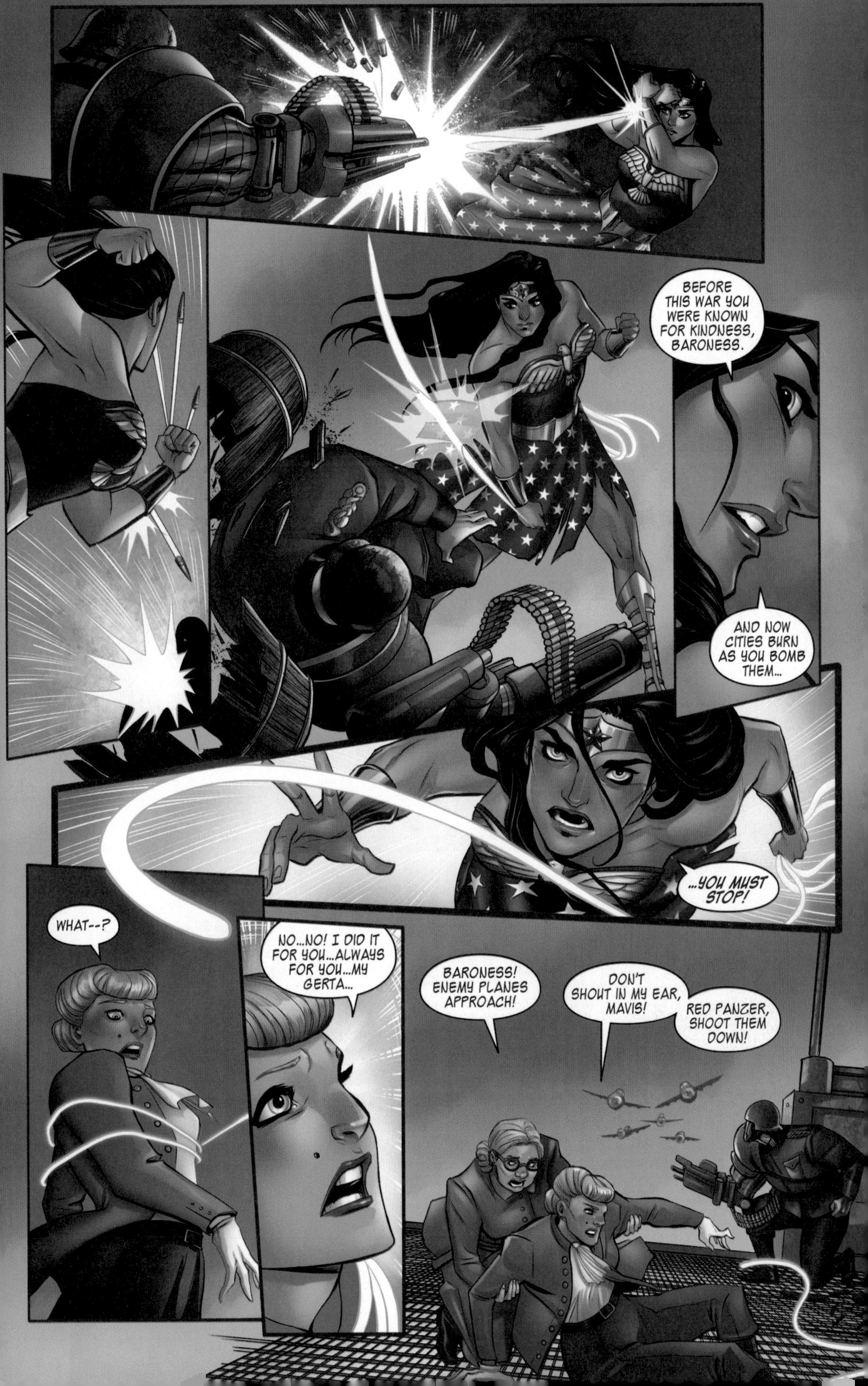
BEFORE THIS WAR YOU WERE KNOWN FOR KINDNESS, BARONESS.
AND NOW CITIES BURN AS YOU BOMB THEM...
...YOU MUST STOP!
WHAT--?
NO...NO! I DID IT FOR YOU...ALWAYS FOR YOU...MY GERTA...
BARONESS! ENEMY PLANES APPROACH!
DON'T SHOUT IN MY EAR, MAVIS!
RED PANZER, SHOOT THEM DOWN!

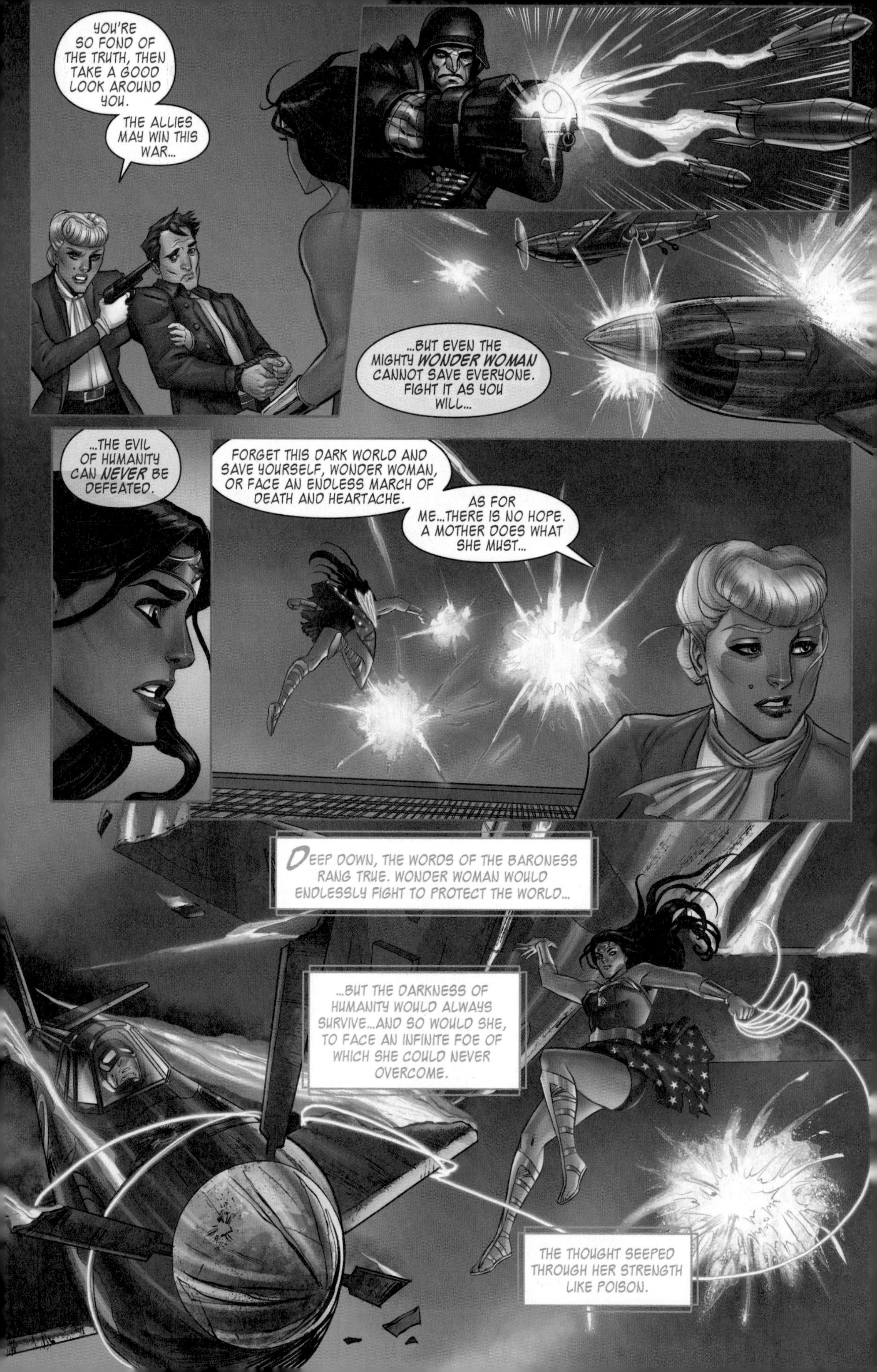
YOU'RE SO FOND OF THE TRUTH, THEN TAKE A GOOD LOOK AROUND YOU.
THE ALLIES MAY WIN THIS WAR...
...BUT EVEN THE MIGHTY WONDER WOMAN CANNOT SAVE EVERYONE. FIGHT IT AS YOU WILL...
...THE EVIL OF HUMANITY CAN NEVER BE DEFEATED.
FORGET THIS DARK WORLD AND SAVE YOURSELF, WONDER WOMAN, OR FACE AN ENDLESS MARCH OF DEATH AND HEARTACHE.
AS FOR ME...THERE IS NO HOPE. A MOTHER DOES WHAT SHE MUST...
DEEP DOWN, THE WORDS OF THE BARONESS RANG TRUE. WONDER WOMAN WOULD ENDLESSLY FIGHT TO PROTECT THE WORLD...
...BUT THE DARKNESS OF HUMANITY WOULD ALWAYS SURVIVE...AND SO WOULD SHE, TO FACE AN INFINITE FOE OF WHICH SHE COULD NEVER OVERCOME.
THE THOUGHT SEEPED THROUGH HER STRENGTH LIKE POISON.

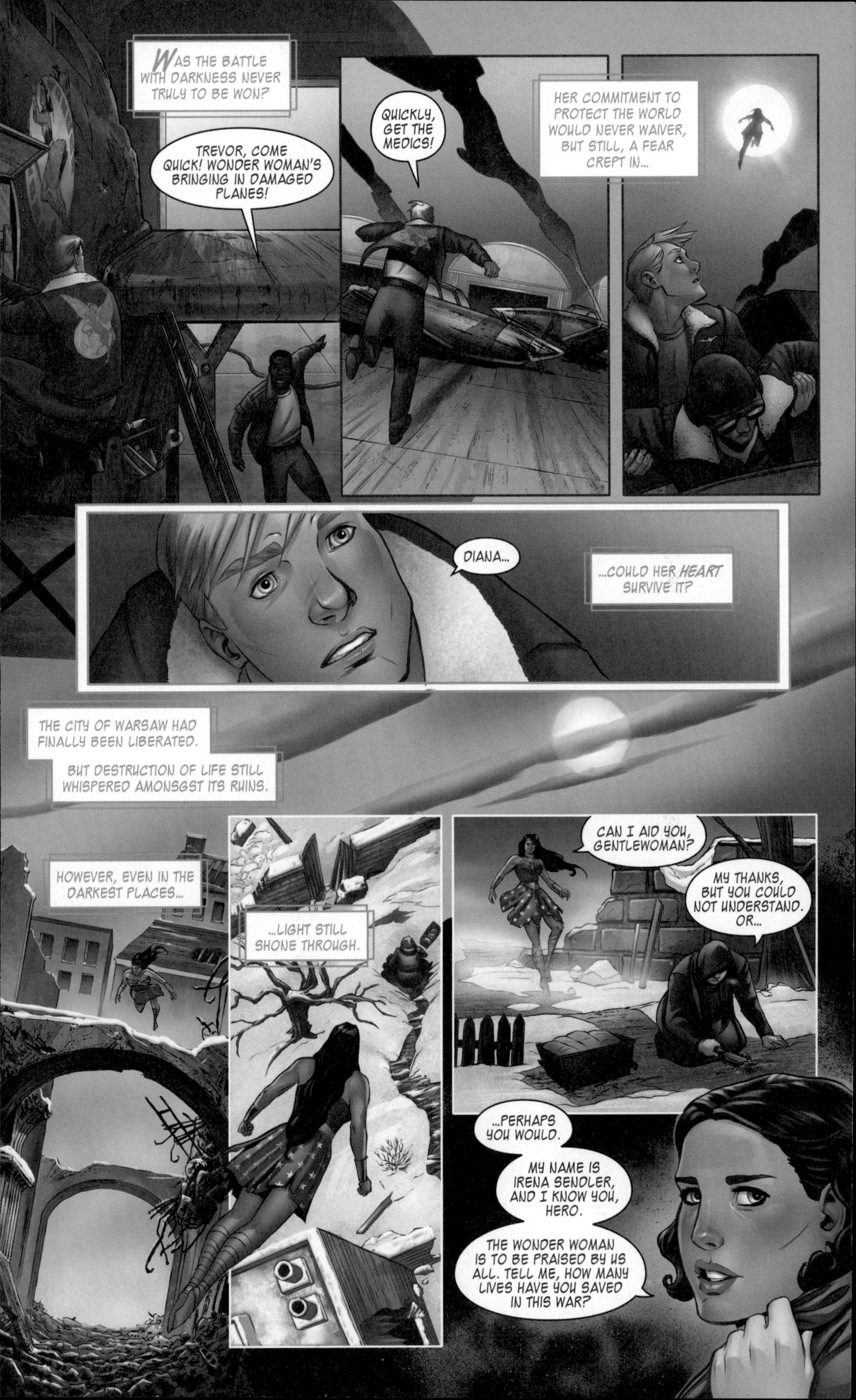

WAS THE BATTLE WITH DARKNESS NEVER TRULY TO BE WON?
TREVOR, COME QUICK! WONDER WOMAN'S BRINGING IN DAMAGED PLANES!
QUICKLY, GET THE MEDICS!
HER COMMITMENT TO PROTECT THE WORLD WOULD NEVER WAIVER, BUT STILL, A FEAR CREPT IN...
DIANA...
...COULD HER HEART SURVIVE IT?
THE CITY OF WARSAW HAD FINALLY BEEN LIBERATED.
BUT DESTRUCTION OF LIFE STILL WHISPERED AMONSGST ITS RUINS.
HOWEVER, EVEN IN THE DARKEST PLACES...
...LIGHT STILL SHONE THROUGH.
CAN I AID YOU, GENTLEWOMAN?
MY THANKS, BUT YOU COULD NOT UNDERSTAND. OR...
...PERHAPS YOU WOULD.
MY NAME IS IRENA SENDLER, AND I KNOW YOU, HERO.
THE WONDER WOMAN IS TO BE PRAISED BY US ALL. TELL ME, HOW MANY LIVES HAVE YOU SAVED IN THIS WAR?

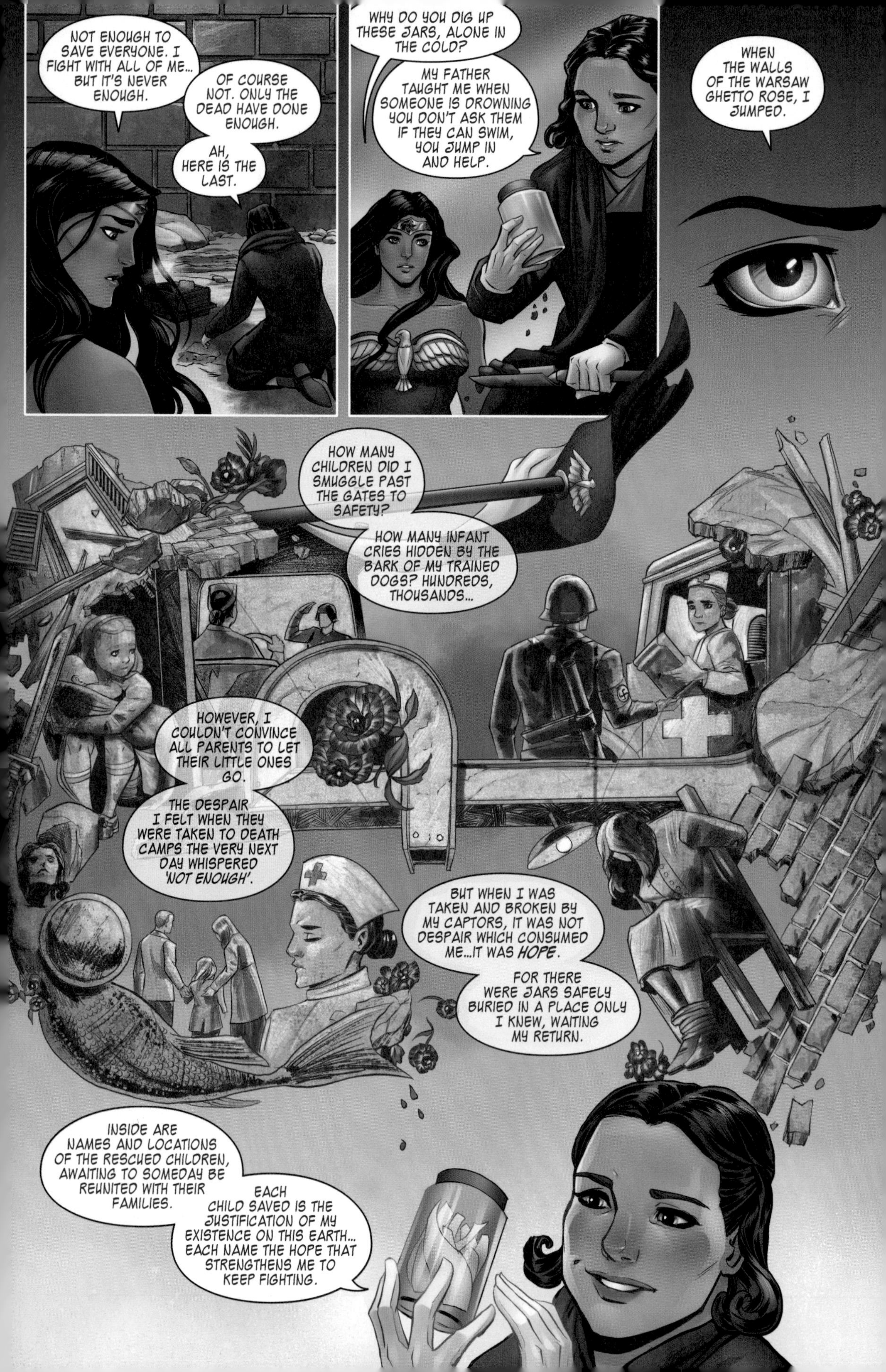

NOT ENOUGH TO SAVE EVERYONE. I FIGHT WITH ALL OF ME... BUT IT'S NEVER ENOUGH.
OF COURSE NOT. ONLY THE DEAD HAVE DONE ENOUGH.
AH, HERE IS THE LAST.
WHY DO YOU DIG UP THESE JARS, ALONE IN THE COLD?
MY FATHER TAUGHT ME WHEN SOMEONE IS DROWNING YOU DON'T ASK THEM IF THEY CAN SWIM, YOU JUMP IN AND HELP.
WHEN THE WALLS OF THE WARSAW GHETTO ROSE, I JUMPED.
HOW MANY CHILDREN DID I SMUGGLE PAST THE GATES TO SAFETY?
HOW MANY INFANT CRIES HIDDEN BY THE BARK OF MY TRAINED DOGS? HUNDREDS, THOUSANDS...
HOWEVER, I COULDN'T CONVINCE ALL PARENTS TO LET THEIR LITTLE ONES GO.
THE DESPAIR I FELT WHEN THEY WERE TAKEN TO DEATH CAMPS THE VERY NEXT DAY WHISPERED 'NOT ENOUGH'.
BUT WHEN I WAS TAKEN AND BROKEN BY MY CAPTORS, IT WAS NOT DESPAIR WHICH CONSUMED ME...IT WAS HOPE.
FOR THERE WERE JARS SAFELY BURIED IN A PLACE ONLY I KNEW, WAITING MY RETURN.
INSIDE ARE NAMES AND LOCATIONS OF THE RESCUED CHILDREN, AWAITING TO SOMEDAY BE REUNITED WITH THEIR FAMILIES.
EACH CHILD SAVED IS THE JUSTIFICATION OF MY EXISTENCE ON THIS EARTH... EACH NAME THE HOPE THAT STRENGTHENS ME TO KEEP FIGHTING.

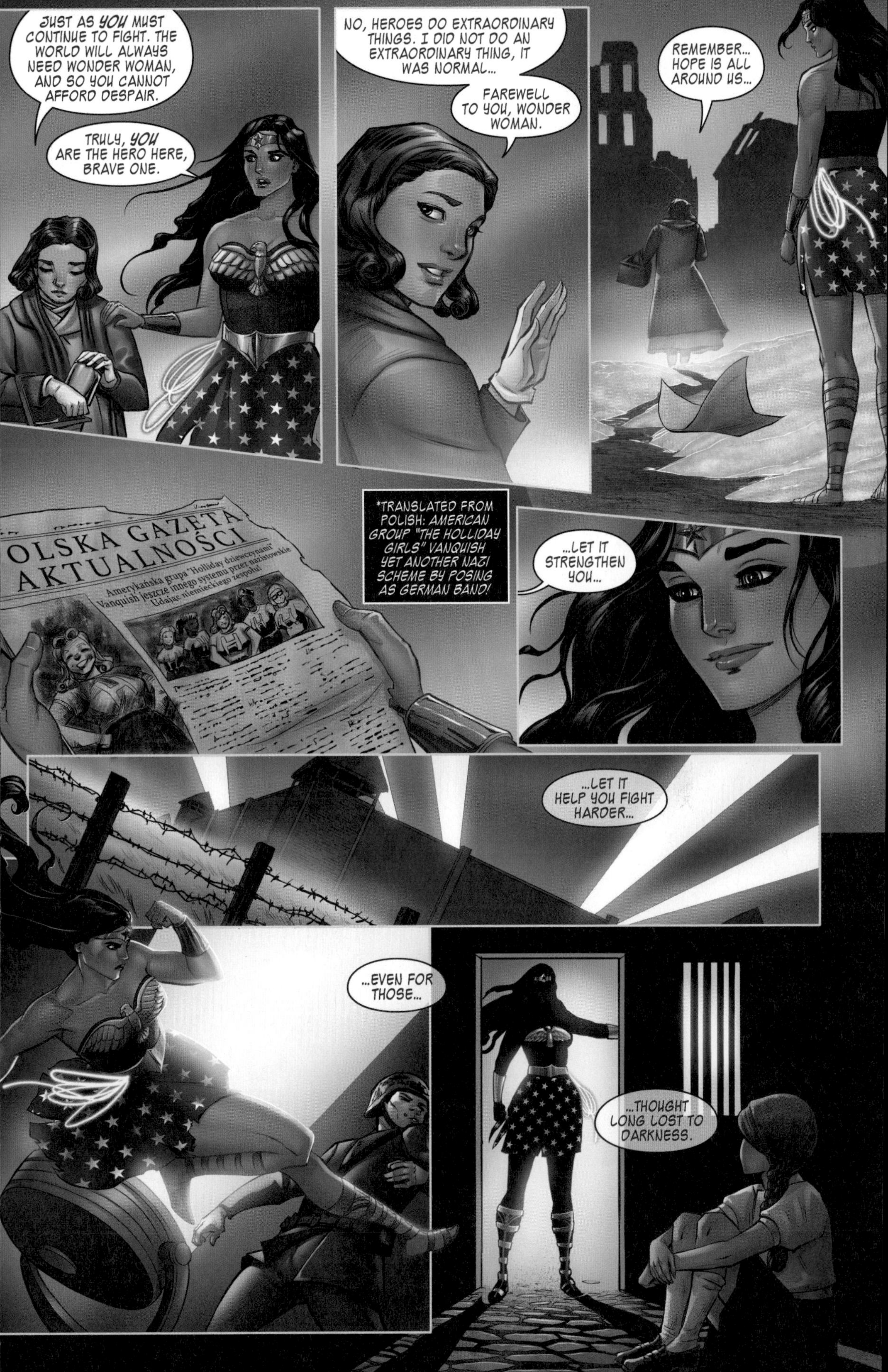
JUST AS YOU MUST CONTINUE TO FIGHT. THE WORLD WILL ALWAYS NEED WONDER WOMAN, AND SO YOU CANNOT AFFORD DESPAIR.
TRULY, YOU ARE THE HERO HERE, BRAVE ONE.
NO, HEROES DO EXTRAORDINARY THINGS. I DID NOT DO AN EXTRAORDINARY THING, IT WAS NORMAL...
FAREWELL TO YOU, WONDER WOMAN.
REMEMBER... HOPE IS ALL AROUND US...
OLSKA GAZETA AKTUALNOŚCI
Amerykańska grupa "Holliday dziewczynami" Vanquish jeszcze innego systemu przez nazistowskie Udając niemieckiego zespołu!
*TRANSLATED FROM POLISH: AMERICAN GROUP "THE HOLLIDAY GIRLS" VANQUISH YET ANOTHER NAZI SCHEME BY POSING AS GERMAN BAND!
...LET IT STRENGTHEN YOU...
...LET IT HELP YOU FIGHT HARDER...
...EVEN FOR THOSE...
...THOUGHT LONG LOST TO DARKNESS.

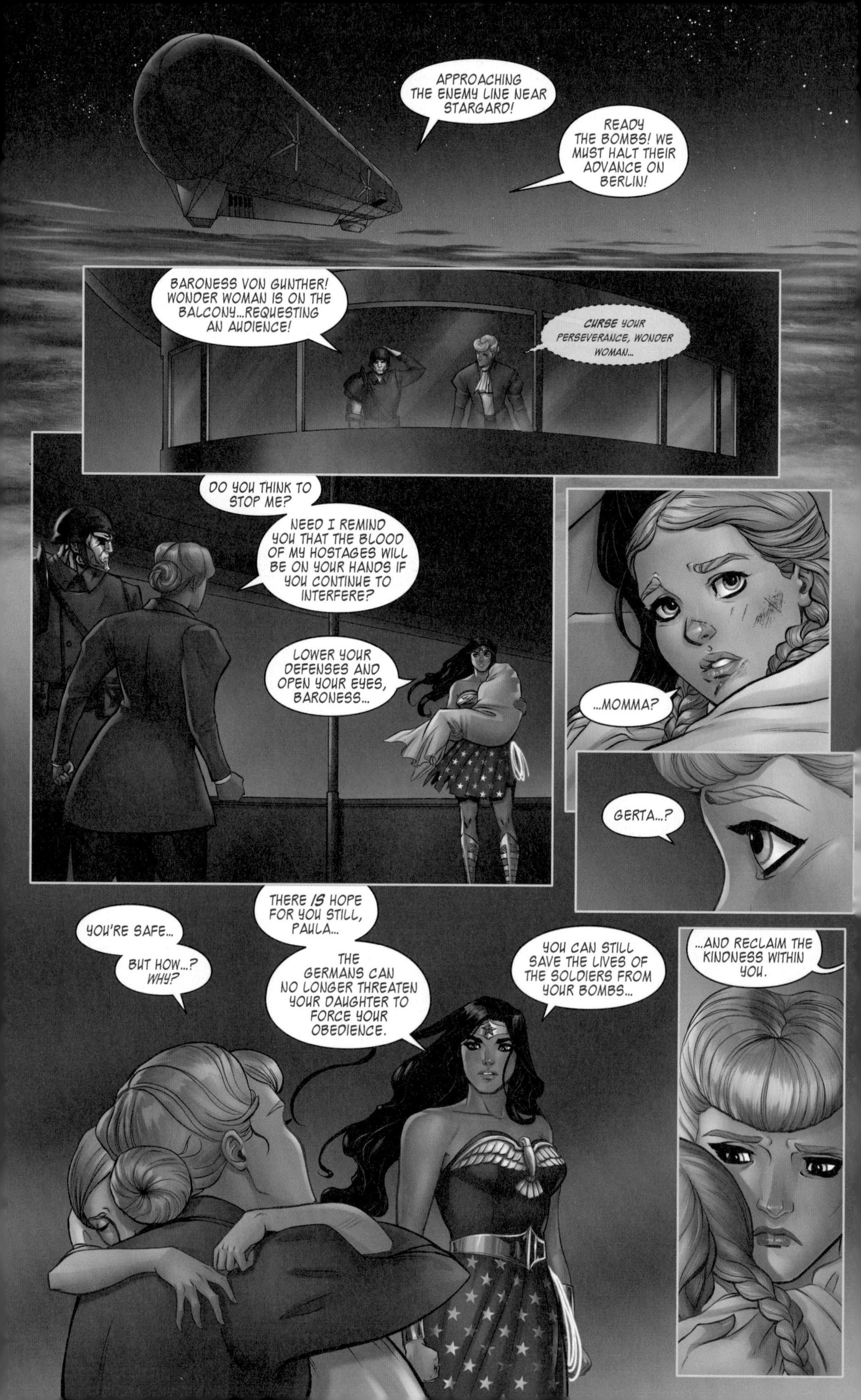

APPROACHING THE ENEMY LINE NEAR STARGARD!
READY THE BOMBS! WE MUST HALT THEIR ADVANCE ON BERLIN!
BARONESS VON GUNTHER! WONDER WOMAN IS ON THE BALCONY...REQUESTING AN AUDIENCE!
CURSE YOUR PERSEVERANCE, WONDER WOMAN...
DO YOU THINK TO STOP ME?
NEED I REMIND YOU THAT THE BLOOD OF MY HOSTAGES WILL BE ON YOUR HANDS IF YOU CONTINUE TO INTERFERE?
LOWER YOUR DEFENSES AND OPEN YOUR EYES, BARONESS...
...MOMMA?
GERTA...?
YOU'RE SAFE...
BUT HOW...? WHY?
THERE IS HOPE FOR YOU STILL, PAULA...
THE GERMANS CAN NO LONGER THREATEN YOUR DAUGHTER TO FORCE YOUR OBEDIENCE.
YOU CAN STILL SAVE THE LIVES OF THE SOLDIERS FROM YOUR BOMBS...
...AND RECLAIM THE KINDNESS WITHIN YOU.

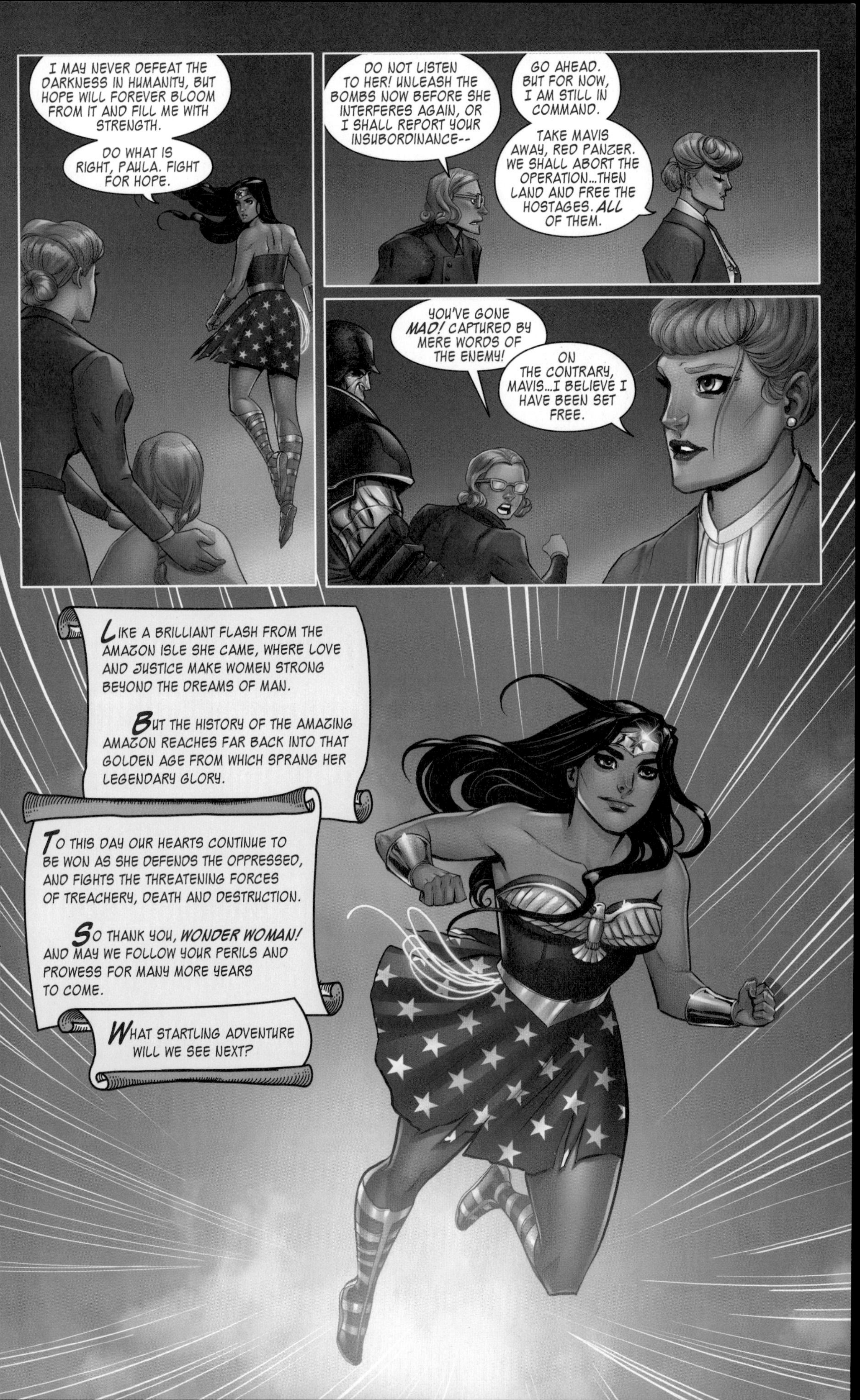
I MAY NEVER DEFEAT THE DARKNESS IN HUMANITY, BUT HOPE WILL FOREVER BLOOM FROM IT AND FILL ME WITH STRENGTH.
DO WHAT IS RIGHT, PAULA. FIGHT FOR HOPE.
DO NOT LISTEN TO HER! UNLEASH THE BOMBS NOW BEFORE SHE INTERFERES AGAIN, OR I SHALL REPORT YOUR INSUBORDINANCE--
GO AHEAD. BUT FOR NOW, I AM STILL IN COMMAND.
TAKE MAVIS AWAY, RED PANZER. WE SHALL ABORT THE OPERATION...THEN LAND AND FREE THE HOSTAGES. ALL OF THEM.
YOU'VE GONE MAD! CAPTURED BY MERE WORDS OF THE ENEMY!
ON THE CONTRARY, MAVIS...I BELIEVE I HAVE BEEN SET FREE.
LIKE A BRILLIANT FLASH FROM THE AMAZON ISLE SHE CAME, WHERE LOVE AND JUSTICE MAKE WOMEN STRONG BEYOND THE DREAMS OF MAN.
BUT THE HISTORY OF THE AMAZING AMAZON REACHES FAR BACK INTO THAT GOLDEN AGE FROM WHICH SPRANG HER LEGENDARY GLORY.
TO THIS DAY OUR HEARTS CONTINUE TO BE WON AS SHE DEFENDS THE OPPRESSED, AND FIGHTS THE THREATENING FORCES OF TREACHERY, DEATH AND DESTRUCTION.
SO THANK YOU, WONDER WOMAN! AND MAY WE FOLLOW YOUR PERILS AND PROWESS FOR MANY MORE YEARS TO COME.
WHAT STARTLING ADVENTURE WILL WE SEE NEXT?

ART BY SEBASTIAN FIUMARA & NATHAN FAIRBAIRN

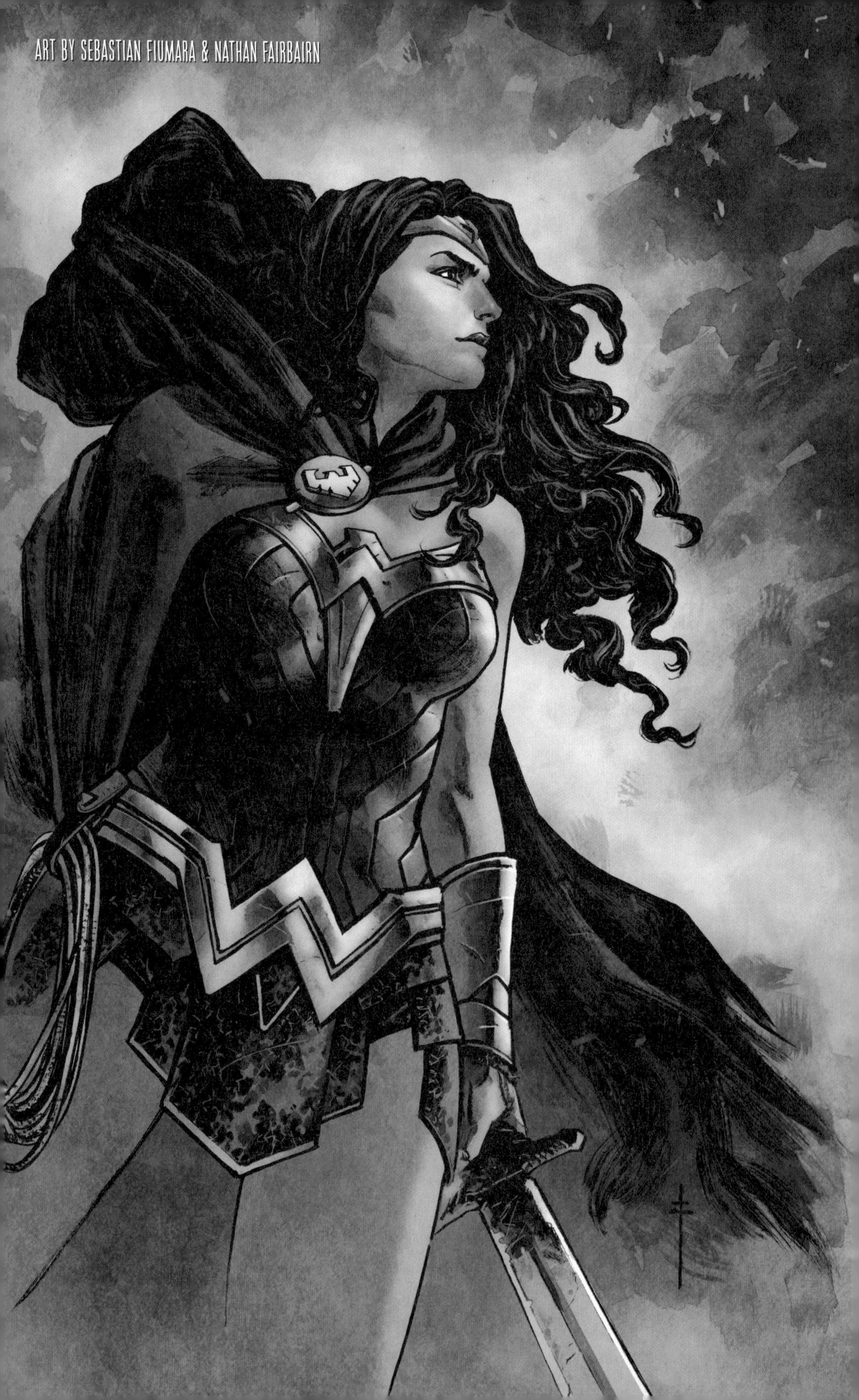

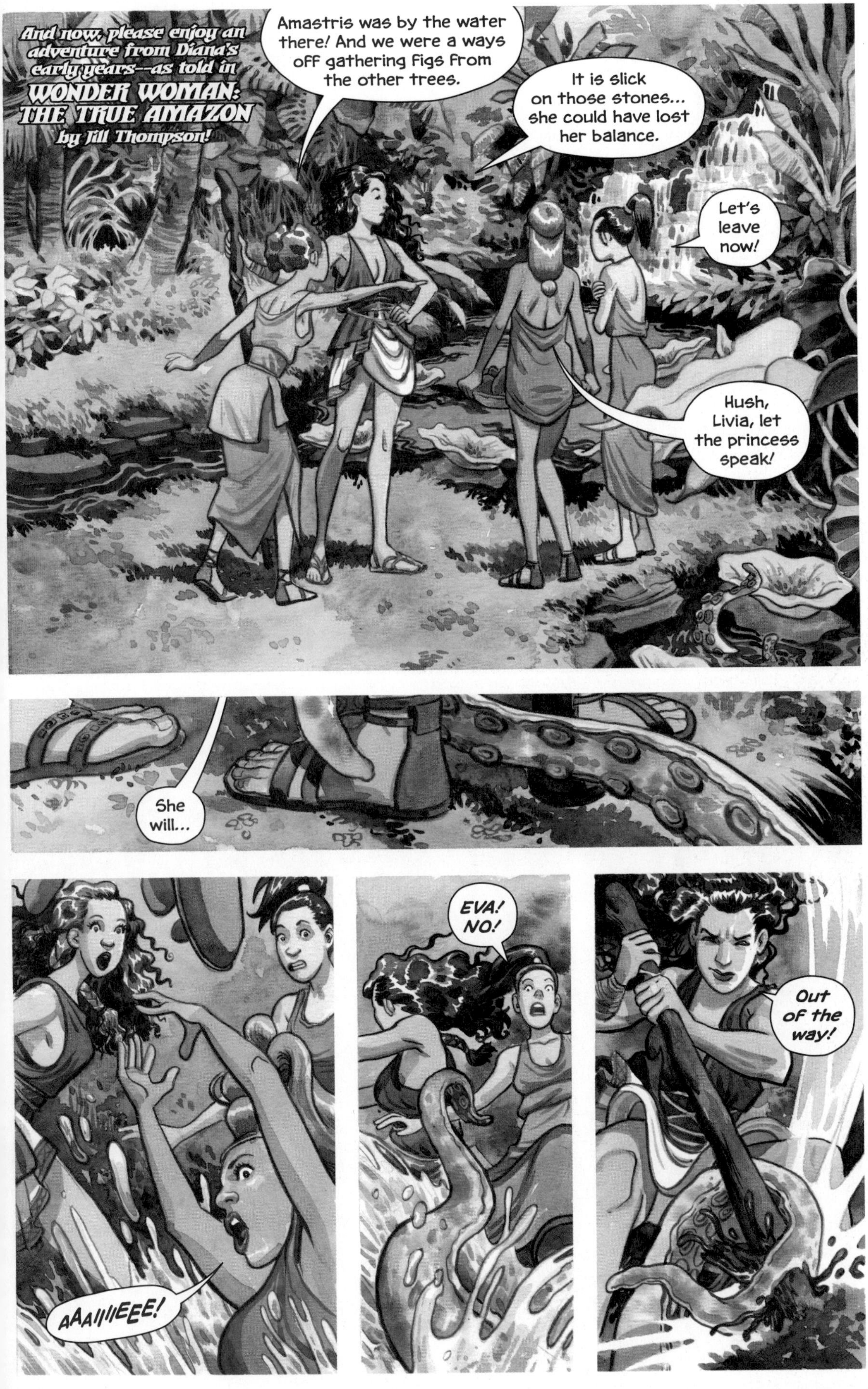
And now, please enjoy an adventure from Diana's early years--as told in
WONDER WOMAN: THE TRUE AMAZON
by Jill Thompson!
Amastris was by the water there! And we were a ways off gathering figs from the other trees.
It is slick on those stones... she could have lost her balance.
Let's leave now!
Hush, Livia, let the princess speak!
She will...
AAAIIIIEEE!
EVA! NO!
Out of the way!

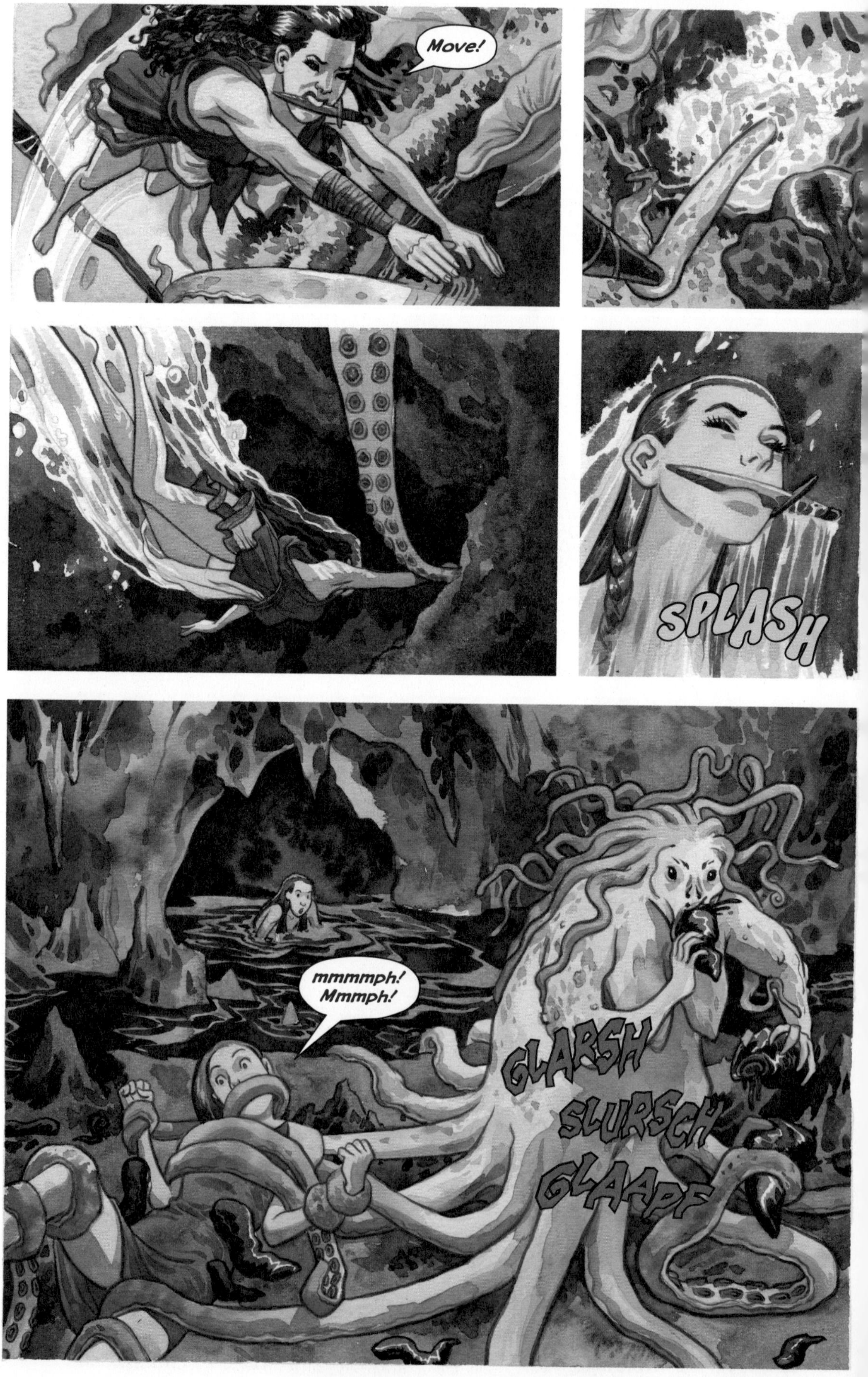
Move!
SPLASH
mmmmph! Mmmph!
GLARSH
SLURSCH
GLAAPF

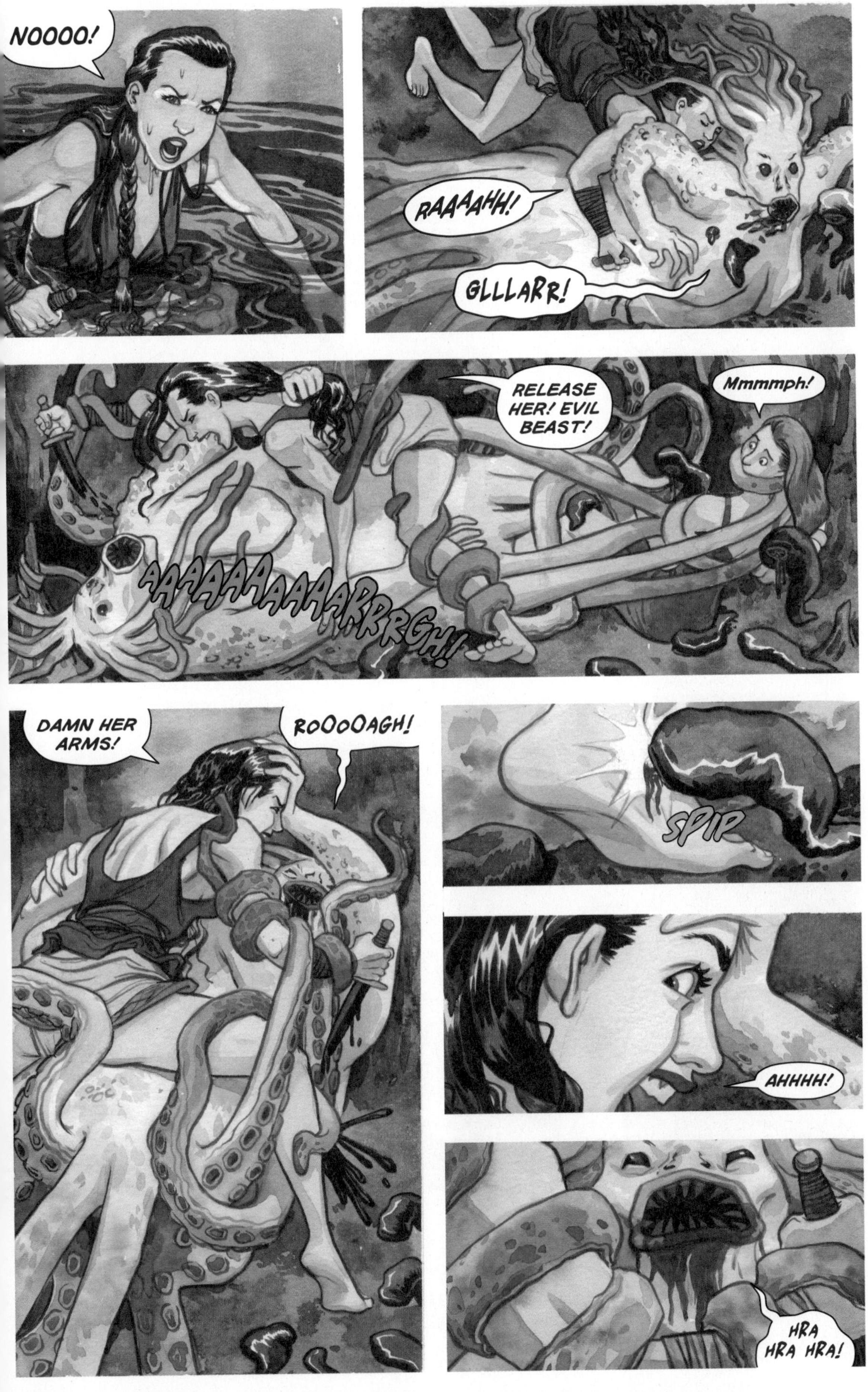
NOOOO!
RAAAAHH!
GLLLARR!
RELEASE HER! EVIL BEAST!
Mmmmph!
AAAAAAAAAAAARRRGH!
DAMN HER ARMS!
ROOOOAGH!
SPIP
AHHHH!
HRA HRA HRA!

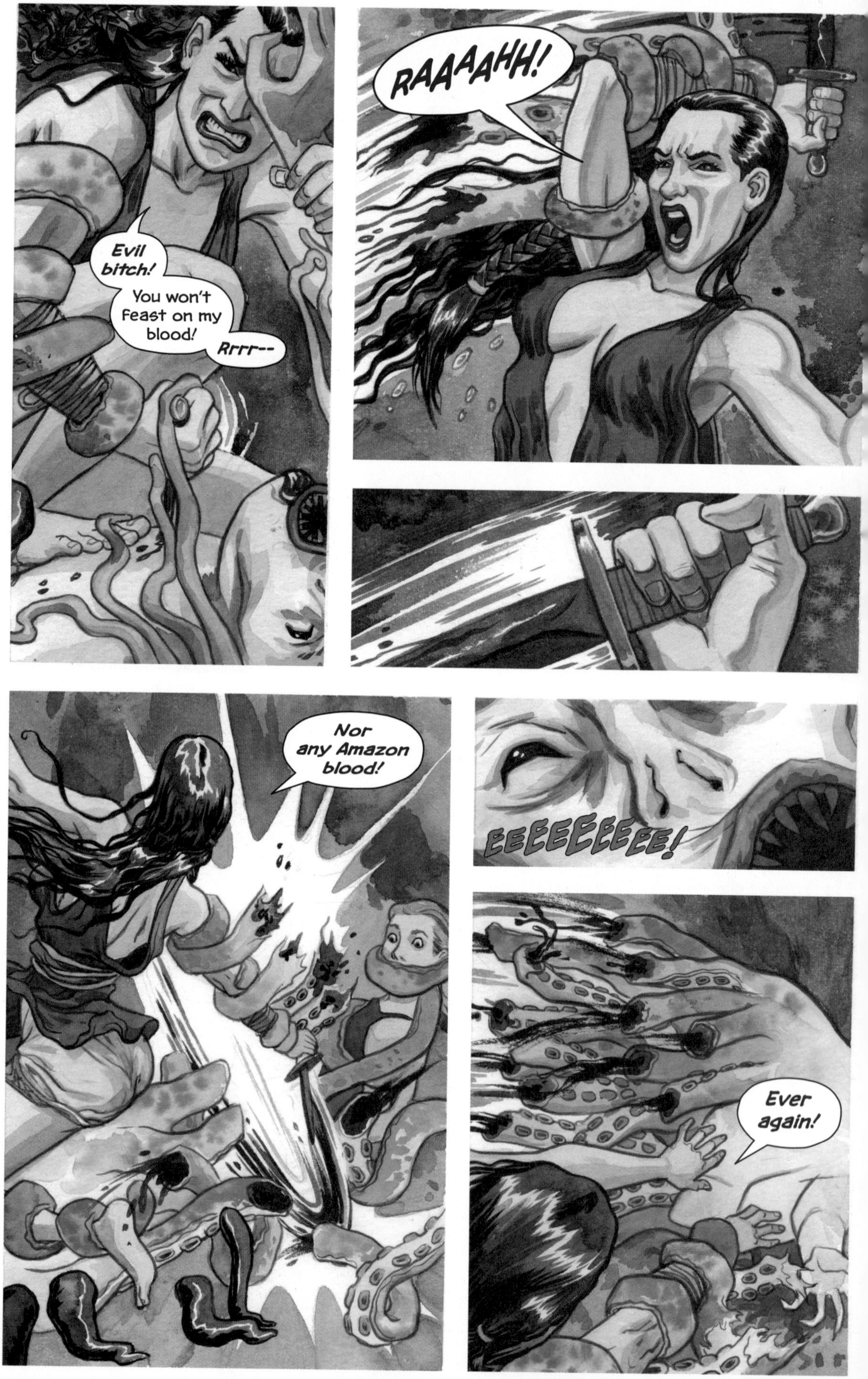
Evil bitch!
You won't feast on my blood!
Rrrr--
RAAAAHH!
Nor any Amazon blood!
EEEEEEEEEE!
Ever again!

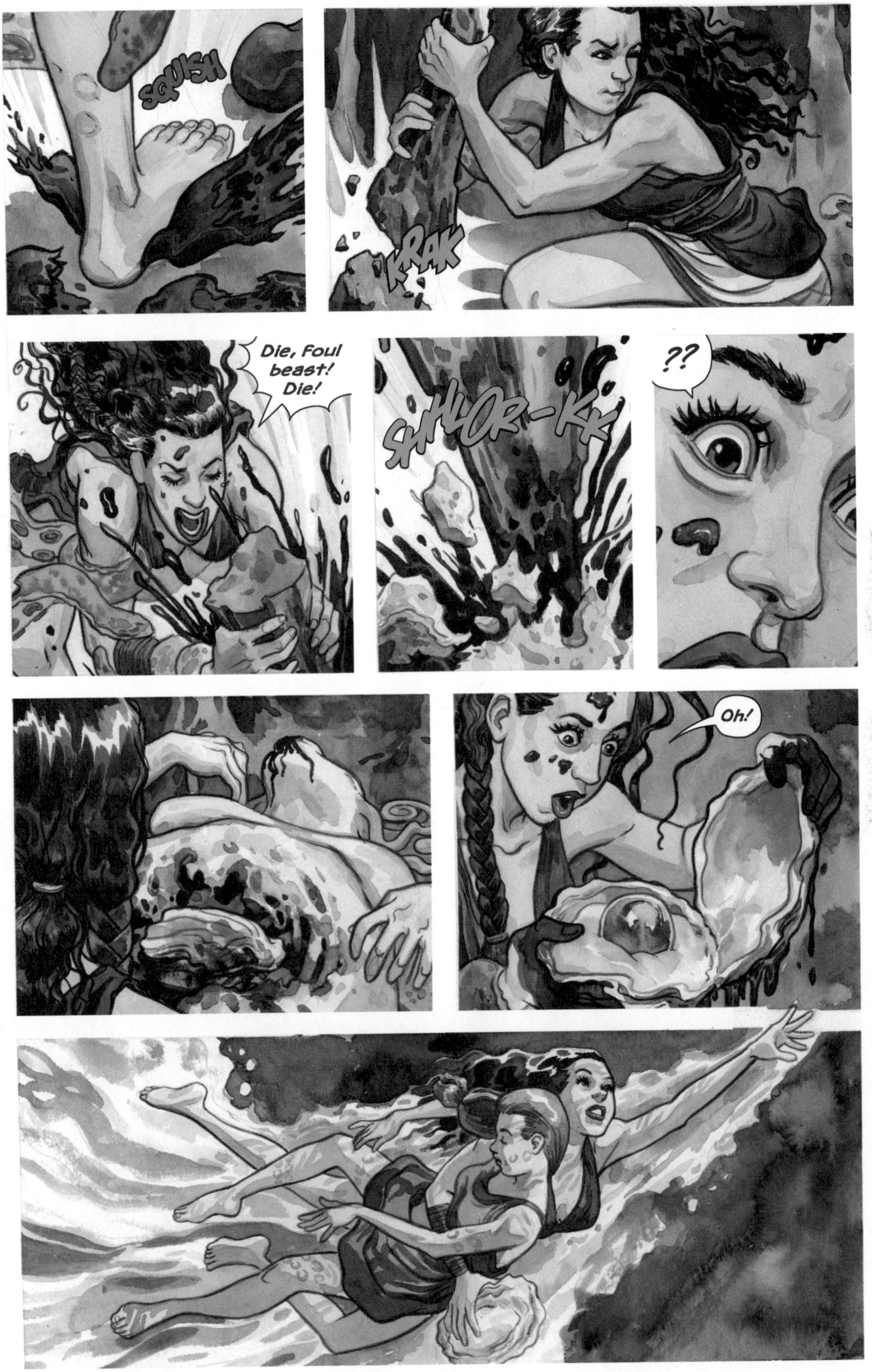
SQUISH
KRAK
Die, foul beast! Die!
SHHLOR-KK
??
Oh!

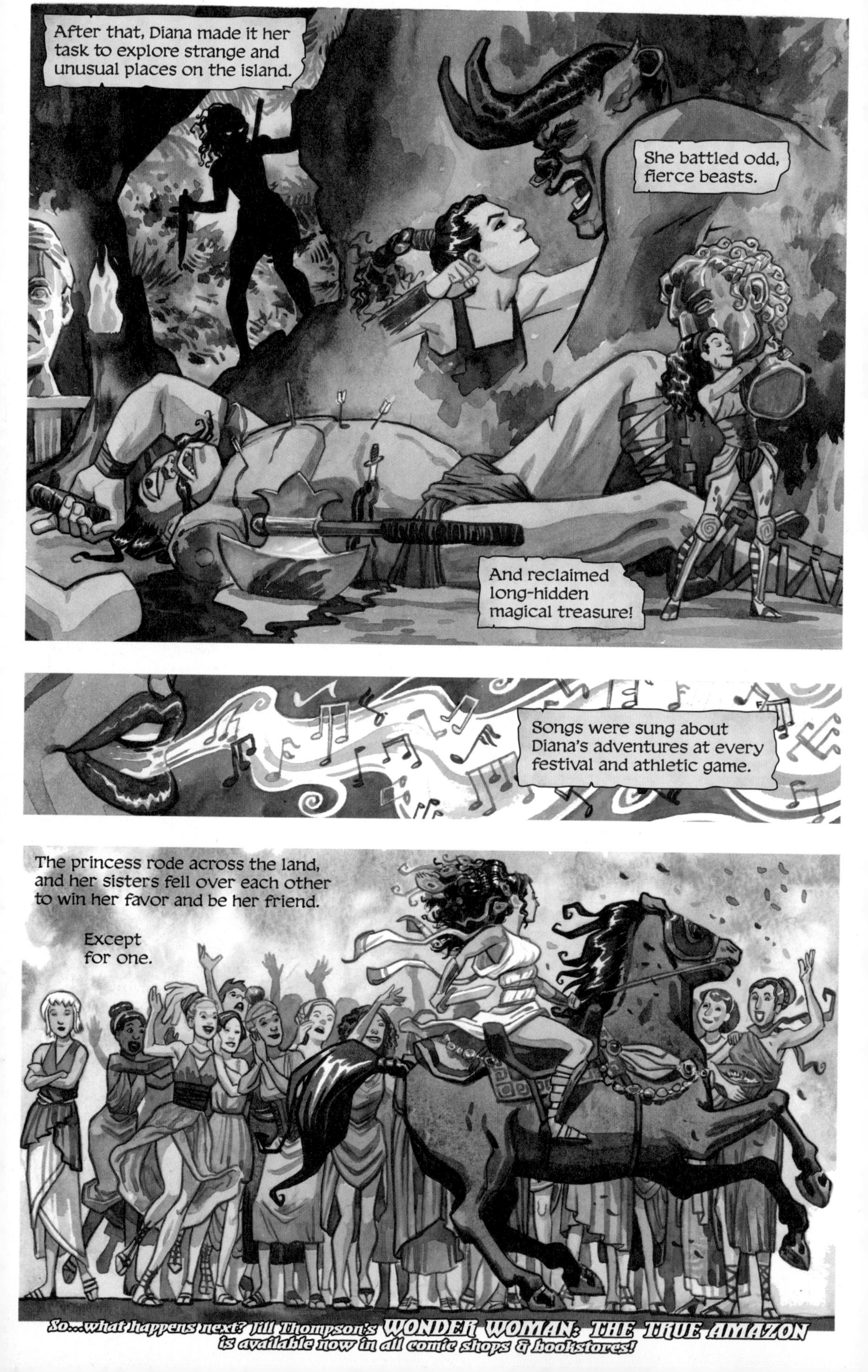
After that, Diana made it her task to explore strange and unusual places on the island.
She battled odd, fierce beasts.
And reclaimed long-hidden magical treasure!
Songs were sung about Diana's adventures at every festival and athletic game.
The princess rode across the land, and her sisters fell over each other to win her favor and be her friend.
Except for one.

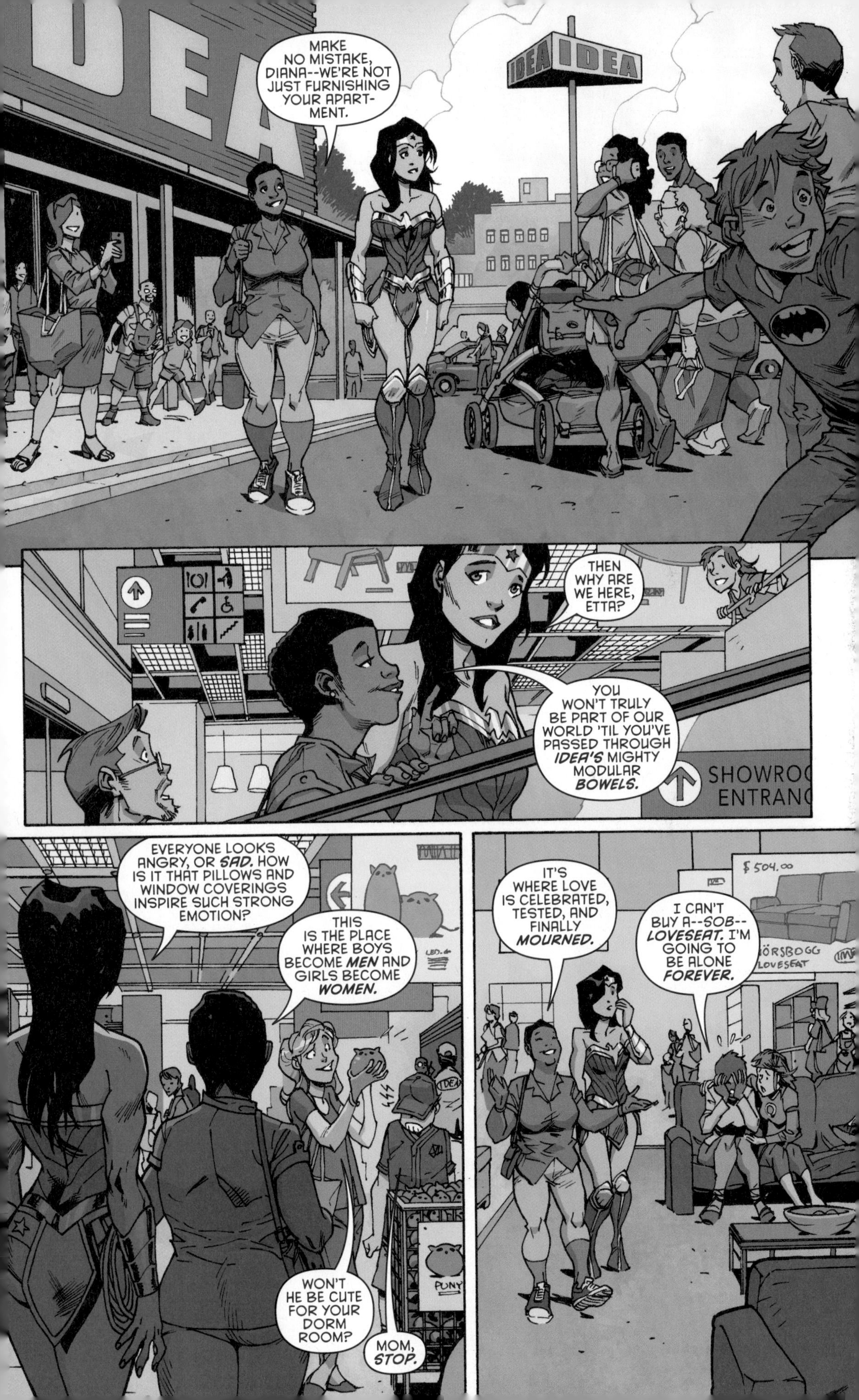
IDEA
IDEA IDEA
MAKE NO MISTAKE, DIANA--WE'RE NOT JUST FURNISHING YOUR APARTMENT.
THEN WHY ARE WE HERE, ETTA?
YOU WON'T TRULY BE PART OF OUR WORLD 'TIL YOU'VE PASSED THROUGH *IDEA'S* MIGHTY MODULAR *BOWELS.*
SHOWROO
ENTRANC
EVERYONE LOOKS ANGRY, OR *SAD.* HOW IS IT THAT PILLOWS AND WINDOW COVERINGS INSPIRE SUCH STRONG EMOTION?
THIS IS THE PLACE WHERE BOYS BECOME *MEN* AND GIRLS BECOME *WOMEN.*
WON'T HE BE CUTE FOR YOUR DORM ROOM?
MOM, *STOP.*
PUNY
$ 504.00
IT'S WHERE LOVE IS CELEBRATED, TESTED, AND FINALLY *MOURNED.*
I CAN'T BUY A--SOB--*LOVESEAT.* I'M GOING TO BE ALONE *FOREVER.*
LOVESEAT

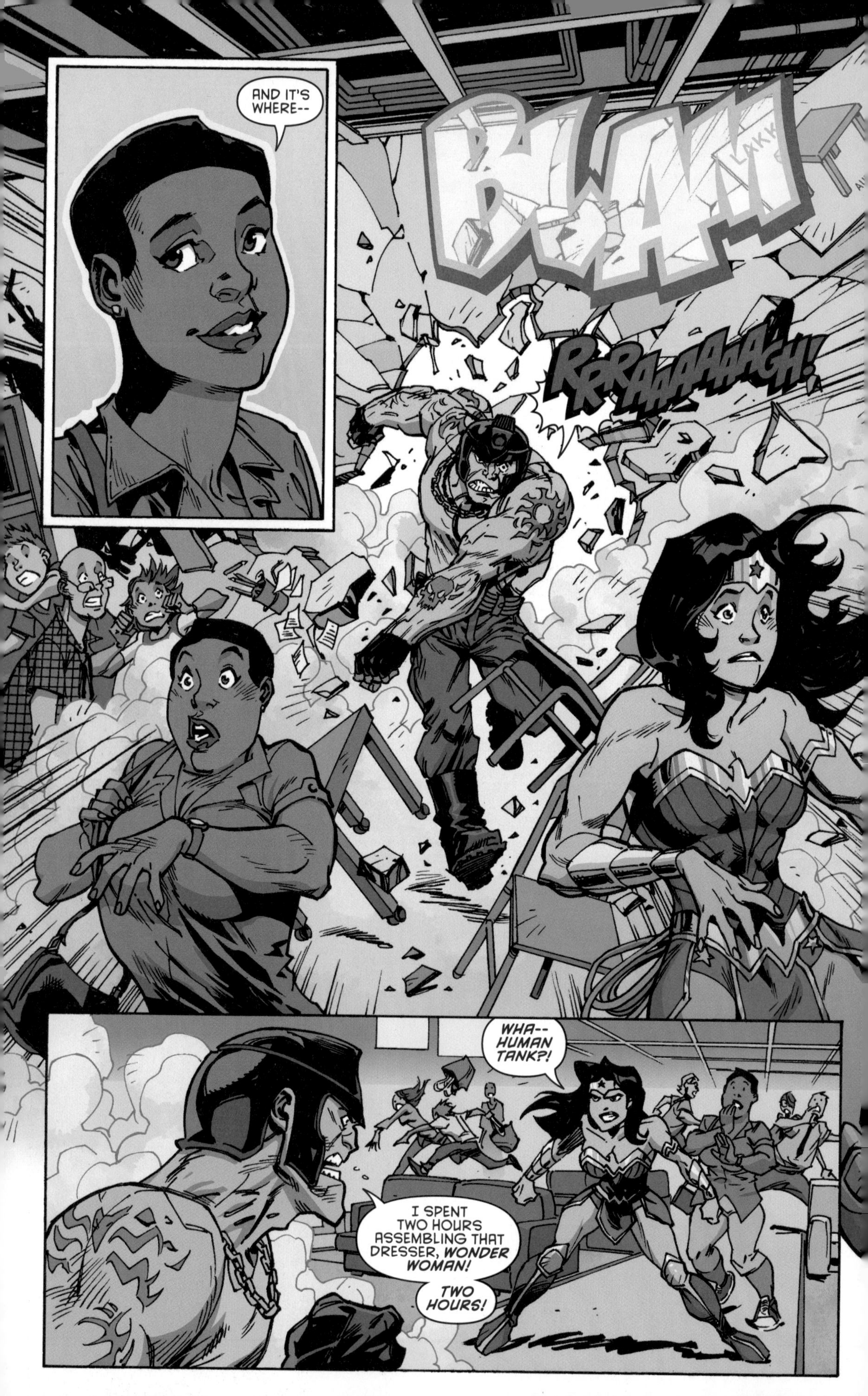
AND IT'S WHERE--
BLAM
RRRAAAAAAAGH!
WHA-- HUMAN TANK?!
I SPENT TWO HOURS ASSEMBLING THAT DRESSER, WONDER WOMAN!
TWO HOURS!

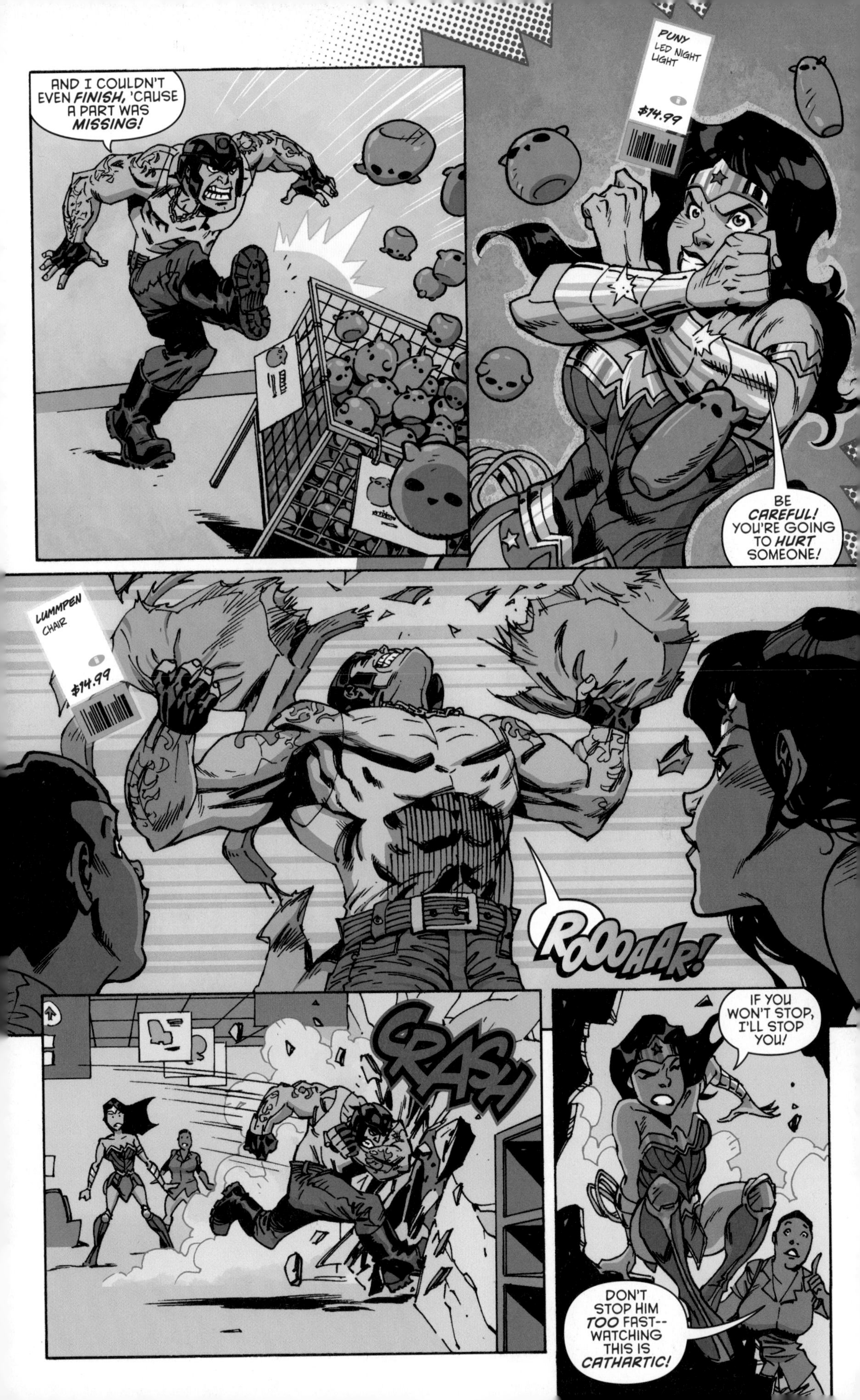
AND I COULDN'T EVEN FINISH, 'CAUSE A PART WAS MISSING!
PUNY
LED NIGHT LIGHT
$14.99
BE CAREFUL! YOU'RE GOING TO HURT SOMEONE!
LUMMPEN
CHAIR
$14.99
ROOOAAR!
CRASH
IF YOU WON'T STOP, I'LL STOP YOU!
DON'T STOP HIM TOO FAST-- WATCHING THIS IS CATHARTIC!

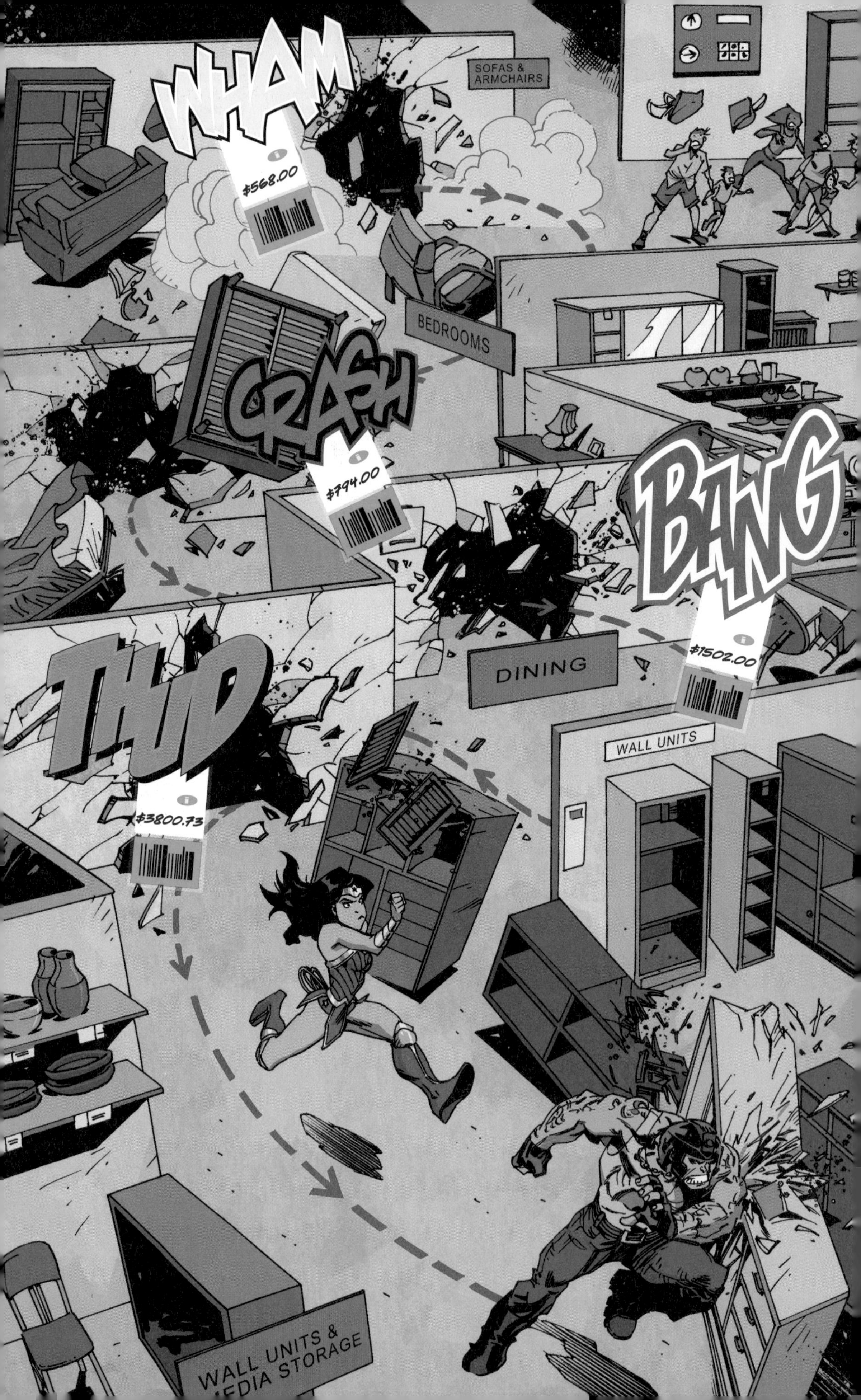
WHAM
SOFAS & ARMCHAIRS
$568.00
BEDROOMS
CRASH
$794.00
BANG
DINING
$1502.00
THUD
$3800.73
WALL UNITS
WALL UNITS & MEDIA STORAGE

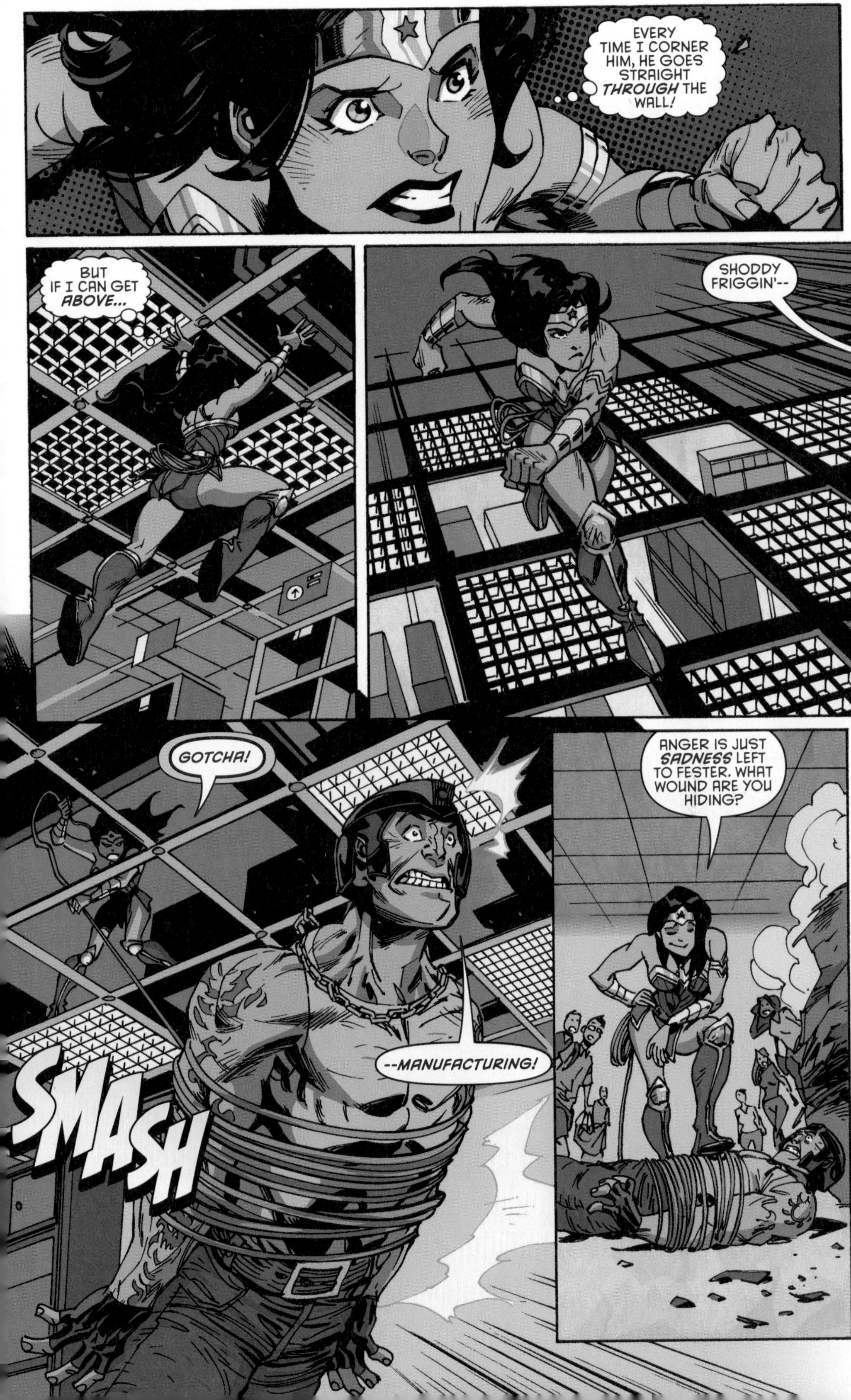
EVERY TIME I CORNER HIM, HE GOES STRAIGHT *THROUGH* THE WALL!
BUT IF I CAN GET *ABOVE*...
SHODDY FRIGGIN'--
GOTCHA!
--*MANUFACTURING!*
SMASH
ANGER IS JUST *SADNESS* LEFT TO FESTER. WHAT WOUND ARE YOU HIDING?

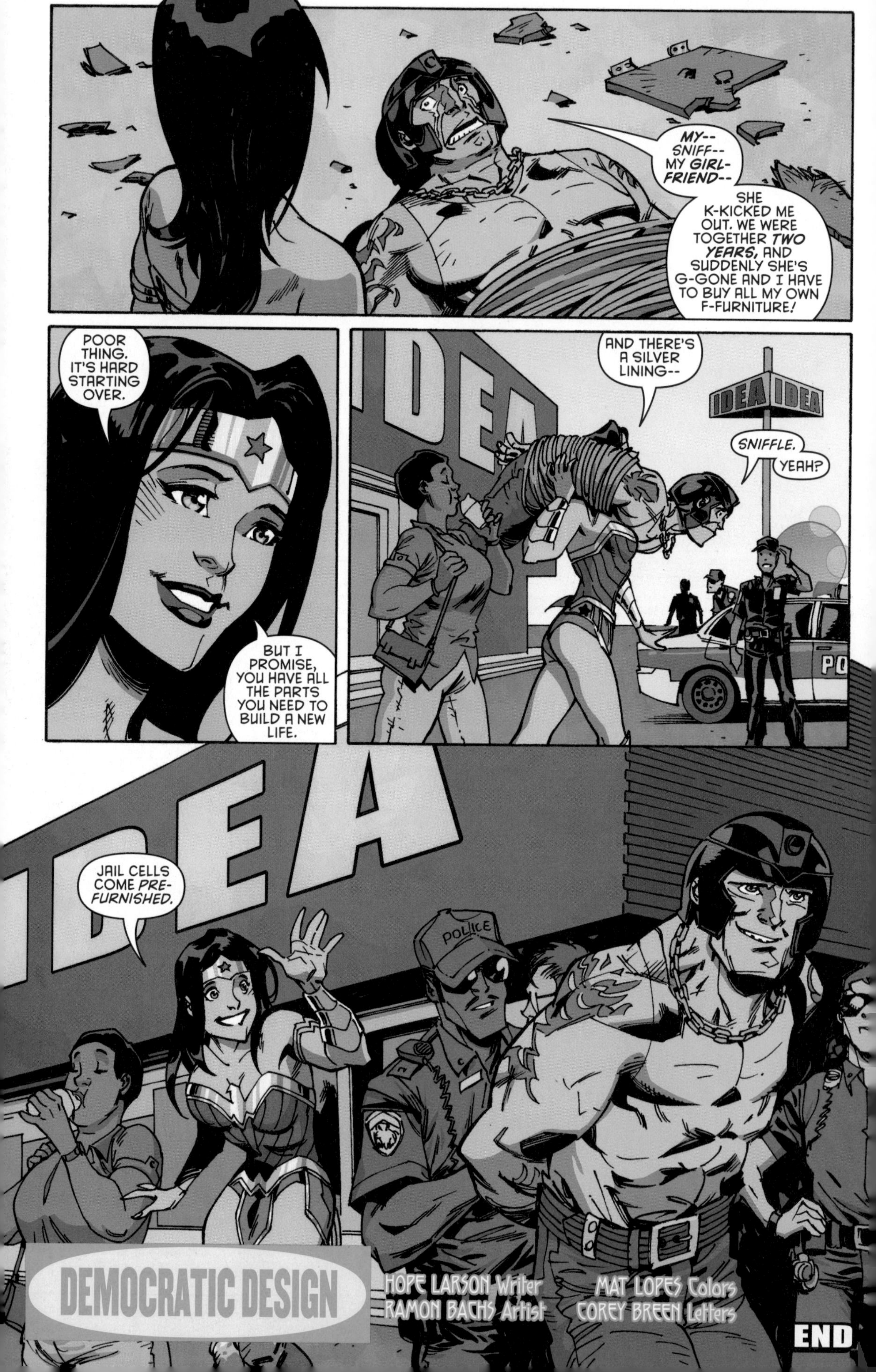
MY--
SNIFF--
MY GIRL-
FRIEND--
SHE K-KICKED ME OUT. WE WERE TOGETHER TWO YEARS, AND SUDDENLY SHE'S G-GONE AND I HAVE TO BUY ALL MY OWN F-FURNITURE!
POOR THING. IT'S HARD STARTING OVER.
BUT I PROMISE, YOU HAVE ALL THE PARTS YOU NEED TO BUILD A NEW LIFE.
AND THERE'S A SILVER LINING--
IDEA IDEA
SNIFFLE.
YEAH?
PO
IDEA
JAIL CELLS COME PRE-FURNISHED.
POLICE
DEMOCRATIC DESIGN
HOPE LARSON Writer
RAMON BACHS Artist
MAT LOPES Colors
COREY BREEN Letters
END

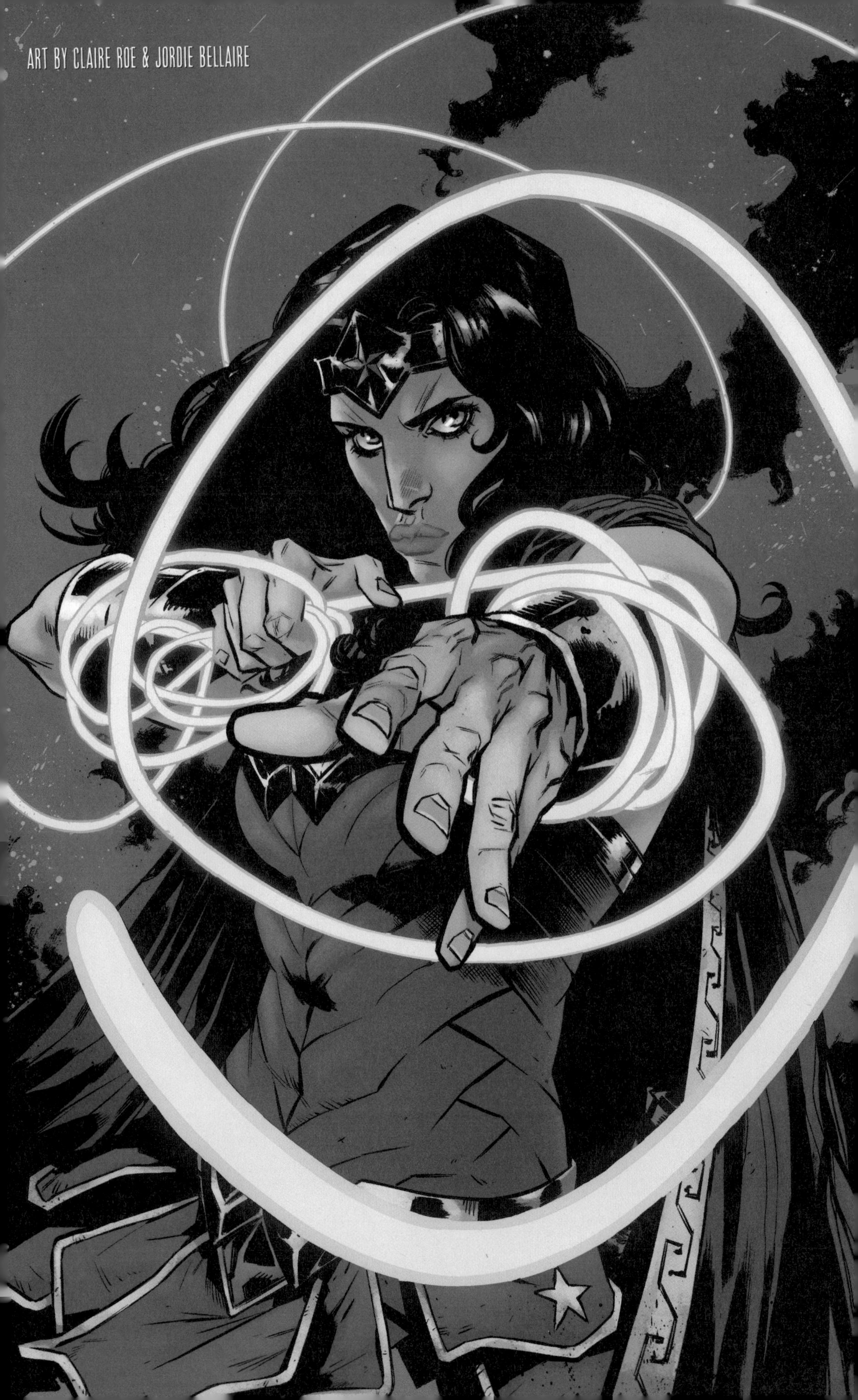
ART BY CLAIRE ROE & JORDIE BELLAIRE

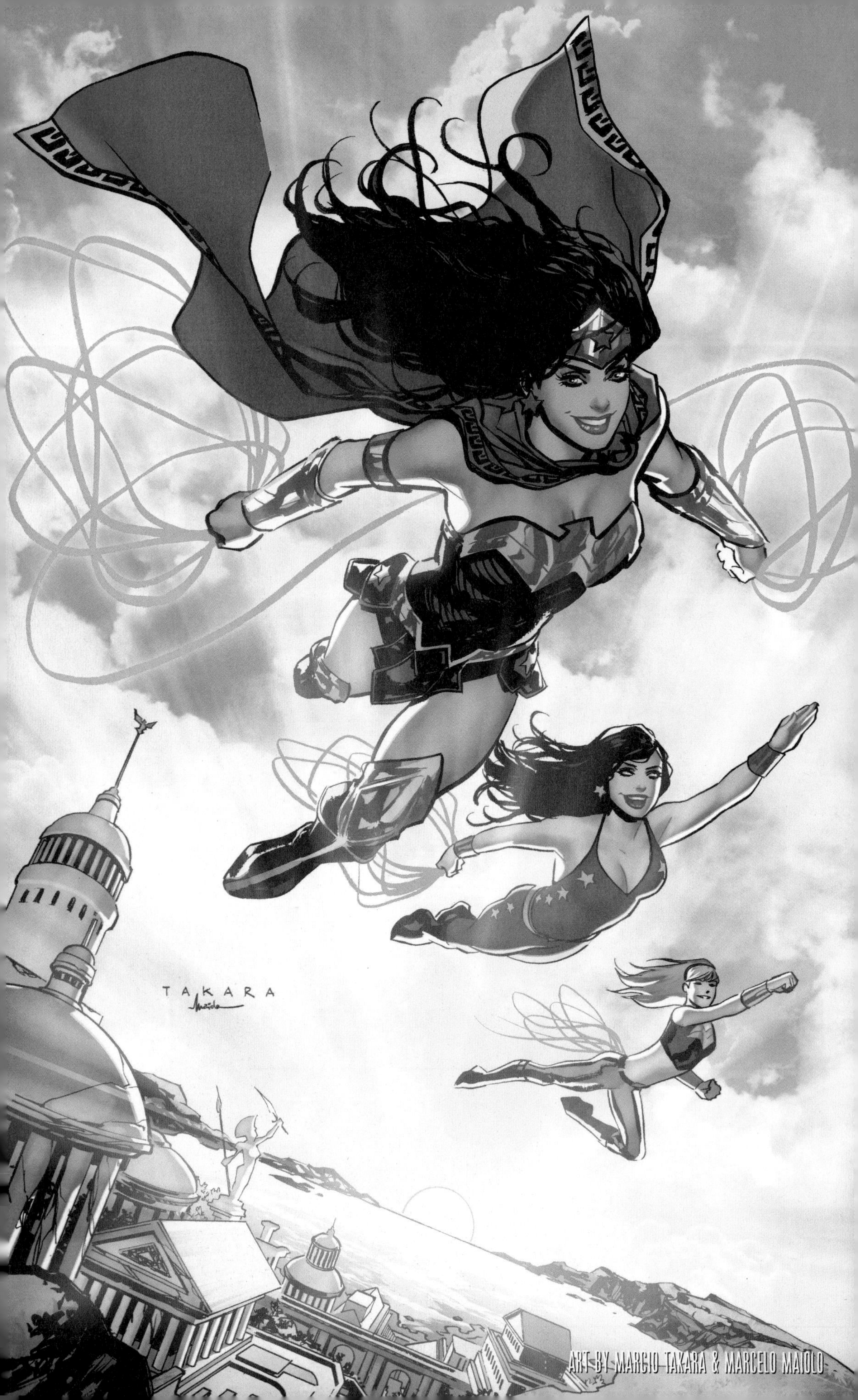
TAKARA
ART BY MARCIO TAKARA & MARCELO MAIOLO

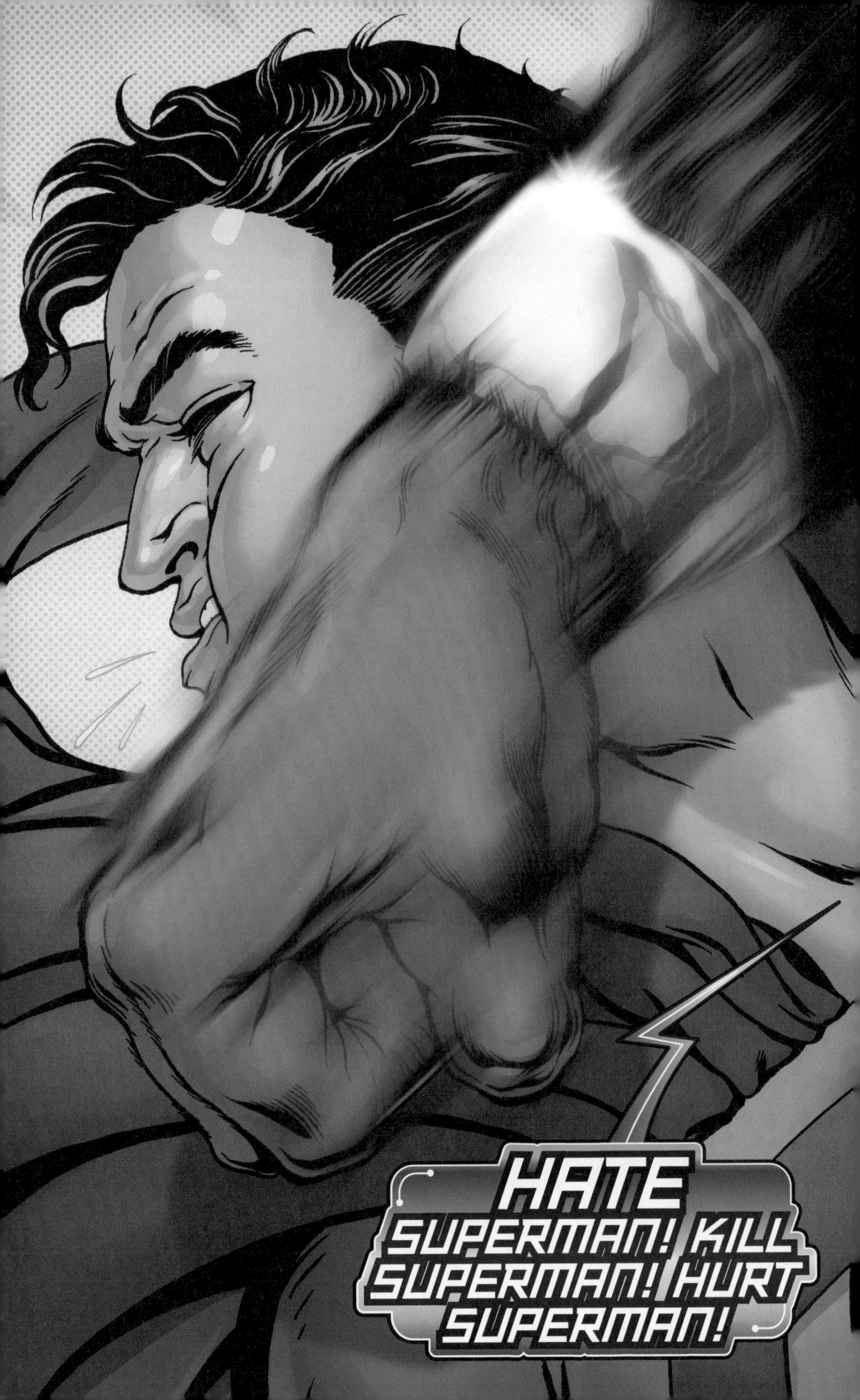
HATE
SUPERMAN! KILL
SUPERMAN! HURT
SUPERMAN!

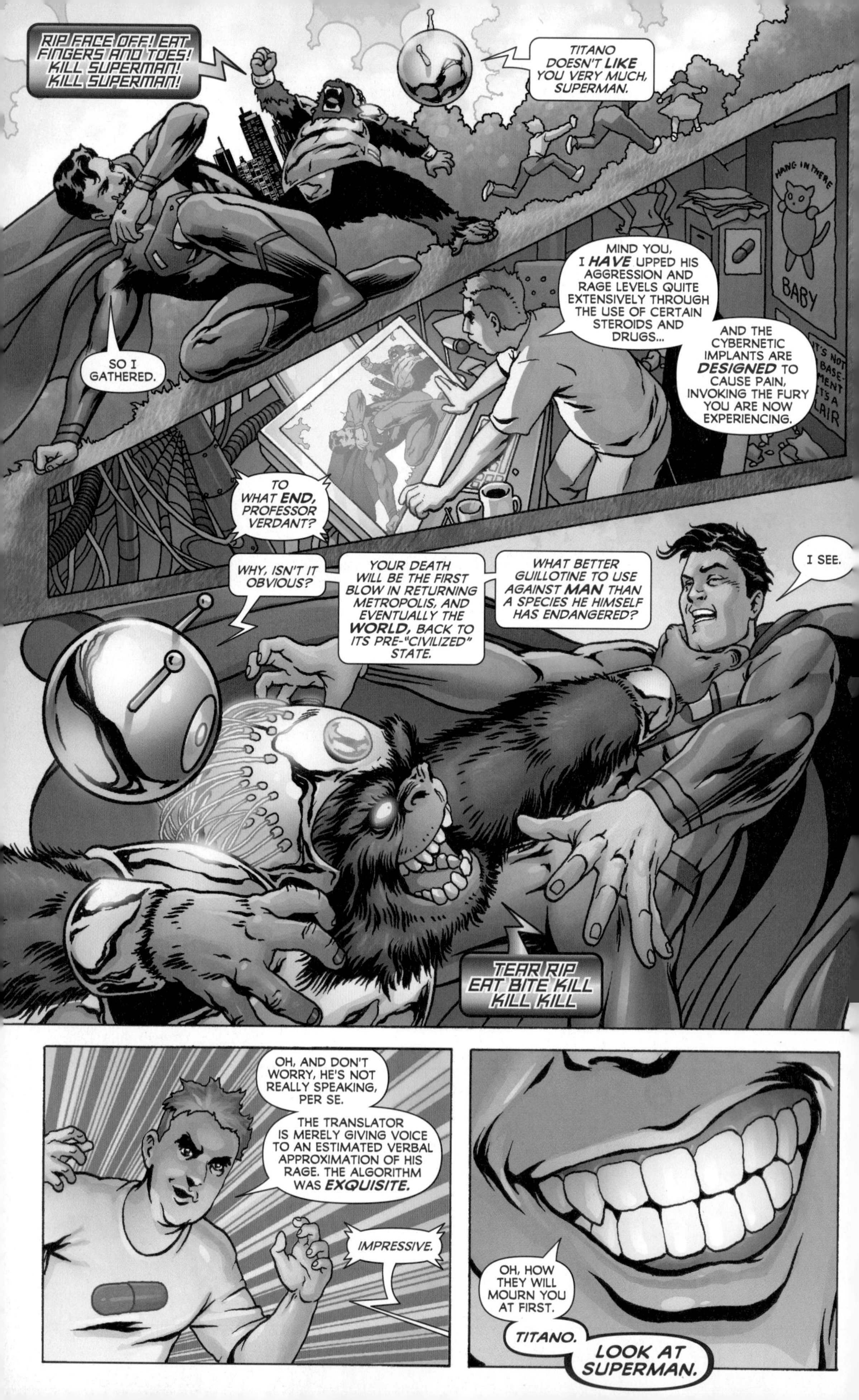

RIP FACE OFF! EAT FINGERS AND TOES! KILL SUPERMAN! KILL SUPERMAN!
TITANO DOESN'T **LIKE** YOU VERY MUCH, SUPERMAN.
SO I GATHERED.
MIND YOU, I **HAVE** UPPED HIS AGGRESSION AND RAGE LEVELS QUITE EXTENSIVELY THROUGH THE USE OF CERTAIN STEROIDS AND DRUGS...
AND THE CYBERNETIC IMPLANTS ARE **DESIGNED** TO CAUSE PAIN, INVOKING THE FURY YOU ARE NOW EXPERIENCING.
HANG IN THERE
BABY
TO WHAT **END,** PROFESSOR VERDANT?
WHY, ISN'T IT OBVIOUS?
YOUR DEATH WILL BE THE FIRST BLOW IN RETURNING METROPOLIS, AND EVENTUALLY THE **WORLD,** BACK TO ITS PRE-"CIVILIZED" STATE.
WHAT BETTER GUILLOTINE TO USE AGAINST **MAN** THAN A SPECIES HE HIMSELF HAS ENDANGERED?
I SEE.
TEAR RIP EAT BITE KILL KILL KILL
OH, AND DON'T WORRY, HE'S NOT REALLY SPEAKING, PER SE.
THE TRANSLATOR IS MERELY GIVING VOICE TO AN ESTIMATED VERBAL APPROXIMATION OF HIS RAGE. THE ALGORITHM WAS ***EXQUISITE.***
IMPRESSIVE.
OH, HOW THEY WILL MOURN YOU AT FIRST.
TITANO.
LOOK AT SUPERMAN.

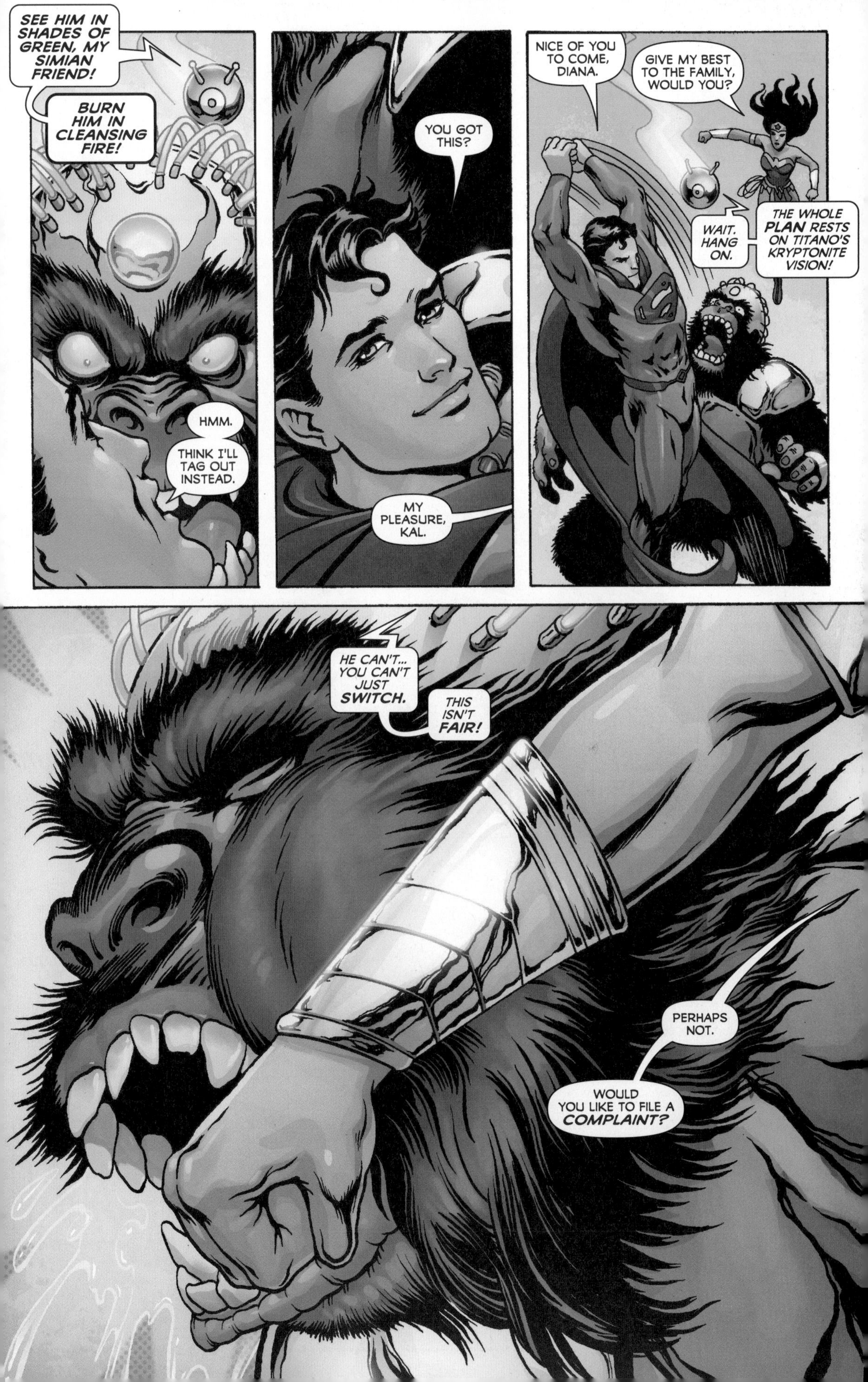
SEE HIM IN SHADES OF GREEN, MY SIMIAN FRIEND!
BURN HIM IN CLEANSING FIRE!
HMM.
THINK I'LL TAG OUT INSTEAD.
YOU GOT THIS?
MY PLEASURE, KAL.
NICE OF YOU TO COME, DIANA.
GIVE MY BEST TO THE FAMILY, WOULD YOU?
WAIT. HANG ON.
THE WHOLE PLAN RESTS ON TITANO'S KRYPTONITE VISION!
HE CAN'T... YOU CAN'T JUST SWITCH.
THIS ISN'T FAIR!
PERHAPS NOT.
WOULD YOU LIKE TO FILE A COMPLAINT?

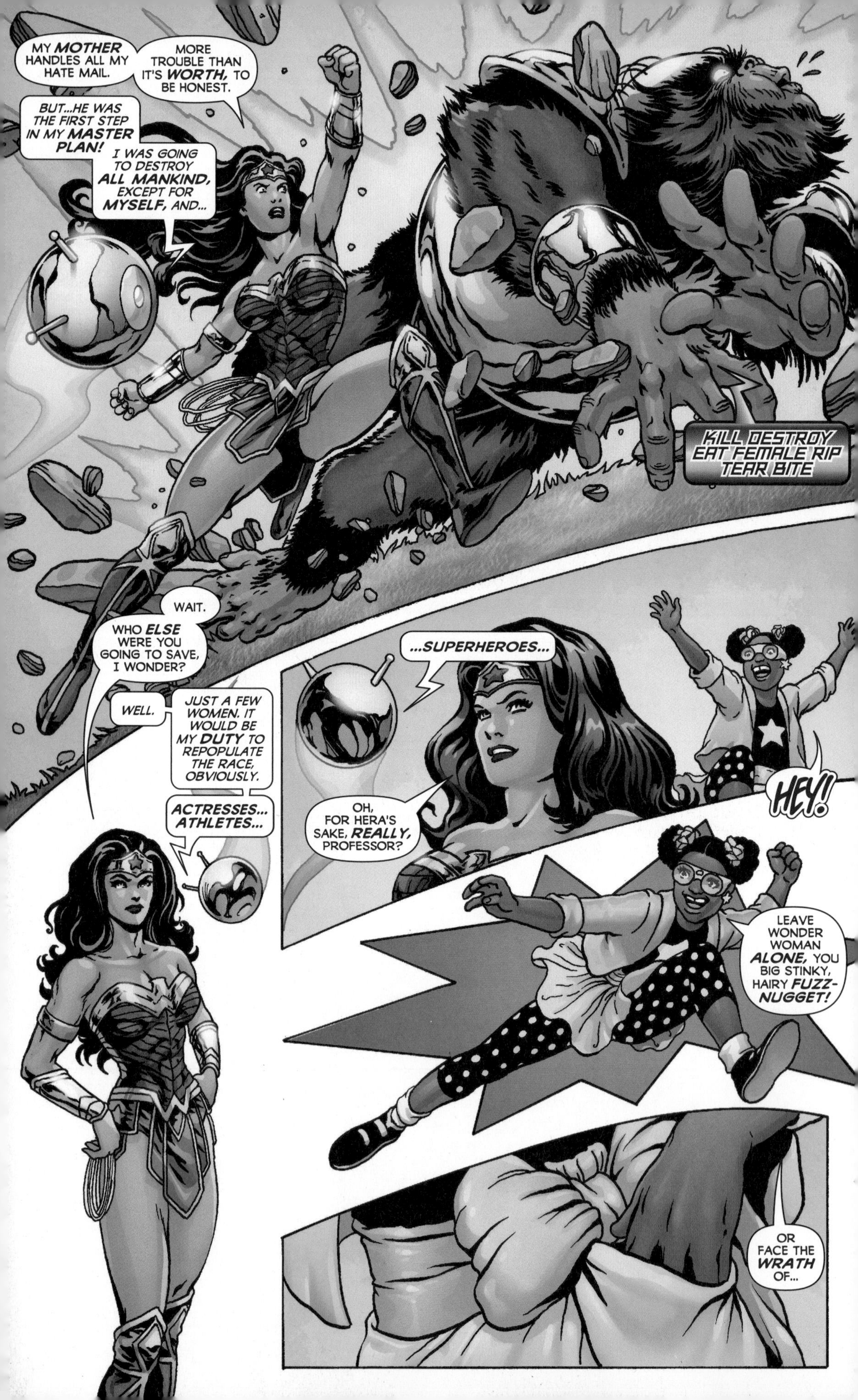

MY MOTHER HANDLES ALL MY HATE MAIL.
MORE TROUBLE THAN IT'S WORTH, TO BE HONEST.
BUT...HE WAS THE FIRST STEP IN MY MASTER PLAN!
I WAS GOING TO DESTROY ALL MANKIND, EXCEPT FOR MYSELF, AND...
KILL DESTROY EAT FEMALE RIP TEAR BITE
WAIT.
WHO ELSE WERE YOU GOING TO SAVE, I WONDER?
WELL.
JUST A FEW WOMEN. IT WOULD BE MY DUTY TO REPOPULATE THE RACE, OBVIOUSLY.
ACTRESSES... ATHLETES...
...SUPERHEROES...
OH, FOR HERA'S SAKE, REALLY, PROFESSOR?
HEY!
LEAVE WONDER WOMAN ALONE, YOU BIG STINKY, HAIRY FUZZ-NUGGET!
OR FACE THE WRATH OF...

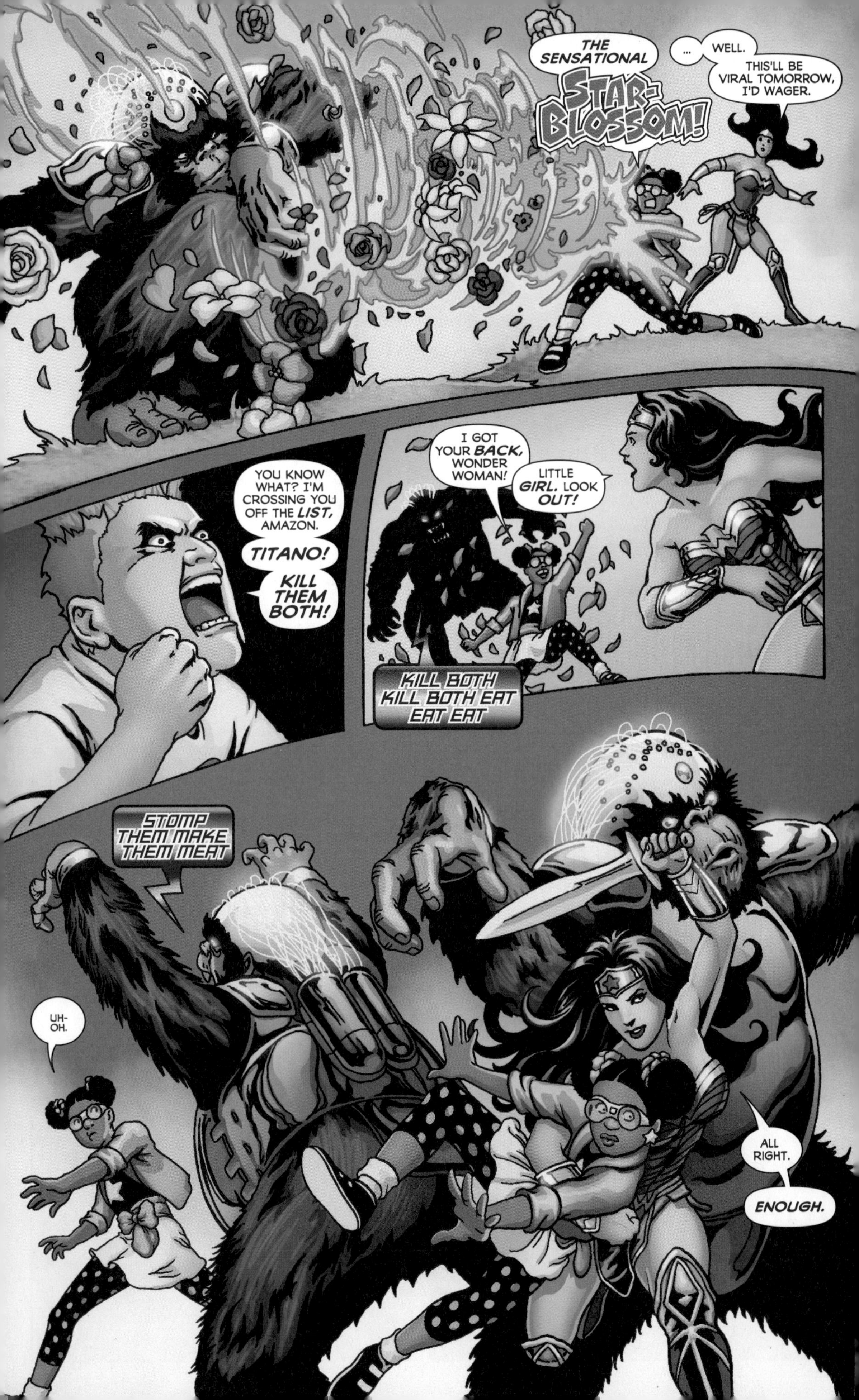
THE SENSATIONAL
STAR-BLOSSOM!
...
WELL.
THIS'LL BE VIRAL TOMORROW, I'D WAGER.
YOU KNOW WHAT? I'M CROSSING YOU OFF THE LIST, AMAZON.
TITANO!
KILL THEM BOTH!
I GOT YOUR BACK, WONDER WOMAN!
LITTLE GIRL. LOOK OUT!
KILL BOTH KILL BOTH EAT EAT EAT
STOMP THEM MAKE THEM MEAT
UH-OH.
ALL RIGHT.
ENOUGH.

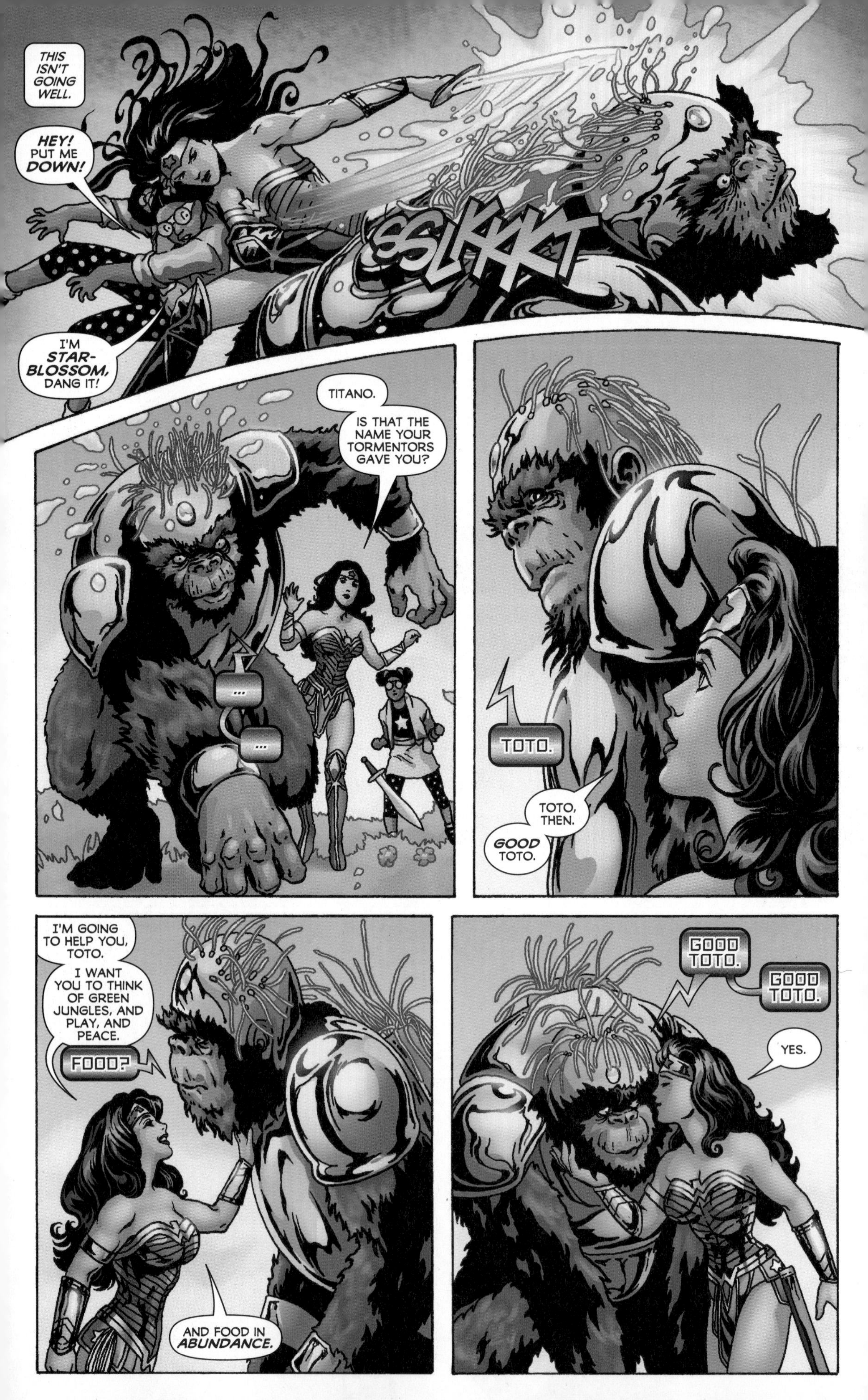

THIS ISN'T GOING WELL.
HEY! PUT ME DOWN!
SSLKAKT
I'M STAR-BLOSSOM, DANG IT!
TITANO.
IS THAT THE NAME YOUR TORMENTORS GAVE YOU?
...
...
TOTO.
TOTO, THEN.
GOOD TOTO.
I'M GOING TO HELP YOU, TOTO.
I WANT YOU TO THINK OF GREEN JUNGLES, AND PLAY, AND PEACE.
FOOD?
AND FOOD IN ABUNDANCE.
GOOD TOTO.
GOOD TOTO.
YES.

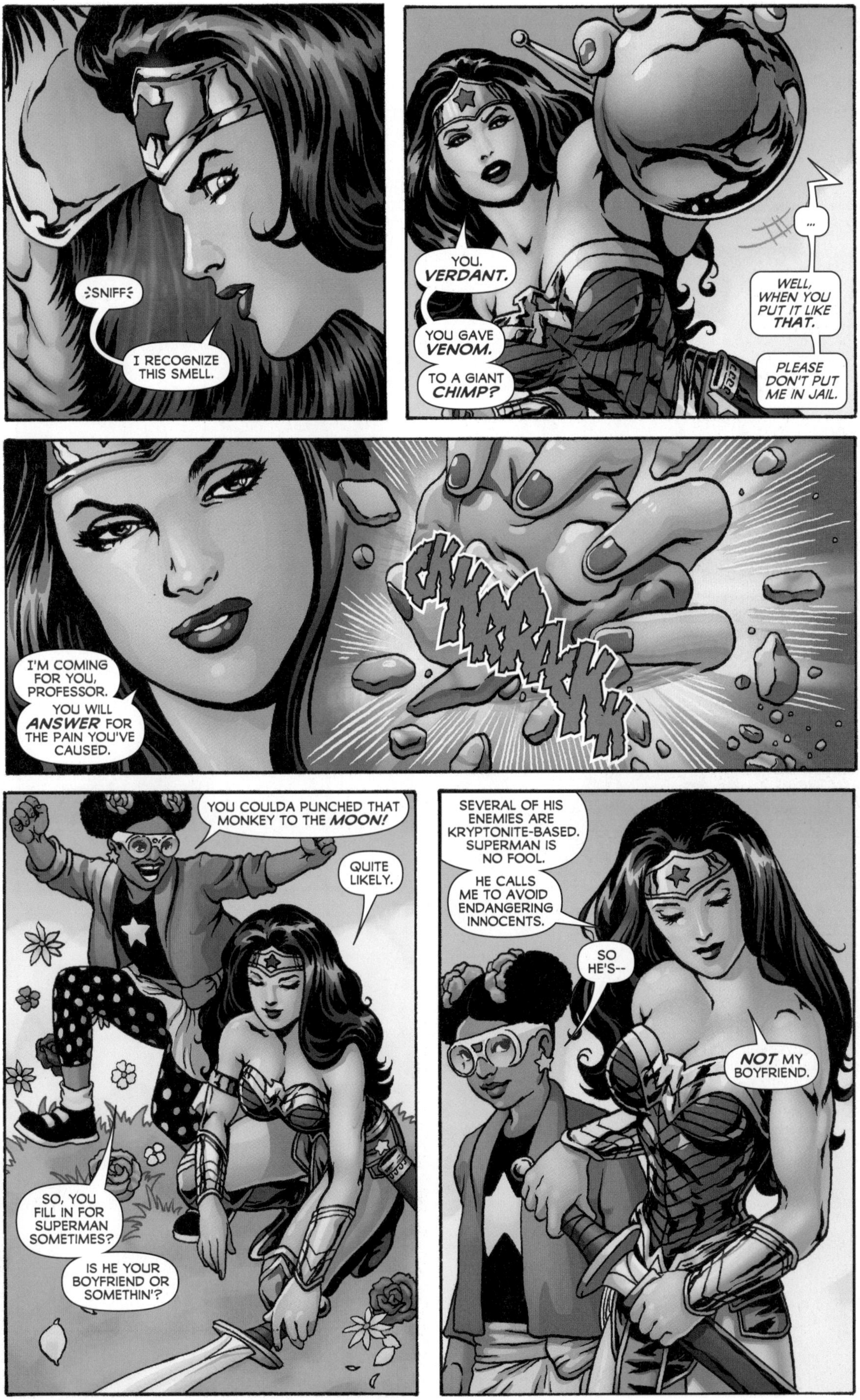
SNIFF
I RECOGNIZE THIS SMELL.
YOU. VERDANT.
YOU GAVE VENOM.
TO A GIANT CHIMP?
...
WELL, WHEN YOU PUT IT LIKE THAT.
PLEASE DON'T PUT ME IN JAIL.
I'M COMING FOR YOU, PROFESSOR.
YOU WILL ANSWER FOR THE PAIN YOU'VE CAUSED.
CKKRRAKKK
YOU COULDA PUNCHED THAT MONKEY TO THE MOON!
QUITE LIKELY.
SO, YOU FILL IN FOR SUPERMAN SOMETIMES?
IS HE YOUR BOYFRIEND OR SOMETHIN'?
SEVERAL OF HIS ENEMIES ARE KRYPTONITE-BASED. SUPERMAN IS NO FOOL.
HE CALLS ME TO AVOID ENDANGERING INNOCENTS.
SO HE'S--
NOT MY BOYFRIEND.

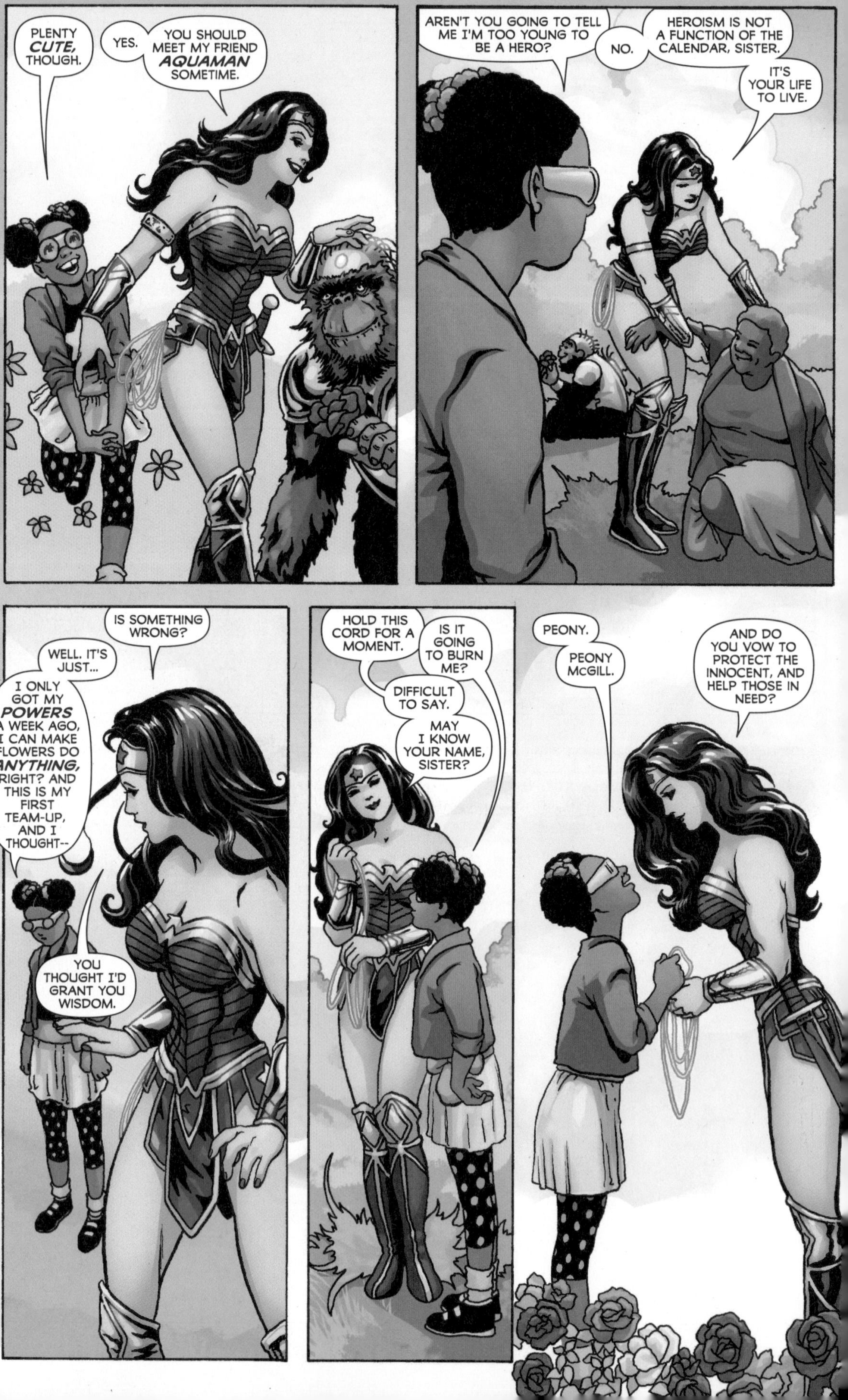
PLENTY CUTE, THOUGH.
YES.
YOU SHOULD MEET MY FRIEND AQUAMAN SOMETIME.
AREN'T YOU GOING TO TELL ME I'M TOO YOUNG TO BE A HERO?
NO.
HEROISM IS NOT A FUNCTION OF THE CALENDAR, SISTER.
IT'S YOUR LIFE TO LIVE.
IS SOMETHING WRONG?
WELL. IT'S JUST...
I ONLY GOT MY POWERS A WEEK AGO, I CAN MAKE FLOWERS DO ANYTHING, RIGHT? AND THIS IS MY FIRST TEAM-UP, AND I THOUGHT--
YOU THOUGHT I'D GRANT YOU WISDOM.
HOLD THIS CORD FOR A MOMENT.
IS IT GOING TO BURN ME?
DIFFICULT TO SAY.
MAY I KNOW YOUR NAME, SISTER?
PEONY.
PEONY McGILL.
AND DO YOU VOW TO PROTECT THE INNOCENT, AND HELP THOSE IN NEED?

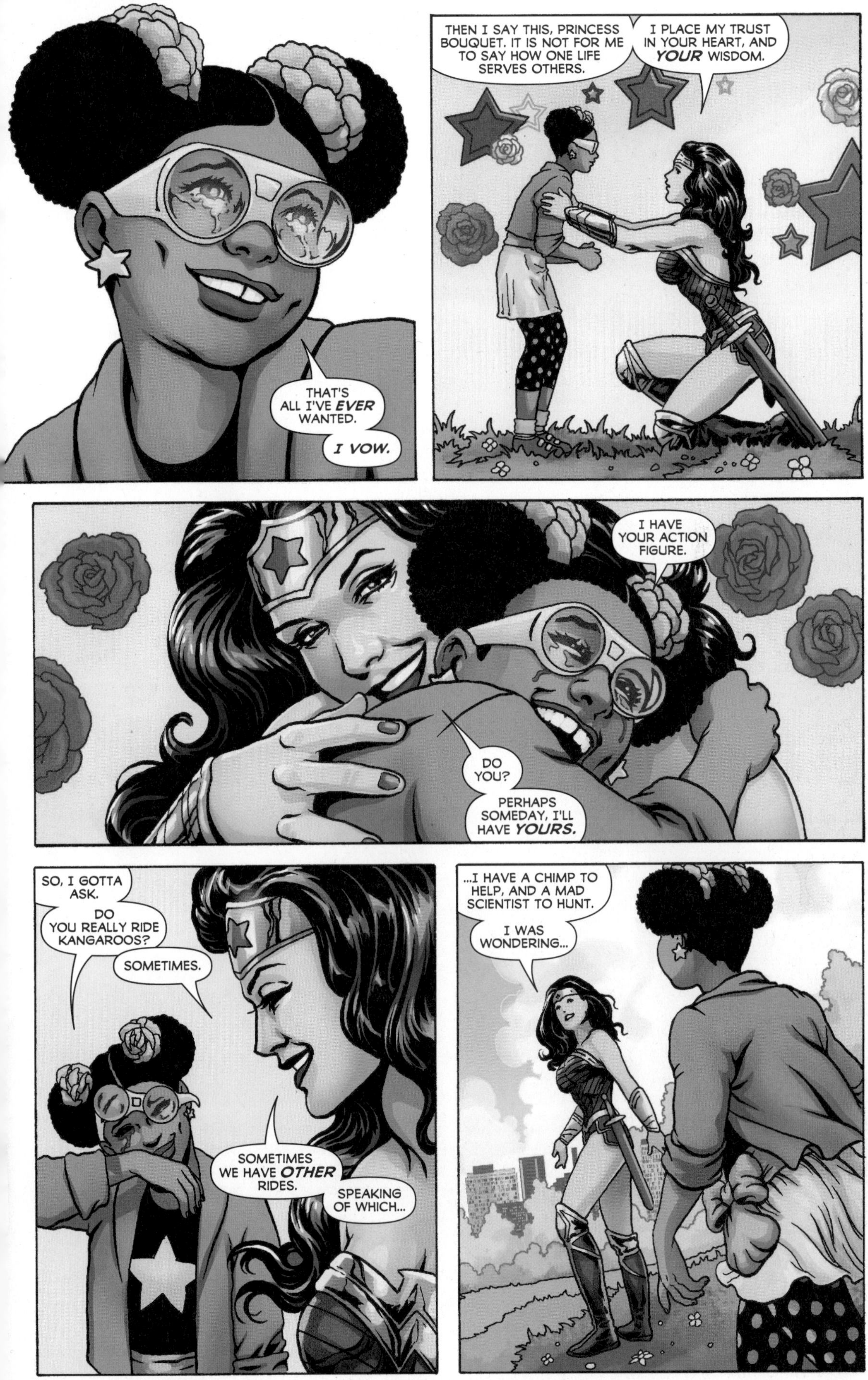
THAT'S ALL I'VE *EVER* WANTED.
I VOW.
THEN I SAY THIS, PRINCESS BOUQUET. IT IS NOT FOR ME TO SAY HOW ONE LIFE SERVES OTHERS.
I PLACE MY TRUST IN YOUR HEART, AND *YOUR* WISDOM.
I HAVE YOUR ACTION FIGURE.
DO YOU?
PERHAPS SOMEDAY, I'LL HAVE *YOURS.*
SO, I GOTTA ASK.
DO YOU REALLY RIDE KANGAROOS?
SOMETIMES.
SOMETIMES WE HAVE *OTHER* RIDES.
SPEAKING OF WHICH...
...I HAVE A CHIMP TO HELP, AND A MAD SCIENTIST TO HUNT.
I WAS WONDERING...

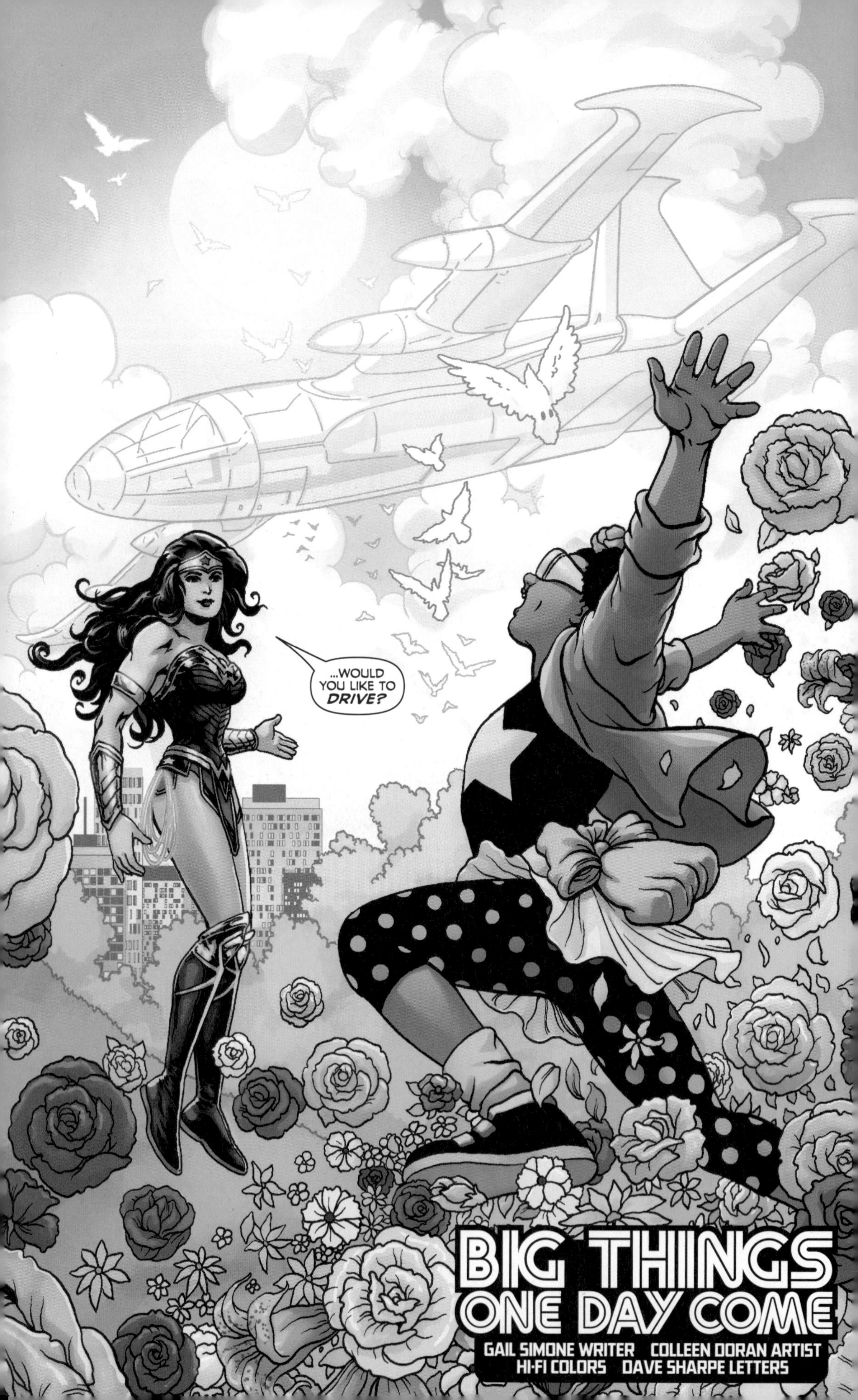
...WOULD YOU LIKE TO DRIVE?
BIG THINGS ONE DAY COME
GAIL SIMONE WRITER COLLEEN DORAN ARTIST
HI-FI COLORS DAVE SHARPE LETTERS

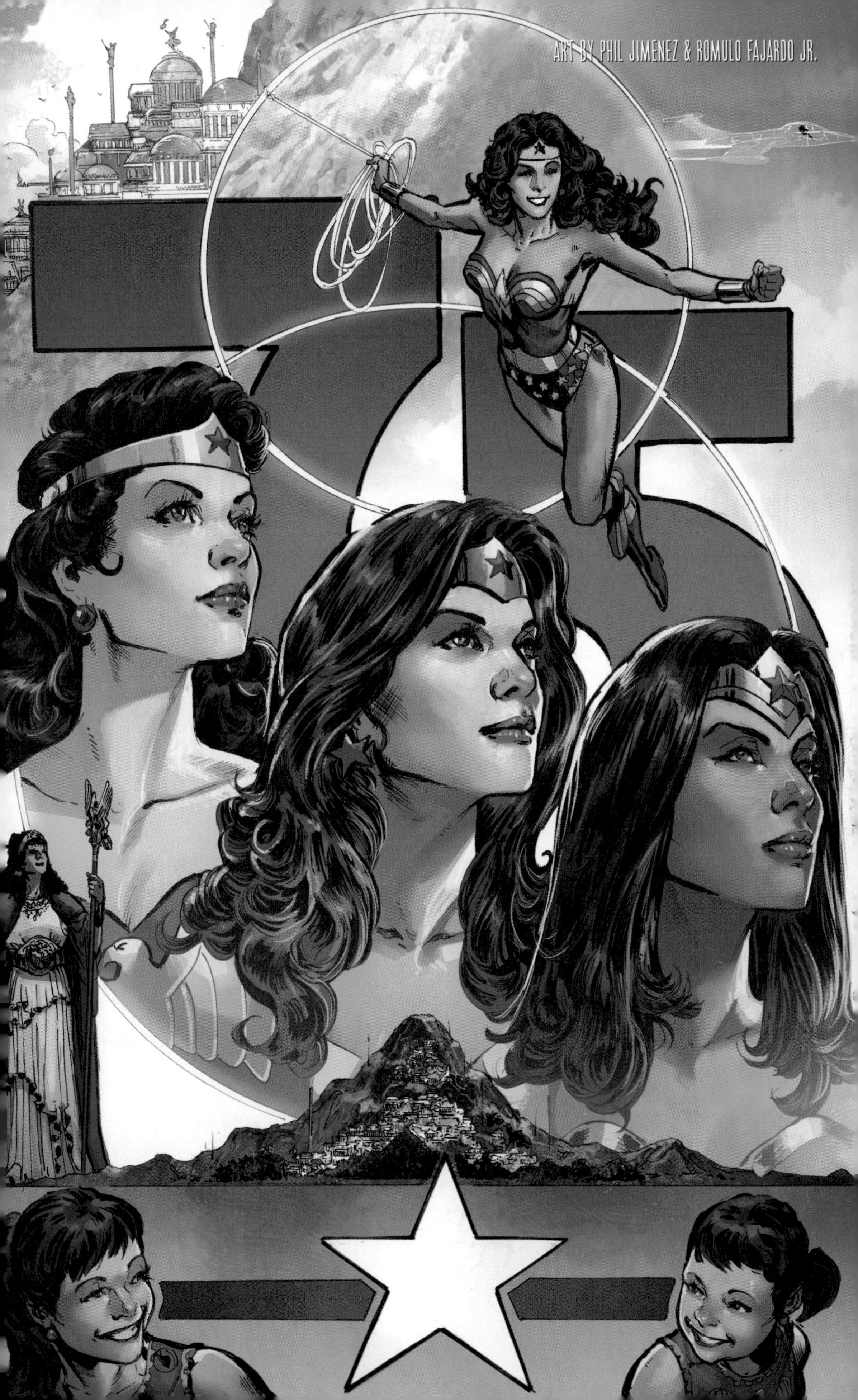
ART BY PHIL JIMENEZ & ROMULO FAJARDO JR.

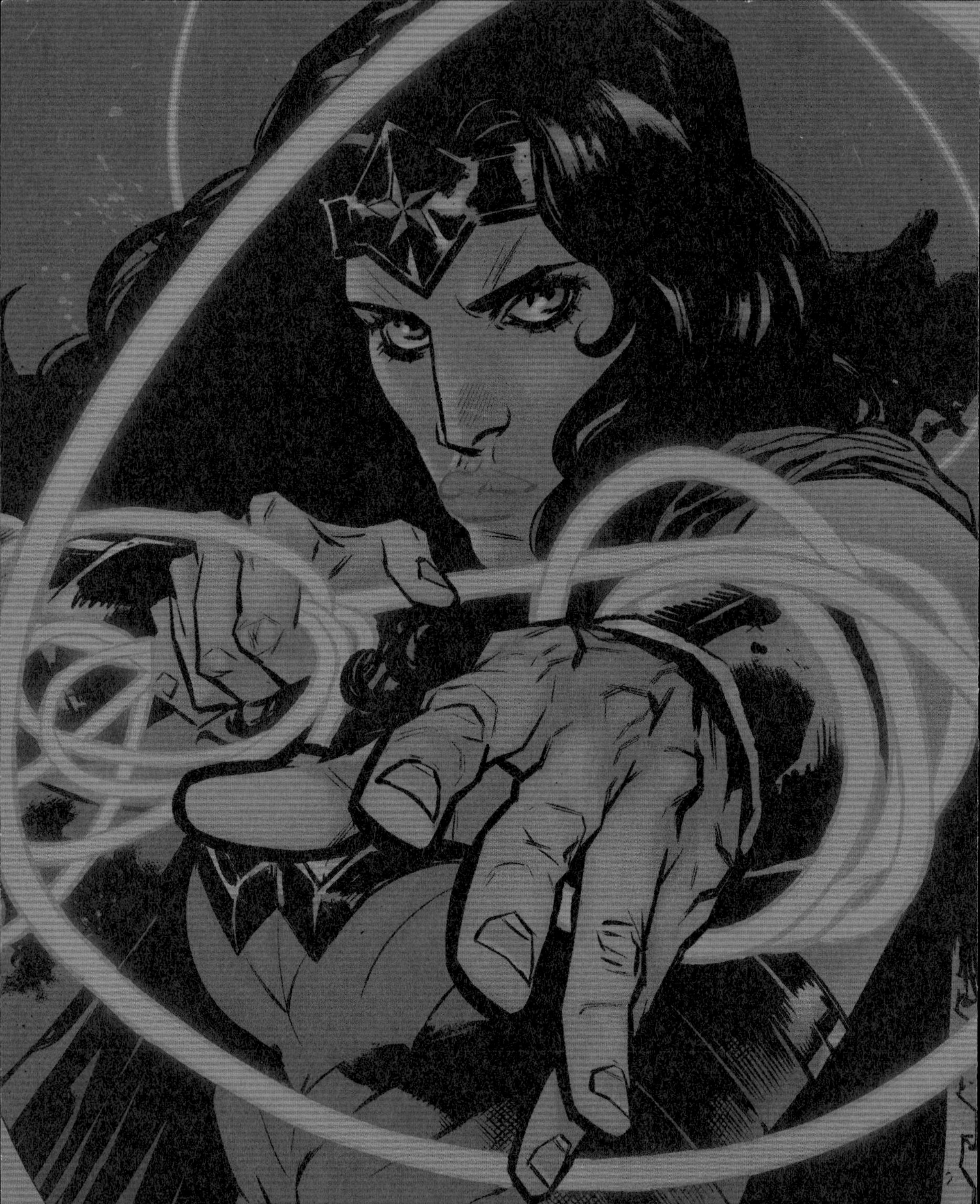

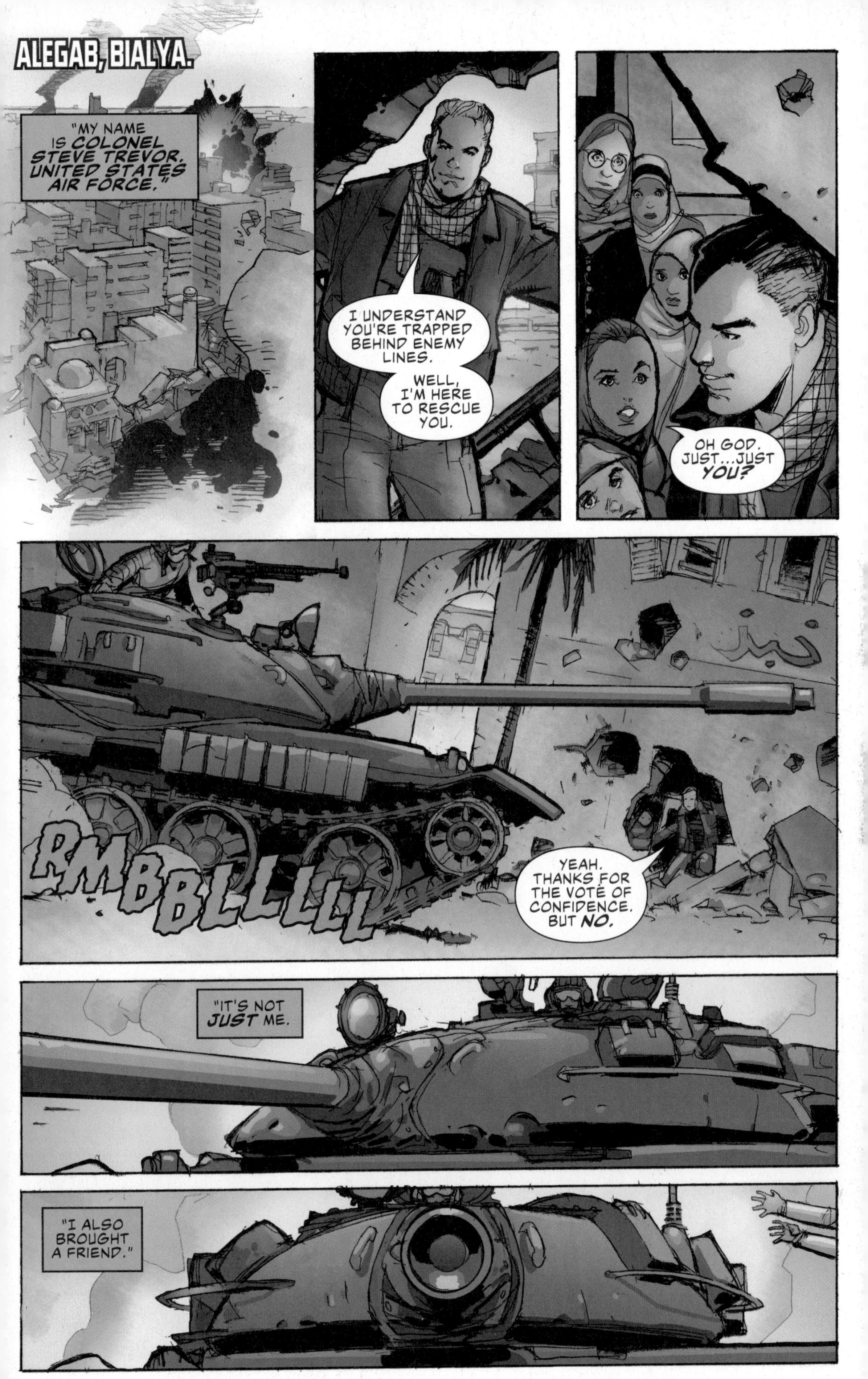
ALEGAB, BIALYA.
"MY NAME IS COLONEL STEVE TREVOR, UNITED STATES AIR FORCE."
I UNDERSTAND YOU'RE TRAPPED BEHIND ENEMY LINES.
WELL, I'M HERE TO RESCUE YOU.
OH GOD. JUST...JUST YOU?
RMBBLLLLL
YEAH. THANKS FOR THE VOTE OF CONFIDENCE. BUT NO.
"IT'S NOT JUST ME.
"I ALSO BROUGHT A FRIEND."

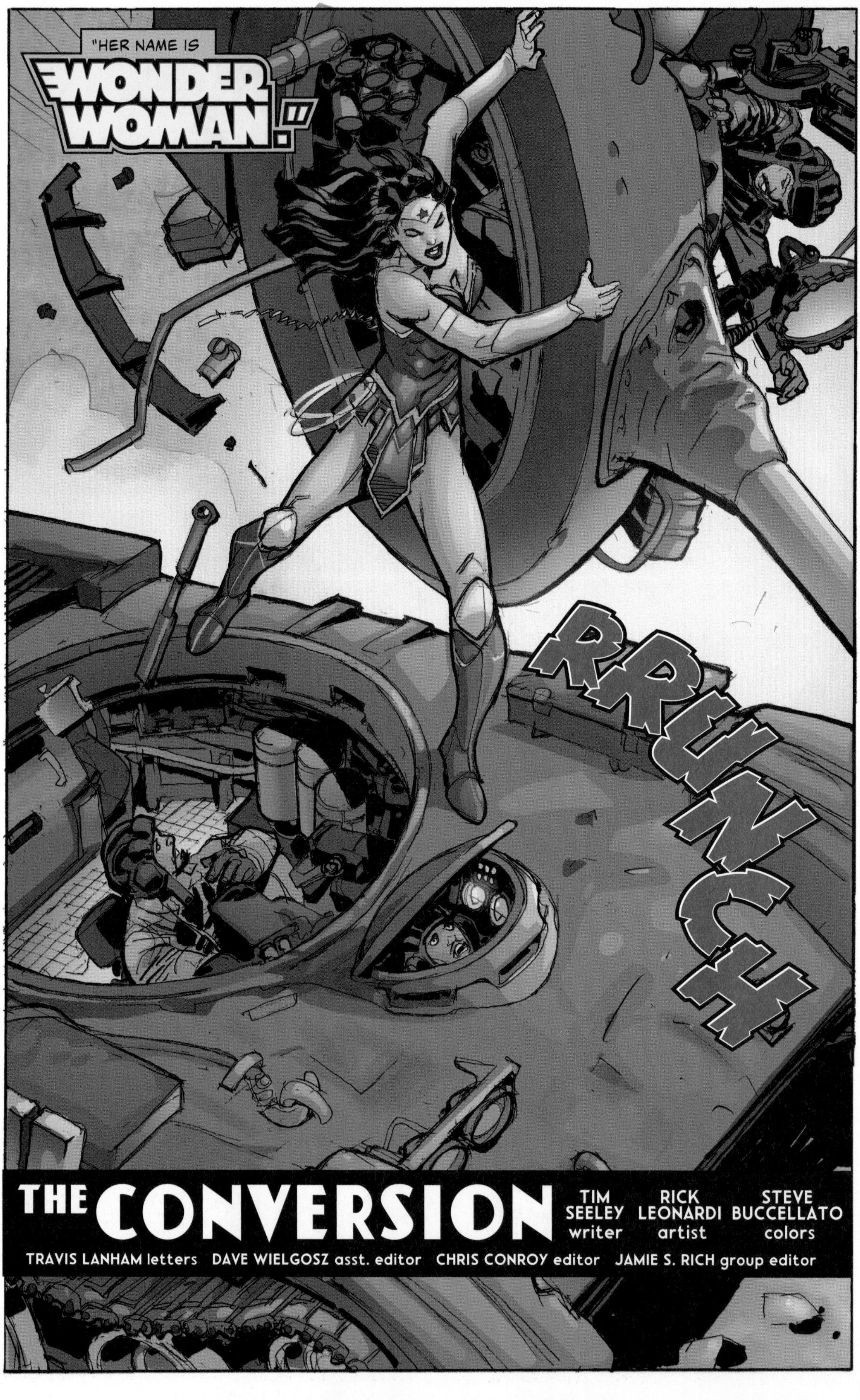
"HER NAME IS
WONDER WOMAN."
RRRUNCH
THE CONVERSION
TIM SEELEY writer
RICK LEONARDI artist
STEVE BUCCELLATO colors
TRAVIS LANHAM letters DAVE WIELGOSZ asst. editor CHRIS CONROY editor JAMIE S. RICH group editor

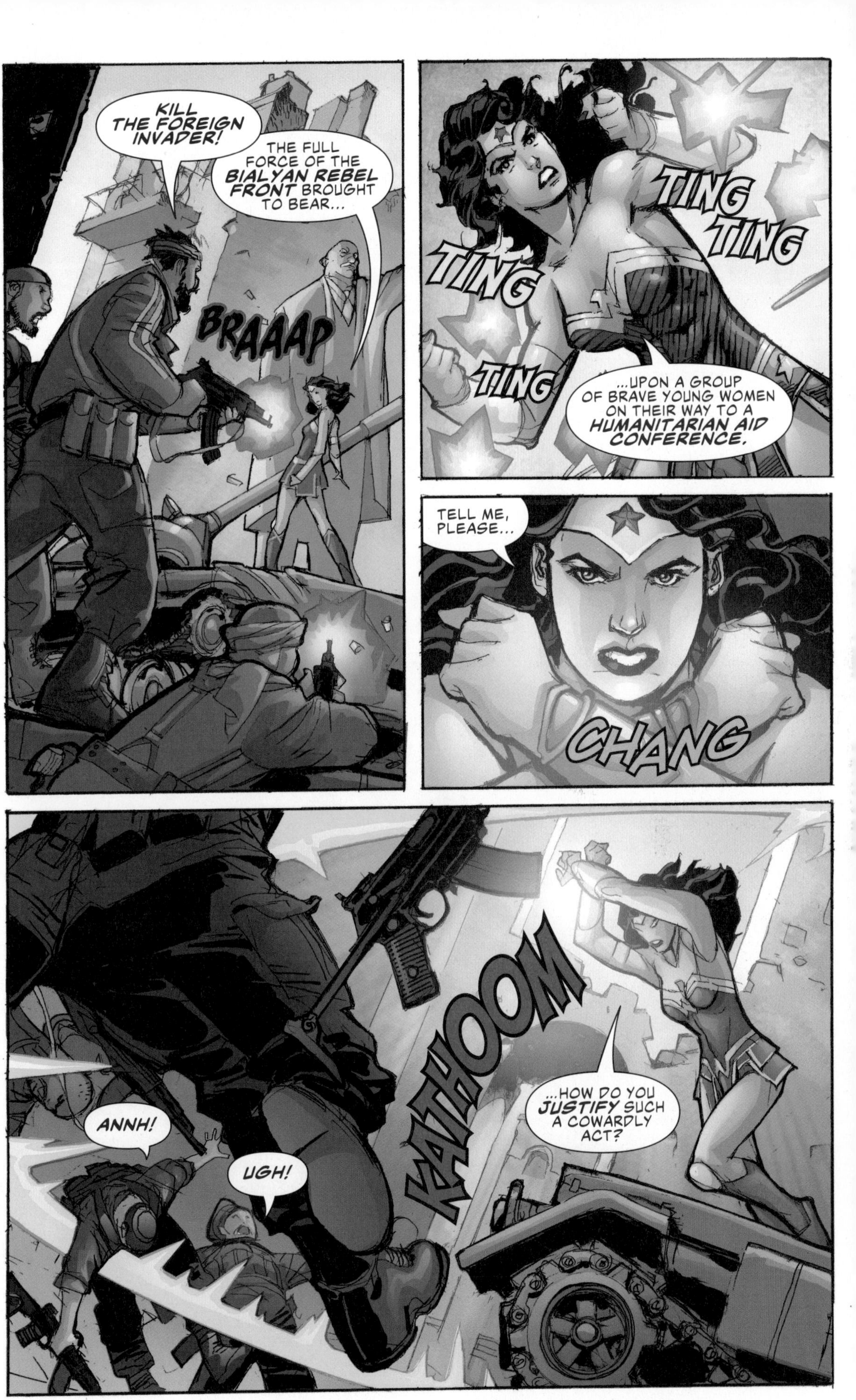
KILL THE FOREIGN INVADER!
THE FULL FORCE OF THE BIALYAN REBEL FRONT BROUGHT TO BEAR...
BRAAAP
TING TING
TING
TING
...UPON A GROUP OF BRAVE YOUNG WOMEN ON THEIR WAY TO A HUMANITARIAN AID CONFERENCE.
TELL ME, PLEASE...
CHANG
KATHOOM
...HOW DO YOU JUSTIFY SUCH A COWARDLY ACT?
ANNH!
UGH!

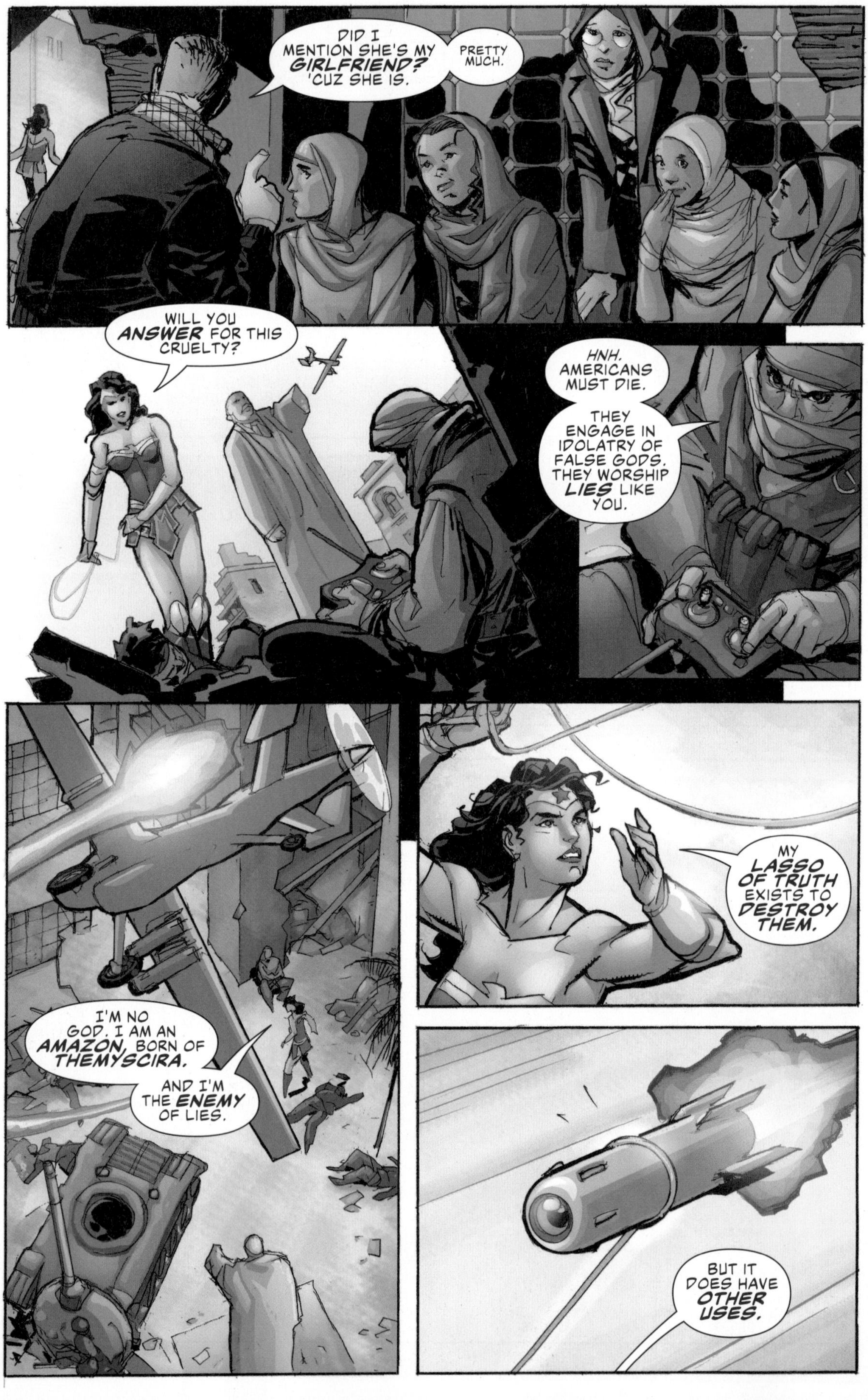
DID I MENTION SHE'S MY GIRLFRIEND? 'CUZ SHE IS.
PRETTY MUCH.
WILL YOU ANSWER FOR THIS CRUELTY?
HNH. AMERICANS MUST DIE.
THEY ENGAGE IN IDOLATRY OF FALSE GODS. THEY WORSHIP LIES LIKE YOU.
I'M NO GOD. I AM AN AMAZON, BORN OF THEMYSCIRA.
AND I'M THE ENEMY OF LIES.
MY LASSO OF TRUTH EXISTS TO DESTROY THEM.
BUT IT DOES HAVE OTHER USES.

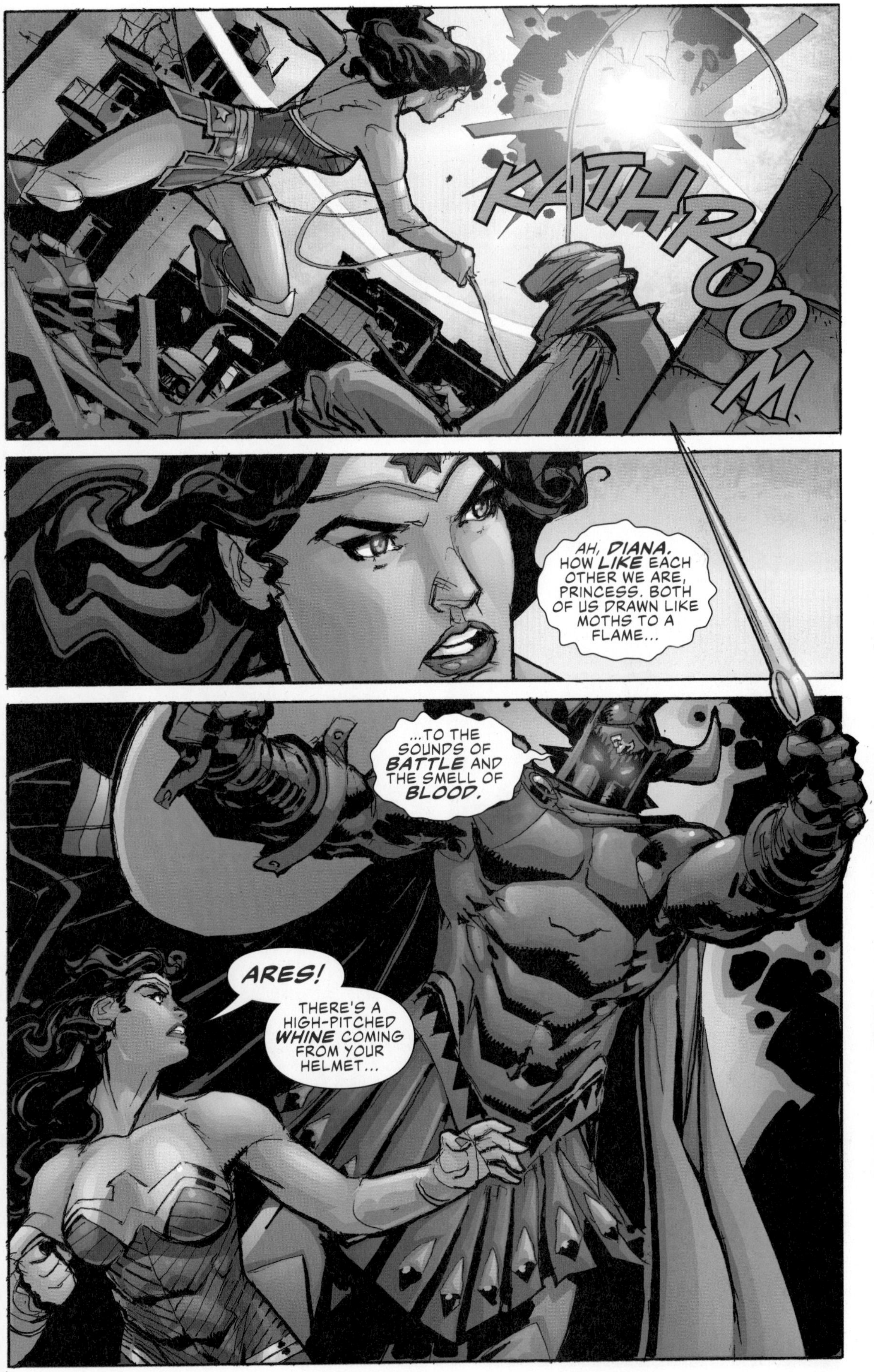
KATHROOOM
AH, DIANA. HOW LIKE EACH OTHER WE ARE, PRINCESS. BOTH OF US DRAWN LIKE MOTHS TO A FLAME...
...TO THE SOUNDS OF BATTLE AND THE SMELL OF BLOOD.
ARES!
THERE'S A HIGH-PITCHED WHINE COMING FROM YOUR HELMET...

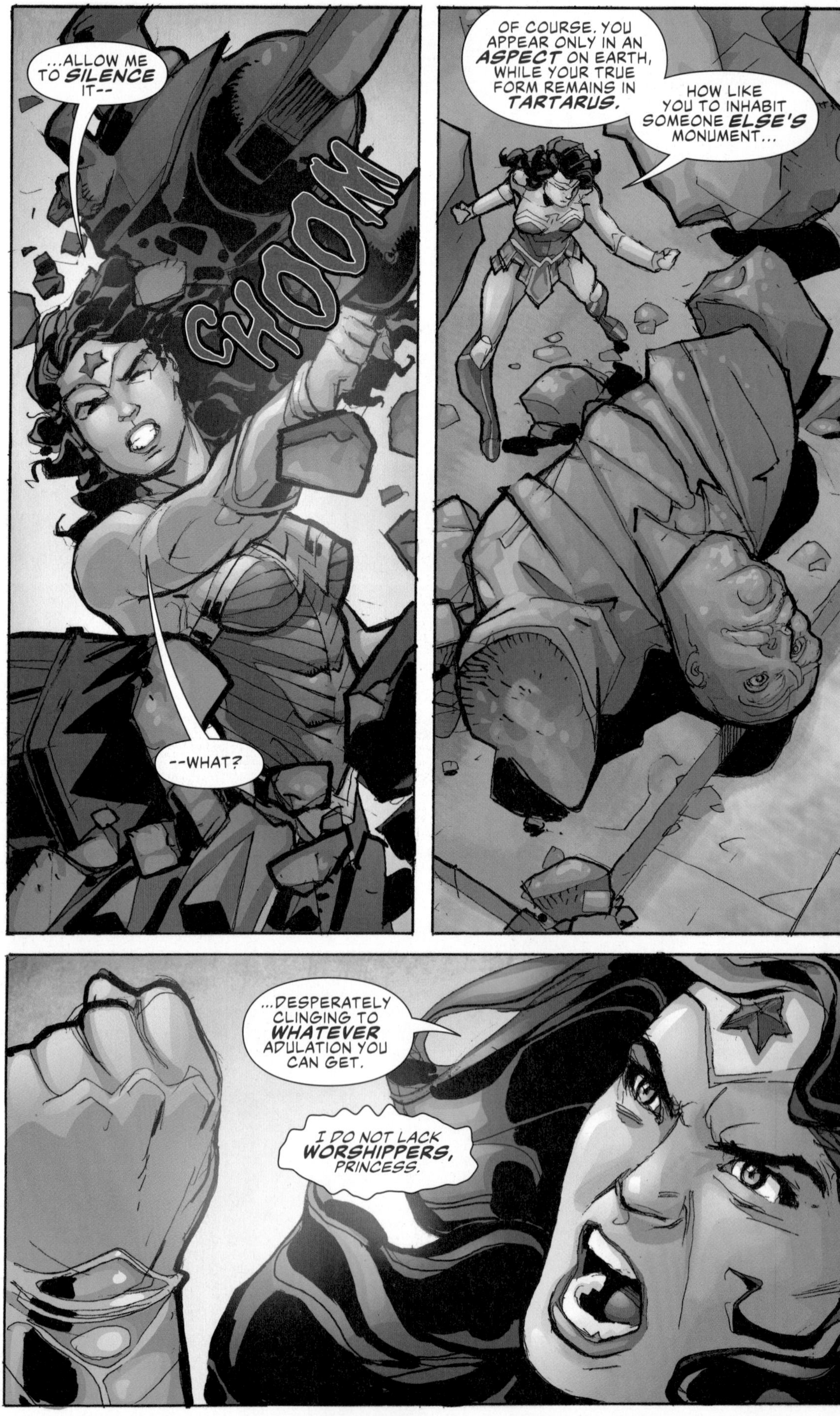
...ALLOW ME TO SILENCE IT--
CHOOM
--WHAT?
OF COURSE. YOU APPEAR ONLY IN AN ASPECT ON EARTH, WHILE YOUR TRUE FORM REMAINS IN TARTARUS.
HOW LIKE YOU TO INHABIT SOMEONE ELSE'S MONUMENT...
...DESPERATELY CLINGING TO WHATEVER ADULATION YOU CAN GET.
I DO NOT LACK WORSHIPPERS, PRINCESS.

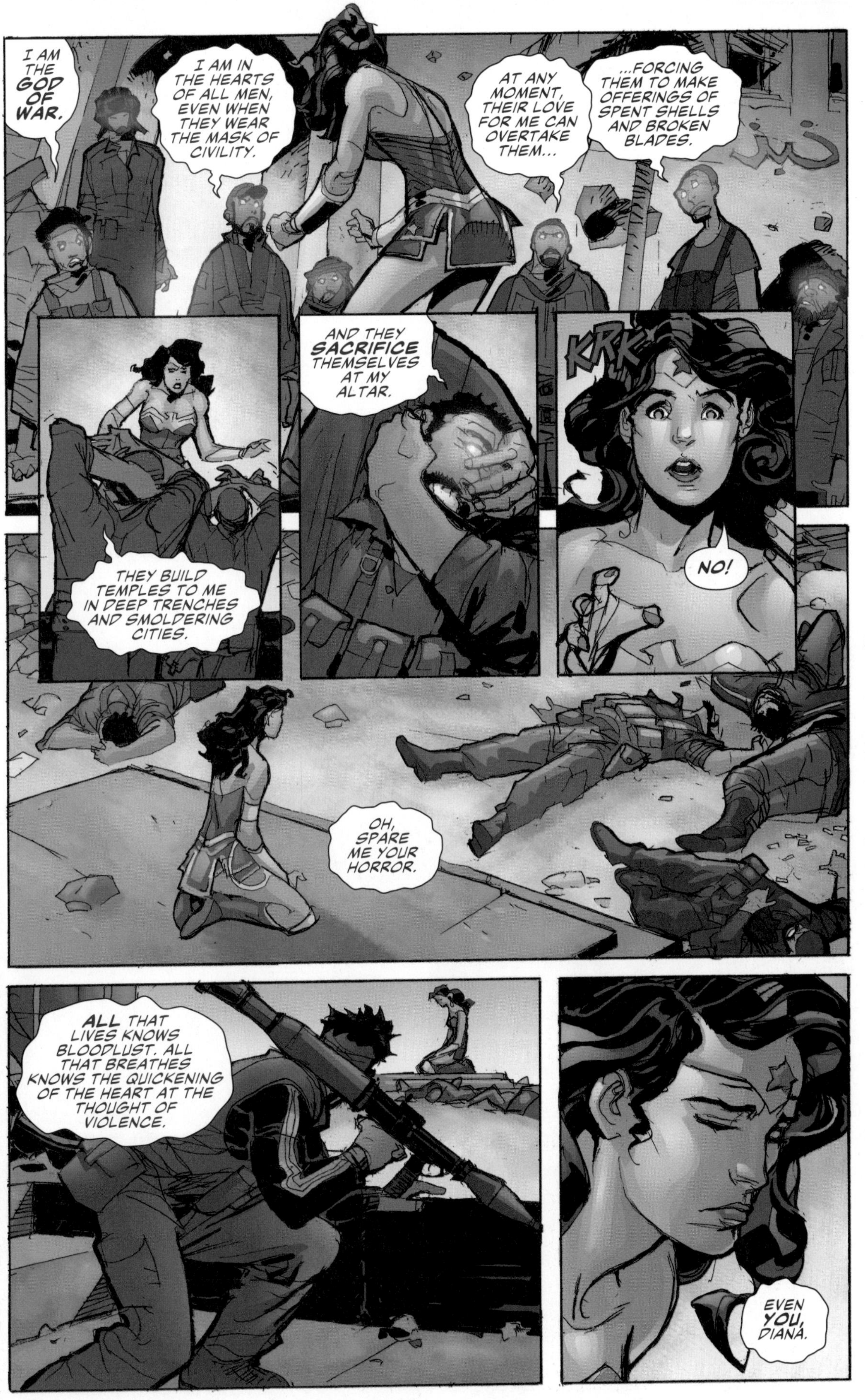
I AM THE GOD OF WAR.
I AM IN THE HEARTS OF ALL MEN, EVEN WHEN THEY WEAR THE MASK OF CIVILITY.
AT ANY MOMENT, THEIR LOVE FOR ME CAN OVERTAKE THEM...
...FORCING THEM TO MAKE OFFERINGS OF SPENT SHELLS AND BROKEN BLADES.
THEY BUILD TEMPLES TO ME IN DEEP TRENCHES AND SMOLDERING CITIES.
AND THEY SACRIFICE THEMSELVES AT MY ALTAR.
KRK
NO!
OH, SPARE ME YOUR HORROR.
ALL THAT LIVES KNOWS BLOODLUST. ALL THAT BREATHES KNOWS THE QUICKENING OF THE HEART AT THE THOUGHT OF VIOLENCE.
EVEN YOU, DIANA.

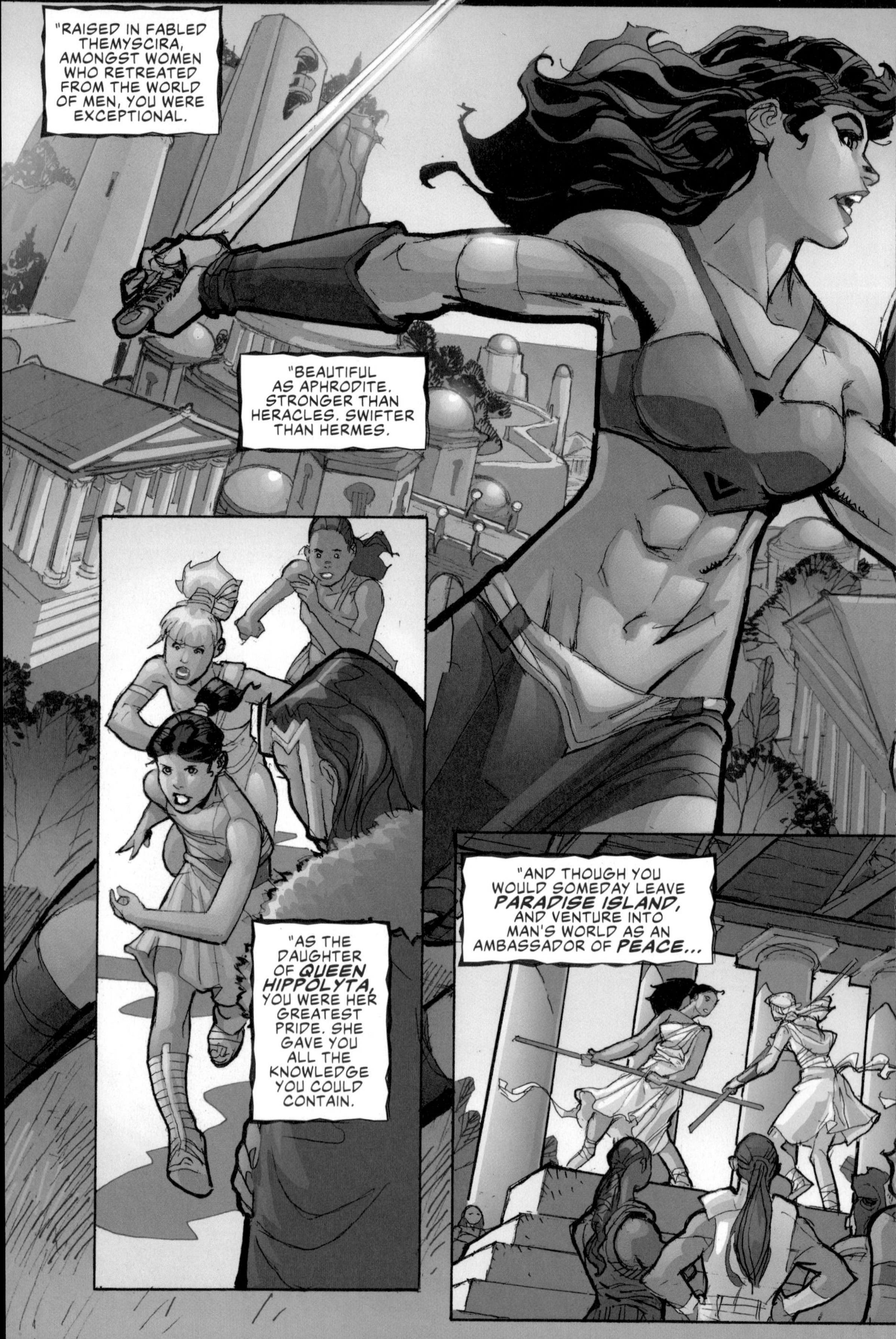
"RAISED IN FABLED THEMYSCIRA, AMONGST WOMEN WHO RETREATED FROM THE WORLD OF MEN, YOU WERE EXCEPTIONAL.
"BEAUTIFUL AS APHRODITE. STRONGER THAN HERACLES. SWIFTER THAN HERMES.
"AS THE DAUGHTER OF ***QUEEN HIPPOLYTA,*** YOU WERE HER GREATEST PRIDE. SHE GAVE YOU ALL THE KNOWLEDGE YOU COULD CONTAIN.
"AND THOUGH YOU WOULD SOMEDAY LEAVE ***PARADISE ISLAND,*** AND VENTURE INTO MAN'S WORLD AS AN AMBASSADOR OF ***PEACE...***

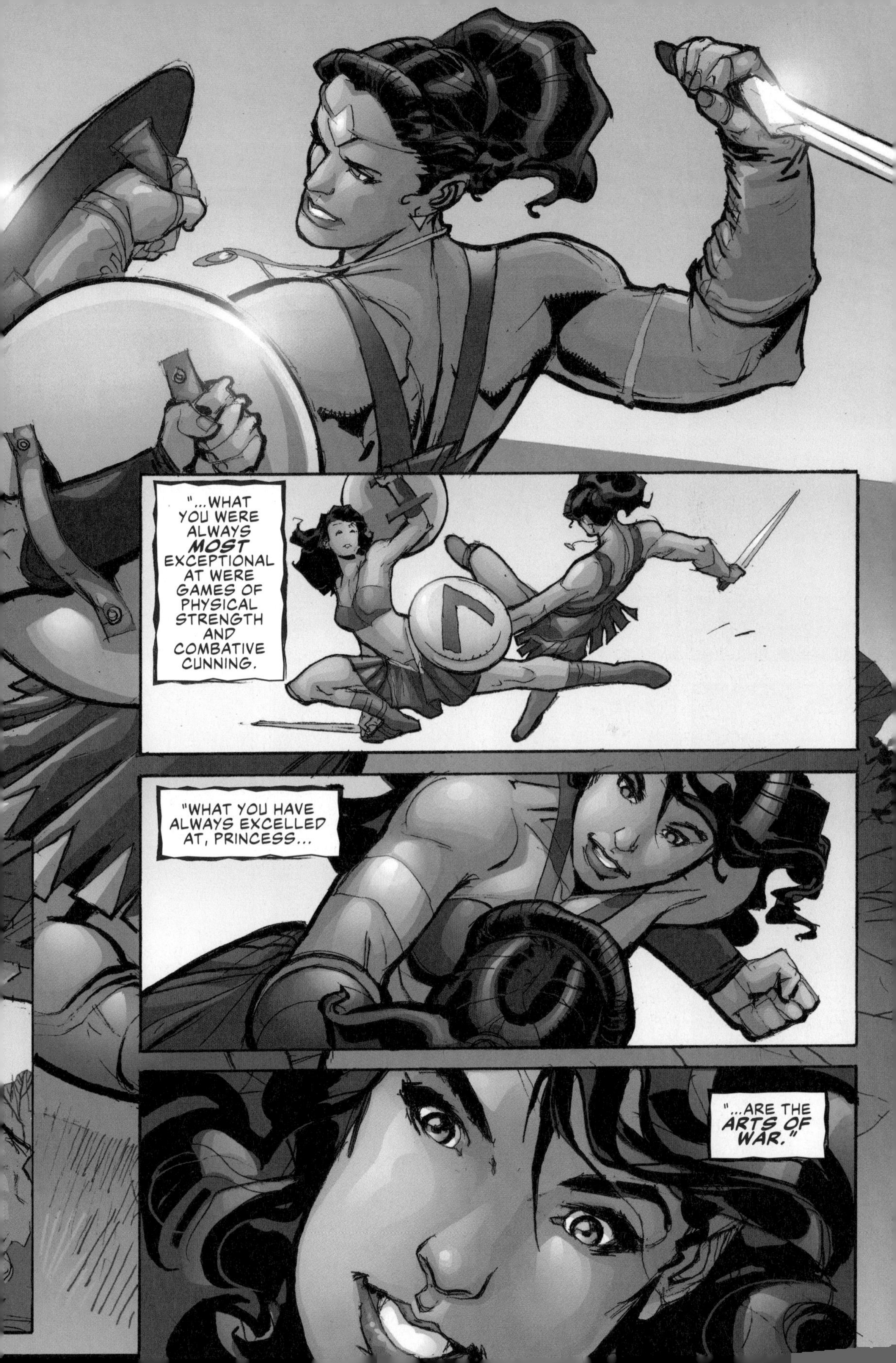
"...WHAT YOU WERE ALWAYS MOST EXCEPTIONAL AT WERE GAMES OF PHYSICAL STRENGTH AND COMBATIVE CUNNING.
"WHAT YOU HAVE ALWAYS EXCELLED AT, PRINCESS...
"...ARE THE ARTS OF WAR."

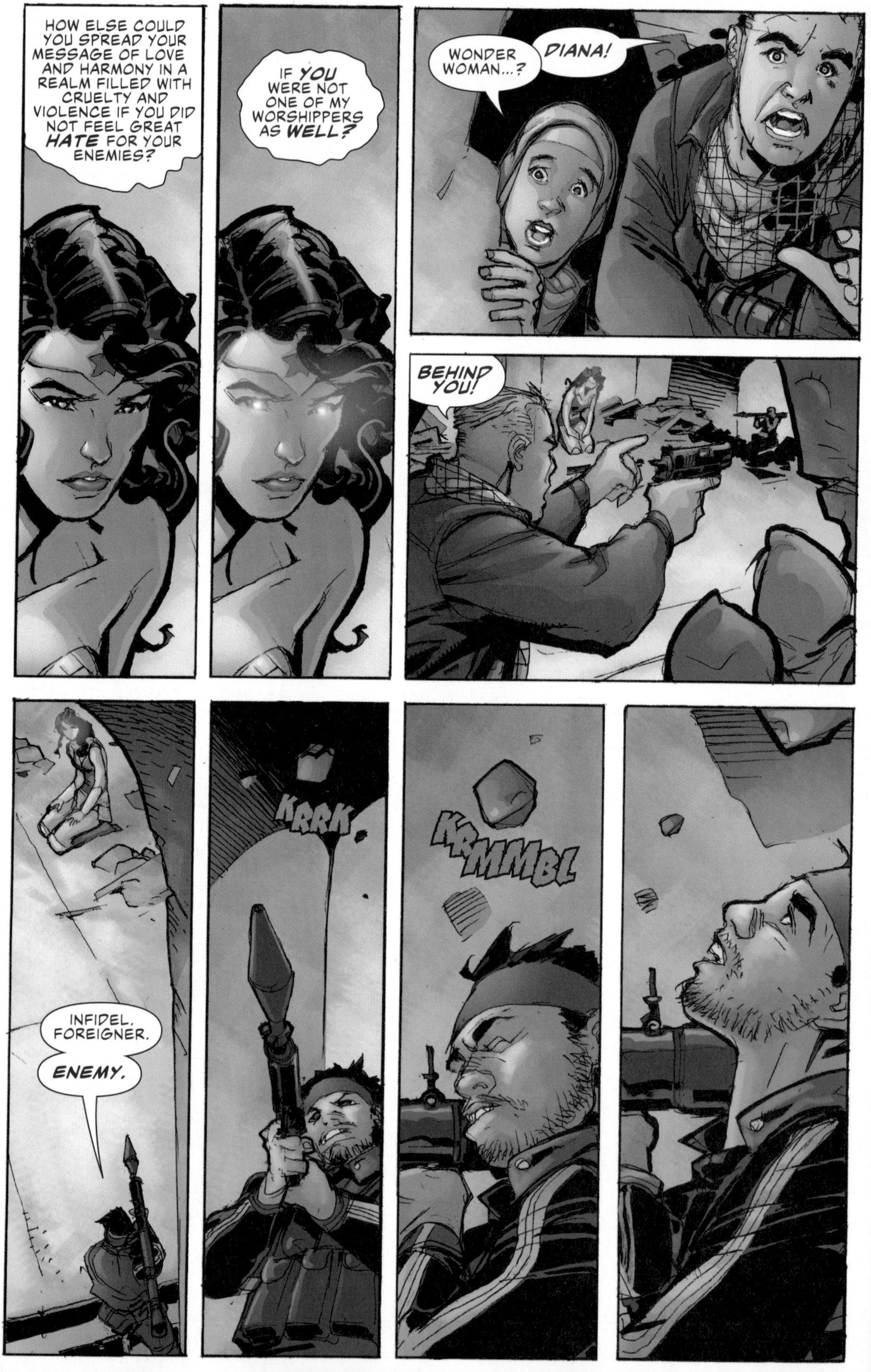
HOW ELSE COULD YOU SPREAD YOUR MESSAGE OF LOVE AND HARMONY IN A REALM FILLED WITH CRUELTY AND VIOLENCE IF YOU DID NOT FEEL GREAT **HATE** FOR YOUR ENEMIES?
IF ***YOU*** WERE NOT ONE OF MY WORSHIPPERS AS ***WELL?***
WONDER WOMAN...?
DIANA!
BEHIND YOU!
INFIDEL. FOREIGNER.
ENEMY.
KRRK
KRMMMBL

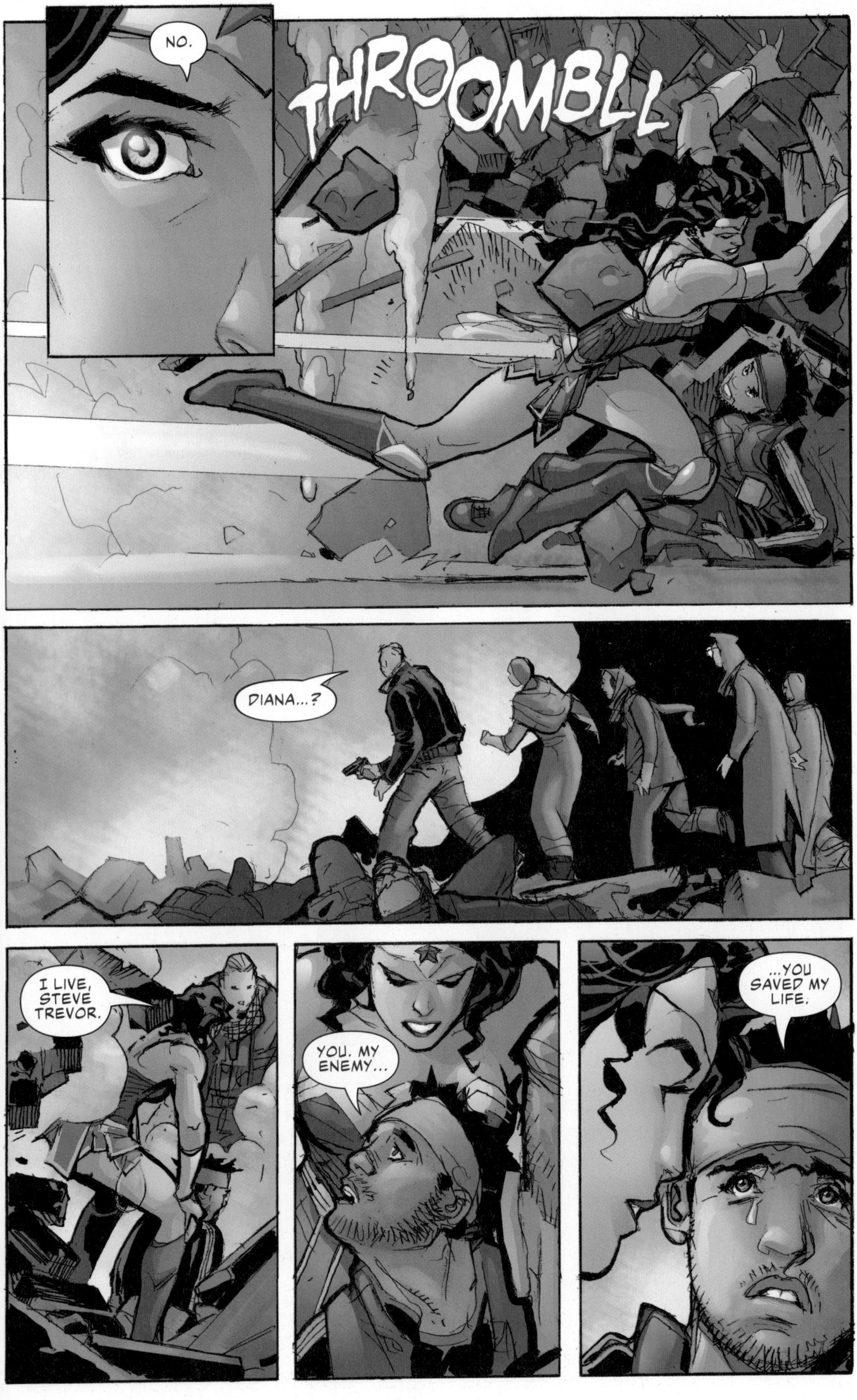
NO.
THROOMBLL
DIANA...?
I LIVE, STEVE TREVOR.
YOU. MY ENEMY...
...YOU SAVED MY LIFE.

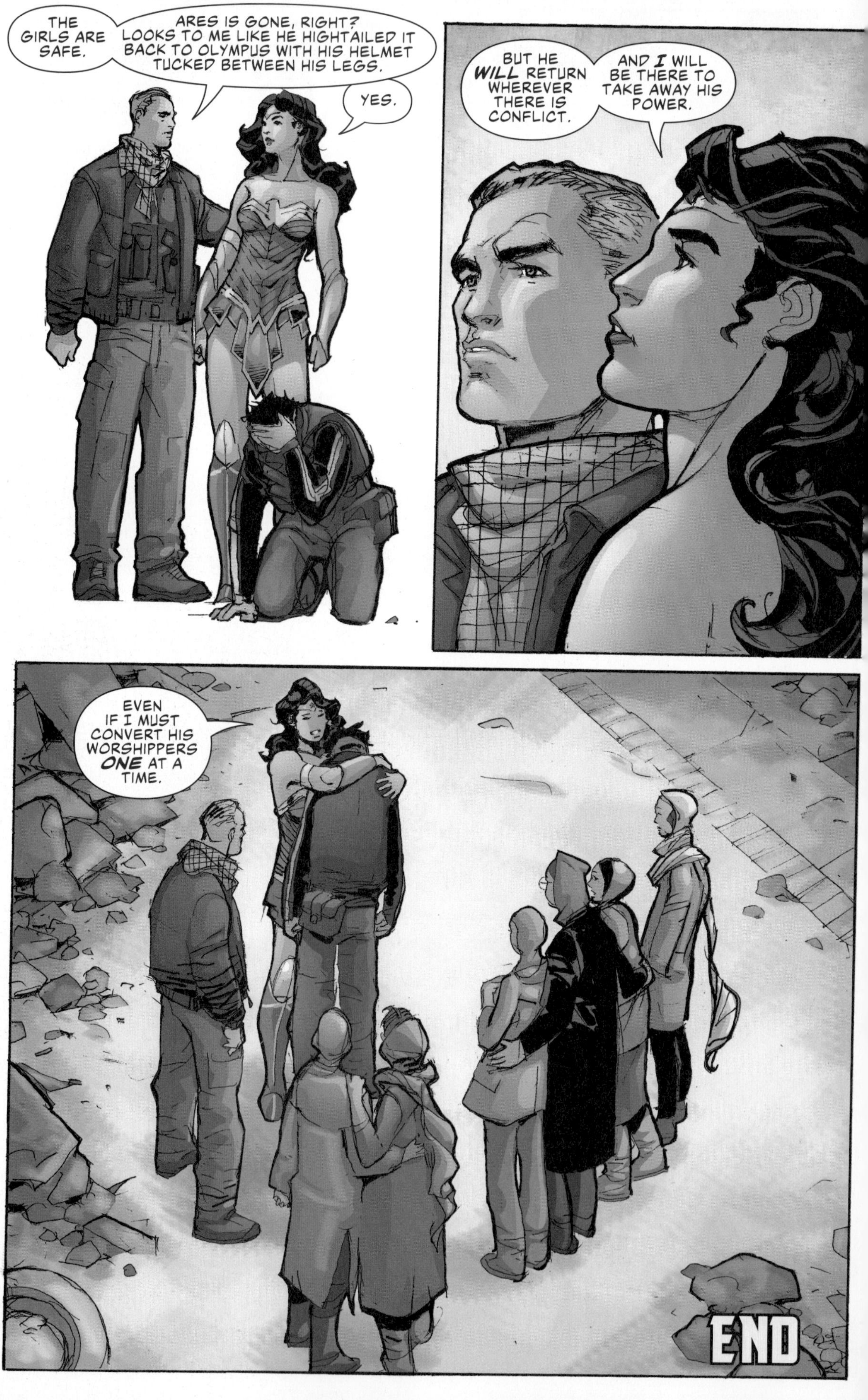
THE GIRLS ARE SAFE.
ARES IS GONE, RIGHT? LOOKS TO ME LIKE HE HIGHTAILED IT BACK TO OLYMPUS WITH HIS HELMET TUCKED BETWEEN HIS LEGS.
YES.
BUT HE WILL RETURN WHEREVER THERE IS CONFLICT.
AND I WILL BE THERE TO TAKE AWAY HIS POWER.
EVEN IF I MUST CONVERT HIS WORSHIPPERS ONE AT A TIME.
END

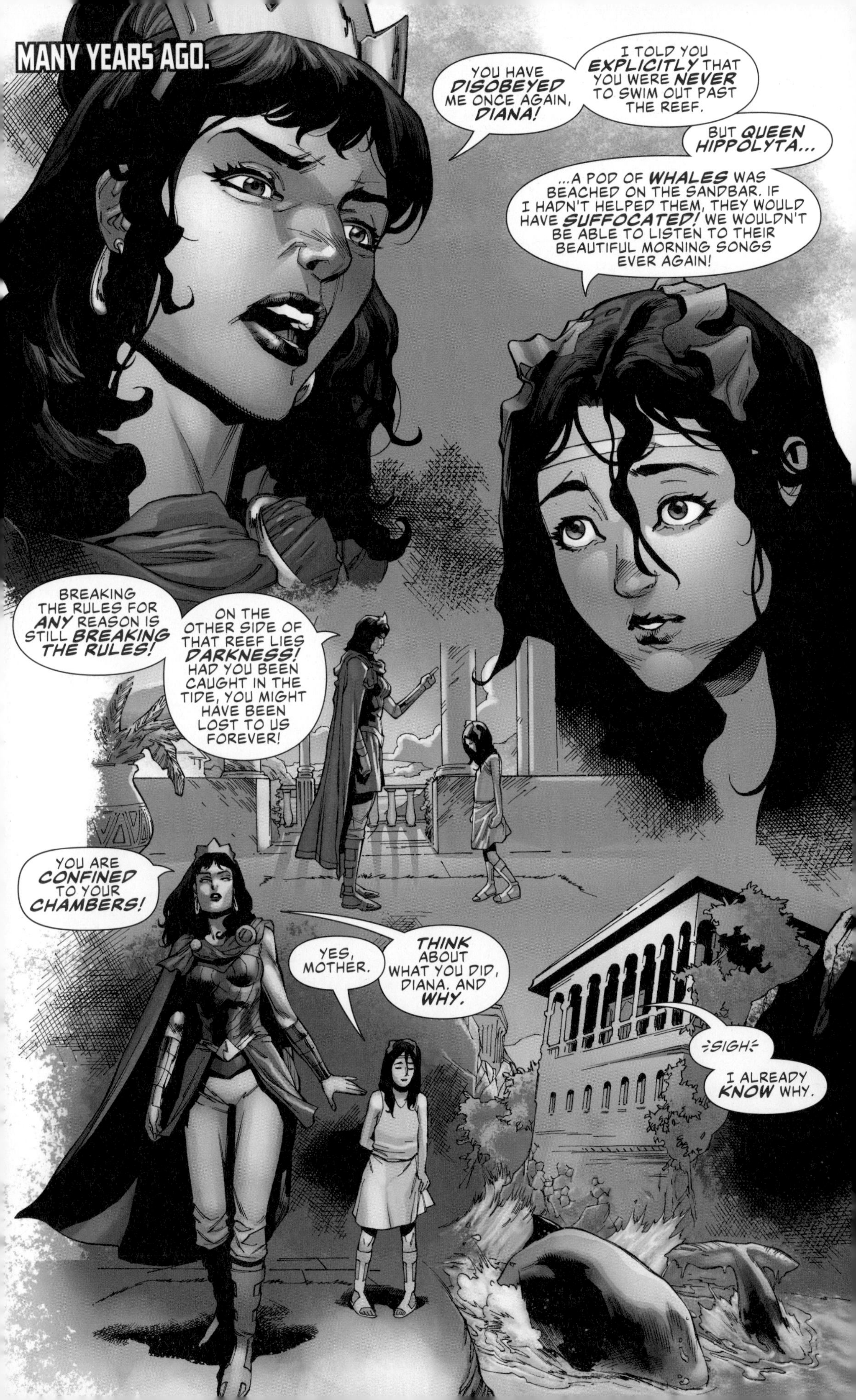
MANY YEARS AGO.
YOU HAVE DISOBEYED ME ONCE AGAIN, DIANA!
I TOLD YOU EXPLICITLY THAT YOU WERE NEVER TO SWIM OUT PAST THE REEF.
BUT QUEEN HIPPOLYTA...
...A POD OF WHALES WAS BEACHED ON THE SANDBAR. IF I HADN'T HELPED THEM, THEY WOULD HAVE SUFFOCATED! WE WOULDN'T BE ABLE TO LISTEN TO THEIR BEAUTIFUL MORNING SONGS EVER AGAIN!
BREAKING THE RULES FOR ANY REASON IS STILL BREAKING THE RULES!
ON THE OTHER SIDE OF THAT REEF LIES DARKNESS! HAD YOU BEEN CAUGHT IN THE TIDE, YOU MIGHT HAVE BEEN LOST TO US FOREVER!
YOU ARE CONFINED TO YOUR CHAMBERS!
YES, MOTHER.
THINK ABOUT WHAT YOU DID, DIANA. AND WHY.
=SIGH=
I ALREADY KNOW WHY.

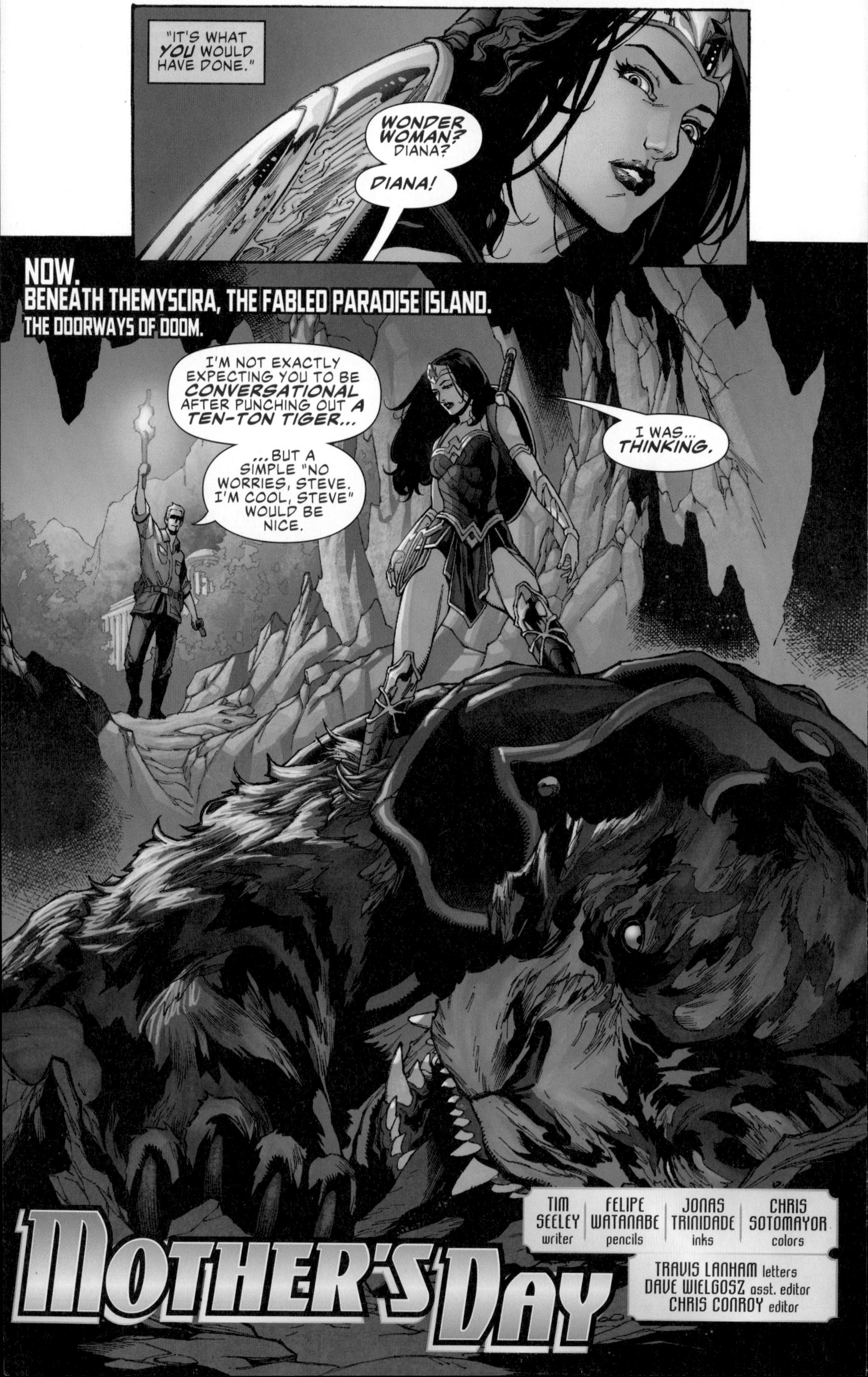
"IT'S WHAT YOU WOULD HAVE DONE."
WONDER WOMAN? DIANA?
DIANA!
NOW.
BENEATH THEMYSCIRA, THE FABLED PARADISE ISLAND.
THE DOORWAYS OF DOOM.
I'M NOT EXACTLY EXPECTING YOU TO BE CONVERSATIONAL AFTER PUNCHING OUT A TEN-TON TIGER...
...BUT A SIMPLE "NO WORRIES, STEVE. I'M COOL, STEVE" WOULD BE NICE.
I WAS... THINKING.
MOTHER'S DAY
TIM SEELEY writer
FELIPE WATANABE pencils
JONAS TRINIDADE inks
CHRIS SOTOMAYOR colors
TRAVIS LANHAM letters
DAVE WIELGOSZ asst. editor
CHRIS CONROY editor

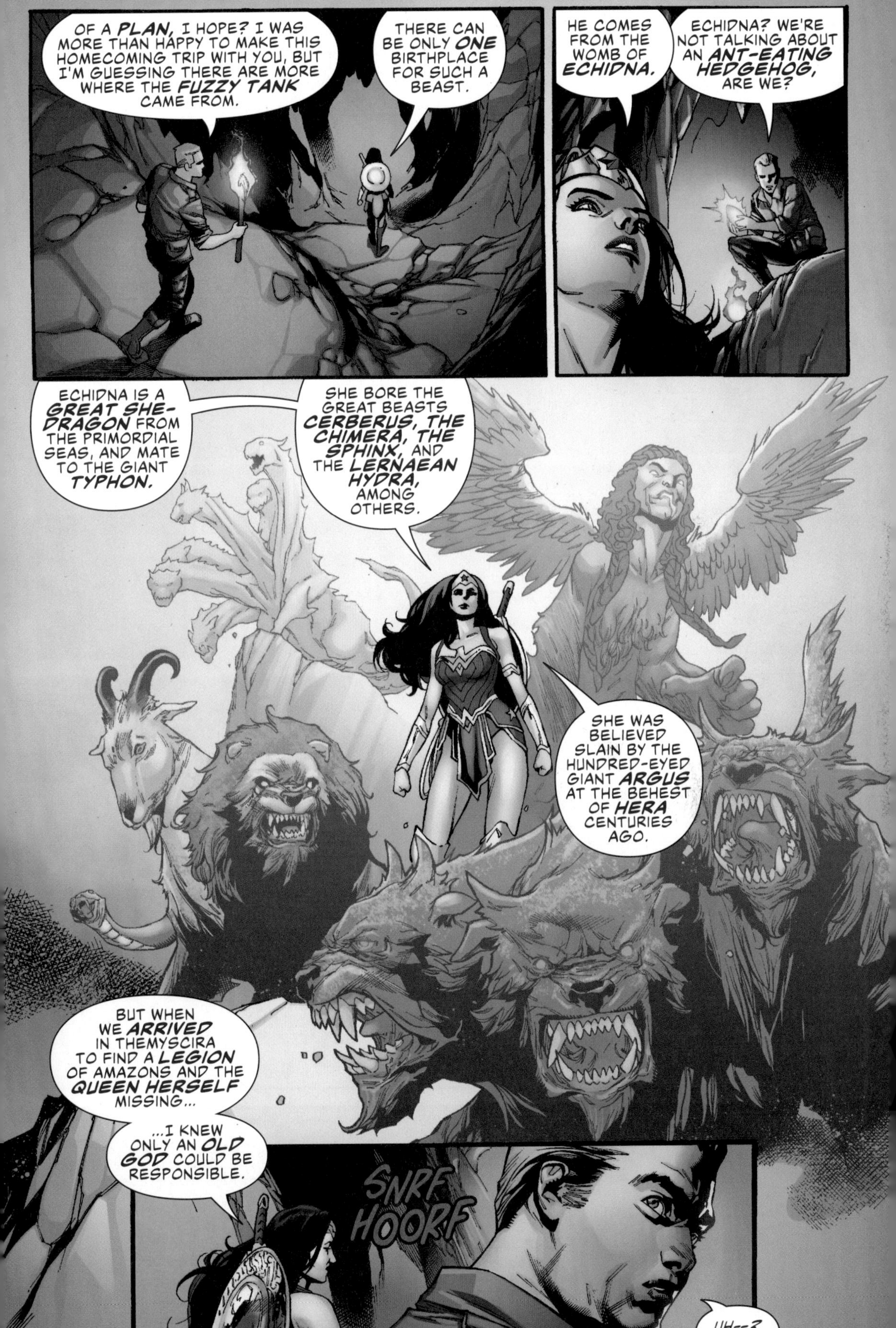

OF A PLAN, I HOPE? I WAS MORE THAN HAPPY TO MAKE THIS HOMECOMING TRIP WITH YOU, BUT I'M GUESSING THERE ARE MORE WHERE THE FUZZY TANK CAME FROM.
THERE CAN BE ONLY ONE BIRTHPLACE FOR SUCH A BEAST.
HE COMES FROM THE WOMB OF ECHIDNA.
ECHIDNA? WE'RE NOT TALKING ABOUT AN ANT-EATING HEDGEHOG, ARE WE?
ECHIDNA IS A GREAT SHE-DRAGON FROM THE PRIMORDIAL SEAS, AND MATE TO THE GIANT TYPHON.
SHE BORE THE GREAT BEASTS CERBERUS, THE CHIMERA, THE SPHINX, AND THE LERNAEAN HYDRA, AMONG OTHERS.
SHE WAS BELIEVED SLAIN BY THE HUNDRED-EYED GIANT ARGUS AT THE BEHEST OF HERA CENTURIES AGO.
BUT WHEN WE ARRIVED IN THEMYSCIRA TO FIND A LEGION OF AMAZONS AND THE QUEEN HERSELF MISSING...
...I KNEW ONLY AN OLD GOD COULD BE RESPONSIBLE.
SNRF HOORF
UH--? DIANA...

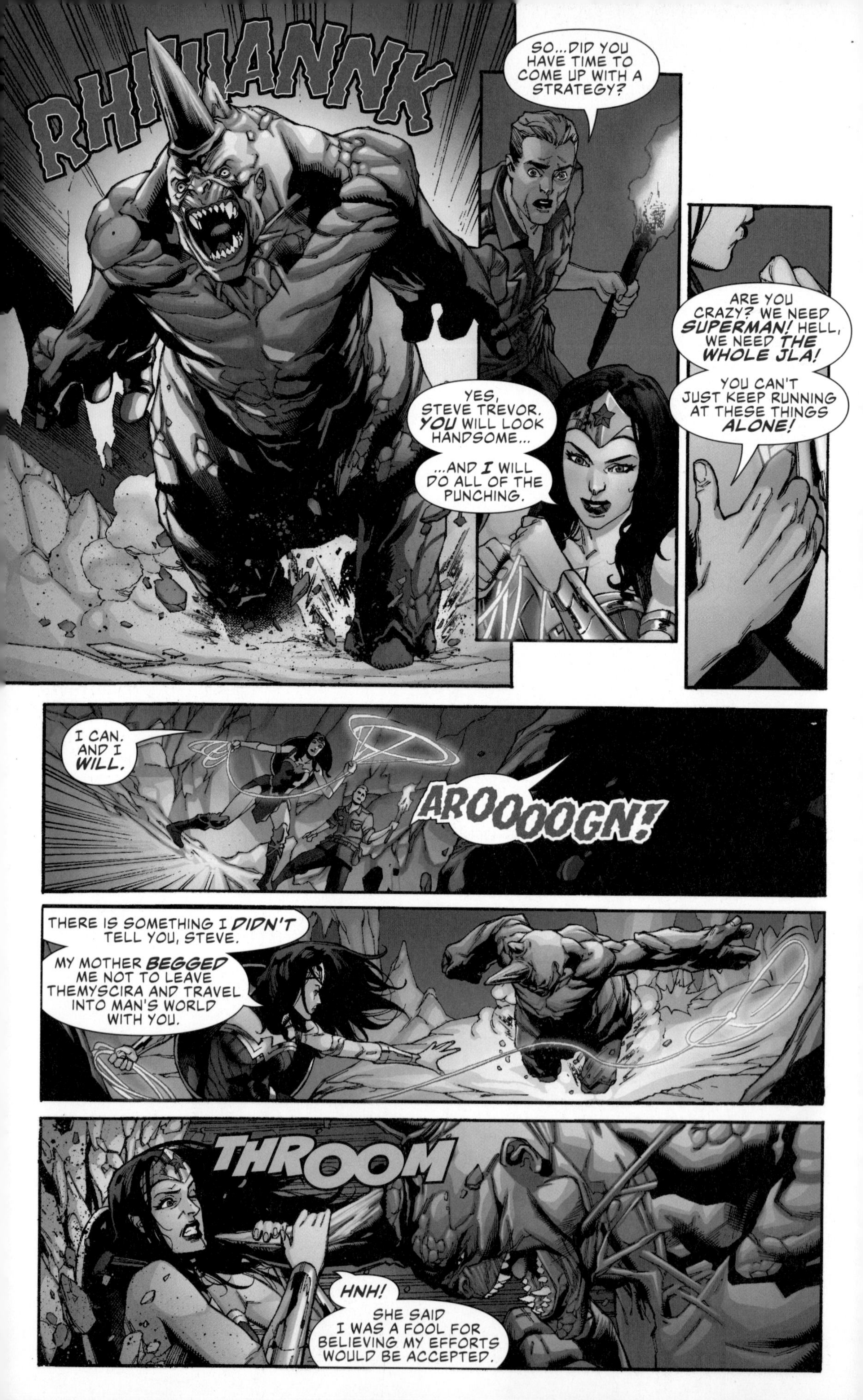
RHHHANNK
SO...DID YOU HAVE TIME TO COME UP WITH A STRATEGY?
YES, STEVE TREVOR. YOU WILL LOOK HANDSOME...
...AND I WILL DO ALL OF THE PUNCHING.
ARE YOU CRAZY? WE NEED SUPERMAN! HELL, WE NEED THE WHOLE JLA!
YOU CAN'T JUST KEEP RUNNING AT THESE THINGS ALONE!
I CAN. AND I WILL.
AROOOOOGN!
THERE IS SOMETHING I DIDN'T TELL YOU, STEVE.
MY MOTHER BEGGED ME NOT TO LEAVE THEMYSCIRA AND TRAVEL INTO MAN'S WORLD WITH YOU.
THROOM
HNH!
SHE SAID I WAS A FOOL FOR BELIEVING MY EFFORTS WOULD BE ACCEPTED.

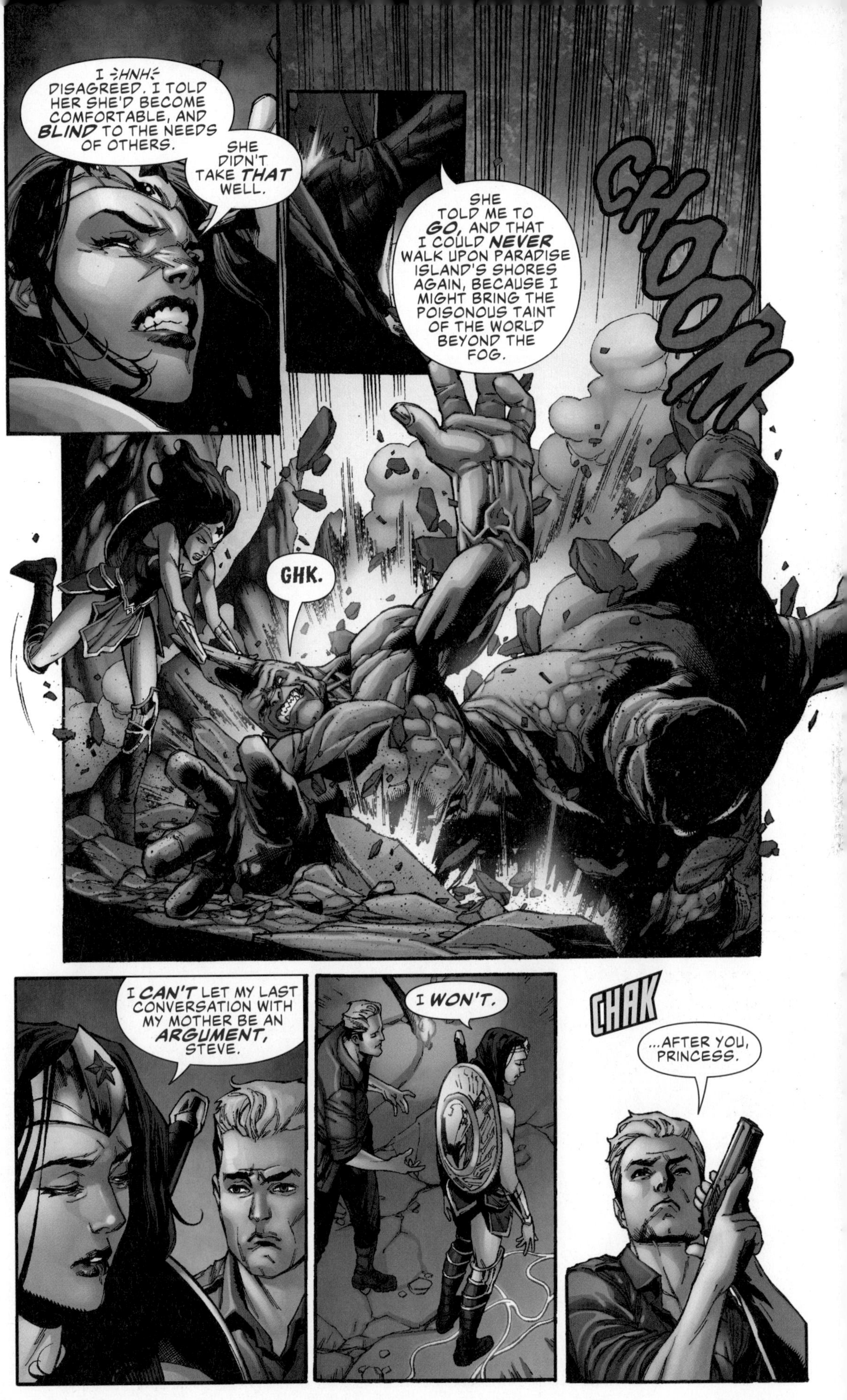
I -HNH- DISAGREED. I TOLD HER SHE'D BECOME COMFORTABLE, AND BLIND TO THE NEEDS OF OTHERS.
SHE DIDN'T TAKE THAT WELL.
SHE TOLD ME TO GO, AND THAT I COULD NEVER WALK UPON PARADISE ISLAND'S SHORES AGAIN, BECAUSE I MIGHT BRING THE POISONOUS TAINT OF THE WORLD BEYOND THE FOG.
CHOOOM
GHK.
I CAN'T LET MY LAST CONVERSATION WITH MY MOTHER BE AN ARGUMENT, STEVE.
I WON'T.
CHAK
...AFTER YOU, PRINCESS.

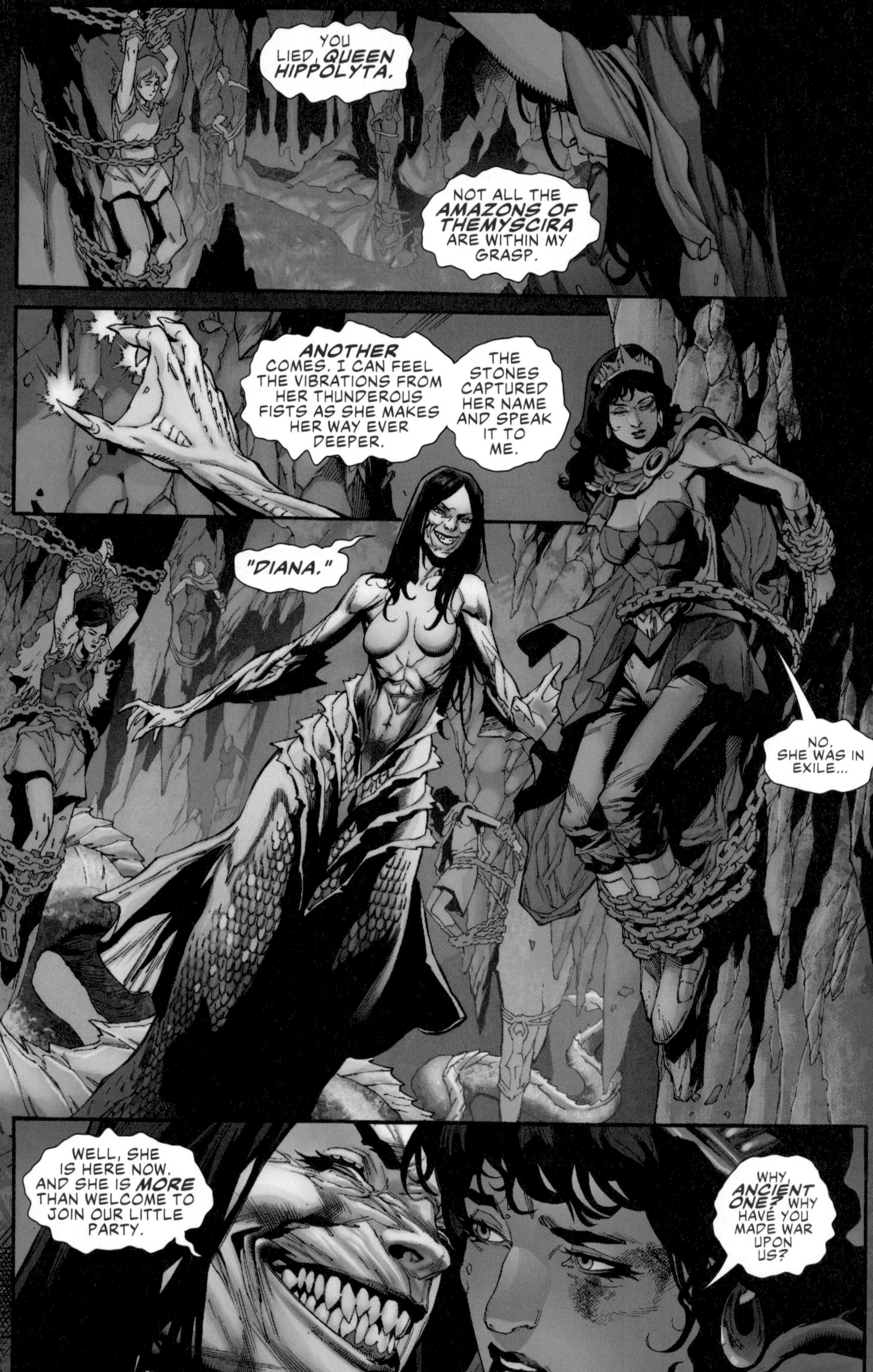
YOU LIED, QUEEN HIPPOLYTA.
NOT ALL THE AMAZONS OF THEMYSCIRA ARE WITHIN MY GRASP.
ANOTHER COMES. I CAN FEEL THE VIBRATIONS FROM HER THUNDEROUS FISTS AS SHE MAKES HER WAY EVER DEEPER.
THE STONES CAPTURED HER NAME AND SPEAK IT TO ME.
"DIANA."
NO. SHE WAS IN EXILE...
WELL, SHE IS HERE NOW. AND SHE IS MORE THAN WELCOME TO JOIN OUR LITTLE PARTY.
WHY, ANCIENT ONE? WHY HAVE YOU MADE WAR UPON US?

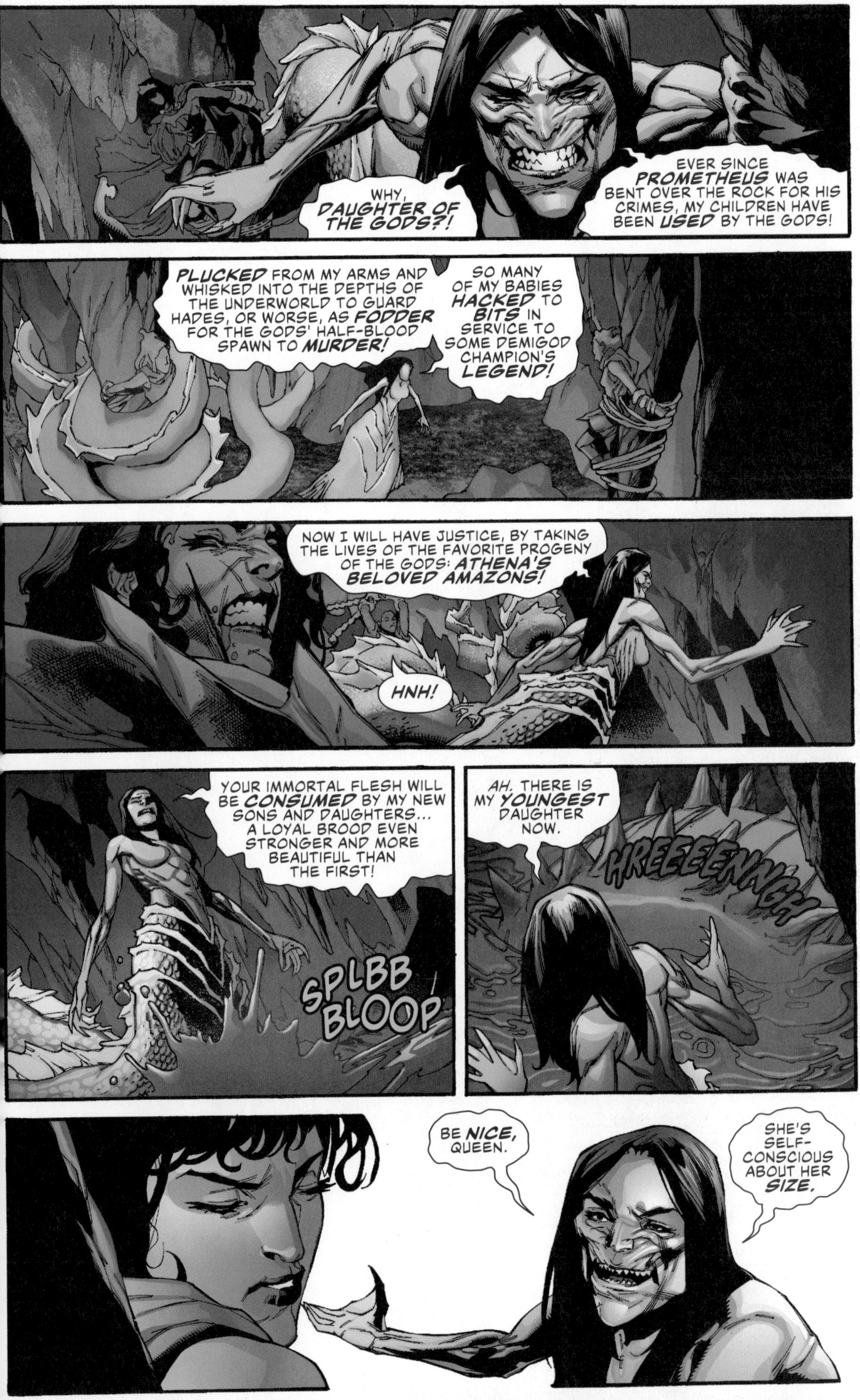
WHY, DAUGHTER OF THE GODS?!
EVER SINCE PROMETHEUS WAS BENT OVER THE ROCK FOR HIS CRIMES, MY CHILDREN HAVE BEEN USED BY THE GODS!
PLUCKED FROM MY ARMS AND WHISKED INTO THE DEPTHS OF THE UNDERWORLD TO GUARD HADES, OR WORSE, AS FODDER FOR THE GODS' HALF-BLOOD SPAWN TO MURDER!
SO MANY OF MY BABIES HACKED TO BITS IN SERVICE TO SOME DEMIGOD CHAMPION'S LEGEND!
NOW I WILL HAVE JUSTICE, BY TAKING THE LIVES OF THE FAVORITE PROGENY OF THE GODS: ATHENA'S BELOVED AMAZONS!
HNH!
YOUR IMMORTAL FLESH WILL BE CONSUMED BY MY NEW SONS AND DAUGHTERS... A LOYAL BROOD EVEN STRONGER AND MORE BEAUTIFUL THAN THE FIRST!
SPLBB BLOOP
AH. THERE IS MY YOUNGEST DAUGHTER NOW.
HREEEENNGH
BE NICE, QUEEN.
SHE'S SELF-CONSCIOUS ABOUT HER SIZE.

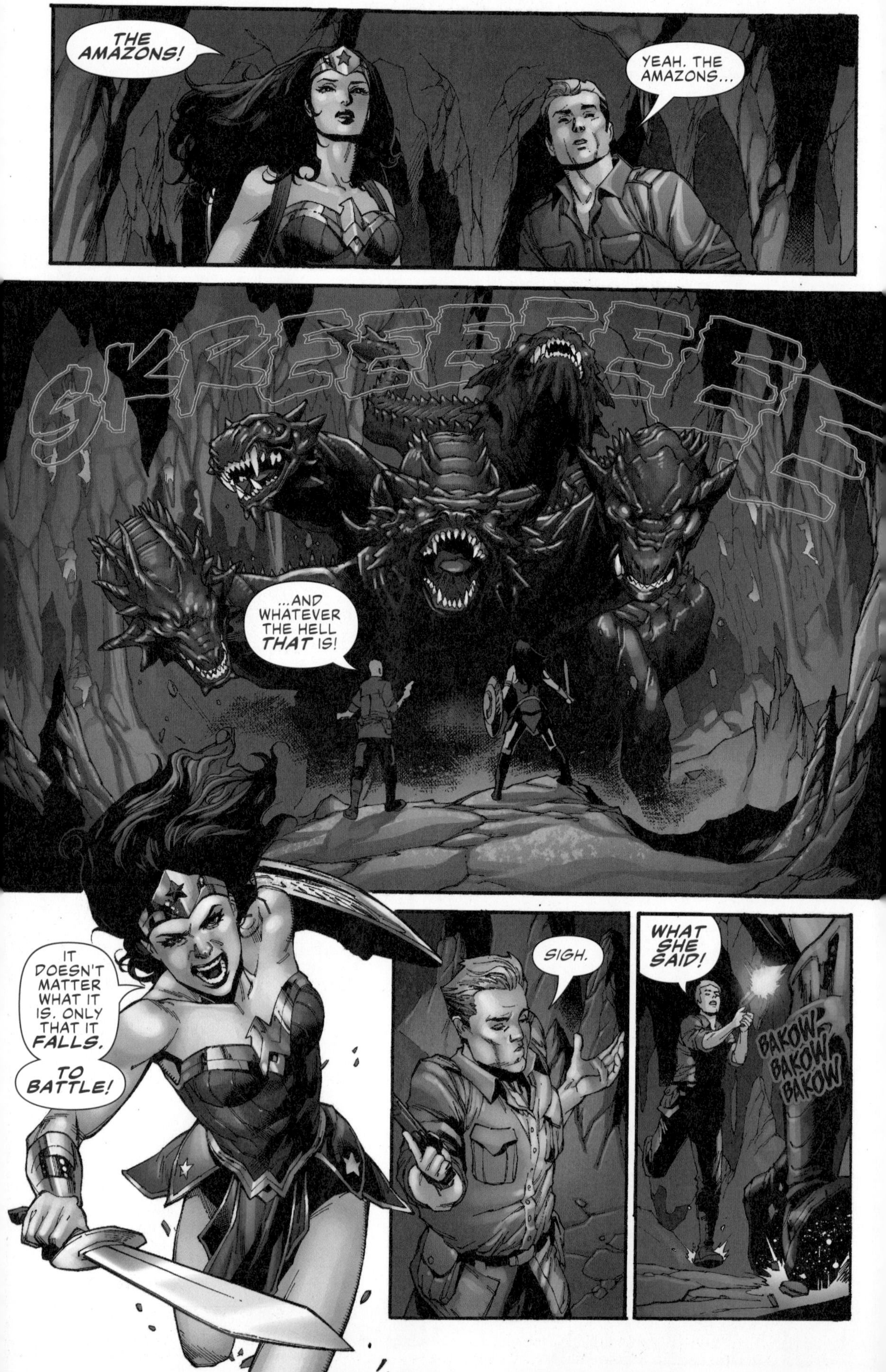
THE AMAZONS!
YEAH. THE AMAZONS...
...AND WHATEVER THE HELL *THAT* IS!
IT DOESN'T MATTER WHAT IT IS. ONLY THAT IT *FALLS.*
TO BATTLE!
SIGH.
WHAT SHE SAID!
BAKOW BAKOW BAKOW

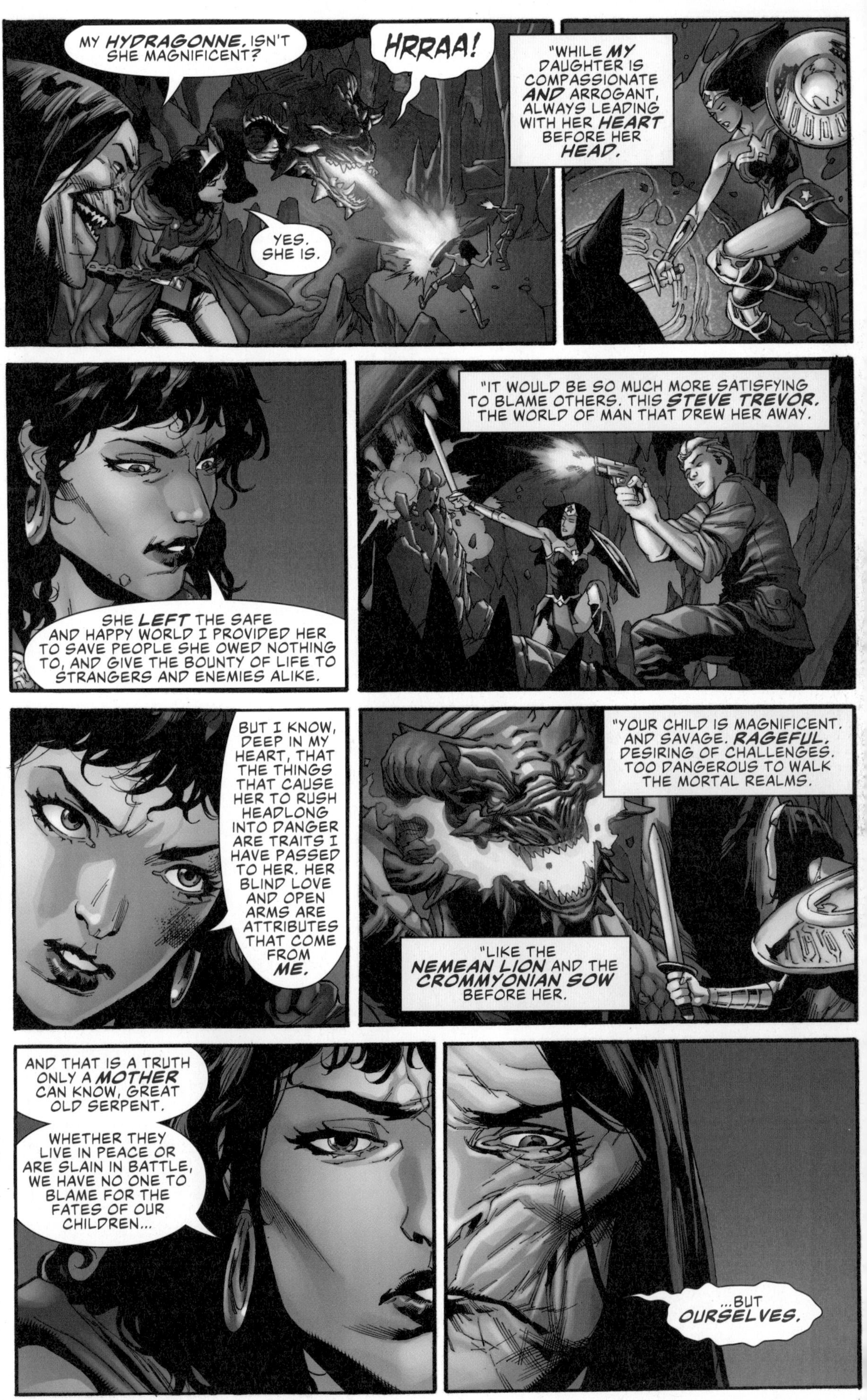
MY HYDRAGONNE. ISN'T SHE MAGNIFICENT?
HRRAA!
YES. SHE IS.
"WHILE MY DAUGHTER IS COMPASSIONATE AND ARROGANT, ALWAYS LEADING WITH HER HEART BEFORE HER HEAD.
SHE LEFT THE SAFE AND HAPPY WORLD I PROVIDED HER TO SAVE PEOPLE SHE OWED NOTHING TO, AND GIVE THE BOUNTY OF LIFE TO STRANGERS AND ENEMIES ALIKE.
"IT WOULD BE SO MUCH MORE SATISFYING TO BLAME OTHERS. THIS STEVE TREVOR. THE WORLD OF MAN THAT DREW HER AWAY.
BUT I KNOW, DEEP IN MY HEART, THAT THE THINGS THAT CAUSE HER TO RUSH HEADLONG INTO DANGER ARE TRAITS I HAVE PASSED TO HER. HER BLIND LOVE AND OPEN ARMS ARE ATTRIBUTES THAT COME FROM ME.
"YOUR CHILD IS MAGNIFICENT. AND SAVAGE. RAGEFUL. DESIRING OF CHALLENGES. TOO DANGEROUS TO WALK THE MORTAL REALMS.
"LIKE THE NEMEAN LION AND THE CROMMYONIAN SOW BEFORE HER.
AND THAT IS A TRUTH ONLY A MOTHER CAN KNOW, GREAT OLD SERPENT.
WHETHER THEY LIVE IN PEACE OR ARE SLAIN IN BATTLE, WE HAVE NO ONE TO BLAME FOR THE FATES OF OUR CHILDREN...
...BUT OURSELVES.

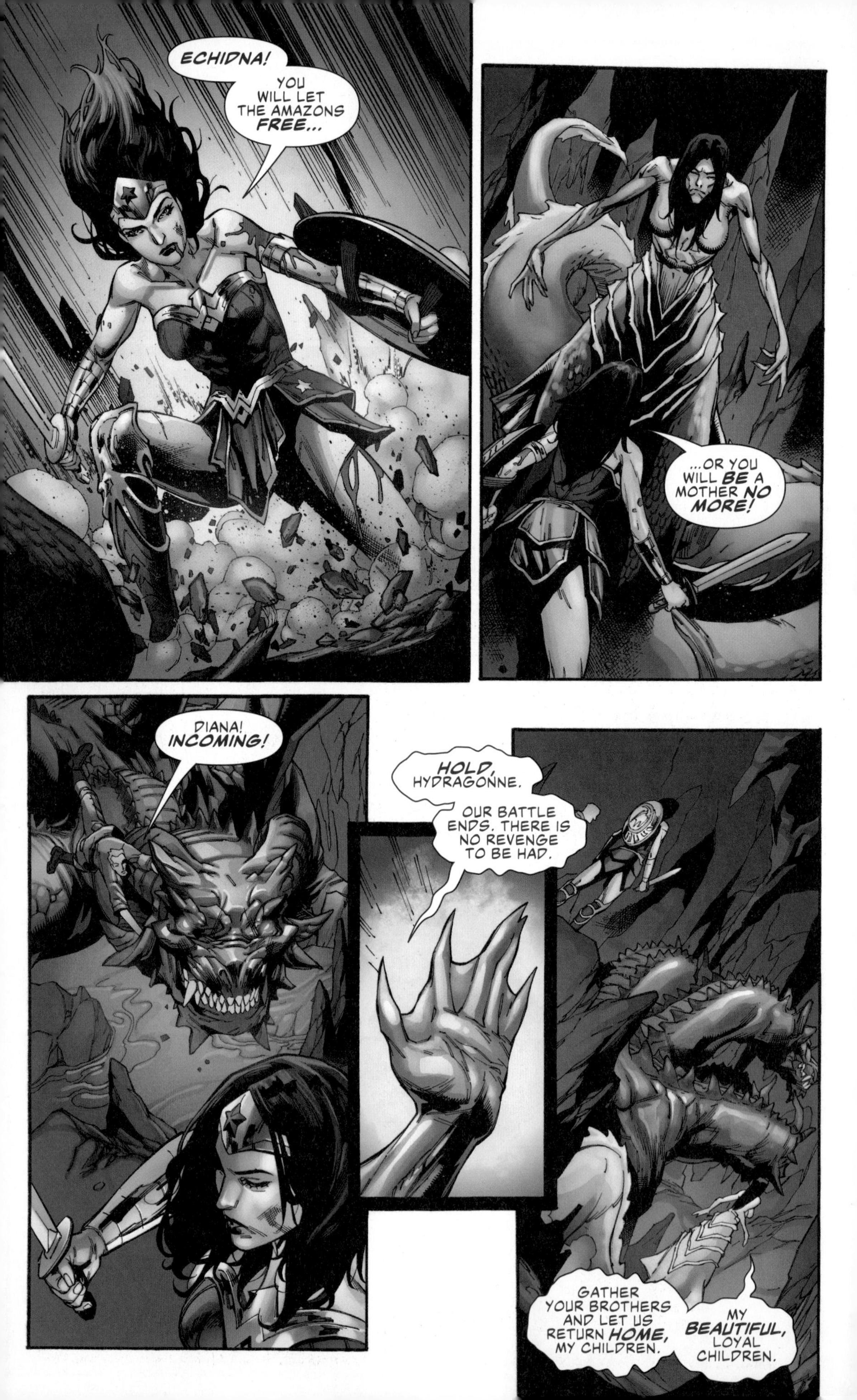
ECHIDNA!
YOU WILL LET THE AMAZONS FREE...
...OR YOU WILL BE A MOTHER NO MORE!
DIANA! INCOMING!
HOLD, HYDRAGONNE.
OUR BATTLE ENDS. THERE IS NO REVENGE TO BE HAD.
GATHER YOUR BROTHERS AND LET US RETURN HOME, MY CHILDREN.
MY BEAUTIFUL, LOYAL CHILDREN.

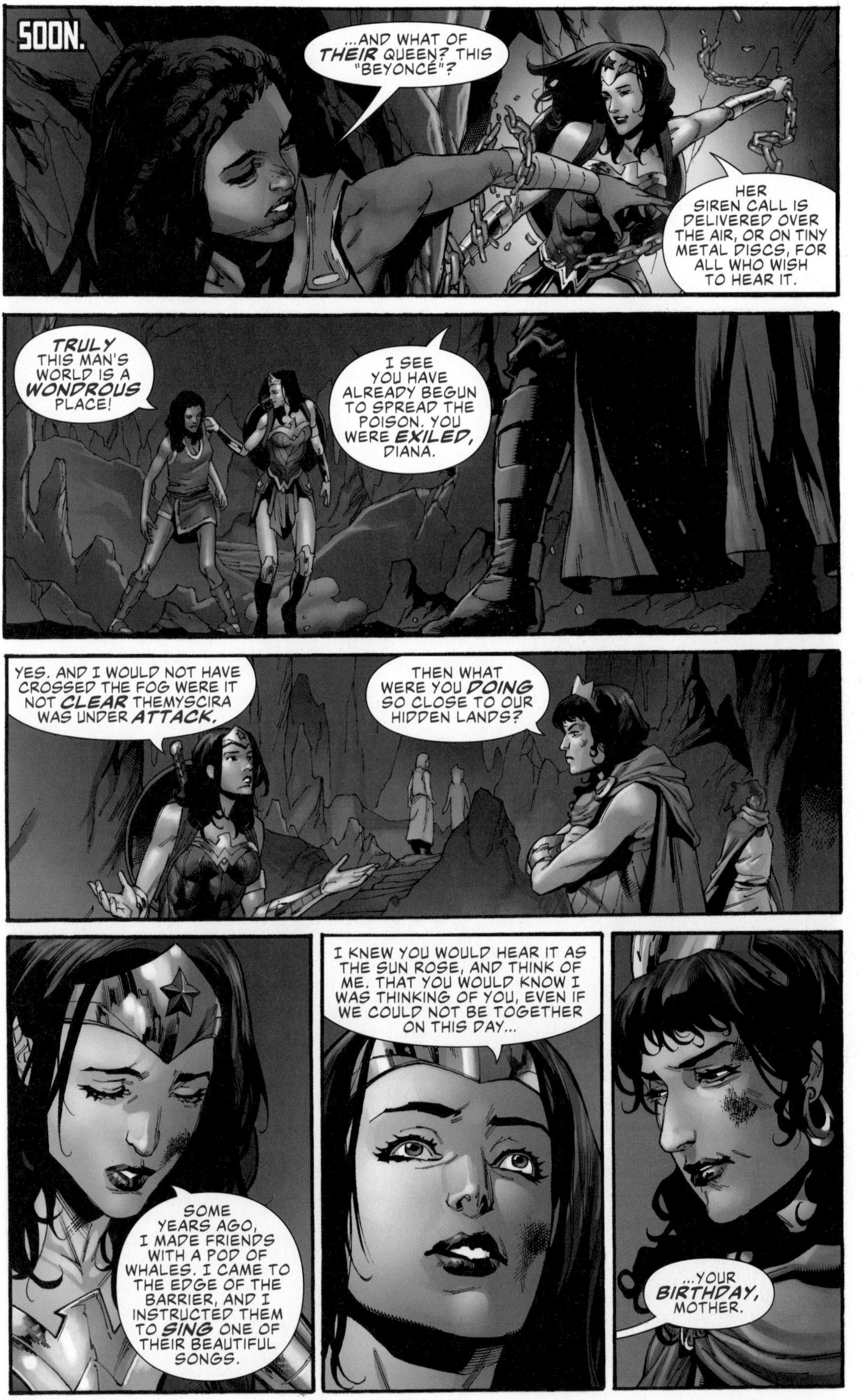
SOON.
...AND WHAT OF THEIR QUEEN? THIS "BEYONCÉ"?
HER SIREN CALL IS DELIVERED OVER THE AIR, OR ON TINY METAL DISCS, FOR ALL WHO WISH TO HEAR IT.
TRULY THIS MAN'S WORLD IS A WONDROUS PLACE!
I SEE YOU HAVE ALREADY BEGUN TO SPREAD THE POISON. YOU WERE EXILED, DIANA.
YES. AND I WOULD NOT HAVE CROSSED THE FOG WERE IT NOT CLEAR THEMYSCIRA WAS UNDER ATTACK.
THEN WHAT WERE YOU DOING SO CLOSE TO OUR HIDDEN LANDS?
SOME YEARS AGO, I MADE FRIENDS WITH A POD OF WHALES. I CAME TO THE EDGE OF THE BARRIER, AND I INSTRUCTED THEM TO SING ONE OF THEIR BEAUTIFUL SONGS.
I KNEW YOU WOULD HEAR IT AS THE SUN ROSE, AND THINK OF ME. THAT YOU WOULD KNOW I WAS THINKING OF YOU, EVEN IF WE COULD NOT BE TOGETHER ON THIS DAY...
...YOUR BIRTHDAY, MOTHER.

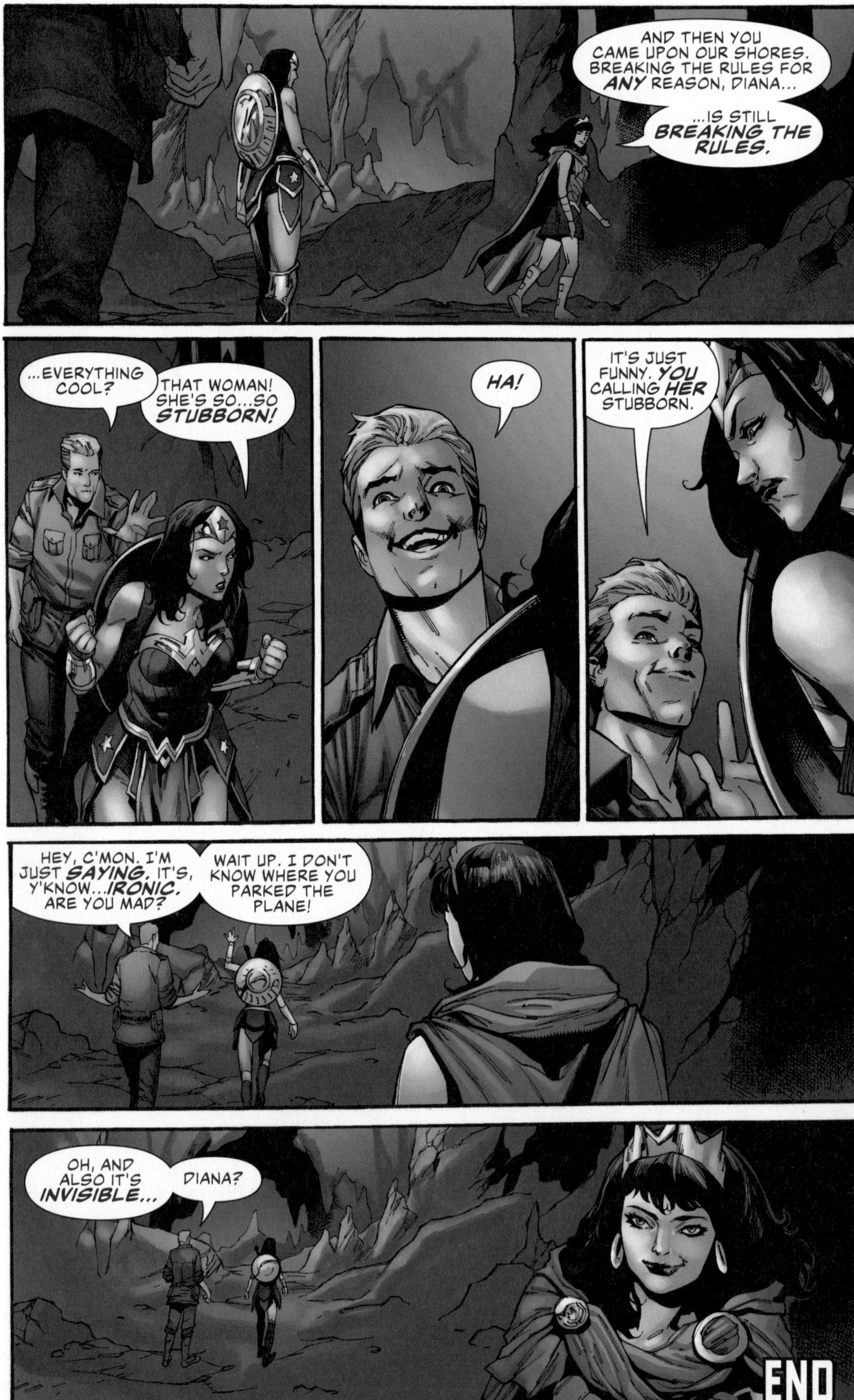
AND THEN YOU CAME UPON OUR SHORES. BREAKING THE RULES FOR ANY REASON, DIANA...
...IS STILL BREAKING THE RULES.
...EVERYTHING COOL?
THAT WOMAN! SHE'S SO...SO STUBBORN!
HA!
IT'S JUST FUNNY. YOU CALLING HER STUBBORN.
HEY, C'MON. I'M JUST SAYING. IT'S, Y'KNOW...IRONIC. ARE YOU MAD?
WAIT UP. I DON'T KNOW WHERE YOU PARKED THE PLANE!
OH, AND ALSO IT'S INVISIBLE...
DIANA?
END

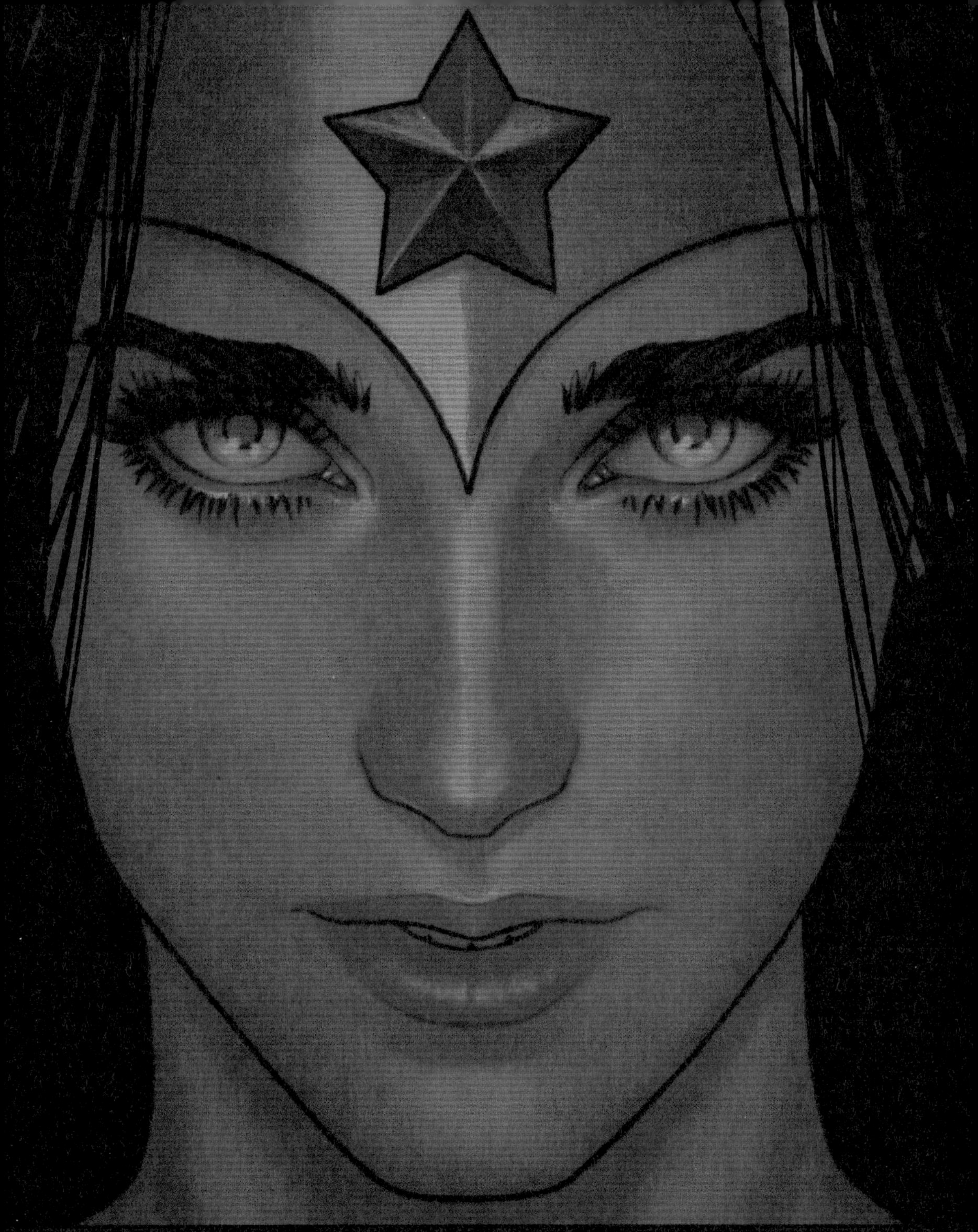

WONDER WOMAN

VARIANT COVER GALLERY

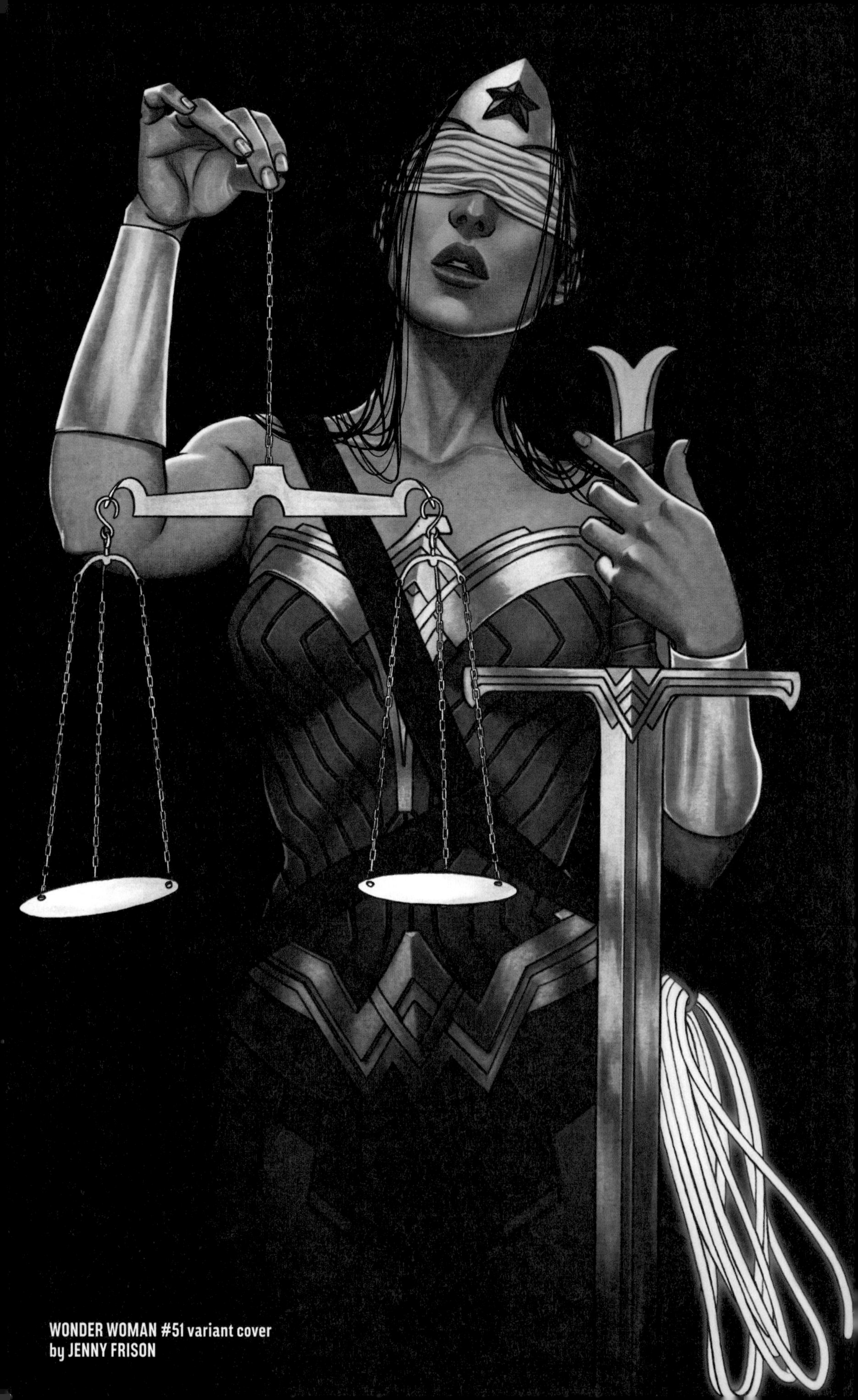

WONDER WOMAN #51 variant cover
by JENNY FRISON

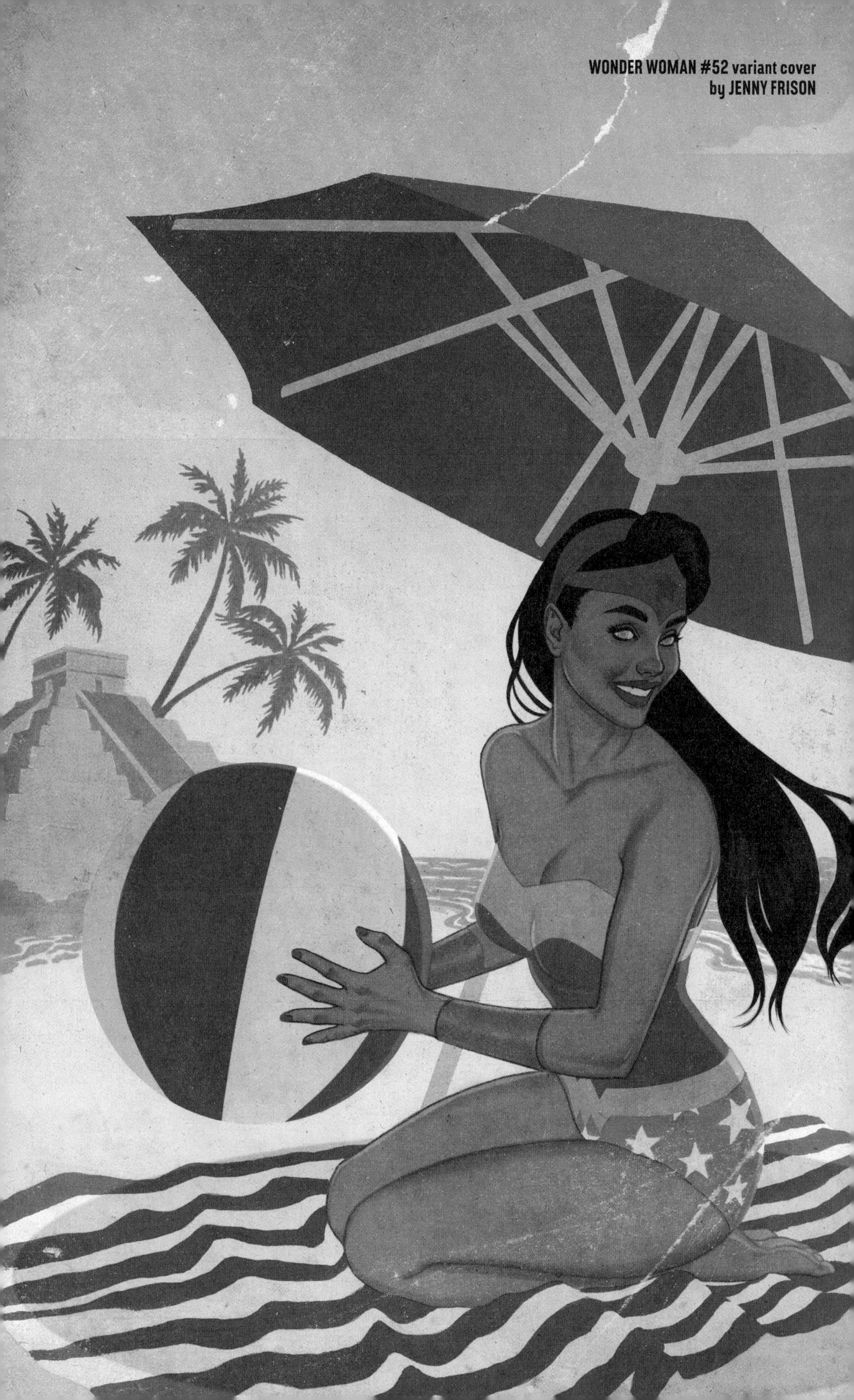

WONDER WOMAN #52 variant cover
by JENNY FRISON

WONDER WOMAN #53 variant cover
by JENNY FRISON

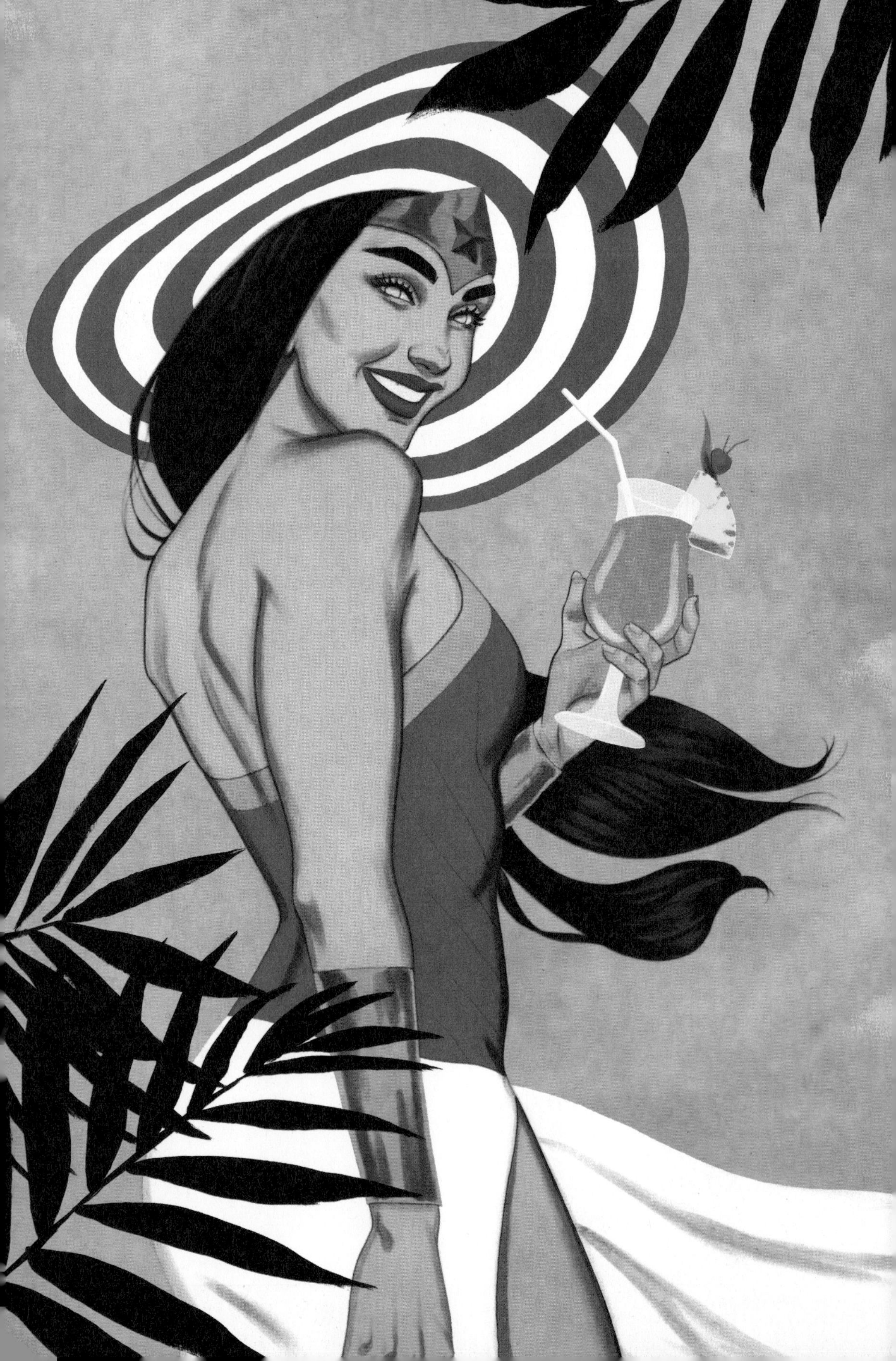

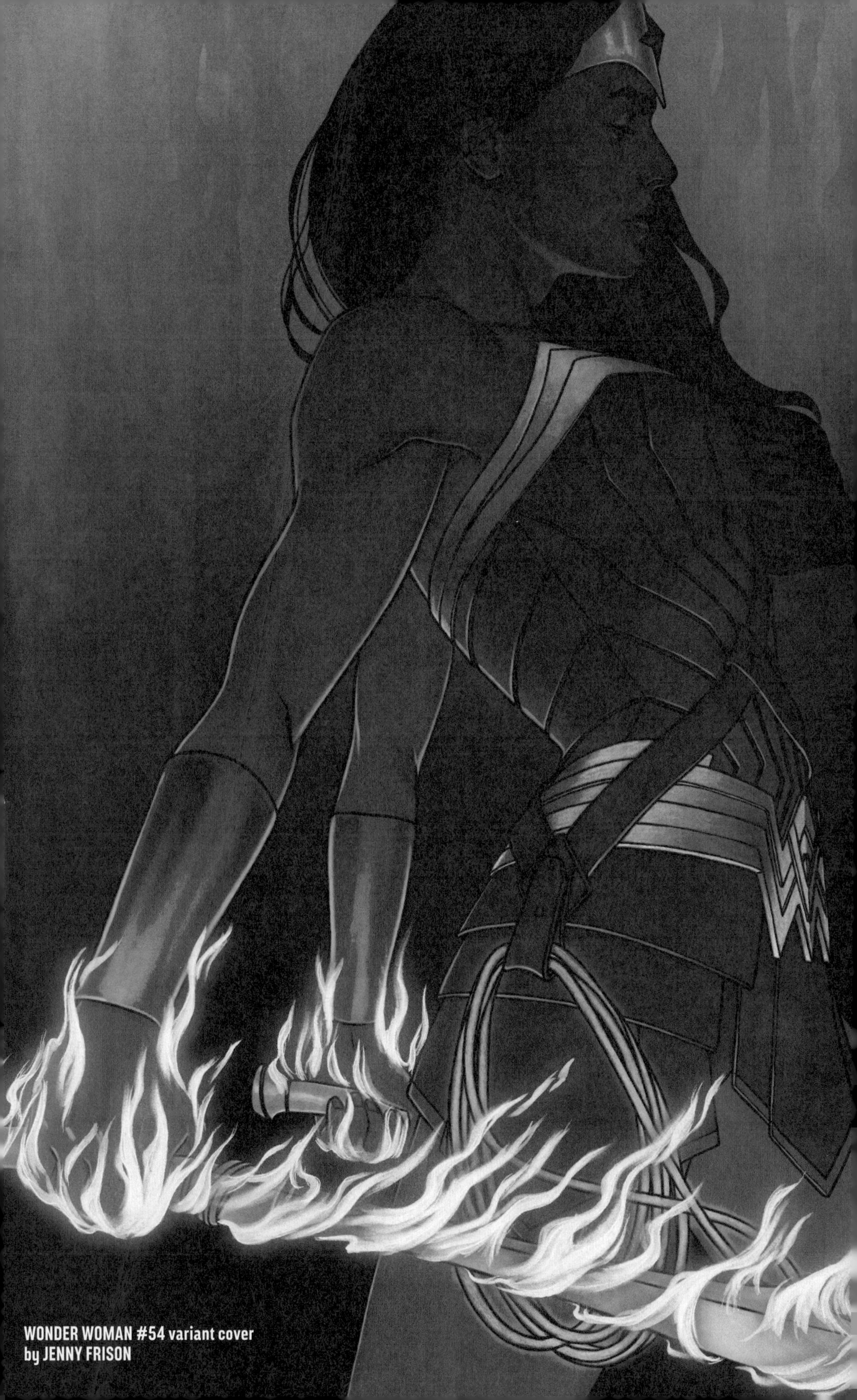

WONDER WOMAN #54 variant cover
by JENNY FRISON

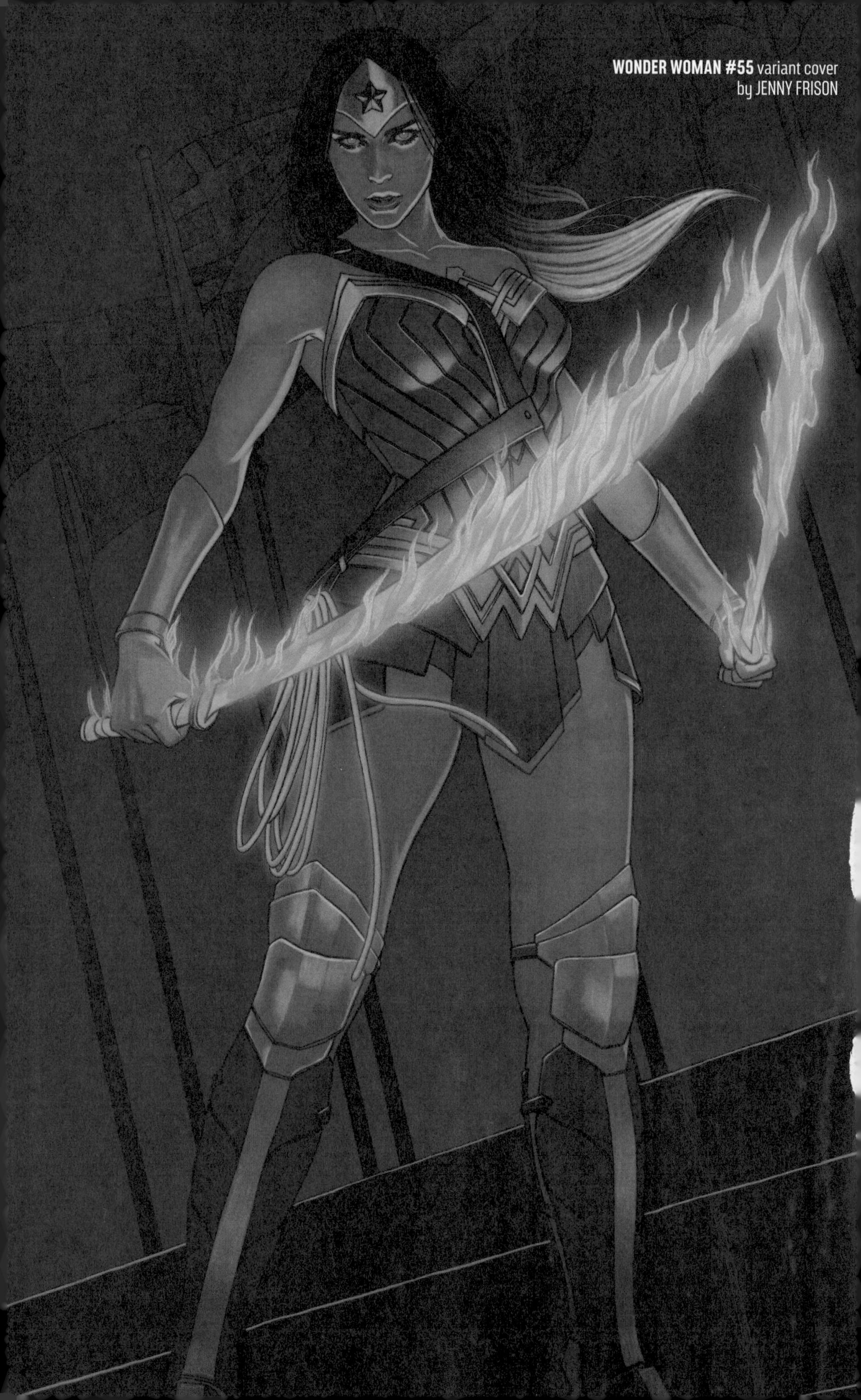

WONDER WOMAN #55 variant cover
by JENNY FRISON

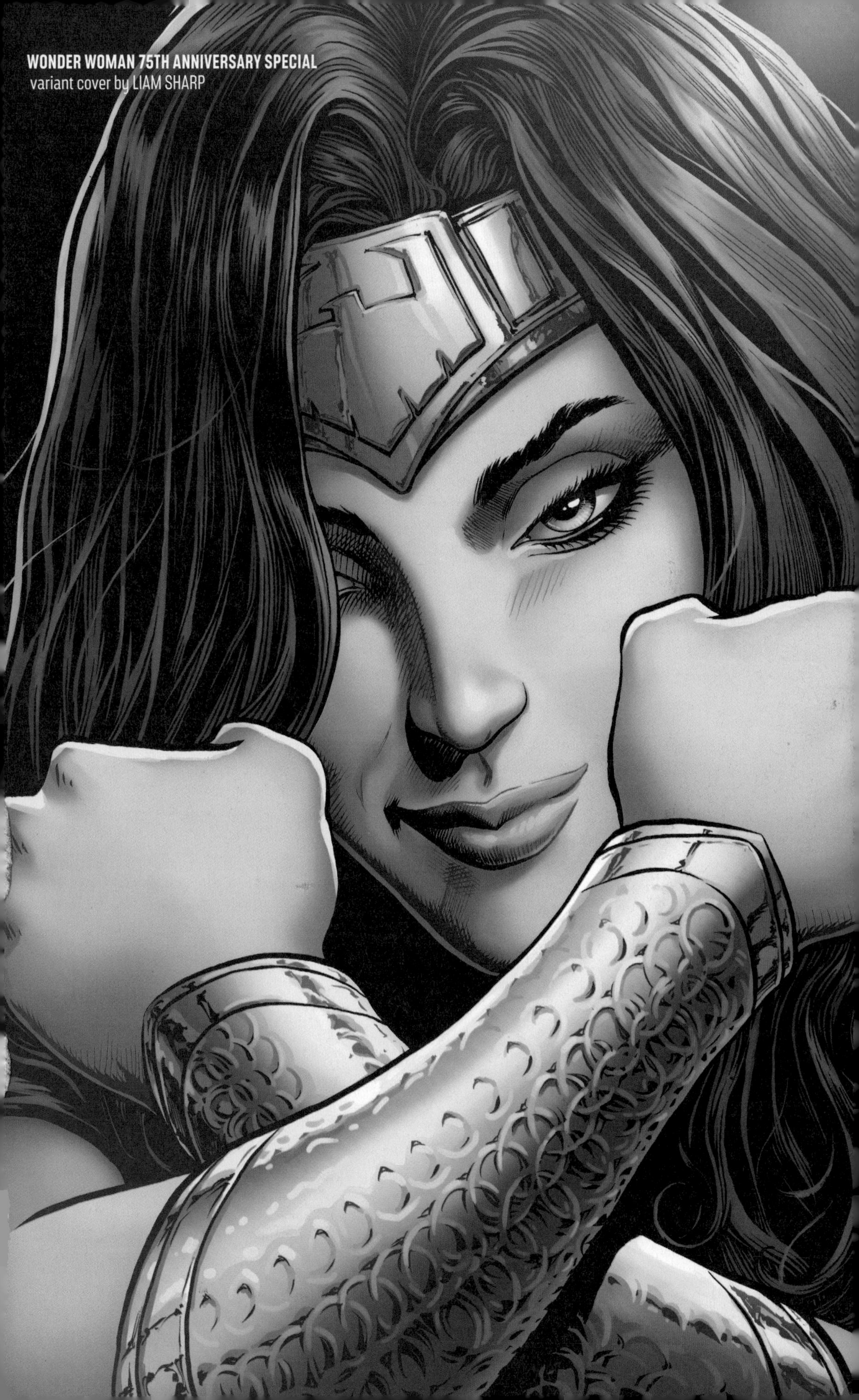

WONDER WOMAN 75TH ANNIVERSARY SPECIAL
variant cover by LIAM SHARP

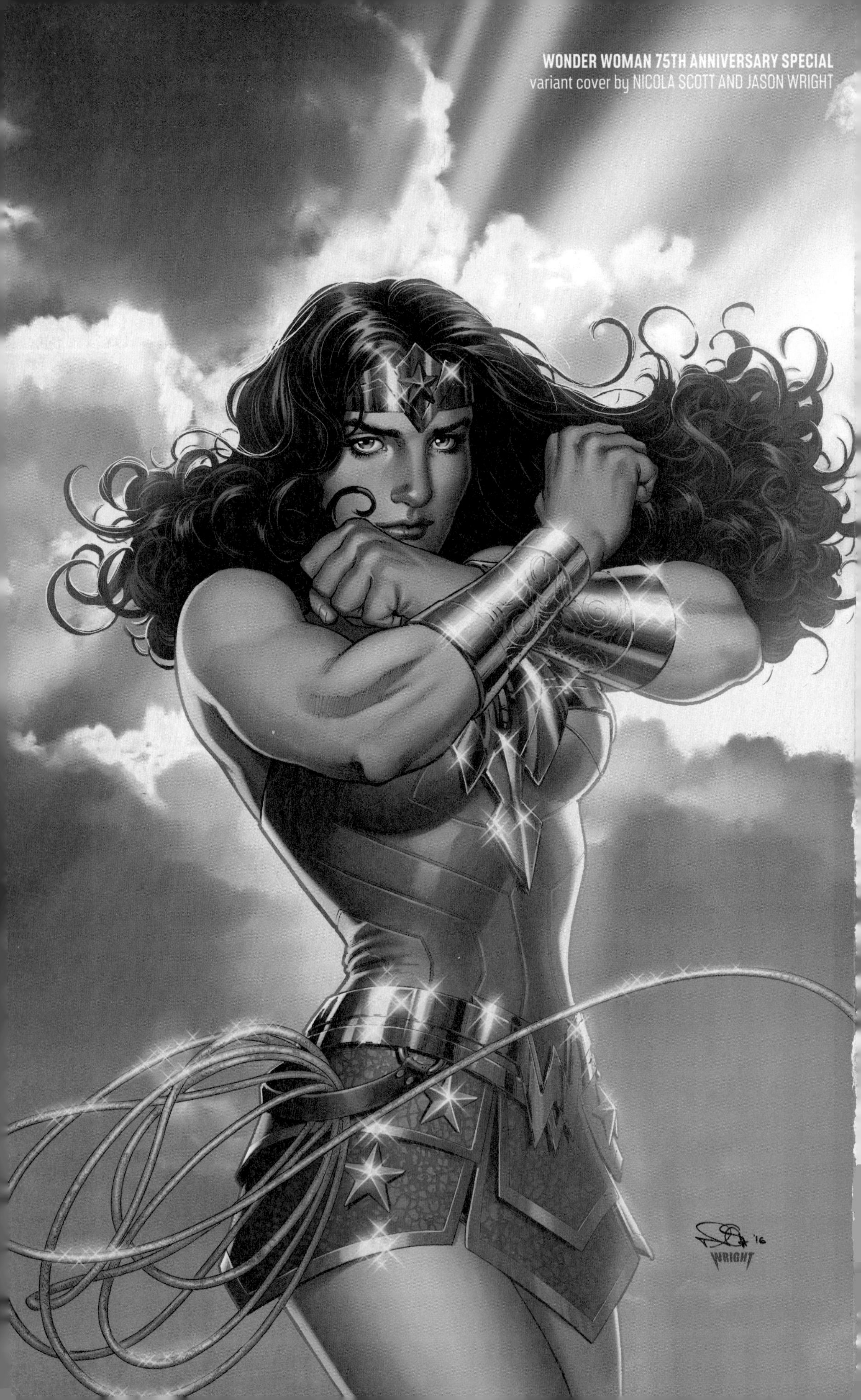
'16
WRIGHT

WONDER WOMAN 75TH ANNIVERSARY SPECIAL
variant cover by NICOLA SCOTT AND JASON WRIGHT